World Politics
in the 21st Century

World Politics in the 21st Century

SECOND EDITION

W. Raymond Duncan
State University of New York, Brockport

Barbara Jancar-Webster
Distinguished University Professor, State University of New York, Brockport

Bob Switky
Sonoma State University

PEARSON
Longman

New York   San Francisco   Boston
London   Toronto   Sydney   Tokyo   Singapore   Madrid
Mexico City   Munich   Paris   Cape Town   Hong Kong   Montreal

Vice President and Publisher: Priscilla McGeehon
Executive Editor: Eric Stano
Senior Marketing Manager: Megan Galvin-Fak
Media Editor: Patrick McCarthy
Supplements Editor: Kristi Olson
Production Manager: Joseph Vella
Project Coordination, Text Design, and Electronic Page Makeup: Shepherd, Inc.
Cover Design Manager: Wendy Ann Fredericks
Cover Designer: Keithley & Associates
Cover Photos: Clockwise from top right: A child soldier, 11, stands by the side of a road at a
Sierra Leone Army checkpoint near the capital, Freetown, Sierra Leone, © Brennan Linsley/
AP Wide World; Afghani women in colorful burqas wait on the side of the road for food to be
delivered, Chris Anderson/Aurora; and Germany holds International conference on Afghanistan,
© Sean Gallup/Getty Images
Photo Research: Photosearch, Inc.
Manufacturing Buyer: Dennis J. Para
Printer and Binder: Courier Corp.—Westford
Cover Printer: Coral Graphics Services

For permission to use copyrighted material, grateful acknowledgment is made to the copyright
holders on p. 578, which are hereby made part of this copyright page.

Library of Congress Cataloging-in-Publication Data

Duncan, W. Raymond (Walter Raymond), 1936–
    World politics in the 21st century / W. Raymond Duncan, Barbara Jancar-Webster, Bob
Switky.—2nd ed.
        p. cm.
    Includes bibliographical references and indexes.
    ISBN 0-321-12959-8 (alk. paper)
        1. International relations. 2. World politics—21st century. I. Jancar-Webster, Barbara,
    1935–   . II. Switky, Bob. III. Title. IV. Title: World politics in the twenty-first century.
JZ1305.D83 2004
327—dc21

                                                                    2003055380

Visit us at www.ablongman.com

ISBN 0-321-12959-8 (Student Edition)
ISBN 0-321-17280-9 (Instructor's Edition)

1 2 3 4 5 6 7 8 9 10—CRW—06 05 04 03

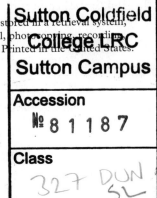

Brief Contents

Detailed Contents

Preface

We live in a world that is both fascinating and terrifying. The list of events that dominate the headlines and our news programs has grown dramatically in the past few years . . . the terrorist attacks on the World Trade Center and the Pentagon . . . a massive U.S.-led worldwide war on terrorism . . . a preemptive military assault by the United States and Great Britain on Iraq.

And with the rush of events, our questions and our need for understanding seem to accelerate as well. Recent events prompt all of us to ask questions like: What is the future for regional stability in the Middle East? What is the long-term outlook for the United States as a superpower? What relations will the United States have with the international community? What will happen to various groups in the Middle East who so fervently wish for independence? What will be the impact of recent events, particularly the war with Iraq, on the U.S. economy?

Such questions underscore that world politics today is in a state of tremendous flux and change. New forces shape our planet at a seemingly faster rate. However, challenges of the recent past also have seemed both daunting and inspiring, and in this book we try to give some perspective to world events. In the last 15 years, for example, we witnessed a revolution in communications technology, the end of a 50-year old Cold War between the United States and the Soviet Union, and the collapse of Soviet communism. We saw the earth from the moon and we came to understand that earth's resources require careful and sustained stewardship if the human race is to survive into another century.

The newest rush of events makes understanding world politics today more challenging than ever. Yet we believe there are keys that will open the doors for us. The main theme of this book is that we can make sense of world politics by finding patterns in world events. This pattern is characterized by forces of *centralization* and *decentralization,* In this new edition we continue our focus on this theme as a way to help students understand the issues and events of world politics. In our discussion of the centralizing tendencies of globalization and global interdependence, we have updated the discussion of the international economy to include the emerging vocal civil opposition to globalization, provided the most recent figures on world poverty, and included coverage of the Johannesburg Environmental Summit (August 2002) in our discussion of the global environment. In our treatment of the decentralizing tendencies, we have expanded and updated the sections on terrorism, nationalism, and ethnic and religious conflict, particularly the Israeli-Palestinian conflict.

Other new coverage includes discussion in the chapters on power and foreign policy on a major change in U.S. war doctrine by the Bush Administration. We also examine the implications of the U.S.-Iraq War, and have added sketches of the foreign policies of three new countries: Egypt, Pakistan, and Saudi Arabia. The subjects of many of the case studies have been changed to make them more relevant to the post-9/11 world, and all of the reading selections in the case studies are updated. Other coverage that reflects recent events includes discussion of increased ethnic and religious tension, as exemplified by East Timor. We also discuss the rise in the number of non-governmental organizations (NGOs), and demonstrate how they have contributed to undermining the traditional authority of the state; in fact, underground terrorist NGOs like *Al Qaeda* are able to penetrate weak states and persuade authoritarian rulers to finance and assist them. We also attempt to demonstrate the difficult concept that perceptions define reality. A Muslim perception of the 2003 U.S.-Iraq war, for example, is distinct from a U. S. perception, which in turn is different from the views of, say, France, Germany, Russia or China.

The problems of poverty in the lesser-developed regions of the world make harsh choices like sexual slavery viable for many women around the world. We attempt to provide a broad picture of the issues faced in such countries.

Within the sovereign state community there remains the seemingly insurmountable difficulty of controlling nuclear and conventional weapons proliferation. We pay particular attention to the spread of ballistic missile technology to states like Iraq, Pakistan and India, as well as chemical and biological weapons.

We hope that this second edition will make it clear that what is happening on the world stage today is so important for our future that it demands every student's attention. To that end, we have included "Why it Matters to You" sections in each chapter—designed to stimulate thinking on the relevance of key issues in world politics.

APPROACH

21st Century Issues

We have written this edition to speak to 21st century realities. We address the centralizing and decentralizing tendencies in the post-Cold War and post- 9/11 world where a wide range of issues are playing new roles—from the proliferation of sovereign states, globalization and interdependence to ethnic nationalism, terrorism, human rights, environmental pressures, political geography, development in the global South, weapons of mass destruction (WMD), and new weapons technology. World politics is increasingly shaped by non-governmental organizations, the social-economic and political consequences of the spread of diseases, advances in technology in agriculture (e.g. genetically modified foods), and fights over scarce resources such as water. And wars still occur for traditional reasons.

But we live in an era in which traditional ways of understanding and analyzing events do not always seem to apply. We have seen the U.S. launch a preemptive military attack on another country without United Nations backing and develop a new national security doctrine to justify such an attack. We live in a world where religious fervor drives some individuals to commit suicide for a cause, killing as many people as possible in the process. Psychology and politics have always gone hand-in-hand, but the scale of today's suicide bombing gives psychology new dimensions in the understanding of world politics. We live in a time when a million people were massacred in Rwanda, and a world where biological and chemical weapons, known as the "poor man" weapons of mass destruction are more likely to be used. For the first time in human history, a disease—AIDS—has become a national and global security issue. A newer disease may pose the same threat. Also for the first time, scientists are arguing whether certain kinds of human activity threaten human existence and the viability of the planet in the form of global warming. We believe our approach is flexible enough to allow analysis of these sobering and challenging issues.

Nontraditional Topics

Today's students are tomorrow's leaders, and we believe they should be exposed to topics that typically receive little or no attention in texts. For example, we include an entire chapter on geographic factors that shape world politics (see Chapter 7), and another dedicated to women, poverty, and human rights (see Chapter 10). We also include a chapter that looks at the environment as a key international issue in itself, rather than as a footnote to the problem of economic development. We believe coverage of these important issues offers an experience attuned to learning for the future rather than remembering from the past.

Active Learning

We concentrate on the realities of the classroom and today's students. We wanted to write this book because each of us felt the need not only for new topics, but also new pedagogical strategies. We had become sharply aware of the wide diversity of learning backgrounds today's students bring to the classroom and the compelling need for diversity in teaching methods if we were going to reach most of them. For this reason, we designed both the book—with its integrated website and chapter-ending case studies—and an Instructor's Manual. The Instructor's Manual contains most of the active learning techniques that have worked well for us in the classroom, but rarely found in available textbooks on world politics. We understand what other instructors face in trying to teach world politics, and we hope this book will help them confront those exciting challenges. Our students deserve multiple learning methods, and we designed this book with that purpose in mind.

The book studies issues in a systematic and logical manner, moving from the more basic concepts and principles toward an understanding of the multiple dimensions of today's world politics arena. Each chapter culminates in a case study that highlights the material presented in the chapter and urges the student to explore the issues more deeply on their own. The inclusion of a case study in each chapter links traditional rote and verbal learning to modern strategies of collaborative active learning. Case studies provide ready environments in which the student learns to think independently. To further the student's development in individual self-exploration, we have given much attention to the Instructor's Manual, wherein instructors will find numerous strategies designed to facilitate student learning. We believe the active learning approach featured there will be extremely useful to students and instructors alike.

Features

This book contains a number of features to aid student understanding. Many of them are borne out of our work in concert with our active learning approach, to make teaching and learning world politics more effective. In addition to the book's rich and extensive map program, each chapter contains the following.

- **Case Study.** Each chapter ends with a case study that combines contemporary readings—many from government sources or from newspapers and journals—along with background text. We attempt to provide coverage of all regions of the world, including case studies on Africa, Asia, Europe, the United States, South America, and the Middle East. The comprehensive readings make library or web searches unnecessary. The case studies provide a rich opportunity for analysis and critical thought. A set of questions follows the readings. The first set checks student understanding of the content of the readings; the second set requires the student to analyze the readings on the basis of material presented in the chapter. A list of websites and literature for further information closes the case study.

- **Key Questions.** These questions, at the beginning of each chapter, prime students for coming material, show them where the information is located in the chapter, and helps them manage information and insights.
- **Boxed Features.** There are three different types of boxed features. "Historical Perspective" boxes provide some additional historical background on important chapter topics. "A View From . . ." boxes give an insider view from a particular country or region. A third type of box, called "Why It Matters to You," shows why a particular issue is relevant to the reader.
- **Concrete Examples.** We believe students need concrete examples in order to understand the concepts involved in studying world politics. Thus, the text includes many real-world examples to make issues and ideas memorable and vivid to the reader.
- **Web Explorations.** Up-to-date Web Explorations, which appear in the text margins alongside related concepts, encourage students to seek additional information from a wide range of sources. In addition to helping students understand critical issues, Web Explorations also give students some experience in seeing which types of websites are most valuable for research. The marginal note directs students to the website for this text, located at **http://www.ablongman.com/duncan.** The Web Explorations can be found within each chapter under Student Resources. Hot links send students directly to the relevant sites.
- **Chapter Summary.** At the end of every chapter is a section that refers students again to the major questions raised in the chapter and reviews the most important points addressed under each question.

For the instructor's benefit, there are learning exercises in the Instructor's Manual that are designed to facilitate different types of learning through individual, paired, and small-group activities.

Supplements for Instructors

Instructor's Manual

Written by the authors, the Instructor's Manual is available as part of the Instructor's Edition (ISBN 0-321-17280-9). Each chapter of the manual features active and collaborative teaching techniques, Internet projects and home assignments, and case study teaching techniques.

Test Bank

This text-specific Test Bank (ISBN 0-321-20242-2) written by the author team contains at least 65 questions per chapter, including multiple choice, true-false, and essay questions.

TestGen-EQ CD-ROM

The printed Test Bank is also available on a cross-platform CD-ROM through our fully networkable computerized testing system, TestGen-EQ (ISBN 0-321-18814-4). The program's friendly graphical interface enables instructors to view, edit, and add questions; transfer questions to tests; and print tests in a variety of fonts and forms. Search and sort features help professors locate questions quickly and arrange them in a preferred order.

Instructor's Guide to the *Microsoft Encarta Interactive World Atlas* CD-ROM

Written by Phil Meeks of Creighton University, this supplement is divided into chapters based on the general topics covered in all International Relations texts. The guide provides an overview of how the Encarta Atlas works more effectively with the text for each given topic, as well as specific suggestions about how instructors can incorporate use of this software into their course for homework assignments, in-class activities, and class projects (ISBN 0-321-08609-0).

Supplements for Students

World Politics in the 21st Century Companion Website (www.ablongman.com/duncan)

On the companion website, students will find chapter objectives and three review quizzes in each chapter to help prepare for the next quiz or test. Through simulations in each chapter, students explore particular issues in greater depth and in a more personalized way. The companion website also contains all the Web Explorations whose icons appear throughout the margins of the book. To find a particular Web Exploration, type the page number where you see the icon into the Search area of the website. The Web Explorations provide specific websites for students to explore various issues in international relations. Rather than just providing a link, the Web Explorations also include context and thought questions to better guide and direct students in their inquiry. For instructors, the companion website allows the download of the Instructor's Manual, an annotated list of helpful web links, and all the maps, graphs and charts from the text.

Student Workbook for *Microsoft Encarta Interactive World Atlas* CD-ROM

This supplement follows the same chapter topics as the instructor's guide. This guide provides Encarta-related activities for students to complete to enrich their study of International Relations and understand course material better (ISBN 0-321-08608-2).

The Microsoft Encarta Interactive World Atlas 2001 CD-ROM

Help students hone their geography skills and give them an unparalleled database of information about countries across the world! This dynamic CD contains thousands of interactive maps in 21 different styles, home pages for 192 countries with more that 10,000 articles and Internet links, statistical data with over 350 indicators, and more. Available for 60 percent off the retail price when packaged with the text! (Give your bookstore ISBN 0-321-21969-4 to order the text + CD package.)

New Signet World Atlas

From Penguin-Putnam, this pocket-sized yet detailed reference features 96 pages of full-color maps plus statistics, key data, and much more. Only $3.50 when packaged (60 percent off retail price) (ISBN 0-451-19732-1).

Longman Atlas of War and Peace

Adapted from *The Penguin Atlas of War and Peace*, this unique booklet contains ten full-color maps with explanatory notes, examining forces changing the world today. FREE when packaged (ISBN 0-321-04195-X).

Research Navigator and Research Navigator Guide

Research Navigator is a comprehensive website comprised of three exclusvie databases of credible and reliable source material for research and for student assignments: (1) EBSCO's ContentSelect Academic Journal Database, (2) *The New York Times* Search by Subject Archive, and (3) "Best of the Web" Link Library. The site also includes an extensive help section. The Research Navigator Guide provides your students with access to the Research Navigator website and includes reference material and hints about conducting online rsearch. Free to qualified college customers when packaged. (ISBN: 0-205-40838-9)

Discount Subscription to *The New York Times*

For only $20, students receive a 10-week subscription.

Discount Subscription to *Newsweek* Magazine

For more than 80% off the regular price, your students can receive 12 issues of Newsweek magazine delivered to their door! Only $6.84 when discount subscription card is order bundled with any Longman text (ISBN 0-321-08895-6).

Writing in Political Science, Second Edition
by Diane E. Schmidt

Takes students step-by-step through all the aspects of writing for political science courses. With an abundance of samples from actual students, the guide also features update information about using new technologies. There is a 10 percent discount when packaged (ISBN 0-321-06998-6).

Acknowledgments

We are grateful to the following reviewers and consultants who provided feedback for the first two editions of this book.

Jeff Dense, Eastern Oregon University
Rado Dimitrov, University of Minnesota
Larry Elowitz, Georgia State College and University
Rick Foster, Idaho State University
Andrea Grove, Westminster College
Nancy Haanstad, Weber State University
Steven Jones, University of Charleston
Guoli Liu, College of Charleston
Richard A. Nolan, University of Florida
Jeffrey Ross, Yale Gordon College
Joseph R. Rudolph, Towson University
Christopher Scholl, Wheeling Jesuit University
Thomas Schrand, Philadelphia University
Charles Sewall, Jr., Robert Morris College
Shawn Shieh, Marist College
Robert E. Sterken, Jr., University of Texas at Tyler
Carol Woodfin, Palm Beach Atlantic College

A special note of appreciation goes to Dr. Nikolai V. Semin of Moscow State University for his invaluable help in PowerPoint design and presentation, and in his ability to reformat for Microsoft Word virtually any text we put in front of him. We would also like to express our thanks to Sue Long of the State University of New York College at Brockport for her efforts to keep us in touch and forwarding chapters and proofs. Our deep thanks as well to the many students who assisted in web research, proofreading, collating, and doing the countless things that a book this size demands. Our thanks goes to Eric Okanović, Paul Ferland, Kara Gable, Alison Schweicher, Mary Buggie-Hunt, Marian Gentzel, and Carrie Labell. Any errors that remain of course are our own.

Last but not least, we must thank our ever-patient and long-suffering spouses without whose constant support and encouragement we could not have brought this book to a successful completion.

And now, *"soyez le bienvenue,"* *"wilkommen,"* *"bienvenida,"* *"vitame vas,"* *"huanying,"* and *"welcome"* to the study of international politics. May you profit greatly from your sharpened understanding of how it works and affects your daily life as we move into the 21st century.

W. RAYMOND DUNCAN
BARBARA JANCAR-WEBSTER
BOB SWITKY

CHAPTER 1

The Importance of International Relations

KEY QUESTIONS RAISED IN THIS CHAPTER

1. Why study international relations?
2. What new forces are shaping the planet?
3. How can I make sense of the changes in the world?

At the beginning of the twenty-first century, the world is both fascinating and terrifying. To understand that world better and to take advantage of its challenges, this chapter gives you three major reasons why the study of international relations is important to you, then identifies the five most significant forces currently at work in the world, and finally explores three theoretical approaches that provide frameworks within which to organize your growing knowledge of the world. The chapter is followed by a case study on one of the most volatile regions in the world—Kashmir—located in the foothills of the Himalayas between India and Pakistan. The case study will draw together the main points made in the chapter and enable you to put into practice the theoretical approaches that were presented. Let's begin with Why Study International Relations?

Why Study International Relations?

To find out more about the terrorist attack on the World Trade Center Go to **www.ablongman.com/ duncan**.

The horrifying events of September 11, 2001, proved that the United States was no longer safe from overseas attacks, while the American-led War in Iraq in 2003 showed that the United States would flaunt world censure to use its military might when its security interests were at stake. The outbreak that same year of the SARS epidemic evoked the terrifying specter of pandemics from earlier times, just as hi-tech medicine seemed nearer than ever to finding cures to humankind's age-old diseases. Americans are living longer and healthier lives at the same time as AIDS is killing off the brightest and best in Sub-Saharan Africa. The world today is a cauldron of change. In 1900, Europe dominated the globe. The European vision was of an increasingly prosperous world where the benefits of science and technology would spread around the globe. Tensions between the major European powers were controlled by diplomacy and the maintenance of a balance of power where one state could not militarily dominate the other. European peace movements called for an end to war. Celebrating this optimism, the American steel magnate, Andrew Carnegie, donated money to build the International Court of Justice in The Hague, Netherlands.

That optimism has been severely tested by two World Wars, and the unplanned side effects of technological development. Daily the media compete for our attention with gory images of human suffering in wars, states torn apart by ethnic conflict, environmental disasters, poverty, rape and disease. 9/11 effectively destroyed the vision of an increasingly harmonious world marching in step toward world peace. We are caught between the threat of global terrorism and our thirst for a just world order, where such threats would become irrelevant.

Relating International Affairs to Your Life

Before 9/11, you might have thought about taking a course in international relations to satisfy some core requirement, or because you wanted to better understand your world so you could choose a career or be directed toward a rewarding job. For example, you might have read about the massive layoffs resulting from the merger of the world's two largest oil companies, Exxon and Mobil, and wondered whether an understanding of the international forces behind such an event could save someone (you) from a similar fate. Or you might have been planning to study or work abroad, and wanted to know more about your country of destination's place in world affairs. The most common reason for studying international relations has always been as preparation for a career in the foreign service or U.S. State Department.

The Fall of the World Trade Tower: At 8:45 Tuesday morning, September 11, 2001, a totally unexpected terror exploded over New York City and in Washington, D.C. In stunned disbelief, witnesses observed a hijacked commercial airliner plunge high up into one of the twin towers of New York City's World Trade Center. Within a short time a second hijacked plane repeated the attack, this time on the second tower. With both towers now engulfed in gigantic flames and plumes of dark smoke, onlookers saw bodies on fire plummet from the upper floors. Not long after, people near ground zero heard an ear-splitting noise as the first tower imploded and came thundering down—followed by the second. In Washington, D.C., an hour after the first attack on the World Trade Center, a third hijacked Boeing 757 slammed into the Pentagon. These terrorist acts, the worst in global history, had been planned, coordinated, and implemented almost exclusively over cell phone, satellite, and Internet!

But perhaps one of the most important reasons for studying international relations is the hard truth that ignorance is not bliss. International affairs affect every aspect of your daily life. Before 9/11, most Americans had so little grasp of international politics that they couldn't begin to understand what had happened. "Why do they hate us?" they asked. Before 9/11, students who had some personal interest looked outside the United States for information on international affairs, but most couldn't have cared less.

Today you need world politics more than ever to enable you to understand the forces at work in the world that are shaping your life and your future. You must literally live and breathe world politics to get a hold on what may be in store for you. The 9/11 attacks were a tragic demonstration of the main theme of this book, namely, the increasing tension between the centralizing forces of globalization and decentralizing forces, such as religious and ethnic conflict, that extend to every corner of our globe. The war in Iraq turns the spotlight on the role of the UN as an effective centralizing force for peace, and the proper exercise of power by the United States and other states to compel regime change in countries ruled by tyrants.

The economic downswing of 2001–2003 provides another example of why the study of international relations is important to you, for it involves one of the new forces dominating world politics in the twenty-first century—the interdependent and transnational character of the issues. In 2002 Enron, a huge global corporation with deep ties to the powerful in Washington suddenly went bankrupt. Its chief executives were accused of fraud, and its employees lost their life savings. Other major American corporations followed Enron into bankruptcy, their chief executive officers exhibiting the same fraudulent behavior as Enron's chief executive officers (CEOs). The news of corruption in the United States economy quickly went out over the TV, radio, and Internet. Europe congratulated itself that its more regulated brand of capitalism had never experienced such fraud, only to see many of its CEOs removed on similar charges. As the value of stocks on the U.S. stock market rose and fell in violent swings, foreign stock exchanges experienced similar confusion. This confusion helped further to reduce the value of stocks on Wall Street. In the meantime, the fall in U.S. stocks made U.S. consumers fearful that their pensions and life savings might disappear, so they decided to buy less. Fewer consumer orders to U.S. companies forced those companies to reduce their orders of supplies from foreign companies. Receiving fewer orders, the Asian and Latin American factories were forced to cut back and fire their employees. Unemployment rose and consumption diminished around the world. International uncertainty about the U.S. economic future was increased by talk of war and fear of oil shortages. In the United States, this international uncertainty translated into higher heating and energy costs, further raising the cost of production in the country and reducing consumer spending.

In this discussion of an economic downswing we have circled the globe and introduced many kinds of issues ranging from local production decisions to world issues of war and peace. The modern world is so complex and interdependent that you cannot begin to know how to act without understanding the connections; and for this understanding you need a solid grounding in world politics.

In this book we address the major areas of international relations (the international system, foreign policy, international organizations, the global economy) and the major issues (political geography, global justice, the environment). Within the chapters, hopefully you will receive the theoretical and factual background to enable you to answer those questions most important to you. These may range from What can be done about terrorism? to What role should the United States play in world affairs? to How can we ensure that the planet will be livable until 2099? and to How can we reduce the huge gap between the rich and the poor in this world? In each chapter, there are three kinds of boxes. The first, called Historical Perspective, contains historical background information; the second (The View from Earth, for example), presents information from a specific area of the world. The third kind of box, Why It Matters to You, highlights why the material under discussion is relevant to your life. Hopefully, when you have finished the text, you will be able to work out answers to your important questions. Good luck.

In summary, the study of world politics helps you make sense of your world. It gives you a set of tools by which to assess the world situation, whatever the crisis or driving forces at work may be. World politics provides methods of analysis to help you understand the diverse positions of the world's leaders and peoples, and it proposes frameworks to help you evaluate the media soundbites that flood the daily news. Last, a look at world politics shows you how the world "out there" is closely tied to the world "at home" and how the interaction between the two affects your life.

Seeing the Interconnections Between International Affairs and the Politics of Individual States

In the modern world, no country conducts its domestic affairs in a vacuum. For the past fifty years, the intertwining of the global and the local has blurred the distinctions between international relations and comparative government. Yet, the differences remain. The central concern of international relations is the interactions between *actors on the international stage*. **Comparative government** focuses on the interactions of actors *within state borders*. It is important to understand that domestic politics and international politics are not part of one continuous policy line. Each has a different agenda, a different audience, and different goals. Comparative government may deal briefly with the foreign policy of an individual state as a matter of internal politics. However, the analysis of how, with whom, where, and why that state conducts its foreign policy is the subject matter of international relations.

Comparative Government
The study of the interactions of actors within state borders.

One substantive example of the interconnectedness of domestic and foreign policy is the question of how the United States should try persons suspected of terrorism. The United States has an independent judiciary and a whole set of rights and precedents that define the rights of the accused and the rules of evidence in civilian courts and in military courts, where U.S. soldiers are tried on charges associated with their military service. When the U.S. military went into Afghanistan as part of its war on terrorism, it took prisoners and detained them at Guantànamo Naval base in Cuba, announcing that they would be tried by a military tribunal. The U.S. legal profession and civil rights organizations immediately objected, saying the accused would not receive a fair trial. This *domestic* outcry played a significant role in the government's subsequent release of a policy statement on the rights of the accused and the rules of evidence in the proposed military tribunals.

The differences between procedure in a civil court and in the proposed military tribunals are small but significant: In the military tribunal, evidence can be admitted "if it would have a probative value (supply proof) to a reasonable person." The government can introduce classified information, including hearsay, and that information is not read out publicly in court so that the accused can respond to it. Conviction requires only a two-thirds vote as opposed to a unanimous vote to convict in a civilian court.[1]

The government's publication of the rules silenced some but increased the protests by civil rights groups and lawyers in the international community. They argued that to try the accused in a military tribunal is contrary to the Geneva Convention which defines the treatment of prisoners of war. They urged the President to try the terrorists in civilian courts where due process of law and civil rights were strictly upheld. The Bush administration answered by stating that the Geneva Convention related to the treatment of captured militants or soldiers in time of war. The Convention said nothing about terrorists and so did not apply. In the United States, civil rights advocates responded by renewing their accusation that the administration was arbitrarily suspending the civil rights of the accused and thus threatening the basic foundation of our legal system and the rights of all Americans.

In this example, domestic judicial practice is intricately enmeshed in international human rights issues where the integrity of the world superpower as a defender of the rule of law and global justice is sharply challenged. This challenge is highly relevant to your life: However the Bush administration decides to try the prisoners, the rights of the accused and the rules of evidence it approves will impact the conduct of future military and civilian trials in the United States, perhaps one day including one in which you are involved. Equally important, the procedure selected will impact on the ability of the U.S. government to keep its intelligence and intelligence sources secret in the prosecution of future international conflicts. In the event of those conflicts your life or the life of a member of your family may depend on highly classified information that risks being made public at a trial of a prisoner of war.

To look at the problem from another angle, what if one day during your junior year abroad, you are arrested in another country at a party where drugs are found, and a judge in that country rules that you do not have the same rights as a citizen of that country? If, to back up his position, the judge cites the precedent of the U.S. treatment of accused terrorists in the War on Terrorism, you are in for tough times. The point here is that a U.S. crackdown on so-called foreign terrorists could mark the beginning of an erosion of civil rights worldwide. Historically, the United States's main selling point to the world is its commitment to freedom and liberty for all peoples. But the identification of one group of people brought before the U.S. justice system as unworthy of equal treatment under the law raises embarrassing questions about the U.S. commitment to human rights around the globe. Understanding the interconnections between domestic concerns, such as the U.S. legal system, and international relations can provide information that makes current events intelligible. We turn to this question in the next section.

Finding Patterns in the Complexity of Current Events

Perhaps most important, you need to study international relations today because the world of the twenty-first century is changing at a more rapid pace than at any other time in history. New forces are shaping the planet. In the final decade of the twentieth century, we witnessed a revolution in communications and technology, and the end of the **Cold War.** The Cold War, between the United States and the Soviet Union, the two major powers in the world at that time, lasted almost 50 years (from 1946 to 1991), and the bipolar world of that era began to seem a permanent fixture of the international landscape. Suddenly the war was over, leaving the international community grasping for clues as to how to define the new era. Too soon, however, **terrorism** supplied some of that definition, as did **religious extremism,** which has become a major ideological factor in world politics.

Giving students tools for understanding the complex, rapidly changing circumstances around us is one goal of this book. And one of its central themes is that despite the seeming chaos of the events portrayed on the nightly news, patterns in them can be found. The principal patterns on which we focus in this book are the centralizing and decentralizing forces in international relations. Forces for centralization are those that bring people together around the world, and they can be seen in the twin processes of globalization and global interdependence. In contrast, forces for decentralization are those that cause division and conflict. They can be found in ethnic nationalism; in individual, group, and state terrorism; and in immediate citizen access to information.

In the preceding sections you found one example of the centralizing/decentralizing tension in the modern world in our discussion of the September 11, 2001, terrorist attacks. In this example, group terrorism was the divisive force, while the rallying of the whole world around the United States in its moment of tragedy was the centralizing force that focused world attention on the need to deal with terrorism. In the

Cold War
The great ideological and power conflict between the Soviet Union and its allies and the United States and its allies, which lasted roughly from 1946 to 1991.

Terrorism
Politically motivated violence usually perpetrated against civilians. Terrorists and terrorist groups normally want to change by force or by threat of force a political context that they do not like.

Religious Extremism
The use of religion to rationalize extreme actions, such as terrorism; militancy against a recognized government.

course of this book, we will bring this theme back again and again in our discussion of the international system, foreign policy, the global economy of industrialized and developing states, women and global justice, and the environmental challenges to our planet.

When you are asked why you have chosen to study international relations, you now can give at least three important answers: You need to study international relations to provide yourself with a framework with which to evaluate and define your life and future. You need to study international relations to enable you to see the interconnectedness of international end domestic politics, and to understand that decisions made in one country can one day profoundly affect you. And finally you need to study international relations to find the patterns that can make sense of those forces that are so rapidly changing our fast-moving world.

What New Forces Are Shaping the Planet?

In this book, we identify five forces as dominant in shaping our world at present: technology, the new global and transnational issues, the increasing inability of the state to solve its problems, the rise of ethnic nationalism and religious fundamentalism, and the new citizen activism. The jury is still out on whether these forces will push the world closer together or further apart. But it is safe to say that at the present time, each of these forces can be either centripetal or centrifugal. They can push either way—toward greater cooperation or toward more global fragmentation and repositioning. Let us look at these forces in turn.

1. Information Technology

Since 1980, the industrialized nations of the world have shifted to what are termed postindustrial technologies. These technologies make distances shorter and increase the speed of communication. They range from currency exchange transactions via the computer to the transfer of ideas and pictures via satellite, fax, E-mail, and the Internet. Our lives have been transformed by the information revolution.

How have these new technologies affected international relations? Let us give a few examples.

In 1989, Chinese students held a sit-in on the huge, central square of the Chinese capital of Beijing. The demonstration was coordinated from Harvard University via E-mail by Chinese students studying in the United States. The progress of the demonstration was filmed by U.S. film crews and transmitted across the world to be seen on the evening news by millions of U.S. families. The comprehensive coverage by the U.S. media was probably a major reason why the Chinese government decided to crack down on the demonstrators and sent Chinese tanks to mow down the students and their supporters. From 1993 to 1995 in Bosnia and in 1998 in Kosovo, the camcorder, Internet, instant transmission, and TV made the whole world participants in the grim ritual of ethnic cleansing. On September 11, 2001, thanks to the array of new information technologies, TV viewers around the world watched in disbelief as two airplanes crashed into the north and south towers of the World Trade Building, causing them to collapse. The CNN film sequence was played over and over again in the days and months that followed. What is even more indicative of the new trends in technology is that Osama Bin Laden and his Al Qaeda organization planned and implemented a whole series of terrorist attacks— in Saudi Arabia in the port city of Aden on the Red Sea, at the Twin Towers of the World Trade Organization, at a Jewish Synagogue in Morocco, and at a vacation

To find out more about the difficulty of making predictions go to **www.ablongman.com/ duncan**.

To find out more about the ups and downs of the stock market, go to **www.ablongman.com/ duncan**.

To find out more about currency fluctuation, go to **www.ablongman.com/ duncan**.

resort in Indonesia—by combining old and established technology such as bombs and airplanes with the new technologies of rapid communication, instant replay, and mass audiences.

In 1987, the U.S. stock market fell more points in a single day than it fell on Black Friday in 1929. In 1998, the stock market went on a roller coaster ride, leaving investors breathless. In 2001 after the terrorist attacks, the U.S. market took a steep plunge before going on a prolonged spin. In each case, computer technology and instant satellite communication of corporate and market news played a role in market volatility. Let's look at how.

In the past, brokers handled all stock dealings. Today, individuals manage their own stock transactions over the Internet; or they can send instructions to their brokers to program the computer to trigger sale of a stock when it rises or falls to a specified amount. When the price of one stock falls rapidly, the downward trend triggers programmed sales of that stock and also of related stocks. To counter such trends after the 1987 crash, Congress passed a law requiring the closing of the stock market if stocks fell too far. Nevertheless, computer programming of stock sales remains a principal player in a roller coaster market. The role of the computer in the buying and selling of securities is tremendously important!

Not only sales are made by computer. The values of stocks are recorded and tracked by computer so that a broker or customer can pull up a stock on the Internet, analyze its performance, and predict its future movements. The computer, with its instant recording and instant replay, has revolutionized how we buy and sell stock. Because of it, thousands of people have entered the stock market who had never been there before. Some even make their livelihood out of tracking the movements of various socks, trading them on the stock exchange for others, and then tracking and selling these.

Instructions to sell or buy stock fly through the Internet at the speed of light. The transfer of money takes a great deal longer. What would happen if there were a simultaneous collapse of the world's stock markets and we all tried to get our money out at the same time?

Nobody knows the answer to this question. One scenario is that the computers would crash under the impact of so many orders coming from all parts of the globe. The crash of the U.S. computer system would be followed by the collapse of other systems, as investors all over the world tried to save their earnings. We would be plunged into a very serious international economic crisis. Without the computer, we have no records of buyers and sellers, no records of who invested in what, no records of where countries might have invested their taxpayers' money. It would take a long while to sort everything out, and it would be extraordinary if things were returned to normal without a major international conflict of some kind.

A third example of the impact of rapid information technology on world events is the tendency for diverse terrorist and ethnic groups to imitate the bombings, shootings, and killings they see reported as news in the media. Another is the use of the Internet by numerous groups to give voice to their points of view and encourage others to follow, whether they are advocating the overthrow of governments or demonstrating on behalf of special interests.

A final example of how the computer revolution affects world events can be seen in the links between new weapons technology and computer technology. You will read more about this advanced weaponry in Chapter 9. Here, we will just say that smart weapons obey instructions programmed into a computer. Pilots no longer have to see their targets. They can bomb targets thousands of miles below them because a computer provides all the information the guided weapon needs to lock onto its target. The new hi-tech weaponry contributes to the depersonalization of war. In times past, war was a matter of one person or division attacking another. Now it is faceless planes dropping bombs on faceless people. The danger is that we may become insensitive to the human tragedy of war.

Today, we find ourselves in the middle of the information revolution and can only begin to assess its impact. Change occurs so fast that we may not be able to understand the dimensions of this revolution until we have experienced its unintended consequences. It is now possible to dial into a server and talk via E-mail to someone on the opposite side of the world. A search on the World Wide Web will locate virtually any information one could want and bring together likeminded people from around the world. The information revolution has liberated individuals from dependence on some authority for information. At the same time, it offers so much information that the individual has difficulty separating reliable and trustworthy information from erroneous hearsay. The revolution risks producing a world of information junkies who lack the tools for finding meaning in the message but who are ready to react to it however they can.

It is still too early to tell whether the new technology is a centralizing or a decentralizing force. Its ability to disseminate information around the globe would appear to be a centralizing feature, as is its ability to unite individuals in one chat room for discussion on a subject of mutual interest. However, the Internet makes it easy for individuals bent on pushing their form of nationalism or religion to organize some major disaster, such as 9/11, without having to go through a telephone or postal system where it has been easier to track their actions. Even in the case of communication among terrorists, the Internet has to be seen as a unifying factor. So we must wait and see before we make a final judgment.

2. The New Global and Transnational Issues

In the twenty-first century, events in one part of the world can reverberate on the global level. They differ from the old issues in that they are **transnational**—freely crossing state borders. For example, in the new global economy, a transnational corporation can use communications technology to run a global business without having a national home. In other words, corporations can invest and locate anywhere on the planet, benefiting the people who live in that location with jobs. However, they can also pull their capital out and move elsewhere, if they so choose. When global capital pulled out of Indonesia in 1997, the Indonesian people were quickly reduced to poverty. In some countries and regions in the world, such as Russia, corporations are reluctant to invest global capital. Other countries seem to attract capital. Without capital, however, countries cannot provide education, health care, or business or job opportunities for their populations. A main feature of our world today is the increasing gap between the world's rich and the world's poor, both within countries and transnationally. At the World Summit in Johannesburg, South Africa, in August 2002, a main topic of discussion on easing the gap between the rich and the poor was how to attract investment to those countries needing it most.

Environmental degradation is another transnational and interdependent problem. The English poet William Blake was among the first to draw attention to the environmental pollution caused by industrialization. In his 1804 poem

Transnational
Going beyond state borders or unstoppable at state borders. Air pollution, for example, may be confined within the boundaries of one state, or it may be transnational, crossing state boundaries. We call this instance transboundary air pollution.

"Jerusalem,"[2] he deplored England's "satanic mills" and called on his readers to build Jerusalem in "England's green and pleasant land." A generation later, the great English poet William Wordsworth wrote that England had become "a fen of stagnant waters."[3] At about the same time, John James Audubon was identifying and painting the birds of America, already aware that the arrival of the Europeans and industrialization had fated many for extinction. The New England philosopher Henry Thoreau, in his celebrated essay, *Walden Pond* (1854), called our attention to the value of wilderness as opposed to the values of the industrial world.

We did not fully understand the prescience of these early environmentalists until we had gone to the moon in 1961 and seen how fragile and small our planet really is. In the industrialized countries, environmental degradation has become increasingly obvious in the death of lakes, the depletion of freshwater fish, and air pollution in the large cities. At first these problems seemed to be solvable by the action of national governments or—where a problem such as pollution of a river involved several states—by a group of states. Now we know that those problems require a transnational approach to their solution.

Global Commons

Areas of the earth's biosphere that are shared by all the world's population, such as oceans and the atmosphere.

The 1980s brought recognition of a new concept: the **global commons.** The global commons are areas of the planet, such as oceans and the earth's atmosphere, which are shared by all the world's population. The environmental health of these commons is affected by what people do to the air, soil, forests, and water where they live and work. Soil erosion, deforestation, and water pollution are all transnational problems. Not only does the cutting down of forests lead to soil erosion locally, reduced rainfall caused by deforestation contributes to global warming. While the jury is still out as to how much our burning of fossil fuels affects the warming of our planet, none of us would wish by our actions to contaminate the global atmosphere in such a way as to risk life on Earth. At the turn of the twenty-first century, protecting and maintaining the life support systems of the earth's environment have become an international priority.

Industrial production has also expanded to encompass the entire globe. In the nineteenth century, most local communities produced all their needs within their borders and imported only luxury goods. Today, production has gone global. One part of a car may be made in Thailand, another in Taiwan, another in China, and yet another in Korea or Japan. Some of those parts may be put together in Mexico. All of them are then imported into the United States, where the car is assembled as a finished product. The gasoline we buy to drive our cars comes from oil purchased from the Middle East but refined in New Jersey. Computer parts are made in Southeast Asia for computer companies headquartered in the United States. The global economy allows corporations of the major industrialized countries to take advantage of low costs and cheap labor in the developing countries in order to manufacture products that they can then market around the globe. People all over the globe benefit from the quantity and quality of goods produced by global corporations. A global market coupled with low production costs leads to lower prices for the consumer.

On the downside, the cheapness of the products produced by global corporations such as Coca Cola and McDonald's can drive out local companies and local products. One result is a global conformity in product choices. A second result is the disappearance from the market of many local products. While there are still a few Adirondack chairs made in the Adirondack Mountains of upstate New York, most are now made many thousands of miles away. Fresh fruit and vegetables produced locally have become a rarity in most supermarkets. The food on your table now comes from an average distance of 2000 miles away. The most negative consequence of globalization is loss of jobs from the closing of local industries, such as textile factories, lumber mills, or farms, when transnational corporations can find what local industry produces at a lower cost somewhere else on the globe. Unemployment has itself become a global problem. Last but not least, one must have money to buy even the cheapest goods. The 1.2 billion people living on less than a dollar a day cannot take advantage of prices or products and must produce what they need with their own hands.

Finally, terrorism recognizes no state borders and has no single source. In recent years, terrorists have come from a diverse set of

McWorld Is Here: At the end of the twentieth century, large corporations produced and marketed literally around the world. McDonald's was the first to market successfully fast food by selling a standardized hamburger and French fries in California. The company expanded operations throughout the United States and prides itself on maintaining the same quality of food service around the world today.

countries—Iran, Libya, Egypt, Saudi Arabia, Afghanistan, and Peru—from drug cartels in Latin America, and from the United States. Fifteen of the nineteen hijackers who commandeered the four planes on 9/11 were Saudi citizens. Identifying terrorists and preventing terrorist attacks are also transnational issues; they necessitate coordinating and making available in a timely fashion large amounts of information from all parts of the world and the coordination of action among countries.

Can you identify other transborder problems? When you do, be sure to include international drug trafficking, the global child and sex trade, and the large migrations of refugees who seek to escape the consequences of global problems. These, as well as the issues that we have identified, have acquired a life of their own, demanding international cooperation and international agency to assure maximum benefits and minimum hardships to all the world's people. The new issues thus operate as a powerful force pushing the world towards cooperation and international community building.

3. The Increasing Inability of the State to Solve Problems

An important theme that runs throughout this book is that no state can solve the new transnational problems on its own. Solutions to terrorism, migration, drug trafficking, environmental degradation, and the global child and sex trade require the cooperation of the major governments around the world, including the exchange of sensitive information, the standardization of laws relating to these issues, and the coordination of national police forces. Even a nation as powerful and wealthy as the United States cannot stop terrorism or drug trafficking by unilateral action. In the case of the environment, it is clear that no one state can undertake the cleanup of the world's oceans or air by itself. Some reduction of domestic levels of carbon or sulfur

TABLE 1.1   Examples of States Where Devolution* or Disassociation⁺ Is Taking Place

Devolution	Disassociation
Canada	Canada
Australia	Rwanda
Great Britain	The Republic of the Congo
Spain	India, Pakistan, Kashmir
Russia	Russia
Israel	Israel
Belgium	Indonesia
Georgia	Mexico
Kazakhstan	Azerbaijan
Mexico	China (Tibet)
Iran	Sri Lanka
Slovakia	Iraq
Romania	Sudan

*__Devolution:__ Power and authority are transferred from the central national government to regional and/or local governments.

⁺__Disassociation:__ The ethnic national group is in the process of breaking away from the mother country by whatever means possible.

dioxide emissions into the air can be achieved through the passage and enforcement of national emission standards. But these reductions generally are limited to local areas. The achievement of a worldwide reduction of emissions requires a global agreement stipulating which country is to do what.

If the state is limited in what it can do to solve the new transnational problems, it is also limited in its ability to solve problems single handedly that were once viewed as purely domestic. Problems such as a fair wage for workers, the right price for wheat, and standards for industry and consumer goods are now also enmeshed in the politics of globalization. The U.S. Congress could raise the minimum wage to ten dollars an hour, but U.S. industries would quickly move south to the Caribbean or to Southeast Asia, where the cost of labor averages a dollar a day. The result would be increasing unemployment in the United States and a further increase in the gap between rich and poor, as more unskilled workers are thrown out of the work force in the United States. In addition, the ten dollars an hour labor cost would increase the cost of products made in the United States to a level where they could not compete with cheaper products on the world market. Globalization has been one of the strongest forces in reorienting state problem solving in the direction of the international organizations (centralizations). On the other hand, the perceived erosion of the state's control of the domestic agenda has contributed to an increase in decentralizing tendencies within state borders.

4. The Rise of Ethnic Nationalism and Religious Fundamentalism

The weakening of centralized state power has encouraged decentralization everywhere from Eurasia and Canada to Australia, Rwanda, the Congo, India, Pakistan, Indonesia, Brazil, Great Britain, and Spain. (See Table 1.1.)

FIGURE 1.1

Do You Know the Difference Between . . . ?

State
- A geographic territory with internationally recognized boundaries.
- An internationally recognized and identifiable population that lives within those boundaries.
- An internationally recognized authority structure or government.

Nation
- A group of people linked together in some manner, such as by a common territory (Estonians, Czechs, Norwegians), although not necessarily by a common territory (Arabs, Tamils, Kazaks).
- Common culture that may or may not be based on religion.
- Common language.
- Common history or understanding of the past.
- General desire for independence.

Ethnic Group
- A group of people linked together similarly to those of a nation, EXCEPT:
  — no expressed desire for independence;
  — most important unifying or identifying factor is language.
- Religion is often a unifying factor.

Multinational state: a state such as China, India, Nigeria, Russia, or the United States, which contains more than one nation within its territory. Most states are multinational.

Multistate nation: a single nation occupying more than one state boundary. The German, Russian, and Kurd nations are classic examples.

Ethnic nationalism: an ethnic group that seeks independence and bases its right to independence on the right to speak its own language (the Hungarians in Slovakia and Rumania, the Kurds in Iraq, Iran, and Turkey, the Basques in Spain and France, the Flemish and the French-speaking populations of Belgium, the Albanians in the Yugoslav province of Kosovo). In contrast to the American fight for independence, which was based on self-rule over a specific territory regardless of language, most modern nationalist movements are language oriented. We call groups seeking independence under such conditions ethnic national groups.

Race: a division of humankind possessing biological traits that are transmissible by descent and are sufficient to characterize it as a distinctive human type.[4] Based on the criteria of pigmentation, color and form of hair, shape of head and nose, and stature, anthropologists generally agree on three major races: the Caucasoid, Mongoloid, and Negroid. To classify humans on the basis of race is highly problematic, for there has been an intermingling of races since earliest human history.

Where state power has dramatically decreased, ethnic nationalist and religious movements have succeeded in breaking that state up into national ethnic entities. (To understand the differences between the state, the nation, and ethnic groups, review Figure 1.1 on p. 13: Do You Know the Difference Between . . . ?)

In 1991, the Soviet Union collapsed when the nationalist majorities of the USSR's constituent republics refused to accept a federal constitution written by Moscow. The country that had been the second pole of the bipolar world created after World War II, and that had been feared as a major nuclear power and an authoritarian state, imploded without a whimper. (See Chapter 4 for details.) The new independent states of the former Soviet Union have had their share of ethnic problems. Each has a multiethnic population. In many cases, the larger ethnic minorities would prefer independence or at least a large share of self-rule. Since 1991, civil wars have raged in Azerbaijan, Georgia, and Tajikistan, as has a war for independence in Chechnya. The fall of the USSR left a power vacuum in Eastern Europe and across the broad expanse of Eurasia. The vacuum was quickly filled by the resurgence of nationalist quarrels. In Eastern Europe the two major nationalities in Czechoslovakia, the Czechs and the Slovaks, split apart peacefully and formed two nations. Yugoslavia was not so fortunate. The wars in the Balkans, particularly the genocide practiced by the Bosnian-Serb Christians against the Bosnian-Serb Muslims, were among the bloodiest of any wars since the Second World War.

Ethnic and religious tension has intensified in other parts of the world as well. The most salient examples are the civil wars in Rwanda and the Republic of Congo, the revolt of the native Mayan minority in the Mexican state of Chiapas, and the war in Kashmir, where Indian Hindu soldiers face Pakistani Muslim soldiers in an unending drama of bloodshed over which country (and religion) is to get Kashmir. In the Ivory Coast in Africa, Muslims from the North face Christians from the South in a deadly fight to see whether Muslim or Christian tribes will dominate. In the Middle East, the conflict between Israelis and Palestinians is now a hundred years old, as is the Kurdish movement for independence that has created political instability in Turkey, Iran, and Iraq. In Indonesia, Malaysia, and Vietnam, the Chinese minority suffers at the hands of the dominant ethnic majority. In Sri Lanka, the Tamils, a minority ethnic group on the island of Ceylon, want independence from the Sinhalese ethnic majority. The Canadian province of Quebec has held several referendums on whether French-speaking Quebec should become independent of Canada.

At the dawn of the twenty-first century, ethnic nationalism and religious fundamentalism have become the preoccupation of groups seeking to find their identity in a globalized world where brands like Nike or Coca Cola bring more name recognition and loyalty than a newly independent state.

5. New Citizen Activism

The fifth and last new force influencing world politics is the resurgence of citizen activism. Citizens around the world are frustrated by what appears to them to be the collapse of domestic order and the seeming weakness of the state to pay attention to their concerns. They may variously blame their government for having abandoned traditional values or traditional religion, or for failing to take sufficiently radical measures to either create or halt change. In Iran, angry citizens in 1978 protested against what they perceived as their government's inhuman and absolutist methods of rapid industrialization. In one short week they ousted the ruling Shah and welcomed home Ayatollah Khomeini, an Iranian cleric urging the return to fundamental Islamic values. In 1984, the population of the Philippines took to the streets to oust the dictatorial government of Ferdinand Marcos in favor of democracy. The Oklahoma City bombing in 1996 is an example from the United States of citizen activism gone out of control. In Indonesia in 1998, thousands of young people—students and unemployed—took to the streets to demand democracy as a solution to the collapse of the Indonesian economy. The mass demonstrations against the World Trade Organization (WTO) in Seattle in November 1999 also vividly illustrated this new level of citizen activism.

A looting mob in Jakarta, Indonesia, May 1998, after the fall from power of Suharto, the 32-year dictator of Indonesia.

Citizen empowerment in the late twentieth century is more than a passing phenomenon. Unlike any other technology, the personal computer or cell phone linked to the Internet gives the individual the ability to seek information and communicate with individuals who have similar views but live in other countries and cultures. Messages flowing across the net provide the infrastructure necessary to support citizens' organizations.

Increase in citizen activism has gone hand in hand with the accelerated growth of **nongovernmental organizations (NGOs).** NGOs (covered in detail in Chapter 6) are organizations of citizens with a common agenda or set of demands they would like a government to implement. Some NGOs go back to the nineteenth century, but most got started in the 1970s or later. NGOs may be organized at the grassroots or at the state and international levels. Grassroots groups commonly organize around a local issue. National NGOs organize to pressure the national governments to adopt certain policies or legislation, while the newest of the NGOs, international NGOs, aim to influence international organizations, such as the United Nations. Existing NGOs are as diverse as Mothers against Drunk Driving (national), Friends of the Earth (international), the Adirondack Mountain Club (local), and El Fatah, an international terrorist organization.

Pressure exerted by global NGOs became so strong that in the late 1980s, the United Nations (UN) agreed to give legal standing to NGOs that registered with them. Legal standing means that the registered NGOs are represented in an official capacity at world conferences and in deliberations about UN activities. Such a practice would have been unthinkable one hundred years ago. The appearance of NGOs as major players in the international arena is considered so significant that a new subspecialty of international relations has come into being: the study of the politics of **global civil society.**

With all these new forces at work in a world that is on a roller-coaster of change, it is difficult to know where to start to make sense of everything (see box Why It Matters to You: New Forces Shaping the Twenty-First Century). Here is

Nongovernmental Organizations (NGOs)
An international organization made up of groups or individuals recruited across state boundaries, either by profession or interest.

Global Civil Society
The term given to the emergence of a great deal of interaction of NGOs with international organizations as they lobby and seek to have their views represented or endorsed by the United Nations and world financial institutions.

WHY IT MATTERS TO YOU

New Forces Shaping the Twenty-First Century

- Postindustrial technology focuses on making distances shorter and increasing the speed of communication.
- Interdependence between nations results from the transnational character of new issues, such as the AIDS pandemic, terrorism, and global environmental degradation.
- Increasing inability of states to solve problems. Interdependence heightens the vulnerability and undermines the sovereignty of the traditional nation state.

- Ethnic conflict and religious extremism are among the most serious decentralizing tendencies
- Increased citizen activism. Mass access to information via the Internet and the rise of the international NGOs has generated new citizen activism in all parts of our globe.

These trends matter to you. They will determine your job, what you wear, and quite possibly what you eat. They will determine whether there is war or peace and, if war, whether you will be involved.

Political Realism
A philosophical position that assumes that human beings are imperfect with an innate desire for power. The international system is composed of states and other actors whose primary interest is to survive and thrive in an anarchic jungle of competing actors where there is no higher authority to mediate their actions. The fundamental purpose of the state is to use its power to further its interests while containing the power of other states that might prevent this from happening.

Idealism
A philosophical position that argues that human beings are basically good. War can be prevented when the proper international institutions are created. States can cooperate to solve problems and improve the existing world order under the right institutions.

where theory can help. In the last section of this chapter we present three basic approaches to the study of international relations. We start by providing a brief description of each approach, followed by an overview of the international relations theories these approaches have generated.

How Can I Make Sense of the Changes in the World?

Whenever you use a theory, you will find it is rooted in assumptions about human behavior and the way humans interact with the world (see Figure 1.2). A group of those assumptions is called a world view or paradigm. The paradigm is the framework from within which we derive theories about the natural and the man-made world.

Three Paradigms

In this section, we discuss three paradigms that underlie theory building in international relations today and that help us understand the international world: **political realism, idealism,** and the **ecological paradigm.** The three paradigms differ dramatically from each other. You must read and decide which world view better suits your outlook on life. Keep in mind that each can offer useful insights into how the world works. Let's look first at political realism.

Political Realism   This paradigm is based on the twin assumptions that human beings are imperfect and that they have an innate desire for power. Realists thus like to theorize about the uses of power, the consequences of power, and the containment of power. The realist approach to international affairs traces its origins back to the ancient Greek historian Thucydides, who wrote what was probably the first systematic analysis of war, entitled *History of the Peloponnesian War.* The work recounted the story of the thirty-year war between the Greek city state of Athens and its great rival, Sparta (421–404 B.C.). In a celebrated passage, Thucydides has the Athenian Assembly debate the fate of a rebel colony, Mytilene. The angry response of the Athenian army to the revolt was to order the whole colony put to death. The Athenian citizens protested that order, and so a popular assembly was called. Using arguments based on political realism, the ruler of Athens, Cleon, urged that the punishment be carried out and the colony be put to death. He claimed that the rebels had known what they were doing and had planned

Theories Help Us To
• Describe things
• Explain things
• Make predictions
• Make policy recommendations

FIGURE 1.2
Theories

the whole thing. Here are three of Cleon's arguments. Each of them, and particularly the last one, reflects a realist point of view.

"One only forgives actions that are not deliberate," (i.e., we should not feel pity for them).

"A sense of decency is only felt towards those who will be our friends in the future," (i.e., give these people what they deserve).

"It is a general rule of human nature that people despise those who treat them well, and look up to those who make no concessions."[5]

One of the earliest proponents of realism in Asia was Kautilya, an adviser and prime minister to the unifier of India and the founder of the Maurya Empire, Chandragupta Maurya (*ca.* 324 B.C.). Kautilya's contribution to the Indian wisdom of his day was his thoughts on the accumulation and exercise of power in a book entitled *Arthashastra,* or "The Science of Material Gain." Some idea of the practicality and realism with which Kautilya saw the role of the king in Maurya society may be gained by the following quote from his work:

> [The king] who does not protect his people or upsets the social order wields his royal scepter in vain. It is power and power alone which, only when exercised by the king with impartiality and in proportion to guilt, either over his son or his enemy, maintains both this world and the next.[6]

From Kautilya the realist path leads to Niccolo Machiavelli (b.1469) and his famous work of advice, *The Prince,* to the ruling prince of Florence, Caesare Borgia. Machiavelli wrote of the realities of state power: "It is better for a prince to be feared than loved," but a wise ruler will take care not to be hated. His central idea was that only "the Prince," the state itself, can be the judge of what is right and wrong in the exercise of state power. Thomas Hobbes (1588–1679), an adviser to another prince—Charles II, Prince of Wales—set forth his realist approach in his treatise on government, entitled *Leviathan, or the Matter, Form and Power of a Commonwealth.* Hobbes's use of the Hebrew word *leviathan,* or sea monster, to connote the reality of state power over its citizens, gave the word a very bad connotation. When we speak of a leviathan state today, we are probably referring to an authoritarian state with a huge bureaucracy to enforce its rule.

Political realism has become synonymous with the practices of Otto von Bismarck, the German prime minister who engineered the unification of modern Germany in 1870. Bismarck in fact coined the term **realpolitik** (real politics) to characterize his foreign policy. Bismarck was a leading supporter of the balance of power principle and did much to build Germany's military so that Germany quickly became a leading European power challenging Great Britain's supremacy.

In the United States, Hans Morgenthau probably made the largest contribution to the development of American political realism after the Second World War. Morgenthau argued that events that occurred between the two world wars, as well as World War II itself, demonstrated that human beings did not come into this world inherently good. They were capable of both good and bad, but the drive for power

Ecological Paradigm
The approach to international relations that assumes that the world of humans cannot be studied apart from its natural environmental contact, and that sees the human world as a subset of the global ecosystem. Central to this paradigm is the view that planet Earth with its surrounding atmosphere represents a finite ecosystem.

Realpolitik
A term coined by the German Chancellor of the nineteenth century, Otto Von Bismarck, to describe his foreign policy for Germany; namely, the building up of Germany's military to make Germany one of the leading European powers, rivaling Great Britain.

The Father of Modern Realism: Hans J. Morgenthau (1904–1977), the leading proponent of realism in America after the Second World War and author of *Politics Among Nations*.

Mutually Assured Destruction (MAD) In the context of the rivalry between the United States and the Soviet Union, both sides were deterred from attacking each other because they believed that the destruction of both countries would be assured if one of them initiated a nuclear attack upon the other.

To find out more about realism and idealism, go to **www.ablongman.com/duncan**.

was innate and instinctive. War was thus a certainty. Government and individuals must deal with the imperfections and devise their actions and responses in the international world based on the worst case scenario. The central event in Morgenthau's life was the onset of the Cold War between the United States and the USSR. If the United States wanted to keep out of a hot war with the USSR, he argued, the United States had to have a superb military and be dedicated to anticommunism.

Realists thus emphasized the primacy of foreign policy over domestic policy, the importance of a strong military force and cutting-edge military technology, and the centrality of national interest. The major player in the international arena was the state. States operate on an international stage where anarchy rules. With no higher power to constrain their behavior, states struggle to increase their power and prestige at the expense of other states. Where idealists argued that we should do away with nuclear bombs because they present a hazard to humanity, realists argued that the only way to keep power-hungry states like the USSR from attacking was through the building of a nuclear arsenal on each side that guaranteed the other, **mutually assured destruction (MAD).**

Many analysts called themselves realists but did not accept all the policy implications of *realpolitik*. New subdisciplines of international relations came into being that sought to maintain what many believed was a more objective approach. Primary among these were foreign policy analysis, game theory analysis, and decision-making theory. Each of these theories builds upon the central tenet of realism, namely that human beings are imperfect in an imperfect world. In an international arena characterized by anarchy, in any and all situations the state will base its action on its national interest rather than on an altruistic fantasy of a better world.

Idealism   Idealism is the second major approach to International Relations. Idealists differ from realists in that they ask what the world could or ought to be and how to get there. In contrast to realists, they believe that human beings are basically good. Therefore, institutions must be developed that will enable them to be the best they can be. At World War I's end (1918), the prewar balance of power system based on *realpolitik* came under sharp attack. Far from preventing war, the two alliances made prior to the war had contributed to starting it. Moreover, the treaties between the alliances were made in secret and kept secret despite the fact that they obliged the contracting parties to go to war if one of the treaty signatories was attacked. When war came, it was a complete surprise to the ordinary citizen, who had not been formally consulted in the declaration of war and knew nothing about the secret treaty obligating his country to fight.

On the eve of the Versailles Peace Conference that distributed the spoils of World War I, American President Woodrow Wilson proclaimed a new vision of the world—his famous fourteen points. These ideas came to be known as *idealism*. The central tenet was that war could be prevented. It was not inevitable if the proper international institutions were created. Rather than the balance of power keeping nations from war, nations would join a League of Nations dedicated to collective security, expressed by the phrase "an attack against one is an attack against all." The League would operate on the principles of international law, would provide a forum for discussion to prevent war, and would threaten potential aggressors by collective military action.

World War II demonstrated that neither international law nor the League of Nations was capable of preventing war. Still, idealists were not disheartened. Human beings may be imperfect, they asserted, but they are perfectible. The League was a badly conceived institution, they argued. It was open only to democratic nations, and unfortunately, the largest democratic nation, the United States, had not joined. After the war, idealists rallied around the formation of a new international organization, the United Nations. This time, membership was open to any duly recognized state, and the United States not only took the lead in the UN's organization, but was one of its founding members. Although some may argue the point, other international institutions and agreements formed after World War II, including the International Monetary Fund (IMF) and the General Agreement on Tariffs and Trades (GATT), owe their founding to the analogous liberal conviction that cooperation can be achieved in the economic sphere and is a rational economic alternative to bankrupting nations and starting trade wars. (The IMF and GATT are discussed in detail in Chapter 11.)

Idealists share the conviction that altruism is as fundamental to the human condition as competition and rivalry. Human beings through the centuries have understood the benefit of cooperation to minimize risks and maximize benefits for all the participants.[7] This understanding, in fact, is what pushes human society to evolve and change. Governments and states can and should work together to develop policies and strategies promoting a more just world order, compassion for the less fortunate, and concern for basic human values because that's the only way forward to the future.

A common concern of many idealists has been the horror of modern war. If the two world wars were terrible in general, the dropping of the atomic bombs on Hiroshima and Nagasaki was especially horrific. Idealists were fierce critics of nuclear war and the nuclear buildup between the United States and the USSR. Throughout the second half of the twentieth century, idealists fought for more international cooperation, more international regulation, and the value of multinational treaties such as the Nuclear Non-Proliferation Treaty and the Montreal Protocol, which limits the emission of chlorofluorocarbons into the atmosphere. You will find idealists to be active members of peace movements, women's movements, and environmental and human rights movements.

Today many idealists center their hopes for a cooperative future on the extraordinary increase in the number of international treaties that have been signed and ratified by the world's governments. These treaties cover a wide range of subjects. Generally, they outline some kind of procedure that the treaty signatories agree to follow. The procedure that is born of a treaty is termed an international **regime.** International Relations specialist Oran Young was the first to look at regime formation resulting from environmental treaties and to ask how we could determine whether a regime would successfully complete or follow the process demanded of it by its treaty. The existence of international regimes challenges the realist assumption that only the struggle for power can characterize international relations. Each state may be out for itself. But the existence of regimes indicates that cooperation between states without coercion from a supranational global authority is not only possible but potentially effective in resolving or promoting international concerns.

The Ecological Paradigm   The third approach to International Relations is the ecological paradigm. It dates only from the late 1970s and was developed by

Regime
The process or procedure that is born of a treaty that the treaty signatories agree to follow. The treaty usually sets up a goal, a process by which to reach the goal, a time line and some kind of permanent organizational framework to monitor progress.

THE VIEW FROM Earth

Pirages's Five Capitals and Three Pillars of Sustainability

Sustainability: community control and prudent use of five types of capital supported by what Pirages calls "the three pillars of sustainability."

The Five Types of Capital

1. *Nature's capital.* Natural resources.
2. *Human capital.* People and the body of knowledge they contribute to community and production.
3. *Human-created capital.* Products and technologies created by humans.
4. *Social capital.* Civic trust and civic involvement in a place; participation in the political life of a particular community, your community, newspaper readership, membership in associations from sports clubs to Lions Club, from unions to choral societies. Social capital defines where you are and the importance of that place to you.

5. *Cultural capital.* A community's culture, including factors that provide it with the means and adaptations to deal with the natural environment and modify it, such as creation myths and dreams of a better world.

The Three Pillars of Sustainability

1. *Economic security.* The control that individuals have over their own economic lives and the degree to which they are capable of shielding themselves from external economic shocks.
2. *Ecological integrity.* Living in harmony with natural systems: clean air; water and land use that meets human needs and maintains the essential elements of the ecosystem.
3. *Democracy.* Citizen participation in community decision making. The three pillars are created and supported by the five forms of capital.[8]

---

political scientists Herman Daly and Dennis Pirages along with many others. The element that differentiates the ecological paradigm from any variant of idealism or realism is its insistence that the world of humans cannot be studied apart from its natural environmental context. The human world in fact is a subset of the global ecosystem; humanity survives or disappears according to its ability to adapt to the global ecosystem. Central to this approach is the realization that planet Earth and its surrounding atmosphere are a finite ecosystem. Most important, the planet possesses finite resources. No amount of money can substitute for the exhaustion of these resources. If humankind is to continue its existence, it must conduct its global transactions in such a way as to sustain or build up the ecosystem and not destroy it.

Sustainable Development

In the interests of its own survival, the human race must not undertake any economic development that leaves a larger footprint on the environment than the ecosystem can successfully accommodate without breaking down. What this concept means in practice is still being worked out.

The buzzword for the ecological paradigm approach is **sustainable development** (see box The View from Earth: Pirage's Five Capitals and Three Pillars of Sustainability). Sustainable development means that, in the interests of its own survival, the human species must not leave a larger footprint on the environment than the ecosystem can successfully accommodate without breaking down. If we overgraze our fields, erode our farmlands, cut down out forests, and use up and pollute our water, our species will disappear from the face of the planet. We will become an historical has-been like the dinosaurs.

In 1988, former president of the Soviet Union Mikhail Gorbachev was the first world leader to put sustainable development at the top of the global political agenda. But it will take some time before every world actor recognizes the need for sustainable development. Many pay lip service to the idea at election time and conveniently forget it until the next vote.

In 1998, Hurricane Mitch brought torrents of rain down on the Central American countries of Honduras and Nicaragua. In the resulting floods and horrendous mudslides, some ten thousand people died. One of the principal reasons that the tragedy was so large was the rapid deforestation occurring in both countries. Another was the pressure of the poor peasants to till marginal land, because the good land had all been dedicated to export agriculture. Deforestation and tilling poor land caused soil erosion and huge bare spots on the hillsides. Torrential rains quickly turned these areas into mudslides. The United States sent millions of dollars in aid to assist the stricken countries. Huge rains in 2002 brought similarly catastrophic flooding to the Yangtze River valley in China, killing thousands and putting millions out of their homes.

Similar tragedies might be avoided in the future if the international community presses forward in its development of sustainable forestry programs and prevails on the nations of the world to agree to them.

Figure 1.3 shows how much of the original forests, termed *frontier forests,* that covered the earth at the dawn of the human race has been cut down. In some places the forest has grown back; however, it is not the original forest, but a secondary or *nonfrontier forest.* In other areas the forests have completely disappeared. Particularly in Southeast Asia, the Middle East, and Central America, population pressures have speeded up the cutting down of trees to plant food crops and thereby have increased the risk of more severe natural disasters. Hurricanes, floods, typhoons, and ice storms are natural phenomena. They become human tragedy when the **anthropogenic,** or human-created, impact exceeds the **carrying capacity**[9] of the at-risk ecosystem, causing the ecosystem to collapse.

In Central Asia improperly planned and executed irrigation resulted in the drying up and salting of the Aral Sea—the main freshwater source in the region. The damage occurred because fertilizers and pesticides flowed down the irrigation canals and were dumped into the shrinking sea, where the wind picked up the particles and blew them back on the newly created desert where the sea used to be. As the sea shrank and the fish died, the fishing industry collapsed and the fish processing plants closed. Out of work, their homes high on the sand, and without drinkable water, thousands of people were forced to migrate. The then Soviet government had known the sea would shrink and could have made contingency plans to do something about it, but the depth and breadth of the consequences came as a huge surprise.

In China the government is continuing to build the Three Gorges Dam on the Yangtze River. This huge dam will flood millions of acres of fields, towns, and cities. Two million people have been resettled and more are waiting for new homes. The government says the dam will be a great energy generator, but the long-term human and environmental price will probably outweigh any immediate energy benefits.[10] We talk more about the Three Gorges Dam project in Chapters 3 and 13.

The proliferation of man-made natural disasters such as these in the twentieth century suggests that the ecological paradigm may well take center stage in the international politics of the twenty-first century.

How do these basic paradigms about the human condition influence the theories that one adopts to explain the international world? Throughout this book we will discuss a variety of global events and issues based on one or more of these paradigms. Table 1.2 sets out these three paradigms and their assumptions, and indicates the political theories that have developed from them.

Anthropogenic
Caused by humans or originating from human actions.

Carrying Capacity
A natural ecosystem is determined by its maximum sustainable yield and this yield is the products of the size of the ecosystem and its ability to regenerate itself.

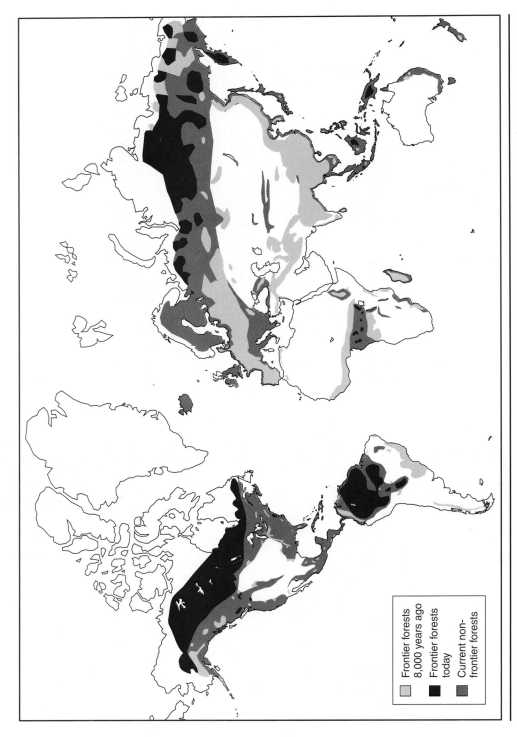

FIGURE 1.3

Eight Thousand Years of Changes in the Earth's Forest Cover: The map compares areas of the planet covered by forests 8000 years ago and in 1998. Which continent has lost the most of its original forests?

SOURCE: World Resources Institute, Forest Initiative Project (http://www.wri.org/ffi/maps/).

Legend:
- Frontier forests 8,000 years ago
- Frontier forests today
- Current non-frontier forests

The Three Gorges Dam on the Yangtze River, China: Research is showing that dams may frequently do more harm than good. On the positive side, they generate electricity from falling water, one of the cleanest ways to generate power. On the negative side, they store water in huge reservoirs, completely changing a river's ecology. Environmentalists all over the world have been protesting the construction of huge hydroelectric projects like this one in China that will be discussed in more detail in Chapters 3 and 13.

TABLE 1.2   International Relations Paradigms, Theories, and Assumptions

Parent Paradigm	Assumptions	Theories Derived from Assumptions
Realism:	Human beings are imperfect. The international world is a jungle characterized by an anarchic struggle for survival and power. War is inevitable. The only thing that stops power is power.	Balance of power Hegemonic stability Neorealism, structural

Idealism:	Utopianism: the world is getting better and better.
	Human beings are perfectible.
	Caring and compassion are innate.
	We can cooperate to build a better world.
	We must restructure flawed institutions and create good.
		Marxism
		  Imperialism
		  Dependency Theories
		Liberalism
		  Collective security
		  Regime theory
		  Neoliberalism

Ecological paradigm:	Human world is a subset of global ecosystem. Resources on Earth are finite. Humans cannot exceed an ecosystem's carrying capacity or that system will collapse. We need sustainable development.	Deep ecology (Arne Naess) Ecofeminism Ecojustice

Theories from Paradigms

In this section, we discuss three bodies of theory derived from the three paradigms previously discussed. In each section we present a brief summary of the theoretical approach and then discuss the most salient of the modern theories derived from the approach. In presenting the realist and ecological paradigms, we identify three modern theories that have evolved from the general approach. There are two main branches of the idealist paradigm—Marxism and Liberalism. From the Marxist branch have sprung two important theories and from the liberal branch, we identify three. To help you keep track of the different theories, refer to the summary Table 1.2.

Realism

Realism's central concerns are about war, peace, and security. War may be inevitable, the theory goes, but we can limit the desire of our enemy to wage war by appropriate military preparedness and by diplomatic maneuvers to redirect that country's interest. Meanwhile, we will use diplomacy as long as it promotes our state interest but will be ready for war if diplomacy fails. In the words of the nineteenth century German general Karl von Clausewitz, "War is the continuation of politics by other means."[11] In every international interaction, the gains of one state come as a loss to another.

Three modern theories that derive from the realist perspective are the **balance of power theory, hegemonic stability theory,** and **neorealism** or structural realism.

Balance of Power Theory According to this realist theory, war is avoided by a condition of equilibrium between the main players in the potential war. Just as we can find out a baby's weight by placing him or her on one side of a scale and adding increments of pounds or kilos to the other side of the balance, so we can measure global or regional equilibrium by weighing the power attributes (such as military and economic potential, the characteristics of a state's leadership, or the extent of international involvement) of one state or a set of states against the power attributes of a second state or set of states. If the power balance goes out of equilibrium, war will break out.

Balance of power theory dominated diplomatic and international military and economic relations throughout the nineteenth century. Using this theory, U.S. Admiral Alfred Mahan and Sir Halford MacKinder argued in the late nineteenth century that power was determined by strategic and geopolitical factors. Mahan and MacKinder's theories gave rise to the discipline of geopolitics, a subdiscipline of international relations that we discuss in Chapter 7. The theory was also used to justify the alliances between both the Allied and Axis powers in World War I (1914–1917). According to this theory, World War I was caused by a breakdown in the rough equality between the Axis powers and the Allies.

Today balance of power theory may not seem very useful, since the United States is now the sole superpower in the international system. However, many scholars still value it. American historian Paul Kennedy, for example, wrote a book in which he asked whether the United States is a declining power and how that decline might affect international power relations. Balance of power theory is also useful in investigating regional conflict, such as the United States led invasion of Iraq, or the difficulties of finding a solution to the century-old Israeli-Palestinian conflict. The balance of power within a region can determine which way a conflict will be resolved. Various indexes of a state's power are described further in Chapter 3.

Balance of Power Theory
Posits that peace and security are best preserved by a state of equilibrium between the major players in a potential war.

Hegemonic Stability Theory
A theory that argues that economic and/or political stability in the world or region is best achieved in the presence of a strong state power, termed a hegemon or leader to monitor and oversee the interactions of the other states.

Neorealism
An approach to international relations developed by Kenneth N. Waltz, which argues that while humans may be selfish by nature and driven by a lust for power, power is not the true end. States really pursue power in order to survive. The end goal is national survival.

Hegemonic Stability Theory   This second theory in the realist paradigm argues that economic and/or political stability in the world or in a region requires a strong power, termed a ***hegemon,*** from the Greek word for leader. Why were the Asian countries of Japan, Korea, and Taiwan able to industrialize as rapidly as they did? Hegemonic stability theory says that they were able to do so because there was a hegemon (the United States) in the region that provided the military and economic security necessary for these states to develop. Moreover, the United States was strong enough economically to keep its markets open to the products of the Asian countries, which was something a weaker power could not do.

On an entirely different plane, suppose we want to investigate why some international treaties produce regimes (organizations and regulations) that are followed and upheld, while others do not. In several cases it has turned out that the presence of a hegemon provided the necessary stability to implement the regime. For example, until the United States decided to participate, peace keeping in the war-torn country of Bosnia in the mid-1990s was virtually impossible. The same could be said for Kosovo in 1999. However, in other cases, the subject to be regulated by treaty seemed to be the rallying point for agreement rather than the influence of a hegemon. One example is the 1973 multilateral agreement on the Conservation of Polar Bears between the United States, the then Soviet Union,[12] Norway, Denmark (for Greenland), and Canada. The polar bear is a symbol of the Arctic, and every signatory to the agreement wanted to cooperate to preserve this much-loved species. In still other conservation treaties, agreement between lesser but more interested powers seemed to provide sufficient impetus for adherence. In general, however, the data tend to show that the participation of a hegemon is critical to treaty implementation.

Neorealism   This third and final theory based on the paradigm of political realism was first formalized by U.S. political scientist Kenneth N. Waltz in his 1979 book *The Theory of International Politics.* Waltz agrees with realism that people are by nature selfish, that they are driven by a lust for power, and that international relations is, to quote Hobbes, "a war of all against all." But Waltz no longer considers power an end in itself. States, in his view, pursue power for the sake of survival. For Waltz the single most important property of the international system is the absence of central governing institutions. In general, neorealists agree with the following points:

- States remain the primary actors on the world stage. However, the main goal of all states is not power but survival in a dog-eat-dog environment.
- The primary difference between states is not different goals but their differing capabilities to influence the course of international events.
- The unequal distribution of capabilities defines the structure of the international system and shapes the ways states interact with one another. We will talk more about this point in Chapter 2.

Neorealists pay little attention to what is going on inside states. For example, to them it is not important whether states are democratic or dictatorial. Regardless of internal beliefs and ideologies, the foreign policies of all states are, in their view, driven by the same systemic factors; they are so many "billiard balls" obeying the same laws of political geometry and physics.[13] Because the structure of the international system is defined by the capabilities of states, neorealists are pessimistic about achieving international cooperation and a world of peace and justice. The anarchic structure of the system compels states to worry about their relative position in the distribution of power and to try at all times to compete to improve or even just

To learn more about how the balance of power theory works, go to **www.ablongman.com/ duncan**.

Hegemon or **Hegemonic State** A country with overwhelming military, political, and economic power, and with the ability to write and enforce the rules of the international system. A powerful state in a region that tries to use its military or economic power to dominate countries in the region.

maintain that position. Driving that competition is concern for what other states may do, lack of trust in their future intentions, and fear of dependence on one or more states. For the neorealists, permanent insecurity is the major impediment to global cooperation, and it is built right into the anarchic international system, whether we admit it or not.

Political realism has its gloomy moments. Its predictions for the future are not hopeful. Realists force us to take a hard look at reality as they see it. That reality is an anarchic world where, in the absence of a central authority or world government, states compete with one another in a fierce and brutal struggle for survival. The only way to contain power is with power. During the Cold War, the *realpolitik* of mutually assured destruction prevented nuclear war. In the post–Cold War world, neorealists argue that the attacks of September 11, 2001, proved without a doubt that the insecurity brought about by the changed landscape of states, the globalization of the economy, terrorism, and regional conflict demand that the state maintain its vigilance to look out for Number One. The United States war in Iraq may be considered a neorealist response to reduce that insecurity.

Idealism

Idealists are nowhere near as gloomy about international cooperation. The assumptions that altruism is innate and that the world is perfectible if we can only get the institutions right lead us to several important theories in international relations. The two great transforming ideologies of the twentieth century, **Marxism** and **liberalism,** stem from an essentially idealist view of the world.

Many scholars would not place Marxism in the idealist camp. However, Karl Marx is an idealist in the sense that he is a utopian. Essentially, you have the liberal and utopian branches of idealism. Both branches believe that change is for the better, and that humankind is perfectible. Both ask, What is wrong with human society? How can it be improved? Both are rooted in the belief that human beings can be perfected through education and by changing institutions and their relationships to one another. Both believe that the right structuring of institutions liberates the altruism in human beings, enabling them to cooperate in building a better world free of greed and envy. Marx himself was convinced that socialism would be the fulfillment of political liberalism. However, his positing of immutable laws of historical development and the adoption of his theories as a recipe for revolutionary action promoted highly dogmatic interpretations of his philosophy among his followers.[14] We will now look more closely at Marx's theory.

Marxism   History, according to Marxist theory, is a one-way street from the past into the utopian future. As we move from the past to the present, we see that certain thresholds in human experience mark turning points, or decisive changes, to a different form of socioeconomic and political organization. The historic instrument of these changes was what Marx called the class struggle. Every major socioeconomic change in the history of humankind, Marx said, occurred as a consequence of the struggle between the two most important socioeconomic groups in that period of time: the property-owning class that controlled the key economic assets and made all the rules (the haves), and the propertyless class that owned none of the assets (the have-nots) and worked for and obeyed the ruling class.

Marx argued that the changes were typically violent because they involved real struggle between the haves and the have-nots. But the changes were always a

Marxism
The theory that history is a one-way street from the past into the future. As history progresses, we find that there have been thresholds in human experience that mark a turning point in terms of socioeconomic and political organization. These changes are always a change forward and indicate a progressive betterment of the human condition. The engine driving the change is the class struggle—the tension between the class that possesses the means of production in a given society and the class that works for the ruling class. Marx identified the human race as having gone through prehistoric society, slave-holding society, feudal society, capitalist society. The end condition of human society was the classless society of communism.

Liberalism
A philosophical approach that argues that human nature is basically altruistic and that human altruism enables us to cooperate. In the international arena, compassion and caring for the welfare of others should motivate state actions. War is not a certainty because violence and selfishness are not the only part of the human condition but rather the result of flawed institutions. In addition, all wars are a matter of collective concern.

The Fathers of Communism: *Karl Marx (left) wrote his* Communist Manifesto *in 1848 and started two movements to improve the conditions of the working class: socialism and communism. Vladimir Ilych Lenin (right), the leader of the Russian Revolution of 1917 and first communist ruler of the Soviet Union, introduced the theory of imperialism into Marxist thinking.*

change forward and indicated a progressive betterment of the human condition. Communism for Marx was the end-state of human social organization. Under communism, he asserted, all exploitation would cease; there would be no rich or poor and no class divisions, and the state would no longer possess coercive and oppressive authority. All humankind would live in harmony, according to the principle, "From each according to his ability, to each according to his need."[15]

The ideas of Marx inspired the democratic socialist democracies in Western Europe and the communist regimes in Eastern Europe, Eurasia, and Asia. A central assumption of communist regimes is that the state can create a "new man" (or woman) who will have all the best qualities. To achieve these goals, capitalism, with its emphasis on individual and private gain, must be abolished and a new system of state ownership of the economy established. Once the revolution has been achieved, the state can then focus its vast powers on the education of the new person and provide work in the new working environment no longer governed by the profit motive but by the worker's enthusiasm for work.

Imperialism   The application of Marxism or neo-Marxism to the international arena produced two corollary theories. The first was developed by the first leader of the Soviet Union, Vladimir Ilych Lenin. Lenin used the term **imperialism** to describe the division of the nineteenth-century world by the European powers into national colonial empires for each state. Imperialism, he said, was the highest stage of capitalism. Imperialism involved the movement of domestic capital abroad in search of cheap raw materials, cheap labor, and new markets that the mother country no longer, or never, possessed. The spread of capitalism and the industrial revolution was supported and heavily promoted by the so-called capitalist states of Europe, which were also the prime movers in imperialism. Lenin was quick to see the disruption of traditional lifestyles brought about by the transfer of the industrial system to the colonies. The class struggle that Marx had identified between worker and capitalist in one country, Lenin saw transferred to the international world. The capital-exporting countries were the imperialists, and the peoples of the colonial countries were the proletariat.

Imperialism
A theory developed by Vladimir I. Lenin, who argued that it was the highest stage of capitalism (see *Marxism*). Under imperialism, national states driven by economic success and the need for more and more raw materials, acquired colonies that they proceeded to exploit for cheap labor and natural resources, and which they used as an expanded market where they could sell their goods.

Until the late 1980s, the Soviet Union and China based their foreign policies on antagonism to imperialism. They endorsed Lenin's view that the institution of private property inevitably led to wars and rivalry for power. Socialism, they believed, would bring the end of private property and thus open the door to peaceful international cooperation. Unfortunately, history proved otherwise. For years, the USSR and China conducted a foreign policy hostile to the world's industrialized countries, and to the United States in particular. For years as well, the Soviet and Chinese leaders each claimed that their country represented the leading edge of the march of the world toward communism. Interstate rivalry produced a mini-cold war for leadership of the so called "Socialist states" that at times broke out into hot wars along the Soviet-Chinese border.

In the new century, the word *imperialism* still resonates in the expansion of the U.S. and European transnational corporations' production, distribution, and retail facilities around the globe.

Dependency Theories   A second derivative of the Marxist branch of idealism is **dependency theories.** In the two decades following World War II, most of the colonies of the European powers became independent states and were admitted as members to the United Nations. The end of colonialism was a major event of the time. One of the big problems of the new states was how to develop their economies, prompting the elaboration of scenarios of how states could become industrialized as efficiently as possible. As time went on, many of the new states seemed to be growing economically, but they were not developing in the sense of becoming industrialized states. A new type of theory, *dependencia* or dependency, was born. The word comes from Spanish, because the concept evolved in Spanish-speaking South and Central America.

Dependency theorists use classifications similar to those of imperialism. They divide the world into the industrial states (core countries) and the developing states (periphery countries). And they also address questions such as, Why don't the developing states becoming industrialized? Why do they only remain sources of raw materials and cheap labor? Dependency theory says that developing states can never develop because they depend on the industrial states for capital and technology. Loans and capital investment come with strings attached. If a country wants a loan from the World Bank or the IMF, it must meet certain criteria in terms of banking and monetary practices and the privatization of industry and agriculture. Some advocates of this theory argue that the developing countries are now so dependent on the industrialized states that they will never become industrialized. Others argue that the only way for developing countries to develop their own economies and to become industrialized is to protect their industries from global competition. While dependency theories have fallen into disrepute, some scholars think they still offer a useful way of explaining poverty in Third World countries. Dependency theories are further examined in Chapter 12.[16]

Liberalism   The philosophy of liberalism derives directly from idealism. Consistent with the idealist approach, the core assumption is that the world is perfectible and that by choosing the right institutions, human beings have the altruism to make the world—if not perfect—at least a better place. In contrast to Marx, who saw the perfectibility of human institutions and human beings rooted in immutable historical laws, liberals emphasize the individual and the fundamental human ability to choose. The liberal argument may be summarized as follows: Human nature is basically good and, more important, altruistic; we care about others. These qualities make us perfectible. Through education we can learn to use our reason. We can learn to consider the whole of humankind and not just our little national or local

Dependency Theories
A set of related theories that have in common the belief that less developed countries can never develop because they are dependent upon the industrial states for capital and technology. An approach that argues that foreign investment in developing countries is a means to dominate and extract capital from weaker states.

problems. Liberals believe that government can create institutions that will train the citizen to greater tolerance and produce a society dedicated to social justice. One of the main goals of a liberal democracy is to provide universal education to all its citizens so that they can make rational choices regarding their leaders and the policies they would like to see adopted.

Participation in government, the liberals argue, further develops our reason. Democracy is the best and ultimate form of government because citizens elect representatives to make decisions for them based on their understanding of the candidate and the issues. The election process makes these officials accountable to their constituents and thus limits their power to act arbitrarily. The result is a more stable political system and a more prosperous economy. Democracy provides sufficient security to its citizens so that they can develop their capacity to care for others.

Liberals also assert that our natural altruism lies at the heart of international cooperation and trust. Since their citizens feel more secure, democratic states are less prone to make war on other states. Because of democracy's greater internal stability, trade prospers between democratic states, improving the standard of living for all. One part of the liberal reform program insists on the merits of free trade to replace the economic nationalism that liberals believe propelled Hitler's Germany into the Second World War.

Compassion and concern for the welfare of all should inform all actions taken on the global stage. One example of the world's compassion is the humanitarian aid given to states experiencing famine or natural disaster. Another example is the enormous outpouring of sympathy for the families of the victims of 9/11 and for the United States from people and governments all over the world.

In addition, according to liberalism, violence and selfishness result from flawed institutions rather than the human condition. Agreement between states in secret—called secret diplomacy—is one example of a flawed institution that can lead to war, as was the case with the First World War. Liberals believe that dictatorships are flawed institutions that promote violence and oppression, and thus they urge the promotion of democracy worldwide. The United States asserts its liberal philosophy when it calls states that have oppressive dictatorships, such as Iraq and North Korea, "rogue states," or states that are worthless and misbehaving.

Finally, liberals assert, war is not a certainty. It can be avoided by perfecting institutions designed to control violence. Thus, liberals are strong advocates of the United Nations, and they seek to extend and strengthen its activities in the world.

Collective Security   The UN action in Kuwait in 1992 provides a fine illustration of the relevance of **collective security,** our first offshoot of liberalism. Most liberals espouse this doctrine, which holds that all wars are a matter of collective concern. The two world wars of the twentieth century demonstrated that agreements between states are no guarantee against war. The best guarantee is when all cou__ries ascribe to the notion that "an attack against one is an attack against all." When Iraq invaded Kuwait in 1991, President Bush immediately called together the Security Council of the United Nations and secured a UN mandate to to drive Sadam Hussein's army out of Kuwait. The UN action against Iraq in 1992 may be viewed as a success story of collective action from the liberal point of view.

Regime Theory   A second derivative of liberalism is regime theory, which we discussed earlier. This theory assumes that international policy making can be organized in such a way as to promote cooperation. It is possible to devise treaties and international agreements that will set up a process or regime to implement the aims of the signatory parties, which the parties may actually carry out. Once the process is

Collective Security
A concept of world order maintaining that aggression could be deterred by promising overwhelming collective retaliation by the combined power of the world's states against any community member that pursued aggression. In other words, an attack against one is an attack against all. Collective security first took form in the League of Nations—which the United States refused to join—immediately following World War I.

initiated, the states can move forward towards the implementation goal of the treaty by making little modifications one at a time over an extended period of time. For example, the 1973 Polar Bear Treaty mentioned previously provides for specific action by the signatory states, a joint research program, and periodic consultation. The U.S.-Russian extension of that treaty in 2000 goes further in establishing a joint commission to supervise and coordinate activities. Regime theorists believe that if states can agree on a general direction of action, subsequent meetings and consultations can refine and direct that action into increasing cooperation between states.

Neoliberalism   A third offshoot of idealism/liberalism is **neoliberalism.** Neoliberalism developed as a response to what liberals saw as the failure of both realism and liberalism. Both proved unable to predict or explain the peaceful downfall of the Soviet Union. More significant, both failed to predict the enormous transformation of global society that occurred in the twentieth century and the emergence of global problems, such as environmental degradation, the AIDS epidemic, mass migrations, population growth, and failed economic development. The neoliberals proposed a new look at liberalism based on the following assumptions:

- Progress in international relations can only be achieved through international cooperation.
- International institutions can help countries resolve their differences peacefully. This is one reason why neoliberals are sometimes called *neoliberal institutionalists.*
- The world may look chaotic, but it has patterns that may be found by studying the dynamics of international relationships.
- Peace and cooperation can be promoted if we focus on understanding the dynamics of the web of relationships and influences driving the international world, such as democratic government, free trade, international law, international organizations, collective security, arms control, and morally based decision making.

Some questions asked by neoliberals are, What kinds of processes promote cooperation? How can negotiations lead to a cooperative solution for all parties? What types of governments or institutions tend toward cooperation rather than isolationism? What are the elements of conflict resolution? In short, neoliberalism is more than just theory. An understanding of negotiation and conflict resolution is very relevant to diplomats such as those seeking to end the Israeli-Palestinian conflict, to find peace in Kashmir, or to build a nation in Afghanistan.

If we look at the theories derived from idealist assumptions, we can see that essentially they all aim to transform the world in some way—to make it better. They provide a theoretical framework that explains how and why the world is badly organized and how and why reforming or modifying the appropriate institutions will bring the desired world harmony.

On the negative side, both Marxism and liberalism have a strong component of utopianism. The end goal for both is a perfect social system where everyone lives in harmony with everyone else. History suggests that that goal will not be achieved anytime soon.

Ecological Paradigm

The main tenet of the ecological approach is that you cannot separate humankind from nature either in theory or in fact. Humankind sprang from nature and depends on nature for survival and sustenance. From a tiny group, homo sapiens gradually

---

Neoliberalism

A philosophical position that argues that progress in international relations can only be achieved through international cooperation. Cooperation is a dynamic rather than a static process. By focusing on understanding the dynamics of the web of relationships driving the international system, states and other international actors can effectively use the international institutions spawned by the system to promote peace and cooperation.

To find more information on the ecological paradigm, go to **www.ablongman.com/ duncan**.

spread out over the globe until the human species dominated the earth. From the ecological approach, then, any theory of global politics that does not put Earth first underestimates interdependence between humankind and planet Earth. From this perspective, three very new theories have emerged; we turn to them next.

Deep Ecology   **Deep ecology** in many ways is more a philosophy than a theory in international relations. Deep ecology developed out of the thinking of Norwegian environmentalist and philosopher Arne Naess.[17] Naess distinguishes between two groups of environmentalists. The first is what he terms the "shallow" environmentalists, concerned about the environment for what it can do for human beings in terms of quality of life and resources. The second are those who are "deeply" concerned about ecological principles: complexity, diversity, and symbiosis, and the way these relate human life to all things on the planet. In the deep ecologist's view, the environment has its own value, independent of human needs. Human beings need to go back to their primordial relationship with nature and see nature as a web of interdependent beings that is wonderful in and of itself. In other words, we must treat nature reverently.

In the United States, Henry Thoreau and John Muir could be considered the forefathers of deep ecology. The deep ecologist sees human beings in a living relationship with their environment. The environment has its own reasons for being. It is not just a hunting ground for raw materials and real estate development. Moreover, it speaks to each one of us and assigns us our identity. Modern society has lost this sense of identity. Many of us are indifferent to where we live. But to the Mohawk, the Huron, or the Navaho, a particular mountain or stream, or a particular lay of land, is sacred. A tribal member finds renewal by going back to the natural home revered by his ancestors. Deep ecology proposes to reconnect modern society to its natural home.

In international affairs, the deep ecologist tends to oppose large earth-moving human projects, such as dam construction, extensive logging, the paving over of swamp land for parking lots, or the destruction of habitat for agriculture or a new factory. You may find the deep ecologists active in international environmental NGOs but you could just as well find them sitting on a log next to a running brook, deep in communion with nature. Partly because of this principled opposition to what both the idealists and the realists call progress, the deep ecologist easily becomes the subject of ridicule or of ill-contained frustration.

Ecofeminism   A second offshoot of the ecological perspective, **ecofeminism** argues that women are more closely associated with the natural world than men because they are the baby bearers and thus actively participate in the renewal of the species. Men, the ecofeminist argues, have an instrumental attitude toward nature, asking questions such as What can nature do for me? Women, on the other hand, have a reverence and empathy for nature, containing within themselves the secrets of birth and regeneration. Ecofeminism holds that capitalism is the last and worst outgrowth of a patriarchal society. The division of labor that capitalism calls efficient separated men and women into two separate worlds, the world of paid work and the world at home. Men, with the aid of male-dominated modern science, rape the world in search of raw materials to satisfy their always hungry industrial machines. As a result, the world at the end of the twentieth century has lost most of its forests and biodiversity; and, the theory continues, if men are allowed to continue this process of industrialization, nothing will be left.

Deep Ecology
A world view that promotes a reverence for nature, a concern for ecological principles such as complexity, diversity, and symbiosis, and that sees human beings in a living relationship with their environment. The environment is not there for human use alone. We gain our identity from it. Deep ecology proposes to reconnect humankind with nature.

Ecofeminism
Argues that women are more closely associated with the natural world than men. Men have an instrumental attitude towards nature and ask, How can I use it? Women have a reverence and empathy for nature, since they contain within themselves the secrets of birth and regeneration.

Ecofeminists relate male domination of nature to male domination of women, arguing that the structure of domination is the same in both cases. Women and nature are considered instrumental to the achievement of male goals, be they pleasure or power, and are treated accordingly.

Some scholars dismiss ecofeminism as irrelevant. But ecofeminists are quick to point out that at the local level, where women are most active politically, women are in the forefront of environmental groups. Women organized the movement in India to save Indian tropical forests. Women were the first to draw attention to the bad environmental conditions of poor families in our major cities. The most vocal opponent of the high dam being built on the Yangtze River in China is a woman.[18] Women were also the principal protesters in Niagara Falls, New York, and maintained their vigilance until the U.S. government agreed to buy the homes contaminated by toxic waste dumped into Love Canal.

Ecofeminists, like the deep ecologists, emphasize the living relationship between humankind—especially women—and nature. They argue that the global environment will remain at risk as long as the international community continues its action-oriented primarily male view of it. For example, at the Fourth World Conference on Women in Beijing in 1995, women NGOs lobbied futilely with national delegates to include a phraseology guaranteeing indigenous peoples the right to benefit as much as the international drug companies from the scientific extraction of useful medicines from local herbs. Unfortunately, the wording never got into the final document. (See Chapter 10 for more details on the women's movement.)

Male ecologists argue that there is nothing special about women's relationship to nature and that males can also feel a special closeness to the natural world. The answer of the ecofeminists is that males who do develop an intimacy with nature are in essence discovering the women's world. They encourage more men to follow this path. In particular they would like to see the major international organizations give up their patriarchal emphasis on development and begin to assess its impact in terms of our place in nature and our spiritual need to connect with it.[19]

Ecojustice
Since environmental quality is not equally distributed around the world, there is a need to develop methodologies and procedures to address the environmental inequalities that are the result of lack of natural resources, poor location, and poverty.

Ecojustice   A third theory derived from the ecological paradigm is **ecojustice.** Ecojustice theory starts from the observation that environmental quality is not equally distributed around the world. Some environments are more desirable than others. Some environments, like the world's forests, belong to a few states but are essential to all humankind to protect our common atmosphere. The ecojustice movement started among working black women in Warren County, North Carolina, on land that had been predominately black since the time of slavery. The movement began when Warren County was selected to be the final burial site for over 32,000 cubic yards of soil contaminated with PCBs (polychlorinated biphenyls); Dollie Burwell demanded that the site be properly clean (see Historical Perspective box: The Origins of the Ecojustice Movement). The merging of race, poverty, and pollution in a single issue rapidly picked up followers all over the United States and around the world, most notably in Kenya, Nigeria, and Russia.

Today political scientists working in the environmental field have made ecojustice an important theoretical tool of analysis. Among the most active is Stephen D. Bullard, director of the Ecojustice Resource Center in Atlanta, Georgia. Ecojustice theory drives the argument of the developing nations that since today's industrial pollution was generated by the industrialized countries, those countries must therefore pay for the clean-up. At the UN Conference on Global Warming in Kyoto, Japan, in 1998, China and other developing countries refused to sign a treaty requiring them to limit emissions from the use of fossil fuels because they considered

HISTORICAL PERSPECTIVE

The Origins of the Ecojustice Movement

In 1981, Dollie Burwell organized black people in her community and demanded that the government pay for decontamination of the soil. In 1991, the First National People of Color Environmental Leadership Summit broadened the movement's focus beyond toxic waste concerns to include public health and safety issues.

The movement spread to Louisiana and Texas, where in 1992, ecojustice grass roots groups catapulted into national visibility over waste contamination issues in low rent, largely Hispanic residential areas, known as *colonias*, near El Paso on the Texan-Mexican border. Subsequent proof that federal money tended to be spent upgrading the environment in predominantly white neighborhoods across the United States led to an explosion of ecojustice groups all over the country and, in 1994, to the formation of an Office of Environmental Justice in the Environmental Protection Agency.

The ecojustice movement quickly spread all over the world, most notably to Kenya, Nigeria, and Russia. In Russia, woman lawyer Vera Mishenko organized an ecojustice legal group, *Ecojuris,* to publicize the inequity of pollution in Russia's major cities. The lawyers filed suit in a number of landmark cases that argued that the principal victims of industrial pollution were women and young children.

the treaty to be unfair. In China's view, the industrialized nations were eager to reach an international agreement on preventing global warming because they had achieved full development by polluting the planet in the past and paying nothing for the mess they had made. By contrast, if China cut back on the consumption of fossil fuels to the extent required by the treaty, the Chinese would be risking the whole course of their economic development.

A similar plea for ecojustice developed at the Earth Summit in Johannesburg, South Africa, in August of 2002. The delegates and NGO representatives from the industrialized world called for better assurances of sustainable development from the developing countries, placing the onus of environmental cleanup on Third World governments. The delegates from the developing states replayed the Chinese argument used at Kyoto. According to Indian Foreign Minister Mr. Yashwant Sinha, low levels of official development assistance from the international community, coupled with low capital investment by the international corporations and high import tariffs, made spending on the environment unaffordable for the developing countries. In his words, "the terms of trade are stacked in favour of the rich."[20] (We will discuss this issue more in Chapter 12.)

Unfortunately, Mr. Sinha's comments fell on deaf ears. The summit ended with no commitment by the industrialized countries for a radical increase in either official development assistance or capital investment to promote environmental remediation.

Ecojustice theory attempts to develop methodologies and procedures to address issues like these by analyzing the connections between poverty and environmental degradation. A leading ecojustice theorist, Andrew Szasz, found, for example, that "toxic victims are, typically, poor or working people of modest means. Their environmental problems are inseparable from their economic condition."[21] In Russia, ecojurists have documented connections between environmental degradation, the living conditions of low-paid workers, and high mortality rates. Critics argue that poverty and poor living conditions have always existed, so the ecojurists are simply reworking old history. However, in accordance with the environmental paradigm, ecojurists believe that justice in human society cannot be divorced from a search for a just distribution of environmental goods within that society. When large-scale agriculture or agribusiness occupies the best arable land in Central America, the great mass of the population is left to eke out a marginal existence on poorer soils. When European Union (EU) subsidies pay EU sugar beet growers more than double the going price on the world market, EU sugar can be dumped on the world market at a rock bottom price. How, ask the ecojurists, can a small sugar beet grower in South Africa beat that kind of competition? The connection between poverty and environmental degradation or scarcity of an environmental resource, such as water, leads to research into the contribution of the environment to social unrest within and between states. We will discuss ecojustice theory in more detail in Chapter 10.

The environmental paradigm is the newest arrival in international relations. Many texts on world politics do not mention it at all. After reading about ecotheories, you may very well ask, So what? Sure, the environment is important, but let's be real. It has nothing to do with power relations between states. The deep ecologist, ecofeminist, and ecojurist will reply, You think so? Then why do the industrialized states use their great wealth to build environmental showcases such as nature preserves, while 2 billion people in the world live on under two dollars a day in conditions of severe environmental degradation? Why does deforestation continue as floods increase in severity? Economic and military power derive from the production of wealth from the environment with human labor. Whose environment is polluted and whose hands create the products that the transnational companies sell and that consumers buy are matters of international economics and politics. It is far more palatable to pollute in a faraway place, unassociated with your family and friends, than to do it in your hometown. If you go into international business, you will learn that the bottom line that benefits your company materializes because production occurs in a land where environmental standards are low, and the people are desperately poor.

There is no good life, say the environmentalists, if the environment is destroyed. Citizens in the industrialized world are living the good life in a clean environment because they have transferred their pollution to the developing world. The industrialized states have not tried, and so far have shown little desire, to try sustainable development. To achieve sustainable development, the industrial states have to recognize the primary importance of the environment to all human society and not just a privileged few.

This chapter has presented three paradigms you can use to build your world view. Only you can decide whether you are a realist and gung ho for power, an idealist with the conviction that you can help make the world a better place, or an environmentalist, believing that the last best hope for human kind is planet Earth. This chapter has also suggested why the study of international relations is important to you. It's not just a subject for diplomats and experts. As a voter, a future player in the global economy, a future professional or businessperson, and as a consumer concerned about your health, your present and future life and lifestyle will be profoundly affected by international relations.

CHAPTER SUMMARY

Why Study International Relations?

The attacks of September 11, 2001, showed us the reality of the world today. It is a world torn by tension between the centralization forces of globalization and the decentralizing forces of ethnic and religious fanaticism.

Before 9/11, knowledge of international relations was important to you in making career choices, deciding where to live, and generally being a well-informed citizen.

After 9/11, world politics is worth studying more than ever to enable you to understand the increasing tension between globalization and fragmentation that underlie the tragedy of 9/11.

After 9/11, you need to study international relations because knowing just about the government of your country or other countries is not enough. You need to know how states are interrelated, which is precisely what international relations is all about.

The world of the twenty-first century is changing at a more rapid pace than at any other time in its history. You have to stay current and up to date in a world increasing in complexity.

What New Forces Are Shaping the Planet?

At least five new forces are shaping our planet:

- Postindustrial technology makes distances shorter and increases the speed of communication.
- Interdependence between nations is increasing as a result of the transnational character of new issues, such as the AIDS pandemic, terrorism, and global environmental degradation.
- The power of the traditional nation state is being progressively weakened as it finds itself vulnerable to events beyond its capability to control.
- Decentralizing tendencies have become stronger as ethnic and religious groups within states seek redress of alleged injustices or outright independence, fragmenting existing states.
- New citizen activism through mass access to information via the Internet has brought international events into our homes the moment they occur, giving them an immediacy and urgency they did not have before and that make people want to respond. The rise of the international NGOs has brought interest-group lobbying to international organizations, creating what has been called a "global civic society."

How Can I Make Sense of the Changes in the World?

Three basic paradigms clarify our assumptions about human behavior in the international arena. These paradigms enable to us generate theory about how states behave in international politics. We examine the paradigms first and then look at the theories.

- The realist paradigm holds that human nature is by definition imperfect. We all have an innate drive for power. National governments, therefore, should concentrate on promoting the national interest through a strong military to defend against aggression and a "what's in it for me" posture in the conduct of foreign policy.
- The idealist paradigm posits that human beings have an innate altruism that makes them perfectible. With the right institutions to guide them, individuals and states can learn to cooperate and prefer peace to war.
- The ecological paradigm posits human society as a subset of the natural environment. This environment has limits and we must learn what those limits are and accommodate our institutions to them if humankind is to survive.

Theories about international relations may be derived from each of these three paradigms:

- From the realist perspective, we derive the theories of the balance of power, hegemonic stability, and neorealism.
- From the idealist perspective come the theories of Marxism and liberalism (the two major theories of the past 150 years) and the more recent dependency theories, collective security, and neoliberalism.
- Within the ecological perspective, we find deep ecology, ecofeminism, and ecojustice.

In this chapter, we have presented the major trends in global politics and the paradigms that you can use as lenses through which to view and understand the trends. The world today is global. You need to know about it, for you feel its influence every day.

ENDNOTES

[1]The difference between a military and civilian court are nicely presented in table form in *The New York Times*, March 21, 2002, at *http://www.deathpenaltyinfo.org/Terr-MilChart.html*

[2]William Blake, "Jerusalem" from "Milton, A Poem in Two Books" (1804–1808), *The Portable Blake*, Alfred Kazin, ed (New York: The Viking Press, 1946), p. 412.

[3]William Wordsworth, in *The Oxford Book of English Verse*, ed. Sir Arthur Quiller-Couch (Oxford: Oxford University Press, 1952), p. 617.

[4]For more discussion see Ruth Benedict, *Race and Racism* (London: Routledge, 1942) or *Race, Science and Politics* (New York: The Viking Press, 1945). See also Thomas Sowell, *The Economics and Politics of Race: An International Perspective* (New York: Quill, 1983), pp. 15–19.

[5]Thucydides, *History of the Peloponnesian War*, trans. Rex Warner (New York: Penguin Book, 1981), pp. 212–217.

[6]Kautilya, Book 1, Chapter 19, *Kautilya's Arthashastra*, (2d ed., trans. R. Shamasastry (Mysore: Wesleyan Mission Press, 1923), *passim*. Scanned by Jerome S. Arkenberg, Cal. State Fullerton. The text has been modernized by Prof. Arkenberg, Fordham University. *http://www.fordham.edu/halsall/india/kautilya1.html*.

[7]For an exposition of this view, see Robert Wright, *Nonzero: The Logic of Human Destiny* (New York: Vintage Books, a Division of Random House, Inc., 2001), pp. 29–44.

[8]From Dennis Pirages, *Building Sustainable Societies* (Armonk, NY: M.E. Sharpe, 1996), pp. 43–48.

[9]The carrying capacity of a natural ecosystem "is determined by its maximum sustainable yield and this in turn is the products of its size and regenerative powers." Grasslands and forests in humid areas have greater capacities of regeneration and hence greater carrying capacities than have semi-arid regions. (Lester R. Brown, *The Twenty-Ninth Day* [New York: W.W. Norton & Co, 1978], p. 13).

[10]A crtique of the Three Gorges Project may be found in Margaret Barber and Grainne Ryder, eds., *Damming the Three Gorges: What Dam Builders Don't Want You to Know* (London and Toronto: Probe International: Earthscan Publications, 1990).

[11]As printed in *Dictionary of Quotations*, B. Bergen Evans, ed. (New York: Avenel Books, 1978), pp. 734–735.

[12]The United States and Russia signed a new bilateral treaty on the conservation of polar bears in 2000. The treaty updates the 1973 Agreement.

[13]Owen Harries, "Realism in a New Era," *Quadrant*, 39 (April 1995), p. 13.

[14]For a thoughtful discussion of Marxism and its relation to political liberalism, see George H. Sabine, *A History of Political Theory*, revised ed. (New York: Henry Holt and Company, 1958), pp. 751–756.

[15]Karl Marx, "Critique of the Gotha Program," *Marx & Engels, Basic Wirtings on Politics & Philosophy*, ed Lewis S. Feuer. Anchor Books (New York: Doubleday & Company, Inc, 1959), p. 119.

[16]Several good references for dependency theories are: Ankie Hoogvelt, *Globalisation and the Postcolonial World: The New Political Economy of Development*, (London: MacMillan, 1997). Ozay Mehmet, *Westernizing the Third World: The Eurocentricity of Economic Development Theories*, London: Routledge, 1995). Tim Allen and Allan Thomas, *Poverty and Development in the 1990s*, Oxford: Oxford University Press, 1992).

[17]Arne Naess's thoughts are best set forth in Arne Naess, *Ecology, Community and Lifestyle* (Cambridge: Cambridge University Press 1989).

[18]Dai Qing et al, *The River Dragon Has Come! The Three Gorges Dam and the Fate of China's Yangtze River and Its People* (Armonk, NY: M. E. Sharpe, 1998).

[19]Good discussions of ecofeminism may be found in Gaard, Greta, ed. 1993. *Ecofeminism: Women, Animals, Nature* (Philadelphia: Temple University Press, 1993); Carolyn Merchant, *Earthcare: Women and the Environment* (New York: Routledge, 1996); and Maria Mies and Vandana Shiva, *Ecofeminism* (London: Zed Books, 1993).

[20]From speech to the Johannesburg Summit by Mr. Yashwant Sinha, Indian Minister for External Affairs, September 4, 2002, downloaded from *http://www.un.org/events/wssd/statements/indiaE.htm*

[21]Andrew Szasz, *Ecopopulism: Toxic Waste and the Movement for Environmental Justice* (London and Minneapolis: Minneapolis University Press, 1994), p. 151.

CASE STUDY

Why Is Kashmir Important to You?

Chapter 1 was about the importance of international relations. As promised at the beginning of the chapter, here is a case study about a part of the world that is probably far removed from your daily life. It is about the fifty-year conflict between India and Pakistan over who owns Kashmir. You may know that the goat that gives the world its beautiful cashmere wool for scarves and sweaters comes from Kashmir and you may think that keeping that wool coming to the West is important to you to maintain your lifestyle. The case study will lead you further down the road to seeing why what happens in the foothills of the world's highest mountains is relevant to you.

Chapter 1 began by recalling the attacks of 9/11 and saying that this tragedy had highlighted the new forces that were shaping our planet, such as the new focus on technology, the interdependent and transnational character of the new issues, the increasing inability of the state to solve problems on its own, the increase in decentralizing tendencies and the new citizen activism. You will find all of these forces at work in this case study. Your task will be to identify these forces to put together the complex picture of what is happening in Kashmir and why that matters to you. You may then put on your liberal, realist, or ecological hat to find out which of those theoretical approaches is most useful in resolving the difficult problem of who owns or should own Kashmir. You will recall that theories help us to explain events and make policy recommendations.

The material for the case study is divided into two parts. The first part is a very brief explanation and analysis of the problem by Simon Jeffery and Mark Tran of the British newspaper *The Guardian*. The analysis will give you background of the situation and provide information on the global importance of the issue. The second part contains official government reactions to the Kashmiri elections by three of the states most interested in the elections' outcome, the United States, India, and Pakistan. Each of the statements reacts to media reports on the violence attending these elections in a different manner, providing good clues to the position of each state on the significance and validity of the elections. Note particularly the differences in the Indian and Pakistani positions.

KASHMIR

Would a Liberal, Realist, or Ecological Approach Be More Likely to Resolve the Tension There?

Part I

As tensions between India and Pakistan escalate in a dispute over the Kashmir region, Simon Jeffery and Mark Tran explain the history of the conflict.

What Is Happening?

By Simon Jeffery and Mark Tran

Tuesday, May 21, 2002
Tensions have risen in recent weeks after a raid on an army camp in Indian-controlled territory that New Delhi blamed on Pakistan-backed militants, just one attack in a 13-year insurgency in Kashmir.

Pakistan denies Indian allegations that it is waging a proxy war through jihadi groups (it says it simply offers "moral support" to them) but the two sides are lining up heavy artillery and a million men along a ceasefire line in what could be preparations for a conventional war.

Abdul Kader Jaffer, Pakistan's high commissioner in London, said today that the international community should be aware of the seriousness of the standoff between the two countries. India and Pakistan almost went to war in January this year after a suicide attack on the Indian parliament building the previous month, and also in 1998-99.

India has stepped up pressure on Pakistan in the last week—following the army camp attack—by firing its big guns across the border and starting an exchange of fire. Indian officials say militants have piled into Kashmir as the winter snows melted, despite a pledge by Pakistan's leader, General Pervez Musharraf, to end "terrorism."

Why is it so alarming?

Both countries have nuclear weapons. India conducted nuclear tests in May 1998 and Pakistan followed suit the following month. While India has indicated it may pursue a limited campaign against training camps used by militants in Pakistan—and in the mountain passes it says they use to enter Indian territory—such acts would almost certainly provoke a response from Pakistan.

Sources in the Foreign Office have told the press that Kashmir is their "number one concern" due to fears that the command and control structures that govern India and Pakistan's nuclear weapons systems are not adequate, and that the two countries could slip into conflict that spins out of control.

How did it start?

The partition of British India into Hindu-majority India and Muslim-majority Pakistan left 580 or so princely states that were free to join either or become independent. One of these was Jammu and Kashmir, a Muslim-majority state in the Himalayas with a Hindu minority of around a third of its population. Its ruler, Hari Singh, had still not made a decision by August 1947 (when India and Pakistan gained independence) and asked the two states to sign a standstill agreement.

Mr. Singh soon accused Pakistan of sending insurgents into Kashmir, and of strangling the state economically by blocking supplies of food and petrol. By October he had announced his decision to join India. Indian troops were sent to protect Kashmir and, by May 1948, they were fighting their first war against Pakistan. Taking Kashmir from India remains official Pakistani policy.

Why does Pakistan dispute India's possession of Kashmir?

Islamabad argues that Kashmir should have become part of Pakistan because the majority of its population is Muslim. It says that numerous UN resolutions mean that Kashmiris should be allowed to vote in a plebiscite to decide between membership of India and Pakistan.

India counters that under the terms of the Simla Agreement of 1972 both countries agreed to solve the Kashmir dispute through bilateral negotiations, not through international forums such as the UN. New Delhi also says a plebiscite should not be held in Kashmir because elections have demonstrated that people living there want to remain part of India.

Are India and Pakistan now on the brink of war?

Two of three wars fought by these bitter regional rivals (in 1947-48 and in 1965) were over Kashmir. There is enormous international pressure on both India and Pakistan to hold back from further conflict, with US and EU representatives holding high level meetings in New Delhi and Islamabad to dissuade the two governments from war. Washington, in particular, needs to keep President Musharraf onside to prosecute its war against al-Qaida in Afghanistan and Pakistan's largely autonomous tribal areas.

But nuclear weapons may yet act as a deterrent to war—India has a no-first use policy while Pakistan has let it be known it would use nuclear weapons in defence of its territory, making an act of war by New Delhi on its neighbour especially dangerous. Restraint, however, cannot be guaranteed.

SOURCE: The Guardian, May 21, 2002, © 2002 The Guardian. Reprinted by permission. (www.guardian.co.uk/kashmir).

Part II

Department of State Press Statement on Jammu and Kashmir: Elections

By Richard Boucher, spokesman

October 10, 2002
Washington, DC—The United States welcomes the successful conclusion of elections in Jammu and Kashmir. Prime Minister Vajpayee's personal commitment to making them transparent and open was a critical factor that helped to take the process forward. We hope that this will be the first step in a broader process that will bring peace to the region. We

applaud the efforts of the Indian Election Commission and commend the courage of candidates and voters who chose to participate despite violence and intimidation. The Kashmiri people have shown they want to pursue the path of peace.

We unreservedly condemn the terrorist attacks aimed at disrupting a democratic process and intimidating the Kashmiri people. We welcome the assurances that reports of irregularities, including alleged coercion by the security forces will be fully investigated by the Indian authorities. It is important that these assurances are followed through.

Following the completion of credible elections in Jammu and Kashmir, we call on both India and Pakistan to make strenuous effort towards an early resumption of diplomatic dialogue on all outstanding issues, including Kashmir. A lasting settlement, which also reflects the needs of the Kashmiri people, can only be achieved through dialogue. We welcome the Indian government's commitment to begin a dialogue with the people of Jammu and Kashmir and we hope this dialogue will address improvements in governance and human rights.

The United States and the international community will continue to make every effort to help India and Pakistan resolve their differences.

SOURCE: U.S. Department of State (www.state.gov/r/pa/prs/ps/2002/14278.htm).

Statement by Indian Prime Minister Shri Atal Bihari Vajpayee on Jammu and Kashmir Elections

September 24, 2002
Maldives—My dear compatriots in Jammu & Kashmir, accept my hearty congratulations for the courage and conviction with which you have participated in the first two rounds of polling in the elections to the Legislative Assembly of your State.

All the people in the rest of our country join me in saying, with admiration and thanks, "Salaam" to you.

We in India have seen many elections. But rarely has there been an election in which the voters have had to brave threats to their very lives just to exercise their fundamental right; in which the vote is not so much for this or that party, not for this or that candidate, but for democracy and national unity. Irrespective of who wins, it is clear to the whole world that, in Jammu & Kashmir, the ballot is winning a resounding victory over the bullet.

Since the elections were announced on August 22, there have been as many as 400 incidents

of terrorist violence, in which 37 political activists, including two candidates, have been killed. Sixty security personnel also have lost their lives and over 100 others have been injured.

The successful anti-terrorist operation in Srinagar this morning was a yet another reminder of the lethal plans of anti-India and anti-democracy forces to sabotage the polls. I take this opportunity to express our appreciation and gratitude to all those security and administration personnel who worked for the smooth conduct of polling in the State.

By answering fear with fortitude, you have foiled the sinister designs of those indulging in terrorism, and their patrons across the border. They did everything to subvert the polls—kill candidates, intimidate voters and threaten polling personnel. Their description of the polling in Jammu & Kashmir so far a "sham" shows nothing but their growing frustration.

Before the start of the electoral process, we had pledged that the elections in Jammu & Kashmir would be free and fair. The first two round of polling are a proof that, with your cooperation, we have redeemed that pledge. I am confident that the remaining part of the election would further reinforce its positive message and open a new chapter of peace and development in the history of your State.

SOURCE: Embassy of India (http://www.indianembassy.org/pm/pm_sept_24_2002.htm).

Comments on the Kashmiri Elections as excerpted from a speech by Pakistani President General Pervez Musharraf at the 7th Summit of the Economic Cooperation Organization, a regional IGO composed of Turkey, Iran and Pakistan

October 14, 2002
Istanbul, Turkey—Unfortunately, our eastern neighbour, India, has sought to exploit the international campaign against terrorism to undermine the freedom struggle of the people of Kashmir and to step up the use of brute force, to silence the voice of the Kashmiri people. The 700,000 strong Indian security forces, stationed in Jammu and Kashmir have used terror as a weapon and have killed eighty thousand innocent Kashmir men, women and children over the last decade alone, in their frenzied attempts to destroy the will of the Kashmiri people and to maintain illegal Indian occupation. There can hardly be a more glaring example of State terrorism than Indian brutality in Kashmir.

India has tried to divert international attention from its reign of terror against the kashmiri people by making spurious allegations against Pakistan of supporting infiltration across the Line of Control in Kashmir. In advancing these baseless charges, India has sought to act as an accuser and a judge. It has refused to accept Pakistan's proposal for the strengthening of United Nations Military Observers Group for India & Pakistan (UNMDGIP) or some other impartial international mechanism to monitor the Line of Control and to objectively assess the veracity of the allegations of infiltration.

Recently India organized farcical elections in the Indian Occupied Kashmir under the bayonets of the Indian troops. The Indian game plan was to justify and legitimize its illegal occupation by claiming that the Kashmiris had spoken through these elections. These elections were boycotted by the Kashmiri people. Despite the coercion employed by the army to force people to the polling stations, the turnout at the elections was abysmally low. There was blatant rigging before and during the elections. Such sham elections can never be a substitute for a fair and impartial plebiscite under UN auspices to ascertain the wishes of the Kashmir people, as decreed by the United Nations Security Council.

Since the beginning of this year, India has deployed almost one million troops on its border with Pakistan, forcing us to move our troops to forward positions as a defensive measure. The resulting tensions along our border with India and the Line of Control have raised fears of an armed conflict between the two countries. We have repeatedly stated that instead of resorting to accusations, threats and dangerous escalation, India should withdraw troops to peace-time locations and return to the path of dialogue and negotiations. We do not want war; we will not initiate war with India. But if war is imposed on us we will defend ourselves with the utmost resolution and determination.

SOURCE: *Islamic Republic of Pakistan Website (http://www. infopak.gov.pk/President_Addresses/President's%20speech %20at%20ECO.htm).*

QUESTIONS

Check Your Understanding

1. According to the analysis in Part I, why are India and Pakistan fighting over Kashmir? Who is most to blame?
2. According to their official statements, what are the positions of the United States, India, and Pakistani on the resolution of the conflict in Kashmir?

Analyze the Issues

3. What examples can you find throughout the reading material of the new forces that are shaping our planet? Which of these forces as presented in the articles do you think is most relevant to you?
4. What data do the articles present that indicates that what happens in Kashmir is important to you?
5. Write a news analysis of the Kashmiri elections and the attending violent in the Indian subcontinent using one of the three paradigms discussed in the chapter.
6. Do you see ethnic unrest, religious conflict, and terrorist actions coming close to your home? If so, what options would you have to reduce their threats to you?

FOR FURTHER INFORMATION

To find out more about the rivalry between India and Pakistan and the situation in Kashmir, consult the following journal articles, newspapers, and Internet sites:

Jonah Blank, "Kashmir: Fundamentalism Takes Root," *Foreign Affairs,* vol. 78, no. 6 (November/December 1999), pp. 36–53
BBC News In Depth: Kashmir Flashpoint.
  http://news.bbc.co.uk/2/hi/in_depth/south_asia/2002/kashmir_flashpoint/ This website gives you almost all the information about Kashmir you need to have to understand its importance in the current international picture.
The Guardian has compiled an excellent research guide to the web for Kashmir, providing Indian and Pakistani perspectives. See *http://www.guardian.co.uk/weblog/special/ 0,10627,720247,00.html.*

CHAPTER 2

The State and Its Role in the International System

KEY QUESTIONS RAISED IN THIS CHAPTER

1. What is the basic unit of analysis in the international system?

2. What is the structure of the International System?

3. How do we use the levels of analysis to understand international relations?

In Chapter 1 you learned that one of the five forces shaping the planet is the increasing inability of the state to solve problems because of decentralizing ethnic, religious, and economic tensions. You further learned that most issues today are transnational and transboundary in character, promoting a centralizing tendency in the international system as, for example, the tendency for states to turn to the UN and other international agencies for regulations and guidelines. What is this entity called a state, and why does international politics seem to revolve around it? How can we understand the centrifugal tensions that are pushing the states toward dissolution and the centripetal tensions that are pushing them toward international cooperation?

This chapter will enable you to address those questions. We will first look at the state—what it is, how it arose, and why it plays such a central role in international relations today. We will then look at the structure of the international system by applying levels of analysis. For example, we may study the international system in its entirety, as we might study the solar system as a whole. That's one level. But we can also study the international system at the regional level, by looking at regional organizations of states such as the European Union or NAFTA. For a third perspective, we can study the international system at the state level, that is, by looking at the world from the standpoint of the behavior of individual states. Or, we can study the international system at the substate level, and look at ethnic conflict or civil wars and how these tensions impact the state and its ability to perform its functions at the regional and international levels. Finally, we can look at the international system through the role individuals play in moving and shaking world politics. We will conclude the chapter by showing that by understanding what the state is and how it functions at these five levels we can begin to get a hold on the centralizing and decentralizing tendencies at work in the world today.

What Is the Basic Unit of Analysis in the International System?

States are the basic building blocks of the international system. In Chapter 1, you were given the following three characteristics that differentiate a state from a tribe, an ethnic group, or a nationality. To review, a state is:

1. a geographic territory with internationally recognized boundaries;
2. an internationally recognized and identifiable population that lives within those boundaries;
3. an internationally recognized authority structure or government.

Let us look more closely at these characteristics.

The State and Its Primary Characteristics

Treaty of Westphalia
The treaty signed at the close of the Thirty Years War in 1648 that called for the recognition of territorial entities that could no longer be dominated as sovereign states and which had fixed borders, a recognized population, and an acknowledged government.

Our understanding of what a state is grew out of rivalry for power and wealth among the rulers of Europe from the fifteenth to the seventeenth century. The concept of "international system" dates from the **Treaty of Westphalia** in 1648, that ended the Thirty Year War about religion and our modern understanding of the term is derived essentially from European experience.

The treaty recognized the fact that none of the rival European powers that had been fighting for some thirty years could win sufficiently to dominate the other

---

Legitimacy

All states have a right to exist and that the authority of the government in that state is supreme and accepted as lawful and right.

Sovereignty

- No higher authority than the state exists.
- No other state or international organization can compel that state against its will to do something it does not want to do.
- The recognized government of a state makes all the decisions for the people in the name of whom it governs.

Obligations

The state must:

- behave according to the rules agreed upon under international law.
- conduct its relations with other states according to the rules of diplomacy.
- conduct war according to the international rules of war.
- implement treaties that it has signed.
- treat diplomatic representatives of other states, prisoners of wars, and refugees according to the generally accepted tenets of human rights.

FIGURE 2.1

Characteristics of a State

---

powers. The treaty thus called for the recognition of these territorial entities as states, with fixed borders, an acknowledged government and a population identified as living within that state's borders. The treaty recognized these states as *sovereign* or self-ruling and promised that the government of one state would not interfere in the affairs of another. Relations between states would be characterized by diplomacy and regulated by international law in the form of treaties and agreements.

The modern definition of *state* is based on the principles set forth in the 1648 treaty. Central to the definition are the concepts of legitimacy, sovereignty, and formal obligations. *Legitimacy* means that all states have a right to exist and that the authority of the government in that state is supreme and accepted as lawful. *Sovereignty* means that no higher authority than the state exists. The United Nations is made up of states, yet it has no authority to compel the member states to take any action or refrain from any action. In the last analysis, each state decides its own course of action. Finally, states have *formal obligations,* or duties, to one another. Rules are laid down according to international law for declaring and fighting a war, for implementing treaties, for continuing to recognize the legitimacy of the governments of other states, and for exchanging and treating diplomatic representatives. (See Figure 2.1).

While the principles of legitimacy, sovereignty, and duty are still in force today, the forces of change discussed in Chapter 1, especially globalization and the increased speed of communications, have undermined the sovereignty of the state. For one thing, the state has become increasingly *vulnerable* to events it cannot control beyond its borders. The attacks of September 11, 2001, vividly demonstrated the inability of the most powerful state in the world to prevent a terrorist attack within its borders that had been planned and directed from outside. Another less obvious example is the Asian financial crisis of 1997–1998. In 1997, the economies of several Southeast Asian countries collapsed. The crisis began in Thailand but quickly spread to the Korean and Japanese economies. Then came Russia's turn. Faced with mounting international indebtedness, the Russian government declared in the summer of 1998 that it could no longer pay

To find out more about the Treaty of Westphalia, go to **www.ablongman.com/ duncan**.

To find out how Europe evolved from the Treaty of Westphalia, go to **www.ablongman.com/ duncan**.

interest on its debt. The Russian economy collapsed. The crisis moved to threaten Latin America. These countries were victims of events well beyond their control.

The 9/11 attacks highlighted two additional important dimensions of a state's vulnerability: *failure* and *insecurity.* Not all states are successful. Some fail to maintain law and order within their borders or to provide the level of economic well-being, education, housing, food, and security their populations demand. Failed states today include Afghanistan, Angola, Burundi, the Democratic Republic of the Congo, Liberia, Sierra Leone, Somalia, and Sudan. In each of these states, economic and political chaos reign. Five out of the eight are in outright civil war. The others are restrained by international peacekeepers from waging war or else have disintegrated to the level of local fiefdoms at the mercy of the reigning warlords. Failed states, such as Afghanistan before 9/11, offer havens for criminals, terrorists, drug trafficking, and cross-border mayhem. In so doing they promote global insecurity. The United States bombed Afghanistan not because it had declared war on the state of Afghanistan, but because this failed state harbored Osama Bin Laden's terrorist organization. In the interests of guaranteeing security at home, the United States, for the first time in the history of the state, declared war against a *nonstate actor,* deliberately violating the internationally recognized *sovereignty* of Afghanistan.

The war in Iraq exemplifies a final and disturbing dimension of a state's vulnerability: the blurring of the distinction between terrorist operations and conventional wars between states. First, the war was preemptive, designed, according to the U.S. government, *to prevent* Sadam Hussein from completing the development of weapons of mass destruction and distributing them to terrorist groups. The only other preemptive war in recent history is the 1967 Six Day War when Israel attacked its Arab neighbors. Second, the stated goal of the attacking coalition was *regime change:* to destroy Saddam Hussein's tyrannical rule and establish democracy in Iraq. Regime change as a purpose or reason for war is new to world politics. When the allied powers fought against Hitler in World War II, the stated goal was total and unconditional German surrender. The war effectively ended the Nazi regime in Germany, but that was not the allies' main objective. Third, contrary to historic practice, particularly in twentieth century wars, the invaders sought to target only regime institutions and military objectives, and to minimize civilian casualties and destruction of civilian infrastructure (such as water supply and electricity). Finally, the war was fought between a new kind of hi-tech, highly trained, mobile and flexible military force, trained to fight terrorists, and enemy troops composed of the Iraqi regular army, the elite Republican Guards, and guerrilla and terrorists groups loyal to Sadam Hussein. While guerrilla units have operated in virtually all wars, this was the first time they were used as a main strategy of defense. What kind of permanent impact the blurring of this distinction will have on the concept of the sovereign state remains to be seen.

Some analysts of the liberal persuasion hail the increased vulnerability of states as testimony to the growing **interdependence** of states. Sovereignty is not coming to an end, they argue; the exercise of sovereignty is simply being modified by new conditions. These analysts consider interdependence a good thing. In their view, states that depend on other states for raw materials and export markets are less likely to go to war to resolve differences and are more likely to cooperate.[1] Neorealist Kenneth N. Waltz and others criticize this position as being too simplistic. We need to look at how states depend on one another, they say, and honestly admit that the United States can probably get along without the rest of the world

Interdependence
States do not live in isolation from one another. Increasingly, the new driving forces in world politics—such as international finance, trade and commerce, environmental pollution, the information revolution, transnationalism, intergovernmental organizations (IGOs), and nongovernmental organizations (NGOs)—are linking states together in a web of wide-ranging interactions.

better than most states can get along without the United States. Waltz argues that the low level of U.S dependence upon other countries is a primary source of its great power status and the relative facility with which a great power can unilaterally control the behavior of less powerful states.[2] We will return to this idea in Chapter 3.

A third position, derived again from the liberal paradigm, is reflected in the work of James Rosenau. Rosenau sees the growing loss of sovereignty as signaling the end of the dominant role of states in the international system. The salient characteristics of the emerging post-Westphalian system, he argues, are the inclusion of non-state actors and the development of global civil society. After the 9/11 attacks, Rosenau's perspective seems most convincing and also most terrifying.[3] How can any state control the behavior of non-state actors whose membership is largely invisible? We will talk more about the behavior of non-state actors in Chapter 6.

The Difference Between a Nation-State and a Multinational State

Our discussion of the state and its characteristics would not be complete without our distinguishing between two kinds of states that will appear frequently throughout the text. The first is the *nation-state*. The nation-state is composed primarily of one ethnic or nationality group or nation. The common definition of **nation** is a group of people who have a common language, common ethnicity, common culture, common territory, and a desire for independence. Ethnic groups like the Kurds and the Palestinians in the Middle East, the Chechens in the Caucasus, and the people of East Timor are nations. All demand independence in a specific territory, based on a common language and common culture. A nation-state is that state once it has gained independence. Examples of nation-states are Germany, the Netherlands, Israel, and Japan.

The second kind of state is the **multinational** or **multiethnic state,** as it is often called. As the name suggests, this kind of state is made of two or more ethnic groups or races. The world's largest states—Russia, China, India, and the United States—are all multinational. But so are some of the world's smallest states, such as Switzerland, Belgium, and many states in Africa. Multinational states sometimes suffer from the desire of the component ethnic groups to live their own lifestyle and/or obtain more power in the central government.

The Origins of the State

How did the world get to be dominated by states where ethnicity and nationalism play such a strong role? The state is both a relatively new arrival on the international scene and an old form of social organization that appeared for relatively short periods of time in antiquity.

The City-State as the Forerunner of the Modern State
At the dawn of human civilization in the Tigris and Euphrates Valley in what is today Iraq, a people who called themselves Sumerians built the first city-states. These city-states had the same characteristics as the modern state. They had a recognized geographic territory, a recognized population that spoke a common language, and a sovereign and legitimate government. The major difference was smaller size.

To get a clear understanding of what a multiethnic state is, go to **www.ablongman.com/ duncan.**

Nation
A group of people linked together in some manner, such as by a common territory, with a common culture that may or may not be based on religion, a common language, a common history or understanding of the past, and a general desire for independence.

Multinational or **Multiethnic State**
A state such as Nigeria, the United States, Russia, or India, which contains more than one nation and/or ethnic group within its territory. Most states are multinational in nature.

The Acropolis: The heart of ancient Athens and the glory of fifth century B.C. Greece.

To learn more about the early city-states, go to **www.ablongman.com/ duncan**.

Pericles: The leader of Athens during its Golden Age in the fifth century B.C.

In Genesis, the first book of the Torah and the Bible, we read of Abram setting forth from the city of Ur to go wherever the Lord God would lead him. Ur was a city-state that reached the height of its independent growth around 2500 B.C. Under Ur-Nammu (ca 2060 B.C.) gave the world its first written code of laws. It fell to the first empire-builder in Mesopotamia, Sargon of Akkad, around 2180 B.C. Once incorporated into a kingdom, Ur and the other Sumerian city-states lost their independence. Ur, however, retained its cultural preeminence.

The next time we read about city-states is in the fifth century B.C. in Greece. Because the Greek peninsula is so mountainous, cross-country travel is difficult. As a result, urban complexes grew and prospered in the valleys between the hills, especially those with access to the sea: Corinth, Sparta, Athens, and Mycene.

The people in these cities all spoke a common language, Greek, and lived in a common territory they called Helas, the Greek peninsula. But there was no national government for the whole of the peninsula. Instead, each city was independent: it made its own laws and conducted its own foreign policy and foreign trade. When the Persians from Asia Minor tried to conquer the Greek cities at the beginning of the fifth century B.C. (490–480), the cities banded together in a formal alliance to defeat them. Herodotus, an early Greek historian, wrote a moving account of how the Greek alliance of free city-states fought the imperial, despotic invader.

The next century, from 400 to 300 B.C., saw the flowering of the Greek city-state, which fostered the beginnings of democratic government, the first Olympic Games, and some of the greatest playwrights and artists the world has ever known. During this period the Greeks created new forms of drama called tragedy and comedy, as well as splendid buildings, sculpture, and other artworks that still remain the standard by which art is judged.

Unfortunately, all this creativity came at a price: dissension between the city-states. Athens soon outgrew the poor land around the city and looked abroad for

Thucydides: "My work is not a piece of writing designed to meet the needs of an immediate public, but was done to last forever." (Thucydides, *The Peloponesian War, Book 1, 22*). The father of history as a literary genre and the first to theorize about international relations.

arable land, food, and trade. Fifty years after the Persian War, Athens had become a merchant trading empire whose inhabitants were mostly slaves. It was roundly disliked by the other Greek city-states, which formed alliances to protect themselves from their proud neighbor. These alliances and treaties may be called the first glimmerings of the modern international system but it collapsed under the weight of intercity rivalry.

As the great Greek historian Thucydides recounts, Athens began to think it was invincible and organized an attack against one of the weaker city states, only to discover that its target had the support of the military might of Sparta.[4] The war between Athens and Sparta raged for almost one hundred years.

At roughly the same time, during what is known as the Spring and Autumn period (722–481 B.C.), ancient China saw the flowering of some 170 states, each with its walled city. Like their Greek counterparts, these states formed alliances and engaged in diplomacy and war. By the period of Warring States (400–221 B.C.), only seven states remained. They were unified under the state of Qin, and China entered its first unification period under the Han Dynasty in 221 B.C.[5]

During the founding of the city of Rome, the Italian peninsula also knew city-states. As the city of Rome prospered, the Romans moved out to conquer first the Italian peninsula and eventually all the lands bordering the Mediterranean Sea. The so-called Roman peace, or *pax romana*, brought a large part of the Middle East and Europe under a single superpower. Under that empire, the city-state ceased to exist. The modern state had its rise in the Middle Ages, long after Rome fell. The history of Europe is the history of rivalry—war and conquest among feudal chieftains, with the periodic ascendancy of a strong man, be he king, duke, or earl. These rulers were eager to expand their domains. To do so, however, they needed to create sufficient wealth to raise an army. The medieval city was just coming into its own as a commercial power. Some cities, like Venice and Florence in Italy, and Dubrovnik in Croatia, flourished as independent city-states. Others accepted the rule of the prevailing strong man. Through patronage, subsidies, and the granting of an imperial or royal charter, these cities became centers of trade, finance, and learning. With the support of the cities, and helped along through marriages of convenience to princesses with large land holdings, the kings gradually became stronger than the

Dubrovnik, Croatia: One of the best preserved of Europe's medieval cities, it was almost destroyed during the fighting between Croats, Muslims and Serbs in 1991—1995.

feudal chieftains, whose power largely resided in the agricultural base of the land they held. The consolidation of royal power in the fifteenth century put Europe well on its way to playing midwife at the birth of the modern state.

Ideology and a Common Culture   We cannot be sure that modern states would have evolved out of this process if it had not been for the long conflict between the rising nation states of France, Spain, and England, on the one hand, and on the other, the Pope in Rome, who called himself Vicar (deputy of Christ) of Christendom, by which he meant Europe. Gradually, the royal powers challenged the spiritual authority of the Catholic Church and carved out a space where they could rule independent of church control. They did this through a policy of granting special privileges to the merchant towns, like Prague, London, or Paris, with their thriving commerce and rising wealth. In return for royal protection and reduced taxes, these towns supported the crown that gave them their liberties. The next step was the breakup of the medieval church into Protestant and Catholic sects. Both kinds of believers saw their king as the guardian of the true faith and their true leader. Thus began the identification of a national leader and, by extension, the nation-state with a particular belief or ideology. The ideology of nationalism replaced Christianity as the glue that bound European peoples together.

The Role of Technology   Perhaps no other development had as great an impact on the rise of the national state as the printing press. (See box Historical Perspective: Impact of the Printing Press with Movable Type.)

HISTORICAL PERSPECTIVE

Impact of the Printing Press with Movable Type

The printing press enabled many copies of one manuscript to be made public and disseminated across a wide area. The more copies of a book that were published, the more money the printer made. Printers quickly shifted into printing books in the vernacular, or language that people spoke, to get a wider readership.

People rushed to learn to read. The arrival of books in the vernacular greatly encouraged people to learn to read. The fifteenth and sixteenth centuries were bloodied by wars about religion. Those people who protested against the authority of the Pope to determine what was the true religion and what was not, said that the true religion was only found in the Bible. The German Protestants read the printed Bible in German, the French protestants in French, and the English protestants in English.

Printing gave nationalism a big boost. In 1453 the international language of Europe was Latin. With the appearance of books in vernacular languages, such as English, French, and Spanish, people began to buy only those books they could read. If bad roads and bad terrain had separated people previously, printing separated them more visibly by the language they read and spoke.

Printing engendered freedom of the press. With the printing press, the making of books moved out of the monasteries, where their production was tightly controlled by the medieval Church as to what the contents of a book should be. The dawn of the printed word brought with it the thorny issue of what people should or should not read.

Individual and priceless artwork was lost from books when printing became widespread. However, quality illustrations, good paper, and well-designed typefaces have remained the hallmarks of great book publishing companies to this day.

In 1215, 43 hand-written copies in Latin of the Magna Carta, each bearing the seal of King John of England, were deposited in key locations throughout England. The Magna Carta is the first document to set forth the rights of English people and is the foundation of the British and United States constitutions. If the Magna Carta had been signed in 1453, Gutenberg's press could have printed hundreds of copies in both English and Latin to carry to all the cities in England; and some would have been put on sale for a price in the new urban bookstores. If the Magna Carta had been signed today, it would be immediately available, as it truly is, at the National Archives and Record Administration website (http://www.nara.gov/exhall/charters/magnacarta/magtrans.html) on the Internet, or in bookstores, where for a few dollars, pounds, yen, or rupees, anyone interested may purchase it in his or her native language.

In one month Gutenberg could turn out more German bibles than the monks could write by hand in Latin in several years. Thus, the printing press made literature in the *vernacular* (the language people spoke in a particular locale) easily available and readily disseminated in the form of the printed book. In the process, some languages were winners. Some were losers. If Dante had not decided to write his *Divine Comedy* in the northern Italian dialect, the people of Italy would be speaking Provençal, the language spoken by some people living in the south of France. With the printing press hundreds of copies of Dante's great epic became available to all

The Inventor of the Printing Press: Printing was actually invented in China, where the Emperors disseminated their edicts and orders through a printed text composed of ideographs or picture symbols. European written languages use an alphabet representing the sounds or phonemes present in the spoken language. The advantage of the alphabet is that many combinations of sounds can be written down using a few letters. Gutenberg's achievement was the invention of movable type. Instead of carving a font of a word or ideograph, as the Chinese had to, Gutenberg used a line of type that could be filled with different letters, depending on the word appearing in the text. Time–Life listed Gutenberg's press as the Number 1 event of the last millennium.

who could read. As a result, that one work became almost single handedly responsible for the creation of modern Italian.

A Common Language   Not only did the printing press make it easy to distribute the printed word in the local language, it prompted kings to standardize the language throughout their domains. If some people in the kingdom did not speak the king's language, then they would learn it—by force if necessary. Other languages or dialects would be suppressed. By the sixteenth century, in part due to having acquired a set of common languages, Western Europeans had developed a strong sense of nationality, territory, and common history. The French Revolution of 1789 spread the ideology of nationalism as far as Russia with the march of Napoleon's armies eastward, thereby awakening the East European peoples to the possibilities of independence and the right to speak their own language. World War I marked the fall of the three remaining empires in Europe—the Ottoman, Russian, and German. They were replaced by nation-states. In the twentieth century the great overseas empires of Britain, France, Germany, Spain, Portugal, and

To find out more about how technology has revolutionized access to information, go to **www.ablongman.com/ duncan**.

Russia were replaced by independent states, the newest being the states formed from the former Soviet Union.

The modern state thus derives from a rich heritage of independent self-governing city-states in classical times to the clash between church and the crown in the Middle Ages, to the emergence of France, England, and Spain as nation-states with a common language, common territory, and common culture in the fifteenth and sixteenth centuries. The concept of the state was given primacy in international affairs at the Treaty of Westphalia in 1648, and the characteristics of the state remain unchanged: sovereignty, legitimacy, and formal obligations to one another in the international system.

The modern state also inherits four centuries of state domination of the international arena. Today, that domination is being challenged by the large number of new states, and by the vulnerability of states to events they cannot control. The 194 large, medium, and tiny princeling states from all over Europe that signed the Treaty of Westphalia made up the entire international system at the time. Today, the **international system** has long outgrown its European origins and expanded to include the whole world, with 187 states and a growing number of nonstate actors, such as IGOs and NGOs.

Let us now take a closer look at the international system, especially its structure, and how we use that structure to analyze the activities of state and nonstate actors.

What Is the Structure of the International System?

With the founding of the United Nations in 1945 at the end of World War II, the victorious Allies formally endorsed the concept of an international system composed of states. The UN began its existence with 50 signatory states, so amazing as it may seem, most of today's states have come into being since then. Of the 187 states today, some are very small like the African states of Burkina Faso or Guinea-Bissau, and the tiny islands that appear on a map as dots in the ocean, such as Comoros in the Indian Ocean or Kiribati in the Pacific Ocean. Others are large land masses, like the United States, Canada, Russia, and Australia. States also extend over water. They include the large *archipelagi,* or groups of islands such as Indonesia or the Philippines, that stretch several thousand miles across the ocean, and smaller groups, like the Marshall Islands. As we will learn in Chapter 7, geography, including size, location, and shape, plays a big role in the ability of states to play international politics effectively.

Because most of the new states came into being as a result of the breakup of the colonial empires, virtually all the borders of the new states were made by the colonial powers. The citizens of the new states had virtually no say. And with the exception of some island states, virtually none of the new states contains only one ethnic group. Most contain many such groups. Consequently, a major problem of the new states is to develop citizen loyalty to the new country and a sense of belonging among people who, just a generation earlier, were living under an entirely different system of government imposed by rulers from somewhere far away.

Under the principles of international law, the new states are as sovereign and independent as the older and more established powers. The principle of equality is recognized through the mechanism of "one country, one vote" in the General Assembly of the UN. In practice, however, the newer states can do little to oppose the power of the major states. The best they can do is to play one power off against

Web Exploration

To see how the international system has changed over time, go to **www.ablongman.com/ duncan.**

International System
A concept that includes a number of key actors (states, nations, IGOs and NGOs) and the patterns of actions among those actors that can be explained by the distribution of power and other factors. The state plays a pivotal role within this system, because the system has no central authority to maintain order and dispense justice.

TABLE 2.1 Levels of Analysis	
Levels	**Actors**
1. International system level	States, IGOs, NGOs, TNC,* individuals
2. Regional level	Regional states, regional IGOs, NGOs, individuals
3. State level	States, state level NGOs, TNC, individuals
4. Substate level	State and substate NGOs, ethnic groups, individuals
5. Individual level	Individuals of all kinds

*TNC: Transnational companies whose production and distribution capabilities circle the globe.

the other to assure that they do not fall under the control of one state permanently. In addition, states at the turn of the twenty-first century are living in a period of U.S. superpower dominance. It is very hard for small, weak states to oppose the United States or larger regional entities, such as NATO, in their part of the world. One reason, then, that Americans are both envied and disliked is that every state leader would probably like his or her state to be in as solid a position in the international system as is the United States.

The dynamics of the modern international system remain the same as in the days of the Treaty of Westphalia—at least in terms of the interaction between strong and weak states. Weak states must decide the merits of forming regional alliances, giving in to the superpower, or going it alone. The difference between 1648 and today is that the international action now covers the entire globe. In 1648 it covered only the continent of Europe.

Levels of Analysis
A method of classifying the players and how they relate to one another in the international system on five different levels.

How are we going to analyze the interactions of 187 countries and various regional governmental and nongovernmental associations? Because doing so is extremely complex, political scientists have developed a tool for getting a handle on the international system, its players, and how they relate to one another. It is called **levels of analysis,** a system for organizing the players into five levels of international activity (see Table 2.1). Let's begin with the highest level.

The International System as a Whole

System level analysis enables us to make generalizations and sometimes predictions about patterns of interaction among the actors in the system. The basic assumptions underlying system level analysis are (1) that the international system is considered as a single whole; and (2) that within this whole, actors interact with and respond to one another in ways that are predictable.

An analogy of the system might be a forest. A forest is composed of trees, but if you're interested in the system, you do not look at each individual tree but rather at the component parts of the forest, such as the deciduous trees and the coniferous trees. By identifying behavior patterns of each component, you then can classify the deciduous trees into oak, maple, larch, or birch. The coniferous trees might be pine, hemlock, and spruce. Through study of the forest, we can make generalizations about the conditions necessary for the survival of all forests—and of species of trees within the forest.

TABLE 2.2	The Four Worlds of the International System
First World	The industrialized states: North America, Western Europe, Australia, New Zealand, Japan
Second World	Countries in transition from communism to a free market economy: Russia, states of East Central Europe and Central Asia, and the independent states formed from the former Soviet Union, in Central Asia and the Caucasus
Third World	States in process of development: states in Latin America the Carribbean, and Asia; most African states
Fourth World	States that are so poor that they may never be able to take the road to development

In similar ways, though with considerable less accuracy, we can consider the international system as a whole and identify its components. Among the most important components to look at are the types of actors within the system.

The Four Worlds   As you already know, the principal actors are the states. We commonly group these states into what are called the four worlds, or sets of states, based on the level of economic and political development a state has attained. As Table 2.2 shows, these divisions are the **First World,** or the *industrialized states,* such as the United States, Western Europe, Japan, and Australia; the **Second World,** consisting of the *former communist countries in transition to a democratic society and market economy:* Russia, the countries of East Central Europe, and the independent states formed from the former Soviet Union and located in Central Asia and the Caucasus; the **Third World,** or the *developing states,* including countries in Latin America, the Caribbean, Asia; and most of the countries in Africa; and the **Fourth World,** the *at-risk states,* or those that may not develop the economic and political institutions necessary for survival. They include Afghanistan, Somalia, Chad, Ethiopia, the Central African Republic, and other African states that are desperately poor and possess virtually no natural resources.

As you can see, the groups of states are not equal in power and wealth. Although in theory all states are defined by the same characteristics, and each has one vote in the General Assembly of the United Nations, in practice we automatically assume differences based on economic and political factors. Indeed, the classification suggests a rank order with the industrialized states at the top and the countries of the Fourth World at the bottom. We thus may expect the leading states of the international system to be found in the industrialized world.

Lead State Actors of the International System   Lead actors at any time in history have always come from the most economically advanced regions. In the first century A.D., India, China, and Rome were the most economically advanced regions and world leaders. In the fifteenth century, China, the Netherlands, Portugal, and Spain were the world leaders. In the eighteenth and nineteenth centuries, the major European powers were the movers and shakers. In the international system of that time, England, France, Germany, Austria, and Russia maintained a fragile balance of power at the top, while they divided the rest of the world between them as parts of their colonial empires.

Web Exploration

To find where the Four Worlds of the International system are found, go to **www.ablongman.com/ duncan**.

As a result of World Wars I and II, the power position of the European countries was substantially weakened. The United States and the Soviet Union emerged as the two superpowers, each possessing the capability to destroy each other and the world. What is fascinating to students of the international system is that neither country sought to emerge as a superpower.

Nonstate Actors   The category of **nonstate actors** conveniently divides into two groups: *international governmental actors* and *nongovernmental, extranational actors.* International governmental actors are international organizations (IGOs) whose members are nation- or multinational states. You will learn more about these in Chapter 5. Examples of IGOs are the United Nations, the World Health Organization, the World Bank, the International Monetary Fund, and the International Court of Justice.

The second group of nonstate actors is called nongovernmental organizations, or NGOs. These are generally described as *not-for-profit organizations,* and their members are individuals rather than representatives of states. Four types of NGOs may be identified. The members of *professional and scientific NGOs,* such as the International Political Science Association or the International Union of Concerned Scientists, are generally professionals with similar education and backgrounds. Members in *religious NGOs,* a second type, share religious convictions. One example is the World Council of Churches. Members in *environmental NGOs,* such as Greenpeace or Friends of the Earth, believe in the goals and purposes of the NGO's charter. The fourth group are what might be called *single-issue NGOs.* For example, women have taken leading roles in not-for-profit activities and have formed NGOs focused specifically on women's issues, such as Virtual Sisterhood, a global communications network with a focus on women and the media, or the Women's Jurist Association/Women's Advocacy Center, that operates at the state level but reaches out to similar women's legal associations across the world.

A third group of nonstate actors are the *transnational corporations* (TNC) doing business in the global economy. These corporations may have headquarters in one country but subsidiary factories or subcontractors all over the globe. Sales also are worldwide. Examples are MacDonalds, Exxon Oil Corporation, International Business Machines, Microsoft, Intel, Nokia, and Toyota. The fourth and final group comprises the various *organizations that promote international terrorism.* The types, organization, and activities of NGOs will be discussed in Chapter 6.

Opinions vary on the assessment of the activities of NGOs in the international arena. Many international relations experts, such as James Rosenau, see the emergence of NGOs as a positive development. In his view they operate as active lobbying groups in the international system as a whole and represent the emergence of global civil society. Others argue that these groups are not representative of any interest as their members are non-elected individuals and as such merely represent themselves. In addition, some of them, like the terrorist NGOs, are dedicated to destroying the international system as we know it.

Relations Between Actors in the International System   A first important generalization that emerges from our previous discussion is that relations between states, and indeed between states and nonstate actors, are characterized by power relationships. At any given time in history, one or several states are on top. Pick any date in the past, and the international system may be characterized by how the powerful states relate to one another and to the rest of the world.

The emergence of nonstate actors does not significantly change the power relationships between the weak and strong states. However, weak states can and do use

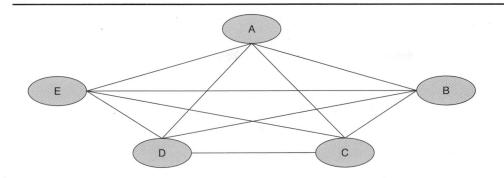

FIGURE 2.2
A Multipolar System

both the IGOs and NGOs as advocates for, negotiators of, or simply extensions to, their foreign policy.

A second generalization derives directly from the notion of power relationships among lead actors, supporting actors, and very weak actors. At the system level of analysis, we define the strong states that attract weaker states into their orbit as the system's *poles of power.*

During most of the nineteenth century, several powerful European states were rivals for power. The international system of the period may thus be described as a European **multipolar system.** As each state sought to prevent another state from acting too aggressively and disrupting the system, it entered into an alliance with what it perceived to be like-minded states (see Figure 2.2).

A so-called **balance of power** was produced through the alliances of two groups of states, one in opposition to the other. Since England was an island apart from the continent of Europe and had by far the largest empire, it saw its role as a balancer of power to prevent France, Germany, or Russia from dominating the European continent.

The European multipolar system gave way after World War II to the **bipolar** (two-pole) **system** of the Cold War, where the two poles were the United States and the Union of Soviet Socialist Republics. But the Soviet Union collapsed in 1991, and as we enter this century, no other country—with the possible exception of China—comes close to challenging the United States either militarily or economically.

We could classify the current system as **unipolar** (see Figure 2.3). However, although there may be only one superpower, many *regional* powers are economically strong. Thus we might redefine our current system overall as unipolar with one superpower but with a multipolar regional structure. We will talk more in depth about the balance of power and power relationships in the next chapter.

As mentioned, interacting with the groups of states are the increasing number of nonstate actors. After September 11, 2001, there is some question as to whether groups like Al Qaeda—and others, such as Friends of the Earth—are eroding the sovereignty of the state, as James Rosenau and other neoliberals contend. For example, the events of 9/11 entailed an attack against the United States—a member of the UN—by Al-Qaeda—a group whose members, numbers, and location are unknown, but which can strike anywhere at any time. No member state of the UN has these privileges. If you recall, states have formal obligations to one another. The UN was founded to keep aggressor states in line and to promote collective peace, but the UN document says nothing about protecting states from NGOs.

Multipolar System

An international system based on three or more centers of power (poles) that may include states or IGOs, such as the European Union. The nineteenth-century international system may be described as *multipolar.*

Balance of Power

A foreign policy principle that world peace and stability is best preserved by way of a basic equilibrium among the world's major actors—typically states.

Bipolar System

A balance of power system in which states are grouped around two major power centers.

Unipolar System

When power in the international system revolves around a single superpower.

FIGURE 2.3

Unipolar World on the International System-as-a-Whole Level of Analysis and a Multipolar World at the Regional Level of Analysis

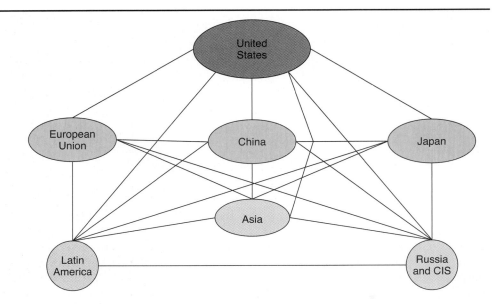

Moreover, NGOs may now apply and receive formal NGO status at the UN. Every major international conference, such as the Johannesburg Summit Conference on Sustainable Development in August 2002, has its set of recognized NGOs in attendance, which lobby the UN delegates and promote their point of view. Do these developments minimize the importance of states in the international system? Many scholars argue that the international system is fast becoming a civil community of state and nonstate actors recruited from all over the globe and who appeal to the UN with multiple proposals for the collective resolution of world problems. What do you think?

You may be thinking that this discussion of poles of power and power relationships looks at the international system solely from the realist point of view. However, you may have noted the idealist perspective in the preceding critique of the response of international relations experts to the states' current perceived loss of sovereignty. The organization of power is an essential component of the systems level of analysis. Whether you see in that organization an opportunity or a challenge to the state system depends on your choice of theoretical paradigm.

The Regional Level of Analysis

The regional level of analysis enables us to compare one region to another, or *across* regions, and to compare *one state with another within a region.* As with the systems level of analysis, we are concerned with the actors that make up the system and the generalizations we can make about them.

At the regional level, we look at the same actors as at the international level. The difference is that at the regional level when we compare, for example, economic growth in Southeast Asia with economic growth in Sub-Saharan Africa, we look at specific states and nonstate actors in those specific regions. At the international systems level, we are concerned with how the actors behave in the overall power structure.

By comparing the combined economic and industrial capacity of states grouped as regions, we may further study the hypothesis made earlier in the chapter

Toronto Skyline: The Great Lakes are the largest source of fresh water in the world, vital both to the economy and ecology of North America. Toronto, Ontario, Canada, is the largest Canadian city on the lakes.

that although we currently have a unipolar system with one superpower, we also have a strong multipolar distribution of economic power across regions. To prove the point, we could compare the wealth of the **European Union (EU)** with that of the continent of Africa, or we might compare the per capita income of Kenya or South Africa to that of Ethiopia or Chad, in northern Africa.

At the regional level, we can also study the dynamics of regional organizations—of IGOs and NGOs—in various parts of the world. We may compare the structure, organization, and activities of IGOs with similar goals but with differing ranges of function and jurisdiction, such as the European Union (Community) and the North American Free Trade Association (NAFTA), or the Organization of African Unity, the Organization of American States, and the Organization of Southeast Asian Nations. Finally, we can look at the international reach of regional organizations, such as the North Atlantic Treaty Organization (NATO) or the European Union, and attempt to predict from the behavior of the most active regional IGOs a general future pattern of regional IGO behavior. (Refer to the colored maps at the beginning of your text for maps of the EU and NAFTA.)

Regional NGOs are not quite as visible as their international cousins. They seem most active in the European Community, where a supranational government has the authority to make laws and regulations binding on the member states. For example, the European Social Action Network focuses on developing coherent European policies on human rights, and the European Union Migrants Forums unite and provide representation at the EU level for some 190 migrant organizations throughout Europe. However, regional environmental NGOs such as the Union de Grupos Ambientalistas—a federation of 38 Mexican environmental NGOs—and the United States-based Sierra Club uniting groups in Canada, Mexico, and the United States, played a decisive role in assuring the attachment of an environmental agreement to

European Union (EU)
A multipurpose international organization comprising fifteen western European countries and that has both supranational and intergovernmental characteristics.

the North American Free Trade Agreement in 1991. Regional women's groups, particularly in Africa and South Asia, have been instrumental in making governments in those regions aware of the problems women face in agriculture and commerce both within the region and in interregional trade.

The State Level of Analysis

As its name suggests, the *state level of analysis* looks at and contrasts the behavior of individual states. But how do we compare and contrast states so that we may better understand their position in the international system? What specific features do states have in common? The four factors most often considered are power, wealth, status and prestige, and population.

When we talk about the way that power is organized and distributed within a state, we are talking about its system of government, the kind of constitution and legal system it has, and its requirements for citizenship and participation in politics, such as the right to vote or the minimum age for holding public office. *Wealth* and its distribution involve all aspects of a state's economic system. Wealth factors include the quality and quantity of natural resources, agricultural and industrial output, labor indicators, external and internal trade, gross national product (GNP), taxation policy, public finance, and technological development. The concept of *status and prestige* relates to a state's social system, health and education policies, and the distribution of justice. When we compare status and prestige among states, we are investigating who's on top—that is, which group influences the conduct of government the most. Status in society thus depends to a large extent on the type of social system the state has. In states with a class society like the medieval states, the highest class, such as the clergy in feudal Europe or the Brahmins in ancient India, had the most prestige and status. In our modern more democratic states, education is a determining factor in the kind of profession or job you will have and your ability to exert influence in your local community or at the national level. In other states with authoritarian forms of government, certain groups are denied status and prestige, such as women in Muslim countries. We shall talk more about education and the status of women in Chapter 10.

Health is also a determinant of status and prestige in today's world. Illness and chronic disease debilitate a person, making it extremely hard, if not impossible, to rise to a high-status position where one may exert influence. Epidemics and serious health problems weaken a state, sometimes threatening its very existence. In determining whether to invest in a state, the international community needs to know how healthy its population is. Does the state have a functioning health system? What major diseases does the population face? Statistics tell us, for example, that most of the world's AIDS cases are found in Sub-Saharan Africa. If we compare the health of the population in Uganda with the health of the population in Thailand—another one of the states most threatened by AIDS—we find that Thailand has started a public health project to educate its citizens about AIDS and also has a more comprehensive public health care system than does Uganda. In comparing these two countries on the health factor alone, we would assign more promise to Thailand than Uganda, where the World Health Organization has predicted that AIDS threatens to wipe out virtually an entire generation from age 20 to age 40.

The last factor used at the state level of analysis, *population,* includes much more than the size of a state's population and its demographic characteristics. Besides such factors as the age profile, the rate of population growth, the birth rate, and age of marriage, an analysis of a state's population is also concerned with the level of unity. What is a state's ethnic and/or religious make-up? How much harmony or disharmony do we find between these groups?

Analysis of a state's population also looks at its level of productivity. If we return to our example of Uganda, deprived of citizens in the prime years of their lives and who could contribute most to the building of their country, we see that it is in a very unhappy situation. Finally, concerning population, we need to know something about the educational level of a state's people. A state whose population has a very low level of literacy is at a distinct disadvantage in comparison with states that invest in education and require high levels of educational achievement from its people.

If we compare just these four factors across states, we can make generalizations regarding the capability of each to be strong and effective players in the international system. For example, one hypothesis we could test is that states with strong government institutions and a more equal distribution of wealth tend to be more active and aggressive players than those with weak government institutions and an unequal distribution of wealth. Or we might want to see if there is any correlation between a state's level of economic development and the health and education of its population. What is the impact of AIDS or any other serious epidemic (health) on the stability of government institutions in such diverse states as South Africa and the United States? In conducting foreign policy, governments make such analyses every day. We will return to these questions later.

The Substate Level of Analysis

Beneath the state level of analysis is the substate level. At this level we find all the units that go to make up a state or that act as players in a regional organization. We will look first at the actors that inhabit the substate level and then turn to the generalizations we can make about them.

The Actors and Their Issues
The subunits of the United States are the 50 states. In Germany the subunits are the länder, or German lands. Belgium is divided between the Flemish-speaking provinces and the French-speaking provinces. The United Kingdom is composed of England, Scotland, Wales, and Northern Ireland. China has its provinces.

The Russian Federation has an array of substate entities: First are the autonomous republics, including the Republic of Tatarstan on the Volga River and the Republic of Sakha in the Siberian Arctic. Then there are the oblasts, or regions, such as Novgorod oblast, Novosibirsk oblast, and Moscow oblast. Among the oblasts are autonomous ethnic oblasts such as the Autonomous oblast of Yamal, or the Autonomous Oblast of Khantia-Mansia. Finally, there are the federal cities with oblast status: the City of Moscow and the City of St. Petersburg.

Figure 2.4, a map of the territorial divisions of Russia, shows how complex the substate unit system can be. The map shows that the country is divided first into republics, then into something called an *oblast* and something called a *kraj*, which are similar to the U.S. states, and finally, into a smaller unit called an *okres*, which is similar to the U.S. county. The perpetuation of two different names, *oblast* and *kraj*, for entities at an analogous administrative level is a holdover from the past. But that already complex arrangement is complicated still more by the existence of *autonomous* oblasts and *autonomous* okres. The reason for this complexity is that over 160 ethnic

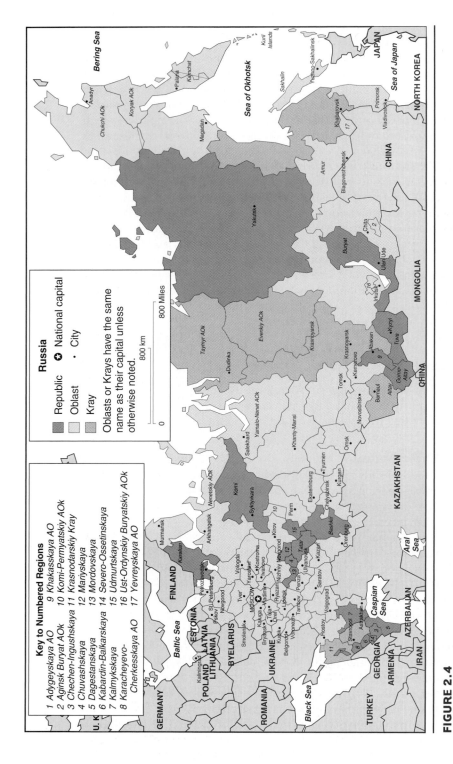

Key to Numbered Regions

1 Adygeyskaya AO
2 Aginsk Buryat AOk
3 Chechen-Ingushskaya
4 Chuvashskaya
5 Dagestanskaya
6 Kabardin-Balkarskaya
7 Kalmykskaya
8 Karacheyevo-
    Cherkesskaya AO
9 Khakasskaya AO
10 Komi-Permyatskiy AOk
11 Krasnodarskiy Kray
12 Mariyskaya
13 Mordovskaya
14 Severo-Ossetinskaya
15 Udmurtskaya
16 Ust-Ordynskiy Buryatskiy AOk
17 Yevreyskaya AO

Russia

⊛ National capital
· City

Republic
Oblast
Kray

Oblasts or Krays have the same
name as their capital unless
otherwise noted.

0   800 km

0   800 Miles

FIGURE 2.4

The Complexity of Russia's Territorial Divisions: If you were going to visit Severo–Ossetinskaya, would you have a clue where to go?

SOURCE: *University of Texas Library Online* (www.lib.utexas.edu/PCL/Map_collection/commonwealth/RussiaAdDivisions.jpg).

groups inhabit the Russian Federation. The Russians have developed an administrative system that tries to satisfy the differing national aspirations of all these groups. When the Soviet Union collapsed, Boris Yeltsin, President of the Russian Republic—a subunit of the USSR at that time—declared the republic to be independent and no longer a part of the Soviet Union. Immediately, the nations and ethnic groups within the new Russian Federation began to ask for either full independence or a large degree of autonomy (self-government) to regulate their own affairs. It may be hard to believe, but the clamor was so loud and strong that President Yeltsin had to reach a signed agreement with virtually every existing province, region, and republic, to define the scope of their power within the infant Federation. He did not sign an agreement with one group, the Chechens, and their status remains unresolved and volatile to this day. We will read more about Chechnya in the chapter's case study. Continued unrest has forced President Vladimir Putin, who succeeded Yeltsin, to revisit agreements with all the ethnic units in the Russian Caucasus—the strip of land between the Black Sea and the Caspian Sea in Figure 2.4 that is full of numbers representing the multiple ethnic subdivisions of the region.

Until recently, scholars paid little attention to the substate level. However, as you saw in Chapter 1, as the new forces shaping the planet have tended to make states more vulnerable, their central governments have come under pressure from both without and within to loosen central control. These decentralizing tendencies have given new life and power to the state's subunits.

Increased activity at the regional level has also contributed to the new vitality at the substate level. For example, over the past forty years, the states of Europe have been gradually harmonizing their markets, their legal systems, and their monetary systems to form a European Union. The EU is a supranational authority. If a law of one state within the Union does not meet the requirements or specifications of EU regulations, it must be revised to meet the standards. The subordination of the state governments to the institutions of the European Union has to a large degree weakened the extent to which they can dictate to their subunits. These, on the other hand, have recognized the transfer of member state sovereignty to the EU as an opportunity to assert their powers and privileges at the substate level.

A similar phenomenon may be taking place in the United States. The United States and Canada have an international agreement binding on both countries regarding the conservation and use of the Great Lakes. Initially, this agreement primarily regulated water use. In the 1970s, the agreement was amended to include the harmonization of pollution control. However, neither the United States nor Canada has taken much action in this regard. Most of the work has been done at the substate level, with U.S. states bordering the Great Lakes forming an organization and inviting the Canadian provinces of Ontario and Quebec to join them. Moreover, substate NGOs, such as the Great Lakes Consortium, are pursuing agendas to link the two countries in a single environmental management effort. The success of the Great Lakes border states and provinces in international cooperation has become a model to other substate actors for the management of international environmental issues. (See Chapter 13 for a general discussion of the management of international environmental issues.)

Can you see why the environmental paradigm is particularly relevant at the substate level? The Great Lakes basin forms a natural ecosystem. The political entities within that basin, both states (here, in the sense of subunits of the United States) and provinces, recognize the vital importance of that ecosystem to their survival and future livelihood. They thus have a greater interest in working out cooperative arrangements than the more distant federal governments, which have a great many other international interests that need to be addressed.

To find out more about China's agricultural problems, go to **www.ablongman.com/ duncan**.

China provides another interesting case of the power and importance of emerging substate actors. China is divided into rich and poor provinces. China's rich provinces are to be found on the country's east coast. These provinces have been granted special rights as free enterprise regions to enter into agreements with foreign corporations and sell directly abroad. As foreign capital has poured into the provinces, the economies have grown by leaps and bounds, the populations have been lifted out of the grinding poverty of the rest of the country, and the provincial governments have grown wealthy through the taxation of an upwardly mobile people. One of the great fears of the central Chinese government is that these provinces will grow so wealthy that they will refuse to pay taxes to the central Chinese authorities and choose to split off from the rest of the mainland.

Russia faces a similar risk of a split, as its center is in the west, while the provinces that make up its huge far eastern area can be thought of as the periphery pulling away from the center (see Figure 2.5). Russian far eastern trade is focused toward Japan and Korea, and communication links are rapidly being built to tie Japan and Korea to Russia's far eastern urban centers. Japanese and Koreans also form a substantial group in the populations of these centers. Also underscoring its distance from the center, the Russian far eastern port city of Vladivostock is linked to Moscow only by air and a two-track railroad that spans the nine time zones across Siberia to Moscow. Russians living on the Kamchatka Peninsula might well choose independence and slide closer to their eastern neighbors.

At issue is what might be called the contract between the national or federal government and the substate units. If the substate units are growing faster and acquiring power, wealth, and prestige in the process, they will question the necessity of remaining tied to a center that seems to lag behind their own development. The arrival of substate actors on the international scene adds yet another dimension to the growth of international civil society. To be players in the international arena, substate entities need to attract and keep the attention of the major players in the international system. To give legitimacy to their push for greater self-rule within the state or for complete independence from the state, these substate units often turn to a superpower like the United States, a regional actor like the EU, or an IGO such as the United Nations, to request recognition and assistance. The Autonomous Republic of Chechnya in Russia is one example; Kosovo in Yugoslavia is another.

In their struggle for international attention, the substate actors play on the same themes that brought the state of which they are a part into being: legitimacy, sovereignty, and the obligation to live up to international rules and laws. The arguments used to support their demands for self-rule are the arguments that people fighting for independence, including the thirteen colonies of North America, have used over the ages:

- The substate refuses to recognize the legitimacy of the mother state's government because the substate does not have adequate representation in the government.
- The substate desires sovereignty because the mother state refuses to let the people in the substate speak and learn their own language; the mother state further prevents them from earning a decent living by excluding them from education or certain areas of the economy.
- The mother state has no right to control the people in the substate because it does not practice or obey the basic rules of international law.

Not surprisingly, these demands often run counter to the interests of the mother state, and conflict results. We will now examine the main causes of this conflict.

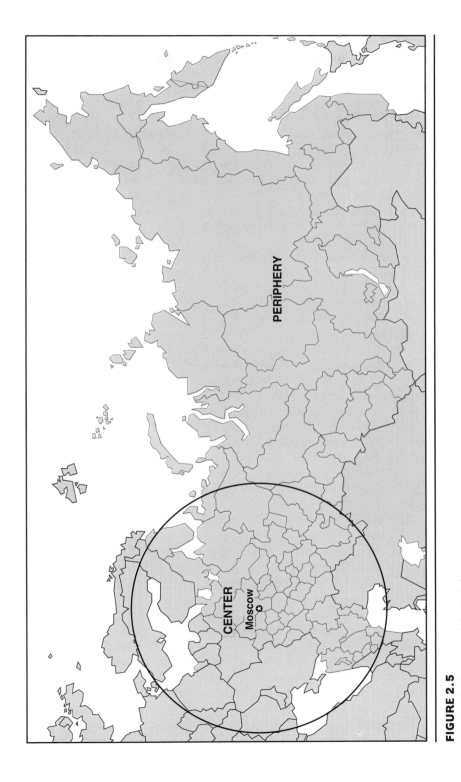

FIGURE 2.5

Russia: The Center and the Periphery

SOURCE: *University of Texas Library Online* (www.lib.texas.edu/maps/commonwealth/russiaaddivisions.jpg).

Conflict at the Substate Level Often the issue that divides a substate from its mother state (Kosovo from Yugoslavia) or one substate from another (Dagestan from Chechnya) flows from disputes over ethnicity, territory, language, and/or religion (see Chapter 1). *Boundaries,* closely related to the issue of territory, can also cause serious problems. In the nineteenth century, the colonial powers—Great Britain, France, and Germany—carved up Africa. They put boundaries where they seemed useful to the colonial powers, but they had little relation to the living patterns of the people who inhabited the area. Today the huge territory known in the nineteenth century as the Belgian Congo and now called the Republic of Congo is in the throes of a civil war over the boundaries set by the former colonial power. Some parts of the territory could well be swallowed up by neighboring states. In Asia, India and Pakistan have been at war since the two states succeeded the British colony of India in 1947. The issue is where to draw the boundary line between them in the Himalayan territory of Kashmir. And neither state appears to care that a large majority of the inhabitants of Kashmir would probably prefer independence. In the Balkan peninsula, Slobodan Milosevic agreed to let NATO peacekeeping forces into the Yugoslav province of Kosovo with the understanding that Kosovo would remain part of Yugoslavia and that the international boundary lines would not change. So, the peacekeeping forces, as upholders of the international agreement, must honor it, regardless of the fact that the Kosovars want independence. United States history, too, includes many boundary disputes both on its northern and southern borders. The settlement of these disputes put us at war with our neighbors, particularly with Mexico over the U.S. southern boundary in the 1840s.

Twentieth-century Europe was also full of boundary disputes. A principal reason why France went rather enthusiastically to war with Germany in 1914 was to regain its lost provinces of Alsace and Lorraine and to return the eastern boundary line of France to the Rhine River. The river had been the boundary for several hundred years until the Germans defeated the French in 1870 and pushed the line west. After the Second World War, as a punishment for Germany's behavior during the war, the victorious allies moved the German border west from where it had been, giving a large chunk of the former Germany to Poland and Russia (Kaliningrad). When West Germany and East Germany voted to unite in 1990, the new united Germany had to sign an agreement with neighboring Poland that it would respect the existing boundaries and not seek to have them revert to the pre-World War II line.

History shows that boundary lines can be very important to the people who live within them. If states are not to be continuously fighting over where the line runs, it makes sense that boundary lines should be recognized by the international community and especially by the UN.

History also shows that not everybody who lives within some particular set of boundary lines wants to be part of the state those lines describe. When a state wants to restore old boundary lines or push its boundary lines farther out to include some people that the state believes are kin to its own population, we call this **irredentism.** When a people or ethnic group within the borders of a recognized state, like the Kurds in Northern Iraq, wishes to carve out a part of the recognized state and set up their own sovereign government, we call this a movement for *self-determination.* In 1991, the Kurds rose up to demand self-determination from Saddam Hussein. The Iraqi regime bloodily repressed the nascent civil war, using poison gas, bombing, torture, mass killings, and deportation. The regime's tactics forced NATO to establish a no-fly zone in Northern Iraq off limits to

Irredentism
When a state wishes to push its boundary lines farther out to include some population that it believes belongs within its boundaries. Irredentism can lead to war when one state claims the people and a part or the whole of the territory of another state.

TABLE 2.3	**Substate Movements**
Independence	**breaking away from the host country** (Slovakia broke away from Czechoslovakia; Slovenia and Croatia from Yugoslavia; East Timor from Indonesia.)
Irredentism	**taking over a part of the neighboring country** (Hungary at one time wanted to get back the province of Transylvania, which was given to Romania after World War I.)
Civil War	**occurs when** (a) ethnic groups in the substate unit disagree over independence or staying with the host country; (b) ethnic groups in the substate unit fight the army of the host country for independence (Kosovo, East Timor).

Saddam Hussein's bombers and protected by NATO troops, where the Kurds could practice a limited form of self-government. The relation of the Kurdish territories to the rest of Iraq is of crucial importance to the consolidation of a new, democratic Iraqi government. (See Table 2.3 for an overview of substate movements.)

Probably the single most significant factor in substate conflict is the presence of a heterogeneous population, meaning that a variety of ethnic groups are represented there. An ethnic group, as we learned in Chapter 1, is a group of people linked by some common bond. Most frequently this bond is language, but it may also be one of belonging to the same tribe or religion. Less frequently, **race** can be a common bond. However, the meaning of race changes with circumstances, geography, and time period, and is nowhere near as common a bond as the others mentioned.[6] For example, the Han Chinese and the Japanese may be said to belong to the "yellow race," although there is no biological definition of "yellow race," so it's even unclear who would be included in the term. Yet, often in their history they have been mortal enemies. In Africa a black army from Uganda fights a black army from Rwanda in the predominantly black state of Zaire.

Language is the most common bond of ethnicity. If you have ever traveled to Europe or are planning such a trip, you will discover when you get to Paris that the Americans tend to group together in one corner of a cafe, the Germans in another, and the French somewhere else. Language is obviously an important reason for these divisions. Few Americans are bilingual, and few French or Germans feel comfortable conducting a conversation in a foreign language. When you visit Switzerland, you will find that it is separated into three distinct areas, each of which is primarily populated by a different ethnic group. In each part—the French cantons, the German cantons, and the Italian cantons—the signs are in the language of the majority population.

This desire for people who speak the same language to want to live together can be seen in the history of the formation of modern Europe. From the thirteenth century on, as Latin increasingly fell out of use as a language of trade and international communication, people began speaking in their own tongue. As leader fought leader, state fought state, and parts of empires fought imperial rule, the continent gradually sorted itself out into the countries we know today—each speaking its own language. Some ethnic groups, such as the Basques of Spain and France, never achieved independence. Others, such as the French-speaking Walloons and the Dutch-speaking Belgians, agreed halfheartedly to try to live together in a multiethnic state.

Race

A division of humankind possessing biological traits that are transmissible by descent and that are sufficient to characterize it as a distinctive human type. Color is the major trait identified with race today.

To find out more about how languages are distributed around the world, go to **www.ablongman.com/ duncan**.

If we turn to Afghanistan, one of the main problems in creating a national state is that the country is composed of seven ethnic groups, each speaking a different language. The largest group, the Pashtuns, would like to control the government and have their language, Pashtun, become the official one. The ethnic Tadzhiks and others disagree. And so tension between the tribes and their chieftains threatens the existence of the fragile state.

A second major reason people want to live apart is *religion*. Religious conflict tends to occur wherever two religions neighbor each other and where the boundaries between the two are *porous* (or not well defined, meaning that people can easily cross the boundary and move from one region into another). The island of Ireland is a prime example. The Irish people in the Republic of Ireland and Northern Ireland, which is part of the United Kingdom, all speak the same language or languages. The 100-year-old civil war in Northern Ireland is over religion. The Republic of Ireland is Catholic and wants to remain so. About half the people in Northern Ireland are Catholic, and most of these would like to join their Catholic relatives and neighbors in Ireland. They also would like to share in the good economic times Ireland is enjoying.

The other half of the people in Northern Ireland are Protestant—descendants of English and Scottish immigrants who moved to Ireland. They are afraid that the Catholic Irish will take over the province and vote to join Ireland. Protestants then would have, in the Protestant Irish view, no rights at all. They would be a permanent minority that would enjoy permanent discrimination. The Northern Ireland accord of November 1999 may be a step toward resolving this conflict—if the agreement holds. Religion can be a source of conflict between Muslims as it is between some Christians. Sixty percent of the Iraqi population belongs to the Shiite branch of the Muslim faith. Yet, under Saddam Hussein, they were considered a danger to his rule, and brutally suppressed. Their uprising against the Iraqi regime in 1991 was put down with the same cruelty as the Kurdish revolt.

Bosnia-Herzogovina is another example of a state divided by religious conflict. Essentially, the Bosnian Croats, the Bosnian Serbs, and the Bosnian Muslims all belong to the same South Slav ethnic group. And although the Croats speak a softer variant of Serbian, slurring their vowels as Southerners tend to do in the United States, the language spoken by both Serbs and Croats is the same. It was named Serbo-Croatian by Vuk Karadzic (1787–1864), the man who developed an alphabet based on the Cyrillic and Latin alphabets, and who wrote the first grammar for what had been up to that time primarily a spoken language. But all that was before 1992 and the Balkan War.

The war was essentially about territory: which group would get how much of Bosnia? But the issue of territory was framed in religious terms: Catholic Croats versus Muslim Serbs and Orthodox Serbs. Each side practiced ethnic cleansing and burned down sacred relics and religious places of "the enemy." When the dust settled, the Catholic Croats had their Bosnia-Herzogovina staked out primarily in Western Bosnia. The Orthodox Serbs had territory adjacent to Serbia and a nice corridor under Serbian control leading straight back to Serbia. The Muslims found themselves with reduced territory in the center of Bosnia. Today Bosnia may be a united nation on paper, but its three peoples live apart and seem intent to live that way permanently. Many observers believe that were it not for NATO's presence, Bosnia would once again erupt into civil war.

At the close of the twentieth century, tensions between Christians and Muslims acted as a catalyst of interethnic war throughout the world. Kosovo serves as one example, as the two peoples have been at each other's throats for the past 25 years.

The Serbs claim that Kosovo is the cradle of the Serbian nation. Here, 700 years ago, in 1389, the Orthodox Serbs believe they saved Christian Europe from the Muslim Turks by decimating the Turkish forces at the *battle of Kosovo,* or Field of Blackbirds even though the Serbs lost the battle. The Albanian Kosovars, who are Muslims, insist that all that history is irrelevant to the present. Today Kosovo is predominantly Muslim and, they say, should remain so.

True to the pattern we described of independence-seeking groups winning outside support for their cause, the Kosovars succeeded in convincing the states of NATO that they were being unjustly persecuted and that Serbian strong man Slobodan Milosevic had overstepped all bounds of legitimacy and international law in trying to cleanse Kosovo of Kosovars. NATO began a horrendous bombing campaign designed to stop Milosevic. After an agreement was reached between Milosevic and the NATO leaders, the Kosovars flooded back into Kosovo and attempted to ethnically cleanse the remaining Serbs in the province, most of whom then fled to Serbia for protection. Whatever the outcome of Kosovo's international status, one thing is certain. Neither of the two ethnic groups will live peacefully with the other for a long, long time.

On the other side of the planet in Indonesia there is a similar problem. The people of Indonesia are multiracial. However, Islam is the state religion. At the extreme eastern end of the Indonesian chain of islands lies the *island of Timor.* Timor was occupied by the Portuguese in years past, and half of the island embraced Catholicism. The Catholic East Timorians fought for independence from the Muslim mainstream for half a century. In 1999 in a UN-monitored referendum, almost 80 percent of the people of East Timor voted for independence. The day after the results were known, Muslim Indonesian militia in the region went on a rampage of violence—including, fire, murder, and rape to prevent the people from realizing their desire. The UN had to intervene to stop the killing and restore order to the new state that finally received its independence in 2000.

In conclusion, when you combine territorial, religious, and ethnic issues into one package, you often discover a substate/state conflict of seemingly irresolvable proportions. This is the case with the Israeli–Palestinian conflict, which is now over 100 years old. For more on this important issue, see the box The View from the Holy Land: The Israeli-Palestinian Conflict.

Independence with a Vengence:

An East Timorese man cries after his entire village was destroyed by anti-independence militiamen.

THE VIEW FROM   the Holy Land

The Israeli-Palestinian Conflict

The century-old conflict between Israelis and Palestinians has religious roots as well as political ones. The two peoples are kindred ethnic groups. The Palestinians are the descendents of the Philistines, whom the Hebrew people, the people of the one God, drove out of Palestine in the early part of their history. The Israelis prospered but were unable to withstand Roman military might. They repeatedly tried to reassert their religious and political autonomy only to be beaten back by the Roman army. In 79 A.D., the Roman Emperor Titus had had enough of Hebrew revolts. He ordered that Jerusalem, the Hebrew capital since the Hebrews first came to Palestine, be destroyed and the Hebrew people driven from the region. The Jewish Diaspora, or dispersion, as it came to be called, sent Jews into Southern Europe, East Asia and the Caucasus, Northern Europe, and Spain. The people who remained in Palestine became known as Palestinians. At the end of the ninetieth century, under the influence of European nationalism, Jews in Germany and Eastern Europe started a movement to return to their homeland. During the First World War, in an effort to mobilize the Jews to fight against the Turks, who were the rulers of the area at the time, the British Prime Minister declared that the Jewish people had a right to a homeland. Over the course of the century, Jews settled in ever greater numbers in Palestine, buying land from Palestinian landowners. It did not take long before the Palestinians became alarmed at the noticeable increase in Jewish settlers in their country. The efforts of the British, who inherited Palestine with the fall of the Turkish Empire, proved unable to bring the two sides to any agreement. World War II only increased the tension. The Jewish people believed they had a God-given right to a Jewish state after the horror of the holocaust and went to war to get it. Thus, throughout the twentieth century the relation between the two peoples on land they both claim as their own has been one of violence, revolt, killing, and war. The Palestinians are using suicide bombers to fight what they call *intifadah* or revolution for their right to live as independent people on two parts of the former Palestine. The Israelis fear the Palestinians want to drive them from their homeland. And so the violence continues, with no easy end in sight.

History offers a rather brutal lesson. Any government that has tried to create one nation from a multiethnic population has in the main had to rely on force to achieve its goals. You encounter this lesson again and again, when reading the history of France, England, and Germany, or when exploring the story of white expansion across the American continent. The native American tribes were beaten back until the few who remained were sidelined onto reservations. The United States prides itself today as a multiethnic state that celebrates cultural diversity. But its history has several chapters on ethnic cleansing, including a significant one about the people who reached America first.

The Individual Level of Analysis

At the individual level of analysis, we examine the role individual human beings play in the international system. In reading this section, you will note that this role can be more important and critical than you may have expected.

The Actors   Some of these actors we consider at this level are powerful government or NGO officials. Others are inventors, artists, actors, or sports people.

Two People Who Have Made a Difference in International Affairs at the Turn of the Twenty-First Century: George W. Bush, President of the United States; and Osama Bin Laden, Saudi terrorist.

When students in world politics classes at the State University of New York (SUNY) at Brockport were asked to name the five most powerful individuals in the world today, the most frequent replies were the president of the United States, Bin Laden, the Pope, Bill Gates, and the chairman of the board of a large U.S. corporation. When pressed, students added Mother Teresa, even though she was no longer alive.

We tend to think of an individual's power and influence based on the role he or she plays. Anyone who becomes president of the United States exercises a tremendous amount of individual influence by virtue of the office. We also tend to associate individual influence with roles played in large established institutions.

But how would you rate the influence of the Saudi financier Bin Laden, alive or dead, who bankrolled the training of terrorists in Afghanistan and has been the mastermind behind Al Qaeda? And how do you assess the influence of Mother Teresa as compared with Bin Laden, Bill Gates, or even Saddam Hussein? Would the U.S. power be more or less if the president today were Teddy Roosevelt, who led a group of volunteer soldiers known as the Rough Riders to defeat the Spaniards in Cuba in 1898? Does President Bush have the influence to persuade the American people to fight the war on terrorism indefinitely? Clearly, the personality and beliefs of a national leader have a decisive impact on both the input and the outcome of an international event. When we work at the individual level of analysis, we are always trying to measure or assess the relative influence on world politics of one individual against another on the basis of his or her personal characteristics.

Generalizations at the Individual Level of Analysis   We can make several generalizations about the impact of individuals on world events. First is the basic proposition that individuals do have the ability to influence world events in a unique direction, although much depends on the time and place. At the beginning of World War II, Winston Churchill galvanized the British to fight rather than capitulate to the Nazis with his rousing speech on "blood, sweat, and tears." However, as soon as the war was won, the British people threw him out of office at the next election. Clearly, they did not think he was the right person to be in charge of rebuilding a peacetime British economy.

Konrad Adenauer was a key figure in rebuilding West Germany after World War II. Under his leadership, West Germany was integrated into the western sphere of influence. West Germany joined NATO and became a founding member of the European Coal and Steel Community, the forerunner of the European Union. Today, however, Germany faces new issues. The wall dividing East and West Germany is no more, nor is the East-West antagonism. In the 1990s, a former member of the German Communist Party, Gerhardt Schroeder, was elected prime minister of Germany, an event that would have been unimaginable a generation ago. In his elaboration of an expanded international role for his country, Chancellor Schroeder is putting his stamp on Germany. For the time being the electorate backs him. But at some point, a new issue will bring a new face to the fore.

Former American President Bill Clinton wanted to stamp his image on world history when he used force for humanitarian purposes and sent the U.S. military into the Balkans. President George W. Bush would doubtless like to go down in history as the winner of the war against terrorism. Clearly, the personality and beliefs of a national leader make a difference in the outcome of an international event.

The second generalization to be made about the role of individuals in world events is that their perceptions and motivations play a key role in their decisions. Political psychology, a branch of international relations, is devoted to understanding these aspects of decision making, and the field has produced testable hypotheses about the attitudes and thought processes of leading international political actors. Two of the leading proponents of political psychology are Robert Jervis and R. Ned Lebow. Based on his study of the Cuban missile crisis, Jervis developed a series of hypotheses on the role of misperception in the management of crisis situations. For example, he claims that "actors tend to see the behavior of others as more centralized, disciplined, and coordinated than they are," and that "actors tend to overestimate the degree to which others are acting in response to what they themselves do."[7] Lebow's work centers on perceptions and misperceptions during the Cold War. In *We All Lost the Cold War,* he argues that what ended the Cold War was Soviet President Mikhail Gorbachev's realization that the Soviet Union had to reform economically. Another Soviet leader might have reacted to the American arms build-up with his own renewed build-up, despite the economic costs and the threat of economic break-down.[8] Gorbachev's perceptions and responses to those perceptions were critical to the ending of the Cold War.

The third set of generalizations we may formulate about individuals has to do with the amount of power they have. Indeed, almost all questions we want answered about individual actors on the international stage center on power: What is it, who has it, and how does he or she use it? (See box Why it Matters to You: What Human Kind Has Said About Power, for several famous sayings about power.)

Power comes from the Latin word *posse,* meaning "to be able, to have the ability to act or to do." When we talk about someone's *potential,* we are talking about that person's as yet unrealized ability to act or to do something. Teachers talk about their students' potential as scientists, scholars, mathematicians, or engineers. In biographies of great individuals, the author usually tells us whether the potential of that individual was recognized in childhood or whether, as with Sir Winston Churchill, his early life gave little indication of what he would actually achieve in his adult life. Power thus involves the ability to act or do, and in politics, it involves the ability to get someone to do something that he or she otherwise would not do voluntarily.

The common way for individuals to acquire power and become powerful has been "out of the barrel of a gun," to quote the father of Communist China and for-

WHY IT MATTERS TO YOU

What Humankind Has Said About Power

The concept of power has been a preoccupation of people in many places throughout history. Some see it as corrupting or violent; some, like Hans Morgenthau, the founder of modern realism (see Chapter 1), see it as the only game in town; and some follow the generally held religious view of power that individuals alone are powerless unless they are empowered by a divine source. How you view power colors not only your theories of how to get ahead and succeed in life, but also your views of what makes a successful politician and how your country should conduct itself in the international arena. In short, how you define power says a lot about your liberal, conservative, or ecological values.

- "Power corresponds to the human ability not just to act, but to act in concert," Hannah Arendt. *On Violence*.[9]
- "All power corrupts and absolute power corrupts absolutely," Lord Acton.
- "Power tends to corrupt, and absolute power corrupts absolutely. Great men are almost always bad men." Lord Action.[10]
- "To be feared is much safer than to be loved," Machiavelli. *The Prince*.[11]
- "International politics, like all politics, is a struggle for power." Hans Morgenthau, *Politics Among Nations: The Struggle for Power and Peace*.[12]
- "Power is A's ability to get B to bring about outcomes favorable to A's preferences or desires." Political scientist Robert Dahl, *Modern Political Analysis* 5th Edition.[13]
- "Power can be taken, but not given. The process of the taking is empowerment itself." Gloria Steinem, American feminist (b. 1934).
- "In democracies, all power resides in the people." Opinion shared by many Americans.
- "Power grows out of the barrel of a gun," Mao Zedong.[14,15]
- "*Kto kovo*" (Who, whom, or who wipes out whom?). Soviet description of power struggle in the former USSR.

mer Chinese dictator, Mao Zedong. The majority of powerful people since the dawn of time have become powerful largely through conquest. Although rare, a few individuals are recognized as powerful for their influence on our way of thinking or for their example of human goodness. Socrates, Shakespeare, Leonardo da Vinci, Francis of Assisi, and Mahatma Gandhi come easily to mind. Gutenberg, who perfected the printing press in Europe, and Bill Gates are examples of people who have influenced the course of human history through their development of powerful technology. Finally, certain people become powerful through their recognized role as head of a people, a nation, or a state. For example, no matter who fills the role, the president of the United States is one of the most powerful persons in the world today.

CEOs, too, are important in defining a vision of the global role of the corporations of which they are head. Thomas J. Watson II, son of the founder of International Business Machines, was listed among *Time Magazine's* 100 business people of the twentieth century because he saw the future of computer technology and pushed the mass distribution of the personal computer. How long would it have been before computers became commonplace in our life if Watson had not seen the future that way? We cannot answer the question. But Watson surely influenced the direction of technology by his vision of IBM's place in the world.

How do individuals *exercise* power? Throughout history we find only two ways: through force or through persuasion. Frequently, the two may be combined. Force is customarily violent: military might, terrorism, or compelling economic means (hostile takeovers, embargoes). Persuasion may be achieved through negotiation and bargaining, propaganda or advertising, by the direct one-on-one influence of a powerful person over someone less powerful, or by persuasive example, as in the case of St. Francis.

Political scientist Theodore White first focused our attention on the notion of power as influence in his studies of the making of the U.S. president in the 1960s. When someone easily persuades others to do something they otherwise would not do, we say that person has *charisma*. Unfortunately, charisma is not a gift given only to good people. Quite often, it seems that charisma belongs to the villains of this world: Hitler, Joseph Stalin, Saddam Hussein, Slobodan Milosevic. But Franklin Roosevelt had charisma. John F. Kennedy had charisma. Winston Churchill and the French wartime leader Charles de Gaulle had charisma. Most elected officials possess some charisma to get elected. It is seldom that an elected official has no charm at all.

Finally, in our explanation of the role of the individual in the international system, we can make generalizations about average people. Believe it or not, many people whose names we don't even know exert considerable influence. For example, many states agreed to give money for the rehabilitation of Kosovo and the Balkan peninsula. Large financial institutions pledged billions of dollars in loans that have taken a long time being processed. In the meantime, individuals from humanitarian NGOs such as the Catholic Relief Organization and the International Red Cross have been working in the region since the beginning of hostilities.

We hear calls to send help to hurricane victims in Nicaragua and Honduras, to give money to assist the refugees returning to Kosovo, to save the starving in Rwanda or Ethiopia, or to help the victims of earthquakes in India. Some of us help by sending a check. Others help by giving personal time to an organization that is raising the money. And still others actually go to the area that needs help and volunteer their labor. In 1995, after the Fourth UN Conference on Women in Beijing, American and Canadian women who had heard about the terrible situation of girl babies in China spent their own money to go to that country, adopt baby girls, and save their lives by bringing them back to Canada and the United States. Individuals can make a difference.

Former U.S. President and Nobel Peace Prize winner Jimmy Carter's work with Habitat for Humanity inspires others to help homeless people all over the world build their own homes with the assistance of volunteers. Those who assist hurricane victims or volunteer to build homes make a huge difference in the international system. Without the involvement of individuals at the grassroots, many international projects that alleviate suffering could not be realized. When individuals care about someone or some problem in the world and act upon their feelings, they have an impact. You too can be a player at the individual level in the world today.

How Do We Use the Levels of Analysis to Understand International Relations?

We have looked at five levels of analysis: the international system as a whole level, the regional level, the state level, the substate level, and the individual level. What is the best use to make of them? Must we look at only one level at a time? Can we combine levels?

Volunteers for Habitat for Humanity Building Homes in the Philippines: Dr. Potter along with 200 other volunteers went to the Philippines to help Filipinos build a home for themselves. Volunteers are found in every NGO and provide the vital services of providing home, food, and clothing to the millions of poor, sick, and homeless in our world today. The global community cannot do without them.

SOURCE: Private Photo, Dr. Robert T. Potter.

By this time in your studies of international relations, you probably can answer those questions on your own. We can use the levels however we want. We focus on a particular level of analysis based on (1) the shape and content of the situation; (2) what it is we want to find out; (3) what paradigm is used to formulate the question, What do I want to find out?

Let us take as an example Kashmir, because Kashmir was the subject of the case study in Chapter 1. How can using the levels of analysis shed light on the problems of Kashmir? Let's start at the state level. In 1948 the Hindus and the Muslims of the Indian subcontinent, worn out from fighting over which religious sect was to have the upper hand in the new state of India, agreed to a partition of British India into two states, Muslim Pakistan and largely Hindu India. At the sub-state level, you will find out that most of the former provinces of India had little difficulty deciding whether to join Pakistan or India. Most wanted to stay with India, because their populations and ruling class were largely Hindu (status and prestige). Kashmir, however, was different. Its ruling class was Hindu and its population predominantly Muslim. The decision to join India or Pakistan was not made by popular referendum in the provinces, but by the government. In this case, the government was one person, an autocratic ruler.

This piece of information tells us about the distribution of power in the province. Further investigation informs us that in the social structure of the day, high-level Hindus enjoyed status and prestige while the Muslims were at the bottom of the social ladder. Provincial rulers in British India were generally very wealthy, and this rajah was no exception. With most of the power, wealth, and status under his control, the rajah definitely had major decision-making power. When asked whether Kashmir should be in India or Pakistan, the Hindu ruler chose India. Immediately our attention shifts from the state to the individual level of analysis. Here is a case where one ruler seems to have made all the difference. Who was this person? What were his beliefs? His education? Who were his advisers? Didn't he know the majority of the population was Muslim, and that Muslims and Hindus had been bitterly fighting each other all over the subcontinent?

In fact, following the decision to join India, war broke out almost immediately between Hindus and Muslims in the territory of Kashmir, and it has continued to this day. The rajah who made the decision is dead. Why hasn't the issue been resolved? As a budding international relations expert, you immediately suspect that something may have been going on at the system level of analysis that prevented the two states from negotiating a settlement. You are absolutely right. From your knowledge of the power relations of the international system as a whole and data we shall assume you got from research, you assemble the following informative picture.

From 1948 to 1991, the international system was bipolar, with a cold war going on between the United States and the Soviet Union. The United States supported Pakistan. The Soviet Union supported India. The bipolar nature of the system put such pressures on Pakistan and India that they were unable to resolve their differences.

In 1991, the Soviet Union collapsed and the bipolar system ended. You might think that the climate would then have been ripe for a settlement. But a new force had emerged on the international stage—the civic community and the NGOs. To understand the role of this force, we must backtrack. During the 1980s, the United States feared that the Soviets would take control of Afghanistan and thus bring together India and Soviet Central Asia. To prevent a Soviet victory, the United States armed and trained Muslim groups in Pakistan to operate in Afghanistan. Many of these groups were associated with Al Qaeda. Pakistan used and may still be using these groups to keep up the pressure on India to cede Kashmir. The result is that even though the bipolar international system gave way to a unipolar system led by the United States, the United States cannot dictate the terms of the Kashmir settlement (1) because of the long-standing regional rivalry between India and Pakistan (regional level), (2) the existing relationship between the terrorist NGOs and the Pakistan military (state level, distribution of power), (3) the U.S. need for Pakistan to wage its war on terrorism in Afghanistan, and (4) the U.S. ignorance of much of Indian politics because of some 50 years of exclusion from direct communication (international system as a whole).

Do you see how an international relations expert can use the levels of analysis like a lens on a camera, zooming into the individual level, out to the system level, and moving freely between the centralizing tendencies of the system level and the decentralizing elements at the state and substate level? With the levels of analysis as structure and the state as the main unit, you now are ready to try to figure out what it would take to end the war in Kashmir. Good luck!

This chapter has been about the building blocks or the fundamental units of the international system. It thus has done more describing than theorizing. We will use theory much more in the coming chapters, but these basic concepts—the levels of analysis and the way power is used within each one of them—will recur as essential themes. In fact, so important is the concept of power that the entire next chapter is devoted to just that one idea.

CHAPTER SUMMARY

What Is the Basic Unit of Analysis in the International System?

The basic unit of the international system is the state.

The state is a relatively new international entity given recognition under international law at the Treaty of Westphalia in 1648.

A state is defined as a common territory inhabited by a people with a common language and a common culture.

The characteristics of the state are:

Sovereignty, meaning that the state is self-governing and that there is no higher authority that has jurisdiction over it. The sovereignty of states is limited in today's world through the vulnerability of states to events beyond their control.

Legitimacy, which refers to international and domestic acceptance of a state's government as the one that reflects the common language and culture of its people.

Duties, referring to the idea that states have *formal obligations* to one another through international treaties, regulatory conventions, and customs regarding the exchange of diplomats.

States are either national, multinational, or multiethnic. Multiethnic states have caused the most problems for the international state system because of the desire of substate ethnic groups for independence or merger with another state of a similar ethnic makeup.

The origins of the state lie in the city-states of antiquity in Mesopotamia, Greece, and Rome. With the fall of Rome in the West and the beginning of the Han Dynasty in China, the city-state virtually ceased to exist, but a new type of state based on kingly power began to emerge in Europe in the fourteenth and fifteenth centuries. Also, the Middle Ages saw a fight for control between the Catholic Church and the feudal monarchs. The fight between church and state ultimately saw the people picking sides. Most of them went with their monarch and so the modern nation-state came into being.

The invention of the printing press enabled royal edicts and royal news to spread rapidly throughout the country, multiplied the availability of books and literature, and encouraged everyone to learn to read. As common people did not read Latin, the international language of the day, the books were printed in the *vernacular* or language of the people to create a mass audience.

The modern state inherits four centuries of state domination of the international arena. Today, that domination is being challenged by the large number of states (187) and the vulnerability of states to events they cannot control.

What Is the Structure of the International System?

With the founding of the United Nations in 1945 at the end of World War II, the victorious Allies formally reendorsed the concept of an international system composed of states. The UN began its existence with 50 signatory states. *Most of today's states came into being over the past forty to fifty years* and are thus newcomers to the international system.

These states are of all different sizes.

The newer states formed from the former colonies of the European powers have arbitrary borders within which people of different ethnic backgrounds live. In these states, many people lack faith in the government's ability to solve problems. Thus they are weak states.

Under the principles of international law, all states are equal in sovereignty. However, in practice the weak states must adapt their behavior in the international arena to the cues of the strong states.

To get a handle on what the international system is, who all the players are, and how they relate to one another, we use what is called **the levels of analysis.**

The discipline of international relations structures the players in the system on five levels of international activity.

1. The system level of analysis. The basic assumptions at this level are (1) that the international system is considered as a single whole; (2) within this whole, actors interact with and respond to one another in ways that are predictable.

The principal actors are the states. We commonly group these states into what are called the four worlds, or sets of states, based on the level of economic and political development that a state has attained. The First World comprises the industrialized states. The Second World includes all the states formed after the fall of the Soviet Union and its satellite countries. The Third World refers to the developing countries, and the Fourth World are the at-risk or failed states.

The other actors are the nonstate actors. These include the intergovernmental organizations (IGOs) whose members each represent a participating state, and the nongovernmental actors (NGOs), whose membership is global and voluntary.

Nonstate actors have become increasingly visible in the post–Cold War world. The attacks of 9/11 brought home the significance of these groups in international politics.

Generalizations that can be made at this level of analysis include:

- Relations between states, and indeed between states and nonstate actors, are characterized by power relationships.
- Strong states that attract weaker states into their orbit constitute the system's *poles of power*. We can thus distinguish between a multipolar, bipolar, and unipolar international system.
- There is now such an increasingly large number of nonstate actors, particularly NGOs, that scholars have proposed the emergence of an international civic community.

2. The *regional level of analysis* enables us to compare *across* regions and to compare states *within* regions. Thus, if we are studying Europe, for example, the actors would include the European states, the European Union as the principal regional IGO, and whatever NGOs had their base in Europe.

We can make several generalizations at the regional level of analysis:

- We can generalize about economic and political capacity across regions.
- We can generalize about the structure of power within a region and across regions.
- We can generalize about the dynamics of regional IGOs and NGOs in various parts of the world

3. The *state level of analysis* looks at and contrasts the behavior of individual states, which are the actors at this level. Common factors to compare and contrast about individual states are power, wealth, status and prestige, and population. By comparing and contrasting the four factors across states, we can make several kinds of analyses:

- We can assess the capability of states to be strong and effective players in the international system.
- We can look for correlations—for example, between a state's level of economic development and the health and education of its population.
- We can consider the comparative impact of a particular event or condition—for example, the impact of AIDS (health) on the stability of governmental institutions in such diverse states as South Africa and the United States.

4. At the substate level, we find all the units that make up a state or that act as players in a regional organization. The actors include such subsections of states as the provinces of Russia, Canada, and other countries or the lander in Germany. They also include any IGO and NGO institutions active at the substate level. The issues around which substate conflicts revolve are most often of an ethnic, religious, or linguistic nature.

Sources of conflict between the state and the substate are similar to those between states.

- The substate refuses to recognize the legitimacy of the mother state's government because the substate does not have adequate representation in the government.
- The substate desires sovereignty because the mother state refuses to let the people in the substate speak and learn their own language; the mother state further prevents them from earning a decent living by excluding them from education or certain areas of the economy.
- The mother state has no right to control the people in the substate because it does not practice or obey the basic rules of international law.

Conflicts at the substate level often involve boundary disputes or ethnic or racial groups that speak different languages, practice different religions, or come from different economic levels.

5. The individual level of analysis investigates the role individual human beings play in the international system. Actors may be powerful government or NGO officials, inventors, artists, actors, sports people, or ordinary citizens.

The individual level of analysis offers several types of generalizations.

- Individuals have the ability to influence world events in a unique direction, depending on their time and place in history.
- A whole branch of international relations is devoted to understanding the role of perception and motivation in the way key individuals make important decisions. Political psychology has produced testable hypotheses that generalize about the attitudes and thought processes of leading international political actors.
- The impact of individuals can be assessed based on the amount of power they have.

- Average people also have an important role to play in the international system.

How Do We Use the Levels of Analysis to Understand International Relations?

We use the levels of analysis like the lens of a camera to zoom in and out of a situation, looking at the international system level of analysis for the broadest view of power relationships, zooming into the state or substate level for an analysis of the variables that explain why a state or substate unit acted the way it did, zooming further in to the individual level to understand the characteristics and abilities of the individuals who seem most involved with the situation under analysis, and returning to the regional level for an analysis of the power relationships at the level that may support or not support the state or substate unit under investigation.

ENDNOTES

[1]Robert Kohane and Joseph S. Nye, *Power and Interdependence: World Politics in Transition* (Boston: Little Brown, 1977).

[2]Kenneth N. Waltz, *Theory of International Politics* (Reading, MA: Addison-Wesley Publishing Company, 1976), pp. 129–160.

[3]James N. Rosenau, *Turbulence in World Politics: A Theory of Change and Continuity* ((Princeton: Princeton University Press, 1990), pp.114–140.

[4]For a complete account of the Peloponnesian (or Peninsular) War see Thucydides, *A History of the Peloponnesian War,* trans. Rex Warner, A Penguin Classic (New York: Viking Press, 1986).

[5]See John King Fairbank, *China: A New History* (Cambridge, MA: Belnap Press of Harvard University, 1992), pp. 49–58.

[6]For a discussion of race from different points of view, the reader is referred to Adalberto Aguirre and David V. Baker, eds.

Sources: *Notable Selections in Race and Ethnicity* (Guildford, CT: McGraw-Hill Textbook Division, 1998); Elizabeth Pathy Salett and Diane R. Koslow, *Race, Ethnicity, and Self: Identity in Multicultural Perspective* (Washington, DC: National Multicultural Institute, 1994); Thomas Sowell, *Race and Culture: A World View* (New York: Basic Books, 1995).

[7]Robert Jervis, "Hypotheses on Misperception," *World Politics,* Vol. 20, No. 3 (April 1968), reprinted in Falk and

Kim, *The War System* (Boulder, CO: Westview Press, 1980), pp. 481–482.

[8]For a brief exposition of this position, see Richard Ned Lebow and Janice Gross Stein, "Reagan and the Russians," *The Altantic Monthly* (February 1994), as printed on *http://www.the atlantic.com/politics/foreign/reagrus.htm.* For a fuller discussion, see Richard Ned Lebow and Janice Gross Stein, *We All Lost the Cold War* (Princeton: Princeton University Press, 1995).

[9]Hannah Arendt, *On Violence* (New York: Harcourt Brace and Co., 1970), p. 44.

[10]Lord Action in a letter to Bishop Mandell Creighton, April 3, 1887), as cited in Dictionary of Quotations, ed by Bergan Evans (New York: Avenel Books, 1978), p. 547.

[11]Niccolo Machiavelli, *The Prince,* trans. and ed. Robert M. Adams (New York: W.W. Norton Company, 1977), p. 47.

[12]Hans Morgenthau, *Politics Among Nations:* The Struggle for Power and Peace, 3rd ed. (New York: Alfred A. Knopf Publisher, 1965), p. 27.

[13]Robert A. Dahl, *Modern Political Analysis,* 5th ed. (Englewood Cliffs, NJ: Prentice-Hall, 1991), p. 32.

[14]Number 55709. Attributyed to Gloria Steinem (b. 1934) as cited in The Columbia World of Quotations, 1996. *http:www.bartleby.com/66/9/55709.html*

[15]"Political Power Grows Out of the Barrel of a Gun." Mao-Tse Tung, "Problems of War and Strategy" (November 6, 1938), *Selected Works,* Volume II, p. 224.

CASE STUDY

A Russian Invasion
of Georgia?
Some International Reactions

In the fall of 2002, Russian President Vladimir Putin let it be known that just as the United States was targeting Iraq for harboring terrorists and producing weapons of mass destruction, so Georgia was harboring terrorists and outfitting them with arms. So serious was the situation, that he, Putin, was considering invading Georgia to put down the terrorists. The following case study contains four articles. They analyze the costs and benefits of the Russian proposal to invade its neighboring state of Georgia to root out paramilitary groups that Russia claims are terrorists who are undermining the Russian attempt to stabilize its breakaway Republic of Chechnya. First, here is some background.

The people of the Caucasus Mountains on the border between Asia and Europe have waged a war for their survival for many centuries. The impenetrability of the region has enabled countless tribes to find refuge there. The Arab historian al-Azizi dubbed the region the Mountain of Languages, recording that 300 mutually incomprehensible tongues were spoken in Daghestan alone, Chechnya's next door neighbor. The Chechens themselves are descendants of an early migration from Europe and one of over a hundred tribes that settled the region. They lead a harsh life, as agriculture is difficult, and the steep slopes require strenuous hiking up and down to bring water where it is needed. Caucasian life has been dominated by the blood-vendetta, the *kanli*, which ensured that no wrong, however slight, could go unavenged by the relatives of a victim. The *kanli* has been waged between all the tribes, and the region has known little peace. The Chechens took up arms against the Russians at the turn of the nineteenth century under the legendary Chechen leader, Shaykh Shamil. The Russians were forced to conquer the mountainous country inch by inch. And the battle has continued on and off between them ever since, gaining in intensity since an open Chechen rebellion in 1995.

Today, the Russians claim that the Chechen rebels have managed to escape the Russian army by holing up in the Panchir Gorge on the border with Georgia. The inaccessibility of the Gorge, says the Russian president, means that the Russians can't get close enough from the air to bomb it, and the Chechens are free to move back and forth over mountain roads between Chechnya and Georgia. In Georgia, the Chechens find sympathetic supporters who help move men and material into the rebellious republic. The way to stop this process, Putin says, is to invade Georgia, just as the United States was planning to invade Iraq.

How should the international community in general, and the United States in particular, respond to Putin's move? The following series of articles looks at the Russian/Georgian standoff from four of the levels of analysis discussed in this chapter. Thus, they will give you experience using the levels of analysis to understand world events and to direct your attention to options for action at each level.

From the Perspective of the International System as a Whole

On the first anniversary of the 9/11 terrorist attacks in the United States, Russian President Vladimir Putin warned the Georgian leadership that if it failed to take effective measures to prevent Chechen guerillas from launching attacks on Russian territory from bases in Georgia, Russia would avail itself of its right—guaranteed by the UN Charter—to take appropriate action in self-defense. Georgian President Eduard Shevardnadze dismissed Putin's threat of military action against Chechen rebels in the Pankisi Gorge as biased and one-sided, and called for international assistance to resolve the issue.

That same day, September 11, 2002, the Russian President sent a letter to the UN Secretary General and to the members of the UN Security Council and the Permanent Council of the Organization for Security and Cooperation in Europe, an agency dedicated to promoting security and cooperation on the European continent. In his letter, President Putin argued that Chechen militants had taken refuge in Georgia with, Putin claimed, the support of the Georgian leadership. Putin accused Georgia of violating the UN Security Council's antiterrorism resolution No. 1373 and said Georgia must be made to comply with its international obligations. Putin said Russia might be constrained to resort to its right under UN Security Council resolution No. 1368 and the UN Charter to individual or collective self-defense to neutralize what it sees as a terrorist threat with or without Georgian assistance.

The following two press releases from the OSCE and the United States provide responses from the international community. They were chosen because the OSCE has been involved in monitoring activities on the Georgian-Russian border while the United States has committed military personnel to train Georgian border guards. Read the articles carefully.   How would you describe the reaction of the two parties to Russia's threat against Georgia? What do the two statements suggest are the stakes the international community has in this regional dispute? Can you identify some international security concerns to which the two statements might be referring? What information does the U.S. statement give you about the status of U.S./Russian relations? How has the United States moved to protect Georgian sovereignty and to assure an American presence in the area?

Excerpts from the Press Release of the Chairman-in-Office, Organization for Security and Co-operation in Europe

NEW YORK, 13 September 2002—The OSCE Chairman-in-Office, Portuguese Foreign Minister Antonio Martins da Cruz, continues to be deeply disturbed by the increasing tension between Georgia and the Russian Federation.

The Minister noted the letter by the President of the Russian Federation, Vladimir Putin, to the Secretary-General of the United Nations, heads of State of the permanent members of the UN Security Council and Heads of State or Government of the OSCE participating States, in which President Putin stated, *inter alia*, that "Russia may be forced to use the inalienable right to individual or collective defense."

Against this background and in accordance with the OSCE's responsibilities as a regional arrangement under Chapter VIII of the UN Charter, the OSCE Chairmanship has initiated urgent consultations with the parties involved, as well as with other OSCE participating States, in order to assist Georgia and the Russian Federation to reduce the existing tension.

The Chairman-in-Office called on the Russian Federation and Georgia to abstain from any action which might further increase tensions in the region and which might have grave consequences for the security and stability of the Caucasus and the whole of the OSCE area. He urged all parties to make full use of OSCE instruments to prevent an escalation in tension and resolve their differences.

The Chairman-in-Office expressed his conviction that the OSCE, including through the activities of its Border Monitoring Operation (BMO) in Georgia, will be able to help to restore confidence between the parties. The Chairmanship had already initiated a review of the current work of the BMO with a view to increasing the efficiency of its activities.

SOURCE: Organization for Security and Co-operation in Europe (http://www.osce.org/news/generate.pf.php3?news_id=2724).

Statement of U.S. Position at OSCE Permanent Council Meeting in Vienna, Austria, September 26, 2002

By Douglas Davidson, Deputy Chief of U.S. Mission to the Organization for Security and Cooperation in Europe

Released by the U.S. Mission to the OSCE

Mr. Chairman, I would like first to reiterate once again the United States' strong support for Georgia's sovereignty and territorial integrity. The United States takes strong exception to President Putin's much publicized September 11 statement threatening unilateral action against Chechen fighters and international terrorists in Georgia's Pankisi Gorge, should Georgia not take more active measures against these fighters. The United States responded immediately to this statement both through public declarations and high-level diplomatic channels, stating our unequivocal opposition to any unilateral Russian military action inside Georgian territory.

Our reaction is similar to the Russian appeal circulated to all OSCE participating States in Vienna two weeks ago. We have strongly urged Georgia to regain full control of the Pankisi Gorge region, where we too believe there are third-country terrorists with links to Al Qaeda. These terrorists threaten not only Georgia's security and political stability, but also that of the Russian Federation. We understand the Russian concerns, but we firmly believe that problems in the Pankisi Gorge should be addressed by the Georgian Government.

We fully support the continuing efforts of the Georgian authorities to clear the Chechen and other fighters from the area. To this end, we are working with the Georgian military, border guards, and law enforcement agencies to enhance Georgia's capacity to provide effective border controls and internal security.

Mr. Chairman, the United States continues to encourage the Georgian and Russian governments to work together on all levels to promote regional security on their own respective territories, and to find negotiated political solutions to their various differences. I believe I can speak for my colleagues around the table in saying that we will all do whatever we can to support such efforts. This includes support for a team of OSCE Experts, including representatives of the Russian Federation, as suggested by the Georgian Ambassador.

Source: U.S. Department of State (http://www.state.gov/p/eur/rls/rm/2002/14111.htm).

From the Perspective of the Regional Level

This article is from a journal published in Armenia, a state that borders on both Russia and Georgia. Since its independence in 1991, Armenia has been closely allied to Russia in its quarrel with a third neighbor, Azerbaijan, over which state owns the predominantly Armenian enclave in Azerbaijan called nagorno-Karabakh. Armenia, a Christian country, has stuck with Russia, also a Christian country, because Russia has traditionally supported Christians against Muslims in the Caucasus. However, Georgia is also a Christian country, while the Chechen rebels are Muslim. Armenia might want to mediate because she sees herself as a Christian country capable of mediating between two Christian neighbors. But if you look on your maps at the beginning of your text, you will see that Armenia is tiny compared to giant Russia. How much influence would such a small country have on its huge neighbor, who has always been the regional hegemon?

The articles gives you a good look at the issues and concerns that have surfaced at the regional level of the proposed Russian invasion. Read the article carefully. Since it is a translation from the original, the English may sound strange to you. Why do the Armenians say the Georgians don't want Russian help to get rid of the "terrorists"? What does the article say are the Russians' intentions in the region? Can you infer what the Armenians hope to get out of mediation?

A few points of information: Schevarnadze is the president of Georgia. Tbilisi is the capital of Georgia and is used to mean the Georgian government. Yerevan is the capital of Armenia and is used to mean the Armenian government.

Can Armenia Mediate to Calm Down Russian-Georgian Confrontation?

By Rafik Hovhanesian

The noise raised by the official Kremlin about the presence of Chechen militants in Georgia's Pankisi Gorge is, of course, exaggerated. The tough announcement by Russian president Putin on September 11, which was timed to the anniversary of tragic events in the United States, and which was described by some Russian mass media as "an ultimatum," contained some elements of theatricality.

It is however, not a secret for anyone that there were and are Chechen militants in the Pankisi Gorge. But this presence is presented by Moscow's propaganda machine as if the biggest threat to Russia is emanating from this gorge, which is just a pretext to prepare an invasion into the Georgian territory.

By the way, some reprimands addressed to Georgian authorities by Moscow are well grounded. President Putin was right when expressing bewilderment. "We are told that Georgia is not capable of fighting against guerillas by its own forces. But when we offer help they refuse it, saying we shall do it ourselves."

It is obvious why Georgia "refuses" Russian offer to help. Simply, Georgians do not want to create a new occasion for Russian military presence in their country, having in mind that the strife to free their country from Russian military bases has become a kind of national idea after the collapse of the Soviet Union. The Kremlin views this all not only as an attempt to take Georgia out from the zone of its influence and interests, but also as a manifestation of helping the U.S. drive to force Russians out of the Caucasus at all. There is no doubt that there is such strife. After the September 11 attacks on the United States, Georgians could have thought that the process of ousting Russians from the South Caucasus might speed up. I think it was one of the big mistakes of president Shevardnadze. Putin unreservedly stood by the United States in fighting against the international terrorism and this will, at least, freeze implementation of the U.S. program on ousting Russia from the region as long as that struggle continues.

Taking advantage of the moment, Moscow in turn is striving to reinforce itself in the region, and for that it is necessary to slap Georgia in the face . This is the secret spring behind the clamor raised around Pankisi Gorge. One can suppose that Putin's calculation is more far-reaching than that of Shevardnadze. In the struggle against international terrorism Moscow is by far a more important ally of the United States than Georgia. President George W. Bush would hardly spoil relationship with Moscow for the sake of Tbilisi. In this regard last week's letter by Bush to Shevardnadze may be interesting. The leader of the most powerful state in the world, who had earlier, on September 14, disagreed sharply with Putin's ultimatum to Georgia, was urging Tbilisi "to cooperate with Russians in Pankisi."

This was followed by an announcement by a senior U.S. official that they "do not have illusions regarding the Georgia's question," and have verified information about international terrorists who are hiding in Pankisi. The official also said that they know that Georgia was more than tolerant towards them.

This sharp change in the U.S. position means that Russian foreign and defense ministers, who had a series of meetings in Washington with most influential persons in Bush's administration, have managed to find a common language in the Georgian issue, meaning that Moscow has free hands in air-striking on Pankisi region.

Under these conditions a statement made by Armenian foreign minister Vartan Oskanian on September 12 that Armenia was willing to mediate in easing the Russian-Georgian tension, takes an exclusive value, as an offer by a country that has friendly relations with both Russia and Georgia. Two weeks have passed but neither Moscow nor Georgia has responded. This proposal may, at a certain point, be pushed ahead, if Moscow and Washington agree on retaining Shevardnadze's regime. In that case Moscow would benefit to demonstrate to the international community that the "dispute" of two "brother" nations was resolved with the help of the third "brother" nation. But if the issue of maintaining the regime of Shevardnadze was not discussed in Washington or was ignored, it means that the Yerevan's proposal will remain unanswered for the time being, as long as Moscow sees that it would be able to achieve the resignation of Shevardnadze through raising the tension in Pankisi Gorge. There is of course this prospect as the anti-Shevardnadze forces would not think twice to accuse the aging president of spoiling relationship with the powerful neighbor to topple him. If that scenario would not work it would never be too late to "remember" about the proposal by Oskanian.

SOURCE: AZG Armenian Daily #171, September 24, 2002. Reprinted with permission of the publisher.

From the Perspective of the State-Level

This article is written by the leader of one of the parliamentary opposition parties in the Russian Duma, or legislature. Take a close look at the first paragraph. What kind of party do you think Yavlinsky heads? A labor party, a party pushing for democratic principles, or a probusiness party? Why does Yavlinsky say the invasion of Georgia is "inadmissible"? What does he think might happen in Russia or happen to Russia's image abroad?

This Could Prove a Costly Escapade

By Grigory Yavlinsky

Russian military strikes against Georgia are inadmissible. The questionable gains of a military operation are completely outweighed by the political damage that Russia would incur both at home and internationally if it spreads the war in Chechnya to the neighboring independent state of Georgia. For 200 years we lived together in a single state, including 70 years under the Soviet regime. The consequences of such a move would be destructive for both nations.

Moreover, the situation in the Pankisi Gorge does not hold the key to ending the war in Chechnya. There are considerably more rebel fighters and terrorists in Chechnya itself and adjoining territories, than there are in Pankisi. Georgia is far from being the main conduit for rebels, terrorists, mercenaries, weapons, and money to enter Chechnya. And we should not forget that Chechnya gave rise to the "Pankisi factor" and not the other way around.

The military, by proposing strikes on Georgia to President Vladimir Putin, is trying to conceal from the president its inability to deal with the task at hand in Chechnya; talk of strikes is also being used as a ruse to divert public attention. This could well prove to be a costly escapade.

It is undoubtedly the case that certain forces in Georgia are providing political support to active adversaries of Russia's constitutional order. Some Chechen rebel fighters have illegally crossed over onto Georgian territory. Instead of prosecuting them, Tbilisi has been giving them a free hand and using them for political purposes.

Chechen insurgents in Georgia should be disarmed and terrorists neutralized and tried. This is what political cooperation between the leadership of Russia and Georgia should be centered on. Russia can and should bring pressure to bear on Georgia to use its law enforcement agencies to this end. But this is not an issue of armed conflict between the two states.

Indeed, Russia's myopic and irresponsible interventions in Abkhazia, Adzharia and South Ossetia have been futile and extremely dangerous. This of course does not refer to the soldiers of Russian peace keeping forces whose duty there is justly acclaimed not only by UN and OSCE, but by President Shevarnadze himself as well. It is in response to the Russian elite's penchant for indulging separatist aspirations, Tbilisi considers it acceptable to give political cover to Chechen terrorists. Counting on backing from the international community, Tbilisi is mistakenly serving up a "symmetrical response" to Russia and as a result is simply repeating Russia's mistakes.

Russia's might is incomparably greater than that of its neighbors. For this reason, it is incumbent upon Russia to show heightened responsibility regarding what goes on in the region.

Putin should reach an agreement with Georgian President Eduard Shevardnadze. And after that, the relevant law enforcement agencies in Russia and Georgia should be left to get on with the job. And that's it.

SOURCE: *Grigory Yavlinsky, leader of the Yabloko party, contributed this comment to* The Moscow Times, *Monday, September 23, 2002, p. 12. Reprinted by permission of the Author.*

From the Perspective of the Individual Level

The *Boston Globe* is a leading Boston paper. The columnist focuses primarily on the two protagonists of the Russian threat, President Bush and President Putin, with a focus on the challenges Putin poses to himself and to Bush. What problems does Putin face as leader of Russia that might hurt him if he invades Georgia? What problems does Bush face if he sides with Putin, or if he says no? This is a good presentation of a problem from the individual level of analysis.

On Iraq, Putin May See a Gain in Backing Bush

By David M. Shribman

WASHINGTON—The gathering Iraq crisis is being portrayed as two grave tests of character and resolve, one for George W. Bush, the other for Saddam Hussein. But this peculiar moment in world affairs, at the end of a period of traditional power politics and at the beginning of a new age of terrorist threats, also presents a momentous turning point for another world leader. It is the biggest international test yet for Vladimir V. Putin.

The Russian president is surrounded by troubles. He faces an insurrection in Chechnya. He fears a terrorist haven in Georgia. He worries about economic instability at home. He is constantly reminded that the end of the Cold War meant the end of his nation's status as a superpower. And now he faces the growing likelihood of an attack on a country [Iraq] where Russia has important political ties and commercial interests.

But one of the laws of geopolitics is that grave moments of peril also present brave moments of opportunity. This is a turning point not only for what the Bush administration has come to call the New Iraq; it is also a turning point for what Western leaders have come to call, more in hope than in reality, the New Russia.

In the old days, the formula for a nation looking for world leadership was simple: Assert yourself as an honest broker, defuse a difficult situation with a dispassionate eye, and approach world problems the way cubist painters approached still lives, by looking at them from all sides. Theodore Roosevelt used that formula to win a peace at the end of the Russo-Japanese War of 1904–1905. For that work, he was awarded the Nobel Peace Prize, and world opinion awarded his nation, which at the time was no superpower, great prestige. That formula is almost certainly not available to Putin this time. The Bush administration is in no mood for mediation.

The Russian opportunity is different in 2002. Here's the menu of the limited choices Putin has:

Take Saddam Hussein's side. The Russians realize that former president Boris Yeltsin missed a great opportunity in the Balkans in the 1990s by hanging on to the losing side, politically and morally, until the last hour, and Putin does not want to be identified with isolated rogue states and failing causes.

Find a safe haven for Hussein outside Iraq. The Iraqi dictator is not the shah of Iran or Jean-Claude "Baby Doc" Duvalier of Haiti, both of whom fled their countries, and there is no indication that the Iraqi leader has got the urge for going. There are fewer places to hide a discredited dictator today than even a decade ago.

Help accomplish unimpeded weapons inspections. The Bush administration is skeptical that weapons inspections can be effective, but this is a legitimate role for Russia. Because so many expect these inspections to break down, it could still lead to U.S. military intervention.

Join Bush in regarding Iraq as a threat to regional and global stability. This option highlights Russia's importance to an international coalition and has the added advantage of letting Putin appear to rush in to rescue Bush, an image that the

Kremlin is unlikely to be able to replicate in the next several years.

Russia is like Britain in the days of empire. It has interests, not allies. One of its interests is world prestige: Putin wants to show that Russia matters and cannot be ignored; he wants to look like a power broker. Another Russian interest is oil contracts. Oil politics matter in Russia, too. They have, for example, driven Putin on issues in the Caspian region involving pipelines. He is now under pressure from his own domestic oil interests not to permit Russia's oil concessions in Iraq to be torn up by a regime that succeeds Saddam Hussein.

That's why the effort to make an international coalition on dealing with Iraq is going to look a little bit like making a deal. There are immense pressures inside Moscow pulling Putin away from Bush, mostly because of Russian worries about the extension of U.S. power, first in Central Asia and now in the Middle East. (The Western analogue to these pressures is the worry among American allies, including France and Canada, about U.S. unilateralism.)

Even so, the United States will probably guarantee the investments of Russia (and, perhaps, of France) in a reconstituted Iraq. In exchange, the United States would win Russian forbearance, or perhaps cooperation, in Iraq. The United States would win one thing more, which has been of assistance in Afghanistan: access to Russian intelligence capabilities, which Washington experts believe are better than U.S. capabilities in the region.

This situation is laced with irony. Perhaps the most compelling irony is embedded in the rationale for an American strike against Iraq. Last week, the Bush administration formalized its policy of preemptive strikes, legitimizing a doctrine that troubled American presidents when it was used by the old Soviet Union in Hungary, Czechoslovakia, and elsewhere.

That acceptance of preemptive action already has been noted in Moscow. On September 12, Putin escalated his rhetoric against Georgia, which he believes is harboring Chechen fighters. Like President Bush, he asked the United Nations for support. Like President Bush, he is threatening what he calls "adequate measures to oppose the terrorist threat." His words are evidence that Putin, who is using common language with Bush as he decides whether to make common cause with Bush, sees not only an opportunity here. He may also see an advantage.

QUESTIONS

Check Your Understanding

1. Who are the major leaders in this international drama, and which country does each represent?
2. Explain the parallels between a U.S. invasion of Iraq and a Russian invasion of Georgia.

Analyze the Issues

1. What do the articles say are the positive and negative impacts of Putin's threat to invade Georgia at the international and regional levels? In your opinion, which kind of impact seems more critical to encouraging or delaying action?
2. Why would Armenia, a state that neighbors Georgia and Russia, be interested in playing mediator?
3. What are the pro and con pressures on the United States at the international level with regard to the invasion of Georgia?
4. Describe what is going on between the actors at each level of analysis. Which level of analysis do you think seems most useful in guiding policy? Which might be most influential in determining the next move? Explain your answer.
5. At which level(s) of analysis does Georgia's state sovereignty become an issue? From the material in the chapter, do you think that in today's climate Georgia's insistence on its sovereignty would meet with a sympathetic hearing at the international level?
6. This chapter has argued that individuals do make a difference. Do you think the positions of the United States and Russia in this matter are determined more by the power they exhibit in the international system or by the strength of their leaders?

FOR FURTHER INFORMATION

To find out more about Chechnya, its struggle for independence, and how Georgia is involved, consult the following journal articles, maps, Internet sites, and films:

For the traditional Russian attitude, read "The Prisoner of the Caucasus" in Leo Tolstoy, *The Prisoner of the Caucasus and Other Stories* (Moscow: Raduga Publishers, 1983) or in Leo Tolstoy, "Short Stories," selected and introduced by Ernest J. Simmons, *Modern Library Collection of the World's Best Books,* (New York: Random House, 1964–1965).

For the Chechen point of view, browse "Chechen Republic Online" at *http://www.amina.com/*

Rajan Menon and Graham E. Fuller, "Russia's Ruinous Chechen War," *Foreign Affairs,* vol. 79, no. 2 (March/April 2000), pp. 32–44.

For an in-depth understanding of Georgia's side of the story, please see the Study Guide on Georgia (*http://www.1upinfo.com/country-guide-study/georgia/index.html* and two analyses of the tension between Russia and Georgia. One is by Georgian scholar and defense analyst Gela Charkviani and entitled "Georgia-Russia: Power of Perceptions" at *http://www.georgiaemb.org/Gela%20-%20speech%2011.htm*. The other, by Russian journalist Vladimir Socor, is entitled "The Russian Squeeze on Georgia," Russia and Eurasia Review, I, 1 at *http://russia.jamestown.org/pubs/view/rer_001_002_004.htm*.

CHAPTER 3

Power Factors in International Relations

KEY QUESTIONS RAISED IN THIS CHAPTER

1. What is power and how is it defined?

2. What are the major elements of objective power?

3. What are the major elements of subjective power?

4. Why is power so difficult to measure in world politics?

5. What patterns of power operate in world politics?

lmost all questions addressed in world politics have something to do with power. As discussed in Chapter 2, power has received much attention over the years, including Lord Acton's notion that "all power corrupts and absolute power corrupts absolutely." Of course, some types of power such as *military force,* seem more self-evident, while other forms are more subtle—an individual leader's charisma, for example, captures popular imagination and inspires human allegiances and devotion. Franklin D. Roosevelt had charisma and used it to pull America out of economic depression in the 1930s, while Adolph Hitler employed charisma to launch the holocaust and territorial expansion in the 1940s.

One key to understanding centralization and decentralization in world politics is to understand power. This is so because policies pursued by the main actors on the world politics chessboard—especially states, nations, IGOs, and NGOs—rest on the power capabilities at their disposal. U.S. military policies such as bombing the Taliban in Afghanistan after 9/11 and Iraq in 2003 rest upon military capabilities. Saudi Arabia's foreign policy influence stems from its vast oil resources—a form of economic power. When countries cooperate or lock in conflict on the world stage, rest assured that available power is a factor driving those policies. The point here is that foreign policies, examined in more detail in Chapter 4, represent power capabilities that have been translated into actions designed to influence others. What makes power capabilities so interesting is the diverse forms they can take and the uses to which they are put.

This chapter will introduce you to the concept of power. First we will examine the nature of power and how to define it, with special attention to the concepts of hard and soft power. Next we will explore the major elements of objective power, with a close look at geography and natural resources, population, wealth, infrastructure, and military power. Once we understand objective power (things you can see, touch, and count), we will move on to subjective power. This type of power includes elements that do not lend themselves to counting but that still are extremely powerful when mobilized. They include national culture (such as population's work ethic), national morale, quality of government, and quality of diplomacy.

Our next task will be to consider why power is difficult to measure and quantify. Here we will study the relative and situational nature of power and its dynamic and changing characteristics. This chapter's case study—which presents America as a country with declining power—illustrates how the question of a country's power capabilities is subject to sharp debate.

All this brings us to some of the classic patterns of power in world politics, such as balance of power and collective security, both of which illustrate different combinations of power alignments among states. By the time you finishing studying this chapter, you should be well grounded in one of the most important elements at work in world politics in the twenty-first century—and a major element in the understanding of centralization and decentralization in the world political arena.

What Is Power and How Is It Defined?

Power literally jumps out of each day's news. On September 11, 2001, members of Osama bin Laden's Al Qaeda terrorist organization hijacked U.S. commercial airliners and used them to crash into New York City's World Trade Center and the Pentagon in Washington, DC, killing thousands of people. Here was a case of raw power, exercised by a group with far less military muscle than its target, the United States. The United States responded with classic military strength by bombing the

WHY IT MATTERS TO YOU

Power

Why is power so important? The answer stares us in the face, because virtually everything that happens in world politics all comes down to power. Power lies behind terrorist attacks and war that threaten us with instability and violence. It permeates alliances and trade pacts that help bring steadiness and prosperity to our lives. It shapes our capability to protect ourselves against adversaries, enjoy a higher standard of living, and exert influence around the world.

Here are two examples. Power matters to you because how the United States conducts its foreign policy bears directly on your life:

- Billions of dollars spent on defense help secure your personal security. Yet it means money and resources diverted from areas that impact your life—such as health, education, and welfare. This is the classic "guns versus butter" dilemma.

- Dependence on foreign oil to provide the energy for industries and consumer products means that threats to oil-producing states directly affect you—as in the Persian Gulf War or war with Iraq. Would more research on renewable resources make a huge difference in your life?

How other countries react to U.S. policies with their own power directly affects your life as well:

- Al Qaeda terrorists—believers in a form of fundamental Islam—have resented the U.S. presence in Saudi Arabia, its ties to Israel, and its role in globalization. The events of 9/11 were powered by this resentment.

- Powerful states like France, Germany, Russia, and China are disenchanted with U.S. unilateralism (do-it-alone) power in world politics. Any war conducted by the United States alone, without allies, will cost more in money and lives—and will drain resources from the U.S. economy.

Power relationships in world politics are all around you. They affect your quality of life and perhaps your very existence.

---

ruling Taliban in Afghanistan, the Taliban being Islamic religious group that had provided a sanctuary for bin Laden and his Al Qaeda forces. The Taliban government collapsed in December 2001, but remnants of the Taliban and Al Qaeda fled into neighboring Pakistan with U.S.–coalition forces in pursuit.

These events, however, are only part of the story of power and how it operates in world politics. Let's take a closer look at the nature of power, its definitions, and an assessment of so-called hard and soft power. Then we will examine power and its role in world politics. This section that follows will give you a general understanding of power and will set the scene for the following discussion of objective and subjective elements of power.

The Nature of Power

Power lies at the heart of world politics. If politics is all about who gets what, when, and how, then power explains the political process as it plays out in the human drama of international relations. To put it another way, when one speaks of the "politics" part of "world politics," one is faced with the issue of power. The politics of almost anything you can imagine—from education, energy, health care, or military spending to conflict management and cooperation on regional disputes—entails

International Organizations (IOs)
A catch all term that refers mostly to intergovernmental organizations but that can also apply to nongovernmental organizations.

power and the human struggle to seize and use it in order to accomplish objectives. It lies behind the foreign policy of states as they pursue their goals in world affairs, it affects **international organizations (IOs)** and international nongovernmental organizations (NGOs), and it shapes the nature of decision making inside states. In a nutshell, power is at work around the globe 24 hours a day.

Power capabilities include a country's assets that can be seen, touched, or measured—such as natural resources, economic factors (like gross domestic product, or GDP), infrastructure, technology, transportation systems, and military forces. We can identify these power capabilities as **objective** sources of power, which will be discussed in more detail later. A second source of power capabilities is **subjective** in nature, for it lies in the domain of human strengths or weaknesses. Subjective sources of power include a country's culture, morale, quality of government, and political stability. These objective and subjective capabilities represent the base of a country's index of power or strength. When translated into action that affects the behavior of a country's population as well as that of other countries, those power assets become what might be called **kinetic power**—or power in motion. When potential power becomes kinetic power, it reaches the stage of **influence.** We speak of influence, because at this point power capabilities are in motion to affect the behavior of others inside a country as well as leaders and followers abroad. How power is used, or translated, into action is a key subject in the study of foreign policy, explored in Chapter 4.

Influence
The capacity of one actor to change or sustain the behavior of another actor in the global system.

Power capabilities and influence take hard and soft forms. **Hard power** generally refers to those tangible, measurable assets—like military and economic strength and geographic location—that give some countries more power than others. Hard power is a coercive kind of power—like economic sanctions applied by the United States to Cuba or the military force used by the Israelis to occupy the West Bank. **Soft power,** which has gained increasing attention lately, is the ability of a country to get what it wants through attraction rather than through coercion and military force. Promoting a successful economic model of development, as did Japan, or electing a new development-oriented political party, as did Mexico with Vicente Fox, are examples of soft power. In the case of the United States, more money diverted to aid, information, educational, and cultural programs—and recognition that the United States operates in a complex arena where mutual interests are worked out through interaction with others—would be forms of soft power. With these aspects of power in mind we now turn our attention to defining power more precisely.

On Defining Power

Power is best thought of as the capacity (or capability) of Party A to influence the behavior of Party B—that is, the ability of A to get B to do something.[1] *Behavior* can be defined here as Party B's thinking, perceptions, or actions. In the case of Israel's massive military occupation of Palestinian cities and refugee camps, including Yassir Arafat's headquarters, in 2002, multiple objectives were in play. First, Israeli Prime Minister Ariel Sharon sought to compel Palestinian leader Arafat to declare and enforce an unconditional cease-fire—and end the Palestinian uprising **(Intifada)** against Israel that dated back to December 1987.

Second, Sharon's diplomatic strategy was to obtain a long-term interim agreement with the Palestinians, rather than a final peace accord. His intention was to offer the Palestinians a state with about 42 percent of the West Bank and Gaza Strip. That was the amount of territory Israel already had turned over to the

Palestinian's under a previous agreement, and which was, in effect, a state of Palestinian enclaves broken up by Israeli settlements. Third, Sharon hoped to push Arafat out of power, because he was viewed as the key roadblock to the type of Palestinian state settlement Sharon desired.

Another definition of power is power in motion (kinetic), which is first and foremost an act of influence. Influence, of course, comes in many forms. If Party A seeks to influence Party B to do something, it may try, for example, to persuade, reward, threaten, coerce, or punish. When a family member tries to influence another member of the family, a variety of influence-seeking tactics may take place; so it happens between states. The family member can beg and plead, cry, or threaten some kind of act, reason, or bargain. Just as a family member may try to coerce another member, so a state may seek to influence behavior in an attempt to get a desired result. Such an example is Israel's attempt to pressure the Palestinian leadership to cease actions that are inimical to Israel's interests.

A number of additional examples illustrate influence seeking—politics—at work. The United States has tried to persuade Israel and the Palestinians to reach a cooperative agreement on their territorial disputes by sending mediators to work with the contending parties. Similar cases of mediation and persuasion are found in U.S. efforts to broker a peaceful solution to problems in Northern Ireland and Bosnia—as in the Dayton Peace Accords of 1995. The International Monetary Fund has attempted to induce Russia to strengthen its western-backed economic reforms by lending Russia over $20 billion since 1992. Compare these influencing efforts with the U.S. embargo imposed on Cuba in 1962—and still in place—which was designed to *punish* Cuba for its brand of communism and to *coerce* the Cuban government to move toward democracy and a free market economy.

Another way to think about power is to view it as a state's capacity to exert influence, through means such as military troops, tanks, aircraft, or guided missiles—as when the U.S.-led coalition bombed and occupied Iraq in 2003 to remove Saddam Hussein from power. Of course, a country may possess certain types of power capabilities (such as chemical, biological, or nuclear weapons) and decide *not* to put such force into operation. In this case it has power potential, unutilized capabilities that can be brought to bear in the future. Meanwhile, although a power capability may not be in use, it still is in play if it affects the perceptions of leaders in other countries. Possession of nuclear weapons, for example, typically deters other countries from launching a military campaign against that country out of fear of retaliation. Such symbolic power is a key ingredient in world politics, especially in terms of how state leaders view each other.

Hard Versus Soft Power

When "power" in world politics comes up for discussion, the first tendency is to think of military power, or brute force. This is not surprising, because on the chessboard of international relations, you see this impressive brand of power dramatically at work in most corners of the world. The instruments of military power command one's attention by their sheer scale and destructive power—from nuclear weapons and intercontinental ballistic missiles to satellite command and control systems, war ships, tanks, and millions of men and women in uniform (see Chapter 9). At virtually any time of day or night, some battle is raging somewhere on the globe, and the news media are there to bring it into our homes. It is no small wonder we think of military power first. Yet, as we shall see, power takes soft forms as well, and many observers make a compelling case that it should be used more effectively to spur cooperation and centralization.

Power's Hard Profile   As noted, the hard side of power is visible around the world on a day-to-day basis. Taiwan, for example, looks across the Taiwan Strait at China's growing military capacity. Beijing's coastal weapons deployment is designed to remind Taiwan that Beijing considers Taiwan part of China, and that it should never declare its independence. By the summer of 1999, China was engaged in a robust buildup of ballistic and cruise missile forces that the U.S. Pentagon declared would give Beijing an "overwhelming advantage" over Taiwan by 2005.[2] For its part Taiwan is unlikely to forget that in 1995–1996, Beijing launched M-19 missiles into the waters off Taiwan. When Taiwan dug in its heels to repudiate the "one China" policy, Beijing resurrected its threat to retake the island by force if it moved toward independence.[3] Still, Taiwan's President Chen Shui-bian has continued to defy China by asserting Taiwan's sovereignty.

A vivid example of raw military power can be seen in the case of North Korea's weapons technology. Although reportedly near economic collapse, North Korea has continued on a path of hard-line, Stalinist communist rule and bellicose posture toward South Korea since the Cold War's end and, not surprisingly, finds itself isolated and out of step with other nations. In an effort to demonstrate its military strength—and thus its ability to defend itself against would-be aggressors—North Korea urged its citizens to "love rifles, earnestly learn military affairs, and turn the whole country into an impregnable fortress."[4]

Meanwhile, with the U.S. focused on Iraq, North Korea—having withdrawn from the nuclear non-proliferation treaty in January 2003—reactivated in February a nuclear plant capable of producing weapons-grade plutonium. North Korea warned the U.S., first, that any decision to build up its troops in the region could lead North Korea to make a pre-emptive attack on American forces, and second, any U.S. attack on North Korea's nuclear facilities would trigger a total war. Among the reasons North Korea pursued this hard line power position may be (1) the desire to negotiate a non-aggression pact and improved economic aid with the U.S, and (2) as a part of the "axis of evil" declared by U.S. President George Bush, it anticipated an attack from the U.S., as in the case of Iraq.[5]

Naked military power abounds in the early twenty-first century. A classic example is the U.S.-British March 2003 attack on Iraq. Shortly after a predawn missile assault, U.S. and British troops began to fight their way toward Basra and Baghdad. By early April both cities were occupied, against fierce Iraqi opposition, as dictatorial power slipped out of Hussein's hands. Iraq then began its transition toward a postwar setting fraught with obstacles to stability and questions about what type of power the U.S. and Great Britain would bring to bear to govern and rebuild the country.

The Soft Side of Power   Whereas *hard power* is a state's economic and military capability to coerce, *soft power* is the state's ability to influence through cultural and ideological appeal. While economic strength and military weapons certainly are needed to advance a state's key security interests (territorial protection and economic well-being), soft power factors also comprise major elements of a country's overall power inventory. Soft power rests on the appeal of a country's ideals and culture, and on its ability to establish an agenda that will persuade others to agree

Deterrence
A defensive strategy to dissuade, without the actual use of force, another country from attacking. Normally used in the context of nuclear deterrence.

For more information of North Korea's weapon's technology, go to **www.ablongman.com/ duncan**.

For more information on the North Korea–South Korea demilitarized zone, go to **www.ablongman.com/ duncan**.

on values, institutions, and behavior.[6] Numerous critics of U.S. foreign policy believe that America has not used its potential soft power adequately.

The U.S. historically has benefited from its substantial soft power. In the words of Joseph S. Nye, Dean of the Kennedy School of Government, Harvard University, "If America can make its power legitimate in the eyes of other countries . . . and encourage others to define their interests in ways compatible with ours, we may not need to expend as much on costly traditional economic or military sources of power."[7] In this view, U.S. soft power—its ideals of democracy, liberty, human rights, freedoms, and vast opportunities for its citizens—should flow across the globe by vast streams of film, television, and electronic communication. U.S. soft power has a negative aspect too. By the early twenty-first century, fundamental Islamists were reacting harshly to America's globalized culture—not its positive democratic freedoms, but its pop culture of McDonalds and consumer materialism—underscored by the terrible attacks of 9/11. Many foreigners perceive the U.S. as arrogant, self-absorbed, self-indulgent, and contemptuous. U.S. policymakers set about to try to improve this image by creating a new Office of Global Communications.[8] America's deteriorating relations with much of the world over its use of hard power in Iraq likely will complicate its job.

The information revolution—symbolized by the Internet and World Wide Web—impacts soft power. By March 2002, 562 million people were using the Internet, a number that could reach a billion by 2005. These relatively cheap flows of information have vastly expanded the number and variety of transnational channels of contact and have made state borders more porous. The Internet and World Wide Web transmit ideals and ideologies to and from all parts of the world—including those of terrorist organizations like Al Qaeda or Hamas.

Power and World Politics

Power, then, both hard and soft, is at work throughout the international system—in state-to-state relations, within regional trading blocs and military alliances such as NAFTA or NATO, and between IGOs and NGOs of all kinds. At any time around the clock, some decisionmaker in a group, organization, or country is trying to influence other decision makers of another group, organization, or state to change or sustain its behavior in ways compatible with the interests of the one applying power. As former President Harry Truman liked to think of it, power is the ability to get someone to do something that they wouldn't otherwise normally do. Power and influence in world politics—like electrical energy in a giant New York City office building, water from the Colorado River, or information flowing through the world's land and satellite-based computer information networks—are constantly flowing in ways that drive international politics toward conflict and cooperation, decentralization and centralization.

Indeed, power arguably has become the single most important subject examined by students of world politics over the years, especially in the United States since the end of World War II. One of the most important books published on the subject was Hans Morgenthau's *Politics Among Nations*. Among other contributions Morgenthau made in this study of world politics was his *realist* notion that international relations, above all, is the struggle for power and peace. According to Morgenthau, power refers to control over the minds and actions of others—a "psychological relation between those who exercise it and those over whom it is exercised."[9]

What Are the Major Elements of Objective Power?

Objective elements of power include those capabilities or assets that can be seen, touched, and measured—or in other words empirically verified. How and where these elements of power are distributed on the global stage set the scene for who will be the big players and who will be the small actors in the drama. Neither Haiti nor Bangladesh have much chance of making their voices heard in the daily political struggle over who gets what, when, and how, whereas the United States, European Union, China, and Russia wield considerable weight. Saudi Arabia has oil that the United States, Western Europe, and Japan need. This gives Saudi Arabia power, for despite its past role in supporting Islamic schools that teach anti-Western Islamic fundamentalism, those states in need of petroleum count Saudi Arabia as an ally. We now turn to a closer view of these elements of objective power.

Geography

Geopolitics
The study of the geographical distribution of power among states throughout the world, with specific attention to the rivalry between the major powers.

Temperate Zone
Two (north and south) areas of the globe that lie between 23 degrees and 60 degrees north and 23 degrees and 60 degrees south. They are temperate in climate and said to be prime territorial areas conducive to economic development owing to temperature and other climatic factors.

Landlocked State
As the term suggests, a state surrounded by other sovereign states and shut off from easy access to the sea—such as Paraguay and Bolivia in South America.

The geographic size and location of a state, as you might imagine, are extremely important as elements of objective power. Indeed, these factors are so important that a whole field of study centered on geography and politics, called **geopolitics,** has emerged over the years. As you will see in Chapter 7, a number of geographic factors affect a country's power capacity. A country with natural harbors and outlets to the sea, for example, is much more favorably located than a landlocked country. A country located in the **temperate zone** (23–60 degrees north latitude and 23–60 degrees south latitude) has a climate more favorable for human and agricultural productivity than a country located near the equator or in the far north or south of the globe. Mountains can deter potential invaders, as in Switzerland, while mountains combined with jungles can impede a country's internal economic development, as in Peru.

As to the territory states occupy, one look at a map tells you that states vary remarkably in their location, size, shape, topography, and resources. Some are **landlocked states** like Bolivia or have few warm-water ports like Russia. Others, such as the United States, China, Great Britain, and Japan enjoy profitable port facilities. The shape of states makes the world map look like a jigsaw puzzle of crisscrossing borders, but it also determines who gets which topographical features, ranging from fertile agricultural land to deserts, mountains, and jungles. Some countries, like Saudi Arabia with its oil or South Africa with its diamonds, are rich in resources. Others, like Bangladesh and Haiti, are pathetically poor. A number of countries are extremely large in land size: Russia, Canada, China, the United States, Brazil, Australia, and India. Others are the size of postage stamps, as in the case of the Pacific Island states.

A number of basic questions come into play when we consider the impact of geographic power. Does the country have huge oil or coal deposits—like Iraq and Saudi Arabia—either for export or to provide energy to run its industries? Can the country feed itself or must it pay dearly to import food? How do mountains, deserts, and jungles affect a country's food-producing limits? This is an important consideration regarding power, because if a country can feed itself, it avoids those big expenditures like the kind that Cuba now faces. Is the country located in a region of natural hazards, where hurricanes and earthquakes threaten its infrastructure? If so, it faces economic consequences when natural hazards destroy buildings, roads, and communications, which is the case in much of Central America. Indeed, the Caribbean basin, South and Southeast Asia, and the Far East are all subject to massive hurricanes, cyclones, and typhoons—typically more than five per year.

Natural Resources

Natural resources constitute a key power capability closely associated with geography. These vital factors make it possible for a country to feed and shelter its population, industrialize its economy, and engage in trade. Access to natural resources like arable land for food production; coal, oil, and uranium; rivers for energy sources to run industries; or iron ore for steel production are the basis for comparative levels of gross national product, levels and balances of trade, and military preparedness. If a country does not have sufficient land to raise food, then it must import it, which means less money for other vital investments. If a country must import its oil, gas, or coal, it has less money to spend on education or health care. So the natural resource base of a country becomes a key ingredient of power—and of course that base can change over time.

For more information on nuclear energy, go to **www.ablongman.com/ duncan**.

Today the United States must import oil, whereas it used to be self-sufficient. Western Europe's states and Japan also import oil, which is one reason why some European countries have turned to nuclear energy. As a country or region's economic growth expands, it brings drastic increases in energy consumption. The Asian Pacific region ranked first globally in energy demand growth at the end of the twentieth century, and was highly dependent on the Middle East for oil. In 1993 China, for example, became a net oil importer to meet its energy demands.

U.S. dependence on oil illustrates how energy resources affect a country's power base. Once self-sufficient in oil, U.S. dependence on imports of foreign oil has been increasing over the years. According to the American Petroleum Institute, the United States will be forced to import around 68 percent of its oil by 2015 in order to meet nationwide demand. This will exceed the U.S. demand for foreign oil in the late 1990s; the United States was then able to supply approximately 50 percent of its own energy needs. Thus, the United States will become increasingly dependent on Middle East oil, as well as on petroleum imports from Latin America. Like the United States, many European countries already rely on foreign oil. Oil and who controls it have driven wars in the twentieth century and were the main reasons for conflicts such as the Persian Gulf War in 1991.

Rivers are another valuable natural resource that can add to a state's objective power. They provide drinking water and are used for transportation, commerce, and energy production (hydroelectric power) through the use of dams. The United States has been blessed with a superlative river system, as have the Western and Eastern European countries and China. Hydropower provides one-fifth of the world's electricity and is second only to fossil fuels as a source of energy. Fourteen percent of that one-fifth of the world's hydropower is in the United States, 10 percent in Canada, and 9 percent in the former Soviet Union. Hydropower has grown steadily in the United States, rising from 56,000 megawatts in 1970 to over 90,000 megawatts by the end of the twentieth century. It accounts for a greater share of electricity than petroleum.[10] U.S. hydropower plants produce the energy equivalent of 500 million barrels of oil per year. When China completes its massive Three

Denying Energy Resources to the Enemy: During the 1991 Gulf War, when the U.N. backed U.S.-led coalition removed Iraq from Kuwait, the Iraqis blew up hundreds of Kuwaiti oil wells as they retreated, letting them burn uncontrollably and polluting the country with fumes and thick black smoke. Here is a photo of those burning oil fields in Kuwait, in front of which you see a destroyed Iraqi tank. Fewer oil wells were set fire in the 2003 Iraq war.

Gorges Dam project, it will move into fourth place and ahead of Brazil, which has more than doubled its hydro capacity since 1970.

The Yangtze River itself is a major source of power for China in several respects. The longest river in both China and Asia, it starts on the Tibetan plateau at 18,000 feet, and its tributaries cover several basins to make a total of 18,500 miles of water transport routes. Oceangoing vessels can travel over 600 miles up the river through Nanjing to Wuhan. The Yangtze River accounts for about 70 percent of China's inland shipping. In addition to serving as one of China's leading transport corridors and as a major source of hydroelectric power, the Yangtze Basin—over 2,000 miles east to west and 600 miles north to south—is the rice bowl of mainland China. Because food is a source of a country's power, the Yangtze's contribution to rice production and its yield of 7 million tons of fish per year make it an outstanding base of power (see Figure 3.1).

Discussion of the mighty Yangtze River also leads to the consideration of freshwater as a key source of power. Without freshwater, a state's population could not survive. The problem in many states is population growth that exceeds, or puts pressure on, its freshwater supplies. At the turn of the century 31 countries with a total population of half a billion people are experiencing chronic water shortages. Within 25 years, 59 countries with three billion people will experience freshwater difficulties.[11] The problem stems not only from population growth but also from increasing demands created by agriculture, industry, and urban growth. A compelling argument can be made that countries should pay much more attention to their freshwater situation as a source of available power within the international system. We will look at the question of the diminishing global supply of freshwater from the perspective of the ecological paradigm in Chapter 13.

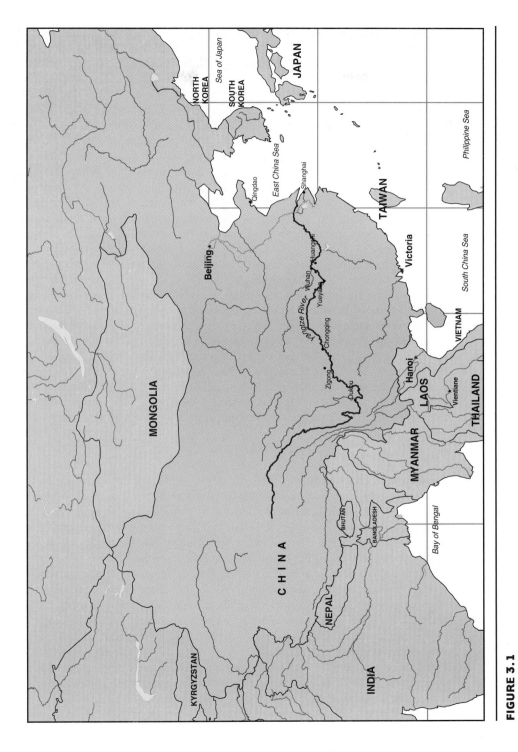

FIGURE 3.1
China and the Yangtze River

Geography and natural resources, then, are key sources of a country's power. The size of a country, its location, and its natural resources go a long way in enabling a country to become powerful. Until recently, the three most powerful countries were also the three largest: the United States, the former USSR, and China. Each of the three has significant natural resources. The former USSR contained significant amounts of untapped oil and natural gas reserves, and large deposits of the world's most wanted minerals, along with one-fifth of the world's forests—stretching across Siberia to the Pacific coast. The United States also has important oil and gas reserves, especially in Alaska, as well as some mineral reserves and large stands of forests. Still, the United States faced a serious energy crisis during the winter of 2001, which led President George Bush to urge oil and natural gas development in the Artic National Wildlife Refuge in northeast Alaska. This approach to the energy problem led to vehement opposition from environmentalists, who wanted no part of drilling in a region where caribou calve.

With regard to location and resources, the United States is better situated than Russia or China. Most of the United States lies in a temperate climate, with accessible coasts on two sides and friendly countries on the other two. The United States also has some of the most fertile agricultural land in the world. By contrast, China has far fewer natural resources. Its main energy resource is coal. It also has far fewer natural mineral resources, forests, and agricultural land. While all three countries contain a substantial share of desert, more than a third of the former USSR (and Russia today) lies above the Arctic Circle, making a large area of the country inhospitable for large settlements and industrial development. The Tibetan plateau to the south and the Central Asian deserts to the west leave little space in China for agriculture or for the expansion of its population.

Population

Population is also a critical ingredient of power. Factors that enter into the population issue include its size (relative to the land size of the state it occupies), age distribution, health, and education. Population size and density vary greatly from state to state, but in general a large population in a large territorial state can be an asset. It provides a base for selecting soldiers for military service and a work force for the economy. Small developing countries that face regional threats, however, may create large military forces despite their small populations. This policy diverts scarce resources from economic development. As to the social aspects of population, countries with a healthy, literate, and socially mobile population as a base for economic and political development are likely to produce more national power compared to those with an uneducated and socially immobile population. (See Figure 3.2 for a map showing global illiteracy rates.)

The bottom line is that the large territorial states with huge populations—like China, the United States, Russia, and India—tend to have substantial military forces and are influential in the world arena. The reason most often given for considering China to be so potentially powerful is its large population of over a billion people. No other country in the world has so many people. The country with the next largest population is India, with over 900 million. India is likely to overtake China in population by 2010. The United States by contrast has a population of 260 million, less than a third of India's. Present-day Russia has only 140 million people. (See Figure 3.3 for a map showing population growth rates.)

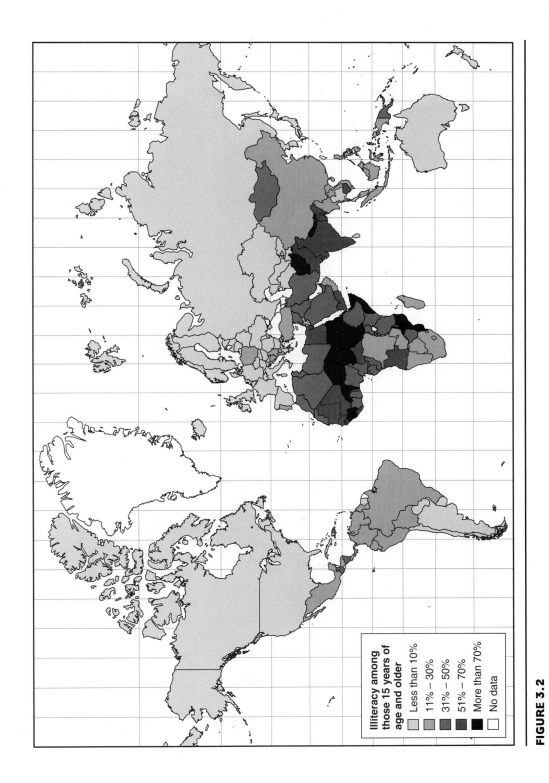

FIGURE 3.2
Global Illiteracy Rates

Illiteracy among those 15 years of age and older
- Less than 10%
- 11% – 30%
- 31% – 50%
- 51% – 70%
- More than 70%
- No data

SOURCE: John L. Allen, *Student Atlas of World Politics, Fourth Edition,* (Guilford, CT: Dushkin/McGraw-Hill, 2000), p. 66.

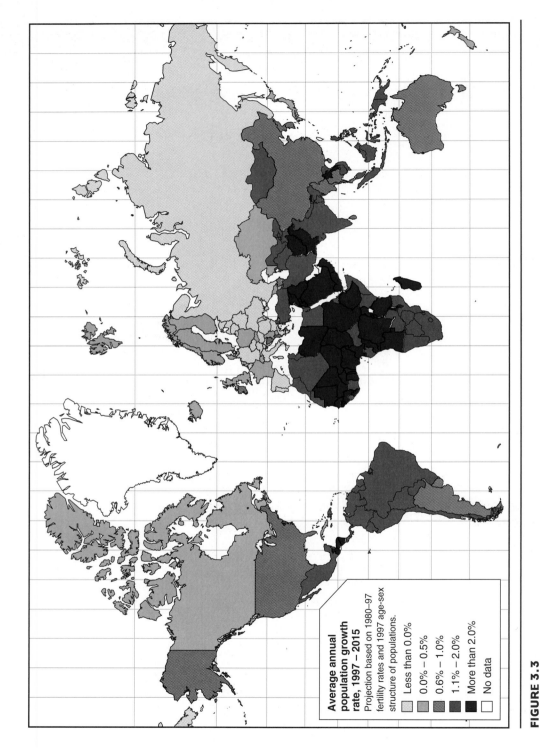

FIGURE 3.3

Population Growth Rates

SOURCE: John L. Allen, Student Atlas of World Politics, Fourth Edition, (Guilford, CT: Dushkin/McGraw–Hill, 2000), p. 60.

Average annual population growth rate, 1997 – 2015

Projection based on 1980–97 fertility rates and 1997 age-sex structure of populations.

Less than 0.0%
0.0% – 0.5%
0.6% – 1.0%
1.1% – 2.0%
More than 2.0%
No data

THE VIEW FROM   China and Japan

A Confucian Culture of Work and Self-Discipline

Research and observation have demonstrated that some cultures have a value system based on Confucian work dynamism characterized by a long-term focus and values of thrift, persistence, and hard work. The cultures of China and Japan embody these values. Such a culture finds expression in working habits of endurance and mental and physical toughness—with many people realizing that a work ethic is the key to job security. The Confucian work dynamism is reflected in the classrooms of China and Japan as well. Asian students tend to be well disciplined and well mannered and to challenge themselves academically. In contrast to China and Japan, countries low on Confucian work dynamism are short-term oriented with a focus on the here and now. You can surmise from the Confucian culture that it is an immense source of power—leading to a highly productive population.

With a large population, a state has many people available to put into the armed forces. China boasts an army of over 3 million men. The United States has always recognized the threat that such a large army poses and has never attacked China directly for fear of what this huge army might do. Mao Zedong recognized the value of large numbers when he declared that the atomic bomb was a paper tiger.

A look at China and India is instructive. It is not China's population size alone that gives it big power status. China, unlike India, is relatively homogeneous in the sense that the bulk of its population is Han Chinese. Likewise, the vast majority of Chinese are able to read the same characters, even though dialects vary from region to region. Of China's approximately 1.3 billion people, 96 percent are Han—despite China's population of 56 ethnic groups. Another factor in China's favor—from a power perspective—is its culture of hard work, thrift, and the high value attached to education (see box The View from China and Japan for more on this aspect of culture). Still, China worries that its huge population will grow out of control and overload the country's carrying capacity (ability to sustain a population). Therefore, China has tried to instill a "one-child" policy to control such growth.

India, the country with the second largest population, appears to benefit less from its large number of people. India's population, as noted, is growing more rapidly than China's. From 1995 to 2010, India's estimated rate of growth is 1.7 percent, compared to China's 0.8 percent. By the year 2010, India's population will be just behind that of China's. This means more mouths to feed, more health care and education demands, and greater demand for employment as young adults enter the work place. Meanwhile, India's rigid caste system, multiple ethnic groups and languages, and its overall cultural diversity tend to inhibit broad scale development and wider income distribution—thus inhibiting India's overall power in world politics.

While such population dynamics suggest that India is less well endowed from a strictly population assessment, we should remind ourselves that India remains the world's most populous country with a democratic government and is moving ahead swiftly on the technological front. Dozens of U.S. computer software companies have established offices in India, where top quality engineers can be hired for one-fifth the cost of salaries in California's Silicon Valley. The reasons for India's high tech take-off is that English is widely spoken, math and science are highly valued in

Busy Shanghai, China, Harbor: Much of China's economic vitality lies on its eastern coast. Shanghai today is one of China's most thriving cities—literally a beehive of modern activity.

India's educational system, and the country turns out around 60,000 electronics engineers yearly—twice as many as does the United States.[12] India also has six institutes of technology, which are among the world's premier technical colleges.

The point here is that population size is just the tip of the iceberg when thinking about power. Literacy, health, age distribution, urbanization, cultural traits, and other factors also enter into the population issue. In terms of literacy, for example, China is 81.5 percent literate compared to India at only 52 percent literate. Indeed, a number of scholars argue that if China becomes fully industrialized with a market economy and a Confucian work-oriented and literate population, it has the potential to become a superpower.

Population demographics also affect a country's power base. For example, if a large sector of the population is under 15 years of age, a substantial percentage of its population has not yet entered the workforce and therefore is unlikely to participate in the country's economic productivity. Such is the case in many developing countries. A state's population in the 65-and-older bracket also typically does not participate in economic productivity, yet it draws on social security and health benefits, as is the case in the United States and other developed counties. Problems of this type are looming for Japan as well.

A large population, as you can see, can be both a blessing and a curse. China is lucky in that the majority of its population is homogeneous. In contrast, India is composed of many ethnic groups, as is the United States. Keeping all the groups happy is a very difficult task. The breakup of Yugoslavia illustrates that when economic and social gaps between groups become very wide, the country faces political difficulties. The fall of the Soviet Union is a prime example of what can happen when ethnic groups become dissatisfied and demand change. The USSR fell with hardly any bloodshed. As the larger and more assertive ethnic groups, including the Russians, demanded and gained independence, few were left to defend or reinforce the old union. The multinational federation disintegrated, revealing an empty core.

Ethnic diversity is not always a disadvantage, however. The United States, for example, has opened its doors to immigrants from every part of the world—including the Middle East. The resulting influx of people is one of the major reasons for the vitality and innovative capacity of America. While racial discrimination still leaves deep scars across the country, the United States is generally viewed as a positive example of interethnic cooperation.

A final aspect of population is its educational level, and basic literacy is only the bottom line of what we are talking about here. To be powerful in today's world, a state must possess an educated population, capable of technological and scientific invention. In the past century, education was not yet a must for technological and economic development. But today, science has advanced so far that a state can only advance if it has a highly educated public. The United States has benefited up to now because it was able to recruit the most talented and educated people from around the globe. In the past century these immigrants came from the many states experiencing political and economic problems: Europe previously, and more recently, Asia, Latin America, and Russia. However, it is probably not wise to rely exclusively on emigration to provide the scientific and cultural innovators of the future. That is why today the United States educational system is under such public scrutiny and why every president in the past 15 years has emphasized the importance of a good education for all Americans. In the future, the most important power aspect of population will be its educational level.

Wealth and Economic Stability

As we saw in Chapter 1, some states are not as wealthy as others, nor are they at the same level of economic development. By far the wealthiest state in the world today is the United States, owing largely to its technological leadership and worker productivity. While the rest of the world was experiencing an economic setback at the end of the 1990s, the United States seemed to be going from one economic high to another. Other wealthy and highly developed states include Japan and the 15 states that make up the European Union (formerly known as the European Community). It must be said, however, that wealth and economic stability do not remain constant—and when they decline they affect a state's power base.

America's Economic Decline in 2001—2002　While the world's wealthiest state, the United States, nevertheless is subject to fluctuations in its economic power. As the twenty-first century began, the U.S. economy moved into recession, with the economy shrinking during 2001—long before the terrorist attacks of 9/11—with recovery slow in coming during 2002. While America's economic decline in 2002 resulted in part from the financial dislocation caused by the September terrorists' attacks, scandals in corporate America also sent a huge shock wave through the economy. Corporate fraud, accounting scams, highly paid executives cashing out of their companies as they sank, and other forms of corporate greed and corruption in effect robbed thousands of investors of their retirement funds and sent the economy into a tailspin.

As scandals spread from the Enron Corporation to Tyco, Merrill Lynch & Co., and the Arthur Anderson accounting firm to Adelphia Communications,

Computer Associates, Qwest Communications, Global Crossing and WorldCom, the U.S. stock market plummeted—along with American and foreign investor confidence. Needless to say, this decline in the U.S. economy did little to strengthen either America's hard or soft power. By the end of the summer of 2002, however, it appeared that America's economy had started to recover. The bottom line is that despite its ups and downs, the U.S. economy—with a GDP of over $ 9 trillion compared to second-ranked Japan at $ 4.3 trillion—remained by far the world's largest and thus still the most powerful.

Post World War II Japan and Germany   In 1945 the United States and its allies defeated Japan. Although much of Japan's economy had been destroyed during the war, ten years later the country was regaining its wealth. Twenty years later the Japanese miracle was held up as a model for other developing countries to follow. Similarly in 1945, Germany was in ruins, its economy destroyed, and its people demoralized. Even the division of Germany into two nations in 1948 did little to quell the drive of the German people to get back on their feet. By 1960 the West German economy was thriving, and by 1980 communist East Germany stood out above its communist neighbors in economic development and social welfare.

Yet we must remember that economic strength is not guaranteed. Like the United States, Germany and Japan have faced continuing economic challenges and problems. As the world's third largest economy ($ 2.1 trillion GDP) and performing as the economic heart of Europe, Germany's reunification in 1989 has cost more than expected, with the east still poorer and less productive than the western area. Since reunification the economy has been sluggish as well, and unemployment has remained high. Japan, for its part, has been in an economic slump dating back to its stock market crash in 1989, which created conditions worse than America's Great Depression. Japan's subsidized state-run corporations have dragged down productivity, with unemployment rising along with a growing government debt. Such economic problems undermine both countries' power bases.

Concentration of Global Wealth   As we noted in Chapter 2, despite all the horrors of World War II and recent ups and downs in the economies of America and Japan, the wealth of the world has remained firmly in the hands of the states that were wealthy prior to the war, and the concentration of this wealth in the highly developed states is steadily increasing. This means that the gap between the wealthiest and the poorest nations is also increasing, as is the gap between the richest and the poorest in any one state. And as demonstrated by the economic crisis that swept Southeast Asia in 1996–1997, economic instability in one region caused economic instability throughout the world. States with chronic economic problems are most vulnerable to financial crises in the regional countries near them.

States with strong economies, like the United States, France, the United Kingdom (UK), and Germany, seem to weather financial crises like these more easily.

Level of Economic Development   A country's level of economic development is a key element of power, because it reflects the ability of a country to sustain itself, engage in finance and trade, and maintain a strong military establishment. A thriving economy typically measured by a country's gross national product—the total value of goods and services produced—indicates the strength of its international power. This kind of power is strikingly illustrated by the United States, with its booming economic indicators at the turn of the century, compared to Russia's near bankruptcy and China's difficulties with economic reforms. Although a high level of economic development does not guarantee national power, it remains a necessary ingredient of both hard and soft power as previously discussed.

A country's level of development is a product of many forces, including its natural resource base, territorial location, political system, and the country's culture and national pride. Political stability and nature of government are also key factors that will be discussed later in this chapter. Here it should be noted that Russia's productivity, never as high as that of the United States for a variety of reasons, fell off precipitously after the Soviet Union collapsed in 1991. Russia's political turmoil and instability since then go hand in hand with an economy where taxes go uncollected, corruption runs rampant, organized crime proliferates, bureaucracy is endless, and money flees the country. Bosnia, another example of a state in political turmoil, is held together largely by international organizations, while, as in Russia, corruption undermines its economic growth. In addition, lack of a legal system in Bosnia hinders investment, and disunity at the top impedes reform and long-range strategic economic planning.

Industrial Base

National infrastructure is a major asset that must be factored into the power equation. This category includes a country's industrial base, technological development, transportation networks (railroads, all-weather roads, port facilities, and air transport systems), and information and communication systems. National infrastructure lies at the base of economic power. When we speak of a country's industrial base, we refer to the quantity and quality of its industries—ranging from steel production to manufacturing and services. Industries lead to exports and thus income-generating activities and the ability either to exert economic pressure on others or to resist their economic pressures. Industrialized states are well situated in this respect compared to developing countries.

Technology   A vital factor in a state's capacity to generate wealth and maintain economic strength and stability, the term *technology* refers to a wide range of factors within the national infrastructure, from computers and computer chips to robotics, synthetic fertilizers, lasers, and weapons. In the latter category, military analysts are projecting a revolution in military affairs—a country's hard power—that will come with improvements in precision-guided munitions and via the speed, memory, capacity, and networking capabilities of the modern computer. With this revolution, a country's ability to establish and maintain overseas bases and deployments may become much less important as a factor in its level of power.

For centuries great empires like those of India, China, and what have become the Arab nations were the world leaders in wealth and technology. Somehow, however, their technological innovations never translated into the type of revolution in production of goods and services that occurred in Europe with the systematic application of technology to production. *Automation,* the replacement of human labor by technology, is the product of Western development. And once embarked on the transformation of production through technology, the West has stayed the leader in new technological developments, with the United States probably the country on the cutting edge of innovation. The exception is Japan, whose threat to overtake and surpass the West in technology (high-speed railways, modern highways and port facilities) was overturned by the very severe Japanese recession that began in 1989.

The retention by the West of technological leadership has meant that if the developing states wish to catch up, they must find a way to obtain Western technology.

From this need springs a variety of conflicts and negotiations about the transfer or sale of Western technology to other states. And from this need also springs the theory of *Dependencia,* which originated in South America and was discussed in Chapter 1. According to this theory, you will recall, developing states are permanently dependent on the developed states because the latter have a monopoly on technology and capital.

China is perhaps the one state that still believes that it can use its own scientists, educated either at home or abroad (preferably in the United States), to jump ahead of the technology in current use in the West. In the late 1990s Chinese leaders categorically denied a U.S. accusation that Chinese scientists working in the United States had stolen U.S. military secrets. According to the Chinese, they were perfectly capable of developing the allegedly stolen military technology themselves. The U.S. accusation, say the Chinese, was a ploy meant to denigrate Chinese education and Chinese science.

Transportation Systems   Transportation systems impact the ability to move people and goods within a state's territory as well as abroad—and thus contribute to a country's overall power. The old Soviet Union (and today's Russia) has been notorious for its ineffective transportation system, which left grain and vegetables stalled and lost. Western Europe and Japan, on the other hand, have efficient high-speed railway systems famous for their precision and territorial scope. A state's transportation system can be evaluated by its mileage of paved versus dirt roads and mileage and condition of railroads. Compare Nigeria's 213 miles of paved roads and 6 miles of railroad track for every 1,000 square miles to the 1,049 miles of paved roads and 45 miles of railroad track for every 1,000 square miles in the United States. Such transportation links are keys to power.

Information and Communication Systems   Information and communication systems are additional indices of a country's power. From radio and television the world has moved to satellites, computers, the Internet, and cell phones—all of which facilitate industrialization, commerce, and military power. Countries with more televisions, radios, telephones, and computers per capita are stronger in these capacities than those with fewer communication and information systems. The United States and Canada, for example, rank higher in industrialization, commerce, and military power than Haiti, Bangladesh, Pakistan, Indonesia, India, and China combined. Still, keep in mind that China and other countries are undergoing a cell phone revolution; today Hong Kong is awash in cell phones. The presence of cell phones is an indicator of a country's technical level of sophistication and thus an element of power.

Military Preparedness

Military preparedness arguably is the most compelling aspect of a country's objective power. This is so because military capacity is the way in which a country protects its territory and people from threats of aggression and furthers its objectives abroad. But military capability also can be used indirectly—as perceived power in the minds of other states' decisionmakers. In this way, it can be used to deter other countries from attack or to persuade a state or ethnic group within a country to desist from undertaking an action not yet taken, as in NATO's occupation of Bosnia to prevent the outbreak of ethnic war.

Military capability is derived from the first three sources of a state's power: (1) energy and mineral deposits to build and power its military (although Japan has

Weapons of Mass Destruction: A United Nations inspector samples air quality inside a monitored chemical facility in Iraq in 1995. Such sites took on new meaning by 2002 as the U.S. and UN pressed for renewed investigations of Iraq's weapons program. Saddam Hussein, Iraq's leader, has continued to pursue a policy of brinkmanship to stop international inspectors from monitoring Iraq's nuclear and chemical facilities and to resume production of weapons of mass destruction. In this way he eluded the cease-fire agreements of the Persian Gulf War—that is, until the U.S. and Great Britain bombed and occupied Iraq in March 2003.

shown us that even a country that lacks basic natural resources can build a great military force); (2) self-sufficiency in agriculture so that the state does not need to import food when it is under attack or when it attacks other parts of the world; and (3) a large, well-educated population, so that the state can both create a large army, navy, and air force, while developing ever-newer, more destructive technology in the race to create the ultimate military machine.

There is no doubt that the technological military capability of a state can be threatening. The world watched in awe and disbelief as bombs rained down on Iraq and Kosovo. How could any leader continue to defy the relentless punishment being visited on his or her territory? Yet we must study history before we accept the notion that military technology is everything in a conflict and that small countries are unable to stand up against a threat of superior force. The United States and its allies did indeed create widespread destruction in Iraq. The Iraqi troops were quickly withdrawn from Kuwait in response to the bombing. But, despite continued bombing from 1991 to 1999, Saddam Hussein, the ruler of Iraq and the author of the invasion of Kuwait, remained in power until the Spring of 2003.

In addition to ending Hussein's rule, military power played a key role in forcing Slobodan Milosevic out of power as president of former Yugoslavia in October 2000. Milosevic had refused to quit as president after 13 years of power, despite September 2000 elections that had named Vojislav Kostunica president-elect. But the public was fed up with Milosevic's many wars and policies of ethnic cleansings in Bosnia and Kosovo, as well as the disastrous losses and devastation those wars had cost in Serbia—and which were intensified by heavy NATO bombing of Serb

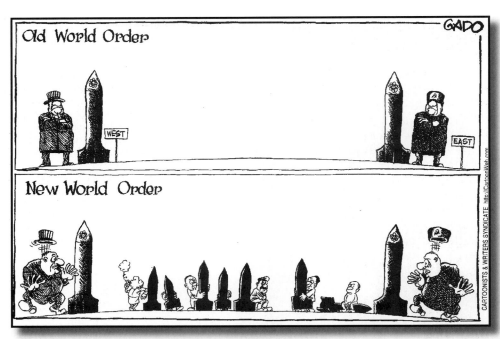

SOURCE: *Gado/Cartoonists & Writers Syndicate* (http://www.cartoonweb.com).

For more information on NATO's use of power in Kosovo, go to www.ablongman.com/duncan.

forces in Kosovo and of Serbia itself. After days of confrontation and unprecedented popular uprising in Belgrade and across Serbia, Milosevic went into temporary hiding and Kostunica became president.

In brief, while not all battles are won by superior military technology, the better weapon is generally a surer test of a state's power than any other measure. We may say that Germany and Japan are great economic powers, but they cannot compare in weapons sophistication with the United States. Although the Soviet Union was a superpower, its economic development was not equal to that of the United States. Nevertheless, the former USSR possessed a very high level of weapons technology, particularly nuclear capability. Under the same criteria, China is generally said to be a potential superpower. However, until the weapons technology of China equals that of the United States, China will remain a potentially great power, rather than a great one.

America currently leads the world in all dimensions of objective power—military, economic, cultural, and scientific—by a margin deeply out of proportion to its population.[13] In some respects the United States is positioned today to reshape the world much like it was at the end of World War II, when Japan and Germany lay defeated and Europe and Asia were on their backs. The question much of the world might ask is, How will America use its awesome power in the early twenty first century? The answer to this question may lie more in the domain of psychology than with economic or military power capabilities—and it is to that world of subjective power that we now turn.

What Are the Major Elements of Subjective Power?

Subjective power factors—those that entail human values, beliefs, perceptions and motivation—are less empirically measurable but remain enormously important in assessing a country's power base. Subjective factors also help us understand why conflict or cooperation arises among states, IGOs, NGOs and other actors on the world politics stage. Such human, subjective factors are expressed in the various ways people participate in government, express nationalism, engage in diplomacy, display their work ethic, react to world events, and in many other forms of political behavior.

Examples of events involving subjective power include the loss of investor confidence in America during 2001–2002, owing in part to corruption in the business world and poor business ethics. These factors in turn helped trigger an economic recession and weakened U.S. economic power. With one chief executive officer (CEO) or chief financial officer (CFO) after another charged with misuse of corporate funds and depriving company employees of their retirement funds, America's image abroad as the land of market capitalist opportunity took a beating.

Palestinian and Al Qaeda willingness to commit suicide for a cause illustrates how human will can lead to human destruction and how a commitment becomes a power factor aimed at others. Suicide bombers underscore how a religious or ideological value can wield power over people or gain power for a nation. Violent street demonstrations in India and Pakistan over the disputed territory of Kashmir highlight mass action as a form of mobilized human power.

If we go back to the twentieth century, we see that the German and Japanese work ethic fueled a remarkable economic recovery in both countries. Vietnam's guerrilla fighters—living in tunnels, existing on small portions of rice, and fighting without heavy weapons—remained tenaciously committed to winning their war with the United States during the 1960s and 1970s. They eventually forced the United States to withdraw, despite its overwhelming military superiority. When we enter this subjective world of power, we have entered human psychology—a potent force indeed, both for cooperation and centralization and for conflict and decentralization. We turn first to the potent energy of national culture, a central factor in subjective power.

National Culture

When we speak of national culture, we refer to qualities of intellect and behavior that are distinctly imprinted on and valued by national groups across the world's stage—Russians, Vietnamese, Germans, and so on. Not only do these qualities set national groups apart. They also distinctly influence a number of attributes associated with power. These include influencing attitudes toward work—as we have seen in the cases of China and Japan—political culture, interethnic national stereotyping, behavior within and between the peoples and cultures occupying state territory, and negotiating styles in diplomacy.[14]

National cultures remain tenacious in world politics, despite what appear to be the homogenization effect of globalization—and by implication the centralizing tendencies globalization would be expected to produce. This fact has deep implications for power relationships in world politics, because looking out at the world through the lenses of a national culture shapes one state's perceptions and expectations about the power of another, conditions how it conducts its diplomacy, and can serve to unite a people in a common cause. The following quote gives insight into the deep imprint of national culture, even when it's not visible.

> The frequency of cross-cultural encounters should not be confused with cultural homogenization at a deeper level. To speak in English is not always to think in English; to wear a three-piece suit rather than a *jalabiya* (a long,

Thriving Downtown Ho Chi Minh City, Vietnam: In Vietnam's brand of market socialism, Ho Chi Minh City is the pulse beat of this country's economic life. Some observers have seen it as Vietnam's version of frenetic New York City, while Hanoi in the north is more like Paris, France, in terms of cuisine and culture.

hooded robe worn by the Bedouin of the Sinai desert and the Egyptians in the teeming metropolis of Cairo, Egypt) is not the same as abandoning cherished Muslim values; to know the ways of the West is not necessarily to wish to emulate them. One of the characteristics of any vibrant society is its ability to assimilate foreign influences while remaining true to its essential beliefs and motifs.[15]

The general aspects of a people's behavior tend to stand out over time. Russians, for example, lived under the historic "groupthink" of government and economic pressure of communist rule for so long that their work ethic may have been stifled in ways that affect Russia's low productivity today. Under communism, the old saying about the relationship between workers and the government was, "we pretend to work and they (the government) pretend to pay us," referring to the low value of the national currency, the ruble. The culture of many countries in Latin America, as Latin American scholars have noted, is less supportive of those who work with their hands than those who work with their intellect, like writers and poets.

By contrast the Chinese, Vietnamese, Japanese, and South Koreans are known for their ethic of work, saving, thrift, and high value given to education. In Malaysia, Chinese dominate the business and financial world, while Malays tend to control the government. Germans are known as extremely hardworking. American and Japanese workers also are recognized for their high productivity. A strong work ethic is correlated with high productivity in the economy and is consequently a key factor of power.

A nation's philosophical, historical, and religious underpinnings may have a deep bearing on the content and values inherent in national culture and hence on national power. East Asia's economic success, as we saw above, may be explained in part by the legacy of Confucianism.[16] A Confucian tradition runs from Japan to Singapore and encompasses the robust economies of Taiwan, South Korea, Hong Kong, and China. The Confucian ethic stresses self-restraint, which might explain this region's high savings rates. A believer in Confucian principles emphasizes scholarship and a tradition of examination to enter the civil service.

This emphasis has produced comparatively strong literacy rates throughout the region. The Protestant ethic of the West stresses work, saving, and thrift. In Japan cooperative behavior and interpersonal relations are highly valued, as is the concept of efficiency. This culture may have deep historical roots, as the Japanese people long ago built an agricultural society from the paddy fields—a task that required cooperation. Another cultural aspect of Japan is that, unlike America, it places society ahead of the economy—a cultural trait that in tending to unify a people becomes a power factor for the state as a player in world politics.[17]

National culture is also expressed via international relations in the following ways:

- *Negotiating styles.* Parties that understand each other's national culture will be more successful in their diplomatic efforts. Chinese negotiators, for example, negotiate on the basis of clearly stated principles and pragmatism that are consistent with the thinking of the top strata of the highly structured Communist Party bureaucracy. Americans have a reputation of wanting to get to the bottom line right away. Latin Americans are noted for engaging in social interaction well before getting to the key points.
- *Perceptions of one national group as distinct from others.* Nationalist Serbs view neighboring Bosnians as abhorrent to their way of life, while the same could be said of Croatians' views of Serbs. This cultural conflict leads to disintegration as the breakup of Yugoslavia illustrates.
- *Protectionism.* This tendency to perceive outside influences as potential corrupters of one's own culture can be seen in Islamic fundamentalism as well as in Vietnam. Such attitudes have produced deep decentralization in world politics.
- *Styles of doing business.* A country's international corporations are likely to be more successful if they understand the cultural underpinnings of the other countries in which they wish to do business. A lack of understanding can breed insulting behavior, insensitivity to cultural mores, and loss of contracts. In doing business in Latin America, a trusting personal rapport between negotiating counterparts is all-important.

National Morale

Although elusive and unstable, national morale reflects the determination of a nation to support the policies of its government. The Vietnam War, noted above, is a classic case in which national morale played a significant role. As the United States became increasingly entangled in Vietnam (1964–1973), morale on both sides increasingly affected its outcome. The Vietnamese, fighting on their own territory against foreign invaders, remained tenacious, while Americans became decidedly demoralized as the body count rose. Despite America's overwhelming hard power (military weapons) superiority, it was Vietnamese resolve that carried the day. The Paris Peace Treaty of January 27, 1973, ended this painful experience for both sides. Today's Vietnamese, as field research and interviews reveal, are surprisingly optimistic about the future, and fascinated and comfortable with foreigners despite past foreign domination.[18] In contrast, *Al Qaeda* terrorists and many Middle East Muslims are bitterly disenchanted with Western globalization, their own governments' ties with the West, and their profound poverty. Palestinian refugee camps in Israel's West Bank and Gaza Strip are filled with demoralized people of all ages—a spawning ground for suicide terrorists.

Quality of Government

The structure of the political system, its cohesiveness, and its effectiveness in decision making are all aspects of a government's quality. Authoritarian governments, such as the Chinese one, are noted for their efficiency in decision making and a high degree of predictability. In contrast, democratic governments shift policy in reaction to swings in public opinion and election of new representatives to Congress—in the United States, every two years. Because democratic foreign policy making involves so many parties—the executive branch, Congress, interest groups, the media and public opinion, and the military—decisions are less predictable and less efficient. Still, democratic governments tend to be more stable in the long run than authoritarian dictatorships and do not typically go to war against each other. There are some states, however, that suffer from a nearly total lack of government, and these so-called weak or failing states have little political and economic cohesiveness. They generally cannot mount a strong foreign policy and therefore suffer a lack of national power. Afghanistan, Angola, and Somalia are cases in point.

The quality of government is undermined by internal conflicts and loss of legitimacy. Internal conflicts can arise from religious differences, ethnic frictions, military infighting, drug traffickers, guerrilla movements, and breakaway efforts by separatist groups either through ballots, as in East Timor versus Indonesia, or through bullets, as in the case of Kosovo. Loss of central government legitimacy is associated with internal conflicts like these, as well as with rising widespread corruption. While no state is immune from corruption, Mexico, Russia, and Bosnia were particularly corrupt at the turn of the century. Northern Ireland's troubles flow from deep religious differences, and Colombia's from drug trafficking and guerrilla warfare. Indeed, just as Colombia's new president, Álvaro Uribe Vélez, was sworn in as president in Bogotá on August 7, 2002, leftist guerrillas opened fire in the center of the capital, killing at least 14 people. And this came in response to his election pledge to crack down on Colombia's leftist guerrillas, who are connected to drug traffickers.

Another quality of government that plays a gigantic role in a country's power base is its ability to foster economic growth and quality of life for its citizens, which includes providing a free and open society where the rule of law prevails, and where change and innovation take precedence over protecting the ways of the past. In this context, a government may be democratic, as in India and the United States, but if it operates with excessive bureaucratic red tape as, for example, when endless forms are required to start new businesses, it stifles freedom of innovation in technology, commerce, and finance. Ineffective government has undermined economic growth and stability in the economies of Argentina and Brazil—despite their vast potential for economic power.

In this sense the United States and Hong Kong have fared better than India. Indians, as well as Swedes, French and German people, and East Europeans, immigrate to the United States just so they will have the freedom to start new businesses. Indeed, Hong Kong fares better than India when it comes to economic and business freedom, with thousands of people immigrating to Hong Kong. Governments play key roles in fostering an open environment and scientific research that contribute to new discoveries and economic vitality. It may come as no surprise that, since World War II, the United States leads by far in the number of Nobel Prize awards in physics, chemistry, and medicine. The United States has had 61 Nobel Prize winners in physics, 43 winners in chemistry, and 71 winners in medicine. The second place winner in these categories is Great Britain, with 11 winners in physics, 19 in chemistry, and 17 in medicine.

Political Stability

What is meant by political stability? On what basis can we say that the more stable a state's political system, the more powerful the state? To understand political stability, it helps to talk about political instability. In high school you may have studied the history of Europe or Japan. Although you may not remember the specifics, you may retain an impression of feudal families warring with one another. History seems to be a record of innumerable wars. Many of these are called wars of succession—wars about who is to follow whom on the throne. When princes or princesses succeed their fathers or mothers on the throne, they are considered legitimate rulers, because in hereditary monarchies the oldest child inherits the leadership of the state upon the parent's death. The population living in the kingdom accepts the new ruler as the rightful ruler. Sometimes it happens that a king or queen may have no heir or that the heir is incompetent. In other cases, the heir may die before succeeding to the throne. When the next ruler is not identified, conflict and instability surface, and wars of succession occur.

Dictatorships are also politically unstable for reasons related to succession. Every dictator has to struggle to be recognized as the ruler, and none has a natural successor. When the first dictator of the Soviet Union, Lenin, died, a number of people struggled to take his place. Stalin eventually won—by liquidating his competition in a series of cruel and bloody purges. Upon Stalin's death, another struggle for power ensued, until Nikita Khrushchev came out on top. He sent his rivals out of the country as ambassadors or into political exile in Central Asia.

In China the death of Mao Zedong occasioned a frantic struggle between the followers of his wife and a group of moderate economic reformers. Mao's wife lost. She and her supporters, known as "the gang of four," were brought to trial and condemned. The winner in the struggle was Deng Xiaoping, who ruled until the late 1990s. A new ruler, Jiang Zemin, succeeded Deng. Jiang has been accepted internationally as China's legitimate head of state. China selected a new head of the Communist Party in November 2002—Hu Jintao. Although Jiang Zemin stepped aside as Party boss, he kept his post atop the Chinese military and stacked the powerful Politburo Standing Committee with many of his allies. By replacing Jiang as party chief, Hu became the favorite to succeed Jiang as president in March 2003.

Democracies solve the problem of succession by holding regular elections every four, five, or even seven years. The winner of the elections is the recognized new head of state. Thus, people who live in democracies do not have to worry about a possible civil war when the current head of state dies, nor do they have to wonder about a breakdown in government that might cause the economy to fall. Democracies have other built-in mechanisms for maintaining stability. For example, a dictator or king may plunge his territory into confusion by making any kind of law that pleases him. People feel insecure because they are never sure what law is in effect at a given time. In democracies, however, we elect representatives to sit in a legislature and make laws for us in our name. Because democracies are generally free of the problems of succession and arbitrary rule, political scientists argue that democratic political systems provide more political stability, which is essential both to economic stability and social well-being—and therefore to a state's power base.

Quality of Diplomacy

Diplomacy
The negotiating process by which states and other international actors pursue international relations and reconciliation of competing interests by compromise and bargaining.

Arguably one of the more critical elements of national power, **diplomacy**—or negotiating either with or without military teeth—translates national power capabilities from potential into policy and influence. As Morgenthau, mentioned earlier in this chapter, states, diplomacy "is the art of bringing the different elements of national power to bear with maximum effect upon those points in the international situation which concern the national interest most directly."[19] While negotiating styles vary from country to country, as requiring negotiating partners to be sensitive to these differences, the guiding principle is that a country use diplomacy to make the most of its hard and soft power capabilities.

Former Yugoslavia under Slobodan Milosevic offers a classic case of poor diplomacy. Since 1991 Milosevic's brand of diplomacy resulted in four bloody wars. Following the classic Balkan negotiating style—deceive, obfuscate, bully, never accept a proposal from the other side without first attempting to change it to fit your own purpose, and agree only when under severe pressure—Milosevic left what remains of former Yugoslavia with a devastated infrastructure and national power base. These wars also undermined the legitimacy of Milosevic's government and ultimately led to his downfall. In February 2003, former Yugoslavia's parliament dissolved Yugoslavia and renamed the country Serbia and Montenegro.

During the latter half of the twentieth century, diplomacy between North Korea and South Korea coupled with U.S.-North Korea diplomatic contacts, eased tensions and improved North Korea's position in the world community. South Korea's President, Kim Dae-jung, won a Nobel Peace Prize for his efforts. Kim Dae-jung's diplomatic efforts lead to the key question: what constitutes high quality versus low quality diplomacy?

Good diplomacy requires diplomats who are discreet, practical, and careful, and who possess a strong sense of responsibility. While all diplomats are out to advance the national interests of their country, a one may argue that good diplomacy means cooperation to advance security and justice in the world and to reduce violence and poverty. This diplomatic style—aimed at positive global governance—is distinctly unlike the diplomacy of the Cold War, which rested not on compromise but on attempts by each side to reach a goal at the expense of the other.[20] The United States and the former Soviet Union began to move in this cooperative direction after Mikhail Gorbachev came to power in 1985, and the two sides started to manage their relations more peacefully in the Third World.

For more information on American diplomacy, go to **www.ablongman.com/ duncan**.

Why Is Power So Difficult to Measure in World Politics?

While power is the major ingredient of political relationships, calculating the circumstances in which power operates can be annoyingly elusive. For example, we know that influence involves party A getting party B to do something it otherwise would not do; however, this endeavor can be less straightforward than it might seem. Let's take a look at the qualifiers that so complicate the measurement of power.[21]

Differing Forms of Influence

Countries have a variety of techniques for exerting influence over another country. They may, for example, use power to punish, coerce, reward, bargain, or cajole. Country A, for example, can try to *coerce* party B, as Israel did when it assaulted Yassir Arafat's headquarters in 2002. Or A may try to *reward* B for good behavior, as in U.S. efforts during the spring of 1999 to convince China to improve its human rights behavior by promising to support China's application to join the World Trade Organization (WTO). Conversely, B—in this case, China—tried to *persuade* the United States that it merited U.S. backing in its bid to join the WTO by pointing out trade concessions it had made and efforts to crack down on internal corruption.

Chinese Premier Zhu Rongji made this argument during his April 1999 visit to the United States. His influence seeking was undermined, however, by serious strains in U.S.-China relations at that time, including U.S. allegations (and a Congressional report) that China had stolen U.S. nuclear secrets during the 1980s. The result of all this back-and-forth influence seeking ultimately led the United States, in September 2000, to approve normalized trade with China, which set the stage for China's accession to the World Trade Organization. Other power and influence efforts were at work during this visit by Premier Rongji. One example is the U.S. computer industry's all-out lobbying effort to convince Congress to loosen export restrictions to China. Thus, depending on contexts, decisionmakers may use different brands of power—and different types of issues—to influence other decisionmakers to act in a favorable manner.

Violent and nonviolent civil disobedience also operates in world politics as a form of influence seeking. On the violent side, Palestinian suicide bombers inside Israel have attempted to apply political muscle in pressing for an independent Palestinian state carved out of the West Bank and Gaza Strip. Human will and strapped-on explosives are their forms of power. In 1947 Mohandas K. Gandhi practiced passive resistance and promoted nonviolent civil disobedience to win India's independence from Great Britain. More recently, communism disintegrated across Eastern Europe in 1989—in many cases with nonviolent demonstrations, as in Czechoslovakia's Velvet Revolution, when the Communist Party responded by simply stepping aside. The nonviolent approach worked in both India and Czechoslovakia. In contrast, the violent approach of the Palestinian suicide bombers has resulted in harsh military reprisals from the Israeli government, so this strategy has yet to produce the desired ends. The problem in measuring power and its effectiveness—vividly demonstrated in suicide bombing—is that psychological perceptions on the part of the target adversary are unpredictable. In this world of emotion and perception, policy responses are often difficult to foresee.

Multiple Power Factors

One big error countries make is to give a single factor overriding importance.[22] The Soviet Union made huge investments in its military technology but neglected its infrastructure, food processing, transportation systems, and other nonmilitary economic factors. After 1991 its economic weaknesses became glaringly apparent. The lesson? To build a powerful country, leaders must orchestrate many elements of

Military Power as Influence: A Topol-12M nuclear missile at one of Russia's strategic bases, ready to be used at any time. Despite the end of the Cold War in 1991, Russia still retains thousands of nuclear weapons—a number of which remain on alert. As time goes on, questions arise about Russia's capability to safeguard its gigantic holdings of nuclear weapons and delivery systems. This is especially true in light of Russia's economic and political instability.

power. Critics of U.S. foreign policy have noted America's concentration on its hard power at the neglect of its soft power. Still, most countries equate military power as a primary source of influence, which has led a number of countries (United States, Russia, Brazil, Israel, European Union states) to produce weapons for sale abroad. Since Russia's economic collapse, it has used military weapons as a primary export to shore up its economic power. We will look at this power and foreign policy issue more closely in Chapter 4.

Dynamic and Changing Nature of Power

As we saw in Chapter 1, and as we are seeing as this century advances, rapid changes in power have occurred due to a number of driving forces. The twenty-first century has witnessed a growing willingness of those who are part of terrorist organizations— or who are simply living in despair—to commit suicide and, in so doing, to kill as many individuals as possible. The attacks of 9/11 and Palestinian suicide terrorism in Israel illustrate this phenomenon. This form of human motivation has produced awesome decentralizing effects in world politics.

The Internet and World Wide Web have created another power shift. This technological power has made all state borders more porous, thus weakening, traditional power capabilities (the military) for maintaining territorial security—as demonstrated in the international communications that lay behind 9/11. On the flip side, the information revolution has contributed to centralization by creating growing state interdependence of financial power—as in banking transactions and stock market performances. Closely related to the information and communication revo-

SOURCE: *By permission of Mike Luckovich and Creators Syndicate, Inc.*

lution is the rise of globalization and state interdependence. Because of the connectedness of international finance, banking, and commerce, what happens in one country's economy can produce a chain reaction in countries around the globe, thereby impacting the economic power of all.

Power shifts are created by other central factors. The military's technological innovations, such as computers and global positioning systems, long-range aircraft, nuclear weapons, ballistic missiles, biological weapons, and chemical warfare, are cases in point. Those states that move forward in acquiring such weapons of mass destruction assume strong power positions on the globe. The U.S. effort to remove Saddam Hussein from power rested on the assumption that he possessed weapons of mass destruction (WMD); given his record of using them on his own people and Iraq's aggressive action in Kuwait, his power and WMDs posed a threat to the United States and the world. Meanwhile, rising numbers of ethnic national movements diminish the power of those states in which they occur, just as the spread of AIDS in Africa—where millions have died from this dreaded disease—undermines the productive power of infected states. Still another power shift may be seen in collapsing economies, as occurred in Argentina during 2001–2002.

Admittedly, some aspects of power appear more static and unchanging than others, such as China's long-standing Great Wall—built to keep northern invaders at bay over the centuries. In contrast, the Berlin Wall—constructed by former East Germany during the Cold War to keep the people in East Berlin from fleeing into West Berlin—lasted only 28 years (1961–1989). Overall, the situation in today's world regarding power capabilities is more like the wall in Berlin than the one in China, for it is remarkably changing in character.

No longer sitting in a defensive posture behind its wall, China's military power, for example, is growing steadily, as the "Sleeping Dragon" awakes. Japan's economic strength waxes and wanes. Cuba's economy and military strength went into

AIDS Epidemic in Zimbabwe: AIDS in Africa has drastically undermined this region's human development capability in terms of numbers of deaths and dying, soaring costs of health care, and human productivity.

For more information on China's growing military power, go to **www.ablongman.com/ duncan**.

a tailspin in the early 1990s with the collapse of its chief supporter, the Soviet Union. Russia's economy also faltered badly during the 1990s as it struggled to replace a state-controlled economy with a market economic system. Asia's once thriving economies were in serious decline during the mid-1990s, but seemed to bounce back by the late 1990s. South Korea's economy appeared to be the strongest, followed by that of Thailand, Malaysia, Singapore, and the Philippines.[23]

The Relative Nature of Power

Any one state's power can only be evaluated in context. For example, China has more economic power when compared to its next-door neighbor Vietnam or Taiwan, but not when compared to Japan or South Korea. Mexico has much greater overall power in relation to Guatemala, which lies to its south, than in relation to its northern neighbor, the United States. Russia is more able to exert its influence on the Ukraine or Kazakhstan in Central Asia than on any member of the European Union, which lies to its west and is safeguarded by NATO. Vietnam worries more about China's power than about Cambodia's, given the power difference in its two neighbors.

Power, then, is relative, not absolute. While Russia has suffered severe economic decline, it still has a powerful military capability, and its presence is felt in those countries that lie close to it geographically, which Moscow refers to as the "near abroad." The near abroad comprises the lost regions of the old Soviet empire, in which some 25 million Russians still live. The United States has vast objective power, but its perceived negative image abroad make it vulnerable nonetheless, as demonstrated by the attacks of 9/11. While the United States might spend more on the Pentagon—well over the amount spent on the next 15 largest militaries combined—its lack of attention to its public image has undermined its overall relative power capability.

Another excellent example of the relativity of power can be seen in the capabilities of Al Qaeda. While this is an organization rather than a state, the will of its members and their readiness to commit suicide while killing as many people as pos-

Riots in Buenos Aires, Argentina, as Banks Failed, 2002: Economic vitality and political stability, factors of power, are closely interconnected. A failing economy often leads to political instability—depicted in this photo of rioting that took place in Argentina in 2002 when the population was unable to recover their money from the country's banks, owning to mounting economic difficulties.

sible have proven enormously effective in posing a threat to western powers. Al Qaeda by no means possesses the colossal power of the United States, nor can it effect change through the use of commerce, finance, trade, or conventional military weapons. Yet, it has demonstrated significant relative power in its ability to cause the United States to shift huge resources to homeland security, increased military spending, and attention to a war on terrorism. Meanwhile, it has produced a situation in which the United States has lost allied support in Western Europe and the Middle East—thus undermining overall U.S. power.

Neither Iraq, Iran, nor North Korea is a great power. Yet their perceived power—at least in the United States—has been profound since 9/11. North Korea has been completely ineffective in feeding its population, while Iraq hardly enjoys admiration—and thus power—around the world or even within the Middle East. Iran is still struggling with internal religious conflict and antimodernization sentiments that have done little to enhance its overall power. Yet in a relative sense, each has achieved a higher power evaluation—at least from the United States—because each is perceived to be in possession of some kinds of weapons of mass destruction (WMD).

The Situational Nature of Power

Power is only meaningful within a specific policy context. Here are some examples to illustrate the point. Although the United States possesses vast nuclear power, it has had little effect in stopping other countries or Al Qaeda terrorists from actions contrary to U.S. interest. Even the U.S. nuclear arsenal failed to deter 9/11 or to prevail in the Vietnam War. Furthermore, U.S. possession of nuclear weapons has not stopped the Organization of Petroleum Exporting Countries (OPEC) from raising oil prices more than once, thus causing U.S. drivers to pay more for gasoline. And Saddam Hussein proceeded to occupy Kuwait, despite knowing that the United States, Western Europe, and Japan would be displeased. Finally, he prevented UN-backed weapons inspectors from entering his country for years violating international law —until the UN, under intense U.S. pressure, approved a tough new resolution in November 2002 (Resolution 1441) aimed at returning UN weapons inspectors to search for weapons of mass destruction. The point? Although U.S. nuclear weapons have not deterred such activities, they have worked quite well in other situations. For example, during the Cold War the U.S. nuclear arsenal deterred Moscow from launching a nuclear attack against the United States out of fear of a devastating counterattack.

Web Exploration

For more information on weapons of mass destruction, go to **www.ablongman.com/ duncan**.

What Patterns of Power Operate in World Politics?

Over the past three hundred years or so, state decisionmakers appear to have been guided by a principle referred to as the *primacy of the state*. By this is meant that states centered their foreign policy on advancing the interests of the state by using power to protect their territorial security, economic vitality, and political independence. In this view, each state had to rely on its own power, precisely because there was no world government (and still is not) to regulate the affairs of territorial states. You will recall that a major reason for the absence of world government—or broadreaching international law—is that states view themselves as sovereign. They try not to recognize any higher legal authority above the state, as discussed in Chapter 1. Consequently, states exist in a situation of semi-anarchy, and they need to be self-reliant to protect themselves. Thus, pursuing power to defend the their primacy becomes a paramount concern of states. As you now know, this theory of power politics is known as *realism*. While states are not the only actors in world politics, they remain the central actors. So let's take a look at the power patterns they have created in the world political system.

Balance of Power

The balance of power theory, about which much has been written, emerged after the Peace of Westphalia in 1648 as a way to promote world stability. The golden age of balance of power began in the mid-seventeenth century and lasted until World War I. The idea was that if each country had sufficient power, in balance with the power of other countries, then peace and stability would follow. The idea here was to check power with power; if one alliance seemed to be gaining the edge in power, then an opposing alliance should increase its power—and vice versa. It should be kept in mind, however, that the balance of power did not work consistently well and had many breakdowns during this period. Balance of power tactics can be seen during the Cold War when the United States and NATO faced off against the Soviet Union and the Warsaw Pact. But many scholars argue that it was not the balance of power that kept war from breaking out between these two alliance systems, but rather the *balance of terror*—the fear of nuclear retaliation if one side attacked the other with a nuclear weapon.

This balance was threatened in early 2000, when the United States announced that it intended to build a system to shield itself against specific types of rocket attacks. This national missile defense (NMD) system—in effect an antimissile shield—would undermine the 1972 Anti-Ballistic Missile (ABM) Treaty, under which America and the former Soviet Union had agreed that neither would build a defense against the other's long-range nuclear missiles.

The ABM Treaty made sense because it guaranteed against a "first strike" by either side; without a shield, neither side could protect itself from the devastation of the other's "second strike" retaliation and, thus, would not risk making a first strike. Opponents of the new U.S. NMD argued that it would initiate a nuclear arms race, because all nuclear powers would now fear the possibility of a U.S. first strike. The United States countered such arguments, stating that its proposed NMD was designed to protect against rogue states like Iraq or North Korea, not the friendly nuclear powers that included Russia. This U.S. position did not, however, put Russian fears to rest, nor did opponents derail the U.S. plan, and ground breaking on silos for six interceptor missiles at Fort Greely, Alaska, took place in August 2002—with completion scheduled for 2004.

In reading today's news headlines or listening to policymaker speeches, you will hear references to balance of power, for an example being that one country or another is seeking to correct the balance of power. The problem is to determine how the speaker or news release is using the term, for it has multiple meanings. The term may refer to one country trying to check and balance another country's growth in military power and perceived threat by adding more weapons to its own arsenal—as occurred frequently in military weapons acquisitions by the United States and Soviet Union during the Cold War. Or it might refer to a country seeking an advantage over another, as when India or Pakistan detonates a nuclear weapon to shift the power lead to that country.

Balance of power can also refer to various structural models by which power is distributed:

For more information on the military balance of forces, go to **www.ablongman.com/ duncan.**

- *A tight bipolar balance,* as during the late 1940s and early 1950s in the United States/NATO vs. USSR/Warsaw Pact face-off.
- *A loose bipolar balance,* roughly beginning in the mid-1950s, as China moved away from the USSR and France from NATO, and the Third World countries began to organize in the neutral and nonaligned movement (see Figure 3.4).
- *A beginning multipolar balance,* referring to the period of the 1970s and 1980s, as North America and Western Europe grew apart economically, Japan and China became more independent and powerful, the Soviet Union remained intact, and the developing countries moved off in different directions.
- *Today's still evolving multipolarity,* as demonstrated in the breakup of the USSR, rise of China, emerging trade blocs, and so on. In this configuration, multiple centers of various types are forming. Whether balance can occur in this configuration is still an open question.

Collective Security

Because balance of power has been so difficult to achieve over the years—which is especially evident by its breakdown in World War I—policymakers have tried other methods to preserve world peace and stability. One such method is *collective security,* a concept introduced by President Woodrow Wilson following World War I, which calls for a system that combines the military power of peace-loving states to create an overwhelming power base capable of deterring would-be aggressors. In this sense,

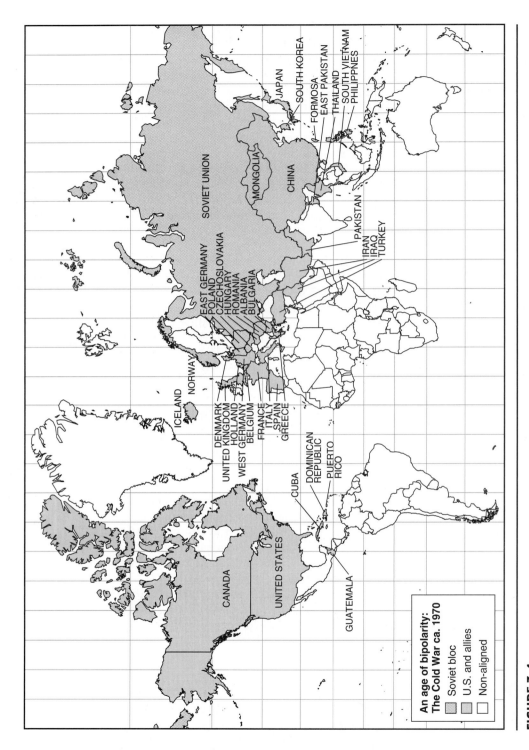

FIGURE 3.4

An Age of Bipolarity: The Cold War ca. 1970

SOURCE: John L. Allen, *Student Atlas of World Politics, Fourth Edition,* (Guilford, CT: Dushkin/McGraw-Hill, 2000), p. 26.

**An age of bipolarity:
The Cold War ca. 1970**

- Soviet bloc
- U.S. and allies
- Non-aligned

any attack on one state would be considered an attack on all states—to be met with collective action. The League of Nations was to be the first such effort of this type. To the dismay of its advocates, the very countries that proposed it, including the United States, did not implement it. Japan invaded Manchuria in 1931 and China in 1937; Italy invaded Ethiopia in 1935, and Germany marched into Czechoslovakia and other European countries from the 1930s onwards—all with impunity. When the strategy of collective security failed to head off World War II, balance of power came back into vogue.

By the late twentieth century, however, UN resolutions legitimizing the use of force in situations like the Persian Gulf War, coupled with its global peacekeeping operations in Bosnia, exemplify a modified form of collective security that has reappeared on the world stage. The 1999 UN-backed effort to bring peace to East Timor—led by Australian forces against Indonesian military forces and antiindependence militias—further illustrates this new modification of collective security. Thus, the message may be that authoritarian governments, militaristic states, or dictators can no longer hide behind their country's sovereignty to conduct acts that grossly violate human rights. Collective security may be expanding from a strategy of stopping acts of aggression by one state against another to stopping such acts by a country's leadership inside its sovereign territory.

Still, the jury is out on how the international community will address systematic violations of human rights, such as genocide, inside sovereign states in the future. Is it legitimate for a group of states in a regional organization like NATO to go into Kosovo without international consensus or clear legal authority? The bombing of Kosovo was a NATO action, not a UN action, which places it more in the realm of *collective defense* (a regional alliance) than in that of collective security (an international or global organization like the UN). Where genocide in Kosovo produced NATO action without UN legitimacy, genocide in Rwanda produced neither NATO nor UN action. Kofi Annan, the UN Secretary-General, argues that the international community must reach a consensus on how to check systematic violations of human rights inside states—especially when one **ethnic national** group goes after another as in former Yugoslavia.[24]

The U.S., meanwhile, struggled with lagging UN Security Council consensus on going to war against Iraq for its material breach of earlier UN disarmament mandates. While the November 2002 UN Resolution 1441 invoked unspecified "serious consequences" for any new failure by Iraq to cooperate with weapons inspectors, Germany, France, China and Russia wanted more time for inspections to take place in February 2003. The U.S., however, pressed for military action. It stressed that the Security must not back down in its demands, allowing a dictator to defy and mock it. So questions also remained about collective security in dealing with a regional hegemon in possession of weapons of mass destruction that threatened world peace.

Power Shifts and Realignments

That power relationships between states change over time is apparent from even a brief reading of history. Immediately after World War II, defeated Germany and Japan were in ruins. Yet each regained much of its lost power during the post-war period. Yugoslavia today is a far cry from the size and strength it was in 1990. At the turn of the century, Russia is a shadow of the once powerful USSR that so dominated news headlines during the Cold War. China and India, with large populations, appear poised to become great powers once they become industrialized.

For more information on NATO and collective defense, go to **www.ablongman.com/ duncan**.

Ethnic Nationalism
Identity of a people—focused essentially on ethnic roots, such as Serb or Russian identity—expressed in behavior ranging from peaceful to violent.

How Power Shifts Over Time States rise and fall in power over time, and as they do their power relationships with other countries shift dramatically—a phenomenon that illustrates not only change in a state's power capabilities, but its relativity of power at any given point in time. Scholars have given much attention to this issue, as in the writing of Paul Kennedy, a historian at Yale University. In his book *The Rise and Fall of the Great Powers* (1987), Kennedy argues that since 1500 great powers have declined when they over-committed themselves to military expenditures and far-flung military operations abroad.[25] In this respect, Kennedy's work may point to the United States, which may be overextending its foreign defense obligations and commitments, thus risking the same fate as Spain in the 1600s, Britain in the 1900s, and Hitler's Germany in the 1940s. U.S. military spending fell dramatically after the Cold War ended. It rose again at the end of that decade—and increased even more after the horrifying events of 9/11. War with Iraq will cost in the billions.

Globalization and Shifting Power John Lewis Gaddis, Yale historian, points out that 9/11 illustrates the dark side of globalization and interdependence, for globalization has spawned deep grievances against the United States as well as the power and means to attack it as demonstrated in the use of civilian aircraft for suicide bombers.[26] Joseph Nye, Dean of Harvard's Kennedy School of Government, points out that while never since Rome has any country loomed so large in power above the others as the United States does today, even Rome eventually collapsed. His point is that America is not invincible; it could undermine its power through unilateralism, arrogance, and parochialism.

This is so, Nye points out, because we live in a globalized world with porous state borders through which pass information, electronically transferred sums larger than most national budgets, weapons and plans of attack by terrorists, and potential cyberspace terrorism by hackers of all stripes.[27] Globalization and the information revolution that has come with it, according to Nye, have created virtual communities and networks that slice through national borders, as previously discussed. This means that transnational corporations (like multinational corporations) and nongovernmental actors (including terrorists) now play larger roles in the international system.

Stanley Hoffmann, professor at Harvard University, has also weighed in on the massive effects of globalization on power in world politics. Hoffman stresses three forms of globalization, each with implications about power: (1) economic—which has recently been undergoing revolutions in technology, information, trade, foreign investment, and international business; (2) cultural—which has led to recent assaults against Western culture (denounced as arrogant, secular, and smacking of U.S. hegemony); and (3) political—which is characterized by a domination by the United States and its political institutions. Hoffman notes that globalization has spread resentment around the world against the United States, produced threats to state sovereignty, stimulated rising violence, and spawned virulent forms of terrorism. Each negative consequence has profound implications for how power now takes new forms in an interdependent globalized world—and how states in a globalized world should mobilize power to combat terrorism. Older concepts of balance of power and collective security become inappropriate in this world of porous borders, and none of America's traditional power capabilities provide protection against future terrorist attacks.

Impact of Change in the Global Distribution of Power Scholars have given much attention to the impact of change in the global distribution of power over time. Change in military technology, for example, affects how war is conducted, and therefore the behavior and perceptions of states affected by weapons innovation. If a state possesses nuclear weapons and missiles to deliver them, it has the power to deter other nuclear-owning countries from attack. Possessing, "the bomb" in effect helps move a country toward great power status, as is the case with the United States, Great Britain, France, and other nuclear powers. The United States emerged from World War II with tremendous power compared to war-torn states, and consequently became a major actor in the international system from the mid-1940s onward.

The ups and downs of who has power and who does not affect the distribution of power in the international system and hence how it operates. Although total agreement among political scientists by no means exists, many studies have reached the following conclusions about patterns of change:

- The world seems most prone to violence during times of rapid shifts in the global distribution of power—as occurred following the collapse of the Soviet Union in 1991.[28]
- Rapid shifts in power distribution tend to create more instability than slower shifts—vividly illustrated in the increased power of international terrorism that led to 9/11 and subsequent instability around the world.
- Bipolar systems (previously discussed) tend to be more stable than a multipolar power distribution in the international system.
- Multipolar systems with four or more poles have the highest probability of war.

By the end of the twentieth century, the world had one superpower, the United States, but power was shifting toward a multipolar arrangement. The USSR suddenly collapsed in 1991, breaking up into many new independent states. The Warsaw Pact fell apart as many of its member states moved from communist to more democratic political systems. While these changes in global power distribution reduced the possibility of nuclear war between the two Cold War superpowers (the United States and USSR), international terrorism, regional instabilities, and civil wars continued to haunt the international system. Two new nuclear-armed countries stood toe-to-toe (India and Pakistan) in conflict, while Al Qaeda terrorists and the Palestinian-Israel crisis added to world instability and decentralization.

Tomorrow's Superpowers and Great Powers   Clearly, states are not equal in terms of power capabilities. While the United States remains the world's superpower, other countries are close behind and in some power categories exceed the United States. From a gross domestic product perspective, for example, the United States ranks number one, with a GDP of around $9 trillion—more than twice as much as second-ranked Japan, and over four times the GDP of country number three, Germany. In per capita income the United States also ranks number one.

The United States, on the other hand, has a huge deficit in its **balance of trade** (the difference between exports and imports of goods and commodities). This and other factors have led some observers to see a decline in America's economic power in the early twenty first century. Immanuel Wallerstein of Yale University, this chapter's case study author, points out that revelations of Wall Street corruption in 2001–2002—insider trading, falsified balance sheets, and other unethical corporate behavior—reveal the weakened dimension of U.S. economic power.[29]

Economic power indicators also show that China is coming on strong as a great power, followed by Germany, India, France, and Great Britain. Hong Kong,

Balance of Trade
An economic term referring to the value of goods coming into, and going out of, a country.

THE VIEW FROM   China

Will China Be the World's Next Superpower?

A number of factors must be calculated to reach a prognosis on whether or not China will become the world's next superpower. The "pro" factors may be summarized as follows:

- Territorial size
- Large population base
- Natural resources
- Work ethic
- Industrialization in progress
- National pride
- Desire for economic growth
- Fascination with money
- Rising military power

Still, numerous negative factors must be cited as factors affecting any assessment:

- Government bureaucracy
- Failing banks
- Sputtering state-owned enterprises
- Massive unemployment
- Under-funded education and health
- Government corruption
- Party disunity on how to modernize
- Weak legal system
- Masses of illegal internal refugees

Which factors do you think are most important? Where do you see China in, say, ten years from now?

now a part of China, has also become a major economic power but not a military one. Its tremendous economic energy will be of major benefit to China. Finally, with the emergence of mega-trading-bloc regions, such as the European Union, NAFTA, and MERCOSUR (South American Common Market) any discussion of power capabilities takes on new dimensions. New poles of economic power in a new multipolar economic global system appeared to be taking shape at the close of the twentieth century.

As we have seen, apart from industrial economic capability, some countries are exceptionally powerful because they control natural resources other states need. Oil reserves and oil production are cases in point, with Saudi Arabia, Iraq, Kuwait, Iran, Russia, the United Arab Republics, and Mexico blessed from this perspective. The box The View from China illustrates this range of resource power. At one time it was thought that Brazil might become a great world power, but its recent economic woes have put such thoughts on the back burner.

When we measure military power by using total military spending and number of military personnel in the armed forces, we get other indicators of superpower and great power ranking. The United States and Russia have dominated in military spending, although Russia and China significantly exceed the United States in numbers of personnel in the armed forces. Ranking countries in terms of military power changes when we add nuclear weapons hard power—or, in the case of Vietnam, the soft power of morale. It changes still again if we try to factor in the component of military leadership. When you come right down to the bottom line, it is extraordinarily difficult to measure a country's war-making and military capabilities.

A New Age of Terrorism Power

President George Bush's 2002 State of the Union Address, delivered to the U.S. Congress on January 29, 2002, vividly illustrates how power in world politics

SOURCE: Toronto Globe and Mail.

comes in different forms and how the terrorist acts of 9/11—in conjunction with weapons of mass destruction—have raised terrorism power to a new level in the arena of international relations. In this new age of terrorism, a newly prominent power issue is not so much which countries will become the next superpowers, but which countries or terrorist groups are in possession—or potential possession—of weapons of mass destruction. The United States has placed Iraq, Iran, North Korea, Cuba, Syria, and Libya on this list—along with terrorist organizations like Al Qaeda.

Al Qaeda is an NGO—terrorist organization committed to suicide bombing in the name of their anti-West cause. Although not a state, it nevertheless possesses organizational and informational capabilities, cyberspace technology, and human will power that can pierce porous state borders—and as such poses a major threat to the nonfundamentalist Islamic world. Because NGOs like Al Qaeda or Hamas are potential recipients of weapons of mass destruction from the so-called evil empire states (North Korea, Iran, and Iraq), they have raised the specter of **terrorist power** to particularly dramatic levels.

The upshot is that while we still use traditional indexes of power defined in terms of objective and subjective factors and according to the concepts of hard and soft power, we also find ourselves in a new age of terrorist power. This new age, in which traditional military, organizational, informational, communications, and human commitment capabilities and influence are combined with terrorist approaches, has raised enormous problems for stability in the world political system and for sustained progress toward centralization.

CHAPTER SUMMARY

What Is Power and How Is It Defined?

Power is a capability that when translated into influence enables one country (or IGO or NGO) to get another state (or IGO or NGO) to do something that it would not otherwise normally do.

- To exert power and influence requires the capability to do so, best thought of as a source of power, such as military strength or economic vitality.
- Power capabilities fall into two general categories: *objective* (geography and natural resources, population, wealth, national infrastructure, military preparedness) and *subjective* (human capabilities, such as culture, morale, quality of government, quality of diplomacy).

Hard power refers to objective capabilities, such as military or economic power. **Soft power** is the state's ability to influence subjectively through cultural and ideological appeal. While economic strength and military weapons certainly are needed to advance a state's key security interests (territorial protection and economic well-being), soft power rests on the appeal of a country's ideals and culture, as well its ability to establish an agenda that will persuade others to agree on values, institutions, and behavior.

What Are the Major Elements of Objective Power?

Objective elements of power include those capabilities or assets that can be seen, touched, and measured—or, in other words, empirically verified. How and where these elements of power are distributed on the global stage set the scene for who will be the big players and who will be the small actors in the drama of global power politics.

Objective power capabilities include:

- Geography and natural resources
- Population
- Wealth and economic stability
- National infrastructure
- Military preparedness

What Are the Major Elements of Subjective Power?

Subjective power factors are human values, beliefs, perceptions, and energy. They come in different forms and are less measurable than objective power factors, yet they remain enormously important in assessing a country's power base. They too help account for conflict or cooperation among states, IGOs, and NGOs in world politics.

Subjective power factors are:

- National culture
- National morale
- Quality of government
- Political stability
- Quality of diplomacy

Why Is Power Difficult to Measure in World Politics?

Power is hard to measure in world politics for a number of reasons. Power capabilities are:

- Different in forms.
- Dynamic and changing over time.
- Relative, not absolute.

New forms of power suddenly emerge to threaten international stability—as in terrorist suicide bombing. A state's power changes over time owing to a host of factors, such as how much it invests in its various power sectors (e.g., research and development in energy and technology).

- Changes in a state's power base can have dramatic effects in the international system, such as changing the overall distribution of power, shifting the system from bipolar to multipolar, producing hegemonic states, or contributing to regional wars or cooperation.
- Globalization has made the task of measuring and understanding power even more complex.

What Patterns of Power Do We Find in World Politics?

Power is expressed in different patterns and distributions within the world political system. The term *balance of power*, normally associated with realist foreign policy, has a variety of meanings. Balance of power differs from collective security. Whereas balance of power refers to individual states that look out for their self-interests, either alone or in alliances, *collective security:*

- Calls for the pooling of power of all states into a single organization, such as the United Nations.
- Has not worked well, largely because of competing state security interests and unwillingness of states to place their military forces under UN auspices.

While the United States is the sole superpower, power in the international arena is shifting. Some observers see China as the world's next superpower. Among the most dramatic forces changing the nature of power is the information revolution—the Internet and World Wide Web—associated with globalization and increasing interdependence.

- Globalization and the information revolution have made state borders more porous and power more relative, as is seen in the rise of anti-U.S. grievances stemming from globalization and in the consequent resorting to terrorist acts.

We now live in a new age of terrorism power initiated by 9/11 that has changed the nature of power—including its use not by states but by NGOs like Al Qaeda.

ENDNOTES

[1]One of the most articulate students of international relations, K.J. Holsti, laid out this formula many years ago, and it still stands as a clear concept model about power. Holsti, *International Politics: A Framework for Analysis,* 7th ed. (Englewood Cliffs, NJ: Prentice Hall, 1995), Chap. 5.

[2]*The Washington Post,* February 26, 1999.

[3]*Yahoo News,* July 15, 1999.

[4]*St. Louis Post Dispatch,* January 5, 1999.

[5]*BBC News,* February 6, 2003.

[6]Joseph S. Nye, "Hard Power, Soft Power," *Boston Globe,* August 6, 1999.

[7]Ibid.

[8]The Associated Press, reported in the *Democrat and Chronicle,* July 32, 2002.

[9]Hans Morgenthau, *Politics Among Nations,* 6th ed. (New York: Alfred A. Knopf, 1979).

[10]Megawatts (MW) are used to measure the output of a power plant or the amount of electricity required by an entire city. One megawatt equals 1,000 kilowatts, which equals 1,000,000 watts. The average output of U.S. power plants is 213 MW, and a 1000-MW power plant is truly large. A watt describes the rate at which electricity is being used at a specific moment in time. One hundred watts describes the amount of electricity that a 100-watt light bulb draws at any particular moment.

[11]*International Wildlife,* September/October 1999, p. 24.

[12]Julie Schmit, "Software Industry Grows in India," *USA Today,* February 24, 1999.

[13]"Survey: America's World Role," *The Economist,* June 27, 2002.

[14]Morgenthau, pp. 146–153.

[15]Raymond Cohen, *Negotiating Across Cultures: International Communication in an Interdependent World,* revised ed. (Washington, DC: U.S. Institute of Peace Press), pp. 3–4.

[16]Nicholas D. Kristof and Sheryl Wudunn, *China Wakes: the Struggle for the Soul of a Rising Power,* (New York: Vintage Books, 1995), pp. 319–320.

[17]Peter F. Drucker, "In Defense of Japanese Bureaucracy," *Foreign Affairs,* vol. 77, No. 5 (September-October 1998), p. 78.

[18]Observations by one of this book's coauthors, W. Raymond Duncan, based on a research trip to Vietnam in the summer of 1998.

[19]Morgenthau, p. 159.

[20]Vladimir Petrovski, Diplomacy as an Instrument of Good Governance, 1998, *http://www.diplomacy.edu/Books/mdiplomacy_book/petrovski/regular/default.html*

[21]While many books and articles have been written about power capabilities and evaluating power, Hans Morgenthau's *Politics Among Nations* stands out as one of the best. It was published first in 1948, and many writers use Morgenthau's analysis as the basis of their own. See *Politics Among Nations,* 6th ed. (New York: Alfred A. Knopf, 1985).

[22]Morgenthau, p. 178.

[23]*The Economist,* August 21–27, 1999, pp. 11, 21.

[24]See *The Economist,* September 18, 1999, pp. 49–50.

[25]Paul Kennedy, The Rise and Fall of the Great Powers (New York: Vintage Books, 1987)

[26]See John Lewis Gaddis in Strobe Talbott and Nayan Chanda, eds. *The Age of Terror: America and the World After September 11* (New York: Basic Book, 2001).

[27]Joseph Nye, "The New Rome Meets the New Barbarians: How America Should Wield Its Power," *The Economist,* March 23, 2002.

[28]John Rourke, *International Politics on the World Stage,* 6th ed. (New York: Dushkin/McGraw Hill, 1997), pp. 74–77.

[29]Immanuel Wallerstein, "The Eagle Has Crash Landed," *Foreign Policy,* July-August 2002, pp. 60–68.

CASE STUDY

Is America's Power on the Decline?

As we have explored in this chapter, scholars and policymakers in recent years have debated the rise and decline of great powers—and the question of America's power has been a part of that debate. Remember that in his best-selling book, *The Rise and Fall of the Great Powers* (1987), historian Paul Kennedy argues that no great power of the modern era has been able to sustain great power status. Great powers typically overextend themselves militarily and economically. In the final analysis, the military and economic costs of their expansion exceed what they can sustain. Without the exercise of skill and insight, this fate could befall the United States.

Paul Kennedy's prognosis of great power decline led Joseph Nye of Harvard University to write *Bound to Lead: The Changing Nature of American Power* (1989). In it, Nye argued that it is highly unlikely that great power decline lies in America's immediate future. America's hard and soft power simply are too strong to wind up in the dustbin of history. Still, Nye reminded his readers that military strength depends on a strong economic base that must be carefully nurtured. As long as this relationship stays in place, America will remain, in his opinion, the world's largest economy and strongest military power. This case study, based on Immanuel Wallerstein's view of this issue, reveals a sharply pessimistic view of America's future.

As you read the case study, keep in mind the points about power made in the chapter. Especially important are the differences between hard and soft power, the major elements of objective power capabilities, and the dynamic and changing nature of power. Ask yourself how power is changing in America and in what direction it is headed. As you read, think about the trends Wallerstein points out and consider whether they might be reversible. Is America doomed, or can we do something about the situation? If Wallerstein is accurate, how will America's decline contribute to decentralization in world politics? Notice what Wallerstein says about economic, political, and military power. Also notice that wars are an important focus.

THE EAGLE HAS CRASH LANDED

BY IMMANUEL WALLERSTEIN

The United States in decline? Few people today would believe this assertion. The only ones who do are the U.S. hawks, who argue vociferously for policies to reverse the decline. This belief that the end of U.S. hegemony has already begun does not follow from the vulnerability that became apparent to all on September 11, 2001. In fact, the United States has been fading as a global power since the 1970s, and the U.S. response to the terrorist attacks has merely accelerated this decline. To understand why the so-called Pax Americana is on the wane requires examining the geopolitics of the twentieth century, particularly of the century's final three decades. This exercise uncovers a simple and inescapable conclusion: The economic, political, and military factors that contributed to U.S. hegemony are the same factors that will inexorably produce the coming U.S. decline.

Introduction to Hegemony

The rise of the United States to global hegemony was a long process that began in earnest with the world recession of 1873. At that time, the United

States and Germany began to acquire an increasing share of global markets, mainly at the expense of the steadily receding British economy. Both nations had recently acquired a stable political base—the United States by successfully terminating the Civil War and Germany by achieving unification and defeating France in the Franco-Prussian War. From 1873 to 1914, the United States and Germany became the principal producers in certain leading sectors: steel and later automobiles for the United States and industrial chemicals for Germany.

The history books record that World War I broke out in 1914 and ended in 1918 and that World War II lasted from 1939 to 1945. However, it makes more sense to consider the two as a single, continuous "30 years' war" between the United States and Germany, with truces and local conflicts scattered in between. The competition for hegemonic succession took an ideological turn in 1933, when the Nazis came to power in Germany and began their quest to transcend the global system altogether, seeking not hegemony within the current system but rather a form of global empire. Recall the Nazi slogan *ein tausendjähriges Reich* (a thousand-year empire). In turn, the United States assumed the role of advocate of centrist world liberalism—recall former U.S. President Franklin D. Roosevelt's "four freedoms" (freedom of speech, of worship, from want, and from fear)—and entered into a strategic alliance with the Soviet Union, making possible the defeat of Germany and its allies.

World War II resulted in enormous destruction of infrastructure and populations throughout Eurasia, from the Atlantic to the Pacific oceans, with almost no country left unscathed. The only major industrial power in the world to emerge intact—and even greatly strengthened from an economic perspective—was the United States, which moved swiftly to consolidate its position.

But the aspiring hegemon faced some practical political obstacles. During the war, the Allied powers had agreed on the establishment of the United Nations, composed primarily of countries that had been in the coalition against the Axis powers. The organization's critical feature was the Security Council, the only structure that could authorize the use of force. Since the U.N. Charter gave the right of veto to five powers—including the United States and the Soviet Union—the council was rendered largely toothless in practice. So it was not the founding of the United Nations in April 1945 that determined the geopolitical constraints of the second half of the twentieth century but rather the Yalta meeting between Roosevelt, British Prime Minister Winston

Churchill, and Soviet leader Joseph Stalin two months earlier.

The formal accords at Yalta were less important than the informal, unspoken agreements, which one can only assess by observing the behavior of the United States and the Soviet Union in the years that followed. When the war ended in Europe on May 8, 1945, Soviet and Western (that is, U.S., British, and French) troops were located in particular places—essentially, along a line in the center of Europe that came to be called the Oder-Neisse Line. Aside from a few minor adjustments, they stayed there. In hindsight, Yalta signified the agreement of both sides that they could stay there and that neither side would use force to push the other out. This tacit accord applied to Asia as well, as evinced by U.S. occupation of Japan and the division of Korea. Politically, . . . [therefore,] Yalta was an agreement on the status quo in which the Soviet Union controlled about one-third of the world and the United States the rest.

Washington also faced more serious military challenges. The Soviet Union had the world's largest land forces, while the U.S. government was under domestic pressure to downsize its army, particularly by ending the draft. The United States therefore decided to assert its military strength not via land forces but through a monopoly of nuclear weapons (plus an air force capable of deploying them). This monopoly soon disappeared: By 1949, the Soviet Union had developed nuclear weapons as well. Ever since, the United States has been reduced to trying to prevent the acquisition of nuclear weapons (and chemical and biological weapons) by additional powers, an effort that, in the twenty-first century, does not seem terribly successful.

Until 1991, the United States and the Soviet Union coexisted in the "balance of terror" of the Cold War. This status quo was tested seriously only three times: the Berlin blockade of 1948–1949, the Korean War in 1950–1953, and the Cuban missile crisis of 1962. The result in each case was restoration of the status quo. Moreover, note how each time the Soviet Union faced a political crisis among its satellite regimes—East Germany in 1953, Hungary in 1956, Czechoslovakia in 1968, and Poland in 1981—the United States engaged in little more than propaganda exercises, allowing the Soviet Union to proceed largely as it deemed fit.

Of course, this passivity did not extend to the economic arena. The United States capitalized on the Cold War ambiance to launch massive economic reconstruction efforts, first in Western Europe and then in Japan (as well as in South Korea and Taiwan). The rationale was obvious: What was the point of having such overwhelming productive superiority if the rest of the world could not muster effective demand? Furthermore, economic reconstruction helped create . . . obligations on the part of the nations receiving U.S. aid; this sense of obligation fostered willingness to enter into military alliances and, even more important, into political subservience.

Finally, one should not underestimate the ideological and cultural component of U.S. hegemony. The immediate post-1945 period may have been the historical high point for the popularity of communist ideology. We easily forget today the large votes for communist parties in free elections in countries such as Belgium, France, Italy, Czechoslovakia, and Finland, not to mention the support communist parties gathered in Asia—in Vietnam, India, and Japan—and throughout Latin America. And that still leaves out areas such as China, Greece, and Iran, where free elections remained absent or constrained but where communist parties enjoyed widespread appeal. In response, the United States sustained a massive anticommunist ideological offensive. In retrospect, this initiative appears largely successful: Washington brandished its role as the leader of the "free world" at least as effectively as the Soviet Union brandished its position as the leader of the "progressive" and "anti-imperialist" camp.

One, Two, Many Vietnams

The United States' success as a hegemonic power in the postwar period created the conditions of the nation's hegemonic demise. This process is captured in four symbols: the war in Vietnam, the revolutions of 1968, the fall of the Berlin Wall in 1989, and the terrorist attacks of September 2001. Each symbol built upon the prior one, culminating in the situation in which the United States currently finds itself—a lone superpower that lacks true power, a world leader nobody follows and few respect, and a nation drifting dangerously amidst a global chaos it cannot control.

What was the Vietnam War? First and foremost, it was the effort of the Vietnamese people to end colonial rule and establish their own state. The Vietnamese fought the French, the Japanese, and the Americans, and in the end the Vietnamese won—quite an achievement, actually. Geopolitically, however, the war represented a rejection of the Yalta status quo by populations then labeled as Third World. Vietnam became such a powerful symbol because Washington was foolish enough to invest its full military might in the struggle, but the United States still lost. True, the United States didn't deploy nuclear weapons (a decision certain myopic groups on the right have long

reproached), but such use would have shattered the Yalta accords and might have produced a nuclear holocaust—an outcome the United States simply could not risk.

But Vietnam was not merely a military defeat or a blight on U.S. prestige. The war dealt a major blow to the United States' ability to remain the world's dominant economic power. The conflict was extremely expensive and more or less used up the U.S. gold reserves that had been so plentiful since 1945. Moreover, the United States incurred these costs just as Western Europe and Japan experienced major economic upswings. These conditions ended U.S. preeminence in the global economy. Since the late 1960s, members of this triad have been nearly economic equals, each doing better than the others for certain periods but none moving far ahead.

When the revolutions of 1968 broke out around the world, support for the Vietnamese became a major rhetorical component. "One, two, many Vietnams" and "Ho, Ho, Ho Chi Minh" were chanted in many a street, not least in the United States. But the 1968ers did not merely condemn U.S. hegemony. They condemned Soviet collusion with the United States, they condemned Yalta, and they used or adapted the language of the Chinese cultural revolutionaries who divided the world into two camps—the two superpowers and the rest of the world.

[The attack on Soviet collusion with Washington plus the attack on the Old Left further weakened the legitimacy of the Yalta arrangements on which the United States had fashioned the world order. It also undermined the position of centrist liberalism as the lone, legitimate global ideology.] The direct political consequences of the world revolutions of 1968 were minimal, but the geopolitical and intellectual repercussions were enormous and irrevocable. Centrist liberalism tumbled from the throne it had occupied since the European revolutions of 1848 and that had enabled it to co-opt conservatives and radicals alike. These ideologies returned and once again represented a real gamut of choices. Conservatives would again become conservatives, and radicals, radicals. The centrist liberals did not disappear, but they were cut down to size. And in the process, the official U.S. ideological position—antifascist, anticommunist, anticolonialist— seemed thin and unconvincing to a growing portion of the world's populations.

The Powerless Superpower

The onset of international economic stagnation in the 1970s had two important consequences for U.S.

power. First, stagnation resulted in the collapse of "developmentalism"—the notion that every nation could catch up economically if the state took appropriate action—which was the principal ideological claim of the Old Left movements then in power. One after another, these regimes faced internal disorder, declining standards of living, increasing debt dependency on international financial institutions, and eroding credibility. What had seemed in the 1960s to be the successful navigation of Third World decolonization by the United States—minimizing disruption and maximizing the smooth transfer of power to regimes that were developmentalist but scarcely revolutionary—gave way to disintegrating order, simmering discontents, and unchanneled radical temperaments. When the United States tried to intervene, it failed. In 1983, U.S. President Ronald Reagan sent troops to Lebanon to restore order. The troops were in effect forced out. He compensated by invading Grenada, a country without troops. President George H. W. Bush invaded Panama, another country without troops. But after he intervened in Somalia to restore order, the United States was in effect forced out, somewhat ignominiously. Since there was little the U.S. government could actually do to reverse the trend of declining hegemony, it chose simply to ignore this trend—a policy that prevailed from the withdrawal from Vietnam until September 11, 2001.

Meanwhile, true conservatives began to assume control of key states and interstate institutions. The neoliberal offensive of the 1980s was marked by the Thatcher and Reagan regimes and the emergence of the International Monetary Fund as a key actor on the world scene. Where once (for more than a century) conservative forces had attempted to portray themselves as wiser liberals, now centrist liberals were compelled to argue that they were more effective conservatives. The conservative programs were clear. Domestically, conservatives tried to enact policies that would reduce the cost of labor, minimize environmental constraints on producers, and cut back on state welfare benefits. Actual successes were modest, so conservatives then moved vigorously into the international arena. The gatherings of the World Economic Forum in Davos provided a meeting ground for elites and the media. The IMF provided a club for finance ministers and central bankers. And the United States pushed for the creation of the World Trade Organization to enforce free commercial flows across the world's frontiers.

While the United States wasn't watching, the Soviet Union was collapsing. Yes, Ronald Reagan had dubbed the Soviet Union an "evil empire" and had used the rhetorical bombast of calling for the destruction of the Berlin Wall, but the United States didn't really mean it and certainly was not responsible for the Soviet Union's downfall. In truth, the Soviet Union and its East European imperial zone collapsed because of popular disillusionment with the Old Left in combination with Soviet leader Mikhail Gorbachev's efforts to save his regime by liquidating Yalta and instituting internal liberalization (*perestroika* plus *glasnost*). Gorbachev succeeded in liquidating Yalta but not in saving the Soviet Union (although he almost did, be it said).

The United States was stunned and puzzled by the sudden collapse, uncertain how to handle the consequences. The collapse of communism in effect signified the collapse of liberalism, removing the only ideological justification behind U.S. hegemony, a justification tacitly supported by liberalism's ostensible ideological opponent. This loss of legitimacy led directly to the Iraqi invasion of Kuwait, which Iraqi leader Saddam Hussein would never have dared had the Yalta arrangements remained in place. In retrospect, U.S. efforts in the Gulf War accomplished a truce at basically the same line of departure. But can a hegemonic power be satisfied with a tie in a war with a middling regional power? Saddam demonstrated that one could pick a fight with the United States and get away with it. Even more than the defeat in Vietnam, Saddam's brash challenge has eaten at the innards of the U.S. right, in particular those known as the hawks, which explains the fervor of their current desire to invade Iraq and destroy its regime.

Between the Gulf War and September 11, 2001, the two major arenas of world conflict were the Balkans and the Middle East. The United States has played a major diplomatic role in both regions. Looking back, how different would the results have been had the United States assumed a completely isolationist position? In the Balkans, an economically successful multinational state (Yugoslavia) broke down, essentially into its component parts. Over ten years, most of the resulting states have engaged in a process of ethnification, experiencing fairly brutal violence, widespread human rights violations, and outright wars. Outside intervention—in which the United States figured most prominently—brought about a truce and ended the most egregious violence, but this intervention in no way reversed the ethnification, which is now consolidated and somewhat legitimated. Would these conflicts have ended differently without U.S. involvement? The violence might have continued longer, but the basic results would probably not have been too different. The picture is even grimmer in the Middle East, where, if anything, U.S. engagement has been deeper and its failures more spectacular. In the Balkans and the Middle East alike, the United States has failed to exert its hegemonic clout effectively, not for want of will or effort but for want of real power.

The Hawks Undone

Then came September 11, 2001—the shock and the reaction. Under fire from U.S. legislators, the Central Intelligence Agency (CIA) now claims it had warned the Bush administration of possible threats. But despite the CIA's focus on Al Qaeda and the agency's intelligence expertise, it could not foresee (and therefore, prevent) the execution of the terrorist strikes. Or so would argue CIA Director George Tenet. This testimony can hardly comfort the U.S. government or the American people. Whatever else historians may decide, the attacks of September 11, 2001, posed a major challenge to U.S. power. The persons responsible did not represent a major military power. They were members of a nonstate force, with a high degree of determination, some money, a band of dedicated followers, and a strong base in one weak state. In short, militarily, they were nothing. Yet they succeeded in a bold attack on U.S. soil.

George W. Bush came to power very critical of the Clinton administration's handling of world affairs. Bush and his advisors did not admit—but were undoubtedly aware—that Clinton's path had been the path of every U.S. president since Gerald Ford, including that of Ronald Reagan and George H. W. Bush. It had even been the path of the current Bush administration before September 11. One only needs to look at how Bush handled the downing of the U.S. plane off China in April 2001 to see that prudence had been the name of the game.

Following the terrorist attacks, Bush changed course, declaring war on terrorism, assuring the American people that "the outcome is certain" and informing the world that "you are either with us or against us." Long frustrated by even the most conservative U.S. administrations, the hawks finally came to dominate American policy. Their position is clear: The United States wields overwhelming military power, and even though countless foreign leaders consider it unwise for Washington to flex its military muscles, these same leaders cannot and will not do anything if the United States simply imposes its will on the rest. The hawks believe the United States should act as an imperial power for two reasons: First, the United States can get away with it. And second, if Washington doesn't exert its force, the United States will become

increasingly marginalized. Today, this hawkish position has three expressions: the military assault in Afghanistan, the de facto support for the Israeli attempt to liquidate the Palestinian Authority, and the invasion of Iraq, which is reportedly in the military preparation stage. Less than one year after the September 2001 terrorist attacks, it is perhaps too early to assess what such strategies will accomplish. Thus far, these schemes have led to the overthrow of the Taliban in Afghanistan (without the complete dismantling of Al Qaeda or the capture of its top leadership); enormous destruction in Palestine (without rendering Palestinian leader Yasir Arafat "irrelevant," as Israeli Prime Minister Ariel Sharon said he is); and heavy opposition from U.S. allies in Europe and the Middle East to plans for an invasion of Iraq.

The hawks' reading of recent events emphasizes that opposition to U.S. actions, while serious, has remained largely verbal. Neither Western Europe nor Russia nor China nor Saudi Arabia has seemed ready to break ties in serious ways with the United States. In other words, hawks believe, Washington has indeed gotten away with it. The hawks assume a similar outcome will occur when the U.S. military actually invades Iraq and after that, when the United States exercises its authority elsewhere in the world, be it in Iran, North Korea, Colombia, or perhaps Indonesia. Ironically, the hawk reading has largely become the reading of the international left, which has been screaming about U.S. policies—mainly because they fear that the chances of U.S. success are high. But hawk interpretations are wrong and will only contribute to the United States' decline, transforming a gradual descent into a much more rapid and turbulent fall. Specifically, hawk approaches will fail for military, economic, and ideological reasons.

Undoubtedly, the military remains the United States' strongest card; in fact, it is the only card. Today, the United States wields the most formidable military apparatus in the world. And if claims of new, unmatched military technologies are to be believed, the U.S. military edge over the rest of the world is considerably greater today than it was just a decade ago. But does that mean, then, that the United States can invade Iraq, conquer it rapidly, and install a friendly and stable regime? Unlikely. Bear in mind that of the three serious wars the U.S. military has fought since 1945 (Korea, Vietnam, and the Gulf War), one ended in defeat and two in draws—not exactly a glorious record.

Saddam Hussein's army is not that of the Taliban, and his internal military control is far more coherent. A U.S. invasion would necessarily involve a serious land force, one that would have to fight its way to Baghdad and would likely suffer significant casualties. Such a force would also need staging grounds, and Saudi Arabia has made clear that it will not serve in this capacity. Would Kuwait or Turkey help out? Perhaps, if Washington calls in all its chips. Meanwhile, Saddam can be expected to deploy all weapons at his disposal, and it is precisely the U.S. government that keeps fretting over how nasty those weapons might be. The United States may twist the arms of regimes in the region, but popular sentiment clearly views the whole affair as reflecting a deep anti-Arab bias in the United States. Can such a conflict be won? The British General Staff has apparently already informed Prime Minister Tony Blair that it does not believe so. And there is always the matter of "second fronts." Following the Gulf War, U.S. armed forces sought to prepare for the possibility of two simultaneous regional wars. After a while, the Pentagon quietly abandoned the idea as impractical and costly. But who can be sure that no potential U.S. enemies would strike when the United States appears bogged down in Iraq?

Consider, too, the question of U.S. popular tolerance of nonvictories. Americans hover between a patriotic fervor that lends support to all wartime presidents and a deep isolationist urge. Since 1945, patriotism has hit a wall whenever the death toll has risen. Why should today's reaction differ? And even if the hawks (who are almost all civilians) feel impervious to public opinion, U.S. Army generals, burnt by Vietnam, do not.

And what about the economic front? In the 1980s, countless American analysts became hysterical over the Japanese economic miracle. They calmed down in the 1990s, given Japan's well-publicized financial difficulties. Yet after overstating how quickly Japan was moving forward, U.S. authorities now seem to be complacent, confident that Japan lags far behind. These days, Washington seems more inclined to lecture Japanese policymakers about what they are doing wrong. Such triumphalism hardly appears warranted. Consider the following April 20, 2002, *New York Times* report: "A Japanese laboratory has built the world's fastest computer, a machine so powerful that it matches the raw processing power of the 20 fastest American computers combined and far outstrips the previous leader, an I.B.M.-built machine. The achievement . . . is evidence that a technology race that most American engineers thought they were winning handily is far from over."

The analysis goes on to note that there are "contrasting scientific and technological priorities" in the two countries. The Japanese machine is built to analyze climatic change, but U.S. machines are designed to simulate weapons. This contrast embodies the oldest story in the history of hegemonic powers. The dominant power concentrates (to its detriment) on the military; the candidate for successor concentrates on the economy. The latter has always paid off, handsomely. It did for the United States. Why should it not pay off for Japan as well, perhaps in alliance with China?

Finally, there is the ideological sphere. Right now, the U.S. economy seems relatively weak, even more so considering the exorbitant military expenses associated with hawk strategies. Moreover, Washington remains politically isolated; virtually no one (save Israel) thinks the hawk position makes sense or is worth encouraging. Other nations are afraid or unwilling to stand up to Washington directly, but even their foot-dragging is hurting the United States.

Yet the U.S. response amounts to little more than arrogant arm-twisting. Arrogance has its own negatives. Calling in chips means leaving fewer chips for next time, and surly acquiescence breeds increasing resentment. Over the last 200 years, the United States acquired a considerable amount of ideological credit. But these days, the United States is running through this credit even faster than it ran through its gold surplus in the 1960s.

The United States faces two possibilities during the next ten years: It can follow the hawks' path, with negative consequences for all but especially for itself. Or it can realize that the negatives are too great. Simon Tisdall of the Guardian recently argued that even disregarding international public opinion, "the U.S. is not able to fight a successful Iraqi war by itself without incurring immense damage, not least in terms of its economic interests and its energy supply. Mr. Bush is reduced to talking tough and looking ineffectual." And if the United States still invades Iraq and is then forced to withdraw, it will look even more ineffectual.

President Bush's options appear extremely limited, and there is little doubt that the United States will continue to decline as a decisive force in world affairs over the next decade. The real question is not whether U.S. hegemony is waning but whether the United States can devise a way to descend gracefully, with minimum damage to the world, and to itself.

SOURCE: Immanuel Wallerstein, "*The Eagle Has Crash Landed,*" Foreign Policy, *July/August 2002, pp. 60–68. Copyright 2002 by Foreign Policy. Reproduced by permission of Foreign Policy in the format textbook via Copyright Clearance Center. Immanuel Wallerstein is a senior research scholar at Yale University and author of, most recently,* The End of the World as We Know It: Social Science for the Twenty-First Century *(Minneapolis: University of Minnesota Press, 1999).*

QUESTIONS

Check Your Understanding

1. What are the most important sources of evidence Wallerstein uses to support his central thesis that American power is in decline?
2. Name two concepts from the chapter on power that are most relevant in Wallerstein's argument.

Analyze the Issues

3. According to Wallerstein, why is this a particularly important time in world politics to reflect on the nature of U.S. power?
4. Apply the theoretical perspective of why power is so difficult to measure in world politics to the case study?
5. From what you have learned about power—and its objective and subjective components—would you say that Wallerstein makes a compelling argument about America's decline? If so, why?

FOR FURTHER INFORMATION

For further information regarding the argument made in this case study, see the following sources:

Terence K. Hopkins and Immanuel Wallerstein, eds. *The Age of Transition: Trajectory of the World System, 1945–2025,* London: Zed Books, 1996.

Joseph Nye, *The Paradox of Power: Why the World's Only Superpower Can't Go It Alone,* New York: Oxford University Press, 2002.

Thomas J. McCormick, *America's Half-Century: United States Foreign Policy in the Cold War and After,* 2nd edition, Baltimore: Johns Hopkins University Press, 1995.

On the question of whether or not America will remain the only superpower in the world, see Paul Kennedy, *The Rise and Fall of the Great Powers,* New York: Vintage Books, 1987; and Joseph S. Nye, Jr., *Bound to Lead: The Changing Nature of American Power,* Boulder, Colorado: Basic Books, 1990.

For more insight on the nature of power and how it changes over time in world politics, you will find the following web pages helpful. The *Foreign Affairs* web page may be found at *http://www.foreignaffairs.org/* and the *Foreign Policy* web page is located at *http://www.foreignpolicy.com*

CHAPTER 4

Foreign Policy Formation and Execution

KEY QUESTIONS RAISED IN THIS CHAPTER

1. What exactly is foreign policy?
2. What factors influence foreign policy?
3. What perspectives explain foreign policy decision making?
4. What traits typify American and Russian foreign policy?
5. How have other countries reacted to America's war on terrorism?

When you read daily newspaper headlines or watch television news, you quickly realize that at any given moment, foreign policy—the translation of power capabilities into action—is a major aspect of world politics. Foreign policy is put into play by decision-makers of the world's states and their governments, IOs, and NGOs—including terrorist organizations like Al Qaeda. Each tries to employ power and influence to achieve its desired goals. When one actor uses foreign policy to integrate and cooperate with other actors, it serves as a centralizing force. Diplomats who met at the UN's August 2002 World Summit on Sustainable Development in Johannesburg, South Africa, illustrated this kind of centralizing influence as they tried to agree on ways to reduce poverty while preserving the environment. In contrast, when foreign policies lead to conflict—as when Iraq and the United States clashed in 2003—they operate as a decentralizing force in the international system.

The following are examples of the manner in which foreign policy translates power capabilities and concerns into action:

- America wants to rid the world of terrorists and control weapons of mass destruction, so it launches a war on terrorism and uses military assets to remove Iraq's Saddam Hussein from power; Hussein allegedly possessed such weapons and President Bush believes Iraq would have used them against the West.
- Russia's Vladimir Putin signs a multi-billion-dollar trade agreement with Iraq, despite its defiance of UN disarmament sanctions and America's anti-Hussein posture; Russia's limping economy needs money.
- Japan declares its support of the U.S. war in Afghanistan after 9/11, but pulls back on its promised financial assistance; Japan needs to keep its business ties around the world intact—even with U.S. enemies—because Japan defines its security goals in economic as well as military terms.

Given foreign policy's enormous role in world politics, this chapter looks closely at its major characteristics and how it affects the international system. We will begin with an examination of foreign policy's close links to power capabilities, discussed in Chapter 3, its principal goals and the kinds of issues it entails. Among the key factors that drive foreign policy are national interests, political and government leaders, domestic economic and political structures, and international influences. We will show how these elements come into play and how and why foreign policies change while basic core goals stay in place.

Of great importance in the study of foreign policy is how decisions are made, and this chapter will delve cogently into that big question by examining four distinct dimensions of foreign-policy decision making. We also will put foreign policy into historical perspective by contrasting how the United States and Russia approached foreign policy during and after the Cold War, with particular attention to their intense competition in the Third World. Finally, given the enormous impact of 9/11, we will conclude this study of foreign policy—with its centralizing and decentralizing pressures—with a look at America's war on terrorism and how 9/11 impacted other foreign policies around the world—with close attention to China, Egypt, Pakistan, and Saudi Arabia.

What Exactly Is Foreign Policy?

To get a grip on why leaders of countries and other organizations pursue all kinds of goals on the world political chessboard, we need to understand the basic elements of foreign policy. Beyond simply trying to understand foreign policy for its own intel-

WHY IT MATTERS TO YOU

Foreign Policy

So why does foreign policy matter to you? The attacks of 9/11, with the destruction, loss of life, and loss of a sense of security that followed, vividly underscore the answer. This tragedy serves as an excellent example of foreign policy hitting us in our own backyard. In this case Al Qaeda terrorists, organizing and planning in Afghanistan under Taliban protection, were extraordinarily hostile to America's foreign policy actions around the world—including its leadership in globalization, promotion of western values, and occuption of territory in Saudi Arabia, the site of Islam's holy cities of Mecca and Medina. Further, it was U.S. military support of the anti-Soviet mujahideen during 1979–1989, followed by U.S. abandonment of Afghanistan after the war, that set up conditions for the Al Qaeda Taliban protectors to come to power, and which led up to 9/11.

Foreign policy, of course, matters to you in numerous other ways as well:

Other countries pursue goals to fulfill their own economic and security needs—policies that in turn affect you—from higher oil prices (Saudi Arabia) to the threat of nuclear war (India versus Pakistan) and its impact on the environment.

- U.S. policy can turn friends into adversaries and thus undermine its ability to capture terrorists planning future attacks on America—as in the case involving America's insistence on going it alone in its determination to attack Iraq.
- U.S. foreign policies and those of other countries affect the quality of air we breathe and the products we buy—as well as the capacity of other countries to buy our products. The result impacts employment opportunities in our country and the health of our environment.
- U.S. foreign policy can affect how you will be received if you travel abroad, as well as where you are able to travel.

Foreign policy and domestic policy—as you can see from the above examples—are interdependent. What happens in one area shapes outcomes in the other—a two-way street with vast implications for your well being, safety, and quality of life.

lectual attraction or because you are taking a course on the subject, it is important to understand the foreign policy of your own country—as well as that of others—because it matters greatly in your life, as the box Why It Matters to You: Foreign Policy attests. With foreign policy's relevance to your life in mind, let us probe this subject by concentrating first on foreign policy as an approach to translating power into policy, and then look at its constant set of core, middle range, and long-range goals.

An Approach to Translating Power into Action

In Chapter 3 we discussed the numerous power capabilities at the disposal of states and other actors in the world political arena. We looked at hard and soft types of power, as well as objective and subjective types of power available to leaders of states, IOs, and NGOs. These kinds of power include possession of valued resources like oil (Saudi Arabia and Russia) or food (America and Canada), as well as economic wealth (high GDP as in the United States) or military capabilities (conventional and nuclear weapons like the United States has). Power assets also include a host of subjective factors like morale (the Vietnamese in the Vietnam War), commitment to particular goals (Saddam Hussein's alleged commitment to acquiring weapons of mass destruction)—or in the case of some terrorists, the willingness to commit suicide for a cause.

To talk about power first and foreign policy—the subject of this chapter—second, makes sense, because without some kind of power, it would be difficult to have an effective foreign policy. This is so because *foreign policy—from diplomacy to armed attack—constitutes the ways in which key actors on the international scene translate available power into specific policies designed to shape positive outcomes.* Foreign policy is a vital aspect of world politics, and power is one of its key components.

Power and Policy Tools   Once foreign policy decision makers know what issues they will pursue as foreign policy goals, they have at their disposal a wide range of tools for translating available power capabilities into specific policies. The United States, for example, used its military power to first bomb, then chase on the ground, the Taliban in Afghanistan in response to the 9/11 attacks—and later to attack and occupy Iraq. The Palestinians have used suicide bombers in their drive for an independent state. India and Pakistan have threatened to use nuclear weapons against each other in their dispute over Kashmir. How leaders translate available power into policies, and the tools they use, will vary from state to state, actor to actor, and situation to situation. History and geographic location of a country also come into play—as we will show later—as do the kinds of power available, and the type of government and political culture of the actors.

The tools for translating power into policy range from benign and peaceful (soft power, information programs, humanitarian aid, and diplomacy) to coercive (embargoes, economic blockades, espionage and sabotage, and military force). Each of these policy options requires underlying power to be put it into play—such as money or goods for humanitarian aid, printing presses and film production for information programs, or ships and naval weapons to establish an effective blockade. Figure 4.1 depicts this range and the types of foreign policy tools available to state leaders.

FIGURE 4.1

Tools for Foreign Policy Implementation

SOURCE: *The United States Naval War College, National Security Decision Making Department, Case Study, 1992–1993.*

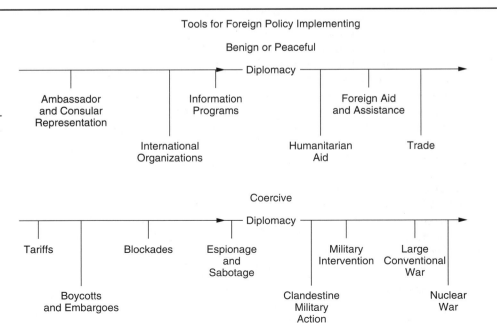

Tools for Foreign Policy Implementing

Benign or Peaceful

Diplomacy

Ambassador and Consular Representation

International Organizations

Information Programs

Foreign Aid and Assistance

Humanitarian Aid

Trade

Coercive

Diplomacy

Tariffs

Boycotts and Embargoes

Blockades

Espionage and Sabotage

Military Intervention

Clandestine Military Action

Large Conventional War

Nuclear War

Changes in the Diplomatic Climate   Note that **diplomacy** is the overarching tool at the disposal of state leaders. By diplomacy is meant the process by which a country negotiates with other countries on everything from trade agreements to military conflict, establishes representation abroad, defends its policies, observes other countries' behavior, exports that behavior back home, and generally conducts political, cultural, economic, and security relationships with other countries. As Figure 4.1 indicates, there are two kinds of diplomacy: benign and coercive; within each category is a range of actions from least benign to most coercive.[1]

The nature of diplomatic negotiations has changed, however, over the years. Before World War I, for example, Europe was the focus of much diplomacy. Few nationalist sentiments complicated the diplomatic process, and ideologies like communism or Nazism had not yet established a footing in world politics. Secret diplomacy was the name of the game, and the diplomats, that is, chief negotiators, tended to have a common aristocratic identity, with French as the key language. They represented governments headed by leaders who knew each other from intermarriage. This period before World War I is referred to as the era of **Old Diplomacy.**

After 1919 the world entered what might be termed the period of **New Diplomacy.** New Diplomacy is more open and public, with less secrecy and more public opinion and public press involvement than during the earlier era. Furthermore, ideologies like Marxism-Leninism became more prominent, and although Marxism-Leninism largely died out in Russia, it continued in mainland China and in Cuba at the end of the twentieth century. National identity and nationalism also became much more pronounced during the mid-to-late twentieth century and were extremely powerful forces at the turn of the century. Europe ceased to be the major dominant geographic pivot of diplomacy, as more and more sovereign states entered the international political playing field, and as diplomacy became globalized.

Other changes are associated with New Diplomacy. The United Nations became increasingly important as a forum for diplomatic representation and exchanges, and it gathered momentum in its global peacekeeping operations, which were backed by diplomatic power. Summit diplomacy—negotiations between heads of states as opposed to embassies, consulates, and diplomats—became more evident. The world also saw the rise of **coercive diplomacy:** the threat and use of force in tandem with diplomatic pressure by an alliance like NATO to influence a war-making state. For example, the NATO alliance used coercive diplomacy to try and get Serbia to cease its military activities in Bosnia and Kosovo. The United States tried coercive diplomacy on Iraq in 2002–2003 to find hidden weapons of mass destruction. Despite these many changes, however, bilateral and multilateral diplomacy continued to operate as in Old Diplomacy, with two states (bilateral) or more than two states (multilateral) negotiating with each other.

America's public diplomacy has gone through a rough patch recently. The agency that has long dealt with public diplomacy, the U.S. Information Agency, has seen its resources reduced over the past decade, and in 1999 it was merged into the Department of State, where its functions have been fragmented and its resources even further depleted. This situation has weakened dramatically America's soft power, as discussed in Chapter 3. The Bush Administration's assertive, unilateralist foreign policy, backed by the U.S. military, has not helped America's public image abroad and, it could be argued, has put America at odds with the international community that it helped build during the post–World War II period and that it needs for security in the post–9/11 period.

Diplomacy
The negotiating process by which states and other international actors pursue international relations and reconciliation of competing interests by compromise and bargaining.

Old Diplomacy
The form of diplomacy that characterized the era prior to World War I. European-centered, it emphasized secrecy and was generally devoid of nationalism.

New Diplomacy
The style of diplomacy that has evolved since World War I, with emphasis on open—as opposed to secret—negotiations, summit meetings, and in which nationalism has a greater impact on the negotiating process.

Coercive Diplomacy
The threat and use of force in tandem with diplomatic pressure by one actor on another. The UN's coercive diplomacy on Saddam Hussein to reveal more information on Iraq's WMD in 2003 is a good example. (Coercive diplomacy failed in this case.)

President Bush Addresses the UN: President Bush spoke before the United Nations in September 2002. His address was designed to win support from the international community to put teeth into its many UN resolutions demanding that Iraq allow inspectors in to verify that it had ended its quest for weapons of mass destruction. The speech marked renewed U.S. attention to the importance of working more closely with the international community in its quest for a regime change in Iraq. Yet U.S. diplomacy in this case failed. The United States and Great Britain, launched a preemptive attack on, then occupied, Iraq in March/April 2003 to bring about regime change.

A Set of Core, Middle, and Long-Range Goals

A sound approach to understanding the goals and objectives pursued by states in the international arena is to begin with the assumption that a country's foreign policy objectives tend to be hierarchical and shaped by many forces. By "hierarchical" we mean that foreign policy goals cover a range of (1) core or vital interest objectives; (2) middle-range objectives; and (3) long-range objectives. These three types of foreign policy goals are defined easily enough.

Core Objectives

A term used in foreign policy to underscore a state's primary objectives (or interests), such as pursuit of its physical (territorial) security, economic vitality, and sovereign political independence.

Core Objectives   A country's most vital national interests guide its **core objectives:** maintaining its (1) territorial security, (2) economic strength, and (3) political independence. If a state is to remain a cohesive actor with some influence and some sovereignty and flexibility within the international arena, it must at all costs use foreign policy to serve its core or vital interests. No matter what a state's central belief system or ideological persuasion—from Iran's and Pakistan's Islamic beliefs to India's adherence to Hinduism and Israel's Judaism—each must attend to these three core interests if it is going to survive in our international political system, which by nature is highly competitive.

We see this pursuit of core national interests in the U.S.-led attack on Afghanistan's Taliban forces—that protected Al Qaeda terrorists—after the events of 9/11. The Taliban and Al Qaeda represented an obvious security threat that had to be met. Core security interests equally were at stake in Israel's military assault on Palestinians as a consequence of Palestinian suicide bombing inside Israel during 2002. The photographs below depict fighting in Afghanistan and Israel's assault on

Fighting in Afghanistan: Following the 9/11 terrorist attack on America, the United States launched a massive military attack on Afghanistan, where the Taliban ruled—and protected Al Qaeda terrorists. Following the formal Taliban defeat in December 2001, remnants of the Taliban escaped and U.S.-led coalition forces continued the fight against these perceived enemies in defense of their core security interests.

Palestinians living in the West Bank—vivid examples of countries focused on protecting their core security concerns.

When you think about the international political system, keep in mind the key points you have learned in earlier chapters. States operate in a global arena that has *no world government* to regulate interstate relations, *no higher legal authority* above the sovereign state actors, *no world executive* to execute decisions, *no world legislature or international legal system* with teeth, and *no world military* to enforce peace within the system. We do have United Nations Peacekeeping Forces and the NATO military forces to try to deal with regional conflicts. But we do not have a global military organization capable of enforcing broad collective security or defending against international terrorists when the fundamental vital interests of the big powerful actors, like the United States or China, are at stake. When the International Court of Justice (IJC) condemned the United States for violating the territorial integrity of Nicaragua in 1986, the United States simply ignored that decision. You can see that states operate within what might be termed a *primitive political system*—not completely anarchic, but still primitive compared to life *within* most states, which have common internal belief systems, legal order, and power to enforce the law.

Two examples illustrate the role of core values in a state's foreign policy. During the Cold War years, the former Soviet Union operated by Marxist-Leninist principles and seemed bent on a foreign policy of expanding communism no matter what the obstacles. Yet in order to serve its vital interests, Moscow traded with states like Egypt, which arrested and punished communists. Why? In the case of Egypt, Moscow needed access to the Suez Canal in order to

For more information about NATO's organization and structure, go to **www.ablongman.com/ duncan.**

Israel's Assault on Palestinians: In response to Palestinian suicide bombing inside Israel during 2002, Israeli military forces—in defense of their basic security concerns—pursued Palestinian forces into Palestinian territory, including refugee camps, on the West Bank.

keep its trading routes open; Egypt's strategic location made it a valuable asset in terms of Soviet vital interests, despite its anticommunist policies. The United States, meanwhile, talked much about expanding human rights and liberal democracy, but supported Caribbean and Central American dictators. Nicaragua's Anastasio Somoza, the Dominican Republic's Rafael Trujillo, and Cuba's Fulgencio Batista (before Fidel Castro) fit this category. The United States backed such dictators during the Cold War, because it saw them as strategic opponents of communism who served U.S. security interests. This U.S. view of dictators changed after 9/11.

Middle Range Objectives   States also pursue a number of mid-range goals as a way of making certain that their vital interests remain primary. For example, states may enhance their prestige and viability in the international system by engaging in foreign aid programs and cultural exchanges; by sponsoring trade shows and conferences of heads of states; by exploring outer space or exchanging diplomatic delegations. They engage in such activities while seeking primary core interests.

Here are some specific illustrations. Norway enhances its vital security interests through the famous Nobel Peace Prizes it grants each year. This effort—dedicated to the arts, sciences, and humanities—improves Norway's image to the outside world as a non-threatening state dedicated to advancing civilized life, all in all a good use of Norway's soft power. China hosted its expensive Fiftieth Anniversary of the Communist Revolution in October 1999, an event designed to portray China's image as a unified political state with a dynamic economic model of development—one way to project the power of perceptions. Russia continued to sponsor its outer space program after the Soviet Union collapsed and despite limited resources.

China's Rising Power: Fiftieth year celebrations in Beijing. China commemorated its fiftieth anniversary of communist rule on October 1, 1999. It threw its biggest ever party in Beijing, although ordinary folk were not invited. Few people complained, however, as they were flushed with national pride at the display of power by the People's Liberation Army in a five-mile long parade—which in effect told the world that China would not be defeated easily. The celebration included a seven-day vacation.

The cooperative effort between Moscow and the United States, which focused on the MIR Space Station, furthered Russia's image as a powerful state on the world politics chessboard. In November 1999, Cuba hosted a trade show in Havana with 70 companies represented, while the Ibero-American summit welcomed the leaders of Spain and Portugal. Both events admittedly were connected with Cuba's vital economic interest in encouraging more foreign investment. At the same time, they highlighted the point that Cuba was still a going concern, despite its poor economic record after Russia withdrew its support in 1991. The point is that when you look closely at what states are doing in foreign policy, you can see many middle-range goals being pursued, and it is useful to consider how they undergird core interests.

Long-Range Goals   As part of their long-range interests, many countries promote their belief systems and overarching basic values abroad. You can see this agenda at work throughout history and certainly into the post–Cold War years. The former Soviet Union, for example, sought to promote Marxist-Leninism, with its unique brand of economic determinism, permanent class conflict, and basic antagonism between communism and capitalism. Toward that end, it sought to promote socialism and socialist-oriented allies in the Third World, like Cuba under Fidel Castro, and to undermine the United States wherever and whenever possible. This ideological prism through which the Soviets viewed the world shaped their long-term view of politics, which included inevitable conflict between the USSR and the West, security threats emanating from the West, and emphasis on how to best mobilize power to combat the West (see Figure 4.2).

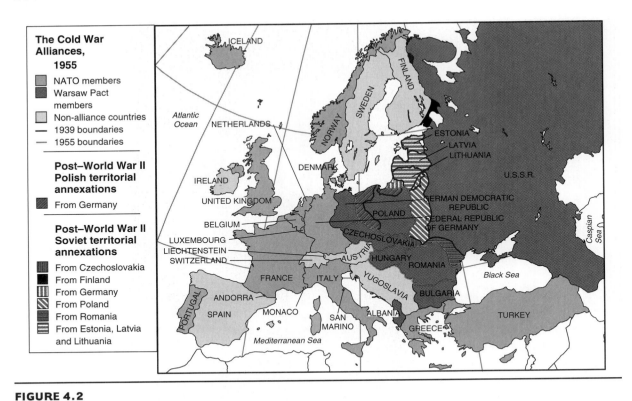

FIGURE 4.2
Map of Cold War Alignments
SOURCE: *John L. Allen,* Student Atlas of World Politics, *Second Edition, (Guilford, CT: Dushkin/McGraw-Hill, 1996), p. 21.*

The United States, for its part, has operated on a different belief system or worldview, one that is centered in a liberal, democratic orientation. This set of perceptions was played out time and again during the Cold War and has emerged strongly in the post–Cold War period. Much of U.S. policy since the collapse of the Soviet Union has focused on the long-term promotion of democratic governments and market economies. We see this objective in U.S. policy toward Russia, Eastern Europe, China, and Bosnia—underscored by the 1995 Dayton Peace Accords, which aimed to bring democratic government to war-torn Bosnia.

As to other countries and their long-term objectives, we can see them in Iran's promotion of Islamic principles abroad, especially under Ayatollah Khomenei in the 1980s and during Afghanistan's Taliban regime in the 1990s. Even tiny Cuba got into the act with Fidel Castro's pursuit of national liberation in Third World countries—including Angola, Ethiopia, Somalia, El Salvador, Grenada, and Nicaragua—during the 1970s and 1980s, when Cuba was backed by the USSR. International terrorists like Al Qaeda are not states, and they operate on unique principles—(in the case of Al Qaeda, a form of Islamic fundamentalism) and objectives designed to undermine Western states like the United States.

A Focus on Key Issues Associated with Goals

Each core, middle range, and long-range goal is tied to a range of issues. In other words, decisionmakers must consider a variety of ways in which to focus their energy,

SOURCE: *Signe Wilkinson/Cartoonists & Writers Syndicate (http://www.cartoonweb.com).*

attention, and power as they plan policies designed to reach their goals. Here is an example to illustrate. Let's assume policymakers are sitting around the conference table
discussing how to defend their country. Defense, of course, is a vital aspect of territorial security. What issues must come into the discussion? Here are just a few:

- Which weapons systems to fund.
- What countries to identify as allies and enemies.
- Where to deploy troops (Army, Navy, Marines, Air Force) around the world.
- Whether or not to go to war, construct an embargo, blockade a territory, or en-
  gage in peace negotiations.
- Whether or not to pursue arms control.
- Whether or not to remove a leader of a hostile state from power.
- Whether or not to engage in military action.
- Whether or not to build a missile defense shield.
- Whether or not to pre-position military assets for an impending attack.

While a country's decisionmakers typically agree that the national interest of
security is paramount for survival in a primitive international political system, the
larger problem is how to translate that need into specific policies. Seeking the national interest is more difficult than it seems, because so many complex issues and
options are associated with it.

Economic vitality is another goal that needs to be promoted by specific policies. Issues associated with economic strength include the following:

- Amount of government control: How much government control should a
  country exert over its economy? The range is wide, from China's market socialism to the market capitalism of the United States.
- Position on trade: Should a country join in a common market or free trade
  organization—like Canada in NAFTA or Germany in the European Union—or
  should it remain aloof from such arrangements? Norway and Switzerland have

For more information about gaining access to petroleum, go to **www.ablongman.com/duncan.**

remained independent of the EU, and North Korea has pursued a unique brand of independent foreign policy.

- What natural resources should be exploited and how best this might occur—either inside the country or abroad.
- Amount of spending on social overhead capital (investments in elements of the economy that enhance the production of goods and services, such as roads, railways, sewerage, electricity, and education): How much of a country's national spending should go to education, communications and transportation, and highways and bridges?

What makes the concept of vital national interests so complex is the fact that policymakers around the world frequently find it difficult to determine the specific policies that will support their agreed-upon interests. The United States found itself in just that kind of bitter internal disagreement when it went into Vietnam back in the late 1960s and 1970s. Some policymakers, like John F. Kennedy, argued that it was in the U.S. national interest to defend Vietnam with U.S. soldiers; others disagreed. More recently, the State and Defense Departments have differed over how best to design a defense policy against Iraq and its alleged weapons of mass destruction that could threaten U.S. vital interests.

In today's global and interdependent world, defining the best way to protect a country's national interests and determining what issues to pursue have become exceedingly complex and difficult. The Soviet Union, for example, assumed it was pursuing its national interests (and communism) in the most effective way possible by engaging in a weapons race with the United States. That quest, in the end, undermined its economy and environment drastically, as the world discovered during the 1990s after the Soviet Union collapsed.

Defining policy priorities is an issue as well. For example, in recent history, investing in weapons and military personnel typically has been of higher priority than investing in UN peace-keeping efforts or in Third World countries during postwar reconstruction to help prevent war's reoccurrence. While the United States did launch a massive reconstruction effort (the Marshall Plan) in Western Europe after World War II to help defend against a perceived communist threat, since then it has demonstrated less inclination to do so in other parts of the world. It helped arm Afghanistan's anti-Soviet mujahideen during their ten-year war with the Soviets (1979–1989), but left them in the lurch when the Soviets departed Afghanistan. This lack of support for postwar reconstruction resulted, as noted above, in the Taliban coming into a war-torn Afghanistan to set up a protectorate for Al Qaeda forces that ultimately attacked America. The United States faces a similar issue today: Will it invest in Afghanistan's post-Taliban reconstruction (schools, roads, telephone systems) or relegate it to a low priority issue as in 1989? How will it handle postwar Iraq?

Keep in mind that the task of ensuring the core interests of territorial security, economic vitality, and political independence affects a state's internal or domestic activities as well as its external ones. Thus, as we have seen, foreign and domestic interests are in many ways interconnected. Examples of this "intermestic" phenomenon (international-domestic connection) include foreign policies in the arenas of foreign trade, defense spending, and the environment—all of which affect the job market, personal incomes of individuals who live in the home state, and quality of life in terms of air and water purity. Remember that the line between foreign and domestic is often blurred.

What Factors Influence Foreign Policy?

Many factors influence foreign policy: a country's self-image (history, beliefs, and values), availability of natural resources, and geographic location (see Chapter 7 on Political Geography) are only three examples. Historically, America's self-image has been composed of a sense of isolationism, moralism, and pragmatism. Russia's historic self-image has focused on conflict between its **Westernizers** (who thought Russia should adopt European practices) and **Slavophiles** (who rejected Western thought in favor of Slavic culture), the drive for territorial expansion, and emphasis on great power status. While national self-images change with time, we still can see elements of these historical self-images operating in America's and Russia's foreign policy formation and execution. America's strong moral tradition with traces of isolationism is evident in its approach to Iraq, while Russia's leaders demonstrate the old conflict between Westernizers and Slavophiles in their attitudes toward NATO expansion.

Whether power resources are available to a country, IGO, or NGO (an example being America's possession of military weapons)—or not available (e.g., Japan's lack of oil)—is another crucial issue in foreign policy. Although Saudi Arabia has oil, other countries—including Russia, Iraq, Nigeria, Mexico, and Venezuela—do as well, which deeply impacts how Saudi Arabia can translate available power into policy. Argentina and Canada have food to export, that earns them hard currency, and Asian countries like China, Taiwan, South Korea, and Japan have cultures that value hard work—a good thing to have when it comes to economic production.

In exploring the many factors that influence foreign policy—with their multiple centralizing and decentralizing impacts—we will look first at the three levels where policy is made: the global, state, and individual levels. We then will look more closely at the dynamics of foreign policies—how they spring from human beliefs, how they clash over core interests, and how they change to keep up with new challenges to vital interests. Finally, we will touch on the need to coordinate foreign policy objectives and take a look at bureaucratic struggles in the formulation of foreign policy.

Global-Level, State-Level, and Individual-Level Factors

As you learned in Chapter 2, a useful frame of reference for analyzing the complex world of international relations involves three levels: the global, the state, and the individual. Working within each level, we can more easily determine which factors affect foreign policy, and how they do so. Let's begin at the global level.

Global-level factors that influence foreign policy include the extensive worldwide impact of **globalization**—how interdependent a country is with the international or regional trade system, such as Mexico's membership in NAFTA or France and Germany's participation in the European Union. Now that China has joined the World Trade Organization (WTO), its foreign economic policies will be affected by the rules laid out by the WTO. In short, countries that participate in regional trading groups, such as the European Union (EU) or North America Free Trade Area (NAFTA), must adapt their foreign policies to the dynamics of these organizations, just as membership in NATO shapes the foreign policies of member countries.

The global arena also shapes the foreign trade and economic development policies of less developed countries, whether or not they belong to trade organizations. Their foreign (and domestic) policies must react and adapt to restrictions imposed by wealthy countries' tariffs on the commodities they would like to export, by their debts to wealthy countries from borrowing, by rules imposed by the

Web Exploration

For an inside look at globalization, go to **www.ablongman.com/ duncan.**

Globalization
The process of becoming worldwide in scope. When we speak of the globalization of industry, we refer to the process of industries going worldwide in scope; the internationalization of industry. The effects or consequences of globalization include the reduction of regional differences in lifestyle and the loss of distinctive regional identities.

international financial community (IMF, World Bank, private international banks), and by lower prices received for their primary products. They are not in an enviable position when it comes to foreign policy, owing to their relative lack of power from their economic base.

State-level factors refer to those elements inherent to a given country. They include such items as its geographic location and natural resources, with attention to its neighbors as well as its size, shape, topography, amount of arable land for growing food, its climate, and a host of other factors that impact its power base. Other state-level factors include a country's type of government (dictatorial or democratic), level of economic development (highly developed and rich or underdeveloped and poor), and military power.

Democratic governments, for example, make policy differently from authoritarian-style governments. The former, like the United States, have a system that includes checks and balances, separation of powers, numerous actors, lobbyists, a free press, public opinion, and many other factors. Authoritarian systems, like those in Iraq, Syria, or Zimbabwe, are more likely to make decisions based on input from a limited number of people and in the context of a controlled press. Saddam Hussein, a dictator, had more individual control over foreign policy than the U.S. president.

As noted, a state's military power is also an important factor in its foreign policy decisions. America's awesome military power has led it since 9/11, in the view of some scholars, to pursue a foreign policy based on a grand strategy of "neoimperialism" (the domination of one state by another by indirect control of its economic and political operations). With regard to Iraq, America's military-based neoimperialism was expressed in the preemptive, preventive use of force—force that is basically unconstrained by the rules and norms of the international community.[2] In effect, then, the United States has decided that its global dominance and the apocalyptic nature of the post–Cold War terrorist threat justify its setting of standards, determination of the existence of threats, and use of force against such threats, in order to bring justice to the world.

Critics of America's new imperialism argue that going it alone on this track is not sustainable for a number of reasons. First, America's allies do not support it. Second, too many other potential hostile states—besides Iraq—are out there with weapons of mass destruction. America does not have the power to deal with all of them. Third, domestic support will fail as costs increase and domestic programs suffer. Fourth, a backlash from other states around the world will threaten America's security—as they refuse to cooperate on matters of terrorism and other central issues. Fifth, the ultimate economic, political, and military costs of this imperialism outweigh the potential gains. As you can see, when a state focuses too heavily on any one foreign policy tool (in this case, military) at the expense of others, it embarks on a risky path.

Individual-level factors include the role of political and government leaders, which is driven in part by their personalities, beliefs, and values. You can see this factor vividly when you consider the monumental role played by Adolph Hitler in leading Germany into World War II, Joseph Stalin's policies of occupying Eastern Europe after World War II—policies resisted by Harry Truman and that resulted in the Cold War. A more recent example is Osama bin Laden's role in orchestrating Al Qaeda's infamous 9/11 attacks. Leaders' approaches to foreign policy also can act as powerful forces for centralization or decentralization—even those of leaders from small states. John Ashe, a 48-year-old engineer and an ambassador for one of the world's smallest countries, Antigua and Barbuda (population 67,000), has become one of the most influential diplomats in the world of international environmental conferences. His mission is to bring together the rich and poor countries in finding ways to reduce poverty while preserving the environment; thus, he exerts a centralizing influence.[3]

Another example of centralizing foreign policies can be seen in the face-to-face meeting in early June 2000 between then South Korean President Kim Dae-Jung and North Korean Leader Kim Jong-il in Pyongyang, capital of North Korea. This historic three-day summit was the first meeting between the two countries since the Korean War (1950–1953). Since 1953 North and South Korea have been divided by the world's most fortified border. That border again became tense in late 2002 into 2003 as North Korea dismissed UN nuclear inspectors, reactivated its nuclear program in defiance of UN sanctions, began activities that pointed toward making weapons grade plutonium, and threatened a pre-emptive attack on U.S. forces if they seemed too close for comfort. In the midst of these tensions, in December 2002, South Korea elected Roh Moo Hyun as the country's next president. Mr. Roh, a former labor lawyer supporting continued dialogue with North Korea, came to power on a tide of public resentment toward the U.S., stemming from frictions with the U.S. military presence in South Korea. He was backed by a younger generation attracted to his pledge to distance Seoul from Washington and deal with America on a more equal basis. In response to Washington's hard line toward North Korea and aggressive stance against Iraq in early 2003, Roh pressed for talks with the North.

For more information about South Korea's president winning the Noble Peace Prize, go to **www.ablongman.com/ duncan.**

Core Objectives

The key point here is that while the ideologies of states come and go, their core (vital) interests remain constant as a factor influencing foreign policy. Examples of this fact may be seen in the collapse of communism in the former Soviet Union in 1991; the emergence and growth of market socialism in China, Cuba, and Vietnam since 1991; and the emergence of democracy in East European countries beginning in 1989. Before and after such ideological transformations, these countries were equally focused on questions of fundamental vital interests. As mentioned earlier, Moscow sought favorable relations with Egypt, despite Egypt's attitude toward communists during the Cold War, because Egypt occupied a strategic position on the Suez Canal. In other words, despite Moscow's ideology, it pursued economic vitality in any way it could. So the big questions guiding foreign policy have always been and likely always will be (1) How do we secure our territorial security? (2) How do we achieve economic vitality? (3) How do we maximize our political independence in the world?

Belief Systems

Despite the example of Russia and Egypt, long-range goals based on ideologies and beliefs do sometimes play a role in policy making when they condition the perceptions and expectations of decisionmakers as to how to protect their country's vital interests. Marxism-Leninism in the Soviet Union and liberal democracy in the United States and the West converted the Soviet Union and United States into natural enemies during the Cold War. Their competing beliefs shaped the world into a bipolar power structure, and as a result, the Soviets became proactive in maximizing their power around the world to undermine that of the United States and the West. In response, the United States, with its moral-legal principles and its emphasis on liberal democratic values and market economics, viewed Soviet Marxist-Leninists as atheistic, immoral, communist enemies.

The Cold War, then, was in many respects a clash of belief systems that shaped the way core goals were defined and pursued. The quest for territorial security on each side led to a world arms race, a struggle for power and allies in the Third World, and an adversarial relationship. The point is that states frequently interpret how they will pursue their **national interests,** or vital interests, through perceptions shaped by the beliefs and values they hold.

National identity and **nationalism** also affect how, and in what ways, a state defines foreign policy in pursuit of its vital interests. National identity, you will remember, refers to a people's sense of connection because of their shared culture, language, history, and political aspirations. Nationalism is the emotive force these shared values generate as state leaders pursue foreign policies crafted to protect their people's aspirations, values, beliefs, and territory. National identity and nationalism have long been powerful in foreign policies and have become dramatically pronounced since the end of the Cold War. One of nationalism's more distinct forms is expressed as **national self-determination,** that is, when a national group seeks to attain self-rule, as is the case among Serbs, Croats, and Muslims in Bosnia-Herzegovina. Figure 4.3 illustrates the complex multiethnic makeup of former Yugoslavia on the eve of its breakup into separate states. Slovenia, Croatia, and Bosnia and Herzegovina broke off into independent states in the early 1990s. The percentage figures tell us what the ethnic national composition is within each of these soon-to-be states at that time. Bosnia had a real problem in trying to reorganize itself as a separate state, given its multiplicity of ethnic national groups. Once it attained independence, its ethnic national groups fell into bitter fighting.

Taiwan's national identity is a classic case in point. Taiwan (the Republic of China [ROC]), you will recall, is a small island across the Taiwan Strait from mainland China (the People's Republic of China [PRC]). The Chinese nationalists fled first to Taiwan and then known as Formosa in late 1949, when the communist Chinese came to power on the mainland. Since then, Taiwan has become highly successful economically. The fifteenth largest trading entity in the world, Taiwan holds the third largest amount of foreign exchange, over $101 billion. A democratic country, Taiwan has a sense of "New Taiwanese" national identity. In the words of Taiwan's past President Lee Teng-hui, the New Taiwanese identity refers to those "who are willing to fight for the survival and prosperity of their country, regardless of when they or their forebears arrived on Taiwan and regardless of their provincial heritage or native language."[4]

The new Taiwanese President, Chen Shui-bian, who took office in May 2000, also accentuates Taiwanese identity. His policy is to enhance Taiwanese national consciousness by emphasizing Taiwanese history and culture in the schools. His inaugural ceremonies featured music, dance, and special guests of Taiwanese heritage as opposed to that of mainland China, and his address highlighted Taiwanese rather than Chinese culture. To underscore his defiance of China, the title of his inaugural address was "Taiwan Stands Up," and he stressed that Taiwan would no longer be a nation subject to insult and humiliation—referring directly to China's threats. The policy objective here is to maintain Taiwan's separation from the PRC while avoiding a war with Beijing. This national identity affects the heart of Taiwan's foreign policy, which seeks to protect its territorial security, economic vitality, and political independence against the geographically proximate and missile-armed PRC with its designs on Taiwan.

National Interests

The principal priorities pursued by states in the international arena. Territorial security, political independence, and economic vitality are a state's key national interests.

Nationalism

A strong emotional attachment to one's nation that can be expressed in a range of behavior from peaceful to violent.

National Self-determination

The right of all people to determine their own government.

For more information about Taiwan's pursuit of independence from mainland China, go to **www.ablongman.com/ duncan.**

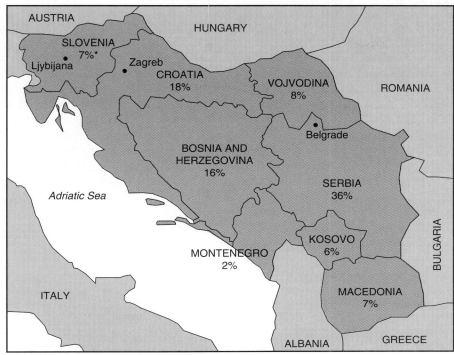

FIGURE 4.3
Ethnic Distribution of Former Yugoslavia

SOURCE: *The International Institute for Strategic Studies; Strategic Survey, 1990/1991.*

* % of national population

	Slovenes	Croats	Serbian	Muslims	Montenegrins	Albanians	Hungarians	Macedonians	Others
Slovenia	90%	3%	2%						5%
Croatia		75%	12%						13%
Bosnia-Herzegovina		18%	33%	40%					9%
Montenegro			3%	13%	68%	6%			10%
Vojvodina			56%				21%		23%
Serbia		2%	65%			20%			13%
Kosovo						90%			10%
Macedonia			2%			20%		67%	11%

In contrast, the PRC calls Taiwan a "renegade province" over which it claims sovereignty. And mainland China seems willing to appropriate Taiwan by force if necessary. So Taiwan's nationalist foreign policy centers on trying to work out a peaceful accommodation with the PRC, based on negotiating together, on a politically equal basis, a reunification of China (a United New China). Taiwan wants the PRC, as you can well understand, to renounce the use of force to resolve the reunification issue. The problem is that in the PRC's national identity and nationalist perceptions, Taiwan is a part of China over which it claims sovereignty. So we have a clash of belief systems regarding national identity.

Foreign Policy Clashes

Typically, on the international political stage, when one country pursues a foreign policy crafted to protect its vital interests, it clashes with another country's perceptions of its own vital interests—most commonly, territorial security, economic power, or political independence. Numerous examples illustrate this principle. When Iraq attacked and occupied Kuwait in August 1990 in quest of its perceived vital economic interests (oil), it violated Kuwait's territorial integrity and political independence. At the same time, that act of Iraqi foreign policy threatened perceived vital oil interests of the United States, West European countries, and Japan, all of which rely on Middle East oil imports for their energy supplies. China's pursuit of its perceived vital interests in Taiwan, as discussed above, threatens Taiwan's political independence, territorial security, and economic well-being. Russia, meanwhile, perceived NATO's expansion to include more East European countries as a threat to its territorial security. And so the story goes over and over again in world politics. One country's pursuit of vital interests can undermine those of another.

Foreign Policy Changes

For more information about Fidel Castro's view of globalization, go to **www.ablongman.com/ duncan.**

States change their policies all the time; it goes with the territory of policy making. While vital interests remain constant, decisionmakers adjust their foreign policies to adapt to changing circumstances. When the Cold War ended, Russia dropped Cuba like a hot potato, the former Soviet Union broke up, and communism sank. It no longer made sense for Moscow to continue costly subsidized trade with Havana— like buying its sugar at above world market prices and selling it oil below world market prices. Fidel Castro in turn dropped support for leftist regimes and movements in Central America and the Caribbean, because in the post–Cold War climate and without Russian support, it no longer made sense to continue. In both cases, Russia's and Cuba's pursuit of vital interests called for a change in policy.

The most dramatic change in policy in the late twentieth century came when Mikhail Gorbachev completely restructured Soviet foreign policy in the period from 1985 to 1990, which in effect contributed to the end of the Cold War. Gorbachev, realizing that the Soviet society and economy were failing under the burden of Cold War military competition with the United States and the West, set about to revitalize his country through what he called "New Thinking" (*perestroika*). Gorbachev's New Thinking also focused on the idea that the Cold War tensions must be reduced, because Russia needed an international environment conducive to economic development. That kind of environment was undermined at the time by costly and unproductive military spending in the arms race with the United States.[5]

Toward this end of lowering Cold War tensions, Gorbachev changed Soviet policy to include:

- *Reasonable sufficiency* in military policy, meaning that the country would possess sufficient military means to defend against attack but not enough to gain victory through aggressive actions
- *Stable coexistence* in East-West relations, meaning an end to the East-West arms race
- *De-ideologized foreign policy,* which would mean moving away from backing leftist Third World regimes and movements focused on using weapons and military technology

- *Cooperative diplomacy* with the United States in the political settlement of Third World conflicts in which Moscow and Washington were backing opposing militant groups—as in Angola, Ethiopia, and Nicaragua
- *Political flexibility and diplomacy in foreign policy,* as opposed to adversarial competition

Gorbachev's remarkable shift in Soviet foreign policy—his New Thinking—went far toward ending the Cold War, and even former United States President Ronald Reagan, who had termed the Soviet Union the "evil empire," came around to working closely with the innovative and charismatic Soviet leader. You can see from Gorbachev's record that a country's leader(s) will change policy when they perceive new circumstances and new opportunities.

Presence or Absence of Coordination Between Policies

Foreign policies are not easily coordinated, which is most notable in democracies. Unlike totalitarian governments such as Nazi Germany or the Stalinist former Soviet Union, democracies speak with more than one voice when it comes to making foreign policy. In the case of the United States, for example, the president is the chief diplomat and major player, but the Senate, House of Representatives, and other groups have a say as well. Each of these political bodies can bring its powers to bear; the Senate, for example, must approve treaties, while the House has investigative and hearings powers.

Democracies have other difficulties, too, in coordinating their foreign policy agendas. One is the clash between the need for secrecy in some foreign policy issues versus the public's right to accurate information. Other factors are the power of the press, public opinion, and interest-group lobbying in democratic systems. At times, as we will see, interest groups are powerful actors in democratic foreign policy decision making—as in the case of ethnic lobbying groups, like Cuban Americans in Miami, who have had a strong hand in shaping U.S. policy toward Cuba. Still another factor, previously noted, is the institutional separation of powers that creates checks and balances in democracies. By contrast, totalitarian leaders and dictatorships do pretty much what they want, without concern for the population's likes or dislikes.

Bureaucratic Struggles

Foreign policies may result from struggles for power within a country rather than from a rationally coordinated process. The point here is that a number of organizations and groups influence foreign policy decision making in most countries. In democracies these include a state's executive leaders, legislative leaders, defense industries and defense leaders, and a wide range of interest groups, such as those revolving around ethnic, city, labor, and business. In democratic systems these organizations frequently are locked in struggles for power over the direction foreign policy should go, the issues that need to be addressed, and the funds that must be allocated in pursuit of specific foreign policies.

Defense spending is a great example of the competing interests that can drive foreign policy. In some cases the Pentagon purchases weapons they do not want because a member of Congress is able to mobilize defense spending for a pet project that will benefit defense workers in his or her district. The V-22 Osprey, a plane capable of transitioning from forward flight to a graceful hover before landing, is a case in point. The Osprey is not a popular aircraft for any branch of the service, owing to its costs and poor safety record. Yet it continues to be produced, thanks in part to Representative Curt Weldon (R-PA), who for years led the crusade to keep the funds coming for the plane's production. The message here is that a variety of actors in the foreign policy decision-making process may define the country's national interests in ways that promote their interests rather than those of the country as a whole.

What Perspectives Explain Foreign Policy Decision Making?

Given the complexity of foreign policy, scholars have wrestled with how to make sense of foreign policy decision making. As you have just learned, if you look at foreign policy from a distance, it may appear that a state's leaders work together in harmony to determine how the national interests of their country should be served. For example, it would seem as if they then choose the best course of action to secure the country's territorial security, economic vitality, and political independence in a complicated and unpredictable world. News headlines might lead to this type of analysis, especially when you read, for example, that Russia did this or that today, or that India made some kind of foreign policy move that upset Pakistan. But also, as you just learned, states are rarely unitary and rational actors pursuing the "right" policy to secure their national interests.

So how can we understand foreign policy decision making? One way is a "systems" approach, which allows you to see the political, organizational, and individual factors that operate. Figure 4.4 depicts the many actors, pressures, and forces

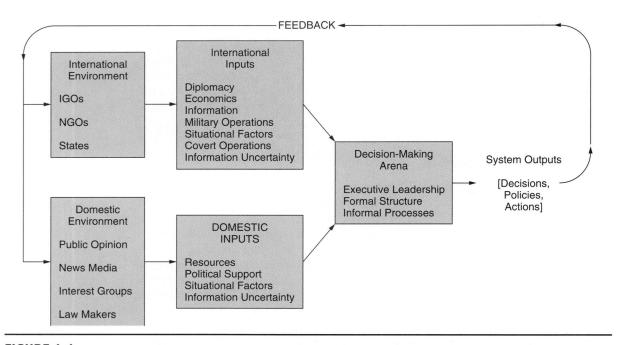

FIGURE 4.4

Foreign Policy Input-Output Model

Source: David K. Hall, "An Introduction to Policy Making and Implementation," The United States Naval War College, National Security Decision Making Department, Case Study, 1992–1993, p. 3.

simultaneously operating to shape a foreign policy decision.[6] Let's take a closer look at this foreign policy input-output model.

Note the so-called "decision-making arena" in Figure 4.4 (Foreign Policy Input-Output Model), where a foreign policy decision is made. You can see immediately that while a country's executive leadership is at work, other forces are pressing on the decision-making arena, such as international inputs and domestic inputs. Also in the decision-making arena are a number of forces, including "informal processes," which refer to the impact of external and internal politics, group dynamics, and individual values and perceptions. Another important force comes from "situational factors," which include the skills of leaders, importance of the event to organizational survival, the time available to make the decision, and the complexity of the issues involved. "Information uncertainty" refers to the fact that one can never be fully certain of the accuracy and/or timeliness of the information available to the decision-making process.

While the model is drawn from policy making in the United States, it is relevant to other types of government. Even totalitarian and dictatorial governments have a kind of "black box" decision-making arena—a realm in which the core processes are hidden and protected, although the number of players inside the box will be more limited. In the former Soviet Union, for example, members of the Politburo were involved in decision making, just as advisors and intelligence networks informed Adolf Hitler's decisions. Questions of accuracy of information, or information uncertainty, and of top level advisors, are at work in all governments.

You can see from the input-output model in Figure 4.4 that other big-time forces operate on foreign policy decisionmakers as well. The international environment—with its IOs, NGOs, and other nations and states—produces a range of international inputs that exert profound pressure on those individuals inside the black box. Decisionmakers also face input from their domestic environments. Public opinion, news media, interest groups, and legislative bodies (in democratic governments) spawn a number of domestic inputs related to resources, political support, situational factors (like pressure from public opinion or influential interest groups), and information uncertainty. As you can see from this model, both international and domestic factors shape foreign policy decisions.

Now let's look more closely at what goes on inside the decision-making arena itself. Scholars have devised numerous methodologies for analyzing the decision-making process. From among these, we will look at four perspectives, each of which gives us a unique view of what happens when foreign policy making is in process.[7]

The Rational Perspective

When we adopt the rational policy-making perspective, we assume that each country acts as if it were a unitary actor with a president who decides what to do in foreign policy on the basis of sound advice from his or her staff, and then influences another state or states to act. Figure 4.5 depicts this model, with state A shown as influencing state B with little or no discussion or disagreement going on within State A. The president is viewed as being on top of the process—coordinating, directing, and making final decisions that translate a country's national interests into rational policy decisions. From the rational policy-making perspective, decisions are related objectively to the country's national interest, and a course of action is selected from various balanced options; it is clear that alternative options and actions will produce consequences with specific costs and benefits relative to the ultimate objective. The president makes a final choice that will maximize benefits and minimize

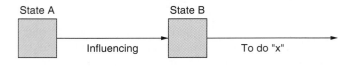

State A   State B

Influencing   To do "x"

Notes:

• The state acts as if it were a unitary actor that rationally decided a policy on the basis of interests and outcomes.

costs for the country. An underlying premise here is that when a country decides on a particular foreign policy, it has the means to execute it.

An example used to support this *rational actor model* is the Cuban missile crisis of 1962. In that case the United States discovered that Moscow and Havana were coordinating their activities to place missiles in Cuba aimed at the United States. When President John F. Kennedy discovered this threat to U.S. territorial security, the question was what to do. President Kennedy determined, with the help of a high-level executive committee of the National Security Council (NSC), to apply a naval blockade on Cuba and tell the Soviet Union that any attack on the United States from Cuba would be considered an attack by the Soviet Union. In response, the Soviet Union kept its ships away, dismantled the missile sites, and avoided a nuclear confrontation with the United States. It was a rational policy from the U.S. perspective, with a limited number of people and organizations providing advice to the president, and the president making the final decision.[8]

The Organizational Perspective

The organizational perspective on decision making emphasizes that large organizations view foreign policy issues as opportunities for or threats to their organization's mission. This means that a large percentage of foreign policy choices flow from the output of large organizations in pursuit of their organizational interests. Figure 4.6 depicts this perspective. Organizations have set ways of doing things, and they tend to focus on selected aspects of problems in terms of their own goals. Thus, foreign policy is the product of a power struggle between organizations. In addition, organizations determine the information and options available to the top leaders, and these too flow from organizational interests. In this sense the U.S. Arms Control and Disarmament Agency might have a different policy recommendation on weapons-spending in the United States than, for example, the Defense Department or State Department. See Figure 4.6 for a look at the organizational perspective on decision making.

Keep in mind, however, that organizations—like the Treasury Department, State Department and Department of Defense—are responsible for implementing the policies decided on by top leaders. Here we run into another aspect of organizational impact on foreign policy. Many foreign policy projects require several organizations to act together to achieve successes. But when organizations are forced to go beyond their standard operating procedures, foreign policy tasks rarely are accomplished as originally intended. If the task assigned to an organization runs counter to its goals, the organization can resist implementation of the policy. Thus, when we adopt the organizational perspective, we see a far more complex and messier pic-

Organizational Model

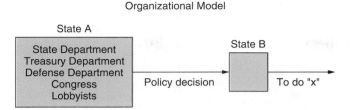

Organizations competing inside State A lead to a policy decision that seeks to influence State B to do "x"

Notes:

- Government is a collection of many organizations.
- Each organization responds to a foreign policy problem in terms of the impact of the problem (threat/opportunity) on the organization.
- Organizations are concerned with avoiding uncertainty.
- An organization's policy decision is shaped by routine standard operating procedures (SOPs), which limit its flexibility.
- A government's foreign policy actions may be viewed as outputs of large organizations employing standard operating procedures and programs.
- Organizations determine the information and options forwarded up to the top leaders, and they implement the policies decided by the top leaders.

FIGURE 4.6

Organizational Model of Foreign Policy Decision Making

SOURCE: *The United States Naval War College, National Security Decision Making Department, Case Study, 1992–1993.*

ture than we do with the rational perspective. For this reason, many experts view the organizational perspective as more "accurate" than the rational one.

The Political Perspective

The key point in thinking about foreign policy decision making from the political perspective is that decisions made by leaders—and organizations—are political in nature. By this is meant that because politics is at heart a bargaining and negotiating process, the final decision on a specific issue, like arms spending, for example, is a compromise between diverse interests represented by powerful individuals. This political process takes place within and between departments and agencies, such as the State Department and Department of Defense—and within and between branches of government, such as Congress and the Executive Branch in the United States. As a political process, foreign policy becomes the product of bargaining and compromises made among individuals who view the country's national interest through their own personal belief systems and preferences relative to what they think is best for the country. See Figure 4.7 for a conceptual overview of the political process perspective.

Differing views of a fighter aircraft are a case in point. An official in the Defense Department might view the F-16 fighter as an issue regarding which weapons should be included in America's military arsenal, while the State Department could view it as a diplomatic issue (don't fool around with us since we have these powerful tools), and the Treasury Department as an economic issue. Or in the case of the V-22 Osprey discussed earlier in this chapter, the Department of Defense viewed it in terms of costs and benefits for each of its separate branches (Navy, Air Force, Marines, Army), while Congressman Weldon saw it in terms of jobs for members of

FIGURE 4.7
Political Process Model

SOURCE: *The United States Naval War College, National Security Decision Making Department, Case Study, 1992–1993.*

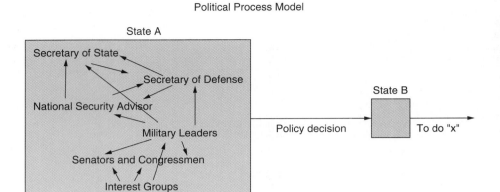

Political Process Model

Political and military leaders competing inside State A lead to a policy decision that seeks to influence State B to do "x"

Notes:
• Decision-making is a bargaining process among key individuals.
• Policy results are a political outcome.
• Individuals have different "states" and "stands."
• Depending on time and influence, individuals pull decisions toward their preferred solution.
• Decisions result from bargaining/compromise.
• No single actor's power is sufficient to "win" every issue; and "win" or "loss" affects the actor's future power.

his constituency working in defense industries. Whether or not the weapon was produced was as much a political struggle over who gets what, when, where, and how, as it was an issue of U.S. national interest.

Many foreign policy scholars like this perspective, because it illustrates how policy often results from bargaining and compromise between individuals with different "stakes" in the game. Figure 4.7 shows that when State A seeks to influence State B to do x, State A's behavior is the consequence of a political process going on inside State A. Still, if we relied strictly on this perspective, we would miss the important organizational aspects of decision making (previously discussed) as well as how much individuals influence decisions, discussed next.

The Individual Perspective

Remember that individual decisionmakers are subject to huge pressures—and among them is the pressure of processing gigantic quantities of often-conflicting information. In dealing with such pressures, decisionmakers—such as presidents and foreign affairs leaders—differ in style, perception, and psychological reactions. The human mind has structures for selecting, sorting, storing, recalling, and comparing information to ease decision making. In essence, the goal is simplicity, consistency, and stability when solving problems. When reality becomes muddled and uncertain, the decisionmaker pushes even harder for simplicity.

U.S. presidents and foreign policy leaders provide many examples of this process. James David Barber, a scholar on presidential personalities, has examined presidents in term of "style" (habitual ways of performing political roles), "world view" (politically relevant beliefs), and "character," or "the way the President orients himself toward life—not for the moment, but enduringly."[9] Barber outlines two dimensions of presidential character: (1) the energy presidents put into the job (active or passive) and (2) their personal satisfaction with presidential duties (negative or positive). *Active presidents* are "can do" kinds of people—energetic and ready to go in accepting their responsibilities. Passive presidents walk a careful walk and avoid conflict if possible. Active-positive presidents are best able to guide the country; they are self-respecting, happy, open to new ideas, and learn from their mistakes. On the basis of this typology, Barber classifies a number of presidents as active-positive. They include Franklin Roosevelt, Harry Truman, John Kennedy, Gerald Ford, Jimmy Carter, George Bush, and Bill Clinton. Active-negative presidents are Woodrow Wilson, Herbert Hoover, Lyndon Johnson, and Richard Nixon.

Scholars have described a wide range of other personality profiles that affect foreign policy orientation. *Nationalists* tend to glorify their own nation and even its superiority, as did Slobodan Milosevic of Yugoslavia and Franjo Tudjman of Croatia. *Militarists,* such as Saddam Hussein in the Persian Gulf War, consider the use of force to be a legitimate means for achieving foreign policy goals. Some leaders seem affected by *paranoia,* a psychoneurotic disorder characterized by high suspicion and fear and distrust of others—as in the case of Joseph Stalin of the former Soviet Union. Others may be sharply moralistic rather than purely rational, which may explain the behavior of former Secretary of State John Foster Dulles toward the Soviet Union. The underlying point is that personality factors—a leader's style, belief system, perceptions, and values—clearly shape foreign policy decision-making behavior and weigh heavily in the arena of foreign policy.

At the individual level, points worth our attention are the following:

- Individual values, beliefs, and cognitive mechanisms influence decisions.
- Our cognitive limitations affect "pure" rationality.
- Human needs seek simplicity, consistency, and stability.
- Under conditions of uncertainty, the mind provides structure when the environment doesn't, inferring relationships and employing "rules of thumb."
- Since the locus of decision making is the human mind, cognitive processes affect all decisions.

As with the other three perspectives, the individual-level analysis offers a useful insight into decision making. Given the role played by powerful individuals, it cannot be ignored. Yet if taken alone as the only perspective, we would miss what is going on in the organizational and political realms. Our best approach is to remind ourselves that decision making—like whether or not the United States should attack Iraq—is a complex process. With these four perspectives in mind, we now have an opportunity to consider them in real world situations. Toward this end, we turn to American and Russian foreign policies.

What Traits Typify American and Russian Foreign Policy?

With the collapse of the Soviet Union and the end of the Cold War between the former Soviet Union and its allies versus the United States and its allies, foreign policy making entered a new era. During the Cold War, each side competed in a superpower struggle between communism and capitalism. The competition deeply affected the alignments of European and Asian states with the United States or the

Nonaligned Countries
A term used to designate those developing countries that tried to avoid siding with either the West or the East during the Cold War years.

Soviet Union, and the conflict spilled over into the Third World and what were then its many **nonaligned countries.** Both the USSR and the United States sought allies in the Third World—from Cuba, North Vietnam, and North Korea, who sided with the Soviets, to much of Latin America, parts of Africa and Southeast Asia, and South Vietnam, which sided with the United States.

With West European countries linked in foreign policy to the United States and Eastern Europe tied to the Soviet Union, Third World countries played the Soviets and the United States against each other in order to protect their own core interests. According to Thomas L. Friedman, reporter for *The New York Times* and specialist on the Mideast, what you had was a world divided into a communist camp, a Western camp, and a neutral camp, with almost everyone's country in one of them.[10] *Security interests* of the key players were paramount during this era, with each side anxious about the possibility of nuclear annihilation; *nuclear and conventional weapons production* proceeded rapidly, with each side trying to deter the other from attack.

When the Cold War ended—and the Soviet Union and its vast communist party structure collapsed in 1991—America and Russia turned foreign policy toward new directions. Both sides were left with, among other things, vast nuclear arsenals that they sought to demobilize, nuclear waste environments that needed cleaning up, and, in Moscow's case, a crumbling economy that required much attention. Then came the terrorist attacks of 9/11, which demanded some kind of coordinated response and brought America and Russia together on a number of issues.

In this section we will look at Cold War trends and then examine the traits that characterized American and Russian foreign policy during the Cold War. Next we will contrast those traits with policies each side adopted after the Cold War, and then look at how America and Russia have responded to 9/11. As you read, think about the previous discussion of factors that influence foreign policy. You will see that American and Russian core objectives (territorial security, economic vitality, and maintaining political sovereignty) have remained constant, although each side's foreign policies have changed dramatically in pursuit of those goals. At the same time, the clash of foreign policies still occurs, as each side puts into place a range of activities, backed by power, to protect its vital interests. You will also see how the Cold War contributed to a decentralized international political system—and how world politics is still decentralized owing to post–9/11 events. Yet it is also marked by zones of cooperation, as in American and Russian cooperation on combating terrorism after 9/11, which illustrates how radically relationships can change, considering tensions between these powers during the Cold War. U.S. policy toward Iraq, however, has undermined that initial cooperation.

For more information about U.S. foreign policy during the Cold War, go to **www.ablongman.com/ duncan.**

Cold War Competition

The Cold War refers to the period 1947–1991 during which the United States and its allies and the Soviet Union and its allies engaged in passionate conflict over ideology and power. The Cold War is characterized by six distinct trends:

1. Alternating periods of intense tension and cautious cooperation—perhaps best illustrated by the Cuban Missile Crisis of 1962, which nearly produced a nuclear war, versus the growing cooperation between Moscow and Washington in managing Third World conflict after Mikhail Gorbachev came to power in 1985.

2. Avoidance of a direct war between the two sides—despite each side's race to acquire sophisticated weapons and the ideological conflict between democratic capitalism and communism.

3. Reliance on high tech nuclear weapons like intercontinental ballistic missiles armed with nuclear warheads to deter the other side from attacking. Deterrence refers to posing costs and risks that outweigh the potential benefits of a first-strike attack by one side on the other. During the Cold War, deterrence took the form of the doctrine of mutual assured destruction, MAD. Mutual assured destruction was the system wherein each superpower possessed the ability to survive a first strike and launch a devastating retaliatory attack.

4. Each side's disregard for its own preferred ideology, when its vital interest could be better served in other ways. For example, Moscow provided aid to many Third World leaders in hopes of expanding its influence while undermining that of the United States, even though such Third World leaders were suspicious of communist parties in their own countries as potential threats (Egypt, Iraq, Sudan, and Iran). The United States, although ideologically championing democracy, backed Central American dictators, because they were anticommunist.

5. Both sides engaged in **proxy wars,** by which is meant that each superpower supported various organizations, movements, and regimes in the Third World that could undermine the organizations, movements, or regimes backed by the other superpower. The United States, for example, provided much economic and military support to right-wing governments in Central America battling revolutionary guerrillas backed by Cuba and the USSR. The Soviet Union, for its part, provided large amounts of assistance to Cuba, because Cuba actively courted Third World movements that advanced the communist cause. The two sides thus avoided a direct armed conflict. The Korean War, the Vietnam War, and the conflicts in Afghanistan, Grenada, Chad, Angola, Cuba, and the Middle East can all be viewed as proxy wars in the context of the Cold War.

6. Each superpower focused on protecting its national security, and this determination—in the tension-ridden Cold War—acted as a strong force for centralization of decision-making power on each side. Since the USSR was already a highly centralized government system, an increase in centralized decision-making power is best seen on the United States side, where presidential power became pronounced during the Cold War.

American Policy During the Cold War   During the Cold War America followed a foreign policy strategy of **containment,** which sought to limit perceived Soviet expansionism. The proponent of this policy, George F. Kennan, Jr., was a leading diplomat during the presidency of Harry S. Truman, and he published his argument for containment in the journal *Foreign Affairs*. Kennan argued that Soviet expansion—as seen in its territorial moves into, and occupation of, Eastern Europe at the end of World War II—could be checked by a counterforce application of military, economic, and political resources. America's fear was that the Soviet Union—by occupying Eastern Europe and rigging elections to favor communist candidates in these countries, by blocking U.S. aid into Berlin, Germany, and by maintaining a high level of military readiness—was bent on expanding communism across the globe. From America's perspective, such tactics must be contained.

Containment
A U.S. foreign policy pursued during the Cold War that aimed at preventing the Soviet Union from expanding into Western Europe, Asia, and other regions of the Third World. President Harry S. Truman announced it in 1947.

A second element of U.S. Cold War foreign policy was the **Truman Doctrine**—a response to communist threats in Greece and Turkey. In an address to Congress in March 1947, Truman proposed that it should be America's foreign policy to support free peoples who were resisting attempted subjection by outside pressures (i.e., communists backed by the Soviet Union). He urged Congress to appropriate $400 million in economic and military assistance for Greece and Turkey, regimes threatened by communism, in order to bolster their economies and military power.

A third feature of America's engagement in the Cold War was the **Marshall Plan,** proposed by then Secretary of State George C. Marshall in a 1947 commencement address at Harvard University. Marshall had returned from a tour of postwar conditions in Western Europe and, on the basis of the devastation and numbers of refugees he saw, he argued that massive economic aid was required for the postwar recovery of West European states—a move perceived as vital in the resistance of Soviet expansionism. Congress allocated around $12 billion in the first four years of the program, and Europe moved steadily to postwar recover. Fourth, the United States established a **string of military alliances** around the Soviet Union as part of its newly developed containment policy. The Rio Treaty (1947) set up a military alliance between the United States and Latin American countries. The North Atlantic Treaty Organization (1947) forged an Atlantic alliance between the United States and its Western European allies. Other key military alliances were forged with Southeast Asia (SEATO—Southeast Asia Treaty Organization), Australia, and New Zealand (ANZUS—Security Treaty between Australia, New Zealand, and the United States). This emphasis on military alliances highlights America's view that it needed to secure its vital security interests during a period of perceived threats to the homeland.

Finally, in gearing up for effective foreign policy decision making during the Cold War, America passed the **National Security Act of 1947.** This important congressional action created the **joint chiefs of staffs (JCS)** and a chairman of the JCS—pulling together America's four military establishments (army, air force, navy, and marines) into a coordinated system of policy making. The Act also created the **National Security Council**—a group of highest-level cabinet officers in the executive branch to advise the president on matters of national security—headed by the **national security advisor.** With the National Security Act came the **Central Intelligence Agency (CIA),** tasked with the job of collecting and analyzing information pertinent to America's security. The National Security Act also spawned universal military conscription, otherwise known as the draft, where American's young men were pulled into military service.

With these policies America became in effect a national security state, with tremendous power given to the president to conduct the Cold War against the Soviet Union. In translating its massive economic and military power into Cold War foreign policies, U.S. defense spending rose enormously, and those groups who had a vested interest in defense spending became increasingly powerful. These groups—defense contractors, the Pentagon, lobbyists for defense contractors, members of Congress whose districts where in defense industry states, and others (scientists and consultants) committed to high defense spending—became known as the military-industrial complex. They maintained a close hold on classified defense-related information, which led to much secrecy during the Cold War. Information they did release—including information on so-called gaps between U.S. and Soviet military capabilities—contributed to an atmosphere in which military spending remained high. Many of these gaps were later proved to be false. Note that before World War II, resources allocated to military purposes were typically no more than 1 percent of the GNP. During the period 1948–1989 military purchases cumulated to over $7 trillion (1982 dollars) and averaged about $168 billion annually, or 7.5 percent of GNP. So the dominant global anticommunism pursued by U.S. policymakers did not come cheap.

Soviet Cold War Foreign Policy   The Cold War got under way largely owing to the expansion of Soviet power into Eastern Europe and the Far East at the end of World War II. In retrospect, it appears that what Joseph Stalin, Moscow's leader at the time, wanted was to improve the USSR's strategic line of defense—against perceived threats from the West—by creating buffer states (Eastern Europe) with a permanent Soviet presence; he was not necessarily bent on world conquest. Once the Soviet Union's Red Army and Communist Party apparatus had pushed into Eastern Europe, it continued to hold this large territorial area by means of military, economic, and political controls. In response to NATO, Moscow created the Warsaw Pact—comprised of the Soviet Union and East European allies. And in response to European economic integration that resulted in part from U.S. Marshall Plan aid, the Soviets forged the Council of Mutual Economic Assistance (CMEA), their own version of economic integration.

The Soviet Union also poured huge amounts of money into strengthening its military prowess—by concentrating investments in heavy industry and military weapons construction, new military technologies (long-range aircraft, outer space satellites, intercontinental ballistic missiles, nuclear weapons, nuclear missile-carrying submarines), and intelligence gathering. It developed the atomic bomb in 1949, tested the hydrogen bomb in 1953, and in 1957 launched Sputnik, the world's first space satellite.

In fighting the Cold War, Moscow created two kinds of economies: (1) a civilian economy that included schools, energy, roads, and other infrastructure projects, and (2) a military economy with emphasis on weapons production. The latter received the most attention, with the best researchers, scientists, economists, workers, and production systems concentrated there—and even with special towns created for this purpose. In contrast, the civilian area was neglected badly—a policy that resulted in poor farm and agricultural management; lack of capabilities for freezing, canning, and transporting food; and unattended road building. As a consequence, Moscow's overall economy unraveled; by the end of the Cold War it found itself in a terrible economic situation. Indeed, it was Gorbachev, as already noted, who saw the need to adopt new policies designed to end the Cold War.

The Soviets were deeply suspicious of the United States after World War II. Stalin mistrusted American motives and believed that the United States entertained imperial ambitions—as expressed in the Containment Doctrine, Truman's efforts to defend free peoples everywhere; in the Marshall Plan aid to resurrect Western Europe's strength, especially since some of that aid would be directed at Germany, Russia's nemesis; and in the string of alliances forged by the United States. Stalin reacted to these policies not only by creating the Warsaw Pact and CMEA but also by investing heavily in military spending. He also established the **Cominform**—the Communist Information Bureau to organize control over communist countries and parties of Europe. Since the **Comintern**—founded in 1919 to coordinate and control communist parties around the world from Moscow's headquarters—had been disbanded during World War II, its resurrection after the war represented an end of accommodation with the West.[11] When added to the revitalization of the Red Army and Soviet intelligence services (KGB), it became clear that adversity would characterize postwar American-Soviet relations for some time to come—as would a highly decentralized world political system.

A key trend in Soviet foreign policy that continued to feed the Cold War—in addition to sophisticated weapons production on each side—was Moscow's Third World strategy. Starting with Nikita Khrushchev in the mid-1950s, Moscow turned to the Third World as an arena where it courted allies, advanced the cause of communism, and undermined the power of the West. Khrushchev launched this dramatic policy change by financing a million-ton steel mill in Bhilai, central India, and then moved on to sign arms transfer agreements with a range of Asian, African, Middle East, and Latin American countries as well as providing them with economic credits and grants.[12]

When Fidel Castro came to power, Moscow's diplomats arrived in Havana, which set the scene for long-term aid, trade, and military agreements between Moscow and Havana. This new Soviet-Cuban relationship brought a Soviet presence into America's strategic back yard and escalated U.S.-Soviet tensions that spread through the Caribbean and Central America, as well as into Africa. Only with the emergence of Mikhail Gorbachev at the helm of Soviet decision making did this trend of U.S.-Soviet adversarial competition in the Third World wind down.[13]

U.S. and Russian Policies After the Soviet Union's Collapse

The breakup of the Soviet Union and end of the Cold War affected U.S. and Russian foreign policies in a number of respects. The world had become far more complex than ever before, due to globalization, the information gathering and processing revolution, terrorism, and a host of ethnic national conflicts. While the United States emerged as a superpower in economic and military terms, Russia found itself in a terrible economic situation, facing ethnic conflicts inside its new borders and a NATO that loomed increasing large and potentially threatening. The United States, moreover, while extending economic help to Russia and cooperation in demobilizing the nuclear arsenal, pressed forward to build its independent shield against ballistic missiles that theoretically would give it an edge in any future nuclear confrontation. The United States was not of course expecting anything like the attacks of 9/11. As we consider the current relations of these two powers, let's look first at the U.S. side of the equation.

U.S. Post—Cold War Policies   When the Cold War ended, the U.S. lost the simplistic concept of "containing" the Soviet Union. **Containment** of the Soviet "evil empire" helped Americans annually to recommit themselves to the principles of liberty, democracy, individualism, and private property; to defend such principles against the communist threat by going to war in places like Korea, Vietnam, and Grenada; and to pay the taxes required for high defense spending.

But if U.S. foreign policy was focused on containing and defeating the Soviet Union in order to defend American and Western values, what happens once the enemy is gone? As one scholar puts it, "The Cold War fostered a common identity between the American people and government. Its end is likely to weaken or at least alter that identity."[14] We can see such an erosion in the rise of right-wing militia groups, including fanatics who fire bomb public buildings, and in the opposition to such international institutions as the IMF, World Bank, and World Trade Organization—as evidenced by the huge demonstrations at the WTO meeting in Seattle, Washington, in November 1999, and elsewhere since then. At the same time, even without the Cold War, America has kept its military power in places like Europe and East Asia, by playing the role of a security presence to help keep the

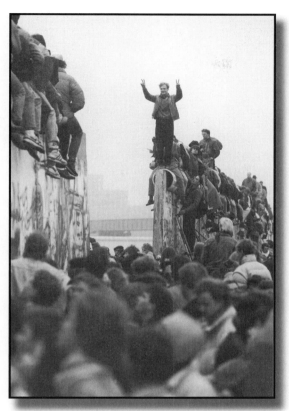

The Infamous Berlin Wall Comes Down: On November 9, 1989, the border separating Western from Eastern Germany was effectively opened. The fall of the Berlin Wall was a key symbol of the ending of the Cold War by uniting West Germany with East Germany.

peace and to act as a regional centralizing factor. Beyond this security role, however, the spreading of peace, democracy, and free trade has proven to be a problem that has demonstrated the limits of U.S. power.

Russia's Post–Cold War Policies   For the Soviet Union, the immediate post–Cold War era was a disaster. To begin with, the Soviet empire broke apart. Russian military units left Germany, came home from Poland, Hungary, and the Czech Republic, and were repatriated by Russia—although there frequently were no homes for officers, 800,000 troops, 400,000 civilian personnel, and 500,000 family members.[15] The last Russian soldier left the Paldiski submarine training base in Estonia in September 1995, which ended Russia's presence in East Central Europe.

Lands possessed for two-and-a-half centuries by Russian and Soviet forces were returned to their captive nations, and Russia returned to its seventeenth-century borders.[16] Boris Yeltsin dramatically reduced the gigantic world of Soviet military power by draconian measures, and in just a few years the Russian defense sector became a shadow of its former self. This shrinking of Russian military power has been a key aspect of its post–Cold War policy—as vividly evidenced in the humiliating defeat of Russia's military in its first war in Chechnya and its continuing problems there since 1999.

Once the Soviet Union collapsed in 1990—1991, Moscow's foreign policy was no longer driven by Marxist-Leninist ideology, dedicated adversarial relations with America, or strategic objectives that sought to undermine U.S. power while advanc-

Hardships of War: The Chechen capital Grozny, February 2000. Wars leave desolation and despair in their wake.

ing that of the Kremlin. Its post–Cold War policy is more pragmatic—cooperating with the United States and the West when it serves Russian interests and not cooperating when it does not. Meanwhile the domestic power base for Russian foreign policy has been seriously eroded since the Soviet Union's breakup. Taxes go uncollected, nuclear warheads and military weapons rust away, the military establishment remains demoralized, the economy spirals downward, and the political system is dominated by friction, back-biting, and fragmentation. Russia has been unable to prevent East European countries from joining NATO, Chechnya from attempting to break away, or civil wars from erupting in the Transcaucasus region. In sum, both powers both lost and gained with the end of the Cold War, and both have struggled with their new political identity. The United States, unfortunately, found a new focus in the shocking attack that struck on September 11, 2001.

America's War on Terrorism and the Bush Doctrine

America's war on terrorism has evolved through several phases since 9/11. In a first phase, much of the world sided with the United States in its war on terrorism—initially directed at the Taliban in Afghanistan who had allowed Osama bin Laden and his Al Qaeda forces to train and plan their attacks. In a second phase of the America-led war on terrorism, the global alliance began to unravel as differences in strategy and tactics widened the distance between the United States and its allies. The Europeans differed sharply with the Americans, as did much of the Middle East, over the interpretation of the Israeli-Palestinian conflict, notably with the U.S. reluctance to intervene directly and for its perceived pro-Israel bias.

In a third phase of America's war on terrorism—as President Bush developed his perceptions of the "axis of evil" (North Korea, Iraq, and Iran) in his January 2002 State of the Union address—cracks between the United States and its previ-

THE VIEW FROM   the United States

U.S. Strategy Shifts to Preemptive Strike Against Foes

In September 2002, the Bush administration declared a new foreign policy strategy of striking first—preemptively—at any foe believed to possess weapons of mass destruction that might be used against Americans or their allies. In a world where terrorists are the main enemy and in one that is still reeling from the 9/11 attacks, President Bush outlined this new military approach to perceived enemies like Iraq in a new national security review. Each president submits to Congress a national security review every four years. President Bush's version marked a radical departure from the strategic concepts of containment and deterrence that had guided U.S. foreign policy since the end of World War II. Some scholars praised the new strategy as realistic in an age of terrorism. Others saw it as an elaborate justification to attack another country in the absence of an immediate threat, thereby violating international law. Perhaps even more dire in its potential consequences is the possibility that such an approach would legitimize "preventive" nuclear strikes by other countries (e.g., Pakistan versus India, or North Korea against U.S. forces), thus leading to nuclear wars.

ous allies opened still wider (see the case study at the end of this chapter). By the end of summer 2002, as Congress returned from its recess, President Bush's talk of attacking Iraq led to sharp splits between the United States and previous worldwide allies as well as to major differences and conflict within Bush's own administration regarding the much discussed plan to initiate military action against Iraq. (For more on this subject (see box The View from the United States).

Then came a fourth phase. Facing opposition from Congress and the international community for his unilateralist, go-it-alone approach to military action against Iraq, President Bush shifted diplomatic direction. In September 2002, he began to build bridges with Congress and the international community. Many observers had been urging him to do this for some time in the belief that any attack on Iraq should have support from Congress, the American people, and the international community as represented by the United Nations. In addition to meeting with high-ranking members of Congress to try to convince them of the threat posed by Iraq, the president delivered a major address to the UN General Assembly on September 12, 2002.

President Bush's UN speech urged the international community to take collective action against Iraq, to stand up to Hussein and not allow him to continue his ten-year defiance of UN demands, and to put teeth into the UN's collective security mission.[17] At the UN he recited past UN resolutions ordering Baghdad to end its weapons programs—to underscore how Hussein's defiance of such resolutions represented nothing less than flouting the authority of the UN and its collective security responsibilities to the world. By agreeing to work through the Security Council—by calling for a UN resolution that would remind Iraq of its obligations under international law, make clear how they would be enforced, and authorizing the use of force should Iraq not comply—the president gave the international community what it was looking for, just as he had begun to do with Congress.

In response, Russia indicated that it might be tilting toward the U.S. position, and even Saudi Arabia indicated that its territory could be used for military action against Iraq if the UN sanctioned that action. Still, many countries hoped that new UN inspectors in Iraq might avert war, while others, Germany and France, for example, remained deeply opposed to military action. When the United States and Great Britain attacked and occupied Iraq in March/April 2003—against the opposition of China, France, Germany and Russia, all members of the U.S. Security Council—this fourth phase of cooperating with the international community ended.

Let's now turn to what has been called by scholars and policymakers the "Bush Doctrine." In early January 2002, President Bush delivered his State of the Union Address, which was reminiscent of President Ronald Reagan's description of the old Soviet Union as the "evil empire." The president identified Iran, Iraq, and North Korea as the "axis of evil." He later added Libya, Cuba, and Syria to the list. They were described as an "axis of evil" because they were so-called "rogue states" actively attempting to develop weapons of mass destruction and/or to pursue "terror." Weapons of mass destruction included biological, chemical, and nuclear weapons. The president and his supporters gave special attention to Saddam Hussein's legacy of producing such weapons and his brutal use of mustard and other poison gases against his own people. For example, he massacred an estimated 5,000 civilians and injured another 10,000 in Halabja, a Kurdish city in northeastern Iraq, in March 1988, in a chemical weapons attack. Today the people of Halabja still suffer from high rates of serious diseases, such as cancer and birth defects.

In light of these tensions, the emerging Bush Doctrine made clear that defense of America's territorial homeland was the top U.S. core interest and that America would consider no measure too extreme to protect it—including a military attack on Iraq, shooting down a commercial airliner if it appeared to have been hijacked by suicide bombers, or using nuclear weapons as a first strike.[18] The basic components of the Bush Doctrine are as follows:

- Keep Al Qaeda undermined and gain sufficient time for a more lasting solution.
- Prevent other terrorist groups from attacking; deny them sanctuaries in states where they might organize, train, and plan.
- Systematically eliminate weapons of mass destruction held by, or in development by, regimes favorably inclined toward terrorist organizations.
- Be prepared to use nuclear weapons as a first-strike option on rogue states like Iraq, North Korea, or Syria.
- Judge allies by their willingness to stand with America not only against Al Qaeda, but against the range of threats that now physically threaten the United States—much as when, during the Cold War, the United States judged its allies by their willingness to stand with America against the Soviets.
- Be ready to consider no measure as too extreme, given the threat that exists to the United States; the United States faces an extraordinary threat, so extraordinary solutions will be implemented.

All this left the United States in a situation of superpower status in the world, yet coming under increased criticism for its declaration of American hegemony and right to preemptively attack anywhere.

Critics of American foreign policy, Before the President's September 2002 United Nations address, argued that the American president appeared disinterested in working with the international community in combating terrorism—giving short

A HISTORICAL PERSPECTIVE

American Foreign Policy on the Eve of War with Iraq

The Bush Administration's frustration with Saddam Hussein's cat-and-mouse game with UN inspectors searching for hidden weapons of mass destruction (WMDs) in early 2003, and its insistence on a pre-emptive war with Iraq to remove Hussein from power and destroy the WMDs, placed the U.S. at a controversial foreign policy crossroads. For its critics, the policy seemed one-dimensional (Iraq) at a time when America faced other more serious threats, such as Al Qaeda terrorism and North Korea's nuclear program. Equally disturbing, the Administration's march to war was out of touch with many former allies.

- The Bush team appeared prepared to go to war against Iraq even without support from France, Germany, Russia and China—members of the U.N. Security Council. None of these countries doubted that Saddam Hussein was evil, but they preferred to contain Iraq with more UN inspectors backed by UN peacekeeping forces rather than initiate war.
- The U.S. and Great Britain believed that Iraq posed an *immediate* threat to the international community that must be addressed by force. France, Germany, China and Russia argued that UN inspectors must be given more time, that Hussein could be kept in the box, and that this approach would avoid the unpredictable conse-

quences of war with massive loss of life (collateral damage).

- The Bush Administration argued that the Iraq war could be won with minimal collateral damage, Hussein removed, WMDs destroyed, and Iraq reconstructed on a democratic foundation. Opponents believed the war's end game would bring rising radical Arab hostility toward a U.S.-occupied Baghdad and its oil fields, escalating Al Qaeda terrorism, deep friction amongst Shiite, Sunni and Kurd communities inside Iraq, and mounting economic and political costs for the U.S.
- Skeptics of the Iraq war were afraid that the U.S. was paying insufficient attention to the war on terrorism, North Korea's nuclear program, rising anti-Americanism across Europe, the Middle East, and South Korea, the reemerging Taliban in Afghanistan, and increasing tensions between India and Pakistan. They were dismayed with the Bush Administration's tendency to see the UN Security Council less as a valuable asset needed in a war against Iraq and more as an obstacle to be overcome.
- All in all, on the eve of war with Iraq, the U.S. post-9/11 Bush Doctrine seemed to be playing a more pronounced role in decentralizing the international system rather than uniting it in common goals.

---

shrift to the opinions of NATO, the United Nations, European Union—that is, much of the international community that previously had worked closely on international problem solving and that the U.S. itself had helped create. Apart from its unilateral orientation, the critics also said, the Bush doctrine lacked clarity.[19]

Finally, the critics point out, the Bush Doctrine underscores how the United States, with its unprecedented power, failed to play the role of global leader at a time when it needed a strengthened international community for its own security in fighting terrorism. Serious division within the international community on whether America should attack Iraq, U.S. failure to use soft power effectively within the international community, and a strong risk of imperial overreach indicate that U.S. foreign policy has entered a new era in the early twenty-first century—one in which the

U.S. acts as a force of decentralization and a far cry from its role after World War II. At that time it worked to forge a United Nations and plan for European recovery and other aspects of a centralized international community. While the Bush Doctrine's fourth stage seemed to return to cooperation with the UN and international community, all that ended—at least temporarily—with the military attack on and occupation of Iraq. To what extent U.S. unilateralism would remain in play in the reconstruction and political governance of postwar Iraq remained an open question—as it did in the future of the "Road Map" to forge a Palestinian state by 2005. The "Road Map" is a plan devised by the U.S., E.U., U.N. and Russia and presented to Israel's Prime Minister Ariel Sharon and new Palestinian Prime Minister Mahmoud Abbas in April 2003. We will look next at several key countries and how they have responded.

How Have Other Countries Reacted to America's War on Terrorism?

This final section of the chapter will provide a brief overview of the foreign policies of Egypt, Pakistan, and Saudi Arabia relative to America's war on terrorism. As you read, you will gain a sense of how each has struggled to advance its core values and beliefs while facing threats to its own security and domestic stability. We focus on these three countries in particular because each played a pivotal role in U.S. foreign policy before 9/11, especially Egypt and Saudi Arabia, and because each country is of pivotal geographic and political significance if the United States is to move forward. We will first look at Egypt, a key U.S. ally in the Middle East and the second largest recipient of U.S. aid, receiving about $1.3 billion annually in military assistance and about $600 million per year in economic assistance. Next we focus on Pakistan, which became a key U.S. partner and staging area for the war in Afghanistan and an essential partner in the war on terrorism. The third country, Saudi Arabia, is the world's largest oil producer.

Egypt

Egypt, the most populous Arab country in the Middle East and a traditionally reliable ally of the United States, is the cornerstone of U.S. policy in the region. The United States has enjoyed close relations with Egypt for almost a quarter century. What makes Egypt so important as a U.S. ally is not only its geostrategic position relative to the Suez Canal, but its remarkable stability, its voice of moderation in the turbulent Middle East, and its cooperation with the United States and Israel in trying to orchestrate a peaceful settlement with the Palestinians. Egypt has continued to observe the terms of the 1979 Camp David accords, Israel's first Arab peace treaty. Egypt was also an active coalition partner in the 1991 U.S.-led military operations against Iraq.

Following the 9/11 attacks, Egypt's President Hosni Mubarak condemned the attacks and supported (but did not join) the U.S. war in Afghanistan, while at the same time calling for a UN conference on terrorism. President Mubarak has worked effectively against Al Qaeda, likely because Al Qaeda's Egyptian roots threaten Mubarak's authoritarian political regime as much as they threaten the United States. One of the 9/11 hijackers, Muhammad Atta—the plot's likely mastermind—was from Egypt, and there is deep grass roots dissatisfaction in Egypt with Mubarak's repressive government. So Cairo has shared intelligence with the United States, permitted U.S. warplanes to fly over Egypt, and strove to undermine terrorist financial networks. In addition, Mubarak has increased arrests and prosecutions of Islamist militants, some of whom have been accused of founding terrorist groups such as Hamas.

Egypt's President Hosni Mubarak Meets with Secretary of Defense Rumsfeld: The two high-ranking officials met in March 2002 in Washington, DC, to discuss the war on terrorism, Israeli-Palestinian tensions, and other regional issues.

On the negative side—from the U.S. perspective—Cairo, along with the rest of the Arab world, has strongly opposed the U.S. invasion of Iraq. Egypt played no key strategic role geographically in that war. In addition, whereas the United States has sided with Israel's military reaction to Palestinian suicide bombing, defined as terrorism, Egypt has criticized Israel during the rising violence with the Palestinians. Yet it has not broken diplomatic relations with Israel, nor stepped away from the Camp David accords. Still, tensions between Egypt and the United States had surfaced by the time of the first anniversary of 9/11. It was clear that public opinion in Egypt was hostile to the U.S. policy on terrorism; indeed, influential Egyptians had praised the 9/11 assaults as punishment for U.S. support of Israel. The United States, moreover, deplored Egypt's human rights record, its heavy-handed crack down on Egypt's Islamic militants, and especially its sentencing of Saad Eddin Ibrahim, an outspoken academic human rights activist and U.S. citizen. The United States has chastised Egypt for not pressing Palestinians hard enough to bargain with Israel.

The bottom line is that while Egypt remains a close U.S. ally, the U.S.-Egypt relationship entered a stage of uneasy cooperation after 9/11 and the U.S. occupation of Iraq. Although both sides still needed each other in their pursuit of core interests—territorial security, economic vitality, and political stability—the U.S. war on terrorism and Egypt's precarious political stability and its own problems with terrorism posed numerous challenges to cooperation and centralization in policy agendas.

Pakistan

Let's examine Pakistan's relevance to the United States and why the United States would take an interest in this country, as it does with Egypt and Saudi Arabia. To begin with, Pakistan has become a key ally in the U.S. war on terrorism. Second, Pakistan's strategic location next to Afghanistan and its possession of nuclear weapons make it a key country in U.S. strategic thinking. On the negative side,

For more information about the Middle East crisis and the Palestinians, go to **www.ablongman.com/ duncan.**

President Pervez Musharraf Meets with His Military Forces: This meeting took place in May 2002 during high tensions with India.

Pakistan conceivably could wind up in a nuclear war with India over Kashmir. On the positive side, it has the potential to become a more democratic, less authoritarian state—a rarity in the Islamic world. It has demonstrated this prospect in the past and has a an educated civilian bureaucracy and a relatively free press. However, the prospect of a Pakistani democracy is somewhere down the line, and much would have to be accomplished before that day.

In the wake of 9/11, President Pervez Musharraf renounced Pakistan's long-standing support for the Taliban and pledged allegiance to the United States in its war on terrorism. This abrupt reversal of policy led General Musharraf to become a key U.S. ally in the campaign against Al Qaeda. Pakistan became a staging area for the war in Afghanistan, granted over-flight rights to coalition aircraft during that war, allowed U.S. forces to use Pakistani airfields, and shared intelligence on suspected terrorists. Musharraf has also cooperated with U.S. security forces in conducting joint raids on suspected Al Qaeda hideouts throughout Pakistan, especially in remote provincial areas that appear to be staging areas for fugitives attempting to regroup in Pakistan. By the time General Musharraf visited the United States in September 2002, Pakistani security forces had arrested 402 suspected Al Qaeda members.[20]

General Musharraf's decision to drop support for the Taliban probably did not reflect a sudden reaction to the events of 9/11. Instead, it indicated a policy shift to adjust to new geopolitical realities that impacted Pakistan's core interests. In view of America's war on terrorism and Afghanistan's Taliban, to have rejected cooperation with America most certainly would have led to U.S. animosity and posed threats to Pakistan's strategic and economic priorities in South Asia. Cooperation with the United States, on the other hand, meant economic and technical aid, which is much needed in view of Pakistan's failing economy, security threats from India, and General Musharraf's precarious hold on political power. In return for its new allegiance to the United States, Pakistan received $600 million in cash, $3.6 billion in projected grants and IMF aid, and a rescheduling of its $12.5 billion debt to a U.S.-led international consortium.

Pakistan, however, remains a troubled U.S. ally in the war on terrorism. It is home to a large number of Islamic militants who have mounted terrorist attacks on Americans and other Westerners in Pakistan since 9/11. These attacks included the February 2002 abduction and murder of *Wall Street Journal* reporter Daniel Pearl and the June 2002 car bombing of the U.S. consulate in Karachi, which killed 12 Pakistanis. In addition, Islamic and ethnic ties have led some Pakistanis to help Taliban and Al Qaeda fighters fleeing Afghanistan. Worth remembering, is that Musharraf heads a military clique that ended Pakistan's short democratic experience, backs radical Islamic terrorist groups in Kashmir, has at times pressed for war with India, has promoted Pakistan's nuclear program, and leads what most observers see as a corrupt and mismanaged economy. General Musharraf faces challenging difficulties in consolidating his government and faces opposition from across Pakistan's Muslim political spectrum—where the Iraq war is universally unpopular.

Saudi Arabia

Like Egypt and Pakistan, Saudi Arabia has enjoyed a favorable relationship with the United States in the years leading up to 9/11. As in all cases where two countries choose close cooperation, each side views the real and potential benefits of close relationships as being greater than the real or potential costs. Through cooperation, each side is able to translate its power into actions that advance its core interests—an axiom that applies to Saudi Arabia as well as to Egypt and Pakistan.

The United States and Saudi Arabia have been friends since the end of World War II, and they fought together in the Gulf War against Saddam Hussein when he marched his military forces into Kuwait. Second, the Saudi government benefits greatly by cooperating with the United States—on whom it depends for U.S. military equipment, advisors, and technical support to modernize and strengthen its military. The United States supplied military power helps Saudi Arabia to maintain its territorial security, protect its economic assets and political system, strengthen its key position on the Arabian Peninsula, and back its efforts to promote solidarity among Islamic governments. In addition, the Saudis need U.S. private investment to expand and modernize their economy.

The United States in turn gains a vital strategic position in the Middle East for the protection of oil reserves, and a valuable trading partner to whom it exports billions of dollars worth of goods and services each year—exports that provide jobs for thousands of American workers. Many of these exports have consisted of military aircraft, such as F-15s, air defense weaponry (Patriot and Hawk missiles), armored vehicles, and other equipment. The U.S. Army Corps of Engineers has also enjoyed a long-term role in military and civilian construction projects in Saudi Arabia. So these historically intertwined relations have helped promote U.S. national security (protecting energy flows) and economic interests (jobs and money for consumer spending), just as Saudi Arabia's core interests benefit from close ties with the United States.

September 11, 2001, however, placed serious strains on the U.S.-Saudi relationship—one that Saudi diplomacy and foreign policy have attempted to reduce, while at the same time promoting their own primary interests. The background facts are as follows:

- Of the 19 hijackers involved in the 9/11 attacks, 15 were Saudi citizens; many Al Qaeda terrorists are Saudis, as is Osama bin Laden.
- U.S. experts have questioned whether the Saudis have been sufficiently supportive in the campaign with military, financial, and diplomatic support.

- A briefing paper presented to the Pentagon's Defense Policy Board on July 10, 2002 (and leaked to *The Washington Post*), described Saudi Arabia as "active at every level of the terror chain," from planners to financiers, cadres to foot soldiers, and ideologists to cheerleaders.
- Saudis have financially supported madrasas in former Taliban Afghanistan, post-Taliban Pakistan, and elsewhere that preaches a brand of anti-Western fundamentalist Islamic beliefs inimical to U.S. national interests. They have done so in part to appease growing domestic opposition to the Saudi royal family, with its close ties to the West—and also due to increasing fanaticism in the Muslim world connected to this opposition. In short, the government is trying to protect itself internally.
- Some Saudis allegedly have extended payments to the families of suicide bombers in Israel.
- The Saudi government has urged the withdrawal of some U.S. troops from their country, and the United States has obliged by quietly moving a number of them to Qatar.

In an effort to promote its fundamental priority interests as a powerful Muslim state in a Muslim world increasingly hostile to the United States, the Saudis have followed a three-track policy in foreign affairs. First, they put forward their own peace plan for the Palestinian-Israeli conflict, which basically calls for Arab states to resume "normal relations" with Israel in exchange for Israeli withdrawal from territories held since 1967. The plan, quickly overcome by rising violence in Israel, was part of the Saudi effort to build an Arab consensus on the Israeli-Palestinian conflict, and to counter U.S. pressure on the Saudi government to root out suspected Al Qaeda militants. Second, Saudi Arabia has lobbied hard in Washington and with President Bush to be more even-handed in the Israeli-Palestinian conflict—an issue that the Saudis and other Middle East governments see as far more decentralizing than the war on Iraq. Still, the Saudi government agreed to allow the U.S. military to use Saudi bases for combat operation against Iraq.

Third, Saudi diplomats have worked the U.S. public media to give their perspective on tensions with the United States—stressing the lack of enmity between Saudi Arabia and the United States and the positive aspects of this relationship. Yet the Saudi monarchy fears a backlash from rising domestic anti-Americanism stemming from the Iraq war as well as America's declared objective to spread democracy throughout the region. It also worries about the possibility of a Shia Muslim leadership coming to power in Baghdad—challenging the Sunni Muslim ascendancy through the Arab world. Perhaps their sentiments led to the U.S. decision to end its military operations in Saudi Arabia and remove its forces from the kingdom following the Iraq war in April 2003.

Web Exploration

For more information about UN sanctions against Iraq, go to **www.ablongman.com/ duncan.**

CHAPTER SUMMARY

What Exactly Is Foreign Policy?

The foreign policy of states involves three elements: (1) an approach to translating power (see Chapter 3) into policy; (2) a set of core, middle, and long-range goals; and (3) a focus on key issues associated with the goals pursued.

- Power refers to all those objective and subjective capabilities we discussed in Chapter 3, and policy refers to how power gets translated into policies, such as using military weapons, engaging in trade to benefit both trading partners, or using soft power such as public relations to create a favorable image abroad. Power can take a variety of policy forms, which means that a country has various policy options at its disposal.

- Diplomacy is the act of making policies work by negotiating with other countries on everything from trade agreements to military conflict.
- A country's core, middle, and long-range goals are its prioritized objectives in the world political system. The highest priority goes to core interests (also known as national interests): territorial security, economic vitality, and protection of the political system.
- Each goal can be achieved by a number of policies. Territorial security, for example, could be achieved via weapon use or acquisition, disarmament, arms control, or alliances. Issues arise because of the various policy options among which leaders and the public must choose.

What Factors Influence Foreign Policy?

A useful way to examine the factors that influence foreign policy is to categorize them into three levels: global, state, and individual-level factors. Global-level factors are those broad international influences on foreign policies; state-level factors are those that are inherent to the country itself, such as its geographic location; on the individual level are such factors as the personality and perceptions of the leader of a country.

Other general principles of foreign policy include the following:

- Core objectives tend to remain constant.
- Belief systems help define how these core objectives will be pursued.
- Foreign policies clash in the world political system as the world's states seek to protect their core interests.
- Foreign policies also change dramatically as states continue to protect core objective. The end of the Cold War illustrates change in the international system that led to change in American and Russian foreign policies.
- Coordinating foreign policy objectives to select the most appropriate policy options is a complicated activity. Bureaucratic struggles are one example of the coordinating problems—

illustrated by disagreement within the Bush administration and the Republican Party over Iraq.

What Perspectives Explain Foreign Policy Decision Making?

- The rational dimension or aspect of foreign policy, which focuses on the state as a unitary actor with no internal forces shaping its decisions.
- The organizational dimension, which focuses on the important role of organizations in shaping policy outcomes.
- The political dimensions, in which decision making is highlighted as a struggle for power and influence among contending individuals, groups, and organizations.
- The individual dimension, in which the focus is people—the unique beliefs, emotions, values, and cognitive processes (how they sift through information and reach conclusions) that each brings to the decision-making table.

What Traits Typify American and Russian Foreign Policy?

- The Cold War (1947–1991) was a period of alternating tension and cautious cooperation between the two superpowers. The tension is perhaps best captured by the Cuban Missile Crisis of 1962, which nearly produced a nuclear war; the growing cooperation is best portrayed in the agreements on arms control culminating in the end of the Cold War during the Gorbachev period (1985–1991).
- American policy during the Cold War centered on containment and the Truman Doctrine—containing Soviet expansion and protecting "free" peoples everywhere. It produced wars (Korean, Vietnam) and many crises in the Third World as America and the USSR used proxies to conduct their Cold War competition. Deterrence and Mutual Assured Destruction (MAD) underscored the intense military competition during the period. The National Security Act (1947) highlighted America's concerns with national security.
- Cold War competition led the Soviets to form their own alliances as a counterpoint to the West's NATO. The Warsaw Pact (Soviets and

Eastern Europe) met this need, just as the Council of Mutual Economic Assistance competed with the West's European Community. Moscow also formed a vast international network of communist parties (the Cominform), courted Third World allies like Cuba and North Vietnam, and used a huge intelligence network (KGB).

America and Russia's Foreign Relations Changed Radically After the Cold War

- America ended containment and concentrated instead on spreading democracy and market economies around the world—notably in Eastern Europe and the Third World.
- Russia struggled to jump-start its economy, deal with Chechnya's ethnic national rebellion, and guard against NATO expansion. It cooperated with the United States on moving toward arms reduction (Cold War's legacy of vast armaments, both nuclear and conventional), while resisting America's move toward a missile defense shield.

September 11, 2001, Produced the Bush Doctrine in America's War on Terrorism

- The Bush Doctrine accentuates defense of America's territorial homeland as the top U.S.

core interest; America considers no measure too extreme to protect it.

- While Russia has cooperated with the United States in its war on terrorism, Moscow pursued its own core interests. Policies designed to promote such interests have included trade and other negotiations with the very countries President Bush has designated as the "axis of evil"—North Korea, Iran, and Iraq.

How Have Other Countries Reacted to America's War on Terrorism?

- Other countries—such as Egypt, Pakistan, and Saudi Arabia—have demonstrated close cooperation with the United States in its war on terrorism. Yet each country has tried to advance its own core interests, and some have clashed with those of the United States. The foremost clash has occurred over President Bush's unilateral approach to military action against Iraq.

ENDNOTES

[1]This model and discussion is adapted from Michael A. Freney, Andrew E. Gibson, and W. Raymond Duncan, "The International System," *The United States Naval War College*, National Security Decision Making Department, Newport, Rhode Island.

[2]G. John Ikenberry, "America's Imperial Ambitions," *Foreign Affairs*, September/October 2002, pp. 44–60.

[3]Dr. Ashe was hard at work on these key issues at the UN's World Summit on Sustainable Development in Johannesburg, South Africa, in August-September 2002. *The New York Times*, August 28, 2002.

[4]Lee Teng-hui, "Understanding Taiwan: Bridging the Perception Gap," *Foreign Affairs*, Vol. 78, No. 6 (November–December), p. 9.

[5]W. Raymond Duncan and Carolyn McGiffert Ekedahl, *Moscow and the Third World under Gorbachev*, Westview Press: Boulder, San Francisco, and Oxford, 1990, Chapter 3.

[6]This model and discussion is drawn from Professor David K. Hall, "An Introduction to Policy Making and Implementation," *The United States Naval War College*, National Security Decision Making Department, Newport, Rhode Island.

[7]William R. Farrell and Mel Chaloupka, "Four Perspectives on Decision Making and Execution in National Security Organizations," *The United States Naval War College*, National Security Decision Making Department, Newport, Rhode Island.

[8]See Graham T. Allison, "Conceptual Models and the Cuban Missile Crisis," in Morton H. Halperin and Arnold Kanter, eds., *Readings in American Foreign Policy*, Boston: Little, Brown, 1973; also Allison, *Essence of Decision*, Boston: Little Brown, 1971.

[9]James David Barber, *The Presidential Character: Predicting Performance in the White House*, 4th ed., Englewood Cliff, N.J.: Prentice-Hall, 1992.

[10]Thomas L. Friedman, *The Lexus and the Olive Tree*, N.Y.: Farrar, Straus and Giroux, 2000, p. 1.

[11]Nicolai N. Petro and Alvin Z. Rubinstein, *Russian Foreign Policy*, New York: Addison Wesley Longman, 1997, Chapter 3.

[12]W. Raymond Duncan, ed., *Soviet Policy in Developing Countries*, Waltham, Massachusetts: Ginn-Blaisdell Publishing Co., 1997, Chapter 1.

[13]W. Raymond Duncan and Carolyn McGiffert Ekedahl, *Moscow and the Third World under Gorbachev*, Boulder, Colorado: Westview Press, 1990.

[14]Samuel P. Huntington, "The Erosion of American Interests," *Foreign Affairs*, Vol. 76, No. 5 (September/October 1997), p. 31.

[15]Testimony by Leon Aron, Resident Scholar, American Enterprise Institute, before the *Committee on Foreign Relations Subcommittee on European Affairs*, US Senate, May 20, 1998.

[16]*Ibid*, p. 2.

[17]See President Bush's speech and reaction to it in *The New York Times* and *The Washington Post*, September 12, 13 and 14, 2002.

[18]*Strategic Forecasting*, March 15, 2002.

[19]Michael Hirsh, "Bush and the World," *Foreign Affairs*, September/October 2002, pp. 18–19.

[20]Rochester *Democrat and Chronicle*, September 11, 2002.

CASE STUDY

How Do the Foreign Policies of China and the United States Fit Together?

As with all states, China's foreign policy stems from its geographic location, its shifting power base, and its historic legacy. Still in control of the economy and the single party state, the Chinese Communist Party nevertheless has moved closer to a market economy and adjusted to the shrinking world made possible by globalization. While inequality, corruption, crime, and human rights concerns still proliferate in China, Beijing [when we speak of China's political center, we say "Beijing," much as we speak of Washington, DC, as the U.S. political center] has pursued a foreign policy of more integration with the outside world, including its entry into the World Trade Organization. It has expanded commercial ties with the world abroad, including the United States, opened its doors to foreign tourists, and been drawn into the sphere of Western values and living conditions as a result of such ties—including exposure to western media. The proliferation of cell phones and Internet use is a case in point. In its increasing westernization, then, China's foreign policy has contributed to centralization in the world political system.

At the same time, the outside world worries about what direction China's foreign policy will take as a result of its hostile attitude toward Taiwan, its weapons development program, its suspicion of Japan, and its historically up-and-down relations with the United States. Chinese nationalistic feelings are profound too, as demonstrated in China's absolute refusal to believe that NATO's bombing of the Chinese embassy in Belgrade in 1999 during the Kosovo crisis was a mistake owing to a faulty map (see Chapter 8 for a discussion of nationalism). Meanwhile, China's military power is growing stronger, while Beijing has cracked down on the Falun Gong spiritual movement as a threat to regime legitimacy, and tried to control public criticism of official policies. The development of China's foreign policy will be extremely interesting to watch as the country tries to keep its political lid on and evolve into more complete market socialism.

In the following article about Chinese (or Sino)-American relations, keep in mind what you have learned about foreign policy and its goals—and the ways in which a country tries to translate its power into action. Global-level, state-level, and individual-level factors can all be seen in this article, as can the concepts of core objectives, belief systems, and changes in how a country identifies and addresses key issues. This case study is particularly helpful in understanding world politics because it highlights the foreign policies of two powerful states—the world's superpower, the United States, and the regional giant in Asia, China—and examines the relationship these policies create between them. How these two countries interact has an enormous impact on centralization and decentralization in world politics.

CURRENT HISTORY

Sino-American Relations Since September 11: Can the New Stability Last?

BY DAVID SHAMBAUGH

"Although Taiwan, missile proliferation, missile defense, and the American military presence in Asia and Central Asia have the potential to upset Sino-American relations over the next year, the current stability is reason for cautious optimism. . . . Neither country needs or seeks a deterioration of relations or a return to the roller coaster of the 1990s. Indeed, both are otherwise preoccupied."

China's Reaction to September 11

When the hijacked airplanes ploughed into the World Trade Center, Pentagon, and a Pennsylvania field on September 11, Chinese President Jiang Zemin watched the tragedy unfold live on CNN. Jiang immediately ordered his government to issue solemn condolences to the American people and to fully cooperate with the United States government's efforts to track down the perpetrators.* For his part, the Chinese president activated the dormant hotline to the White House to personally convey condolences to President George W. Bush (Jiang was reportedly the second foreign leader, following Russian President Vladimir Putin, to get through). Thereafter the Chinese government took a number of steps to offer tangible assistance to the United States:

- helping draft and pass two key resolutions in the UN Security Council and General Assembly;
- supporting, in principle, the coalition attacks on the Taliban regime in Afghanistan (Beijing's vote on Resolution 1368 marked the first time that China had voted in favor of—rather than its usual practice of abstaining from—authorizing the international use of force);
- diplomatically working quietly behind the scenes with its close partner Pakistan to persuade General Pervez Musharraf's government to support the war against the Taliban regime;
- sharing intelligence with the United States on Al Qaeda and the Taliban;

- initiating a series of exchanges with the United States on counterterrorism, leading to a practical working relationship in this field;
- sealing China's short border with Afghanistan to prevent Al Qaeda or Taliban fighters from migrating into the Xinjiang Autonomous Region;
- inspecting bank accounts in Hong Kong and China for links to terrorist groups;
- offering aid for Afghan refugee resettlement in Pakistan and some reconstruction aid in Afghanistan.

China took these steps to unambiguously support the United States in the aftermath of September 11, but it has not done as much as other neighboring nations or other countries in the world. For example, China did not offer military overflight or basing rights—as did every nation surrounding Afghanistan (except Iran). China claims it has problems doing so because of longstanding sensitivities regarding sovereignty. Other nations, however, overcame such sensitivities and rose to the occasion. Nor did China commit any military units to the multinational force in Afghanistan. China's reluctance to become militarily engaged in the Afghan conflict tarnishes its otherwise positive record in the war against terrorism. Even more troubling and mystifying is China's failure to grasp the opportunity to contribute to the postconflict reconstruction of Afghanistan. China has pledged $150 million in reconstruction aid, but it has chosen not to become involved in training the new Afghan army or police forces, nor has it sent engineers, construction workers, or equipment to help rebuild the country. China's decision to send civilian police to East Timor proved to be an effective contribution to the maintenance of security and nation building there. China could—and should—contribute to these initiatives as a concrete expression of its international responsibilities as a major world power and member of the UN Security Council.

A Return to Engagement

China's cooperation with the United States in fighting terrorism certainly helped improve bilateral relations,

---

*Author interview with senior Chinese Foreign Ministry official, October 9, 2001, Beijing.

but it only added momentum to the strengthening of ties that had been evident over the three months prior to September 11. The EP-3 incident in April and May 2001 certainly increased tensions and strained relations between the two countries, but once it was resolved both sides moved quickly to put it behind them and begin a dedicated process of engagement with each other. Immediately following the release of the EP-3 crew, the United States administration began to signal a shift in tone and policy toward China. Despite the bitter taste left by the Chinese government's handling of the incident, President George W. Bush, in a Rose Garden speech announcing the release of the detained crew, put Beijing and his bureaucracy on notice that he sought an improvement in relations. By using such terms as "constructive and productive relationship" and avoiding the standard refrain of "strategic competitor," the president signaled his willingness to improve ties. Keenly aware of the fissures in the administration's thinking about China, and the president's previously neutral stance toward the contending factions, the Chinese government saw a silver lining in the speech and was quick to grasp the opportunity to improve ties.

The responsibility for implementing the new and more positive policy fell to the State Department, which initiated a series of reciprocal official visits during the early summer, culminating in Secretary of State Colin Powell's own trip to Beijing in late July 2001. The tone of these visits was positive; both governments were looking forward to the first meeting of the two presidents at the Asia-Pacific Economic Cooperation conference in Shanghai in October. Thus, improvement in the United States-China relationship was evident before September 11.

While the Bush administration and Bush himself came to office arguing that China was a "strategic competitor," and while many members of his administration saw China as a potential adversary, a coalition of key officials (including the president, secretary of state, and national security adviser Condoleezza Rice) sought to establish a more stable, cooperative, and enduring relationship with Beijing. The rationale behind the shift in tone and policy was not dissimilar from the strategic logic that had guided the China policies of the six previous administrations: a China that is positively engaged with the world, and not withdrawn into a nationalistic cocoon, is conducive to the stability and security of the Asia-Pacific region and to American national security interests.

This realistic approach was soon to pay dividends after September 11. Sino-American cooperation against terrorism paved the way for Bush's visit with Jiang in Shanghai. The two presidents met again in February 2002, when Bush paid a two-day official visit to Beijing. Two American presidential trips to China in the space of four months are unprecedented, and the two leaders have also spoken by telephone a number of times during the past year. Although their chemistry is reported to be businesslike but not warm, such high-level contact is an important element in the overall relationship. It provides a personal sense of the other leader (an important criteria in Bush's worldview) and a channel of direct and uncensored communication on sensitive issues; it also energizes the two governments' bureaucracies to generate areas of joint cooperation.

The past year has not only witnessed this set of high-level meetings but also the full reinstitutionalization of bilateral exchanges. Virtually every United States cabinet official (with the notable and glaring exception of Secretary of Defense Donald Rumsfeld) has now met his or her Chinese counterpart for discussions—some several times.

The lack of military-to-military exchanges is a notable exception to the reinstitutionalization of bilateral relations. Secretary of Defense Rumsfeld suspended all bilateral exchanges with the People's Liberation Army (PLA) following the EP-3 incident. Any such exchanges were to be approved on a case-by-case basis and by the secretary personally. Rumsfeld and other senior officials in the Defense Department are deeply suspicious of the value of these exchanges to the United States. They have the perception that past exchanges have benefited the PLA much more than the United States military, and have primarily been an avenue for Chinese military espionage. Because of the lack of Chinese transparency and reciprocity, the United States, they believe, receives little tangible benefit from military exchanges. Despite this predisposition at the Pentagon, Bush has proposed on two occasions to Jiang Zemin that the two militaries should resume exchanges. The State Department is also pushing for a resumption.

The "Armitage–Wolfowitz Vision"

While some officials in the Bush administration do not even favor the engagement element of the administration's China policy, a consensus seems to have emerged early in the administration that China had to be engaged and not ignored, confronted, or contained. Secretary of State Powell, national security adviser Rice, and the president himself were key in forging this consensus. China was, in their estimation, a "major power" (like Russia) with which the United States had important equities and national security interests that mandated as much engagement and cooperation as possible. Yet, as part of this recognition, the administration also strongly believes that the approach to China must include other regional elements and that the United States should place much greater priority on these regional actors than it places on China.

Today Wolfowitz and Armitage—now the deputy secretaries of defense and state, respectively—have played the dominant roles in conceptualizing the administration's broad Asia strategy. In their view, America's China policy should be embedded in a broader Asia policy, rather than vice versa. This basic conceptualization is not tantamount to a policy of containing China, although it certainly does have the effect of strengthening America's strategic and military ties all around China's periphery (which, to many in China, is precisely a form of neocontainment). While no existing public document describes it, what can be described as the "Armitage-Wolfowitz vision" for China and Asia policy involves at least the following core elements:

- Emphasize Japan. America's entire relationship with the Asia-Pacific region is anchored to the United States–Japan alliance—an alliance that, in Armitage's view, needs substantial strengthening and redefining so that it bears a closer resemblance to the United States–Britain alliance (an unrealistic desire if, for no other reason, Japan does not seek such a relationship);
- Stress and strengthen America's other four regional alliances (South Korea, Thailand, the Philippines, Australia) and its security partnerships (especially Singapore);
- Work to build security ties with Malaysia, Indonesia, Brunei, and possibly Vietnam;
- Vastly enhance overall relations with India—political, commercial, and military;
- Build security partnerships with Central Asian states (this was true September 11 and has become actual policy since then);
- Rebuild relations with Pakistan and help keep Pakistan from becoming a failed state that encourages and exports terrorism;
- Strengthen political and military ties with Taiwan;
- Maintain a robust forward military presence throughout Asia.

On Taiwan the Bush administration has also undertaken many new initiatives aimed at giving the government and people on the island greater confidence and dignity. In 2001 it approved the largest arms sales package for the Taiwanese military since the previous Bush administration agreed to sell 150 F-16 fighters in 1992. While it did not include the hotly debated Aegis-equipped naval cruisers, it did involve a number of weapons previously denied to Taipei (including submarines). The Defense Department has also moved to upgrade other forms of military assistance to Taiwan's armed forces in a variety of areas (an initiative begun during the second Clinton administration but intensified by the Rumsfeld Pentagon). The administration also broke with past policy by authorizing Taiwan's leaders (president and vice president) to make occasional "transit" visits to major American cities. It also permitted an unprecedented visit by Taiwan's minister of defense, who attended a conference in Florida where he met with Deputy Secretary of Defense Wolfowitz and Assistant Secretary of State Kelly. In another unprecedented move, former Taiwanese vice president and leader of the Kuomintang (Nationalist Party), Lien Chan, was invited to a conference and dinner at the White House. With the exception of former President Lee Teng-hui's controversial trip to the United States in 1995, these moves by the Bush administration are unprecedented in the 23 years since the United States derecognized the government on Taiwan. President Bush contributed the most notable policy departure of all by announcing in a nationally televised interview that his administration "would do whatever it takes to help Taiwan defend itself."

Beijing is deeply concerned about and vigorously protests these initiatives, but they have not led to a major rift in the Sino-American relationship. For its part, Beijing is also recalibrating its relationship with Taiwan. The mainland's policy toward the island appears to have four main thrusts: economic integration, political co-optation, military intimidation, and international strangulation. All four elements work in tandem and are collectively intended to make Taiwan increasingly more dependent on the mainland, while sowing seeds of division in the island's domestic politics and closing Taiwan's international options. While official cross-strait dialogue remains suspended and hung up on disagreement over the "one China" issue, interchange of all kinds is rapidly deepening and accelerating.

Potential Problems on the Horizon

Although the Sino-American relationship has experienced newfound stability over the past year, difficulties and potential problems remain. These fall in the areas of relations with Taiwan, nonproliferation, missile defenses, and the American military presence in Asia.

In particular, the Bush administration risks a confrontation and serious deterioration in relations with

China if it continues to upgrade military relations with Taiwan, sell more advanced weapons to it, and permit senior Taiwanese officials to visit the United States. At present, Taipei is pushing hard for a possible visit by President Chen Shui-bian to Washington, and some members of Congress are interested in inviting him to address a joint session. That would be a profound affront to China and would likely trigger a major political crisis in Sino-American relations.

The United States is similarly risking a deterioration if it proceeds to further link the Taiwanese and American militaries in "joint" ways with integrated communications systems, command and control, and intelligence, along with joint force planning, logistics, training, or exercises. Any or all of these acts would, in the eyes of Beijing, reconstitute de facto the military alliance with Taiwan that the United States terminated in 1979 as a condition for the normalization of diplomatic relations with the People's Republic.

The arms buildup on both sides of the Taiwan Strait is also dangerous and destabilizing. An action-reaction arms-race dynamic has developed in the last few years, with Beijing buying specific weapons from Russia to counter those sold by the United States to Taiwan, while the United States selects weapons for sale to the island specifically designed to counter those sold by Russia to China. This escalatory dynamic is costly and risky.

The second concern, China's proliferation of ballistic missiles and missile components to other countries—particularly Iran, Iraq, Libya, and Pakistan—has been a longstanding problem. Despite years of negotiations, a bilateral agreement in November 2000, and countless Chinese denials and pledges, China's ballistic missile proliferation apparently continues.

The missile defense issue has also been an irritant for several years now, with China repeatedly expressing its opposition to the United States withdrawal from the Anti-Ballistic Missile Treaty in 2002 and development and deployment of such defenses. For China the issue centers on the number of ballistic missile interceptors deployed in Alaska as part of a national missile defense system. If a "minimal architec-ture" of 100 or fewer interceptors was deployed, Chinese military and civilian strategists suggest that it would not endanger their present "second-strike" nuclear retaliatory capability—and, hence, China could probably live with it and not undertake major increases in its own intercontinental force. But if a more robust architecture were deployed, China will be forced to build up its intercontinental ballistic missile and submarine-launched missile forces so as to ensure its deterrent. In its *Annual Report on the Military Power of the People's Republic of China* that was released July 12, 2002, the United States Department of Defense predicted that China's force of approximately 20 intercontinental ballistic missiles will likely grow to "around 30 by 2005 and may reach 60 by 2010."

The final potential problem on the horizon of Sino-American relations concerns the growing United States military presence around China's periphery. Deployments in Pakistan and Central Asia as part of the war in Afghanistan, along with the rapidly improving United States-India military relationship; five bilateral alliances and improved security partnerships between the United States and several Southeast Asian states; and the already existing 100,000 forward deployed forces in Northeast Asia give China pause for concern. Many Chinese strategists perceive American encirclement and believe that China's national security environment has significantly deteriorated since September 11. If this perception grows and hardens among Chinese officialdom, and if China perceives these deployments as oriented against China, this military presence could become a problem in the Sino-American relationship. It is a positive sign that Chinese officials have told their American counterparts over the past year, for the first time, that China does not seek to evict the United States from East Asia and respects American interests in the region. This is not quite the same as saying that China agrees (with the United States and other countries) that the American presence is, in itself, a stabilizing force in the region, but it is reassuring.

Source: David Shambaugh, "Sino-American Relations Since September 11: Can the New Stability Last?" Current History, September 2002, pp. 243–249. Reprinted with permission from Current History Magazine, September 2002, © 2002, Current History, Inc.

QUESTIONS

Check Your Understanding

1. What does this author see as positive signs in U.S.-China policy?
2. What did China's reaction to the attacks of 9/11 reveal about relations between the two countries?

Analyze the Issues

1. How do you account for the change in America's shift from a competitive to a cooperative relationship with China? Use the "Four Dimensions of Foreign Policy Decision Making" discussed in the chapter to organize your answer.
2. How do the foreign policies of China and the United States contribute to centralization and decentralization in world politics?
3. How, and in what ways, do Chinese and U.S. core interests conflict over the issue of Taiwan?
4. Ballistic missile programs figure prominently in the pursuit of core interests for China and the United States. In what respects do these programs generate tensions between the two countries?

FOR FURTHER INFORMATION

For additional information on Sino-American relations—and the foreign policy priorities that shape this relationship—see the following sources:

Aaron L. Friedberg, "11 September and the Future of Sino-American Relations," *Survival*, Spring 2002, pp. 33–50.

David M. Lampton, "Small Mercies: China and America after 9/11," *The National Interest*, Winter 2001–2002, pp. 106–113.

http://newton.uor.edu/Departments&Programs/AsianStudiesDept/china-us.html

Nick Smith, "Grand Delusions," *Harvard International Review*, Fall 2002, pp. 7–8.

Parris H. Chang, "The Curse of the Shanghai Communiqué; A Look at the Past and the Future in Sino-American Relations and the Taiwan Issue," *Newsweek*, March 4, 2002, p. 11.

Daniel C. Lynch, "U.S. Shouldn't Indulge China's Taiwan Fantasy," *The Los Angeles Times*, February 14, 2002.

CHAPTER 5

Intergovernmental Actors

KEY QUESTIONS RAISED IN THIS CHAPTER

1. Why do countries join intergovernmental and supranational organizations?
2. What does the United Nations do and how well does it do it?
3. What is the European Union and how does it work?
4. What are the global financial and trade organizations?
5. How does the Organization of Petroleum Exporting Countries (OPEC) differ from other IGOs?

Realism, you will recall, teaches us that the world is dominated by nation-states, that no entity in the world is more powerful than a nation-state, and that nation-states rarely give up any sovereignty to international organizations (IOs). In short, for realists and their contemporaries, the most important unit of analysis in world politics is the nation-state. As we have seen in the first four chapters of the book, to a large extent the realists are correct. However, a quick glance around the world reveals a diverse array of nonstate actors (organizations) that have transformed international affairs. Most members of these organizations would probably take issue with the realist perspective of the world. Many believe that the idealism or ecological paradigm better explains how the world does works and should work.

In general, we can divide up the nonstate actors into two groups. One group consists of IOs whose members are states; these are called international **intergovernmental organizations,** or **IGOs.** Some of the more important ones include the United Nations, the European Union, the Association of Southeast Asian Nations, and the Organization of American States. Membership in the second group of IOs consists of individuals or groups; these are known as international nongovernmental organizations or NGOs. Greenpeace, Amnesty International, international businesses, and even terrorist groups are all examples of international organizations whose members are individuals or groups—not countries. For a comparison of IGO and NGO membership, consider the following example. As an individual interested in human rights around the world, you can join an NGO like Amnesty International. However, as an individual, you *cannot* join the United Nations because only recognized states can become members of an IGO. Although IGOs and NGOs differ in some ways, they do share many common traits, including the following:[1]

Intergovernmental Organizations (IGOs)
An international grouping of states.

- Voluntary membership
- A basic instrument (or charter) stating goals, structure, and method of operation.
- A representative consultative conference system.
- A permanent secretariat to carry on administrative, research, and information functions.
- Procedures based on consent and recommendation rather than compulsion or force.

As discussed in Chapter 1, the weakening of centralized state power has encouraged decentralization everywhere. Part of this decentralization process has made it possible for many NGOs to thrive. At the same time, the centralizing forces at work around the world over the past five years have encouraged greater cooperation among countries, and this has facilitated the rise of IGOs. The International Telegraph Union, started in 1865, was one of the first modern IGOs, but the number of IOs—both IGOs and NGOs—grew enormously in the twentieth century. In 1909 there were about 37 IGOs and 176 NGOs. Since World War II, the number of IOs has ballooned, and today there are over 400 IGOs and over 5,000 international NGOs.[2]

Intergovernmental organizations undertake extremely varied tasks. Some IOs are *global* in scope. The UN, for example, is involved in many places around the world, and most of the world's countries are members of the UN. NAFTA is an example of a *regional* IO comprising the US, Canada, and Mexico. Another feature that varies among IOs is that some have *many purposes,* such as the European Union, while others are designed for a *specialized, limited purpose,* such as the Organization of Petroleum Exporting Countries (OPEC).

Since the world has so many—and so many kinds—of nonstate actors in international relations, we have placed them into two separate chapters. In this chapter we explore several important IGOs: the United Nations, the European Union, international monetary and trade organizations, and OPEC. NGOs are the subject of Chapter 6. The first main section of this chapter raises the question of why countries would join IGOs. The next two sections explore the two most important IGOs and how they function: the United Nations and the European Union. The following section of the chapter covers IGOs designed to deal with global finance (the World bank and International Monetary Fund) and international trade (the World Trade Organization). The last main section of the chapter explores the international role of the Organization of Oil Exporting countries (OPEC).

The aim of both this chapter and Chapter 6 is to enhance the reader's knowledge of the major players in world politics and to remind the reader that although states do drive international relations, they do not do it alone. Ignoring IGOs and NGOs would leave us with an incomplete understanding of the world. The twentieth century moved well beyond the state system that evolved from the Treaty of Westphalia, which envisioned sovereign countries as the key players in international relations; the twenty-first century is not likely to resemble that system either. The chapter case study—which provides the pros and cons of the International Criminal Court—taps into many of these ideas.

Why Do Countries Join Intergovernmental and Supranational Organizations?

Depending on the type of IGO—multipurpose, single-issue, global, or regional—countries consider membership in an IGO for a variety of reasons. In every case, countries must weigh the costs and benefits of membership. One clear cost of participation in an IGO is the potential loss of national sovereignty because a country must sometimes go along with the other IGO members when it may not completely want to. As for the benefits, we suggest several economic, political, and security reasons for joining an IGO.

Economic Rewards

Some countries join an IGO because membership yields positive *economic* rewards. The North American Free Trade Agreement (NAFTA), for example, was formed in part because of the perceived economic benefits that would accrue to its three member states: the United States, Canada, and Mexico. As a member in NAFTA, Mexican companies get better access to the lucrative U.S. market and vice versa. Chinese membership in the World Trade Organization (WTO) offers a similar example. China knows that membership in the WTO will allow it to buy—and more important, sell—goods more freely on international markets to all the other WTO members. And similarly, France originally joined the European Union (EU) to improve its economic status following the devastation wrought by World War II. As we will describe later in the chapter, most countries in the world belong to some type of regional trade organization because of the potential economic benefits.

Political Influence

Another reason countries join IGOs is because they gain *political* influence. The Netherlands and Portugal, for example, are too small to influence the course of world affairs on their own, but as members of the European Union, they can acquire real political clout. The same argument holds for Uruguay and Paraguay in MERCOSUR, a NAFTA-like arrangement in the southern cone of South America. And one reason that Germany and Italy supported the creation of the European Union in the 1950s was that they wanted to show the world—especially the French and other Europeans—that they could be trusted as a cooperative political partner and that they were not likely to start another world war in the heart of Europe.

Security

A country may also join an international organization because it can provide *security*. The North Atlantic Treaty Organization (NATO) is the most influential security organization in the world. It is made up of the United States, Canada, and many Western European countries. Like many security organizations, NATO guarantees members protection if attacked. Another example of a security organization is the Organization for Security and Cooperation in Europe, comprised of over 50 countries including all European states and the United States. Its aim is to provide a forum for discussing the security concerns of NATO and non-NATO countries, as well as for those who were not aligned to either the United States or the Soviet Union during the Cold War.

Cooperation and Reciprocity

As we stated earlier, national leaders must cope with the ever-present tension between the *benefits* of cooperative membership and the *risk* of lost national sovereignty. Let's now take a closer look at the power relationship between sovereign states and the international organizations they belong to. Most IOs are *intergovernmental* in nature, that is, nation-states dominate their direction. Intergovernmental organizations consist of representatives of national governments, and they promote *voluntary* cooperation among those governments. The central administrative authorities of IGOs, often called secretariats, tend to have *very restricted* responsibilities or authority to make decisions on their own, and they tend *not* to have any coercive power to enforce their will.[3] Since national sovereignty is such a highly guarded commodity, governments cooperate with each other but try to minimize the influence of their joint international institutions.

However, if these international institutions gain considerable powers of their own, they become *supranational* actors because in some ways they are above the state. **Supranationalism** describes an arrangement whereby national governments transfer a significant amount of sovereignty to an international governing body. This body is an autonomous authority that is above the state and that has designated powers of coercion that are *independent* of the member states. Supranationality, however, does not mean that these institutions exercise *total* authority over national governments.

Supranational institutions can influence their members in several ways. First, in the case of decisionmaking, *voting rules* can be structured in such a way as to reflect the balance of power among the IGO's member states. In addition, voting

Supranationalism
An arrangement whereby national governments transfer a significant amount of sovereignty to an international governing body. This body is an autonomous authority that is above the state and that has designated powers of coercion that are independent of the member states. Supranationality, however, does not mean that these institutions exercise *total* authority over national governments.

rules in an IGO can force countries to act more cooperatively than if they had full sovereignty and did not have to vote at all. We will see an example of this later when we consider the European Union. Voting can also affect the behavior of states in nonsupranational organizations such as the United Nations. For example, in order for the UN to use military force, all five permanent members of the Security Council must agree—that is, there must be a unanimous vote. Thus in some ways, international rules can constrain states from acting in ways that they might otherwise choose.

Second, supranational IOs can have *legal authority* over the member states. You will soon see, for example, how the European Union's European Court of Justice can overrule the national court of an EU member state (such as Germany or Italy).

Third, supranational institutions may gain considerable influence when a totally new policy issue arises. Instead of national governments dominating the new policy issue, supranational IOs can take advantage of the situation by leading or taking what is called an *entrepreneurial role* in developing new policies. In some respects, environmental policy in the European Union has advanced in such a way.[4]

Fourth, IOs can also be supranational in that they help *foster cooperation* among interest groups from member states. Interest groups such as labor organizations or business associations (made up of representatives of different businesses) may do this on their own, of course, but they may be encouraged to do so by IOs as well.

Another important reason why countries join IOs is because of the actual work they can do. As Robert Keohane has shown, international institutions can teach countries how to cooperate in mutually beneficial ways.[5] This is possible for many reasons. First, IOs can lower the administrative and political costs of making and enforcing agreements. For example, instead of having to "reinvent the wheel" of cooperation every time two or more countries wish to resolve a problem, IOs can serve as permanent arenas where diplomats can meet on a routine basis. Thus, international institutions can also act as neutral participants who monitor how well governments comply with their commitments. Second, international institutions can help reinforce positive behavior, as when one country's responsible behavior is reciprocated by others. *Reciprocity* thus gives states the incentive to keep their commitments so that others will too. To put it another way, international institutions help dampen the fears of defection by others. Finally, general conformity to the rules of the international organization makes the behavior of other states more predictable. As you know, predictability is highly prized in a dangerous—and as some would say, "anarchic"—world.

Now that we have a better sense of what IGOs are, why countries join them, and what their intergovernmental and supranational features are, we can explore several of the world's major IGOs. After reviewing these IGOs, you will have a better understanding of their diversity in both scope and purpose. When reading about the IOs in the rest of this chapter, you will note that we examine each of the following:

- The type of IO: political, security, economic, or some combination
- The power relationship among members of an IO
- The power relationship between the IO and its member states
- The existence of a supranational body within the IO
- The extent of the IO's legal authority over the member states
- The type of voting rules, for example, unanimity, majority, qualified majority

Let's look first at the United Nations, one of our most important intergovernmental organizations, and one that is global in scope.

What Does the United Nations Do and How Well Does It Do It?

The UN's geographic scope and diverse activities are unmatched by any other international organization. This is demonstrated in Table 5.1 below, which lists the UN's nonmilitary activities. The comprehensiveness of the UN is reflected in its many specialized agencies, including the International Labor Organization (ILO), the

TABLE 5.1   Nonmilitary Activities of the United Nations

The United Nations is an intergovernmental organization with an almost endless number of tasks to perform. While it certainly deals with military matters, especially in the Security Council, it also handles many nonmilitary activities, as the list below suggests. You are probably already familiar with some of them.

Branch of the UN	Function
The United Nations International Children's Emergency Fund (UNICEF)	Establishes child health and welfare services around the world
United Nations Conference on Trade and Development (UNCTAD)	Promotes international trade
The United Nations Development Program (UNDP)	Provides technical assistance to stimulate economic and social development
The United Nations Educational, Scientific, and Cultural Organization (UNESCO)	Promotes cooperation in education, science, and culture
The United Nations Environment Program (UNEP)	Promotes international cooperation on all environmental matters.
The United Nations Industrial Development Organization (UNIDO)	Promotes industrial development, especially among the members
The United Nations Institute for Training and Research (UNITAR)	Assists the UN to become more effective through training and research.
The United Nations High Commissioner for Refugees (UNHCR)	Promotes humanitarian treatment of refugees and seeks permanent solutions to refugee problems
The United Nations Population Fund (UNPF)	Assists both developed and developing countries in dealing with their population problems
The United Nations Research Institute for Social Development (UNRISD)	Conducts research into the problems of economic development during different phases of economic growth
The Universal Postal Union (UPU)	Promotes international postal cooperation
The World Health Organization (WHO)	Improves health conditions in developing countries
The World Intellectual Property Organization (WIPO)	Provides protection for literary, artistic, and scientific works

UN International Children's Emergency Fund (UNICEF), and the World Bank and International Monetary Fund.

People who do not know much about the United Nations make two common mistakes about it. One mistake is to *overestimate* its importance; the other is to *underestimate* it. In this part of the chapter, we will explore the power and limitations of the UN, the areas where it is active, and the way it makes decisions.

Managing Global Peace Through the Security Council

The UN is an institution devoted primarily to peace and security in the international system. Known as a collective security organization, the UN seeks to prevent war through the threat, or actual use, of collective action against countries that violate international peace. If the UN wishes to use military force, the **Security Council** must authorize it. In fact, the Security Council is the only UN body that can make decisions that are binding on all UN members.

The Security Council consists of 15 members; 5 of the countries are permanent members while 10 other countries are elected by the General Assembly for two-year terms. The 5 permanent members are the United States, the United Kingdom (i.e., Britain), France, China, and Russia (which inherited the Soviet Union's seat). The other Security Council members are chosen not by a strict rules-based formula but by a political arrangement that tries to ensure that both big and small countries are selected, and that countries from different parts of the world have a more or less equal chance of serving.

For the Security Council to authorize the use of military force, 9 of the 15 members must approve. However, the UN founders recognized that some elements of realism's balance of power needed to be combined with the notion of collective security and thus created a special voting rule for the permanent members. In order to accommodate the status of the world's most powerful countries (and consistent with realism), the Security Council uses **unanimity voting:** a unanimous decision is required among the permanent members to authorize the use of UN force. And even if all the non-permanent members agree to the use of military force, any one of the permanent five can *veto* the proposal. In short, unanimity among the permanent five is required for using force, but only one veto will prevent the use of force.

With the existence of the veto rule, one might predict that the Security Council would rarely authorize the use of force. After all, the 5 permanent members differ significantly in their interests, and at least one of them is bound to use its veto. In fact, the Security Council was virtually paralyzed during much of the Cold War because of the common use of the veto—especially by the United States. But this condition was actually built into the United Nations. The UN founders deliberately wanted to make it difficult for the organization to use military force. They understood the dangers inherent in waging war—especially by an international organization, and they recognized that a political consensus among the world's great powers was needed for the military force to be politically successful as well as victorious on the battlefield.[6]

The entire UN does not use unanimity voting, however. The General Assembly uses **majority voting:** a majority of states must agree to an action or policy. In the General Assembly each country—no matter how big or small—is allotted one vote. A different form of voting is used in other parts of the UN. For example, in the World Bank and International Monetary Fund, variations of *weighted voting* are

Security Council
The most important branch of the United Nations. It deals primarily with peace and security issues, and can authorize the use of military force. The Security Council consists of 15 countries: 5 permanent members (Britain, China, France, Russia, and the United States) and 10 others that rotate periodically.

Unanimity Voting
A voting rule that requires a unanimous decision. This type of voting rule gives each person (or country) a veto; that is, it takes only one "no" vote to nullify the vote.

Majority Voting
A voting rule in which the majority of states (or individuals) must agree.

League of Nations
An international organization established in 1918 to maintain peace and security. Although it did not prevent the outbreak of World War II, it did have a significant influence on the creation and structure of the United Nations.

HISTORICAL PERSPECTIVE

The Origins and Rationale of the United Nations

The idea for creating the UN did not happen all of a sudden at the end of World War II. Roots of the idea can be found in the early part of the twentieth century, in the political idealism that influenced many world leaders (see Chapter 1). The deeper roots actually go back much further. Jean-Jacques Rousseau, for example, argued that the principle of state sovereignty (as recognized by the Treaty of Westphalia) was partially responsible for wars. The influence of Rousseau and others generated the idea that there needed to be curbs on sovereignty and increased international cooperation. In the nineteenth century, the major European powers became more accustomed to frequent (and often cooperative) interaction in order to keep peace in Europe.

At the start of the twentieth century, many political leaders sought to create a cooperative community of nation-states that would ensure the collective security of members. The idea behind collective security organizations was that the chances for maintaining peace would be enhanced because an aggressive act against any member of the collective security organization would met with a collective response. In short, an attack against one is an attack against all. The notion of collective security (also discussed in Chapter 3), combined with the harsh lessons of World War I, led to the formation of the **League of Nations** in 1918. Consequently, the main mission of both the League of Nations and the UN is to maintain peace and security.

Political realists were quick to denounce the idea of a League of Nations as a pie-in-the-sky attempt to control sovereign states. Many argued that even a shallow understanding of history would reveal that the League of Nations was almost completely ineffective. After all, the League of Nations did not prevent the outbreak of World War II. At critical times during the 1930s, when Adolf Hitler's Germany began re-arming (in violation of the Versailles Treaty that ended World War I) and seeking territorial gains, the League of Nations was unable to stop it.

Despite the League's inability to prevent World War II, many political leaders after World War II did not conclude that IGOs were useless in preventing war. On the contrary, with the nuclear age upon them, they saw even more clearly the need for international cooperation.

The critics of realism interpreted the failure of the League of Nations differently. They said the League failed because a key country (the United States) was not a member, and they believed that different decisions by France and Britain could have prevented World War II. This helps explain why the idea of a global security organization (the United Nations) survived and thrived on the ashes of World War II. In more limited ways, political idealists and liberals could even point to some successes of the League. For example, it helped clarify a border dispute between Germany and Poland, and resolved a number of other border disputes involving, for example, Russia and Finland, and Bulgaria and Greece.

The UN that evolved after World War II is best known for its role in maintaining international peace and security. Article 1 of the UN Charter, however, describes an IO that goes much further than a mere security organization. According to its Charter, the UN seeks to develop friendly relations among nations based on respect for the principle of equal rights and self-determination of people. It seeks international cooperation in solving international problems of an economic, social, cultural, and humanitarian character, and in promoting and encouraging respect for human rights and for fundamental freedoms for all.

FIGURE 5.1

Relationship of Assessments to Voting Strength in the General Assembly

SOURCE: Lawrence Ziring, Robert E. Riggs, and Jack C. Plano, The United Nations: International Organization and World Politics. Third Edition (Orlando, FL: Harcourt Brace & Company, 2000), p. 61. Reproduced by permission of the publisher.

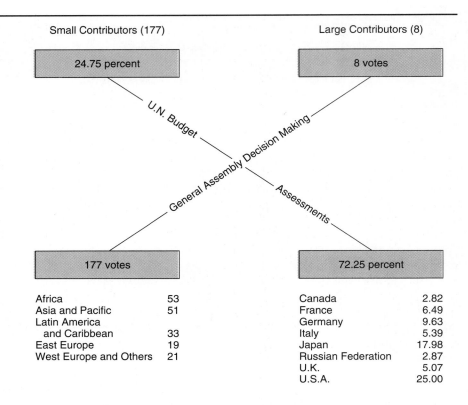

Small Contributors (177)

| 24.75 percent |

Large Contributors (8)

| 8 votes |

U.N. Budget

General Assembly Decision Making

Assessments

| 177 votes |

| 72.25 percent |

Africa	53
Asia and Pacific	51
Latin America and Caribbean	33
East Europe	19
West Europe and Others	21

Canada	2.82
France	6.49
Germany	9.63
Italy	5.39
Japan	17.98
Russian Federation	2.87
U.K.	5.07
U.S.A.	25.00

used. That is, a country gets more voting weight if it makes a larger financial contribution. With this voting rule, the United States has much more influence than, for example, Kenya, because the United States is one of the largest financial contributors to these institutions.

The first time the Security Council authorized military force was during the Korean War, which pitted UN members, led by the United States, against North Korea, which was supported by China. It is interesting to note that the Soviet Union backed the North Koreans and Chinese, but the Soviets did not use their veto to prevent the UN (and thus the United States) from using military force against North Korea. The Soviet Union, it turned out, made one of the worst tactical diplomatic decisions of the Cold War era by boycotting the Security Council over the failure of the UN to consider Chinese membership. When the vote to use force against North Korea came up, the Soviet Union was not there to veto the decision.

Peacekeeping, Peacebuilding, and Peacemaking

A much more common use of UN force these days is that of **peacekeeping.** Although peacekeeping is not in the UN Charter, it has become an increasingly important and controversial part of UN activities. The idea behind peacekeeping is that the UN steps in as a buffer when warring parties agree to allow a neutral UN force to carry out peace plans. In all, roughly 45,000 people from 87 countries now serve in UN peacekeeping operations around the world. **Peacebuilding** is a term used to describe peacekeeping plus additional UN efforts to oversee the development of democratic institutions. Sometimes the UN has been called upon to enforce a

Peacekeeping
A military operation, normally associated with the United Nations, whose aim is to provide a buffer between warring parties who allow a neutral force to carry out peace plans.

Peacebuilding
A peacekeeping operation that includes UN efforts to oversee the development of democratic institutions.

The United Nations Building: New York City

peaceful solution to a conflict when one or more sides do not wish peace. This situation, often called **peacemaking** or *peace enforcement*, became more common in the 1990s, sometimes with unfavorable results.

Peacekeeping operations have become quite controversial in part because of disasters or near disasters. The UN often got involved in highly complex situations and sometimes with terrible results. The debacle of Sierra Leon in 2000, for example, demonstrated the dangers of UN military missions to areas where peace must be *imposed*. One scholar, Michael Ignatieff, has argued that such operations have become so complicated and dangerous and so poorly managed that they are destroying the United Nations itself.[7] One of the most problematic UN peacekeeping operation in the 1990s was in Somalia. Originally, the UN mission was designed to end the country's severe famine. In the midst of the famine, Somalia was dangerously fragmented politically. The UN peacekeeping force in Somalia was initially charged with processing and distributing humanitarian supplies that came from foreign countries. But before long, lawlessness intensified, and in 1992, the UN pleaded for more peacekeeping forces from the major powers. The United States responded by leading an intervention task force. U.S. forces successfully regained control of key transportation links and began withdrawing so that the UN could resume its relief operations. But things got worse when the UN then tried to broaden the scope of its operations—from humanitarian relief to demilitarization of the country's militants and reduction of the military power of competing clans. These efforts resulted in several clashes including one involving U.S. forces battling with clan guerrillas. In the battle that inspired the film *Blackhawk Down*, the fighting led to many thousands of Somali casualties and the deaths of 17 Americans with another 77 wounded. U.S. forces ultimately withdrew in 1994 leaving a tenuous political situation behind them.

Web Exploration

For more information on UN peacekeeping missions, go to **www.ablongman.com/ duncan**.

The United Nations Takes on a Large Number of Political, Economic, Social, and Military Tasks: Not everyone is convinced of the UN's efficiency in one or any of these areas. The UN has been particularly criticized for its inability to deal with contemporary peacekeeping operations.

SOURCE: *Michael Ramirez/Copley News Service.*

The Somalia case demonstrates, among other things, that when UN operations move into highly volatile places, peacekeeping can evolve into even more dangerous peace enforcement. The Somalia case, however, does not typify the UN's peacekeeping experience. In many battered countries, including Cambodia, Namibia, Nicaragua, South Africa, and East Timor, the UN has sent impartial observers to ensure that free and fair elections are carried out successfully. In general, peacekeeping operations are more likely to succeed when the warring sides agree to allow the UN to help resolve their differences.

Since the UN has no army, how does it get troops for its peacekeeping and other operations, and where do the troops come from? Member states voluntarily supply the troops and other personnel. Many Americans get the impression that the United States is always the world's police force. If one takes a closer look at U.S. participation in UN peacekeeping operations, however, one gets a very different picture. Since 1948, roughly 750,000 military and civilian police personnel and thousands of other civilians have given their service to UN peacekeeping. The countries contributing the largest number of peacekeepers have been Pakistan, Bangladesh, Jordan, Poland, the Russian Federation, and Canada, in that order.[8] The United States actually plays a small role in peacekeeping operations. For example, more than 1,580 UN peacekeepers from 85 countries have died in the line of duty. Fewer than 3 percent of these were American.[9] On the Iraq-Kuwait border, a UN peacekeeping force of 1,200 monitors Iraqi troop movements; only 1 percent of the force is American. And in 2001–2002, only 700 to 800 U.S. personnel served in worldwide UN peace operations, accounting for only 1.8 percent of the total number of UN peacekeepers.[10]

Another security concern about the UN, particularly for Americans, is who is in charge of UN peacekeeping troops. Some Americans, for example, are very hesitant about committing U.S. troops to the UN because they fear that non-Americans will be commanding U.S. soldiers. In actuality, the arrangement between the United States and the United Nations is that the command authority over U.S. troops will always be the U.S. commander-in-chief, that is, the president of the United States. U.S. forces, however, may be under the operational command of a "trusted ally" such as a NATO member. When a foreign commander is in charge of U.S. troops, he or she does not have the right to change the mission agreed upon by the president, or to divide U.S. units, allocate their supplies, administer discipline, or change a unit's organization. The UN Charter (Articles 43 and 47) envisions a UN force that operates by agreement with individual states that could function under the collective chiefs of staffs of the permanent members and report to the Security Council. Again, however, as a permanent member of the Security Council, the United States has never agreed to any such arrangement.[11]

Managing Global Economic and Social Issues

The UN has developed special agencies to manage the diverse nonmilitary activities of the organization. Some help save children from starvation and disease while others provide help for refugees and victims of disasters. The UN has also advanced international rights to protect children and migrant workers, and it has been a major global force for the advancement of the equal rights of women. Furthermore, the UN is involved in countering global crime and drugs. In some places, the UN's job is primarily to build democratic institutions. As noted earlier, the UN has sent impartial observers to ensure free and fair elections in many countries. It has also helped armed opposition movements transform themselves into political parties in El Salvador, Mozambique, and Guatemala. Typical examples of UN agencies or missions include the United Nations Angola Verification Mission (UNAVEM III), the United Nations Assistance Mission for Rwanda (UNAMIR), and the United Nations Disengagement Observer Force (UNDOF), which continues to observe a 1974 cease-fire agreement between Israeli and Syrian forces on the Golan Heights.

The most important body in the UN for dealing with this diverse array of issues is the **General Assembly.** The General Assembly is the only UN body that directly represents all member states. It is heavily involved in social welfare and economic matters, and it acts as the focal point of activity for the many agencies, committees, and institutes that deal with United Nations matters. The General Assembly also serves the following functions, typical of national parliaments:

- a forum for airing ideas and complaints from constituents
- an arena for debate among member states
- an environment for evaluating and approving the UN budget

From a political perspective, the General Assembly has its own internal challenges. As the European colonial era ended in the 1960s, more and more newly created countries joined the UN. As a result, in many General Assembly debates, vocal opposition to the United States and other advanced industrial countries grew to such an extent that many Americans viewed the General Assembly as a place to bash U.S. foreign policies. Some UN opponents from the U.S. even complained that the UN was still largely "in the grip of a substantial majority of dictatorial, authoritarian and statist regimes."[12]

General Assembly
A branch of the United Nations in which each member state of the UN is allotted one vote, regardless of size. It is heavily involved in social welfare and economic matters, and it acts as the focal point of activity for the many agencies, committees, and institutes that deal with United Nations matters.

North
A term loosely referring to the advanced industrial democracies of the northern hemisphere.

South
A term loosely referring to the less developed countries of the Southern hemisphere.

The clash within the General Assembly between many of the world's developing countries and the United States reflected a more profound division among United Nations members: the split between the industrialized countries of the **North,** and the mostly poor, often politically unstable countries of the **South.** This division is also related to how different countries view the mission of the United Nations. Southern countries (sometimes referred to as the *Group of 77*) have complained that the rules of the international systems—established by the wealthy countries of the world—are structured against them. From their perspective most of the world's problems, from political instability and ethnic conflict to the AIDS epidemic and population pressures, occur in the Southern states. Some of these problems, they argue, result from policies of Northern countries, especially the United States (see Chapter 12 for more details). In their view then, the UN's mission should emphasize solutions to the problems in the South.

The United States and other Northern countries have resisted giving the UN greater influence for addressing Southern concerns. Some Northern states are reluctant to grant the UN significantly more powers for political or financial reasons. Many Americans in particular have resented the anti-American rhetoric of many General Assembly members, and others simply feel that the UN is not the right vehicle for effecting change in the South. This North-South split within the UN is likely to persist well into the twenty-first century.

The "voice" of Southern countries is enhanced by the voting system in the General Assembly. As we noted earlier, every country in the General Assembly is given one vote regardless of size. This puts very small countries like Peru and Cambodia on the same level as the United States or China. (The U.S. Senate works in a similar way; regardless of the size of the state, each gets two votes. California has no more influence than Rhode Island.) Since the poor countries of the UN vastly outnumber those of the North, sheer numbers give the advantage to the South.

Two important points about the General Assembly's influence need to be made. First, unlike the Security Council, the General Assembly is weakened by the fact that, for the most part, *it can only make recommendations.* Even though it is involved in a wide variety of activities, it cannot issue binding legislation, and it does not have the legal clout to bring violators to justice. This, of course, also hurts the efforts by Southern countries to achieve their goals. Second, the General Assembly is weakened by the widely *diverse interests of its members.* Besides the North-South split, the General Assembly is fractured by countries with different religions, cultures, languages, and traditions, as well as different territorial, political, and economic interests. General Assembly members even disagree on something that the UN claims to uphold: human rights. In the early 1980s, for example, some Islamic countries argued that UN principles related to human rights fit Western standards and not theirs. Religious and cultural splits are particularly evident over issues involving the treatment of women (see Chapter 10).

Besides the General Assembly and the Security Council, there are many other UN "bodies" designed for specific tasks. As mentioned earlier, the UN's Secretariat is the primary administrative organ that runs the UN on a day-to-day basis. Based in New York City and with offices in Geneva, Switzerland, the Secretariat is a clearing house of information for the UN and the principal overseer of all UN activities. It is headed by the *Secretary-General* (currently Kofi Annan), who acts as the UN's chief spokesperson and diplomat. The Secretary-General is appointed by the General Assembly upon the recommendation of the Security Council for a five-year term. The Secretariat is also supported by a large staff from over 150 countries.

The Economic and Social Council is another one of the UN's main organizational bodies. As mandated by the UN Charter, the Economic and Social Council is responsible for promoting higher standards of living, full employment, and economic and social progress; identifying solutions to international economic, social and health problems; facilitating international cultural and educational cooperation; and encouraging universal respect for human rights and fundamental freedoms. In carrying out its mandate, the Council consults with academics, business sector representatives, and more than 2,100 registered nongovernmental organizations.[13]

The final principal body of the UN is the International Court of Justice (ICJ). Located in The Hague, the Netherlands, the ICJ handles cases brought by states, not by groups or individuals. The ICJ also gives advisory opinions on legal questions referred to it by other international organs and agencies. The Court is composed of 15 judges elected to nine-year terms of office by the United Nations General Assembly and Security Council sitting independently of each other.[14] The ICJ will be discussed in greater detail in Chapter 10.

Managing Its Own Affairs

Like many large organizations, the UN employs thousands of people. Think of the UN as a huge bureaucracy designed to tackle many issues, and as with many bureaucracies, managing those thousands of people and other resources can be quite a challenge. In the following pages, we discuss several management challenges facing the UN. In the 1990s, and continuing today, the UN came under intense pressure in managing its budget and streamlining its administrative organs. Let's now turn to these two issues.

The UN's Funding and Its Controversies   In order for the UN to undertake any of its operations—military or otherwise—it needs money. Unlike a sovereign country, however, the UN does not raise taxes. The UN relies on dues and voluntary contributions from UN member states. The UN budget has three main elements: the regular budget, the peacekeeping budget, and voluntary contributions for specific UN programs and activities. In addition, a separate budget exists for international tribunals. The General Assembly's Committee on Contributions assigns each member state a percentage share of the budget, ranging from a minimum of .01 percent to a maximum of 25 percent (the United States). The top seven contributors to the UN are the United States (25 percent), Japan (just under 20 percent), Germany (almost 10 percent), France (6.5 percent), Italy and Britain (over 5 percent each), and Canada and Spain (about 2.5 percent).[15] In the past, the smallest contribution made by a country was about $100,000. The largest amount paid was by the United States (over $300 million).[16] Only the United States has paid the maximum amount, and more than eighty countries generally pay the minimum amount.

This kind of payment schedule may seem unfair to Americans, but how much a country pays depends on the size of the country's population, the size of its economy, and its per capita income. Since the United States is the wealthiest country in the world, it is expected to pay a higher share. In return, the United States is given more UN Secretariat jobs than any other member state. Recently, for example, the United States held the top posts at UNICEF, the UN Development Program, the World Bank, the World Food Program, the International Court of Justice, and the Universal Postal Union. The UN has no legal obligation to provide specific jobs to the major contributors; it is more of a political bargain. The political nature of running the UN is also reflected in who gets contracts from the UN (known as *procurement*). For example, of the roughly $327 million worth of contracts approved by the UN Secretariat in New York in 1997, American companies got almost 60 percent of the business.[17]

The budget for the core *administrative* functions of the UN is about $1.3 billion a year. This covers the Secretariat operations in New York City and Geneva as well as offices in Nairobi, Vienna, and five regional commissions. While this figure may sound large, it is not—in relation to the tasks demanded of the UN. The UN, in fact, can be quick to point out how little $1.3 billion really is. By comparison, the UN budget amounts to about 0.5 percent of the U.S. military budget, and less than 0.2 per cent of global military spending. In addition, the UN's $1.3 billion is only 4 percent of New York City's annual budget, and about a billion dollars less than the yearly cost of Tokyo's fire department. It is roughly $3.5 billion less than the annual budget of the State University of New York system.[18] The *total* operating expenses of the entire UN system are much higher, however, because they include the World Bank, the IMF, and all of the UN funds, programs, and specialized agencies. When all of these are considered, the UN's expenses amount to more than $18 billion a year.[19]

As with any large organization or business, deciding who will pay the bills can be an extremely political process. For example, in the 1990s, the UN was pressured to put a lid on the UN's overall budget because members of the U.S. Congress (mostly Republicans) opposed waste and mismanagement at the UN, and because they were concerned about sovereignty issues related to the UN's articles. Many Americans resent the situation in the General Assembly, where countries that pay only about 2 percent of the budget get 100 votes. Some even favor U.S. withdrawal from the UN. One U.S. Congressman, although clearly not part of the mainstream, argued in 1991 that U.S. participation in the UN infringed on U.S. sovereignty. The UN, he said, was made up of people "who genuinely believe that our interests are best served if we become weaker and weaker and the UN becomes stronger and stronger so that [the UN will] ultimately have a bigger army than we do."[20]

Many countries fail to pay their dues to the UN for political reasons (e.g., the U.S.) or for reasons of real or supposed economic hardship. The UN's budget situation was particularly bleak in 1999 when member states owed the UN almost $3 billion in dues: $1.7 billion for peacekeeping, almost $1.1 billion for the regular budget, and $148 million for international tribunals—notably, those established to deal with crimes committed in the former Yugoslavia and in Rwanda. In order to pay regular budget expenses, the UN often borrows from peacekeeping funds, which means that the UN has been unable to reimburse those countries that have provided peacekeeping troops and equipment. The amount the UN owes can reach into the hundreds of millions of dollars.[21]

The largest debtor has been the United States, which at one point owed the UN $1.67 billion, or two-thirds of the total due. The United States actually risked losing its vote in the General Assembly by not paying its $350 million bill by the end of 1999. According to Article 19 of the UN charter, if a country fails to pay its dues for two full years, it automatically loses its right to vote in the General Assembly. This predicament was resolved by a last-minute compromise. The U.S. pressure on the UN to reduce its contributions from 25 percent of the UN budget to 22 percent finally worked in early 2001. In September 2001, the United States finally agreed to pay its UN dues of $862 million, although as of 2002, the United States was still late in making its payments. Many Third World countries did not understand why the world's most prosperous country, in the midst of unprecedented economic growth, should demand making fewer UN contributions. But the compromise of allowing the United States to pay less at least resulted in the United States starting to pay.

The UN's Administrative Reforms   As controversial as the UN budget is, the bureaucracy of the United Nations may be even more so. We now turn to the politically charged, but unrelated, issues or mismanagement and membership in the Security Council—both of which have been subject to reform.

Examples of UN waste and mismanagement are not hard to find. For instance in the late 1990s, the Committee on Missing Persons in Cyprus hadn't found a single missing person in over 20 years. The Committee was kept alive in part because Cyprus has considerable influence in the U.S. Congress.[22] Also, in Bosnia in the early 1990s, cases occurred in which UN troops sold fuel and food on black markets. In one instance, a UN battalion commander (from Ukraine) accepted a Mercedes from a local Serbian leader, presumably as a bribe for favorable treatment. In 1995 a UN mid-level accountant made $84,000, a UN computer analyst made $111,500, and a UN assistant secretary-general made $140,256. By contrast, in 1995 a non-UN mid-level accountant made $41,965, a non-UN computer analyst made $56,835, and the New York mayor made only $130,000. Finally, in 1994 the UN inspector general, Karl Paschke, revealed that $16.8 million in outright fraud and egregious waste had occurred within the UN.[23]

It was primarily at the insistence of the United States that the UN cut down on waste, fraud, and mismanagement. From the U.S. perspective, reform essentially meant cutting back on UN staff resources and budgets. Throughout much of the 1990s, the unofficial policy of the United States toward the UN was to withhold its dues to the UN as a means to get the UN to clean house. Secretary-General Kofi Annan said in an interview in 1997 that after "50 years of existence, like all organizations, we've picked up some excess baggage that we are trying to shed."[24] By the end of the 1990s, the UN had in fact made major cuts in its labor force, and budget levels were frozen.

Another administration issue, reforming membership in the UN Security Council, has also been politicized for some time. The basic problem is that some countries that don't have permanent seats in the Security Council play significant roles in international relations and make important contributions to the United Nations. Japan and Germany in particular feel they should be among the permanent members. Granting these countries the special status, however, doesn't sit well with many other countries. The complaints center on the lack of representation of developing countries and on poor geographic distribution of permanent members (there is none from Latin America or Africa). One solution is to provide a permanent seat to a representative country from each region of the world. Three countries, one each from Africa, Asia, and Latin America, could then have a permanent seat. The seat could rotate among countries in each region. Another solution is, of course, no solution. Often when countries cannot agree among themselves on how to reform their joint organization, they make no changes at all. For the time being, the Security Council may remain with 15 members, only 5 of which are permanent.

In spite of the sometimes obvious flaws in the UN administration, public support for this IO remains strong around the world and in the United States. In the late 1990s for example, the vast majority of those polled in the United States— 72 percent—thought that the United States should not act alone to reduce international crises without the support of its allies; 57 percent supported U.S. involvement in UN peacekeeping.[25] Support today remains as strong.

Assessing the UN's Effectiveness

An assessment of the effectiveness of the UN often depends on one's expectations. The number of wars since the founding of the UN has increased, and violence is still a core component of world politics. Social and economic problems around the world seem worse today than ever before. Thus, one might get the impression that the UN is relatively ineffective regarding both its security and non-security missions.

However, one should not overlook the many contributions the UN has made, especially given the scarce political and financial resources devoted to it. In 2001, the UN and its secretary-general Kofi Annan were given the Nobel Peace Prize in recognition of their work for a more peaceful world. Annan was singled out for his commitment to human rights, his campaigns to take on new challenges such as the AIDS crisis and international terrorism, and his efforts to bring new life to the UN.[26] This was the first Nobel Prize for the UN as a whole, but the UN has received seven previous awards for individual programs. UN refugee operations offer a good example. In 1998 the United Nations High Commissioner for Refugees (UNHCR) estimated that more than 27 million people were refugees. This specialized UN agency, with a staff of about 5,500, has been awarded the Nobel Peace Prize twice (1954, 1981) for providing humanitarian assistance to millions of people around the world. The scope of the problems faced by UNHCR is often overwhelming if one takes into consideration the many natural disasters and political problems in Africa, and the turmoil in Central America, Asia, and elsewhere. The UNHCR has even come under severe criticism, including for its handling of the Kosovo crisis of 1999. Many people felt that the UN was ill-equipped to tackle the massive refugee emergency that developed from Serb advances in Kosovo and the NATO air strikes that followed. David Hannay, the former British ambassador to the UN, rejected this criticism by arguing that the UN actually did quite well considering its limited resources. "Despite an acute shortage of funds," he said, "it has escaped the attention of many that the UN did a remarkably good job. Extreme malnutrition and epidemics were avoided in the overcrowded refugee camps. . . . [I]t must be asked how many of the UN's failures and weaknesses were due to the unwillingness of member states to stump up resources and to draw operational conclusions from previous crises."[27]

This case raises a key point about the UN, and indeed about all IGOs: when member states essentially have full control over the actions of the international organization, *they should share both the credit and the blame for the successes and failures* of the IO. Moreover, the UN should not be blamed for every war that breaks out; that implies unrealistic expectations about UN capabilities.

If we can't expect the UN to prevent all wars from breaking out, what *can* we expect? The UN does have influence to foster peaceful relations between countries that previously were at war, thanks in part to its *legitimacy* among the nations of the world. Since 1945 the United Nations has been credited with negotiating over 170 peaceful settlements that have ended regional conflicts. One must also remember the UN's extensive measures to address vital social and economic problems facing the people of the world. For example, the UN Development Program has supported more than five thousand projects in the areas of agriculture, industry, education, and the environment. UNICEF offers another example. The UN's children organization spends about $800 million a year on immunization, health care, nutrition, and basic education in more than 135 countries. The World Health Organization has also been instrumental in helping to eliminate contagious diseases in many parts of the world. Polio, for example, is on the verge of being wiped out worldwide.[28] You will learn more about this organization's work in eradicating disease in Chapter 13.

Web Exploration

For more information on how the UN helps refugees, go to **www.ablongman.com/ duncan**.

What limits the ability of the UN to act much more forcefully is that it is an intergovernmental organization (IO) with member states who have very different interests. Remember, one of the important defining elements of *supranational* institutions is that they have significant powers or autonomous authority that is above the member states. The UN, however, is *intergovernmental* in part because the member states (especially the five permanent members of the Security Council) still retain almost all decision-making power over what the UN does. In fact, within the basic principles of the UN is the recognition of the primacy of the nation-state.

It is thus worthwhile reviewing the options that UN member states have, especially the large ones, for preventing the UN from doing something they don't like. First of all, General Assembly resolutions are nonbinding, meaning a country can ignore its resolutions. Second, in the case of the permanent members of the UN Security Council, a veto is sufficient to prevent the UN from using military force. Taking the first two points together produces our third point: only the Security Council may make decisions which are binding on all UN members. However, the permanent members can, of course, veto any decision they do not like. Fourth, member states can also withhold payment to the UN with a *de facto* "financial veto" that can prevent the UN from carrying out certain programs. This option is not available to UN members who make very small financial contributions to the UN.

What will be the role of the UN in the near future? The war in Iraq in 2003 may have permanently altered the role of the UN. Some observers argue that when large states wish to act against Security Council wishes—such as the United States waging war against Iraq—the UN becomes politically irrelevant. And there are some in the United States who demand ending UN membership altogether. The UN's demise, however, is unlikely. The UN will likely play a role similar to its role in the past. It will struggle along with scarce resources and a divisive set of member states to address security, and social and economic problems. The UN will remain an ambitious but restricted international organization. The UN's influence in the twenty-first century could also be limited by the fact that so many other actors are on the international stage, particularly NGOs (see Chapter 6).

What Is the European Union and How Does It Work?

While the UN is a *global* IGOs, many *regional* organizations exist as well. The main example of a regional IGO that we present in this chapter is the European Union. The other regional organizations—such as the Organization of American States or the Association of South East Asian Nations (ASEAN)—have much more limited scope.

The European Union is a unique phenomenon in the history of the world. What began primarily as an economic-oriented organization of six West European countries has evolved into the most complex and integrated set of institutions anywhere in the world.[29] The 15 wealthy, democratic Western European countries that now make up the EU have developed common trade and agricultural policies and have even established a single currency, the *euro*. Table 5.2 lists the current and potential members of the EU. The economic aspects of the EU make up the first of three pillars in the EU's framework. As part of a second pillar, a focus on *justice and home affairs,* the EU aspires to establish common policies to tackle immigration and drug trafficking problems and to cooperate more on border controls. And third, as part of the *common foreign and security policies* pillar, the EU seeks cooperation in foreign policy and military matters. The EU is also unique in that it has the only popularly elected transnational assembly in the world: the European Parliament.

TABLE 5.2 Membership in the European Union			
Current Members		**Countries That May Join Soon**	
Austria	Italy*	Poland	Slovenia
Belgium*	Luxembourg*	Hungary	Cyprus
Denmark	Netherlands*	Czech Republic	Latvia
Finland	Portugal	Estonia	Slovakia
France*	Spain	Lithuania	Malta
Germany*	Sweden	**Notably Missing**	
Greece	United Kingdom (Britain)	Switzerland	
Ireland		Norway	

* The founding six member states.

Functionalism
A theory that states can promote cooperation by working together in selected areas (such as coal and steel industries) and that the ties they build will compel them to cooperate in other areas as well.

Thus, no other IO can match the EU in terms of the depth of its institutional structure or the scope of policies under its jurisdiction.

The Main European Union Institutions

The functioning of the European Union is based on a shifting balance among the 15 member states and intergovernmental and supranational actors. Five institutions together handle most of the EU's affairs. In some respects, some of these may appear to act like the main institutions in a typical country that has judicial, executive, and legislative branches. Appearances, however, can be deceiving. We will address each of these institutions in turn:

- The European Council
- The Council of Ministers
- The European Parliament
- The European Commission
- The European Court of Justice

Of these, the two that are primarily *intergovernmental* are the European Council and the Council of Ministers. Let's now take a quick look at each.

The European Council The European Council is a meeting that consists primarily of the HOGS (the *heads of government and state*) and foreign ministers. Every six months (or more frequently if there is a crisis), the leaders of the 15 member states gather to discuss major political issues and practices. This is really the only time that national politicians (prime ministers and presidents) *directly* affect the direction of the European Union.

The Council of Ministers Responsible for day-to-day operations of the EU, the *Council of Ministers* is known more formally as the Council of the European Union. This legislative body has considerable influence because it has final say on most important pieces of EU legislation—although its powers have weakened over time, as we will discuss shortly. The Council of Ministers is made up of at least one minister from each of the 15 member states; thus, each meeting should have at least 15 people. In actuality, many "councils" exist, depending on the policy area. For example when the topic involves monetary policy, a council will consist primarily of

HISTORICAL PERSPECTIVE

The Origins and Rationale of the European Union

After centuries of warfare between empires and states, why did European countries create the most comprehensive set of international institutions of all time? We can offer five main reasons for why traditionally aggressive countries chose to work together. The first three are primarily economic; the others are more political and military in nature. First, European cooperation began in the late 1940s with the need to rebuild war-torn economies. Many European countries realized that going it alone would not be sufficient to transform their struggling economies. Assistance from the U.S. Marshall Plan was very helpful in this regard. Second, a lesson from the depression era and from World War II was that when states create significant barriers to trade, economic conditions worsen and international relations become more tense. Thus, the Europeans sought to lower internal trade barriers and enhance economic competition. Third, the six founding EU member states, as well as the later ones, also recognized the benefits of *economies of scale*. That is, they saw the advantages of combining their resources in order to become more competitive internationally. Recently, this issue has become particularly important in terms of competition with the United States, Japan, and the newly industrializing countries (NICs) of Asia. Fourth, a more cohesive Western Europe was viewed as being better able to prevent the spread of communism, which was threatening on two fronts. In the 1950s Western Europe was concerned about an invasion by the Soviet Union and its allies. In addition, communist parties had made strong inroads in the *domestic* politics of some European countries, notably France and Italy. During World War II, French and Italian communists had fought heroically against the enemy, and the postwar electorate rewarded them with many votes. Fifth, in the immediate post–World War II period, many feared a resurgent Germany—the country that had been fully or partially responsible for three major wars in Europe in two generations (1870–1945). By integrating

Germany economically and militarily into the EU, it was hoped that German militarism and World War III would be less likely to occur.

Jean Monnet and Robert Schumann—considered the fathers of the European Union—and others recognized these factors and believed that a cooperative and peaceful Europe could be built step by step. They supported the notion of **functionalism,** which later inspired many supporters of European integration.[30] According to functionalism, a shared transnational technical problem—such as the need to rebuild the war-torn industries of Europe—can lead to the formation of common institutions that perform important economic, social, and technical functions to solve the problem. If these institutions succeed, the theory goes, it puts inevitable pressure on states to yield sovereignty. The early decisions and experiences in one functional context were expected to "spill over" into other functional areas regardless of territorial borders, eventually involving interest groups, parties, and greater interbureaucratic contact.[31] In turn, political leaders would begin to press for a strengthening and expansion of the functions of supranational institutions to perform those tasks.[32] As a result, it was predicted, European states, industries, and individuals would shift their political loyalties and look increasingly to the EU.

One of the most important first steps in the creation of the EU was the establishment of the *European Coal and Steel Community* (ECSC). Created to manage the commercially and militarily important coal and steel industries, the ECSC also showed that the French and Germans could actually get along. German and Italian motivation for supporting the ECSC was to demonstrate to the international community that the two states could be trusted partners. The ECSC was also important because it created a set of institutions that would later evolve into the institutions of the EU that we know today: the Council of Ministers, the Court of Justice, the High Authority (today's Commission), and a Common

(continued)

(continued)

Assembly (today's European Parliament). The ECSC thus taught its member states, some with historically deep animosities, that they could cooperate in a vital sector and that the new international institutions with independent political power could function to the benefit of Europe.

The ECSC did have its problems (such as member states failing to abide by the High Authority and the failure to establish a true single market in coal and steel), but the ECSC nevertheless encouraged the formation of the EU. With the signing of the Treaty of Rome in 1957, France, Germany, Italy, and the Benelux countries (Belgium, the Netherlands, and Luxembourg) formed three European "communities": the European Atomic Energy Community (Euratom), the European Defense Community (EDC),

and the European Economic Community (EEC). Unlike the EEC, both Euratom and the EDC proved to be ineffective, which is one reason why many old timers continue to call the European Union the "EEC" or "European Economic Community" for short.

Membership in the EU has increased since 1957. In 1973, it grew from the original six members to nine with the admission of Britain, Ireland, and Denmark. In the 1980s the Mediterranean countries of Greece (1981), Spain, and Portugal (1986) joined. Austria, Finland, and Sweden were admitted in 1995. Although not technically considered an expansion of the EU, East Germany became part of the EU in 1990 after it merged with West Germany. Thus, the EU now has 15 member states. Poland, Hungary, and the Czech Republic as well as several other East Central European countries, and Malta and Cyprus, could join soon.

one finance minister from each member state. When farm policies are up for discussion, the council will consist of agricultural ministers. What helps give the Council of Ministers its intergovernmental flavor is that the ministers' main responsibility is to the *home government first*. The Swedish fisheries minister, for example, tries to push forcefully for what is best for Sweden at the fisheries council meeting.

Leadership in the Council of Ministers rotates every six months among the member states. The country that holds the "council presidency" at any time is responsible for providing overall direction of the EU agenda but also for chairing all the council meetings. The six-month period was chosen in part because it allows many countries the opportunity to lead council activities. The time frame, however, is too short for any one country to dominate the others. A drawback, of course, is that the progress made by one council presidency may not be maintained in the subsequent presidency. This often happens because the country taking over the council presidency has a different agenda. The EU tries to get around this problem by having a *troika*, that is, cooperation among the current, past, and in-coming council presidencies. In the first half of 2002, Spain had the council presidency while Denmark had it during the second half. In 2003 the presidency is split between Greece and Italy. In 2004 Ireland gets the first half and the Netherlands the second.

The Commission Most of the executive power in the EU resides with the *Commission*. It is made up of 20 officials from all the member states, and each commissioner is responsible for a different policy area, such as foreign policy, agriculture, fisheries, relations with Third World countries, and so on. The responsibility of Commission members is to Europe first; this contrasts with the Council of Ministers, whose members push what's best for their own country first. Like all EU institutions, the membership of the Commission is very international. What are the functions of the Commission?

- The most important role of the Commission is *proposing legislation*. By law, the Council of Ministers cannot pass legislation unless it is proposed by the Commission.

- Another important function of the Commission is ensuring that treaties are being followed.
- The Commission also plays a key role in ensuring that EU legislation is implemented. Most of the policy implementation is handled by the member states (because they have the personnel and resources, and the Commission does not), but the Commission oversees the entire process.
- The Commission is a key player in the EU's budget process.
- An additional Commission function is to help varying sides (be they governments, companies, interest groups, or individuals) reach compromises when they have a dispute.
- The Commission often mediates differences between the other institutions of the EU.
- The Commission represents the EU as a negotiating unit in trade negotiations such as those with the WTO.

For more information on the international makeup of the EU Commission, go to **www.ablongman.com/ duncan**.

All in all, the Commission has enormous responsibilities and is viewed by the public as the key supranational institution in the EU. This perception has positive and negative consequences for the Commission as we will see.

The European Parliament   The legislative responsibilities of the EU are shared between two bodies: the Council of Ministers and the European Parliament, to which we now turn. The 626-seat *European Parliament* (EP) is the most visible part of the EU to average citizens. Members of the EP (or MEPs) are the only EU officials for whom citizens actually get a chance to vote, which makes the EP a unique body. The EP is also unique in that it is organized in ideological or party units called groups. There is a Socialist party group, a Christian Democratic group (EPP), the Green group, the Liberal, Democratic, and Reformist group, and others. In each of these party groupings are citizens of different EU countries who are supposed to speak to their *party group's agenda rather than to their country's national interests.* By contrast, the Council, as we have seen, is based on national representation first and functional area of expertise second. MEPs are supposed to be loyal to their *party ideology and Europe first.*

Some powers of the EP are similar to those of national legislatures.

- The EP provides an arena for airing the concerns of EU citizens.
- It issues oral and written questions to the Council and Commission.
- It clarifies, criticizes, and reviews proposed legislation.
- It can also dissolve and censure the Commission with a two-thirds vote. The EP almost dissolved the Commission in early 1999 (because of mismanagement and corruption), but the Commission, under pressure, chose to resign instead.
- The EP also plays an important role in EU budgetary matters.

The EP differs from national parliaments in many important respects. The most important difference is that the EP is the weakest of the EU institutions. Since its founding, the advice of the EP has often been ignored by Council and Commission members, in large part because the EP's opinions were not legally binding. Another important difference, as we have seen, is that the EP's political parties have members from different countries. The two largest political groups are the Christian Democrats (i.e., the European People's Party) and the Socialists, whose members come from every EU member state. The Green political group consists of MEPs from Germany, the Netherlands, and France, among others. The EP also differs from national parliaments because it does not have a fixed location.

For more information on European Parliament elections, go to **www.ablongman.com/ duncan**.

MEPs (and researchers of the EP) have to travel between Brussels (Belgium), Strasbourg (France), and Luxembourg. This situation is both costly and time consuming. A final difference is that EP business is conducted in eleven different languages: Danish, Dutch, English, Finnish, French, German, Greek, Italian, Portuguese, Spanish, and Swedish. The language challenge will worsen when the EU adds new members from Poland, Hungary, the Czech Republic and so on.

As noted, compared to the other EU institutions, the EP remains relatively weak. But its influence has grown steadily as EU officials and the public have recognized the need for more democratic input into how the EU functions. The EP has gained influence using pre existing powers. The landmark decision by the Commission to resign in early 1999 reflected the EP's determination to force the Commission to acknowledge and fix problems of mismanagement, corruption, and nepotism. When the Commission did not address these problems, the EP began proceedings to throw out the entire Commission (because it couldn't impeach individual commissioners). New EP power has more frequently come from new treaties. For example, the Maastricht Treaty called for a new co-decision (legislative) procedure. This procedure allows the EP three different places to affect legislation and make the EP an equal with the Council of Ministers. The Amsterdam Treaty, which took effect in 1999, made the EP the legislative equal with the Council of Ministers in certain policy areas.

The European Court of Justice   The EU's judicial branch helps make the EU unique among all international organizations. World War II taught many Europeans that international relations should be driven by law, not by power. The Europeans also came to understand that common policies (in agriculture, coal, and steel, for example) needed a common legal framework. As a result, the EU has built up an impressive body of legal documents, although without a constitution in the American sense. EU "law" consists of treaties and acts that have accumulated since the founding of the EU in 1957.

At the apex of the EU's legal system is the *European Court of Justice (ECJ)* made up of 15 judges. The ECJ is assisted by 9 advocates general. They are all appointed by the member states and serve renewable six-year terms. The EU's legal system also consists of the Court of First Instance, the Court of Auditors, and a parliamentary ombudsman (who hears complaints made against EU institutions).

The ECJ is the ultimate arbiter of laws made by the EU. As with rulings from the U.S. Supreme Court, there are no appeals from ECJ rulings. The ECJ's rulings are binding on citizens of the EU as well as on the governments of the EU. When EU law conflicts with the laws of a national government, EU law takes precedence.

The ECJ is also more than a toothless body of judges unable to impose their will. Member states or companies that do not comply with ECJ rulings can be fined. Sometimes these fines can be rather large. In 1997 for example, Germany and Italy were fined by the ECJ for not complying with EU environmental legislation. For not complying with laws protecting wild birds, groundwater, and surface water, Germany was fined $31,420 and had to pay about $15,000 each day it delayed implementing EU law. Italy did not implement legislation on waste and radiation protection and had to pay a fine of about $125,000 plus $100,000 for each day it delayed.[33] When countries create such an international legal structure, it of course implies that member states have given up a lot of sovereignty. To put this in perspective, consider the following question. Would the United States be willing to accept such an arrangement, where the United States, its states, and its companies agreed to abide by an international legal body when the international legal body rules against the U.S. constitution? Remember this question as you explore the case study on the International Criminal Court at the end of the chapter.

How Voting Matters in the EU and IOs in General

Voting in the European Union is just as important as it is in any country. There are also some interesting parallels with voting in the United Nations. Since the Council of Ministers often has final say on most EU legislation proposed by the Commission, its voting system takes on considerable importance. As you have learned with UN Security Council voting, unanimity voting means that if just one country vetoes a proposal to use military force, the UN cannot use military force. Unanimity voting is also used in the Council of Ministers in a limited number of circumstances when a member state fears its vital national interest is at stake. It is used, for example, on decisions to add new countries to the EU. Just as with the five permanent members of the UN's Security Council, each member state of the EU has veto power when the unanimity voting rule is used.

Over time however, EU member states have come to realize that too many vetoes were hurting the ability of the EU to get important legislation passed. The problem was summed up nicely by former Belgian Prime Minister Jean-Luc Dehaene in late 1999: "If you keep unanimity, you have immobility."[34] As a result, the EU has tried to use other voting rules for a growing number of policy issues. Sometimes, simple **majority voting** is used. A simple majority is achieved with support from 50 percent of the countries plus one more (that is, 50 percent + 1).

The most common voting rule, however, is **qualified majority voting (QMV).** Under the QMV rule, the larger countries have more votes than the smaller countries. Ten votes, for example, go to big countries like Britain and Germany, while Spain gets 8 votes; others get 5, 4, or 3; only 2 go to Luxembourg. There are a total of 87 votes, and for a legislative measure to *pass*, 62 votes, or 71 percent of the total, is needed. (In a variation of QMV, in certain circumstances, 54 votes must be achieved by 8 states.) Why does QMV matter so much? The key aspect of QMV compared to unanimity voting is that it forces states to compromise in order for them to get what they want. The box The View from the Decision Room: Why Different Voting Systems Matter, on p. 208, contrasts the differing goals and outcomes of these two voting systems and summarizes the three major voting methods and their implications.

Qualified Majority Voting (QMV)
Associated with the European Union, a voting rule in which the larger countries have more votes than the smaller countries and no country has a veto.

The Future of the European Union

If one plots the trend of political and economic integration in EU history, one might get the impression that we will soon see a "United States of Europe," or "U.S.E." Since its founding in 1957, the EU has integrated more and more. An increasing number of policy areas are within the EU's jurisdiction, including monetary policy, and others are being addressed (e.g., common foreign and security policies). In addition, EU decision making is occurring more often at the supranational level (e.g., more power to the European Parliament and more use of QMV). One scenario for a U.S.E. envisions the following governmental arrangement:

- Judiciary: European Court of Justice
- Executive: Commission
- Legislative: Council of Ministers (similar to the U.S. Senate) and the European Parliament (similar to the U.S. House of Representatives)

THE VIEW FROM   the Decision Room

Why Different Voting Systems Matter

In IGOs, states behave differently when voting rules change. In addition, some voting systems are "better" than others if the IGO wants to get work accomplished. In general, for an IGO to get things done, it may need to have voting rules that limit na-

tional control. Think of voting systems as falling along a continuum, with ease of decision making at one end and safeguarding of national sovereignty at the other.

Consider the following diagram.

Voting Method	Implications for Sovereignty	Implications for Efficiency	Benefits for Big vs. Small Countries	Used by (examples)
Unanimity Voting	Best voting system for maintaining sovereignty.	Since every member has a veto, it is often hard to get things accomplished.	Since this is the best system for maintaining sovereignty, it is helpful to small as well as big states.	• UN Security Council • EU Council of Ministers • Organization for Economic Cooperation and Development
Majority Voting	Not very good for preserving national sovereignty.	Very good, since it takes many countries to vote "no."	Small countries tend to benefit most because they are much more numerous.	• UN General Assembly • EU Council of Ministers
Qualified Majority Voting	Not as good as unanimity voting but better than majority voting.	Not as efficient as majority voting but better than unanimity voting.	Big countries are given more votes, but small states may actually come out the winner (e.g., compare Luxembourg's population with Germany's.	• EU Council of Ministers • The IMF and World Bank (based not on population but on level of financial contribution)

In support of such a plan, Joschka Fischer, the German foreign minister, proposed in April 2000 the creation of a European federation with a directly elected president and parliament sharing real executive and legislative powers. Such a scenario is possible in the future, but it is hard to say under what circumstances it will actually happen. First, one should be cautious about assuming that the EU will inevitably "progress" with one policy area spilling over into another until all policies are handled by the EU. Historically, Europeans have always been reluctant to give up national sovereignty to the EU. Many Europeans are very unhappy about the

EU Members Britain and France Disagree Over the Health of Imported Food: Amid increasing integration among European countries, disputes still surface over a variety of issues. In this picture, EU members Britain and France disagree over the safety of imported meat and produce.

powers that have shifted from their own governments to the so-called Eurocrats in Brussels, Belgium (the quasi capital of the EU). It is thus possible that the integration of EU countries will reach a certain level and then stop. Another possibility is that the EU could experience a backlash from people unhappy with EU influence and from people demanding that national governments reclaim some of their powers. Nationalist feelings run deep in Europe, and people easily identify more with their own country than they do with the complicated and seemingly remote institutions of the European Union.

Second, when the Commission was forced to resign in 1999 over corruption and incompetence, the member states became increasingly concerned about granting it more powers. Their reluctance undermines the idea of "the Commission as executive branch." Third, even though the European Parliament has gained considerable influence since the founding of the EU, there is still significant resistance to making it a truly effective legislative body. A fourth point is related to the third: the EU has exhibited and will continue to exhibit a serious legitimacy problem. To put it bluntly, the EU does not have very democratic institutions. It is often mentioned with irony that if the EU were a state and applied to join the European Union, it would be turned down on the grounds that it was not a democracy.[35] As you know, the only democratically elected institution in the EU is the EP, but the EP does not have much relative clout. If the EU can't resolve this so-called *democratic deficit*, the European public may be unwilling to grant more powers to the European Union as a whole.

Finally, the EU often does not act as a coherent organization. See the box The View from Brussels: A Constitutional Convention to Remake the EU, on p. 211. It is sometimes easy to forget that the EU consists of 15 countries, and that those

* Eastern *Länder* joined with German unification in 1990

FIGURE 5.2

Europe: Distinguishing EU Members, Applicant States, Date of Joining/Application, Non-EU States

SOURCE: *European Commission from "Europe" Survey,* The Economist, *October 23, 1999, p. 4.*

15 voices do not always say the same thing. Differences might increase as the EU widens to include more countries (recall Figure 5.2). The EU institutions also compete with one another. The Commission may be at odds with the Council, whose ministers represent the often parochial interests of their home country. Perhaps most important of all, the EU has had trouble establishing policies in critical areas such as defense. To take two examples of this failure, the EU responded incoherently in the early 1990s as the former Yugoslavia disintegrated, and then later exhibited similar divisions when the crisis in Kosovo grew in 1999.

THE VIEW FROM   Brussels

A Constitutional Convention to Remake the EU

From 2002 to 2003, the EU is undergoing a fundamental reevaluation of how it will function in the future. A constitutional convention is underway to address several existing shortcomings of the EU, such as complicated voting procedures and a lack of democratic accountability. Giuliano Amato, vice-chairman of EU's constitutional convention, recently gave a rather unflattering description of how the various EU institutions function. In calling for reform, Amato called it "a crazy system, totally inefficient." He proposes, among other things, an EU president "who remains long enough not to change the priorities every six months."[36] Other proposals envision national governments dealing with foreign and defense issues while the EU Commission handles the day-to-day operations of government. Some countries want the states to have more power, while others want the supranational institutions (e.g., the European Parliament) to have more power. In some ways, a core issue of the constitutional convention—how much power should the states have compared to the central (EU) institutions—is very similar to the debate among the founders of the United States between the antifederalists (supporters of strong states) and federalists (supports of a relatively strong central government).

The EU's constitutional convention is also designed to prepare the EU for up to ten new member countries. Issues on the convention's negotiating table include how much power the Commission and European Parliament should have, how the EU will maintain financial stability with the inclusion of ten relatively poor countries from Central and Eastern Europe, and who should control the Council of Ministers and for how long (remember, it currently has a six-month rotating Council presidency). Smaller but no less important issues are also being debated—such as how agriculture policy will be adjusted with the inclusion of several new, agriculturally dependent countries. The EU will probably look quite different in ten years, but much will depend on the debates taking place today in Brussels and the national capitals across Western *and Eastern* Europe.

Thus, it is probably safe to conclude that the EU won't, any time soon, look like a "United States of Europe," but it is also unlikely that the EU will backslide much or at all. In other words, it is unlikely that the Europeans will decide to give up on the cooperative arrangements that are already in place.

Comparing the EU with NAFTA and Other Regional Trading Blocs

The European Union is the most highly developed regional trading bloc in the world. No other trade bloc has a common parliament; few have a common external tariff; and none is seriously contemplating a common currency or common defense policies. Because of the highly integrated nature of the EU, it is sometimes described as having "deep regionalism." By contrast, the vast majority of the world's trade blocs are more intergovernmental than they are supranational. The North American Free Trade Area, consisting of the United States, Canada, and Mexico, demonstrates this point nicely. NAFTA is a regional trading arrangement—often referred to as trade bloc—that seeks to facilitate the free flow of goods and investment across the borders of the three member states. Canada, the United States, and Mexico have already eliminated or plan to eliminate hundreds of barriers (including tariff and quota barriers) to trade as part of the NAFTA agreement. Each country expects to gain from membership in NAFTA, although not necessarily in the same way.

Like the EU, NAFTA has a set of institutions and an international regulatory body. NAFTA also has a Commission for Environmental Cooperation that grants individuals the right to bring cases against corporations and countries that fail to keep the environmental regulations of the treaty. In addition, NAFTA shares with the EU similar rules that apply to all members. Mexico, the United States, and Canada, for example, have agreed to bring their commercial standards and environmental legislation into harmony so that a truck licensed in Mexico and going from Mexico to Canada will presumably meet safety and emissions standards in all three countries.

Nevertheless, NAFTA and many other regional trading arrangements around the world differ in many ways from the European Union. First, as noted earlier, NAFTA is intergovernmental in nature, although it has the possibility of becoming more supranational if it succeeds in sychronizing more standards and regulations. Second, the EU has many common policies such as agriculture, monetary policy, social policy, regional policy, and environmental policy; NAFTA does not. A third difference between NAFTA and the EU is that NAFTA has no elected assembly. Fourth, as we have seen, the EU's judicial branch has considerable influence in the affairs of member states; NAFTA does not have its own judicial branch per se. Fifth, unlike NAFTA, the EU has a common external tariff (CET).[37] With a CET a company exporting to the EU faces the same tariff barrier no matter where in the EU the product is shipped. Under NAFTA, the United States, Canada, and Mexico maintain their own unique tariff rates. In short, the EU influences the politics and economics of its members much more than does NAFTA. More will be said about NAFTA and trade blocs in Chapter 11.

One of the more interesting recent developments related to regional groups like the EU or NAFTA is the formation in the summer of 2002 of the African Union (AU). The AU replaces the 39-year-old Organization of African Unity (OAU) and takes on a very ambitious agenda: to replicate many of the features found in the European Union. The AU is to have a parliament, a security council, and a peacekeeping force with the authority to intervene in national conflicts. The AU also hopes to create a court of justice, an African Monetary Fund, an African Central Bank and even a single currency. Supporters of the AU deliberately chose the EU as a model in order to promote democracy, the rule of law and respect for human rights. Whether the AU will succeed in any of these endeavors is hard to say at this point. But for the first time, many former OAU members seem willing to give up some of their sovereignty—as EU members have—in exchange for the eventual benefits of international cooperation. The commitment toward democracy is an encouraging sign for a continent with a history of dictatorships and military rule.

What Are the Global Financial and Trade Organizations?

The three most important international financial and trade intergovernmental organizations in the world are the World Bank, the International Monetary Fund (IMF), and the World Trade Organization (WTO). Each has a particular function, but they are all designed to help manage the international political economy. Shortly after World War II, most of the world's major states felt that a national strategy of "going it alone" in an anarchic world was ultimately destructive. Instead, states sought cooperative ways to rebuild themselves after the destruction of the war, and to build institutions and long-term rules that could guide their international political and economic life into the distant future. Britain and especially the United States took the lead in setting up IMF, the World Bank, and WTO (formerly known as the General Agreement on Tariffs and Trade, or GATT).

The International Monetary Fund and the World Bank

Both the IMF and the World Bank (formally known as the International Bank for Reconstruction and Development) are part of the United Nations framework. Although the roles of these two organizations have increasingly overlapped, their missions have traditionally been quite distinct. The IMF is responsible for overseeing the entire international monetary system by *promoting exchange rate stability* and orderly exchange relations among its member countries. The goal of the World Bank, by contrast, is to *promote the economic development of the world's poorer countries*. It assists these countries through long-term financing of a variety of development projects.[38] We will reserve a more detailed explanation of the functions of the IMF and World Bank for Chapter 11. For now however, it is appropriate to discuss the relationship between these institutions and the countries of the world.

In many ways the IMF and World Bank have played a positive role in helping maintain a smooth international political economy since World War II. Like the UN and EU, however, both the World Bank and IMF have had their share of political problems. The aims of these organizations may sound commendable, but not everyone is happy with them. One general criticism is that they are tools used by the Northern industrialized countries to dominate the poorer countries of the South. The World Bank, for example, typically requires countries receiving its loans to "fix" their economic problems, which often leads governments to cut back on programs that help the poor. Other common complaints include the inability of these institutions to meet the demands of serious crises like the Asian financial crisis that began in 1997, the failure to address the role of women in the development policies of Third World countries, and the disregard for the environment in favor of economic growth.

The World Trade Organization

Another of the main IOs to evolve in the immediate post–World War II era was the General Agreement on Tariffs and Trade (GATT).[39] GATT was later transformed in the 1990s into the World Trade Organization. GATT facilitated the smooth functioning of trade rules by creating a permanent forum where countries and companies could discuss issues that concerned them. This forum was (and is) multilateral in nature, that is, many countries were involved in order to avoid the more cumbersome and historically protectionist unilateral or bilateral discussions. GATT, and later the WTO, thus came to be associated with a *multilateral approach* to international trade.

Another means of establishing a productive global economic environment was fostering freedom of trade by the systematic and long-term strategy of lowering barriers to trade. GATT focused at first on the most serious and common barriers to trade: tariffs and quotas. For nearly two decades (the 1950s and 1960s), thanks in part to GATT, the world experienced a historically unprecedented economic boom. By the early 1970s, GATT could confidently say that its basic aims had been achieved. Although it faced rising protectionism after that, it still had played a significant role in freeing up international trade. Between 1950 and 1996 for example, world exports rose 16 times and world output rose 5 times. World export of manufactures rose 31 times, while manufacturing output rose by a factor of 9.[40] In addition, GATT had only 23 countries when it was founded in 1947; now WTO membership stands at 132 with 31 countries waiting to join.

The WTO was given many new responsibilities in the early 1990s, making it potentially a much more influential IO than GATT. The WTO has an expanded scope of responsibility that includes not just goods but services as well (e.g., such things as restaurants, hotels, travel agencies, banking, insurance, intellectual property rights, advertising, and data processing). Another major new development in the WTO is a much more effective and timely *dispute-resolution mechanism*—that is, a more efficient way for companies and countries to resolve their problems quickly and in an orderly way. Finally, and in connection with the dispute-resolution mechanism, the WTO is being given greater powers to enforce its own rules. Like GATT, the WTO can rule against a country for unfair trade practices, but now the WTO's ruling cannot be negated by the offending country's veto of retaliatory action.

As individuals, NGOs, and states have come to realize the influence of trade on many other aspects of society, opposition to the WTO has grown. In late 1999 leaders from WTO member states met in Seattle to set an agenda for a new round of trade liberalization. However, massive demonstrations—some violent—marred the atmosphere of the talks, which ended in failure. The combination of extremely complex trade issues, member states who failed to agree on key issues, and some states that went to Seattle unwilling to compromise all contributed to derailing the talks. After Seattle, most WTO members expressed optimism about furthering the WTO's agenda, but opposition to the WTO is likely to be stronger in the future. You will learn more about all these issues in Chapter 11.

How Does the Organization of Petroleum Exporting Countries (OPEC) Differ from Other IGOs?

Thus far we have discussed IOs whose membership is *global* in scope (like the UN), IOs that are *regional* in scope (like the EU and NAFTA), and *multipurpose* IOs (such as the UN and the EU). The UN, for example, is an IO that addresses a huge number of political, social, economic, and security issues. The European Union is primarily an economic organization, but we have seen how it has evolved to include an equally impressive number of policy areas like those of the UN. The WTO, World Bank, and IMF were designed for more limited financial and economic jobs, but their membership is globally widespread. The final category of intergovernmental organization discussed in this chapter includes IOs created to handle *single* issues. Usually the single issue is a commodity like oil or coffee. Note that *companies* sometimes band together to manage trade in one or more goods. These are **oligopolies** and not IGOs, because their members are companies, not states. In this section of the chapter, we offer an overview of the world's most important single-issue IO: the Organization of Petroleum Exporting Countries (OPEC). We will explore its origins, its powers, and why its influence in the international political economy (IPE) fluctuates over time.

OPEC is *a cartel* built around the single commodity of oil, and it does not aspire to develop the complex web of policies and institutions that we saw with other IOs. The central aim of OPEC is to manage the international trade in oil so that

Oligopoly
A limited number of companies that can control most of the supply—and hence price—of one or more products.

HISTORICAL PERSPECTIVE

The Origins of OPEC's Power

How did OPEC gain such an important role in the international political economy? To answer this question, we must take a quick historical look at the oil industry. Until the early 1970s, the international oil industry was dominated by seven major western multinational corporations, known as the *Seven Sisters*. These included Standard Oil of New Jersey (now Exxon), Gulf (Chevron), Standard Oil of California (Chevron), Mobil, Anglo-Dutch (Royal Dutch-Shell), Texaco, and British Petroleum. The countries that hosted these Seven Sisters, however, resented the fact that the foreign oil companies were benefiting from oil profits more than they were. As part of an effort to gain greater national control over domestic oil production, these oil producing countries eventually took control of the industry from the American and European oil-producing companies by creating OPEC. In the early 1970s, OPEC countries were able to band together so effectively that the United States and other major industrial powers were forced to pay almost what-ever OPEC decided to charge for oil. OPEC members had created an *oligopoly* situation in the world oil industry. Oligopolies are similar to monopolies in that they can control most of the supply—and hence the price—of one or more products. As a result of OPEC's oligopolistic power, two so-called oil shocks hit the world in the 1970s. In the first, in 1973, OPEC sent oil prices sky-rocketing from $3 to $12 dollars a barrel. A second oil price shock came in 1978, and it seemed that OPEC was clearly in the driver's seat in this most critical of economic sectors.

OPEC's enormous influence in the 1970s did not last, however. Through the 1980s and especially the 1990s, things got so bad for OPEC that by 1999, it was losing $65 billion in revenue as a result of lower oil prices.[43] It wasn't until prices seemed to hit rock-bottom in 1998–1999 that OPEC finally began to work more effectively and to play a more prominent role again. As a result, world oil prices more than doubled within a twelve-month period.[44]

---

prices remain stable—and preferably high. Its members are countries: Saudi Arabia, Iraq, Iran, United Arab Emirates, Venezuela, Kuwait, Libya, Nigeria, Algeria, Indonesia, and Qatar. Two important points are worth making related to OPEC's membership. First, most of OPEC's members come from the region of the world where there is, by far, the most oil. Europe has only about 19 billion barrels of proven oil reserves, Asia 44 billion, North America 64.4 billion, Africa almost 75 billion, South and Central America over 95 billion, while the Middle East has over 683.5 billion barrels of proven oil reserves.[41] Second, it is important to remember that, contrary to most people's impressions, OPEC is not just made up of Middle Eastern countries—Venezuela and Indonesia are the obvious stand outs.

Even though OPEC may look like a purely economic organization, its activities are very political indeed. In general, the international oil industry impacts the international political economy in at least three ways. First, it wields significant power in a world dependent on oil. OPEC countries supply more than 40 percent of the world's oil and possess about 78 percent of the world's total proven crude oil reserves.[42] Second, developments in the oil industry have had profound influences on the relationship between the industrialized First World and the less developed countries of Third World (see Chapter 12). Third, the extensive use of oil among the developed countries and increasingly among the developing countries has

Web Exploration

For more information on the global flow of oil, go to **www.ablongman.com/ duncan**.

TABLE 5.3 Oil Import Dependence			
Country/Region	1997	2010*	2020*
North America	44.6	52.4	58.0
Europe	52.5	67.2	79.0
Pacific	88.8	91.5	92.4
OECD**	54.3	63.3	70.0
China	22.3	61.0	76.9
East Asia	53.7	70.5	80.7
India	57.4	85.2	91.6
Rest of South Asia	87.2	95.1	96.1

Oil import dependence is defined as the ratio of net imports over total primary oil demand.

*Forecast

**OECD: the countries of the Organization of Economic Cooperation and Development, most of the world's rich, democratic, industrialized countries.

SOURCE: International Energy Agency, in David Buchan, "Reliance on Middle East poses problems," *Financial Times*, February 1, 2002.

caused serious environmental problems. This aspect of the oil industry will be discussed in Chapter 13.

What accounts for the fluctuations in OPEC's political and economic clout? A satisfactory answer to this question requires a look at the issue from both the *supply* side and the *demand* side. First, from the supply side, after the 1970s new oil was discovered in several parts of the world. In addition, non-OPEC countries helped push global supply levels to the point where prices started to drop. For example, oil production in Mexico, China, Egypt, Malaysia, Britain, Norway, and other countries all helped increase global supply. Today even more oil is expected to be pumped from wells in the Caspian Sea and other locations around the world, including Eastern Siberia, the Gulf of Mexico, Canada's tar sands deposits, and Venezuela's Orinco Belt.[45] With the new non-OPEC sources of oil, OPEC's influence has diminished. For example, in early 2002, output from Brazil, Russia, Canada, and other non-OPEC countries reduced OPEC's hold on the global oil market to 32 percent of the world supply, the lowest level since the mid-1980s.[46] Table 5.3 lists the oil import dependence of different regions. Figure 5.3 illustrates the estimated proven oil reserves by country. In the first graph, note the vastly superior reserves held by Saudi Arabia. Not surprisingly, Saudi Arabia is the most influential member of OPEC. In the pie chart of Figure 5.3, notice that the Middle East is the most important location of the world's oil reserves. This matters, of course, because the Middle East is often the most politically turbulent part of the world.

Second, technological developments in the oil industry have made it much easier to extract oil for less cost. In the past 20 years, the cost of finding and developing oil wells has dropped from $20 a barrel to about $6 a barrel. During this time, the overall cost of producing oil has fallen by half, to under $4 a barrel.[47] So, with lower extraction and production costs, oil deposits that were technically out of reach in the past are now being tapped.

Third, by the 1990s, most OPEC members were pumping out more oil than they were supposed to (thus increasing supply). This occurred in part because most of the world's oil-rich countries were struggling economically. The economies of the

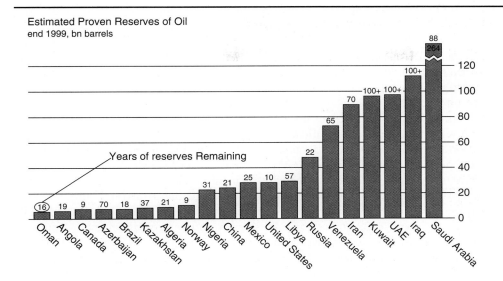

Estimated Proven Reserves of Oil
end 1999, bn barrels

FIGURE 5.3
**Estimated Proven
Reserves of Oil**

SOURCE: *From "BP Amoco
Statistical Review of
World Energy, 2000."
The Economist,
July 15, 2000.*

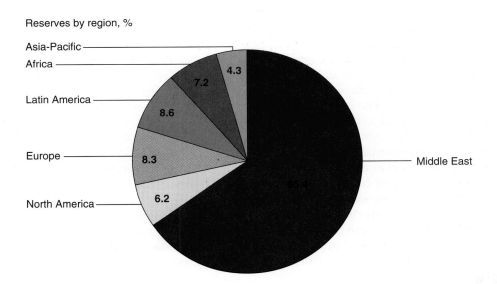

Reserves by region, %

OPEC countries relied—and continue to rely—almost exclusively on oil; for many, oil accounts for 75 percent of their national incomes. In the case of Kuwait, over 90 percent of its revenues were coming from oil. Even Saudi Arabia, the leading oil producer in the world and the political leader of OPEC, faced debt problems and economic recession. In 1997 for example, Saudi Arabia earned about $45 billion from oil exports. In 1998 it earned only about $30 billion. This helped put the Saudi budget $13 billion in the red.[48] As a result of the economic difficulty in oil-producing states, each individual OPEC member had an incentive to sell more oil. According to the dynamics of supply and demand, if countries produce more oil (thus increasing supply), then world oil prices should drop. This is exactly what happened in the 1980s and especially in the 1990s. In short, many OPEC countries simply couldn't afford *not* to pump more oil. This phenomenon is related to the more common and

Free Rider Problem
A form of cheating, like an individual riding a bus for free, associated with countries benefiting from a stable international system or from membership in an international organization without having to pay any of the political, military, or economic costs.

For more information on gasoline prices, go to **www.ablongman.com/ duncan**.

enduring problem of maintaining unity in many international organizations: the free rider problem. The **free rider problem** refers to the situation in which a country tries to take a free ride on a "bus" that is being run by the rest of the members. In terms of OPEC, free riding refers to a member state *cheating* on the cartel's agreement to keep world oil supplies low and prices high. In essence, an OPEC member selfishly sells more oil than it is supposed to (to earn more money), and the resulting lower oil prices end up hurting every OPEC member.

Four key issues are relevant on the *demand* side of OPEC's weakness and, more recently, strength. First, the worldwide recession that followed the two oil shocks of the 1970s helped dampen the demand for oil. Another economic slowdown that reduced demand resulted from the Asian financial crisis, which began in 1997. Second, the greater use of substitutes for oil, including coal, natural gas, and nuclear power, since the 1970s has decreased the overall demand for oil. Third, Western countries have gotten better at conserving energy, thus lessening the demand for oil. Between 1973 and 1982, for example, Western countries became roughly 31 percent more efficient in their energy use.[49] Fourth, significant divisions within OPEC have emerged since the glory days of the 1970s. OPEC members can't completely control global oil prices when they cannot agree among themselves on output targets. Throughout most of the 1980s, for example, two of OPEC's members, Iran and Iraq, were actually at war with each other. Cheating on production targets, mentioned earlier, is another symptom of the lack of unity within OPEC.

In the second half of the 1990s, oil prices remained relatively low until a significant upsurge in 1999. OPEC members agreed to—and essentially stuck to—cuts in supply. Their efforts were enhanced when non-OPEC countries (Mexico, Norway, and Oman) followed OPEC's lead by limiting oil supply. By 2000 the world had again become aware of the vast impact OPEC can have when its members cooperate. The Clinton administration even allowed parts of the U.S. strategic oil reserve to be released with the aim of increasing supply to lower prices. According to one estimate, every $10 increase in the price of oil has the same impact on the U.S. economy as a $50 billion tax hike.[50] The release of the strategic oil reserve was nevertheless seen by many as a ploy to bolster Al Gore's chances in the presidential election only six weeks later.

The enormous rise in oil prices in 2000, however, cannot be completely attributed to the ability of OPEC countries to agree among themselves to control oil production. Many countries were already producing at capacity. In recent years, many Western oil companies have failed to make significant investments; this has hurt their capacity to produce more oil and increase supply. In addition, there had been problems at oil refineries (especially in the United States) and problems of getting the refined oil products to the right place at the right time.[51] And, of course, the non-OPEC countries' failure to boost production complicates matters further. OPEC countries also insist that high prices result from high taxes on gasoline in the United States and especially in European countries.

Given the fact that gas prices essentially tripled between 1998 and 2000, one might wonder why the United States and the world didn't face the same economic turmoil it did in the 1970s. As stated previously, oil substitutes and conservation played important roles. In addition, oil prices in the summer of 2000 were still about a third below what they were in 1990 and half of 1981 prices. The fact that prices tripled is also a bit misleading; in 1998, prices were unusually low. It also helped the United States and the world that inflation was relatively low to start off with—as compared to the 1970s.

The long-term prospects for OPEC are generally not very good. The U.S. Department of Energy's *Annual Energy Outlook 1998* concluded that oil prices will stay, on average, at less than $20 per barrel for the next decade and that supplies will be maintained beyond 2020.[52] This could change, of course, with a crisis in one or more of the major oil-producing countries. If this estimate holds, however, consumers will certainly benefit. Several other important political and economic consequences exist as well. First, when oil prices are low, there is less incentive to undertake risky and expensive exploration for new oil sites. Second, the oil industry is undergoing a consolidation phase. Consider, for example, the recent mergers between British Petroleum and Amoco, between Royal Dutch Shell and Texaco, and between Exxon and Mobil. It is unclear what the impact will be from these mergers, but one effect is that an even smaller number of companies will dominate this important sector and control prices.[53] Third, countries that have relied too heavily on oil can face serious budgetary problems. As noted above, even OPEC members are facing budgetary problems; social services and investment projects are being curtailed. So, while being an "oil-rich" country has its advantages, oil is not a panacea for all of a country's ills.

Another key aspect of the international oil industry is its impact on foreign and security policy. Thanks to the abundance of oil in the Middle East, the world is always attentive to political developments in that region. The United States and its UN allies went to war in the early 1990s against Iraq in order to ensure the free flow of oil. Since Israel remains the main U.S. ally in the region, the United States is almost automatically at odds with most of the countries in the Middle East. Another consequence of the U.S.-Israeli relationship is that even some U.S. allies—those much more dependent on Middle East oil than is the United States—are often at odds with U.S. policy in the region (e.g., France and Italy). Finally, if the potential of the Caspian Sea region (exceeding Russia's entire oil reserves of 6.7 billion tons) can be exploited, the foreign policies of Russia, Iran, Kazakhstan, Azerbaijan, and Turkmenistan will be profoundly affected (refer to the case study at the end of Chapter 7 for more on developments in this region).[54]

In short, while most people are familiar with the international oil industry only in terms of what price they pay at the pump, the political and economic implications of OPEC are enormous, both domestically and internationally.

CHAPTER SUMMARY

Why Do Countries Join Intergovernmental and Supranational Organizations?

- International affairs are usually dominated by nation-states, but nonstate actors are playing an increasingly important role as well. Governments sometimes yield some of their national sovereignty to international organizations because they perceive that international cooperation is in their national interest.
- The political, economic, and military benefits of membership in a supranational IO, even if its institutions are powerful, are often perceived as outweighing the costs. But states always face the tension between their desire to cooperate internationally and their desire to retain as much independence as possible.

What Does the United Nations Do and How Well Does It Do It?

- The United Nations is primarily an intergovernmental organization. It has many functions, including the preservation of peaceful relations among nations, running programs to help poor children around the world, and supporting agencies devoted to world health.

- The two most important UN bodies are the Security Council and the General Assembly. The Security Council, as its name indicates, deals with the UN's military matters. It consists of 15 members, 5 of whom are permanent (Britain, China, France, Russia, and the United States). A veto from any one of these 5 members will prevent the use of UN military force. The General Assembly deals with security issues as well, but it deals primarily with all of the nonmilitary UN activities. Every country, regardless of size, has one vote. This voting method gives tiny countries the same weight as large ones like the United States or India.

- Although the UN gets a lot of press for many of its positive contributions, one should not overestimate the influence of the UN in world politics. For example, the UN cannot act militarily unless it has sufficient support from the permanent members of the Security Council. The UN is also hurt by a lack of funding and by organizational problems.

What Is the European Union and How Does It Work?

- The European Union is a unique IGO in terms of its membership (rich, democratic countries), the depth and influence of its institutions, and the number of policy areas for which it is responsible (such as a single currency, common trade policies, common regional policies, an emerging common foreign and defense policy.).

- The EU has both intergovernmental and supranational features. Countries have decided, first of all, that they want supranational institutions and second, that following supranational institutions and rules brings more benefits than costs to the loss of national sovereignty. Many countries in Central and Eastern Europe agree, and that is why so many of them want to join the EU.

- The main EU institutions are the European Council (meetings between the national leaders), the Council of Ministers (meetings of specific government ministers), the Commission (the semiexecutive branch of the EU), the European Parliament, and the European Court of Justice. These institutions could potentially evolve and create a "United States of Europe," but this is unlikely. EU citizens still place their loyalty in their home government first, and many are worried about too much power being shifted to Brussels.

- NAFTA is a regional intergovernmental organization that, like the EU, is designed to improve trade relations among its members (Canada, the United States, Mexico). NAFTA, however, lacks the scope of policy coverage of the EU and does not have the supranational institutions that the EU has.

What Are the Global Financial and Trade Organizations?

- The World Bank and IMF (both associated with the UN) help manage global financial relations. Politically and economically they depend on their member states, thus helping to make them quite intergovernmental. Although their activities sometimes overlap, the World Bank generally deals with specific projects in poor countries while the IMF is responsible for overseeing the entire international monetary system by promoting exchange rate stability and orderly exchange relations among its member countries.

- The World Trade Organization is an intergovernmental organization that helps manage global trading relations. The WTO is an outgrowth of GATT, which was set up after World War II by governments willing to be bound by international rules and procedures with the aim of opening up global trade. The WTO now not only seeks to lower barriers to trade in goods, but in financial services and intellectual property as well.

How Does OPEC Differ from Other IGOs?

- OPEC is an IGO inspired by the desire for cooperation around a single commodity. Its only real function is to manage the global trade in oil. Its member states cooperate to determine the global price of oil and the amount of world production, normally with the aim of keeping prices relatively high.

- OPEC's influence peaked in the 1970s, but has fluctuated since then. Its members control about 40 percent of the world's oil, which means that they do not control 60 percent. Thus, what non-OPEC countries (e.g., Russia,

Mexico, Norway) do can weaken OPEC influence. So can greater energy conservation efforts.

- OPEC's influence also depends on cooperation among its members (OPEC is more effective when there are no "free riders") and on unforeseen events, such as the Gulf War.

ENDNOTES

[1]Adapted from A. LeRoy Bennett, *International Organizations: Principles and Issues*, Fifth Edition, (Englewood Cliffs, NJ: Prentice Hall, 1991), p. 2.

[2]Mark W. Zacher, "International Organizations," in *The Oxford Companion to World Politics* (New York: Oxford University Press, 1993), p. 451.

[3]For a more thorough description of IGOs, NGOs, and supranationalism juxtaposed with confederalism, federalism, and consociationalism, see John McCormick, *The European Union: Politics and Policies* (Boulder: Westview Press, 1996), pp. 10–13.

[4]See, for example, "Environmental Policy in the European Union," in Helen Wallace and William Wallace, *Policy-Making in the European Union* (London: Oxford University Press, 1996), pp. 236–255; Michael G. Huelshoff and Thomas Pfeiffer, "Environmental policy in the EC: neo-functionalist sovereignty transfer or neo-realist gate-keeping?" *International Journal* XLVII (Winter 1991–1992): pp. 136–158; Rüdiger Wurzel, "Environmental Policy," in Juliet Lodge ed. *The European Community and the Challenge of the Future* (New York: St. Martin's Press, 1993), pp. 178–197.

[5]Robert O. Keohane, "International Institutions: Can Interdependence Work?" *Foreign Policy,* Spring 1998, pp. 83–96.

[6]Another IO that uses unanimity voting is the Organization for Economic Cooperation and Development (OECD).

[7]Michael Ignatieff, "A Bungling U.N. Undermines Itself," *The New York Times,* May 15, 2000.

[8]Lawrence Ziring, Robert Riggs, and Jack Plano, *The United Nations: International Organization and World Politics,* 3rd ed. (Orlando: Harcourt Brace & Company, 2000), p 201.

[9]United Nations, as quoted by the Public Broadcasting Systems, *http://www.pbs.org/tal/un/budget.html.* See also U.S. State Department web site, *http://www.state.gov/p/io/rls/fs/2001/4842.htm.*

[10]Carola Hoyos, "US takes chance to target peacekeeping," *Financial Times,* July 2, 2002.

[11]United Nations Bureau of International Organizational Affairs, U.S. Department of State, April 1997, *(http://www.state.gov/www/issues/iofaqs2.html#ONE)*, and The Charter of the United Nations.

[12]Paul Lewis, "U.S. Panel Splits on Ways to Improve the U.N.," *The New York Times,* (September 13, 1993), p. A13.

[13]For a nice summary of the Economic and Social Council, see the Council's web page, *http://www.un.org/esa/coordination/ecosoc/about.htm.*

[14]For an overview of the International Criminal Court, see the ICJ's web page, *http://www.icj-cij.org/*

[15]"Fact Sheet," U.S. State Department, Bureau of International Organization Affairs, Washington, DC, September 7, 2001, *http://www.state.gov/p/io/rls/fs/2001/4842.htm.*

[16]United Nations, as quoted by the Public Broadcasting Systems, *http://www.pbs.org/tal/un/budget.html.*

[17]United Nations Department of Public Information, DPI/1753/Rev.16, October 1998.

[18]Ibid.

[19]Ibid.

[20]*Time,* December 23, 1991, p. 29.

[21]United Nations Department of Public Information, DPI/1815/Rev. 15, March 1999.

[22]Edward Mortimer, "Tight hand on the purse," *Financial Times,* May 8, 1996.

[23]Ted Carpenter, *Delusions of Grandeur: The United Nations and Global Intervention* (Washington, DC: Cato Institute, 1997), pp. 128–129.

[24]*The Washington Times* (February 25, 1997), p. A15.

[25]The poll was conducted between October 15 and November 10, 1998. The Chicago Council on Foreign Relations, as quoted in *http://www.clw.org/pub/clw/un/399chicagopoll.html.*

[26]Colum Lynch, "U.N., secretary general awarded Nobel Peace Prize," *The Washington Post,* October 13, 2001.

[27]David Hannay, "Balkan scapegoat," *Financial Times,* July 16, 1999.

[28]David Pilling, "WHO in sight of wiping out polio worldwide," *Financial Times,* January 7, 2000.

[29]R. O'Donnell, "Economic Union," in B. Laffan, R. O'Donnell, and M. Smith, *Unsettled Europe: European Integration in a Transformed World* (London: Routeledge, 1997), p. 17.

[30]John McCormick, *The European Union: Politics and Policies,* 2nd edition (Westview Press, 1999), p. 295.

[31]See Leon Lindberg and Stuart Scheingold, *Regional Integration* (Cambridge, Mass.: Harvard University Press, 1971); and Ernst Haas, *Uniting of Europe* (Stanford: Stanford University Press, 1958).

[32]See David R. Cameron, "The 1992 Initiative: Causes and Consequences" in Alberta M. Sbragia, Ed., *Europolitics* (Washington: The Brookings Institution, 1992), pp. 25–30.

[33]Emma Tucker, "Germany and Italy fined for abuses," *Financial Times,* January 1, 1997.

[34]"Veteran politicians hand over EU reform blueprint," *Reuters,* October 18, 1999.

[35]Quoted in Simon Serfaty, *Imagining Europe After the Cold War* (St. Martin's Press, 1992), pp. 162–163.

[36]Daniel Dombey, "Amato calls for strong president to lead EU," *Financial Times,* July 8, 2002.

[37]Although NAFTA does not have a common external tariff, its trade bloc neighbor to the south does. MERCOSUR, like the EU, is technically a customs union.

[38]World Bank, http://www.worldbank.org/, August 1998.

[39]A more comprehensive International Trade Organization (ITO) had been proposed in the late 1940s, but it was opposed by the U.S. Congress. The ITO was never submitted for ratification, and the less substantial GATT emerged by default. See Don Babai, "General Agreement on Tariffs and Trade," in Joel Krieger, Ed., *The Oxford Companion to Politics of the World* (Oxford: Oxford University Press 1993), pp. 342–348.

[40]Martin Wolf, "Wealth of Nations," *Financial Times,* May 19, 1998.

[41]British Petroleum, as quoted in "A dangerous addiction," *The Economist,* December 15, 2001.

[42]OPEC, *http://www.opec.org.*

[43]Edmund L. Andrews, "Kuwaitis Are Exasperated by America's Oil Politics," *The New York Times,* March 27, 2000.

[44]While prices did indeed double in a twelve month period, it is important to remember that prices were, after adjusting for inflation, still relatively low compared to prices in the 1970s during the oil shocks.

[45]Robert W. Fisher, "The Future of Energy," *The Futurist,* September/October 1997, pp. 43–46.

[46]"Opec 'imperils market share' by output cut," *Financial Times,* January 19, 2002.

[47]"Sunset for the oil business," *The Economist,* November 3, 2001.

[48]"The Suffering Gulf," *The Economist,* October 24, 1998, p. 41.

[49]Joan E. Spero and Jeffrey A. Hart, *The Politics of International Economic Relations,* 5th Edition New York: St. Martin's Press, 1997, p. 290.

[50]James C. Cooper and Kathleen Madigan, "Sure, the New Economy Gospel Is Winning More Converts," *Business Week,* September 25, 2000, p. 35.

[51]Robert Corzine, "Opec's increase seen as damage control," *Financial Times,* September 11, 2000.

[52]Mike Charnley-Fisher, "The crisis is confidence, not supply," *Financial Times,* World Energy Supplement, September 10, 1998, p. 4.

[53]Exxon and Mobil, for example, will hold a 14 percent share of the U.S. gas market. They also refine more oil than any other company in the world. The 14 percent market share, however, does not compare with Standard Oil's monopoly of the U.S. market when it was broken up by U.S. antitrust authorities. At the time, Standard controlled 90 per cent of the U.S. market. James Flanigan, "Exxon-Mobil merger could signal a big plus for oil and for consumers," *Los Angeles Times,* November 27, 1998.

[54]Thomas Orszag-Land, "How to Divvy Up Caspian Bonanza," *The Christian Science Monitor,* October 15, 1996, p. 18.

[55]"Nations approve first permanent world war crimes tribunal," *Associated Press,* April 11, 2002.

CASE STUDY

Assessing the Merits of the International Criminal Court

In July 2002, after the sixtieth country had ratified the treaty to create it, the International Criminal Court (ICC) officially came into existence. UN Undersecretary-General Hans Corell said that with the creation of the ICC, a "page in the history of humankind is being turned. May all this serve our society well in the years to come!"[55] The ICC is designed to prosecute individuals accused of genocide, war crimes, and crimes against humanity, notably "widespread and systematic" atrocities. In many ways, the ICC is a natural extension of the war crimes tribunals set up after World War II to prosecute Germans and Japanese who had committed the worst abuses of power during the war. Those who support the ICC hope that future political leaders will refrain from committing atrocities because they know that sooner or later they will be hauled before the new court. If Corell is correct, and a new page in the history of mankind has in fact turned, the atrocities that took place in Rwanda or Bosnia in the 1990s, for example, should occur with much less frequency in the future.

Not everyone, however, is convinced of the merits of the ICC. The strongest, and most important, opponent is the United States. The two articles that make up this case study spell out why the United States opposes the ICC and why the failure of the United States to ratify the ICC treaty might be a mistake. The case raises several important points made in this and other chapters. For example, should a sovereign nation-state (the United States) submit its citizens to a higher authority—in this case, the international court? Should the international community be guided by laws that, theoretically at least, benefit all humanity regardless of nationality, or should nation-states continue to be the main vehicle for determining violations of the law? The case study also helps show how international bodies, despite widespread support, can still be hampered by the political opposition of nation-states, particularly powerful ones.

ARGUING AGAINST THE ICC

Vote About the International Criminal Court

Mr. President,

This resolution represents the culmination of weeks of work by my government and many of the other governments represented here. Some members of this Council are members of the International Criminal Court while others, including the United States, are not and never will be. The United States has therefore sought a resolution that would allow those in the Court to meet their obligations to it, while it protected those of us who reject the jurisdiction of that institution. At risk were the peacekeeping activities of the United Nations, in the first instance in Bosnia but ultimately throughout the globe. The United States is therefore very pleased that we have successfully reached agreement. It offers us a degree of protection for the coming year.

For the United States, this resolution is a first step. The President of the United States is determined to protect our citizens—soldiers and civilians, peacekeepers and officials—from the International Criminal Court. We are especially concerned that Americans sent overseas as soldiers, risking their lives to keep the peace or to protect us all from terrorism and other threats, be themselves protected from unjust or politically motivated charges. Should the ICC eventually seek to detain any American, the United States would regard this as illegitimate—and it would have serious consequences. No nation should underestimate our commitment to protect our citizens.

Our government was founded by Americans to protect their freedom. Our Declaration of Independence states that and I quote "governments are instituted among men, deriving their just powers from the consent of the government" end of quote, "from the consent of the governed," excuse me, in order to secure their rights. We have built up in our two centuries of constitutional history a dense web of restraints on government, and of guarantees and protections for our citizens. The power of the government is very great, but those restraints are equally powerful. The history of American law is very largely the history of that balance between the power of the government and the rights of the people.

We will not permit that balance to be overturned by the imposition on our citizens of a novel legal system they have never accepted or approved, and which their government has explicitly rejected. We will never permit Americans to be jailed because judges of the ICC, chosen without the participation of those over whom they claim jurisdiction, so decide. We cannot allow that Americans who have been acquitted of accusations against them in the United States shall be subject to prosecution for the same acts if an ICC prosecutor or judge concludes that the American legal proceedings were somehow inadequate. We know that prosecutors who are responsible to no one constitute a danger, and we will not expose our citizens to such a danger. We cannot accept a structure that may transform the political criticism of America's world role into the basis for criminal trials of Americans who have put their lives on the line for freedom.

The American system of justice can be trusted to punish crimes, including war crimes or crimes against humanity, committed by an American—and we pledge to do so. But we do not believe the International Criminal Court contains sufficient safeguards to protect our nationals, and therefore we can never in good conscience permit Americans to become subject to its authority.

The power to deprive a citizen of his or her freedom is an awesome thing, which the American people have entrusted to their government under the rules of our democracy. Thus does an American judge have the legal and moral right, founded in our Constitution and in democratic procedures, to jail an American. But the International Criminal Court does not operate in the same democratic and constitutional context, and therefore does not have the right to deprive Americans of their freedom.

The United States does not oppose special tribunals to prosecute international offenses, and indeed has been a key supporter of them. But we believe that these existing mechanisms, within the framework of the UN Charter and the Security Council and already accepted by the international community, are adequate.

Once again I thank the members of the Security Council for their hard work in reaching a successful agreement today. I would also like to pay a special tribute to our President, Sir Jeremy Greenstock, who led us through this very difficult debate. This resolution respects those who have decided to submit to the International Criminal Court, and for one year it protects those of us who have not. We will use the coming year to find the additional protections we need, using bilateral agreements expressly contemplated in Article 98 of the Rome Statute. We will seek your cooperation, that is to say, the cooperation of the Council in achieving these agreements, so as to provide the protection that our understanding of the rights and freedoms of our citizens requires.

With that, I would be pleased to entertain any questions that you might have.

Reporter: Ambassador, once you have sort of established this network of bilateral agreements, Article 98 agreements and status of forces agreements, will you then end your efforts to renew this resolution every July 1st, or is this something that you see that the U.S. would like to be enforced for many years to come—forever?

Ambassador Negroponte: As you know, our initial drafts provided for virtually automatic extension of those provisions on an annual basis. That turned out not to be acceptable to other members of the Council, and we reached the compromise that is reflected in the resolution that you have before you. Yes, indeed, it is our intent, in accordance with the second paragraph, the operative paragraph, of the resolution, to seek renewal of this resolution on an annual basis; but the resolution is clear that this will be an annual decision and no doubt there will be debate within the Council prior to actually taking action, so I wouldn't want to try to prejudge or predict the outcome of any such discussion at this point.

Reporter: Ambassador, those of us who have covered this for many years know that the American bottom line has always been a cast iron guarantee that no American would ever come before this court. You haven't achieved that result in this resolution; why did you give up on that principle?

Ambassador Negroponte: Well, I think that we certainly achieved in operative paragraph one a request to the Court that no investigation or prosecution start before this one-year period. So, in effect, I think for practical purposes it achieves the kind of protection for a one-year period that we were seeking.

We would have preferred that this protection be for an indefinite period of time.

Reporter: But obviously, in the situation where somebody were to commit an atrocity, hypothetically in that one year, it would obviously be hard for you to get a renewal of the deferral and therefore the jurisdiction would attach to that atrocity.

Ambassador Negroponte: Well, I think that perhaps we ought to take this on a stepwise basis. We have achieved these protections for a one-year period, as Sir Jeremy pointed out in virtually in any hypothetical situation of this kind. I don't think either the United States or Great Britain or other countries doubt that we ourselves would administer the requisite justice to the accused individual. But yes, I think it adds an important measure of protection for the year ahead and then we are going to seek through a multifaceted approach to also build additional protections under Article 98 of the Rome Statute and other mechanisms that I referred to in my statement. Thank you very much.

Sources: *"Vote About the International Criminal Court," John D. Negroponte, U.S. Permanent Representative to the United Nations, New York, New York, July 12, 2002. U.S. Department of State (http://www.state.gov/p/io/rls/rm/2002/ 11846.htm.) Remarks at stakeout following UN Security Council vote on Resolution 1422, including text of explanation of vote. Released by the U.S. Mission to the United Nations.*

A Rebuttal: America Is Not So Special

Part of a diplomat's business is to reconcile the irreconcilable—or at least create the illusion that irreconcilables have been reconciled. But even this latter will be difficult to achieve in the confrontation between the United States and its closest allies over the new international criminal court, set up under the aegis of the United Nations, which came into formal being yesterday.

The ostensible argument is over the future of the UN's peacekeeping force in Bosnia. Washington is demanding blanket immunity from the tribunal's jurisdiction for U.S. peacekeepers, on the grounds that they might be liable to politically motivated prosecution. Such at any rate was the argument put forward by John Negroponte, the US Ambassador to the UN, as he wielded his veto in the Security Council to prevent a routine six-month extension of the Bosnian force's mandate. Instead the Council approved a three-day extension, allowing the diplomats an extra 72 hours to find a compromise. But the dispute is not, as Mr. Negroponte claimed, about protecting U.S. peacekeepers from frivolous prosecution. For one thing, ICC rules provide ample safeguards against this happening. Moreover, several participants in UN peacekeeping operations have been expressly afforded immunity under specific agreements. And as Jeremy Greenstock, Britain's envoy to the UN, pointed out, U.S. forces have been serving in Bosnia, despite the existence of the war crimes tribunal for the former Yugoslavia in The Hague, under which they could theoretically have been prosecuted.

Moreover, even if there was the odd unjustified attempt to prosecute U.S. personnel, it would almost certainly have gone nowhere. So why the fuss? Why is the United States unable to accept a minimal risk which is of no bother to Britain, France, and Germany, who play a scarcely less important role in international peacekeeping operations, and have welcomed the ICC?

No, this is not about the safety of U.S. peacekeepers. Washington's obstinacy reflects its visceral opposition to the ICC, as a threat to the supremacy of its own judicial system. That hostility is of the same coin as America's refusal to submit to other international treaties, including those covering global warming, nuclear testing, landmines, and chemical and biological weapons. Essentially, the United States is arguing that its special role in world affairs makes it a special case, entitled to different treatment.

But this reasoning simply will not do. Certainly, the United States occupies a unique position, in which unchallengeable power brings unparalleled responsibilities. That, however, makes it all the more important that America should play by the international rules—above all when Washington is exhorting all and sundry to join its "war against terrorism". Many will be tempted to draw a parallel between the refusal of the United States to observe international norms in its treatment of people rounded up in this "war" and its rejection of the ICC, and conclude that it sees itself as above the law.

Washington's behaviour is both arrogant and unacceptable. Its attempting to use the Security Council to change a properly ratified international treaty would in itself set an appalling precedent. Worse still, in the pursuit of this ignoble end, it is attempting to hold hostage peacekeeping operations in Bosnia and possibly in a dozen other countries, where the UN presence can make the difference between a laborious return to normality and a fresh descent into anarchy. With or without the United States, the peacekeeping operations must continue. And so must the new international court.

Source: *"America is not so special that she can be allowed to shirk her obligations," The Independent (London), July 2, 2002. Reprinted by permission of the publisher.*

QUESTIONS

Check Your Understanding

1. Describe the purpose and role of the ICC.
2. What arguments does Ambassador Negroponte make against the ICC?

Analyze the Issues

3. Ambassador Negroponte says that the United States is a unique country and that because of its uniqueness, it should be exempt from the ICC's jurisdiction. What are the unique features of the United States? What does the second article of the case study have to say about this uniqueness?
4. Based on ideas from both articles of this case study, assess the claim that the ICC represents a threat to U.S. sovereignty.
5. If the ICC does threaten state sovereignty, do you believe that this a good thing or a bad thing for the world community and for individual nation-states?
6. Which theoretical approach described in Chapters 1 and 5—such as neo-liberalism, realism, Marxism, the ecological approach, etc.—best describe the U.S. approach to the ICC? Explain.

FOR FURTHER INFORMATION

To find out more about the International Criminal Court, consult the following sources:

Payam Akhaven, "Beyond Impunity: Can the International Criminal Court Prevent Atrocities?" *American Journal of International Law,* Vol. 95, No. 1, January 2001, pp. 7–31.

"Not (quite) strangled at birth," *The Economist,* July 6, 2002.

Philip Stephens, "America breaks the global ties," *Financial Times,* July 5, 2002.

Zsuszanna Deen-Racsmany, "The Nationality of the Offender, International Criminal Court," *American Journal of International Law,* Vol. 95, No. 3, July 2001, pp. 606–623.

Robert W. Tucker, "The International Criminal Court Controversy," *World Policy Journal,* Vol. XVIII, No. 2, Summer 2001.

U.S. House of Representatives. Committee on International Relations. *The International Criminal Court: A Threat to American Military personnel?* Hearing, July 25, 2000. Washington, DC, Government Printing Office, 2000.

CHAPTER 6

Corporate and Nongovernmental Actors

KEY QUESTIONS RAISED IN THIS CHAPTER

1. What is the significance of Nongovernmental Organizations (NGOs)?

2. What are examples of important NGOs?

3. Why is there political opposition to NGOs?

4. What kinds of business do NGOs operate in the international arena and how powerful are they?

5. What is the power relationship between nation-states and NGOs?

FIGURE 6.1

Growth of NGOs (1956–1999)

SOURCE: *Union of International Associations as quoted in "Swarming: Non-governmental International Organizations," The Economist, December 11, 1999, p. 20. Copyright © 1999 The Economist Newspaper Ltd.*

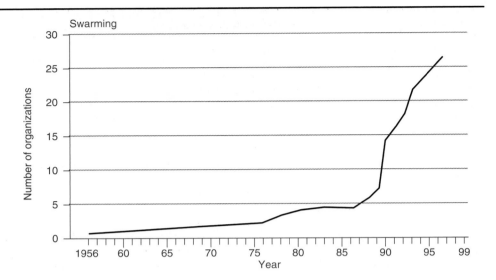

Swarming

Corporate Actors

Businesses and business associations; a catchall term for multinational and transnational corporations.

Chapters 2 and 5 introduced you to the growing visibility in international relations of international nongovernmental organizations (NGOs) without going into much detail about them. That is the task of this chapter. Recall that international NGOs are organizations whose members are groups and individuals but *not* countries. Just as intergovernmental organizations (IGOs) vary in scope and mission, so do NGOs. To most people, the typical NGO is a large organization of individuals who seek to transform a political, economic, or social condition in one or more countries. While that is certainly true for most NGOs, special consideration needs to be made for two highly visible kinds of NGOs: terrorist organizations and transnational businesses (or, **corporate actors**). Terrorist organizations are discussed at length in Chapter 9. In this chapter we will briefly describe the role of corporate actors, but reserve a more lengthy discussion of them in Chapters 11 and 12. For now, it is useful to remember that corporate and noncorporate NGOs can be distinguished by their membership and goals. An international business seeks to maximize profit and consists of traditional employees who receive wages as compensation. Noncorporate NGOs are typically staffed by volunteers who seek change that may be economic in nature but often is not.

Besides the headline-grabbing NGOs like Greenpeace, Oxfam, and the Red Cross, there are rarely publicized NGOs that are increasingly altering the landscape of international relations. For example, the Women in Development Movement and Women for a New Era have gotten the UN to focus on the role of women as an integrated part of a country's overall development process. Around the world, there are over 40,000 (noncorporate) NGOs,[1] including humanitarian, scientific, environmental, women's rights, and religious organizations (see Figure 6.1 for the growth in NGOs over time and Table 6.1, which describes types of international NGOs). A Johns Hopkins University Study found that NGOs employed 19 million people worldwide, and had an income of about $1,100 billion. Some countries have particularly high numbers of NGOs. Brazil, for example, has roughly 210,000 NGOs, while India alone has some 1 million.[2] The large number of NGOs is matched by their diversity. Some NGOs are single-issue oriented, while others deal with a wide variety of political, economic, and social problems. NGOs are funded

TABLE 6.1 Types of International NGOs	
Type of NGO	**Example**
Humanitarian	Catholic Relief Services
Human Rights	Amnesty International
Environmental	Greenpeace
Scientific	International Council of Scientific Unions
Women's Rights	Women for a New Era
Business	Exxon-Mobil
Business Association	International Federation of Airline Pilots' Associations
Terrorist	Islamic Jihad
Religious	World Council of Churches

by individuals, unions, nation-states, local governments, and even the UN and multinational corporations.

In the first part of the chapter we discuss how there got to be so many NGOs and how influential they can be in world politics. The second part looks at three highly visible noncorporate NGOs. Our review of Greenpeace, Amnesty International, and Doctors Without Borders will drive home the point that, under certain circumstances, NGOs can have an important impact on a particular country or on the world as a whole. After exploring these three NGOs, the reader should have a feel for the diverse missions of NGOs. The subject of the next section of the chapter is corporate actors. Corporate actors—such as Exxon-Mobil or SONY— are businesses that have varying degrees of international scope and influence. For this chapter, an important issue to track is the *relationship between NGOs and sovereign states.* For example, the combined impact of NGOs provides evidence that the nation-state may be in retreat. In addition, decentralizing forces in world politics that encourage the growth of NGOs, and the sometimes centralizing effects of NGOS, can undermine the ability of nation-states to control their destiny. It is hoped that by the end of the chapter, you will appreciate the variety and influences of NGOs on the world stage.

For a list of NGOs on the Internet, go to **www.ablongman.com/ duncan**.

What Is the Significance of Nongovernmental Organizations (NGOs)?

The international system established by the Treaty of Westphalia enshrined nation-states as the most important unit of analysis in world politics. As we saw in Chapter 5, intergovernmental organizations play an important role as well. The significance of NGOs cannot rival that of nation-states, but NGOs are now a permanent part of the global landscape. Some have even suggested that NGOs are a crucial force in world politics. Michael Edwards of the Ford Foundation, for instance, sees NGOs as becoming "a force for transformation in global politics and economics."[3] In this respect, NGOs contribute to the centralizing forces at work in world politics by, for example, creating a transnational sense of identity. In an era of increasing globalization, or at least regionalization, NGOs have helped establish or nurture links not just across national borders, but across cultures as well. In the following pages, we will address this issue of NGOs as a centralizing force further and explore why there are now so many NGOs on the international stage.

Reasons for the Rise of NGOs

Several reasons explain why NGOs have become so visible in world politics today. These reasons are rooted in politics, economics, and technology. First, NGOs tend to thrive in democratic environments because democracies allow freedom of expression and association. By contrast, when states (governmental organizations) dominate societies—as in communist countries—it may be impossible for members of an NGO to meet and organize.[4] In China, for example, one of the main problems for NGOs is that they fall into a legal gray area and are often unable to register as legal organizations. According to Nick Young, this unclear legal status leaves many organizations open to government criticism or worse.[5] Since the collapse of communism around 1990, more and more countries have opened up politically and opted for democratic reforms—thus creating a more favorable climate for NGOs.

Another political reason we have so many NGOs is that more and more states are either falling apart or struggling to provide services that people have come to expect from the state. NGOs, for example, have been very active in Bosnia, Kosovo, and Rwanda. The HIV/AIDS crisis in much of southern African has resulted in an abundance of NGOs. NGOs in Russia, perhaps surprisingly, are also becoming more visible as the government increases its restrictions on the new media. Vladimir Orlov, founder of the Moscow-based Center for Policy Studies, says that NGOs are influencing Russian policy in arenas from environmental to security affairs and providing an increasing amount of information to the Russian public.[6] We should expect, then, that as states—especially in the developing world and the former Soviet Bloc—continue to face political, social, and economic upheaval, NGOs are more likely to step in as long as they are allowed to.

Yet another political explanation for the rise of NGOs is that some governments prefer to receive aid directly or indirectly from NGOs instead of other governments. Sometimes, for example, a struggling country may not have the administrative capacity to carry out humanitarian assistance, or a country like China may be unwilling to provide assistance or requisite training for relief workers. In addition, in some instances, political leaders in countries that receive outside aid find a way of keeping it for themselves without sending it to the people who need it. NGOs are often perceived to be more trustworthy and efficient at allocating funds from a donor state.

Second, more open economic environments help NGOs in several important ways. The work of NGOs always entails money and sometimes a lot of it. Getting money from the donors to the international NGO and then to the recipient almost always takes place across borders. Open economic systems facilitate the transfer of money across international borders. Open economies also allow national governments to funnel money through NGOs to people or groups in other countries. In societies dominated by authoritarian or Marxist governments, NGOs do not tend to crop up, in part because of the competition they would face from governmental agencies or from political opposition.

Third, advances in telecommunications and computer technology have been a boon for NGOs around the world. The reverberations of the information age—including global news, the Internet, and faxes—have rendered national borders meaningless in some circumstances. This revolution in telecommunications has benefited NGOs in a critically important way: members of NGOs can communicate much more easily than ever before, both within the same country and across the entire globe. Modern technology and rapid communications

WHY IT MATTERS TO YOU

NGOs and Citizen Activism

Much of international relations, especially for Americans, can seem out of reach and driven by grand forces beyond our control. People often feel they have little chance to influence world events. But, as we have discussed in many sections of this book, the role of the individual can, under certain circumstances, play an important role in world politics. NGOs offer a special opportunity for citizen activism and for individuals—including students—to become players in the international arena.

Students, for example, have been active in pressuring some of the world's largest companies based in the world's rich countries to end sweatshop practices in the world's poorer countries. Through human rights NGOs, students have helped raise awareness of abuses that take place in many countries around the world. Student participation in environmental NGOs like Greenpeace and the World Wildlife Federation can impact the debate at both the local and international levels. And students in NGOs have helped raise the public's consciousness through antiwar protests and demonstrations against international organizations like the WTO and World Bank.

Other, very different kinds of individual involvement exist as well. For a small financial contribution, for instance, an individual can contribute to microloan organizations. Such NGOs provide small-scale loans (as low as $50) to help people in developing countries make crucial investments that can raise them out of poverty (see Chapter 12 for more information). Thus, by now you should realize that world politics can influence you, but that you can also have an impact on world politics.

can, for example, link scientists in virtually any part of the world who are committed to the eradication of a worldwide disease. It can link student protesters with their supporters in other countries. It can also link aid workers in a remote village to their NGO headquarters in New York, London, or any other city. Two of the more recent, successful NGO-led campaigns, Jubilee 2000 and International Campaign to Ban Land Mines, probably would not have succeeded without the Internet.[7] Taken together, these three elements—politics, economics, and technology—have contributed to the enormous growth in the number of NGOs over time.

NGOs: Linking Cultures and Divisive Force

An important result of the activities of international NGOs is connecting like-minded people in different countries. Where political, economic, and technological forces encourage open discussion, NGOs can flourish among peoples from different countries and cultures. This centralizing phenomenon may come in the form of transnational religious, environmental protection, or human rights movements.

NGOs can also be a divisive force in world politics. The best example can be seen in international terrorist organizations, a specific form of NGO that seeks political change through violent means. (Chapter 9 will provide a more thorough treatment of international terrorism.) As many parts of this chapter will show, NGOs can be very unpopular with the world's nation-states. Many NGOs directly challenge government policies, and often NGOs are perceived as threats to a country's national interests. In addition, foreign NGOs may be viewed with suspicion because of their ideas, values, or in the case of international businesses, their products, particularly cultural products such as films and TV programs. The result may be local resistance to NGOs. As some scholars have demonstrated, exposure to the globalization process that is associated with or nurtured by NGOs can challenge old beliefs and social identities. People often react defensively to the global force by trying to hold on even tighter to local customs and beliefs. And contact with corporate and noncorporate NGOs can increase a people's awareness of social, political, and economic discrepancies around the world.[8]

The next section of the chapter describes three major NGOs and shows how NGOs can challenge political authorities and the people of many countries. We will also explore how NGOs can bridge cultural and national divides among peoples and contribute to a global civil society.

What Are Examples of Important NGOs?

To see how these broad concepts work in practice, let's now take a closer look at some specific NGOs. We will present an overview of three NGOs and then describe challenges they face in achieving their goals. The NGOs presented here—Greenpeace, Amnesty International, and Doctors Without Borders—are well-known and global in scope. But keep in mind that hundreds of thousands of smaller NGOs operate internationally, nationally, or even locally. These three NGOs differ in their aims, but all three can be highly controversial because their missions clash with the cultural, political, or economic interests of many countries.

Greenpeace

Greenpeace is a not-for-profit organization made up of a network of national and regional offices in over 30 countries. Its membership consists of roughly 3 million individuals worldwide, and it operates with a considerable budget of $100 million. Originally called the "Don't Make A Wave Committee" from Vancouver, Canada, this NGO was reorganized and renamed *Greenpeace* with the aim of creating a *greener* and more *peaceful* world. The "green" refers to the support of environmental protection, and the "peace" stands for the nonviolent resolution of differences. Like many NGOs, Greenpeace was founded on the idea that a few individuals can make a difference in the world. As a result, one of its main goals is to bring public opinion to bear on policymakers. The organization has been heavily influenced by the nonviolence philosophy of Mahatma Ghandi of India as well as by the Quaker tradition. Greenpeace's goals include the following[9]:

- Promote peace, global disarmament, and nonviolence.
- Prevent pollution and abuse of the earth's oceans, lands, and fresh water.
- End all nuclear threats.
- Protect biodiversity in all its forms. Biodiversity refers to the protection and conservation of the diversity of plant and animal species in an ecosystem.

This philosophical background pervades Greenpeace's tactics and strategy. Greenpeace members are advised earnestly to achieve change through civil disobedience, peaceful demonstration, and educational campaigns. Greenpeace pioneered peaceful civil protests in many places including Lebanon, which was ravaged by civil war in the 1970s; in the Soviet Union and later Russia; in China; and in Turkey.

Tactics used by Greenpeace include holding demonstrations in front of prominent public buildings; publishing scientific, economic, and political research; and lobbying politicians. The tactic that gives widespread publicity to Greenpeace is its blocking of nuclear, whaling, sealing, or other vessels engaged in what Greenpeace calls "the extinction-for-profit" of a species. Greenpeace also carries out boycotts of companies, such as the 2002 consumer boycott of Esso fuels. In this case, Greenpeace argued that Exxon-Mobil helped destroy the implementation of the Kyoto agreement on climate change. Sometimes, Greenpeace's tactics are very unusual. Recently in Belgium, for example, Greenpeace activists broke into a nuclear power plant to protest the Belgian government's subsidies to the nuclear power industry. In 2002, Greenpeace activists gathered on the rooftop of the Japanese embassy in Australia to protest a shipment of plutonium to that country. With the hope of raising money and gaining greater publicity, Greenpeace Spain sold desktop diaries with some of the world's top models posing in the nude. The pictures include one of a woman lounging naked on a mountain of empty mineral water bottles to highlight the hazards posed by nonrecyclable plastic. Feminists from many countries protested the diaries, arguing that it represented a descent into sexist advertising, but *Greenpeace Spain* said the diary had been "well received" in Spain.[10]

The environmental (that is, "green") goals of Greenpeace have sent its members around the world in an attempt to preserve the Earth's oceans, land, and atmosphere. Greenpeace has specifically protested the devastation caused by nuclear and toxic pollution. In 1999, for example, Greenpeace tried to convince Ukraine to replace its Chernobyl nuclear power plant with a natural-gas power plant. According to Greenpeace, the new plant would be cheaper and less dangerous to the environment than the Chernobyl plant. You will recall that in 1986, an explosion in one of the Chernobyl nuclear reactors sent clouds of radioactive material over much of Eastern and Western Europe. Unfortunately for Greenpeace, Ukrainian President Leonid Kuchma rejected Greenpeace's proposal, partly because nuclear plants account for nearly half of Ukraine's electricity production. Nevertheless, Greenpeace continues to press its case before other nuclear power plants are built to replace the one at Chernobyl.[11]

Greenpeace also helped publicize the dangerous connection between the use of chlorine-based chemicals and the destruction of the ozone layer. And Greenpeace is partially responsible for the ozone-safe refrigerators that are now standard in the United States and in many other parts of the world. Greenpeace also claims credit for more than 26 international treaties and conventions of the United Nations and other international bodies on issues such as toxic trade, ozone depletion, climate change, biodiversity, and endangered species.[12] According to Michael Bond, an editor with *New Scientist*, Greenpeace has shown that it can make a difference when a group stands up for principles and challenges the decision makers.[13] Greenpeace was nominated for the Nobel Peace prize in 1986 for its efforts in the environmental area. Here we have enumerated many of Greenpeace's accomplishments. Later in the chapter, we will explore some of the controversies that surround this NGO.

Amnesty International

The mission of Amnesty International (AI) differs dramatically from that of Greenpeace. AI promotes the human rights enshrined in the UN Universal Declaration of Human Rights and other international standards (see Chapter 10 for

Prisoners of Conscience

People imprisoned because of peaceful expression of their beliefs, politics, race, religion, color, or national origin.

a more thorough treatment of human rights in the context of international justice). In particular, Amnesty International campaigns to free all **prisoners of conscience;** to ensure fair and prompt trials for political prisoners; to abolish the death penalty; to end torture and other cruel treatment of prisoners; and to end political killings and "disappearances."[14] The London-based AI has over one million members and supporters in 162 countries and is operated by more than 300 permanent staff and 100 volunteers from more than 50 countries. Amnesty International also has specialist networks—groups of medical professionals, lawyers, and others—who use their expertise to campaign for victims of human rights violations. (See box The View from Portugal: The Origins of Amnesty International).

Like Greenpeace, AI attempts to remain impartial and independent of any government, political persuasion, and religion. AI believes that part of its strength comes from being perceived as an *unbiased* champion of human rights. In fact, one of its principles is that people have fundamental rights that *transcend* national, cultural, religious, and ideological boundaries.

The tactics used by Amnesty International to achieve political change are similar to those of Greenpeace. Its activities include public demonstrations and human rights education programs. To raise money, AI has even sponsored concerts with popular music groups. *The Eurythmics,* for example, played on behalf of both AI and Greenpeace in July 1999 in London on the Greenpeace ship "Rainbow Warrior II." One of AI's most common techniques involves letter-writing campaigns on behalf of prisoners of conscience. In these campaigns, AI members "adopt" a prisoner and write letters to officials in that prisoner's country calling for the prisoner's release. AI also helps the prisoner's family. Since letter campaigns focus on individuals and not countries or political systems per se, AI is able to maintain a measure of political neutrality. Prisoner mistreatment is commonplace and widespread throughout the world. A recent AI paper noted that in 117 countries people were reportedly tortured or ill-treated by security forces, police, or other state authorities. In 41 countries, torture or ill-treatment, lack of medical care, or cruel, inhuman, or degrading prison conditions were confirmed or suspected of leading to deaths in custody.[15]

THE VIEW FROM   Portugal

The Origins of Amnesty International

In 1961 London lawyer Peter Benenson read about a group of students in Portugal—then a dictatorship—who were arrested and jailed for raising a toast to "freedom" in a public restaurant. The incident prompted Benenson to launch a one-year campaign called "Appeal for Amnesty 1961" in the *London Observer,* a local newspaper.

The "Appeal for Amnesty" called for the release of all people imprisoned because of peaceful expression of their beliefs, politics, race, religion, color, or national origin. Benenson called these people prisoners of conscience.

His plan was to encourage people to write letters to government officials in countries that had prisoners of conscience, calling for their release. The campaign grew enormously, spread to other countries, and by the end of 1961 the organization Amnesty International had been formed.

Source: Amnesty International (http://www.web.amnesty.org/), May 28, 1999.

According to the AI executive-director of the U.S. branch, William F. Schulz, human rights violations are increasing because we have no consistent mechanisms or policies for dealing with them. "There is as yet no permanent international criminal court. We have seen a massive military intervention in Kosovo, while the world has done nothing about massive violations in the Sudan and Sierra Leone. We continue to coddle China, and then crack down on Burma and Cuba. There is no consistency in U.S. human rights policy or the response of the international community. That leads to thugs and tyrants believing they can get away with murder."[16] In the wake of humanitarian disasters in Africa and Asia, and more recently in Kosovo, Amnesty International stepped up its demands for a permanent international criminal court.

AI considers its work accomplished when conditions in a prison are improved, when torture is prevented, and when prisoners are given real hope by the knowledge that they have not been forgotten. For its work in pursuing human rights around the world, AI was awarded the Nobel Peace Prize in 1977. AI also has official standing in the UN and frequently presents testimony to the U.S. Congress. We will return to AI, and its more controversial aspects later in the chapter.

Doctors Without Borders

In the past 10 to 15 years, the world has witnessed a growing number of armed conflicts that have been extremely complex politically. For a variety of reasons, political leaders from the international community are often reluctant to get involved. In addition to the International Red Cross, which has been a well-known player on the international stage, a growing number of other international humanitarian relief agencies are trying to fill this political vacuum. Often, they are the first "outsiders" to arrive with help. One such organization is Doctors Without Borders (DWB). A private, nonprofit, humanitarian organization, DWB was started by a group of young French doctors in 1971. (That is why many people know this organization by its French name: *Médecins Sans Frontières*). The founders recognized that a downside to the end of colonialism after World War II was that millions of people worldwide had become refugees. They also believed that the problems of refugees were likely to get worse; and they did. In 1976, for example, there were 2.7 million refugees; in 1979 there were 5.7 million; and in 1996 there were 15 million. For DWB such numbers demand a new level of emergency aid, particularly when nation-states are unwilling or unable to provide the aid.

Since the early 1970s, DWB has become the world's largest independent international medical relief agency. It helps victims of epidemics and of natural and man-made disasters. It also helps those who lack health care due to geographic remoteness or ethnic marginalization. In addition, Doctors Without Borders helps victims of armed conflict. Its first major mission was in 1976, in war ravaged Lebanon. For seven months, 56 doctors and nurses worked in a Beirut hospital caring for Shi'ite civilians under fire from Christian fighters.[17] DWB has also gone to war zones in Somalia, Chechnya, Bosnia, Burundi, Rwanda, Sierra Leone, and most recently, Kosovo.

Every year more than two thousand volunteers from about 45 nationalities work in over 80 countries in front-line hospitals, refugee camps, disaster sites, towns, and villages. They provide primary health care, perform surgery, vaccinate children, rehabilitate hospitals, operate emergency nutrition and sanitation programs, and train local medical staff. DWB also speaks out against human rights abuses and violations of humanitarian law that its teams witness in the course of providing medical relief.

A humanitarian NGO like DWB has to be careful about being perceived as partisan in any conflict. NGOs are frequently used by donor governments to distribute financial aid, to administer medical services, or to distribute food. In the process, NGOs can lose their legitimacy—and their effectiveness—if they are viewed as favoring one side or the other. As the title of this very international NGO would suggest, DWB has few ties to national governments. DWB has offices in 19 countries, and its charter stipulates that members observe strict neutrality and maintain complete independence from all political, economic, and religious powers.[18] For its efforts throughout the world, Doctors Without Borders was awarded the Nobel Peace Prize in 1999.

Why Is There Political Opposition to NGOs?

Tensions often exist between nongovernmental actors and sovereign states. One of the most controversial ideas held by many humanitarian NGOs is that the international community has the *right of interference* in countries that violate the rights of minorities.[19] Recall that national sovereignty as enshrined in the principles of the Treaty of Westphalia suggests that states have the right to govern their territory as they see fit. The notion that organizations outside the sovereign territory have a "right" to interfere represents a serious breach of "sovereignty," which has been the cornerstone of international relations for over 350 years. However, sometimes the very nature of the problem an NGO is trying to fix requires that it get around a sovereign state.

The issue of a right to intervene in a sovereign state has very wide implications, of course. For example, many NATO supporters claimed that the humanitarian disaster that unfolded in Kosovo in 1998 and early 1999 warranted NATO's bombing of Serbian (Yugoslav) targets. None of the NATO members had a direct quarrel with Yugoslavia, and yet Yugoslav territory was attacked with the aim of forcing Yugoslav Slobodan Milosevic to alter his policies toward Yugoslavia's Albanian Kosovars. After Milosevic agreed to withdraw forces from Kosovo, many people wondered whether these events in Kosovo represented a new trend that would play itself out in the twenty-first century.

NGOs are also controversial in that many of them are not transparent or accountable. They can have a large impact on countries, but how they make decisions and finance their activities are not always apparent, and they do not have democratic accountability. To help demonstrate these issues further, let us take a second look at the three NGOs just discussed. This time, however, we will focus on national opposition to these groups. We will follow the same order: Greenpeace, Amnesty International, and Doctors Without Borders.

Political Opposition to Greenpeace

The mission of Greenpeace can clash with countries and companies whose activities or interests differ from those of Greenpeace. We offer several examples that highlight the many obstacles this NGO faces in achieving its mission. Opposition to Greenpeace has existed since its very first project. In 1971 the organization sent a ship to Vancouver, Canada, to stop the United States from conducting an atmospheric nuclear test in the Aleutian Islands. Greenpeace argued that the island location for the test (Amchitka) was the home to bald eagles and peregrine falcons, and was the last refuge for endangered sea otters. The area is also one of the most earthquake-prone in the world. Only five months later, the United States announced an end to nuclear tests in the Aleutian Islands "for political and other reasons," suggesting that the negative publicity generated by Greenpeace had had an impact.

Perhaps the most publicized confrontation between Greenpeace and a sovereign state came in July 1985 when French commandos bombed the Greenpeace ship "Rainbow Warrior," killing a Dutch citizen. Greenpeace had been protesting French nuclear testing in the South Pacific. France, however, wanted to avoid the negative publicity that often comes with Greenpeace exposure by destroying the "Rainbow Warrior" while it was harbored in Auckland, New Zealand. Since someone was killed in the incident, the publicity turned out to be almost all negative for the French, both in New Zealand and internationally. At one point, for example, Australia's foreign minister said, "Every French defense ship or airplane seeking to visit this country will need to give us a guarantee that it is not, and will not in any way, be involved with . . . the nuclear tests in the Pacific. If they do not give that assurance, they will not be allowed to land nor will they be refueled or in any other way assisted by Australia." The Pacific Council of Churches said that "if it is safe to carry out nuclear tests, do it in France and keep our Pacific nuclear-free."[20]

Two agents of the French Directorate General of External Security—Major Alain Mafart and Captain Dominique Prieur—were prosecuted in New Zealand on charges of manslaughter and willful damage to a ship by means of an explosive. The two agents were sentenced to ten years in prison in New Zealand. Unhappy with this decision, however, the French government put economic pressure on New Zealand, and the case finally ended up in the lap of United Nations Secretary-General Javier Perez de Cuellar. Under his mediation, the French paid New Zealand $7 million, issued a formal apology, and pledged not to use the European Union's (then the European Community) influence to limit New Zealand's exports to the EU.[21] In the end, France went ahead with its nuclear testing in the Pacific.

A decade later, Greenpeace sent its replacement ship, the "Rainbow Warrior II," to the French Moruroa Atoll when French President Jacques Chirac announced his decision to do more testing. Exactly ten years after the first "Rainbow Warrior" was sunk, the French navy stormed "Rainbow Warrior II" when it sailed inside the 12-mile exclusion zone around the test site. Commandos fired tear gas at the crew, cut the boat's communications links, and towed it out of the test area.[22]

Greenpeace has faced considerable political opposition from other countries as well. For example, it has been locked in a contentious struggle with Japan and Norway over whaling. Japan and Norway cite scientific and cultural rationales for allowing whaling while Greenpeace claims that the economics of whaling should not justify these countries being exempt from a worldwide ban. See the case study at the end of the chapter for more information on this issue.

Greenpeace protests and other activities can lead to lawsuits by companies and arrests by governments. For example, Greenpeace activists were fined for their role in a protest against genetically modified foods in Hong Kong in 2002. And Greenpeace was recently sued by France's "America's Cup" team, le Defi Areva, after Greenpeace rammed its yacht and blockaded the boat's naming ceremony (attended by 400 guests, including New Zealand's ambassador to France). Greenpeace claimed that the nuclear conglomerate Areva sponsored the yachting team with financial support of more than $10 million. From Greenpeace's perspective, Areva was "trying to 'greenwash' its business by linking itself to the clean, green image of sailing."[23]

Norwegian Whaling: Despite international efforts to ban whaling, Norway resumed whaling in 1992 and lifted restrictions on the trade in whale products in 2001. In this photo, Norwegian whalers haul up one of their catches.

Greenpeace has often tried to work through international organizations to change individual states' domestic policies. Recently the Russian Greenpeace organization appealed to the International Monetary Fund not to give Russia any more money until it guaranteed that factories on the shores of Lake Baikal had the requisite pollution controls. Lake Baikal is one of the world's largest fresh water lakes. It is a mile deep and contains species dating back to the earliest periods of Earth. But Greenpeace faced an uphill battle. The guilty cellulose paper factory was fined $4.5 billion over a 12-year period, but the fines were never paid. The town of Baikalsk depends heavily on the factory, which provides 17,000 jobs—and jobs are extremely hard to come by since the collapse of communism. Complicating matters is that the cellulose company is owned by the Russian military, which does not want the factory closed either. The Russian court decided that employment considerations outweighed the eventual ecological damage.[24]

Look-out, Greenpeace: Like other NGOs, Greenpeace can face stiff political opposition while carrying out its activities. In the case of Greenpeace, sometimes the activities are downright dangerous.

Greenpeace has also been active in opposing genetically modified (GM) foods, in part on scientific grounds but also because it believes that the large biotech companies that produce GM crops exploit farmers who become dependent on GM crops and consumers who unwittingly consume them. While the Greenpeace stance on GM crops has drawn the ire of many companies, many countries in the Third World are also upset with Greenpeace. Developing countries look upon GM foods as a partial solution to widespread hunger, and they also recognize many of their nutritional benefits. "Golden rice," for example, is enriched with vitamin A. Some observers—including (ironically) Patrick Moore, a founder of Greenpeace—have been critical of Greenpeace for ignoring the possibility that genetic modifications could increase yields while reducing pesticide use. Greenpeace, however, dismisses this argument in general and Moore in particular as someone who sold out the NGO's ideals for personal gains made in industry.[25] You can see how complex these issues are—and how difficult it is to arrive at "the truth."

Greenpeace's scientific claims have also been challenged on other issues. Greenpeace has opposed nuclear power plants on several grounds, including that they harm plants and animals from radioactive emissions. But, according to Ross Clark of *The Daily Telegraph*, when Greenpeace was charged with the simple challenge of citing one case of a plant or an animal that has been harmed by radioactive emission from a nuclear plant in western Europe, it could not. "Lobsters have been found off Sellafield with twice the levels of radioactivity allowed in European food regulations," says nuclear campaigner Peter Roach. "But no one has ever looked at whether the lobsters have suffered as a result. In fact, the evidence suggests that more birds have been sliced in two by wind farms than creatures have been harmed by British nuclear power stations.[26]

Greenpeace has also gotten into trouble with countries and companies because of its own mistakes. For example, in 1995 Greenpeace claimed that the deliberate

THE VIEW FROM   China

Confrontation with AI

One of the most notorious events from Amnesty's perspective was the so-called Tienanmen Square massacre in 1989. AI documented 241 cases of people imprisoned for their involvement in the pro-democracy protests just prior to Tiananmen Square, and AI believes that the real figure is much higher.[31] However, according to William F. Schulz, "In China, it is not only the political dissent that we think about when we think about Tiananmen Square. There are hundreds of labor riots, demonstrations, and actions going on in the in-

land provinces," he said. "Uighurs in Xinjiang Province, who are Muslims, feel they have been very seriously discriminated against. China has executed 33 people among them this year." According to an Amnesty report in 1998, about 200,000 people in China were imprisoned without trial and 3,500 were executed, mostly for petty crimes like stealing bicycles.[32] In general, AI has documented a pattern of arbitrary and summary executions, torture, arbitrary detention, and unfair political trials in many parts of China.

sinking of the Royal Dutch/Shell oil platform, Brent Spar, would endanger marine life. But Greenpeace later admitted that its claims were scientifically unfounded.[27] As Michael Edwards, a Ford Foundation researcher and former NGO official, said, NGOs are often less concerned with righting specific wrongs than with stirring up controversy. John Clark, who deals with NGO relations at the World Bank, has said that NGO campaigners sometimes gloss over facts because they are in a hurry to make their point. An even more unflattering evaluation of some NGOs comes from Caroline Harper, a research director at UK Save the Children fund: Harper explains how few NGOs have the in-house resources to master complex issues. "Coming from an activist tradition, NGOs have generally neglected rigorous policy analysis, seeing such research as costly, a luxury and impractical. NGO advocates have tended to leap from the local to the global, armed only with highly contested anecdotal evidence."[28]

Greenpeace faced serious political opposition from the United States in 2001 when it protested the Bush Administration's national missile defense program. Greenpeace activists, and two journalists, drove an inflatable craft into restricted waters near the Vandenberg Air Force base in California to try to disrupt a missile test. They were arrested and sentenced for six years on felony charges of conspiracy and violating a safety zone. The two sides reached an agreement by which the charges were lessened to misdemeanor trespassing, but Greenpeace had to pay the U.S. government $150,000 and cease protest campaigns on U.S. military bases involved in missile defense for five years. William Peden, Greenpeace's disarmament campaigner, said, "The whole deal was politically motivated to stop us carrying out peaceful protests in America. They charged our people with felonies in the first place, which is completely unprecedented, then used the threat of jail to bring us to the table. . . . It was political blackmail." Tom Morozek of the U.S. Attorney's Office in Los Angeles said that it was true that no one had been charged with felony offences for civil protest before, "but no one had done anything as serious as these protesters before."[29] Despite the controversies, Greenpeace shows no signs of diminishing its efforts worldwide, and it has clearly played an important role in raising environmental consciousness.

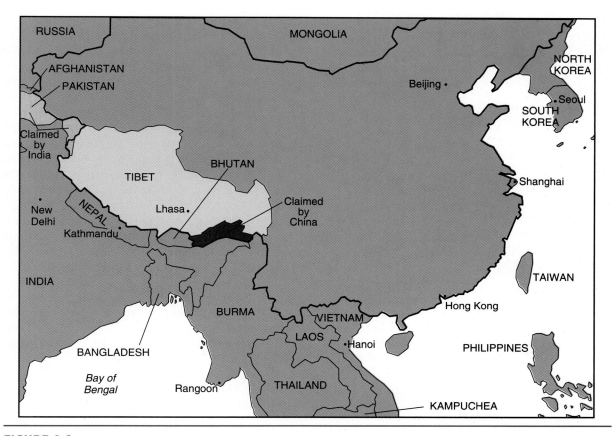

FIGURE 6.2
Map of China and Tibet
SOURCE: *A. Tom Grunfeld, The Making of Modern Tibet (New York: M.E. Sharpe, Inc.) 1997, p. ix.*

Political Opposition to Amnesty International

The very nature of Amnesty International's work makes it liable to confront opposition from sovereign states. In the paragraphs that follow, we offer many such examples, with particular attention paid to China and the United States.

Amnesty International has been highly critical of the Chinese government for a long time and on many accounts. (See box "The View from China.") Consider the following examples in terms of the scope and variety of human rights abuses.

- Amnesty International has reported widespread human-rights violations in Tibet. AI's findings are consistent with those of other organizations, including the Boston-based Physicians for Human Rights.[30] The region of Tibet is in the Himalayan mountains between the northeast part of India and the southwest part of China (see Figure 6.2). Tibet has historically never been a part of the Chinese empire or of China. But in 1949—as the communists led by Mao Zedong gained control of China—the Chinese invaded the area, and today they have no plans to give it up. According to AI, the occupying Chinese forces are guilty of torture and ill-treatment of prisoners. Tibetan nationalists and Buddhists appear to be special targets. In addition, hundreds of prisoners of conscience, among them monks and nuns, remain in prison in conditions that are often cruel and degrading. In addition to imprisonment, China is using Chinese immigration to maintain control of the area. According to the Tibetan government in exile, Tibet is now home to 6 million Tibetans and approximately 7 million Chinese immigrants, making the Tibetans a minority in their own country. Most UN members condemned the Chinese invasion, and the UN General Assembly has passed several resolutions condemning human rights abuses in that country. China's behavior is noteworthy because China has signed several international human rights conventions, including the Convention against Torture and Other Cruel, Inhuman, or Degrading Treatment or Punishment. In addition, China's own criminal law (e.g., Article 136) states that it is strictly forbidden to extort confession by torture.[33]

- Amnesty International and other NGOs, such as Human Rights Watch, have criticized China for using psychiatry to detain and institutionalize political dissidents on a scale that could surpasses similar practices in the Soviet Union.[34]

- Amnesty International is a vocal opponent of the death penalty. Executions were carried out in 40 countries in 1998, and prisoners were under sentence of death in at least 70 countries.[35] The country that carries out more executions than any other is China. China executes more people than the rest of the world put together and sentences on average 60 people to death each week.[36] Today, corruption and theft can be grounds for the death penalty. AI does not single out China for its use of the death penalty, however; AI is critical of many countries, especially those that increasingly use the death penalty for nonviolent offenses: homosexuality in Saudi Arabia, adultery in Nigeria and Sudan, and drug trafficking in southeast Asia.[37]

- Another human rights issue in China involves Falun Gong, a movement that mixes traditional Chinese breathing exercises with a synthesis of Buddhist, Taoist, and folk beliefs. According to historian John Killigrew, Falun Gong may be seen as a modern version of "a long tradition of messianic sects that at times of social discontent surface from clandestine roots and challenge the government."[38] In July 1999 China began a crackdown of Falun Gong practitioners. Falun Gong's founder, Li Hongzhi, claims that with 70 million people, Falun Gong has more members than the Chinese communist party (60 million).[39] Hongzhi, who lives in New York, poses an interesting foreign policy challenge for the United States, especially since China has issued an arrest warrant for him (although there is no extradition treaty between the United States and China). According to official Chinese sources, about 750 people have died as a result of Li's teachings and Falun Gong's "malicious fallacies." Li has denied that there is any connection between the movement and the deaths of members who might already have been ill or unstable.[40] How China reacts to Falun Gong has implications for how much the government will tolerate opposition in general. If the Chinese government uses many of the repressive techniques that it uses in other areas, it is bound to attract the scorn of Amnesty International and other human rights groups.

It is perhaps surprising to many Americans that the United States has often been targeted by Amnesty International as a country with systematic human rights problems. The most visible clash is between AI and those American states where

Amnesty International Monitors Countries Around the World, Including the United States:
One of AI's complaints about the United States is its support for the death penalty. In this
photo, opponents of the death penalty protest against this American policy.

the death penalty is legal. Amnesty International particularly opposes the U.S. practice (in 24 states) of allowing the execution of persons under 18 who commit capital crimes. Ironically, such legislation puts the United States in the same company
as Iran, Nigeria, Pakistan, Yemen, and Saudi Arabia as the only countries that have
the death penalty for minors. The United States is also faulted by AI on a number
of other issues. Consider the following.

- In 2000 Amnesty International accused NATO (and hence the United States
  indirectly) of war crimes for not taking enough precautions to prevent civilian
  casualties during the war in Kosovo.
- In a major report in 1998, AI was critical of the United States for many aspects
  of its criminal justice system. "Across the country thousands of people are subjected to sustained and deliberate brutality at the hands of police officers.

Cruel, degrading, and sometimes life-threatening methods of constraint continue to be a feature of the U.S. criminal justice system."[41] For example, women inmates in U.S. prisons and jails are routinely subjected to sexual abuse by male guards.[42]

- AI has been very critical of U.S. treatment of prisoners from the Afghan war and the war on terrorism. In its view, the United States has not lived up to its commitment to the Geneva Convention because the United States refuses prisoners the right to be informed of the reasons for detention, the right to prompt and confidential access to counsel of one's choice, and the presumption of innocence.

China and the United States, of course, are not singled out by Amnesty International as the world's only violators of human rights. AI find itself at odds with virtually every country in the world. The following examples help demonstrate the geographic scope of AI as well as the types of political opposition it faces.

- Israel: AI has disputes with Israel for being the only country with a law that allows torture.
- Egypt: AI criticizes Egypt for failing to protect minorities such as the Coptic Christians.
- Chile: AI has collided with Chile over the Amnesty campaign to extradite former Chilean leader Augusto Pinochet to Spain.
- Sierra Leone and Sudan: Amnesty International has been particularly forceful in its opposition to the mass killings in Sierra Leone and the Sudan. In Sudan about 1.5 million people have been killed, and children have been sold into slavery. Amid the civil strife in Sierra Leone, 1 million people have died and another 1.5 million have been displaced. According to AI, rebels in that West African country have chopped off the arms of innocent noncombatants.
- France: AI denounced France's president, Jacques Chirac, for meeting with Togo's President Gnassingbe Eyadema in 1999. Eyadema has been accused of instigating mass political murders. For his part, Eyadema was so angry at Amnesty International that he sought an international arrest warrant for its secretary-general, Pierre Sane of Senegal, for "spreading lies."[43]
- Mexico: The Mexican government has been targeted by AI because Mexican citizens continue to disappear in police custody despite President Vicente Fox's promises to end such abuses.[44]
- Uzbekistan: AI opposes the jailing of 7,000 Muslims in Uzbekistan for their political opposition to the government.[45]
- Nigeria: In 2002, AI began a campaign to acquit Amina Nawa, a woman sentenced to death by stoning in Nigeria.[46]
- Pakistan: AI has denounced the plight of Pakistani women who suffer "physical abuse, rape, acid attacks, burns and slayings which have prompted us to call on Pakistani authorities to protect women and take concrete steps to prevent a repetition of situations such as these."
- The G8: AI has opposed the high levels of weapons sales from the G8 (the seven leading industrialized countries plus Russia) to developing countries. According to Kate Allen, Amnesty International's British director, "The G8's proliferating trade in arms and military aid undermines fundamental human rights and sustainable development. If weapons are easier to get hold of than food and medicine, people will often resort to them as a way of realizing their aspirations. This results in an escalation of violence in countries where human rights are not respected and economic opportunities are non-existent for the majority."[47]

These many examples show not only the diverse nature of AI's complaints but also the diversity of AI's targets as well.

Political Opposition to Doctors Without Borders

Like AI and other NGOs, Doctors Without Borders can get into trouble for not being politically neutral. Since its founding, DWB has chosen to take a firm stand even it if goes against the political climate. In Biafra in 1971, a group of French doctors working with the Red Cross was outraged "that it was not possible to speak out against what was essentially a state-planned and state-directed policy of forced starvation."[48] DWB thus made a commitment to speaking out against egregious crimes against humanity, in situations where populations are targeted by their governments or other groups in a way that affronts their fundamental human dignity. This stance has put DWB at odds with the policies of dozens of countries. Even the UN has been pressured by DWB. For example, Doctors Without Borders recently demanded that the UN improve the deteriorating conditions for 180,000 Chechen refugees spending their third winter homeless.

Like AI and other NGOs, Doctors Without Borders has an extensive list of grievances directed at countries in almost every corner of the globe. In 2002, for example, DWB defied South African patent law by importing inexpensive generic AIDS drugs made in Brazil. A daily supply of the medicines costs $3.20 in South Africa, too much for many poor people, according to AIDS activists. Generic versions of the drugs produced in Brazil cost only $1.55. The South African Department of Health responded to DWB's action by saying it would dispatch investigators to see whether the NGO was in compliance with the country's medical regulatory rules.[49]

In the Middle East, DWB was highly critical of Israeli in 2002 for setting up curfews and roadblocks that prevented sick and injured Palestinians, as well as medical staff and supplies, from reaching hospitals and clinics. Joanne Liu, a Quebec pediatrician attached to DWB, said, "We deplore this violation of the human right to access to medical care," upon her return from a medical mission to the Palestinian territories. In response, Israel says that it must take special measures when, for example, Palestinian ambulances have been used "to transport armed gunmen, terrorists and people whose aim is to kill civilians and destabilize the peace process."[50]

DWB also confronted opposition from the United States and its allies in Afghanistan in 2001 and 2002. DWB has complained about the violations of the Geneva Convention, particularly the failure to uphold the principle of distinguishing between soldiers and civilians. In the Afghan city of Kandahar, DWB observed military personnel from the international coalition wearing civilian clothes with or without concealed guns, and driving civilian cars. The soldiers claimed, however, that they were on a "humanitarian mission" to assist NGOs in their work. According to Michelle Kelly, a nurse, and Morten Rostrup, head of DWB, "Despite wearing clearly marked white vests with our logo and name we have been directly asked by Afghans whether we are American soldiers. People suspect us of carrying hidden guns. We were repeatedly warned by Afghans not to go to specific places outside town since people might not be able to distinguish us from western soldiers."[51] DWB is thus very concerned that humanitarian workers will be seen as politically partisan, thus complicating the task of DWB members and other aid workers.

The experience in Afghanistan highlights the most obvious challenge that members of DWB and other humanitarian NGOs face in carrying out their work: They can become targets of attacks. DWB has seen its members kidnapped in the Caucusus regions of Dagestan and Ingushetia. And the efforts of DWB to do its work have not always been helped by the Russian government, which has said that "corruption and irresponsibility displayed by officials of the international human-rights movement in the North Caucasus are the main reason for the crisis in the international human rights activities in this region."[52] To protect themselves, then, DWB workers have avoided going to places that are too dangerous. Other aid organizations face similar challenges. The Liberty Institute, for example, an NGO funded by the U.S. government and the Soros foundation, has criticized the former communist country of Georgia for its lack of concern at the harassment of religious groups. In Georgia, however, a dozen people beat up members of Liberty Institute. According to Archil Gegeshidze, a senior fellow of the independent Georgian Foundation for Strategic and International Studies, the attack on the Liberty Institute represents "a fight between entrenched corrupt interests and forces for . . . establishing democracy, and the Liberty Institute is a major watchdog for this process. This is a life and death struggle, a critical moment for Georgia's future."[53] Red Cross, to offer another example, lost six medical workers in 1995 when they were shot dead in Chechnya. Another two Red Cross staff members were killed there in 1999 when Russian aircraft bombed a column of refugees.[54]

Another problem for DWB and many other relief agencies is that humanitarian aid often does not get to its destination. Instead, it ends up supporting groups that are responsible for creating the crisis in the first place. For example, the outpouring of aid and long-term assistance to the Rwandan refugees in Eastern Zaire inadvertently ended up providing support for the warlords and their genocidal armies.[55]

As this section of the chapter has tried to show, international NGOs address a wide variety of problems. In addition, we have seen that the impact of NGOs can range from insignificant to important, from short term to long term, and from direct to indirect. The next section of the chapter focuses on a special kind of NGO: the corporate actor. We will again want to describe different kinds of corporate NGOs and look at how influential they can be.

What Kinds of Business Do NGOs Operate in the International Arena and How Powerful Are They?

Since World War II, international corporations have played an increasingly powerful role in the world. By the early 1980s, these nonstate actors accounted for about 80 percent of the world's trade in noncommunist block countries. By the same time, the 25 largest banks accounted for about $3.7 trillion.[56] And, the worldwide sales of foreign subsidiaries of local companies are now 1.5 times greater than total world exports. In 1997 some 53,600 international businesses controlled nearly 450,000 foreign companies affiliated with the parent company around the world.[57] There are basically three kinds of international corporate actors behind all this business activity: multinational corporations (MNCs), transnational corporations (TNCs), and business alliances. The following paragraphs describe them and the differences between them.

Multinational Corporations

Multinational corporations (MNCs) are loosely defined as businesses with operations in more than one country. Some MNCs have foreign subsidiaries that are clones of the parent company. For example, an American company with a German *subsidiary* would consist of a self-contained operation in Germany that makes almost everything it sells in Germany, that buys supplies in Germany, and that employs mostly Germans. MNCs are based on the idea that there is only one economic unit—the world. These MNCs, sometimes referred to as transnational companies[58], generally have a local perspective when it comes to sales, service, public relations, and legal affairs, but they have a global perspective when it comes to parts, machines, planning, research and development, finance, marketing, pricing, and management. Transnational companies usually view themselves as nonnational entities. For example, one of the best-known management consulting firms, McKinsey and Co., has been headed by an Indian. Citibank's second most important executive for many years was Chinese, and the top executive at Coca Cola is Australian. In short, the term *MNC* encompasses any large company with operations in two or more countries.

International Business Alliances and Consolidations

Another type of international business arrangement exists in a loose form of cooperation among companies from different countries. By banding together in an alliance, companies gain more control over a market in one or more countries. In the late 1990s, for example, the international airline industry witnessed the creation of a series of such alliances. The Star Alliance involves United Airlines (United States), Air Canada, Lufthansa (Germany), SAS (Denmark), and others from Thailand, New Zealand, Australia, and Japan. The Oneworld Alliance includes American Airlines, Quantas (Australia), British Airways, Canadian Airlines, Cathay Pacific (China), and others from Finland, Chile, and elsewhere. In 2000 yet another alliance—SkyTeam—was announced between Air France, Delta, Aero-Mexico and Korean Air Lines, making it the world's fourth global airline alliance. Other alliances include Wings (KLM and Northwest) and Qualiflyer (Swissair and Sabena).

Business alliances differ from *international business consolidations,* which are basically the merging of two or more businesses into one. Sometimes such consolidations occur between companies from different countries. In the late 1990s, for example, the international oil industry witnessed mergers between BP and Amoco and between Royal Dutch/Shell and Texaco. The merging of international businesses can create huge economic actors in world politics. The Exxon-Mobil merger, for instance, took place through a $75.3 billion takeover of Mobil by Exxon.[59]

Before describing the influence of international businesses, it is worthwhile to ask what motivates a company to go abroad in the first place. There are actually several good reasons. First, by going abroad a company can often lower its costs of production. Sometimes, for example, the cost of labor in the company's **home country** is too high. An American company may want to set up shop in a **host country,** such as Mexico, because there it can pay Mexican workers four or five times less than what it would have to pay American workers. Another reason for a company going abroad is to gain better access to the foreign market. Often companies have little knowledge of the foreign market where they want to sell products. By being on the scene, the company can learn what consumers want and how best to market their products. Other reasons for a company going abroad include establishing market dominance in the host country, avoiding high taxes in the home country, evading tougher environmental standards—which increase production costs—in the home country, and avoiding trade barriers in the host country.

Web Exploration

For more information on huge U.S. industries, go to **www.ablongman.com/ duncan**.

Home Country
The country of origin, or home base, for an international company.

Host Country
The country that hosts an international company. For the company, it is a foreign country.

TABLE 6.2   The World's Top 50 Economic Entities

Rank 2000–2001	Economic Entity	Market Value (Billions of US$)
1	United States	9,837.4
2	Japan	4,841.6
3	Germany	1,873.0
4	United Kingdom	1,414.6
5	France	1,294.2
6	China	1,079.9
7	Italy	1,074.0
8	Canada	687.9
9	Brazil	595.5
10	Mexico	574.5
11	Spain	558.6
12	Korea, Rep. (South Korea)	457.2
13	India	457.0
14	Australia	390.1
15	Netherlands	364.8
16	Argentina	285.0
17	Russian Federation	251.1
18	Switzerland	239.8
19	Sweden	227.3
20	Belgium	226.7
21	**Wal-Mart Stores**	219.8
22	Turkey	199.9
23	**Exxon Mobil**	191.6
24	Austria	189.0
25	**General Motors**	177.3
26	**British Petroleum**	174.2
27	Saudi Arabia	173.3
28	Hong Kong, China	162.6
29	**Ford Motor**	162.4

(continued)

The Influence of Corporate Actors

As more companies become international in scope, there have increasingly been calls for international laws and rules for the global economy. As we will see in Chapters 11 and 12, however, getting control of the huge transnational companies is a very difficult task. Many international businesses control vast economic resources. For example, only three companies produce at least 90 percent of the entire world's vitamins (Roche, BASF, and Rhône-Poulenc). Regardless of the brand of vitamin you take, chances are that it comes from one of these three companies (and, that it contains exactly the same raw materials).[60] Some transnational *companies* have more economic clout than most of the *countries* of the world. General Motors, for example, controls more economic resources than Indonesia, Denmark, and Saudi Arabia. In Table 6.2, you can see that a number of companies are represented among the world's top 50 economic entities. Since economic clout often translates into political influence, such large companies can have a tremendous impact on the political economies of both host and home countries.

TABLE 6.2   The World's Top 50 Economic Entities (continued)

Rank 2000—2001	Economic Entity	Market Value (Billions of US$)
30	Denmark	162.3
31	Norway	161.8
32	Poland	157.7
33	Indonesia	153.3
34	**Enron**	138.8
35	**DaimlerChrysler**	136.9
36	**Royal Dutch/Shell Group**	135.2
37	**General Electric**	125.9
38	South Africa	125.9
39	Thailand	122.2
40	Finland	121.5
41	**Toyota Motor**	120.8
42	Venezuela, RB	120.5
43	Greece	112.6
44	**Citigroup**	112.0
45	Israel	110.4
46	**Mitsubishi**	105.8
47	Portugal	105.1
48	Iran, Islamic Rep.	104.9
49	**Mitsui**	101.2
50	**ChevronTexaco**	99.7

SOURCES: *Adapted from the following sources: For company data, representing total earnings in 2001, see "Global 500" Fortune, July 22, 2002, (http://www.fortune.com/lists/G500/index.html); For country data, representing GDP for 2000, see "World Development Indicators database," World Bank, April 2002.*

The Relationship Between NGOs and Corporate Actors

A common impression is that NGOs, even the large ones described earlier in the chapter, cannot possibly compete for influence with corporate giants like General Motors or Sony. But the relationship between NGOs and businesses is quite complex. NGOs that are critical of many international corporations often demand actions from them that typically have little to do with "traditional" business activity. For example, the International Business Leaders Forum, a noncorporate NGO, argues that corporations have the responsibility to resolve conflicts and foster socioeconomic development in the countries where they are located. Oil companies, for instance, must "proactively create positive societal value by engaging in innovative social investment, stakeholder consultation, policy dialogue, advocacy and civic institution building."[61]

NGOs can and do actually influence how MNCs operate in some countries. Shell, for example, extracted oil from Nigeria for over 50 years without much concern for the local population or environment. But due in part to pressure from NGOs, the company has made important strides in helping its host country. Even Human Rights Watch, one of Shell's harshest critics, admits that "development spending by the oil companies has also brought schools, clinics, and other infrastructure to remote parts of the country that might otherwise be far more marginalized by the Nigerian government."[62]

As another example, in April 2000, Starbucks announced it would buy coffee beans from importers who pay above market prices to small farmers (so-called fair trade beans) and sell them in more than 2000 of its shops across the United States. In August of the same year, McDonald's sent a letter to the producers of the nearly 2 billion eggs it buys annually, ordering them to comply with strict guidelines for the humane treatment of hens or risk losing the company's business.[63] Similarly, public pressure forced Amoco, Texaco, ARCO, and Petro-Canada to withdraw from Myanmar in 1998.[64] And as Edward Aden of the *Financial Times* explains, Home Depot, the world's largest retailer of timber products, agreed to stop buying wood cut from old-growth forests after the Rainforest Action Network and other environmental groups held a series of protests in front of Home Depot stores and ran advertisements denouncing the company. This in turn affected Weyerhaueser to pledge an end to cutting of old-growth forests in British Columbia.[65]

As NGO and public pressure have increased, MNCs have increasingly begun implementing "certification" arrangements. These are "codes of good conduct," production guidelines, and monitoring standards that govern corporate behavior and even the behavior of companies that supply MNCs. The certifications can take several forms. First, they may be written by a single company as in the case of Johnson & Johnson, which wrote its first environmental health and safety report in 1993. Second, certifications may be organized by industry or trade associations such as the chemical industry's global Responsible Care program. Third, certification can involve an external group, often an NGO, imposing its rules and compliance methods onto a particular firm or industry. The NGO Center for Responsibility in Business, for example, designed auditable standards and an independent accreditation process for the protection of workers' rights. By mid-2001, the Center had certified 66 manufacturing facilities around the world that mainly make toys and apparel. A fourth kind of certification involves government or multilateral agencies, as in the case of the UN's Global Compact, which lists environmental, labor, and human rights principles for companies to follow. To be certified, companies must submit online updates of their progress for NGOs to scrutinize. These certifications are now common in many industries, including the chemical industry, coffee, forest products, oil, mining, nuclear power, transportation sectors, apparel, diamond, footwear, and toy industries. They even influence buying strategies of sports organizations. The International Federation of Football Association, for instance, created a licensing program in 1996 to prevent members from using soccer balls made with child labor.[66]

The record of certification so far is mixed. In some economic sectors, the impact is noticeable, particularly in the forest products and clothing industries. The World Wildlife Federal and Greenpeace, for example, created the Forest Stewardship Council (FSC). Companies that meet the Council's requirements can put the FSC logo on their products. Lumber companies have responded with their own version of certification. Likewise, because of pressure from NGOs such as the National Labor Committee, GAP, Inc. became the first retailer to agree to independent monitoring of a foreign contractor.

While certifications may lead to the improvements that NGOs seek, critics of certification are concerned that, in the end, certification will be a weak substitute for a stronger political (state) role in addressing a country's problems. In addition, some observers believe that NGO demands of MNCs can be inappropriate, or that NGO criticisms can be misplaced. According to Marina Ottaway, a senior associate at the Carnegie Endowment for International Peace, no matter what it does, Shell cannot pacify its Nigerian and international critics, because what they want is beyond any single actor's capacity to deliver.[67] Fareed Zakaria of *Newsweek* has also argued that environmental and labor NGOs and anti-corporate demonstrators often choose the wrong target. Attacks on the World Trade Organization as a tool of large corporations, for example, are inappropriate because there "are other methods, treaties, and organizations aimed at pursuing environmental and labor goals."[68]

Typically, NGOs are critical of MNCs, and the bigger the company the greater the criticism. But, sometimes, the world is more complicated than the "you're either with us or against us" attitude would suggest. For example, in 2002 the United Nations chose corporations as the main resources in tackling health problems in Southern Africa mostly because the companies—not local governments or NGOs—had the necessary resources. The Britain-based mining group Anglo-American, for example, plans to offer HIV/AIDS drugs to its workers and provide medicine regimens in the rural communities from which the company finds its miners. While the motive may be seen as purely economic—the Anglo-American estimates that about 23 percent of its 134,000 employees in Southern Africa are HIV positive—the end results may be very positive indeed.[69]

"A few years ago it would have been unthinkable that a board of directors of a company would have considered treating HIV/AIDS. But now it's hitting the bottom line and there must be a good economic argument (for providing drugs). It's a very important development, if not a breakthrough," says Peter Piot, executive director of the UN Program on HIV/AIDS.

In the future, companies and governments may find it to their advantage to work more closely with NGOs, even if the companies and governments may be criticized for pandering to the NGOS, and even if the NGOs themselves get criticized by hard-core activists who argue that the NGOs are "selling out" to the enemy.

Still, the record thus far shows that NGOs often make only superficial progress with big businesses. Oil companies, for example, have sometimes shown a willingness to improve communication and consultation with outside groups, and they even produce reports on company social and environmental performance—but all without changing central company policy. When NGOs were critical of UK Minnow Premier Oil for its investment in Myanmar, the company responded with a detailed description of its social and environmental performance and commissioned an independent social audit, but it remains in Myanmar. Likewise, British Petroleum keeps its Petrochina stake, despite criticism from and a dialogue with the Free Tibet Campaign.[70]

Turning now to nation-states, their relationships with NGOs are often turbulent, as many of the examples of this chapter have demonstrated. But sometimes a symbiotic relationship can exist—a relationship that is beneficial to both parties. In some cases, governments wishing to tap into popular support of NGO issues even seek cooperative alliances with the NGOs. For example, the Brazilian government's Environmental Agency asked Greenpeace to monitor the Amazon rainforest for environmental violations such as illegal logging. A debt relief campaign for heavily indebted poor countries, Jubilee 2000, was designed specifically to change the perceptions of governments, the IMF, and World Bank so that they would be more environmentally friendly. And through its cooperation with Jubilee 2000, the British government gained popular international legitimacy. This debt relief program managed to collect 25 million signatures supporting the program from across the globe and encouraged banks to cancel $30 billion in debt.[71]

What Is the Power Relationship Between Nation-States and NGOs?

The goal of this section of the chapter is to review the many ways in which NGOs can shape international events and nation-states. In general, NGOs can affect nation-states in the short, medium, and long term, and the relationship between NGOs and nation-states can range from complete hostility to peaceful coexistence to overt cooperation. Keep in mind, though, that regardless of the relationship, some NGOs may have no impact whatsoever on nation-states.

In the short term, NGOs' successes occur, but they are rare. The impact of NGO activity on a sovereign state may be immediate, as in the case of UN mediators forcing France to pay for its attack on the Rainbow Warrior. Thereafter, although the French continued their nuclear testing program, they reduced the number of tests. A medium-term success case is Amnesty International's Campaign Against Torture begun in Mexico in October 2001. It led to an increase in Amnesty Mexico membership by 50 percent and to an agreement with a popular radio station to promote human rights issues.[72] While this achievement has not transformed Mexican society over night, AI considers it an important step along the way.

Most NGOs do not succeed in the short run because their demands typically include making large political or economic entities change the fundamental way they operate. So when the interests of these entities are entrenched, short-term successes are likely to be rare. It is over the long run that NGOs may have a more important impact on nation-states and world politics in general. This is because the impact of NGOs can be indirect and subtle. People who have only recently learned about the missions of Greenpeace or Human Rights Watch, for example, may not act at the time of a particular humanitarian crisis, but their new-found awareness may bring them to political action in the future.

As Professor Craig Warkentin of the State University of New York at Oswego has shown, NGOs are facilitators of attitudinal changes, and shapers of norms and values.[73] In other words, for nation-states or other large organizations (e.g., MNCs) to alter their behavior, a change of attitude is often required, and NGOs contribute to a long-term change in public attitudes. For example, NGOs can identify transnational problems that might otherwise be ignored. They may help establish international-level values and norms that can guide future international policies taken by nation-states or international organizations such as the UN.[74] Although Greenpeace is still struggling in its campaign to ban whaling, for example, it is thanks to *sustained* Greenpeace pressure that the International Whaling Commission was transformed from an organization allocating whaling quotas into an organization protecting whales.[75]

Of course, if NGOs are unable to change enough people's minds, they will continue to face formidable political obstacles. For instance, Amnesty International and other human rights organizations face a long, uphill struggle to get countries (including China and the United States) to end the use of the death penalty. In China, the AIDS Action Project, an NGO that is partially funded from international sources, publicized government incompetence in the sale of HIV-tainted blood that may have killed over one million people. The government's response was to evict the NGO from its offices in an effort to silence the group.[76] In the case of whaling, since Norway reauthorized whaling in 1993, making it legal in Norwegian waters, Greenpeace continues to face serious legal challenges should it try to prevent hunting in Norwegian waters.

As for corporate actors, we have seen how multinational corporations can have a major impact on both the *host* and *home* countries. Recall the vast economic resources that MNCs control and the political clout that can accompany such economic power. Some regulation of MNC activity is possible, but no country can completely rein in international businesses without threatening to lose whatever benefits were derived from the international businesses in the first place. The problem is worse for countries that are politically and economically weak.

Clearly, the impact of NGOs on nation-states—when in fact there is an impact—can be quite varied. Sometimes the relationship is hostile, sometimes it is cooperative, and sometimes the relationship is young and evolving. For example, according to Vladimir Orlov, founder of the Moscow-based Center for Policy Studies (PIR), Russia's growing NGO community is stepping into a policy vacuum created by the Russian government's crackdown of press freedoms, and therefore is in a position to influence Russian policy in arenas from environmental to security affairs, and to provide an increasing amount of information to the Russian public.[77]

The relationship between NGOs and multinational corporations is as varied as the relationship between NGOs and nation-states. The stereotypical image is of NGOs protesting the behavior of rapacious MNCs in some Third World country. The NGO complaint usually centers on the MNC's environmental, labor, or human rights record. While this stereotype applies to many NGO-MNC relationships, it does not apply to all of them. As with NGOs and the oil industry, for instance, there have been cases when the two sides have chosen to cooperate instead. According to John Browne, the chief executive of British Petroleum, oil "companies no longer dismiss the NGOs as simple troublemakers, and the NGOs are less inclined to vilify oil companies as 'malign forces doing damage by design or neglect.'" British Petroleum says, "Don't be afraid of NGOs. Listen to them, hear their concerns and challenges, look for areas of mutual advantage. It is important that we understand the business environment in its entirety."[78]

In short, then, NGOs can have both a short-term and long-term impact on nation-states and corporate actors. And the relationship between NGOs and nation-states and corporate actors is often hostile but need not be. When NGOs confront entrenched interests—such as nation-states that pursue their perceived national interest as the expense of the environment, or companies that seek short-term profit regardless of NGO complaints–progress is likely to be slow or nonexistent.

We conclude this chapter by returning to one of the main questions raised in both Chapter 5 and here. How influential can corporate and nongovernmental actors be in a world dominated by states? From one perspective, it would appear that IGOs and NGOs are indeed chipping away at the sovereignty of nation-states. If one looks at the power wielded by international corporate actors, the influence that some international organizations have on countries, or the actions of international terrorists, the nation-state seems to be in retreat.

In terms of sheer numbers, the future looks bright for corporate and noncorporate actors, NGOs and IGOs. Global capitalist relations are encouraging an expansion of the powers of corporate actors on a regional level—as in NAFTA and the European Union—and on a global scale. The NGOs such as Doctors Without Borders are likely to be active as long as people are threatened in unstable or repressive countries. And as long as environmentally harmful substances, nuclear weapons, and civilian nuclear power are used, NGOs like Greenpeace will also be active. Finally, NGOs are likely to prosper as more countries open up their political systems and allow for greater freedoms of expression and associations.

CHAPTER SUMMARY

What Is the Significance of Nongovernmental Organizations (NGOs)?

- International NGOs, organizations whose members are groups and individuals but not countries, are very diverse and have rapidly grown in number, especially in the past 15 years, thanks to technological advances and more open political and economic conditions.
- NGOs are likely to be active as long as states, particularly in the developing world, struggle to stay intact. And as long as environmentally harmful substances, nuclear weapons, and civilian nuclear power are used, NGOs are likely to be very active.
- NGOs can have immediate or delayed influences on specific countries or the entire world.
- Many NGOs try to gain legitimacy by being impartial and independent of any government, political or ideological persuasion, or religion.
- The influence of NGOs can be limited not only by their available resources but also by political opposition. This is especially true when NGOs tread on the interests of sovereign states.

What Are Examples of Important NGOs?

- The NGO Greenpeace promotes global disarmament and nonviolent approaches to resolving political differences. Greenpeace seeks to prevent pollution and the abuse of the earth's oceans, lands, and fresh water. It opposes nuclear weapons and nuclear power and seeks to protect the biodiversity of the planet.
- Amnesty International is a human rights NGO. It opposes the imprisonment of individuals for their political views, it seeks to ensure fair trials for political prisoners, and it opposes the death penalty, torture, and political killings.
- Doctors Without Borders (DWB) is an international medical relief agency. It helps not only victims of epidemics and natural and man-made disasters, but victims of armed conflict as well. DWB also helps those who lack health care due to geographic remoteness or ethnic marginalization.

Why Is There Political Opposition to NGOs?

- NGOs often fail because their objectives collide with those of nation-states or companies whose priorities do not include addressing NGO concerns.
- Opposition to NGOs like Greenpeace or Amnesty International can come from any country (democratic or nondemocratic) as well as from international businesses.
- Although NGOs typically advocate peaceful means of protest, when political opposition is very strong, working for certain NGOs can be life threatening.

What Kinds of Business Do NGOs Operate in the International Arena and How Powerful Are They?

- International corporate actors are business NGOs whose activities take place in more than one country. Some of these multinational corporations (MNCs) have simple subsidiaries designed to address a particular country's market while others MNCs look at the world as a single huge market.
- Corporate actors have become major players in international affairs, especially since World War II. The economic power of some corporate actors rivals that of most countries of the world.
- Corporate actors can have an important impact not only on the home country's political and economic situation but also on that of the host country.

What Is the Power Relationship Between Nation-States and NGOs?

- Sovereign states can be influenced by NGOs such as Greenpeace and Amnesty International. NGOs are highly controversial in some countries since their missions are counter to the existing social, political, or economic order in those countries.
- Sometimes the NGOs are able to publicize government activity they oppose, thus helping to effect short- or medium-term change (such

as shutting down a polluting factory), or long-term change that involves people's attitudes and, eventually, state policies.

- While much of this chapter described examples of political opposition to NGOs, the relationship between NGOs and nation-states and companies can be quite varied, ranging from hostile to cooperative.

ENDNOTES

[1] The Union of International Associations as quoted in Maryann K. Cusimano, Mark Hensman, and Leslie Rodrigues, "Private-Sector Transsovereign Actors–MNCs and NGOs," in Maryann K. Cusimano, ed., *Beyond Sovereignty: Issues for a Global Agenda* (Boston: Bedford/St. Martin's, 2000), p. 256.

[2] Quentin Peel, "How militants hijacked NGO party," *Financial Times*, July 13, 2001.

[3] Ibid.

[4] This section borrows from the nice summary laid out in Maryann K. Cusimano, Mark Hensman, and Leslie Rodrigues, "Private-Sector Transsovereign Actors–MNCs and NGOs," in Maryann K. Cusimano, ed., *Beyond Sovereignty*, pp. 257–261.

[5] Virginia A Hulme, "250 Chinese NGOs: Civil Society in the Making," *The China Business Review*, Vol. 29, No. 1, January/February 2002.

[6] Jon B. Wolfsthal, "Russian NGOs go nuclear, "*Foreign Policy*," No. 129, March/April 2002, pp. 90–92.

[7] Quentin Peel, "How militants hijacked NGO party."

[8] A nice summary of NGOs and the globalization process is written by L. David Brown, Sanjeev Khagram, Mark H. Moore, and Peter Frumkin, "Globalization, NGOs, and Multisectoral Relations," in Joseph S. Nye Jr. and John D. Donahue, eds., *Governance in a Globalizing World* (Washington, D.C.: Brookings Institution Press, 2000), pp. 271–296.

[9] Greenpeace Canada, *http://www.greenpeacecanada.org/*.

[10] Matthew Campbell, "Greenpeace nudes have toxic effect on feminists," *Sunday Times* (London), May 12, 2002.

[11] "Greenpeace urges Ukraine to replace Chernobyl with natural gas," *The Associated Press*, July 6, 1999.

[12] Greenpeace, *http://www.greenpeacecanada.org/*

[13] Michael Bond, "A new environment for Greenpeace," *Foreign Policy*, November/December 2001, No. 127, pp., 66–67.

[14] Amnesty International, *http://www.amnesty.org/web/about ai.nsf*

[15] "Facts and Figures about Amnesty International," Amnesty International, *http://www.web.amnesty.org/web/aboutai.NSF/*

[16] Nora Boustany, "Rights Violators Know No Boundaries," *The Washington Post*, June 16, 1999, p.A25.

[17] Doctors Without Borders website: *http://www.doctors withoutborders.org/*

[18] Doctors Without Borders website: *http://www.doctors withoutborders.org/*

[19] Lara Marlowe, "Advocate of 'right of interference' chosen to restore Kosovo's civic life," *The Irish Times*, July 5, 1999, p. 15.

[20] Keith Suter, "Nuclear Testing: Paradise Lost," *Bulletin of American Scientists*, September/October 1995, Vol. 51, No. 5.

[21] See Conciliation Proceedings: Ruling by UN Secretary-General Javier Perez de Cuellar, New York, 5 July 1986; text

in International Legal Materials 26 (1987) 1346. 12A: Ruling Pertaining to the Differences Between France and New Zealand Arising from the Rainbow Warrior Affair (*http://www.jura.unimuenchen.de/tel/cases/Rainbow_Warrior.html*); and Keith Suter, "Nuclear Testing."

[22] Keith Suter, "Nuclear Testing."

[23] Tim Jeffery, "Protesters ram French boat," *The Daily Telegraph*, May 20, 2002.

[24] "Greenpeace vs. Moscow, *Agency WPS: What the Papers Say*, June 17, 1999. Russian Television (RTR), "Vesti" program, June 16, 1999.

[25] Tom Abate, "Greenpeace founder defends biotech," *The San Francisco Chronicle*, June 10, 2002.

[26] Ross Clark, "Let's really go nuclear," *The Daily Telegraph*, May 11, 2002.

[27] Guy de Jonquières, "The truth, the whole truth and nothing but . . ." *Financial Times*, July 20, 2001.

[28] Ibid.

[29] Steve Boggan, "Greenpeace Agrees to Halt Protests at U.S. Missile Bases," *The Independent* (London), April 15, 2002.

[30] Cesar Chelala, "Torture in Tibet," *The Boston Globe*, June 22, 1999, p. A15, OP-ED.

[31] "China: Ten years after Tiananmen—and still waiting for justice," Amnesty International News Release—ASA 17/27/99, May 26, 1999, *http://www.amnesty.org/news/1999/31702799.htm*.

[32] Nora Boustany, "Rights Violators," p. A25.

[33] Chelala, p. A15.

[34] Richard McGregor, "Attack on China's use of 'political' psychiatry," *Financial Times*, August 13, 2002.

[35] "Facts and Figures about Amnesty International," Amnesty International, *http://www.web.amnesty.org*

[36] "Amnesty International releases 1997 death penalty statistics," *Amnesty International—News Release*, September 9, 1998.

[37] "Number of reported executions around world doubled last year, Amnesty International says," *Associated Press*, April 10, 2002.

[38] John Killigrew, "Quasi-religious movement challenges Chinese Communism," *Democrat and Chronicle* (Rochester), November 24, 1999, p. 11A.

[39] "China's trial by faith," *The Economist*, November 6, 1999, p. 41.

[40] Henry Chu, "New York-Based Leader of Banned Group Targeted by China for Arrest," *Los Angeles Times*, July 30, 1999, p. A4.

[41] Barbara Crossette, "Amnesty Finds 'Widespread Pattern' of U.S. Rights Violations," *The New York Times*, October 5, 1998.

[42] Barbara Vobejda, "Abuse of Female Prisoners in U.S. Is Routine, Rights Report Says," *The Washington Post*, March 04, 1999.

[43]Paul Webster, "Chirac supports 'killer' dictator; African leader seeks Amnesty chief's arrest over mass murder allegations," *The Observer,* July 4, 1999.

[44]Sisam Ferross, "Amnesty: Mexico police victims still vanishing," *The Atlanta Journal and Constitution,* June 29, 2002.

[45]"At Least 7,000 Muslims in Prison in Uzbekistan, Radio Quotes Rights Group," *BBC Monitoring International Reports,* June 27, 2002.

[46]"Spain-Nigeria: Half a Million Spaniards Ask Nigeria Not to Stone Woman to Death," *EFE News Service,* July 5, 2002.

[47]Richard Norton-Taylor, "Arms deals hinder war on terror, says Amnesty," *The Guardian* (London), June 24, 2002.

[48]James Orbinski as quoted in "1999 Nobel Peace Prize," *NewsHour with Jim Lehrer,* October 15, 1999, *http://www. pbs.org/newshour/bb/international/july-dec99/peace_10-15.html.*

[49]See "Group is Illegally Importing AIDS Drugs to South Africa," *The Associated Press,* January 30, 2002, and Mark Schoops, "Doctor's Group Defies South Africa AIDS Policy," *Wall Street Journal,* January 30, 2002.

[50]See Ann Carroll, "Israel blocking aid: doctor," *Montreal Gazette,* June 8, 2002, and Irwin Block, "Stop attacks on medical workers, Israel urged by occupation critics," *Montreal Gazette,* March 20, 2002.

[51]Michelle Kelly & Morten Rostrup, "Identify yourselves," *The Guardian* (London), February 1, 2002.

[52]According to Russia's official news agency Tass as reported in Yasmin Sati, "Feature: Humanitarian crisis in Chechnya," *United Press International,* August 8, 2002.

[53]Ken Stier, "Post-Soviet Georgia struggles to find democracy," *The Christian Science Monitor,* July 24, 2002.

[54]Andrew Jack, "Red Cross chief seeks meeting with Putin," *Financial Times,* March 10, 2000.

[55]Andre-Jacques Neusy, "A call away from arms," *The Lancet* (London), April 1997.

[56]Joan E. Spero and Jeffrey A. Hart, *The Politics of International Economic Relations,* 5th edition (New York: St. Martin's Press, 1997), pp. 96–148.

[57]R. Alan, Hedley, "Transnational corporations and their regulation: Issues and strategies," *International Journal of Comparative Sociology;* Dharwar; May 1999.

[58]A short description of the distinction between transnational and multinational corporations is made in Peter Drucker, "The Global Economy and the Nation-State," *Foreign Affairs,* September/October 1997, Vol. 76, No. 5, pp. 159–171.

[59]Daniel Yergin, "Bigger oil," *Financial Times,* December 2, 1998.

[60]*Wellness Letter,* The University of California, Berkeley, Volume 15, Issue 11, August 1999, p. 1.

[61]International Business Leaders Forum, "The Business of Peace," as quoted in Marina Ottaway, "Reluctant missionaries," *Foreign Policy,* No. 125, Jul/Aug 2001, pp. 44–54.

[62]Marina Ottaway, "Reluctant missionaries," *Foreign Policy,* No. 125, Jul/Aug 2001, pp. 44–54.

[63]Gary Gereffi, Ronie Garcia-Johnson, and Erika Sasser, "The NGO-industrial complex," *Foreign Policy,* No. 125, July/August 2001, pp. 56–65.

[64]Marina Ottaway, "Reluctant missionaries," pp. 44–54.

[65]Edward Alden, "Brands feel the impact as activists target customers," *Financial Times,* July 18, 2001.

[66]Gary Gereffi, Ronie Garcia-Johnson, and Erika Sasser, "The NGO-industrial complex," pp. 56–65.

[67]This discussion of corporate certification draws primarily from Gary Gereffi, Ronie Garcia-Johnson, and Erika Sasser, "The NGO-industrial complex." See also Bennett Freeman, "Drilling for common ground," *Foreign Policy,* No. 125, Jul/Aug 2001, and Marina Ottaway, "Reluctant missionaries," pp. 44–54.

[68]Fareed Zakaria, "After the Storm Passes," *Newsweek,* December 13, 1999, p. 40.

[69]See James Lamont, "Summit accused of ignoring Aids," *Financial Times,* August 30, 2002; James Lamont, "UN Looks to businesses for help in fight against Aids," *Financial Times,* August 30, 2002; and James Lamont, "Business plea for greater investment in poor nations," *Financial Times,* August 29, 2002.

[70]"NGOs Refine Ways To Go After Big Oil," *Petroleum Intelligence Weekly,* April 24, 2002.

[71]See Quentin Peel, "How militants hijacked NGO party," and Alan Beattie, "Campaigners offer integrity for influence," *Financial Times,* July 17, 2001.

[72]"Putting an End to Torture . . . Nation by Nation," *Amnesty International* brochure, 2002.

[73]Craig Warkentin, *Reshaping World Politics: NGOs, the Internet, and Global Civil Society* (Lanham: Rowman & Littlefield Publishers, Inc., 2001).

[74]L. David Brown, Sanjeev Khagram, Mark H. Moore, and Peter Frumkin, "Globalization, NGOs, and Multisectoral Relations," in Joseph S. Nye Jr. and John D. Donahue, eds., *Governance in a Globalizing World* (Washington, D.C.: Brookings Institution Press, 2000), pp. 271–296.

[75]Michael Bond, "A new environment for Greenpeace," pp. 66–67.

[76]Cindy Sui, "Chinese NGO that probed village AIDS deaths evicted," *Agence France Presse,* July 3, 2002.

[77]Jon B. Wolfsthal, "Russian NGOs go nuclear," *Foreign Policy,* No. 129, March/April 2002, pp. 90–92.

[78]"NGOs Refine Ways To Go After Big Oil," *Petroleum Intelligence Weekly,* April 24, 2002.

[79]See "Three Greenpeace militants arrested in Norway," *Agence France Presse,* June 12, 1999; and "Greenpeace Blamed for Environmentalist Injury," *Nordic Business Report,* June 21, 1999.

[80]Dan Goodman, "Blubber banned," Letter to the Editor, *The Economist,* September 30, 2000.

[81]"Greenpeace blasts new Japanese whale hunt," *Reuters,* November 9, 1999.

[82]"The politics of whaling," *The Economist,* September 9, 2000. The Institute of Cetacean Research in July 2002 put more than 2200 tons of minke whale meat on sale that could bring the institute $31.7 million. "Whale meat sold," *Associated Press,* August 1, 2002. In addition, see "For watching or eating?" *The Economist,* July 28, 2001.

CASE STUDY

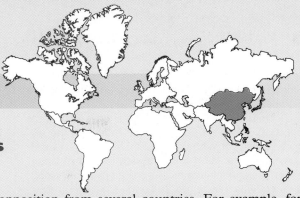

The Power and Limits of NGOs

Greenpeace has encountered serious political opposition from several countries. For example, for years it has had a contentious relationship with both Japan and Norway over whaling. In 1986 a United Nations-approved organization—the International Whaling Commission—instituted a moratorium on whale hunting. But in the summer of 1999, when Greenpeace attempted to prevent ships from hunting minke whales near Norway, one of its boats collided with a Norwegian coastguard ship. One American and two British Greenpeace members were arrested, while others escaped and returned safely to the "Rainbow Warrior." Since Greenpeace was in Norwegian waters and because Norwegian law allows whaling, the coastguard felt justified in thwarting the efforts of Greenpeace.[79]

Greenpeace has also criticized Japan for resuming whaling in an area near Antarctica designated by the International Whaling Commission as a sanctuary. Japan claims that the whaling was for scientific research into the relationship between whales and fish in the north Pacific.[80] But Greenpeace claims that about $100 million in whale meat harvested by Japanese "research hunting" was sold on the market in 1998.[81] In addition, it claims that the Japanese government keeps about 20 percent of the whale meat bought by the government-linked Institute of Cetacean Research for, among other things, promoting the consumption of whale meat.[82] The scientific opinion on the legitimacy of the research program is divided, complicating efforts by Greenpeace and other antiwhaling organizations. Japan's decision in the summer of 2001 to allow fishermen to kill and sell whales caught by mistake in their nets has done little to appease critics.

The two articles that make up this case study provide the arguments for and against lifting the whaling ban. You will notice the intricate political, economic, and even cultural elements to this issue. Note also the pressure Greenpeace can put on nation-states and the lengths to which nation-states will go to try to resist this NGO.

GREENPEACE TAKES ON JAPAN

Japanese Opposition to Greenpeace

(Shimonoseki, Japan, May 19, 2002) Some 700 right-wing activists from across Japan paraded through downtown Shimonoseki on Sunday afternoon blaring slogans like "Greenpeace get lost!" ahead of an international whaling plenary.

"Whale meat is part of Japanese food culture!" the activists shouted from loudspeakers mounted on about 160 trucks and buses in a noisy procession through the former southern Japanese whaling port.

The parade crawled down the main street while men in fatigues and military dress stood on the streets and saluted, some holding Japan's Hinomaru flag. "Reopen the whale hunt!" the trucks screamed. Police

said the group, originally numbering 180 vehicles, came from all over Japan, but did not cause any problems other than the noise.

The parade moved near to the Kaikyo Messe Shimonoseki, the convention centre where delegates from 47 member nations of the International Whaling Commission will gather to discuss whaling for a week-long plenary beginning Monday.

Some of the hundreds of officers lining the streets held up signs warning the group to pipe down. "They were over the legal noise limit, but there were lots of vehicles so we weren't able to identify which ones were breaking the law," said Motoaki Tanaka, spokesman for the Shimonoseki police. "We gave them a warning to lower the volume as a group."

Shimonoseki residents said the support was welcome but a little heavy-handed.

"There's a part of me that wants their voice to be effective," said a 65-year-old housewife with the slogans blaring behind her. "I wouldn't say we exactly welcome the commotion, but if they say it's part of Japanese culture, I think that message is pretty convincing."

"I'm glad they're here to support," said a 68-year-old man out for a bike ride, who said he used to take part in whale hunts himself. "But couldn't they be a little bit quieter?"

SOURCE: *"Some 700 Japanese right-wingers demand reopening of whale hunt," Agence France Presse, May 19, 2002. Reprinted by permission of Agence France Presse.*

Greenpeace Protests Whaling

Jonathan Watts

To allegations of Japanese vote-buying, the International Whaling Commission opens its annual meeting today with a vote that could give whaling states a majority for the first time for almost 20 years.

The balance of power seemed to shift further towards the whaling lobby on the eve of the conference when it emerged that Mongolia, which is said to sympathize with Japan, had joined the commission.

Three other sympathetic states, Palau, Cape Verde and Gabon, have joined in the past week, giving Japan the chance of victory in Shimonoseki, the historic centre of Japanese whaling.

"The votes in favor of a return to commercial whaling are fast approaching those who are against it," the president of the Japanese Whaling Association, Keichi Nakajima, said. "Our benchmark for success at this meeting will be whether we can secure a majority." The first test is expected this morning, when delegates will vote on whether to let Iceland join the IWC, even though it refuses to recognize the moratorium on commercial whaling introduced 17 years ago.

Most delegates said it was impossible to predict the result because two conservation states, Portugal, which has a growing whale watching industry, and San Marino, have also joined recently.

"It is on a knife-edge," the British fisheries minister, Eliot Morley, said. "If Iceland loses the vote, then it will be hard for the pro-whaling nations to make progress. But if they win, then it is going to be a very difficult IWC for us."

It needs three-quarters of the votes to overturn the moratorium, but a simple majority would let the whalers change other aspects of the way the IWC is run.

Japan has long sought the introduction of secret balloting, which would make it easier for delegates to vote in favor of whaling without fearing a backlash from their domestic electorates or a consumer boycott by conservation groups.

"If people could cast their ballots in secret, then we could get more votes in favor of sustainable whaling," Mr. Nakajima said.

A majority would also enable the whaling lobby to expel non-governmental organizations, such as Greenpeace, and change the fee structure, so that joining would be cheaper for small countries, which have tended to support Japan, and more expensive for bigger states, deterring eastern European countries, which are expected to support the moratorium.

The conservationists accuse Japan of buying votes. Greenpeace says that Tokyo has spent $220 million of its fisheries aid in the past two years on securing the support of 10 countries, including Morocco, Guinea and several Caribbean states.

"They have tied aid to votes," New Zealand's minister of conservation, Sandra Lee, said. "If this continues, then we will reach a point where countries that give the most aid in international forums will be able to swing issues their way. Instead, we should be debating on merit."

Japan and its supporters deny using economic aid to secure votes.

"This is a malicious accusation," the chairman of the conference preparatory committee, Nishio Yonezawa, said.

"It is insulting to Caribbean nations to say that they can be bought by a very small amount of money. Such claims are hypocritical. In the late 1980s, Greenpeace and other NGOs recruited many countries to join the IWC."

Greenpeace was the target of a huge contingent of rightwing extremists who drove about 200 lorries [trucks] daubed with nationalist slogans through Shimonoseki yesterday.

Shouting slogans such as "This is our dietary culture. Resume whaling now!" and "Fight off Greenpeace and the ego-eccentric anti-whalers!" they made a great deal of noise but caused little actual trouble at the conference centre, which was protected by riot police.

Most residents were appalled by the raucous nationalist contingent, but many in the town, which is often used by whaling vessels, said the anti-whaling states were practicing a form of imperialism in preventing a resumption of the industry even though minke whale stocks are abundant.

"They should stop telling us what to do. How would people in Britain like it if we told them not to eat cow?" said Keiji Fujino, who runs a whale meat stall at the Karato wholesale market.

"But, at the same time, I am sorry that the Japanese government wastes my tax money buying IWC votes from overseas nations. This is a battle we can never win."

If the balance of power shifts today, however, the picture may look different.

SOURCE: "Whaling ban in danger as Japan's influence grows," by Jonathon Watts from The Guardian, May 20, 2002. Copyright © 2002 by Jonathon Watts. Reprinted by permission.

QUESTIONS

Check Your Understanding

1. From the two articles in this case study, what are the main arguments for allowing whaling to proceed?
2. What are the counterarguments given by Greenpeace?

Analyze the Issues

3. In what ways do nation-states seek to limit the influence of Greenpeace? Consider, for example, how countries try to influence the operation of the International Whaling Commission by exploiting the voting rules of the IWC.
4. Which levels of analysis are most useful for understanding the dynamics of this case study? Explain.
5. Do you agree with the claim that Greenpeace is practicing a form of imperialism in its quest to ban whaling? Either way, do you agree with the Greenpeace goal of banning whaling?

FOR FURTHER INFORMATION

To find out more about the Greenpeace and international whaling, consult the web pages of *Foreign Affairs* (*http://www.foreignaffairs.org/*) and *Foreign Policy* (*http://www.foreignpolicy.com*) in addition to the following sources:

The Greenpeace website: *http://www.greenpeaceusa.org*
The International Whaling Commission website: *http://www.iwcoffice.org/*
Bryan Shih, "We see whales as a fish for hunting," *Financial Times*, September 30, 2002.
Craig Warkentin, *Reshaping World Politics: NGOs, the Internet, and Global Civil Society* (Lanham: Rowman & Littlefield Publishers, Inc., 2001).
Robert Whymant, "Japan accused of using aid to end whaling ban," *The Times* (London), May 17, 2002.
See also the textbook's website for Internet links related to NGOs:
    http://www/ablongman.com/duncan

CHAPTER 7

Political Geography

KEY QUESTIONS RAISED IN THIS CHAPTER

1. What are the basic elements of political geography?
2. What geographic factors impact world politics?
3. How does geography shape human perceptions?
4. How are maps used in political geography?
5. What is the recent history of geopolitical thinking?
6. What political geographic factors help explain the terrorist war against America?

Wars Always Leave Refugees: The U.S. war on terrorism has been no exception, as this photo of Afghan refugees depicts. Refugees constitute a significant global geopolitical fact of life.

As you begin this chapter on political geography, stop for a moment and think about all the connections between land and politics in play around you—in your hometown, village, and state and even in the country at large. Local issues that may come to mind include heated debates over property taxes, land fills, zoning restrictions, strip malls, water rights, or a host of issues about off-campus student housing. Within your state you might find political hot potatoes in the form of conflicts between green space proponents (those who believe in open space) and real estate developers, between political parties arguing over arrangement of the territorial boundaries for congressional districts, and between corporations and individuals with competing views of where to dump nuclear waste. These issues fall distinctly within the domain of political geography.

The study of political geography illustrates the many ways in which the world is becoming both more united and more divided at the same time. At the international level geographic factors frequently lead to conflict and decentralization with profound life and death significance. Countries torn apart by guerrilla struggle (Colombia), by gangs who control swaths of a country's territory (Brazil), by warlords who usurp the power of a country's legitimate government (Afghanistan and Somalia) or by conflict over holy land (Palestinian versus Jews in Israel) are cases in point. International terrorism generated by Middle East Islamic fundamentalists aimed at the United States and other western states, territorial claims that lie at the root of ethnic civil wars, tensions over political boundaries that do not correspond with cultural and ethnic boundaries, and competition for strategic resources such as petroleum divide the world in conflict.

Still, various forces of centralization are at work as well. Civil wars do end (El Salvador, Nicaragua, former Yugoslavia), bitter boundary conflicts are resolved (Eritrea-Ethiopia), disputes over shared rivers and waterways are settled

(United States-Canada maritime boundaries) and compromises are made over interstate transportation (United States-Mexico; within Western Europe; Slovenia-Hungary). Forces for centralization include international intergovernmental organizations (IGOs such as the United Nations and the European Union), international nongovernmental organizations (NGOs such as Greenpeace and Doctors Without Borders), and international law that can unite the world.

In this chapter we begin by taking a look at what political geography is all about—its particular focus, assumptions, and actors. Then we look at key geographic factors that impact world politics, such as location and boundaries. We next examine the kinds of human perceptions geography can shape, followed by an overview of how geography has affected foreign policy, with a special look at the use of maps. Finally we explore the geographic factors that help explain the terrorist war against America.

What Are the Basic Elements of Political Geography?

To understand the news that floods us through our television, newspapers, and magazines, we need at least an elementary understanding of world geography. Just as geography has played a vital historic role in determining the growth of civilizations and empires—due to location and waterways, climate, trade routes and towns, frontiers and boundaries, habitat and economy—so it does today in the dynamics of world politics.[1] Geographic forces underpin all the dangerous headline news and have done so since World War Two—from wars in Korea, Vietnam, the Persian Gulf (two wars against Iraq), and the former Yugoslavia to the Cuban missile crisis and the 9/11 terrorist attacks on America. Geography is also prominent in today's oil pipelines politics around the Caspian Sea (see Case Study at the end of this chapter), in India-Pakistani tensions over Kashmir, in Palestinian-Israeli conflict in the Middle East, and in Northern Ireland's woes, to cite only a few contemporary international tensions. So what exactly is political geography all about, and what is its particular focus?

A Particular Focus

Political Geography
A field of study that looks at the geographical consequences of political decisions and actions, the geographical factors that were considered during the making of any decisions, and the role of any geographical factors that influenced the outcome of political actions.

Political geography—or *geopolitics* as some observers prefer to call it—looks at how geography and world politics interact. While political geography does not have a generally accepted single definition, its central theme is sufficiently clear to allow it to make unique contributions to the study of world politics. A political geographic framework allows us to analyze the many ways geography affects politics and foreign policy—from its impact on national identity and nationalism to the manner in which it impinges on a state's power and development or how it affects political decision making.

Those who look at political geography as a way to inform them about world politics are concerned, as one observer puts it, with "the geographical consequences of political decisions and actions, the geographical factors which were considered during the making of any decisions, and the role of any geographical factors which influenced the outcome of political actions."[2] In other words, spatial features of international politics are the heart of political geography. Think of political geography as a field of inquiry that studies the numerous geographic forces that drive world politics, including the following:

WHY IT MATTERS TO YOU

Political Geography

The political geographic dimension of world politics has profound implications for your life. The resource most often, but not exclusively, directly implicated in the geography of international politics is land.

Land is a source of tension because it contains **vital resources** used in your life. Oil—with its attached price of gasoline in our U.S. pumps—is a case in point. The United States went to war over oil in the Persian Gulf in 1991.

Land entails **strategic location** like Mexico's geographic proximity to the United States Mexico, the United States, and Canada form the regional North American Free Trade Association (NAFTA) with all its economic consequences in your life.

Land is a **nationality-identified piece of the earth's real estate.** The Palestinian-Israeli conflict is in part over disputed territory that both sides consider historically their own. Palestinian suicide bombers in Israel and Israeli occupation of Palestinian land have escalated this quarrel into something closely linked to the world political geographic setting.

The United States has been drawn into this conflict—one of vital interest to you. Much of the Middle East and Western Europe back the Palestinian side. They rightly or wrongly view the United States as unfair to Palestinians and as pro-Israel. This perspective has left the United States increasingly isolated in its war on terrorism and in its relations with Arab and European countries. Egypt and Saudi Arabia's masses have become sharply anti-American, and anti-American terrorists cite America's "pro-Israel tilt" as yet another reason for them to continue to mount attacks against the United States.

- Location, size, and terrain of a country to the extent that they influence development, national power base, foreign policy, security concerns, and territorial disputes.
- Control of key resources—such as arable land, energy, water, and other commodities—that drive national priorities and foreign policy decision making.
- Spatial relationships—for example, borders—to the extent that they affect human perceptions and decision making by key actors in international politics, such as states, ethnic nations, IGOs, NGOs, and international terrorists.
- The diversity of states and regions in the world—for example, differing ethnicities, language groups, belief systems and territorial disputes—and how, in light of all their differences, they interact to affect international economic, political, social, and military relations.

Political geography is all about the overlap of geography and politics. As we shall see in the discussion that follows, geographic/spatial factors play a huge role in who gets what, when, and how in the game of world politics.

A Set of Premises

Three basic premises of political geography stand out. First, *Where humans live and what territorial states they occupy in great measure condition their level of development and power base vis-á-vis other humans in other states in other parts of the world.* In other words, the impact of geography and geographic location on human development is profound. Jared Diamond, Professor of Physiology at the

For more about animal and human aggression, go to **www.ablongman.com/ duncan.**

Ethnology

The branch of anthropology that deals with the comparative cultures of various peoples, their distribution, characteristics, and folkways.

For more about your own geographic roots, go to **www.ablongman.com/ duncan.**

UCLA School of Medicine and Pulitzer Prize–winning author, sets out a clear argument for this point.[3] Diamond stresses that since the beginning of humankind, geography—especially in terms of the plant and animal species available for domestication in a given location—has shaped each human society's culture and competitive position.[4] This means that continental differences in levels of civilization—for example, Western Europe as compared to Australia—arise from geographical differences.[5] We return to this ecological perspective in Chapter 13.

Geography, however, does more than set the ground rules for human development. A second premise—spelled out in Diamond's research as well—is that *humans—like most animal species—compete with each other for territory and have been doing so since their inception.* Indeed, Diamond makes a compelling case for the theory that human behavior is close to animal behavior in terms of territoriality, especially given the fact that we humans share 98 percent of our genetic program with the pigmy chimp of Zaire and the common chimp of the rest of tropical Africa.[6]

This comparison of animal and human behavior is called **ethnology.** Its proponents include Konrad Lorenz (*On Aggression*, 1969), Desmond Morris (*The Naked Ape*, 1967), and Robert Ardrey (*The Territorial Imperative*, 1961). Supporting this theory from another perspective, Jane Goodall, the primatologist, notes that chimpanzees from one tribe in Tanzania have waged war on neighboring chimps, due to a territorial need for food and mating.

Territorial conflicts have been ever-present in human history and world politics. Diamond argues that such conflicts generally take the form of wars between adjacent groups, marked by hostility and mass killing.

A third premise of political geography is that *human perceptions of the world comprise a kind of prism through which we interpret realities around us.*[7] Recall Chapter 1, where the point is made that policymakers and their followers in the world's diverse states and organizations act on their perceptions whether or not they are accurate. This third premise underscores that the unique characteristics of each territory on which humans live—defined by its topography, resources, climate, location relative to neighboring states, and ethnic/cultural diversity—shape the perceptions of their inhabitants. When we look at territorially based perceptions, we find clues to how population groups define their national identity and national interests (territorial security, economic vitality, political goals) and why they utilize different kinds of power and diplomacy to pursue those interests. Their perceptions shape the conflict and cooperation between states, acting as either centralizing or decentralizing forces that in turn define the political geography of foreign policy making.

Major Terms and Concepts

Political geography has a host of terms and concepts that illuminate geographic-political relationships—be they of a decentralizing (conflict) or centralization (cooperative) nature. The following are among the more important ones. Try not to be overwhelmed by the number of "geos" in this list. They go with the territory, so to speak. Most of these terms center on the conflict side of political geography; cooperative aspects are discussed in the section on IGOs, NGOs, and international law.

- **Geopolitics**—mentioned earlier—is the study of geographic distributions of power among states with attention to rivalry between the major states. The global contest between the United States and Soviet Union during the Cold War is a good example.

- **Geostrategy** is a territorial-based foreign policy concept associated with geographic factors such as potential alliance partners, location, and terrain. America's war on terrorism has distinct geostrategic overtones. The Bush Doctrine of eliminating weapons of mass destruction (WMD) in Iraq; citing Iraq, Iran, and North Korea as the "axis of evil"; and adding Cuba, Libya, and Syria as additional "axis of evil" states illustrates geostrategic thinking, because it focuses on particular states. Al Qaeda terrorists, meanwhile, have used a geostrategy of suicide attacks aimed at U.S. and Western countries' territorial assets by penetrating weaknesses in their defense systems.

- **Geoeconomics**—economic geography—studies how geography influences economics and economic development. Geography's impact on economic development can be seen in poor countries that suffer from lack of resources, poor arable land, and climatic problems (lack of rain, for example). A good example of geoeconomics is the use of offshore (Caribbean Islands) tax havens by private U.S. citizens and corporations. By parking their earnings in offshore accounts they avoid paying U.S. taxes and, many argue, their responsibilities for helping pay for all the benefits of living in a democratic country with many government-provided services.

- **Shatter belt** refers to a region of chronic political splintering and fracturing—a highly unstable area in which states appear, disappear, and reappear with numerous changing names and boundaries. Central, Eastern and southeast Europe—with its age-old rivalries and animosities—have given this part of the world a shatter belt identity. The breakup of former Yugoslavia, beginning in 1991, into sovereign states illustrates shatter belt effects of colliding ethnic identities (Slovene, Croat, Bosnian, Serb, Albanian, Montenegrin, and Macedonian) and Christian, Eastern Orthodox, and Muslim religions.[8] The geographic region in and immediately surrounding Israel is a Middle East shatter belt where Islam, Judaism, and Christianity collide.

- **Balkanization** is a related term that refers to the typical consequence of shatter belt activity, for it refers to the breakup of a region or state into smaller and frequently hostile political units. This concept is associated with the Balkan region, where the states of former Yugoslavia are located.

- **Buffer state or states** refers to a country or a group of countries that separate other ideological or political rivals—and which consequently come in for a good deal of buffeting from power-competing neighbors. Jordan is a buffer state between rival Middle Eastern states, just as Eastern Europe was a buffer region between Western Europe and the former Soviet Union during the Cold War. As buffer states, Hungary and Czechoslovakia launched movements to become independent in 1956 and 1968, only to have them squashed by Soviet military forces. Poland has suffered dramatic consequences from its territorial buffer-state situation in Eastern Europe and in fact, has been carved up territorially more than once by rival power contenders.

- **Hegemonic states** are powerful countries that seek to dominate nearby states. The Soviet Union acted as a hegemonic state between 1945 and 1990. The efforts of states seeking to break out of another's hegemonic grip—as Hungary and Czechoslovakia did—frequently have been put down with brutal force, as demonstrated by action on the part of the former USSR. Iraq was

Geostrategy

Foreign policies pursued by states or intergovernmental organizations (such as NATO) that focus on territory and the geographic distribution of power. The U.S. post–World War II policy of containment of the Soviet Union illustrates geostrategy.

For more information on Kosovo and the Balkan shatter belt, go to **www.ablongman.com/ duncan.**

seen as a would-be hegemon in the contemporary Middle East, given the actions of Saddam Hussein against Kuwait and his alleged posession of weapons of mass destruction. Undoubtedly, Pakistan views India as playing a hegemonic role; and likewise, Taiwan—and other neighboring states—view China as a potential hegemon. Similarly, Mexico, Cuba, and other Caribbean and Central American states have viewed the United States, the "colossus of the north," as a hegemonic power.

- **Weak (or failing) states** are those countries frequently found in geographical zones of turmoil that have virtually collapsed from internal forces, such as starvation, tribal warfare, and loss of centralized governing control. Weak states breed internal conflict and invite external intervention. Examples include Afghanistan, Angola, Sierra Leone, Somalia, and Colombia—where rebel guerrilla forces controlled about two-thirds of the country in 1999. Weak states are characterized by corruption in the ruling classes, high civil instability, ethnic and tribal conflict, crime, terrorism and/or drug trafficking. State failure is a prime mover in global instability and decentralization, as the anarchy related to the failure is frequently projected across borders.[9]

State and Nation

Let's turn to a closer look at the geographic aspects of the **state**—that primary, but not exclusive, actor on the world stage for over four centuries. Remember our discussion from Chapter 2 that explored the state's evolution and primary characteristics. A state occupies a portion of the earth's territory with generally recognized limits, even though some of its boundaries may be undefined or disputed. States—which vary dramatically in size, shape, resources, topography, and above all in power—generally are viewed as **sovereign.** To be sovereign means that a state's government exercises power over the people within its boundaries unrestrained by laws orchestrated outside that area. States, then, among other things, are geographic phenomena. They occupy territory within which we find a resident population, a government, and an organized economy of one type or another.

Although the territorial/political state has dominated the world political scene since the Treaty of Westphalia in 1648 (see Chapter 2) and is recognized by other states for its legitimacy and sovereignty over a spatially defined territory and population, this is not the complete story. While states make and conduct foreign policy, form cooperative alliances, and comprise the membership of the United Nations, a state's territory rarely contains a homogeneous cultural population, all of whom share a single national identity.

Our globe has many more national groups than it has territorial states—as we will explore in Chapter 8. And, the world's present territorial states do not necessarily represent the aspirations of the several thousand national groups found around the world.[10] This situation has been one of the leading sources of civil wars— conflict within states as opposed to between states—in the post–World War II period. For example, state governments seeking to preserve traditional state-defined territorial control and boundaries, have repressed ethnic national groups that have their own territory-focused nationalistic aspirations. The breakup of former Yugoslavia and today's Palestinian aspirations illustrate this state-national territorial dilemma.

A striking feature of international political geography is the increase in the number of states since World War II, which greatly complicates the chessboard of world politics. While this process of creating new states has been in progress for some time, the dramatic disintegration of failed states like the former Soviet Union and Yugoslavia in the decade of the 1990s produced a rash of new countries. The number of states in the United Nations grew from 166 in 1991 to 187 in 2000. Yet some countries are not UN members, such as the Holy See (Vatican City) and Switzerland—which has only "observer" status in the UN. East Timor is in the process of making a full transition to the status of a sovereign state, while some territories, like Puerto Rico (a U.S. territory) and Taiwan meet many requirements of independent states, yet are viewed as dependencies. In addition, the number of sovereign states occupying real estate on the globe conceivably could grow dramatically in the future. If today's fragile failing states, which include Afghanistan, Angola, Liberia, Rwanda, the Congo, and Somalia, were to break up into new states, or if today's multiethnic national states were to disintegrate into new states to match the vast number of ethnic nations, then the number of states in the international system could increase to over 800 by year 2025. Many states have but a tenuous hold on their territory. The key point is that states are in constant flux, with state boundaries shifting dramatically as a result of war, self-determination movements, negotiation, arbitration, or even by the sale of territory—as in the case of Russia selling Alaska to the United States. This constant emergence of new states in a vast range of locations on the globe deeply affects state-to-state relationships and foreign policy. A quick review of Chapters 3 and 4 will remind you that geography's imprint on a state's power and foreign policy is profound. To understand the imprint of geography on any state, nation, or region, however, we need to answer the following questions:

- Where is the state located (positioned) on the globe?
- What is the nature of its multinational composition?
- How large or small is it compared to other states?
- Who are its neighbors? Are they friends or adversaries?
- What is its size and shape?
- What natural resources are contained within its boundaries and that impact its power?
- What does its topography and climate look like?
- How do topography and climate facilitate or deter security, economic development, and acquisition of power?
- What strategic role, if any, do waterways—such as the Panama Canal, the Suez Canal, Southeast Asia's Malacca Straits, or the Middle East's Straits of Hormuz—play in the lives of states?

Keeping in mind these thoughts and questions about states and nations—many of which center on conflict and decentralization—let's take a look at how political geography can inform us about cooperation and centralization.

IGOs, NGOs, and International Law

Cooperation and centralization—stemming from spatial relationships among people, territory, and politics—are a part of political geography. In Chapter 5 we looked at a great variety of international intergovernmental organizations both global and regional, like the United Nations and the European Union, and in Chapter 6 we spotlighted international nongovernmental organizations such as Greenpeace and Amnesty International. These IGOs and NGOs foster cooperation on issues of a people/territory/political nature in order to promote geographic/political zones of

Relief Programs Needed: Regions in Africa are well known for poor food production and ineffective government policies that spawn the need for international food relief programs.

centralization and cooperation. A key role of IGOs is to promote and facilitate cooperation among territorial states and other international actors on issues where their mutual interests can be served.

This point is vividly demonstrated by the wave of antiterrorism cooperation sponsored by the United Nations (UN), European Union (EU), North Atlantic Treaty Organization (NATO), and the Association of Southeast Asian Nations (ASEAN) following the 9/11 terrorist attacks on North America. This more or less united antiterrorism front, however, began to break apart during 2002 as the United States increasingly acted independently of its European allies—as we discussed in Chapter 4—and as Washington seemed more often than not to side with Israel in the Palestinian-Israel conflict, thereby alienating the Arab world.

Beyond attempts to counter terrorism, IGOs have promoted cooperation and centralization in a number of ways: via peacekeeping in civil war settings, environmental management, transportation and trade across oceans and territorial borders, and dealing with hunger crises and international refugee problems, to name just a few.

NGOs, for their part, have addressed economic, social, and environmental issues that have political geographic roots. The World Council of Churches, for example, greeted the worldwide Muslim community at the beginning of Ramadan in November 2001, and called for genuine cooperation and joint efforts to assist Muslim victims of human rights violations, to defend human rights and humanitarian law, and to intensify dialogue between religions and cultures."[11] The message was intended as an expression of solidarity with the Muslim community in the aftermath of 9/11. Other NGOs include the Organization of Petroleum Export Countries (OPEC), which controls petroleum prices and supplies; Green Peace, whose mission has been an improved global environment; and Doctors Without

Borders, which cooperates on medical problems in developing countries. Like IGOs, NGOs promote cooperation in many ways on issues with a political geographic dimension.

International law also plays a vital role in stimulating cooperation and centralization within the domain of political geography. Remember that the sources of international law are common practice and custom over time, international treaties, general practice of law as recognized by civilized states (represented by the International Court of Justice), and international law that emanates from the many United Nations declarations and resolutions. International law began to develop with the rise of the territorial state. In the twentieth century it grew rapidly, owing to the need for rules and regulations to manage complex issues associated with security, trade, finance, travel, and communication stemming from spreading interdependence.

While international law by no means always works smoothly, nor is it always obeyed, it still contributes greatly to cooperation and centralization. In the wake of 9/11, a host of antiterrorist UN declarations—and hence international laws—were passed. In today's world of political geography, international law has also focused on antidrug trafficking, the environment, women's rights, human rights, social justice, refugees, trade, and child labor, among other issues.

Legacy of the Past

The concept of political geography dates far back in time. Over 2300 years ago, Aristotle designed a model state based in part on the relationship between population and territory.[12] Some three hundred years later, the Greco-Roman scholar, Strabo, produced a 17-volume description and history of what was then the known world—and which was a tremendous contribution to politics and geography. Political geography blossomed in the Muslim world during the fourteenth and fifteenth centuries, and French writers in the sixteenth and seventeenth centuries followed in the tradition of studying relationships between political units and physical environments. Not least of these individuals was Montesquieu (1689–1755), who looked at the roles of territory and climate in shaping government systems. His ideas helped shape the American Constitution.[13]

Political geography and geopolitics kicked into high gear in the nineteenth century with the work of Friedrich Ratzel (1844–1904), who became known as the "father" of political geography. Stimulated by Ratzel's work, Rudolf Kjellén (1864–1922), a Swedish political scientist and lover of Germany, went well beyond Ratzel's notion that the state is like a biological organism by claiming that the state *is* a living organism.[14] Alfred Thayer Mahan (1840–1914), a naval historian and admiral in the U.S. Navy, argued persuasively that because sea power was critical in terms of the power of a state, the United States should have a large navy.

While Mahan stressed sea power in strategic thinking, other students of geopolitical thinking turned their attention to technology and land power, believing them to be more important than sea power. One such geopolitical thinker was Sir Halford Mackinder (1861–1947), a professor of geography at Oxford and Director of the London School of Economics. Perhaps his best-known contribution to geopolitics was his **heartland theory,** presented in a paper entitled "The Geographical Pivot of History" in 1904 to the Royal Geographic Society in London. Mackinder identified a Eurasian core, the "heartland," that was protected from sea power, could be defended easily, and from which any power could dominate the world. One can imagine how Mackinder's deterministic thinking about the heartland came into play after

Heartland Theory
A geostrategic theory first constructed by Sir Halford Mackinder, which states that Eurasia will have ultimate strategic advantage over sea power in competition for control of the world.

"The Geographer" by Vermeer
Source: *Städelsches Kunstinstitut*, Frankfurt, Germany.

For more on Sir Halford Mackinder and the Eurasia heartland, go to **www.ablongman.com/ duncan**.

World War II as the Soviet Union moved into East Europe, and the United States moved toward its post–World War II **containment strategy.** Some political geographers see today's oil-rich Persian Gulf region as a new heartland.

A critic of Mackinder's heartland geopolitics was Nicholas J. Spykman (1893–1943).[15] Spykman argued that Mackinder had overstressed the power of Eastern Europe and the heartland, in part because of the heartland's huge internal transportation problem, which a look at the map confirms. The best way to protect the Western World, Spykman said, was to control the **rimland**—those regions outside the heartland that include the Middle East, Africa, South America, and Southern and East Asia. The rimland could be seen as a barrier that under the control of friendly forces could deter aggressive action aimed at the Western Hemisphere. According to both Mackinder's and Spykman's writings, **realism, and power politics** (see Chapter 1), and **balance-of-power** thinking had entered into geopolitical strategy.

In newly developing America, geographical strategy lay behind President George Washington's eighteenth-century warning to future U.S. diplomats to avoid "entangling alliances" with European countries engaged in political power maneuvering. President Thomas Jefferson's determination to acquire the Louisiana

Purchase from France in 1803 in order to expand the American West and his commissioning of Lewis and Clark to explore that territory are examples of geostrategic thinking in action.

Later in 1823, President James Monroe warned Spain not to recolonize the Western Hemisphere—a warning that became known as the **Monroe Doctrine.** Thus was born a geostrategic concept. The Monroe Doctrine spelled out that the Western Hemisphere was closed to any further colonization and that the United States opposed any European interference with the independent countries of the New World (Latin America). This geographic doctrine shaped U.S. policy making in the Western Hemisphere for many years. As you can see, the concept of political geography has been around for a long time, although it has taken many forms and served many purposes. Later in the chapter, we will look at the more recent history of political geography.

What Geographic Factors Impact World Politics?

Earlier we raised a number of questions about the imprint of geography on a state's power and foreign policy. Among the issues addressed in those questions are location, access or lack of access to water, size and shape of states, transportation routes and communication channels, boundaries, and air space. A state's location, for example, brings with it a certain type of topography, resources, climate, and exposure to natural disasters—all of which affect the state's development and security prospects. If a state has access to ocean ports, it is better off than if it does not, for land-locked countries operate under serious disadvantages. Size and shape of states are important factors in their ability to thrive within the world political setting. Boundaries and boundary conflicts continually plague the world political setting, while ocean and air space are considered parts of a state's territory—thus leading to additional problems that must be worked out in international relations. We will now look more closely at each of these factors.

Location and Development

Geography dramatically impacts a society's economic and political development. Tied to location are such factors as climate, topography, natural resources, and other elements. As noted earlier, in his book *Guns, Germs, and Steel*, Jared Diamond points out that a society's location determines how readily it can facilitate the spread of agriculture, disseminate and receive technology, and share knowledge.[16] On Figure 7.1, note the North-South axes that runs from North America to South America and within Africa—compared to the East-West axis that runs through Eurasia.

The geographic effects of this axis orientation are enormous, because, according to Diamond the East-West axis generally facilitated transmission of goods and knowledge more readily than a North-South axis. In terms of food, for example, Diamond notes that "Eurasia's East-West axis allowed Fertile Crescent crops quickly to launch agriculture over the band of temperate latitudes from Ireland to the Indus Valley, and to enrich the agriculture that arose independently in eastern

FIGURE 7.1

Major Axes of the Continents

SOURCE: *Jared Diamond, Guns, Germans, and Steel: The Fates of Human Societies (New York: W.W. Norton, 1998), p. 177*

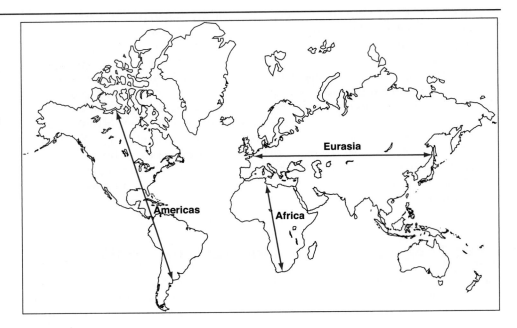

Asia."[17] (See Figure 7.2.) Such a "spread effect" was blocked in the Americas and Africa by huge differences in latitude, climate, topographical barriers (deserts and jungles, for example) and other geographic features.

As you might expect, the world's great empires—Arab, Chinese, Greek, and Roman—developed along the East-West axis. The area was the scene of the Renaissance, the center of the modern agrarian and industrial revolutions, the place where the democratic political state originated, and the setting for the birth of the modern powerful territorial state. Relative location along the East-West axis was a determining factor in these developments.

The Americas, to be certain, developed empires—Aztec, Mayan and Incan—of no small significance in that part of the world. Yet these empires succumbed to Spanish and Portuguese conquest and colonization. The Americas—with their mountains, deserts, and jungles—became known as the "hollow continent," and urban life developed along the coastlines rather than within. Thus, the interior area remained isolated from much of the world, and many of its countries faced problems involving agricultural and the availability of arable land.

Climate The East-West axis lies in the temperate zone, which illustrates the important role played by climate in a society's development and power. Where a state is located affects its climate and arguably its potential for development. The temperate zones lie in the north from the Tropic of Cancer to 60 degrees north latitude and in the south from the Tropic of Capricorn to 60 degrees south latitude. A theory known as the "*temperate zone theory*" holds that in these temperate zones a number of forces favor economic development. They include an average mean temperature of around 70 degrees, a four-stage seasonal pattern, and adequate rainfall. The temperate zones include the United States, Canada, Europe, Middle East, part of South Asia, Southeast Asia, and much of the Far East (China, Japan, and South Korea).

In contrast, as we have seen, countries located near the hot and humid equator have a less favorable record in terms of economic development—as measured by

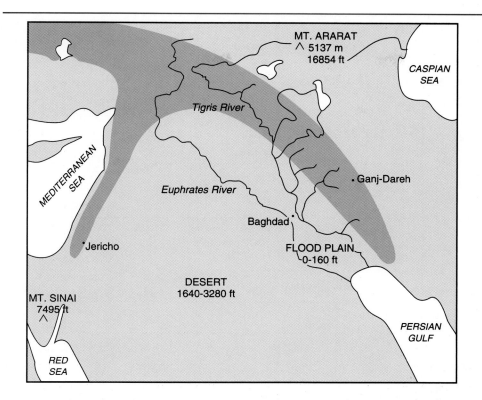

FIGURE 7.2

The Fertile Crescent, 9000–4500 B.C.

SOURCE: www.fsmitha. com/hl/map00- fc.html

rates of increased gross national product and equality of income distribution. Latin America, the geographic region of the world with the highest income inequality, stands out in this regard. Recent research by the Inter-American Development Bank demonstrates that countries that lie near the equator have systematically higher income inequality than countries in more temperate zones of the world.[18] Indeed, research indicates a high correlation between latitude and inequality in this part of the world. One reason cited for this inequality is that life in tropical regions near the equator is complicated by disease and by problems connected with pests and with soil and water quality.[19] Another is that work is often to be found on trop- ical plantations where unskilled laborers must accept low pay.

As illustrated in Figure 7.3, the geopolitics of income distribution disparities— the largest of which are found in Latin America—also help account for low rates of democratic political development, where political power tends to remain in the hands of the wealthier income groups. While some groups may become wealthier over time, it is difficult to state that a country is experiencing high rates of economic development when large sectors of the population do not share equitably in income.

Natural Resources   A state's natural resources—a factor of major geopoliti- cal significance—play a big role in conditioning a country's development and power base and therefore its capacity to find territorial security and exert influence within the international system. You will recall that Chapter 3 discusses the importance of power factors in shaping foreign policy and international affairs. Does the state have strategic resources, like oil, to meet its own energy requirements or to export, or arable land to feed its population? If not, it will have to import food and energy resources. From this geopolitical perspective, the world's large oil-producing and

Natural Resources
A state's basic resources that spring from its physical setting, such as oil, gas, uranium, coal, and arable land so vital to agricultural productivity.

FIGURE 7.3

a. Income Received by the Wealthiest 5 Percent of the Population (Percent of Total Income)
b. Income Received by the Poorest 30 Percent of the Population (Percent of Total Income)

SOURCE: *IDB calculations based on Deininger and Squire (1996).*

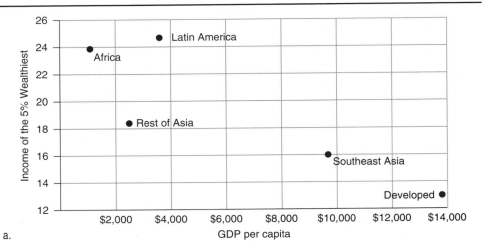

a.

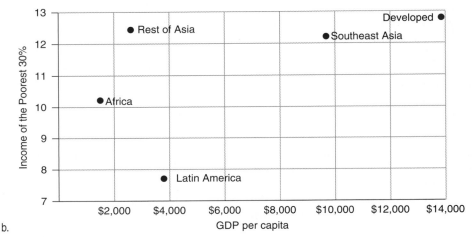

b.

food-producing countries are better off in terms of territory than those countries that must import oil for energy and food to feed their populations. Saudi Arabia, Kuwait, and Iraq, who have oil, are better off than Haiti, Bangladesh, or Somalia, who do not. The United States, Canada, and Argentina are food exporters; India, Russia, and North Korea are not. Japan is an interesting counter example. While Japan imports some of its food and basically all of its oil, it has managed to remain a rich country, thanks to its extraordinarily hard-working population.

The location of strategic natural resources can lead to both significant conflict and cooperation in world affairs. When Iraq invaded Kuwait in 1990 for example, world oil prices rose sharply because Iraqi and Kuwaiti oil disappeared from the market. This caused serious alarm among the oil-importing countries, such as the United States, West European states, and Japan. Even more fearful was the specter of a possible Iraqi invasion of Saudi Arabia, with Iraq's leader, Saddam Hussein, in a position to control world oil prices. As a consequence, the United States took the lead in a huge military buildup designated *Operation Desert Shield* and then led *Operation Desert Storm*, the war to expel Iraq from Kuwait. So great was the perceived threat to oil supplies that many countries cooperated with the United States in the 1991 military action against Iraq. The geopolitics of this region will be covered more thoroughly in the case study at the end of the chapter.

Topography The physical and natural features of a region or country affect its opportunity to integrate itself politically and protect its political sovereignty. Peru is less well endowed than Argentina from this perspective. Two-thirds of Peru lies on the eastern side of the Andes Mountains, much of which is unexplored even today. This makes two-thirds of Peru's territory difficult to integrate politically. Although it also lies to the east of the Andes, Argentina, in contrast, has a more forgiving territorial configuration that lends itself to a nationally unified state by way of telephone, telegraph, and transportation links. Economic integration of countries in trade groupings is likewise affected by topographical relationships. Argentina, Brazil, Paraguay, and Uruguay are territorially more accessible to each other, allowing greater economic ties within their trade organization (MERCOSUR) than with Chile, which lies on the other side of the Andes from them. Members of the European Union enjoy geographic-proximity links similar to those of MERCOSUR members.

Size and Shape The world's small states, many with less than 200 square miles, do not carry much weight in world politics. Think of Andorra (180 square miles), Barbados (166), or Grenada (133). Bigger countries tend to be far more powerful, although some formerly big countries—such as the former Soviet Union and Yugoslavia—have broken up. Remember, however, that large countries also have their own set of problems: multinational people living inside their borders, more than one language spoken, borders to be defended, people to be fed, and communication and transportation links to be maintained. The largest land-area countries include Russia, Canada, China, the United States, Brazil, Australia, and India.

The size and shape of a state help or hinder its unity, development, and overall power. States come in five basic shapes: compact, elongated, perforated, fragmented, and protruded. **Compact states** are those where distances from the center to boundary do not vary greatly—as in Belgium (Figure 7.4a). They tend to be easier to manage than **elongated states** like Chile or Vietnam (Figure 7.4b), or **perforated states** (when one state completely surrounds another one) like South Africa (Figure 7.4c)—which has Lesotho in its midst—and Italy, which surrounds both Vatican City and San Marino. **Vietnam's elongated status** led to the formation of two countries during the Vietnam War of the 1960s: North (with Hanoi as the capital, Communist, backed by Russia and China) and South (with Saigon as the capital, non-Communist, backed by the United States). States that are **fragmented**—also called **archipelagos**—countries like Indonesia with its over 13,000 islands (Figure 7.4d), or the Philippines, are extremely difficult to manage as demonstrated by self-determination movements and terrorist activities in both these states.

Finally, some countries are **protruded** in that they have a panhandle or extended arm such as Myanmar or Thailand. Benefits include possible access to water—demonstrated by the Belgians when they assumed control of the Congo, and created a westward proruption of about 300 miles that followed the Zaire (Congo) River and provided the colony with access to the Atlantic Ocean. A proruption can be formed for other strategic reasons—for example, to separate two states that might otherwise share a common boundary. The British did this during the nineteenth century when they controlled Afghanistan by creating a 200 mile, 12 mile wide corridor (proruption) to the east to prevent their geopolitical competitor, Russia, form sharing a border with Pakistan (Figure 7.4e).

FIGURE 7.4
Shapes of States
a. Belgium: A Compact State

SOURCE: http://www.cyber.vt.edu/geog1014/topics/108States/shape.html

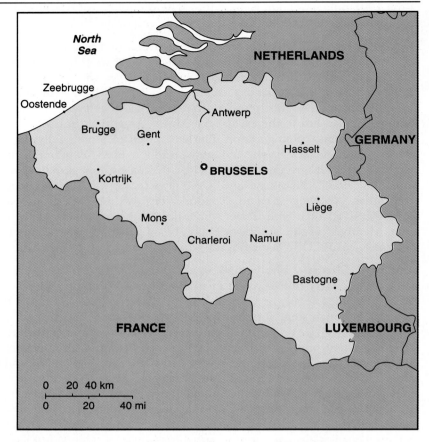

a.

b. Vietnam: An Elongated State

SOURCE: http://www.mapquest.com/altas/main.edp?print=vietman

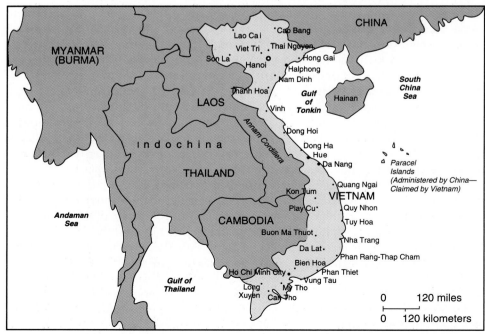

b.

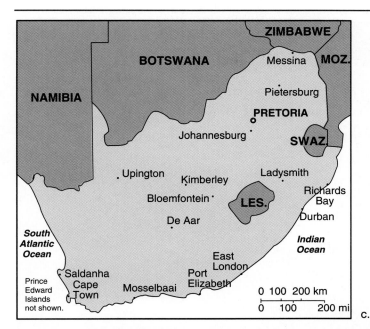

FIGURE 7.4

**c. South Africa:
A Perforated State**

SOURCE: http://www.
cyber.vt.edu/geog
1014/topics/
108States/shape.
html

c.

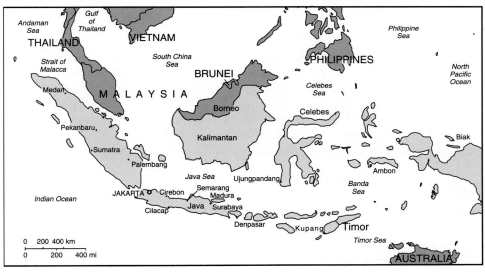

**d. Indonesia: A
Fragmented State**

SOURCE: http://www.
cyber.vt.edu/geog
1014/topics/
108States/shape.
html

d.

Natural Disasters   Location can create obstacles to a country's development and overall economic and political power in the global arena when it exposes a state to natural disasters. Without over-dramatizing the importance of a country's location and its vulnerability to natural disasters, a word or two on the subject is in order. Those countries that lie in the world's dangerous natural disaster areas face the constant problem of major damage from earthquakes, typhoons, and hurricanes, which can sap financial resources needed for economic development (see Figure 7.5).

For example, Hurricane Mitch ravaged Guatemala and Honduras in October 1998, killing more than 9,000 people and causing $8.5 billion damage in infrastructure alone. That single storm probably set back the region's development for years.

FIGURE 7.4
(Continued)
e. Afghanistan:
A Protruded State
Source: http://www.
mapquest.com/
altas/main.adp?
print=afghanis

e.

Similar natural disasters, such as earthquakes and typhoons, have been known to cause huge damage in the Pacific rim countries, not only in Latin America but in Asia as well. India, Japan, Bangladesh, and Turkey have been particularly hard hit. The devastating 7.4 magnitude earthquake that rocked Turkey in August 1999 killed at least 14,000 people. Some estimates of the damage predicted that the cost to Turkey in reconstruction expenses would top $30 billion. The January 2001 earthquake in India left over 17,000 dead, and many thousands more homeless.

Location and Territorial Security

In addition to its effects on development, a state's *location* on the face of the globe is a powerful factor affecting its basic national interests (see Chapter 4): territorial security (physical security), economic vitality, and political control over its territory in defense of its sovereignty. Let's first take a look at the issue of territorial security. If a state is located near a stronger threatening neighbor, it will have to use resources to defend itself. China's weaker status vis-à-vis Japan and the West in the nineteenth and twentieth centuries illustrates this point. Western powers carved out spheres of interest for themselves in China in the late 1800s as did Japan in the twentieth century. In the Western Hemisphere, Mexico, Cuba, and Caribbean states like the Dominican Republic, Haiti, and Nicaragua have long been concerned about the power of the United States. Cuba's location at a strategic point in the Caribbean and Mexico's border ties with the United States historically have placed both countries on the defensive in a lopsided power relationship with the United States. Cuba's proximity to the United States, moreover, led Nikita S. Khrushchev to use the island as a base for missiles aimed at the United States during the Cold War in 1962, an action that brought the USSR and the United States to the brink of nuclear war. In

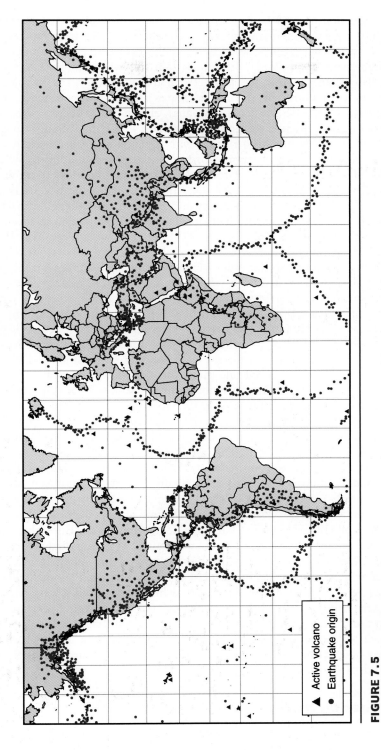

FIGURE 7.5

Volcanoes and Earthquakes

Source: H. J. de Blij and Peter O. Miller, Physical Geography of the Global Environment, Second Edition (New York: John Wiley and Sons, 1996), p. 341.

Active volcano

Earthquake origin

contrast, Khrushchev had no interest in placing missiles onto the Falkland Islands, because they were not strategically located from the Soviet perspective.

In terms of spatial location and territorial security, the United States is in some respects similar to Great Britain. Britain has what amounts to a big moat—the English Channel—that has protected it from land and sea invasion from Europe over the years. Similarly, the United States is protected by water on its east and west coasts (the Atlantic and Pacific oceans), although the oceans provide no defensive barrier against nuclear weapons or terrorists. The United States further enjoys relative safety on its northern border with Canada and on its southern border with Mexico. While U.S. contiguous border ties with Mexico admittedly have led to new types of security concerns, namely, drug trafficking and illegal immigration, separation from Europe and Asia by the Atlantic and Pacific oceans has provided the United States with relative security and isolation from turbulent parts of the world.

This geographic setting helps explain U.S. isolationism in foreign policy up to the beginning of the Cold War (1947–1991) following World War II. Until roughly 1947, the United States avoided entangling military alliances with far-flung countries and did not go to war unless directly challenged, although it did pursue a robust policy of commerce and trade worldwide, and engaged in economic and cultural expansionism.[20] The terrorist attacks of 9/11, however, illustrate that even the territorial security enjoyed by the United States is not immune from committed terrorists who can penetrate porous territorial borders through air space or by other means.

Contrast the U.S. or British security situation with that of Russia or Poland. Russia has no natural territorial buffer between its territory and the outside world. For centuries Russia faced one threat after another from nearby neighbors. Among the more notorious threats were France's Napoleon Bonaparte and Germany's Adolph Hitler. You can see why, in the face of hundreds of years of attacks from foreign powers, a persistent suspicion of foreigners permeates its foreign policy. No wonder that policymakers in Russia have feared an expanded NATO or that, after World War II, Joseph Stalin occupied East European countries as a way to set up buffers against future attacks from the West. Poland, without topographical features to block invasion, lies between Russia and Germany. Its territory has been partitioned numerous times as a consequence of great power struggles between these giants.

Concerns over territorial security have always been a natural a part of the global chessboard. Ancient China built its Great Wall, European medieval castles had their moats, and France built an elaborate system of heavy fortifications before World War II on its eastern frontier—a system that failed to prevent invasion by Nazi armies. Since 9/11, the United States has worried about renewed terrorist attacks across its porous borders. Meanwhile, it has built a long fence on its southwestern frontier with Mexico, which does not deter illegal Mexicans who cross over into the United States. In fact on the Mexican side, vendors have set up little stands to sell tortillas and beans to the intrepid illegals about to dart through one of the many holes in the fence. China's Great Wall was far more successful in keeping out would-be invaders.

For more about the geopolitics of China's Great Wall, go to **www.ablongman.com/ duncan.**

Access to Water

A state's access or lack of access to water has a powerful impact on its ability to develop and acquire power in the international system. In this respect, land-locked states, or those that have no natural access to the seacoast, are not in an enviable position. The 42 countries in the world that are in this situation face huge economic

China's Great Wall

and logistical difficulties in trade and transportation that entail taxes and impediments by neighboring states—and which, in effect, nearly cutting them off from the world. Land-locked states are found in Africa, Latin America, Europe, Central Asia (Mongolia), and Southeast Asia. The gross national product (GNP) of land-locked countries typically is low.

While one might think a land-locked state simply could resort to flying its goods in and out of the country, think again. Most goods in daily life—food, clothing, and other commodities—arrive by ship, because this is the least expensive means of transportation. With no coastline or ports for countries as shown in Figure 7.6, you can see the problem. To complicate matters, some countries are doubly land-locked, that is, other land-locked countries surround them. Uzbekistan and Liechtenstein are cases in point. Other countries are known as "transit states," that is, states with or without a seacoast that are situated between a land-locked state and the sea, and through whose territory traffic in transit passes. Uganda in Africa is such a transit state; it provides transit routes for both land-locked and other transit states.

The situation of land-locked countries illustrates the way that geopolitical realities generate not only development problems but also conflict in world politics. **Afghanistan** is a good example. A mountainous land-locked country located in Asia and home of the infamous and recently defeated Taliban, its turbulent history and culture go back over five thousand years. Often called the crossroads of Central Asia, Afghanistan has been under the control of Alexander the Great and later the Persian Empire. Its many invaders have included the Huns; the Turks; the Arabs, who introduced Islam in the seventh century; and the Mongols who invaded in the early thirteenth century, led by Genghis Khan. In the eighteenth century Afghanistan was caught between the competition and collision of the expanding British and Russian empires, which produced intermittent foreign control into the

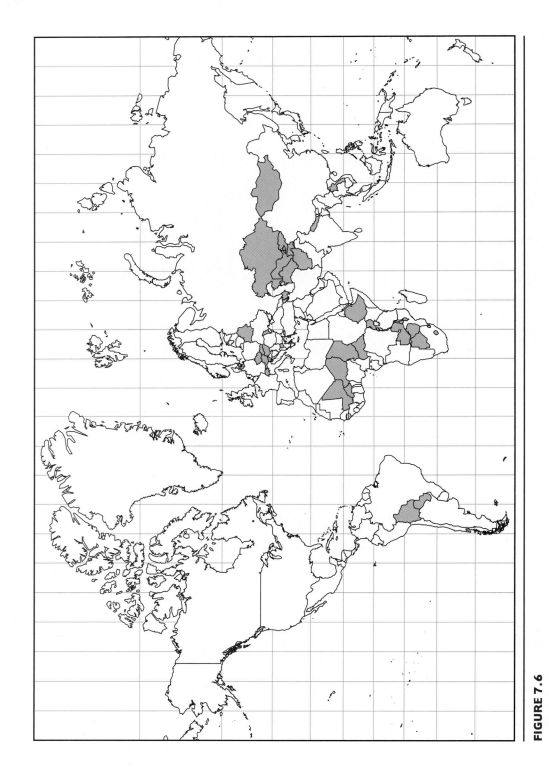

FIGURE 7.6
Land-locked Countries

Source: http://www.cyber.vt.edu/geog1014/topics/108States/neighbor.html

twentieth century. While the story of foreign intrigue goes on, it may be said that after so much war and civil strife, Afghanistan's economy and environment today are in shambles. Newly independent Central Asian states—Azerbaijan, Kazakhstan, Kyrgyzstan, Tajikistan, Turkmenistan, and Uzbekistan—are also involved at different levels of intensity in the political evolution of Afghanistan.

Boundaries and Boundary Disputes

Political boundaries have long characterized how humans organize the turf on which they live. Prominent physical features such as rivers or mountain ranges, as might be expected, frequently serve as boundaries. The Rio Grande River, which divides the United States and Mexico, is a classic example. The Andes Mountains that run down the length of western South America, dividing Chile from Argentina, also illustrate the point. As for how far a state's territory extends out into the sea, most coastal states claim 12 miles for their territorial sea. Several Latin American states claim a 200-mile limit. The United States also claims control over all economic resources in the sea within a 200-mile limit.

For more information on political geography in border conflicts, go to **www.ablongman.com/ duncan**.

Boundaries are sources of conflicts between states as well as between ethnic national groups inside states, who are sometimes in quest of land to create their own state. The **Kurds** and Palestinians provide two examples. In another kind of scenario, national groups divided by a state political boundary may wish that boundary removed so that they can form one state. Witness the unbridled enthusiasm of East and West Germans in 1989 as they dismantled the Berlin Wall, which divided them. Porous borders, on the other hand, can also cause tensions, as with illegal immigrants and drugs pouring into the United States from Mexico. Among the prominent boundary disputes during 2002 were:

Kurds
A stateless nation of people, who live in four states: Turkey, Iraq, Iran, and Syria. They have strived for years to create a state of Kurdistan.

- Russian-Iranian friction over a formula to divide the Caspian Sea floor, with its rich petroleum deposits.
- Contentious debate over thousands of disputed square kilometers in Central Asia that represent borders involving Russia, China, Afghanistan, Uzbekistan, Kyrgyzstan, Tajikistan, Kazakhstan and Turkmenistan—thorny issues marked by strong-arm politics, economic pressure, backroom deals, nationalist sentiments, and mutual mistrust.
- Long-standing friction between Japan and Russia over the Kurile Islands—four small islands off northern Japan.

Numerous border conflicts at present plague peace and stability in the world; they are more the norm than the exception in world politics, a significant feature of international relations. The disputes vary in kind, and many organizations intercede to move contending parties to cooperation and conciliation. These organizations range from the United Nations and other **international organizations** (like the European Union) or **nongovernmental organizations** (like the International Committee of the Red Cross, International Crisis Group, and Carter Center for Conflict Resolution) to governmental bodies, such as those in the U.S. (Departments of Justice, Defense, and State, as well as committees in the U.S. Congress), and a host of foreign governments like those of Australia and Canada.

For more information on Central Asian border conflicts, go to **www.ablongman.com/ duncan**.

There are numerous examples of unsettled boundary conflicts, including those between Peru and Ecuador, and disputes over island territories in the East and South China Seas. Other examples include disagreements owing to ethnicity, religion, and migration, as in Bosnia and Kosovo at the turn of the twentieth century,

Palestine Liberation Organization (PLO)
The major Islamic national liberation movement dedicated to achieving a Palestinian state in what have been Israel's Gaza Strip and West Bank.

and in East Timor in the Indonesian chain of islands. When East Timor's 800,000 people voted for independence from Indonesia in a 1999 UN-supervised referendum, pro-Indonesian militia groups torched homes and slaughtered civilians. Observers reported that the Indonesian military and police were tacitly, and perhaps even actively, working with the militia groups. The underlying message is that governments do not give up territory and existing borders easily or without a fight.

Israeli border security priorities—coupled with rising numbers of Palestinian suicide bombers—led Israeli Prime Minister Ariel Sharon to send Israeli military forces into Palestinian territory in early 2002. Instead of withdrawing military forces and dismantling Jewish settlements in Palestinian territory, Sharon began construction of a security wall along the Green Line that separates the West Bank from Israel in order to stop suicide bombers. Suicide bombing poses an enormous economic, political, and territorial security problem for Israel, for the Palestinians have endorsed this approach as a kind of strategic weapon, a poor man's "smart bomb" that can counter Israel's technological superiority and military dominance. Thus, suicide bombing has become a legitimate tool of war for the Palestinians, one that is awfully difficult to guard against and deter.[21]

Ocean and Air Space

Keep in mind that boundaries are *three-dimensional*.[22] They have land, water, and air dimensions. And airspace over countries also has boundaries. Planes that wander into the airspace of another country—despite the international rules of *innocent passage*—run the risk of being shot down. Such an event occurred on September 1, 1983, when a South Korean civilian airliner, a Boeing 747 on a flight from Alaska to South Korea carrying 269 passengers, entered Soviet air space. A Russian Air Force fighter shot down the plane, which crashed into the international waters of the Sea of Japan, killing all aboard. Another incident of this type occurred on February 24, 1996, when two small planes from South Florida wandered into Cuban air space and were shot down by Cuban MiG fighter jets. Because states claim and exercise sovereignty on, above, and below their territory, as well as over adjacent coastal sea waters, international rules governing civilian use of national airspace and coastal waters have been set forth. They articulate the principle of free international airspace. A 1944 convention created an airspace monitoring body: the international Civil Aviation Organization.

Transportation and Communication

Stop for a moment and think about global transportation and communication links within and between the world's states as key aspects of geopolitics. These systems provide for the flow of commodities and people, which make them key sources of development and power; they play a major role in the political world of who gets what, when, where, and how.[23] Transportation and communication arteries include roads, railroads, waterways (canals, rivers, straits), pipelines (gas, oil, water), bridges, tunnels, maritime transport routes, air transport, and communications networks (telecommunication, satellites, and the Internet). Such transportation and communication routes take on strategic significance when they connect population centers, thus opening opportunities for trade and commerce, high-stakes financial advantages, and access to or denial of energy sources. Canals illustrate the geopolitical importance of waterways. The Panama Canal is a good example of a major waterway

THE VIEW FROM   Panama

The Panama Canal

Although Panama depends on the Canal for only 7 percent of its economy, almost 100 percent of its self-image is connected with the idea that the canal is one of the world's most important trade routes. A cargo ship traveling from the U.S. east coast to Japan saves 3,000 miles by not going around South America. In 1997 a Hong Kong company was awarded a 25-year contract to run terminals at both ends of the canal. Some policymakers fear the company is connected with the Chinese government.

Over 825,000 ships have passed through the Panama Canal since it opened in 1914. Panama now depends on its revenues from the Canal, since it assumed control of it on December 31, 1999.

Today's Panama Canal

For more on the geopolitics of the Panama Canal, go to **www.ablongman.com/ duncan.**

that remains of importance to a number of Latin American countries. The Suez Canal figured prominently in power struggles in the twentieth century and today plays a major role in international commerce as a major point of entry and exit to and from the Mediterranean Sea.

Turning now to other kinds of waterways, the Straits of Hormuz (located between Iran and Oman) carry a huge volume of oil trade vital to the economies of the United States, Western Europe, and Japan. And thanks to the Great Lakes and the Mississippi, Missouri, and St. Lawrence rivers, the United States has achieved great economic development. Transportation and communication routes deeply affect the power of states and the power relationships between states, thus contributing to cooperation and conflict in world politics.

How Does Geography Shape Human Perceptions?

At the beginning of this chapter we noted that human perceptions comprise a kind of prism through which we interpret the world. Let's look at this assumption more closely and see how it applies to geography. To begin with, perceptions refer to the **mental processes of leaders and followers** from past to present—decisionmakers at the highest levels in government and leaders of IGOs, NGOs, national groups, guerrilla and terrorist organizations, and warlords in places like Afghanistan or Somalia. Perceptions are what people think is true about the territorial world around them and their underlying assumptions about that world.

The Power and Problem of Perceptions

Perceptions about territory—whether or not they reflect objective realities—have a potent impact on the actions of leaders and their followers. How Al Qaeda terrorists perceive America has strongly driven them to suicidal missions, just as how President Bush perceived Iraq resulted in the United States attack on Iraq. Similarly, India's and Pakistan's perceptions of Kashmir lead them into a conflict relationship. The problem with these perceptions is that they may or may not correspond with reality. How can this be?

Unfortunately, human beings are not as rational in interpreting the outside world as they may think they are, because they have a limited capacity for remembering and processing information accurately—including geographic information. Humans are nowhere near the equal to computers when it comes to high-speed information processing. Because humans are limited by what they know or can know, their perception and cognitive processes lead them to simplify the outside world—including geographic information. An example of this kind of simplicity would be Al Qaeda's perception that all Americans who live on America's territory are anti-Islamic; therefore, America must be attacked.

The limits to human perception and cognition mean that much of the thought and action taken in world politics is out of touch with reality in one of the following ways:

- Seeing the geographic world through the lenses of one's own national identity and past.
- Behaving on the basis of biases, stereotyping, and prejudices relative to those who live elsewhere on the planet.

- Ignoring information about people living in another territory if it is inconsistent with one's own core values.
- Oversimplifying the outside territorial world of states, nations, and people.

These misperceptions and errors in cognition have a great deal to do with human decisions that lead to centralization and cooperation, as well as to decentralization and conflict in world politics. In the following sections, we will look at perceptions with regard to national identity, region, and religion and will consider how these perceptions drive world politics.

Perception and National Identity

A key aspect of perceptions of territory is the way in which humans have come to identify themselves as "a nation" or "a people" who share a common past and present, language, customs, religion, and territory. In fostering national identity, territory serves a number of purposes.[24] It plays a political role in generating loyalty and a sense of belonging to a piece of land occupied by a people through history. It helps to clarify national identity by giving all members of the national group a common tangible focus—the homeland. It gives the nation an identifiable place on the earth, a piece of territory with boundaries. These functions of territory apply to Americans in America, as they do to Russians in Russia or Germans living in Germany. We see these ideas clearly etched in President Bush's creation of an Office of Homeland Security in the wake of the 9/11 terrorist attacks on America.

Territory-based ethnic national identity has become a major factor in world politics in recent years—and is often the cause of conflict and disintegration. Ethnic national groups make decisions based on perceptions of territorial space and terrain, and on the political relationships such factors breed. The Serb ethnic cleansing of Bosnians in Yugoslavia's bloody civil war of the early 1990s is one of many examples to be found across the global spectrum.

Another is the desire for self-determine the Kurdish people, who have been striving for years to create a state of Kurdistan and who live in four states: Turkey, Iraq, Iran, and Syria. Other national self-determination groups seeking territory for statehood have included **Basques** and **Catalans** in Spain, Quebecois in Canada, Sikhs in India, Eritreans in Eritrea on the Horn of Africa, and Chechens in Russia's Chechnya republic.

Over time Kurd guerrillas have fought the military forces of Iraq and Turkey, and resorted to terrorism and political activities through their Kurdish Workers Party (PKK by the Kurdish initials). In northern Iraq, in the no-fly zone designed to protect the Kurds from Iraq, by the summer of 2002 the Kurds had created a small territorial area that came close to their centuries-old dream. The area they ruled was about 250 miles wide and roughly 125 miles deep, bordered by Syria, Turkey, and Iran. Within this area Kurds claimed to have created freedoms unknown in Iraq since that state's founding in 1921.[25] What will happend to the Kurds during Iraq's postwar reconstruction?

Conflict in Multinational States   Because the leaders of multiethnic national states have little interest in giving up territory or its resources to ethnic nationalist breakaway movements, they typically come down hard on such groups. Why lose land and resources if you don't have to? When Tehran encouraged nationalist Kurds in Iraq to rise up in protest during the Iran-Iraq war, Baghdad used poison gas against its own Kurdish citizens! The struggle for a Palestinian state in

Basques
An ethnic group with its own language and cultural roots located in northern Spain and southern France.

Catalans
A self-identifying ethnic group in Spain.

Israel has produced horrendous bloodshed in recent years. The Chechen secessionist movement from Russia led to the destruction of Grozny, the Chechen capital, and considerable bombing by the Russians in civilian areas. Yugoslavia's breakup in the 1990s as a result of ethnic national secessionist movements produced monumental loss of life and the massacre of thousands of people. The perceptions that lead to ethnic nationalist secessionist movements, then, have been one of the more grisly aspects of geopolitical relationships.

Internal Unrest and Refugees Territory-based identity and its resulting civil wars have produced an extraordinarily large number of refugees in recent years. Refugees are civilians who have been displaced by persecutions and armed conflict. They may wind up living in camps or wandering in their own country, where they are not protected under international refugee law. Indeed, their own government may attack them while they remain inaccessible to outside monitors or providers of humanitarian assistance. By 1997 the number of internally displaced persons equaled more than 17 million.

For more information on the escalating numbers of worldwide refugees, go to **www.ablongman.com/ duncan.**

Displaced persons may also seek asylum in other countries. The largest numbers of refugees by 1997 came from Palestine (3,743,000) and Afghanistan (2,622,000). The Web Exploration gives a broader picture of the number of refugees worldwide. Keep in mind the enormous problems caused by refugees who have either been displaced within their own country or forced to cross the border into other countries. The problems range from financial to logistical—where to put the refuges and how to pay for their needs. The world's refugees, then, are a direct product of human perceptions and consequential territorial conflicts.

Perception and Regional Identity

Territory shapes regional identities as well as national identities—as illustrated by European countries' membership in the European Union or America's participation in NAFTA. Perceptions of regions have political outcomes—as in Islamic fundamentalists' anger at U.S. occupation of parts of Saudi Arabia wherein lie Mecca and Medina, holy cities in the Islamic world. That occupation is one reason that drove Osama bin Laden and his Al Qaeda terrorists to attack the United States Regional identity also shapes Russian foreign policy in terms of how Russian leaders perceive NATO expansion or Eurasian or Central Asian political frontiers. Russian leaders are acutely conscious of threats from Central Asia (flows of narcotics and refugees across unprotected borders), and the always-present China, with whom Russia has a long border.

During the Cold War the United States believed that if the Communists controlled one country, adjacent countries would also inevitably fall to communism. This **domino theory** also prompted U.S. intervention in Vietnam during the 1960s, and the U.S. fear of similar consequences from Soviet-Cuban intervention in Central America and the Caribbean during the 1970s and 1980s. European Colonialism during the nineteenth and twentieth centuries also produced much conflict, as one colonized state after another sought to break away from colonial control—most notably from 1947 onwards after India's break with Great Britain. In each of these cases human perceptions of territorial regions led to major foreign policy decisions.

Perception of Territory and Religion

A brief look at the interplay between geography and religion indicates another impact of geography on perceptions. Millions of people across the globe adhere to any number of religious practices—variations in beliefs regarding one's conduct in accordance with divine commands.[26] What captures one's imagination from the perspective of geography is the interplay between territory, religion, and politics—and how religious identification can produce conflict and cooperation associated with territorial space.

One powerful example surrounds the terrorist attacks on America on September 11, 2001. Those who planned and implemented these acts came from the Arab world—comprised of 23 states and territories (Palestine) located in North Africa and Southwest Asia. Within the Arab world are found wealthy elite rulers of countries (such as Saudi Arabia and Egypt) who have strong connections with the United States and the West. Yet among the poverty-ridden, demoralized masses over which they rule, many are attracted to a brand of anti-Western Islam. They resent their governments' ties to "the West," especially to what they see as an uncaring, rich United States; they also resent the failure of their governments to improve their lives, as well as the general decline of the once powerful Arab Empire. Osama bin Laden, the inspiration for Al Qaeda terrorism, is from Saudi Arabia. Thus you can see how perceptions of injustice, undergirded with religious ideology, have fomented deep-seated discontent with the West and hero worship of the man who masterminded the Al Qaeda terrorist acts.

Religion is often a key element in national identity, which in turn is a force for conflict or cooperation. For example, Eastern Orthodoxy is a part of today's Serb national identity, which has spurred conflict with neighboring Bosnians, where the religious heritage is Islamic. As a consequence, Bosnia is divided into land controlled by Muslims and Catholic Croats on the one hand, and on the other by Serbs. Russia, with its own Eastern Orthodox roots, initially backed the Serbs in their power struggle with the Bosnians, while the Bosnians found backing from Islamic states. Religious tensions are equally strong on the Indian subcontinent, where Indian Hindus clash with Pakistani Islamic believers over Kashmir. That conflict dates back at least to 1947, when India broke free from British rule, leading to tens of thousands of deaths as Muslims struggled to set up East and West Pakistan. Religious perception, then, has a powerful impact as a geopolitical force at work in world politics.

How Are Maps Used in Political Geography?

Geopolitical concepts about world politics take us into the world of maps—of which many kinds are to be found. They range from general geography maps that show states or countries and major cities to road maps that depict transportation routes between cities and towns. Others are special purpose, showing earthquake regions, military installations, natural resources, or population density. Some maps include space satellites and remote sensing, while nautical charts are used in maritime traffic. As representations of geographic areas, maps provide us with a wealth of information—from location, size, and shape of states to territorial and topographical features, such as jungles, deserts, and mountains.

A map is a way to learn about the size and density of a country's cities, electrical power sources, location of natural resources like oil and coal, climate, and environmental problems. Borders with neighboring countries are easily identified, including contested border areas, as well as the location of major waterways. A map, in short, is a quick way to get a handle on a country's physical features and key aspects of its human inhabitants, including their overall living conditions. Maps can also help us understand spatial and power relationships.

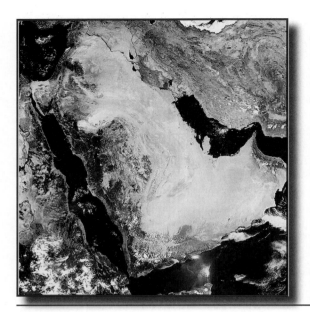

FIGURE 7.7
Satellite Images: Straits of Hormuz (left) and Straits of Gilbraltar (right).

For more information
on remote Sensing with
space satellites, go to
**www.ablongman.com/
duncan.**

But what is truly exciting about today's maps are the advances in cartography that have been made by computer technology, including sophisticated optics, satellite imaging, digital processing, global positioning systems (GPS), remote sensing, and Geographic Information Systems (GIS)—complex databases that store data and create graphic outputs. Satellite images, for example, give us views of the Straits of Hormuz (left) and Straits of Gibraltar (right)—two important shipping lanes noted earlier—from outer space. Satellite, remote sensing, and GPS maps have become vital tools in finding resources like fish and oil, projecting crop production, identifying climate change and environmental deterioration, tracking the AIDS epidemic, or following refugee flows stemming from civil wars and repressive regimes. The field of map making is experiencing revolutionary innovations in terms of attention to detail, visual quality, and accessibility.[27] As Figure 7.7 shows, digitization has made possible easy revision as well as greater accuracy and innovative perspectives, and with computer cartography now available on the World Wide Web and on computer discs, the quality, quantity and accessibility of maps are greater than ever before. They provide extraordinary insights into the spatial world and allow us to "see" geopolitics in action. Military personnel use these improved maps as they always have—for planning and executing wars, gathering intelligence on foreign forces, weapons locations, and tracking maritime traffic carrying troops or weapons. We will now take a more focused look at how maps are used to shape perceptions.

Maps and Perception

Maps are constantly used in foreign policy to shape public perceptions. U.S. relations with Cuba are a case in point. During the Cold War, when Cuba had established close ties with the Soviet Union, Havana became a major thorn in the side of U.S. foreign policymakers. Because the sea-lanes of the Caribbean and Gulf of

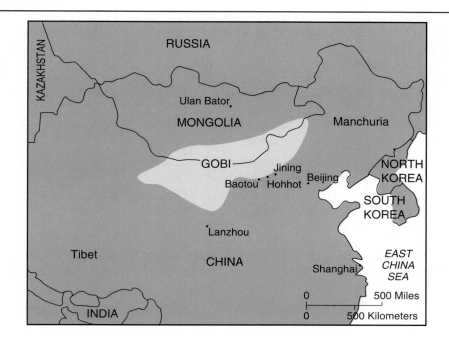

FIGURE 7.8
The Gobi Desert: Much of the Gobi is mountains. Only a small part is a sandy desert. Archaeologists believe that there are many undiscovered cities in the Gobi. Severe sand storms occur yearly and may engulf Beijing in a matter of years.
Source: http://chinapage. com/map/map.html

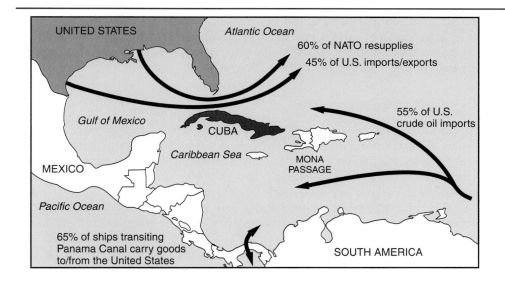

FIGURE 7.9
Cuba's Proximity to the United States
Source: Department of State and Department of Defense, The Challenge to Democracy in Latin America, *Washington, DC, 1986, p. 5.*

Mexico, as we see in Figure 7.9, have long been considered to be vital security interests to the United States, Washington, D.C., policymakers perceived Soviet influence in Cuba as a major threat. Maps were utilized time and again to illustrate to Congress and the American people Cuba's proximity to the United States and the threat it posed to U.S. interests. The Cold War map that follows illustrates how Cuba's location—coupled with its Soviet ties—cast it in the role of a giant warship controlled by the Soviets, conducting operations inimical to the well-being of the United States.

The Cuba map illustrates a key point about maps. Most people think of maps as unbiased reference objects, although they actually depict, like a photograph, a subjective point of view. This Cuba map is designed to convey the sense of Cuba as a geographically proximate security threat to the United States—a strategic extension of Soviet power directly into Americas' backyard. The map legitimizes the U.S. foreign policy position vis-à-vis Cuba and the Soviet Union, depicted as adversaries that must be confronted with power.

Maps, then, can be quite arbitrary in terms of what they illustrate, showing us what the mapmaker wants to emphasize. As one map specialist reminds us,

> Eighteenth–nineteenth-century maps embodied the commercial and political interests of European nation-states. In the increasingly common atlases of the nineteenth century, a distinctly Euro centric world appeared. The borders, markings, illustrations, and notations on these maps graphically express the European states' political, commercial, or scientific interests; colonial possessions were prominently displayed . . . maps are centered on Western Europe, North America, or the North Atlantic. The resulting configuration has become so familiar that few people notice just how arbitrary it is.[28]

In his classic book, *The Power of Maps*, Denis Wood reveals what many maps are: a way to communicate selected perspectives and biases of the mapmaker.[29] For example, Israeli policymakers like to make the point of just how small and vulnerable democratic Israel is compared to the rest of the Arab World.

A map can be, like a painting, an expression of a point of view—an instrument of communication, persuasion, and power. As the leading producer of maps, the United States has a distinct advantage in projecting soft power (see Chapter 3), for it can produce and disseminate maps that portray its best sides to the world and de-emphasize its worst—from colonial America to the present.

Danger of Inaccurate Maps

Maps, however, must be accurate to be useful. Inaccurate maps can strain relations between countries and even cost lives. A classic case of "bad map" geopolitics occurred in May 1999, when the United States confessed that its Central Intelligence Agency officials in charge of selecting bombing targets in the NATO military campaign against Yugoslavia had used a map of Belgrade from 1992.[30] This map was too old to show that Yugoslav arms agency had been replaced by China's embassy. As a result, U.S. airplanes mistakenly bombed the embassy, causing the death of Chinese embassy officials.

In the wake of this "bad map" bombing incident, a scene of violent anti-American sentiment rapidly unfolded in Beijing. Beijing students and other residents gathered outside the U.S. embassy, chanted slogans against the United States, burned American flags, and pelted stones and eggs at the Embassy. In effect they held the U.S. ambassador and staff hostage while the police and soldiers stood by. Chinese leaders blasted U.S. "gunboat diplomacy," and the U.S. State Department published a warning to travelers to avoid China until the situation stabilized. This gigantic intelligence and map gaff reminds one of the U.S. invasion of Grenada in 1983, when U.S. forces found themselves on the tiny Caribbean Island without accurate road maps. It's one thing to look at an inaccu-

Chinese Students demonstrating in front of the U.S. Embassy in Beijing: This event occurred in May 1999 after the U.S. incorrectly bombed China's embassy in Belgrade.

rate map in your university library and chastise the mapmaker, but quite another to use a poor map to wage war.

Maps in the U.S. War on Terrorism

The 9/11 terrorist attacks on America, which led to U.S.-led bombing of the Taliban in Afghanistan produced—and was aided by—a plethora of satellite images and digital terrain modeling and mapping of Afghanistan. The Russians produced some of the best maps of Afghanistan, showing the topography of this country.

The maps make obvious Afghanistan's formidable terrain—in particular, the terrifying Hindu Kush, which contains some of the highest mountains in the world, as well as the country's constricted valleys and its overall exceptionally defensive nature. Military leaders could see that these topographical factors, coupled with the warlike tendencies of Afghanistan's many tribal groups, would make hand-to-hand fighting with the Taliban extremely difficult. Air strikes consequently became military strategy.

When you look at all the dimensions of world politics discussed in this book—from key actors to driving forces and major issues—you come to understand how maps are basic tools of understanding, powerful instruments of foreign policy and international relations, and omnipresent images of perceived reality. They help the militaries of the world as noted earlier, and certainly the U.S. military to plan combat strategy, assess enemy capabilities and weaknesses, plot battle successes and failures, and to shape impressions of the public so they will support military operations. In the U.S.-led war against Iraq in 2003, you can imagine the number and types of maps of Iraq utilized by the military.

What Is the Recent History of Geopolitical Thinking?

As noted earlier in the chapter, leaders of countries and their advisors historically have perceived land space—and who controls it—as a possible threat or opportunity. Major foreign policy concerns have centered on defense against perceived security threats from other states and pursuit of economic priorities. Strategies for achieving these goals have varied from one country to the next, depending on the state's location on the face of the globe—and how its location shapes the perceptions and expectations of its policymakers regarding friends and enemies, trade opportunities, and other factors relevant to its national interests. Geopolitical strategies, then, are territorial-based policy concepts associated with geographic factors. A good example of a geopolitical foreign policy is the UN-enforced no-fly zone applied against Iraq to protect the Kurds in 1991. Let's now look more closely at the recent history of geopolitical thinking that lies behind cases like the no-fly zone. First, we will look at geopolitical concepts that emerged after the Cold War and then take a close view of the U.S. war on terrorism with its geopolitical strategic underpinnings.

During the Twentieth Century

Geopolitics became tainted under Nazi influence during the buildup to World War II. In particular Karl Haushofer (1869–1946), who lectured on geopolitics at the University of Munich as the Nazis came to power, drew on Ratzel's notions of the organic state and on Mahan and Mackinder. Using these theorists, Haushofer developed a theory of **Lebensraum,** or living space, that Hitler adopted to justify German territorial expansion into neighboring states. The organic state must expand or die. German geopoliticians under Haushofer's influence, drawn to the heartland theory and imbued with Hitler's notions of pure Aryan race and a heavy dose of German nationalism, undoubtedly played a role in German aggression. Their ideas also spread through Germany's educational system during the Nazi era. Happily, they ended with Nazi Germany's demise in 1945.[31]

Lebensraum
The German word for "living space." A geopolitical concept touted by Adolph Hitler, it was one justification given to Nazi territorial expansion.

During the Cold War

A great example of geostrategy—the use of geography in strategic ways—in the mid-twentieth century was the U.S. **containment** policy that played a part in the Cold War. A number of scholars have concluded that Spykman's rimland thesis may have been the key foundation of George F. Kennan's containment strategy (1947) for U.S. foreign policy after World War II as a way to stop perceived Soviet expansion. As such, it was even more influential than Mackinder's writings.[32] Kennan directed the newly created Policy Planning Staff of the State Department in the early post–World War II period. He also had observed Soviet behavior firsthand while serving as deputy chief of mission at the American embassy in Moscow.

Kennan influenced President Truman's thinking decisively. Truman adopted Kennan's idea that Russia's drive to expand Soviet power was based on a geographic sense of insecurity and must be checked and contained. Also known as the **Truman Doctrine** after President Harry Truman who proposed it in 1947, it was designed to "contain" Soviet communism, that is, to prevent it from expanding beyond Eastern Europe. To achieve this objective, the United States first pumped bil-

Truman Doctrine
A foreign policy announced by President Harry S. Truman in 1947, which declared that the United States would defend free people everywhere against the threat of communist aggression.

lions of dollars into a post–World War II European economic recovery plan (the **Marshall Plan**) to put West European economies on a solid footing in order to counter the appeals of communism. Secondly, the United States forged an anti-Soviet military alliance—the **North Atlantic Treaty Organization (NATO)**—with West European countries in 1949 as a power block to check expanding Soviet power aimed westward. Containment also went into practice in the Far East in 1950, when the UN sought to prevent Soviet-backed North Korean pressure on South Korea. NATO's decision to expand its membership after the Cold War ended underscores that organization's continued geopolitical dynamic.

The Soviet Union had its own form of geostrategy during the Cold War. In its brand of power projection, Moscow engaged in a struggle for world influence with the United States. It formed the Warsaw Pact (a military alliance of the Soviet Union and East European Countries) to counterbalance the West's NATO alliance and forged the Council of Mutual Economic Assistance (an economic union) to check the European Economic Community in Western Europe. Moscow then moved toward strong economic, military, and political competition with the United States in the Third World. Once the Soviet Union had linked up with Cuba in 1961, Soviet geostrategic competition with the United States became especially pronounced. The imprint of geopolitically based power alignments sought by the Soviet and Cubans was etched sharply in world politics, as Moscow and Havana joined with leftist groups in Angola, Ethiopia, and Somalia. Similar inroads occurred in the Caribbean Basin—the strategic backyard of the United States. The Soviet-Cuban connection in El Salvador, Grenada, and Nicaragua during the 1970s and 1980s also illustrates the point.

Since the Cold War

After the Cold War ended, NATO expanded its membership and its area of operations to Bosnia and Kosovo. In 1999 NATO admitted Poland, Hungary, and the Czech Republic, and in May 2002 it formally welcomed Russia as a participant in NATO discussions. The question of more members remained open at the outset of 2001, owing to a number of strategic considerations. These included the potential for increased disagreement among NATO members over military strategy, as occurred when Greece and Italy almost ended their support for the Kosovo intervention owing to domestic opposition. Another issue is the European Union's initiatives in building its own defense system independently of NATO and Washington—and how this effort will impact NATO members. In addition to these issues, many NATO states depend on trade with Russia; they do not wish to undermine relations with Moscow by expanding membership in ways that would pose an even greater perceived security threat to the Kremlin.

President Bill Clinton pursued a strategy of global geoeconomics as he sought expanded free trade across the globe, which he hoped would create market democracies and, in turn, greater global stability.[33] You can see Clinton's strategy of geoeconomics at work in his pursuit of NAFTA, the **Free Trade Area of the Americas (FTAA),** and the WTO. As it turned out, however, President Clinton was unable to expand NAFTA into a larger trade group because the U.S. Congress would not give him the negotiating power to do so. By the end of the Clinton term of office, Latin America had become a low priority, but the election of George Bush, with his Texas background and knowledge of Mexico, brought a new policy focus on the region. Terrorist attacks on America on September 11, 2001—and

Web Exploration

For more on the Marshall Plan and containment, go to **www.ablongman.com/ duncan.**

Free Trade of the Americas (FTAA)
A proposed free trade area extending throughout the Americas, first announced at a Summit of the Americas in Miami in December 1994. Signatories designated 2005 as the deadline for conclusions of negotiations for the FTAA. Implementation was to follow in subsequent years.

subsequent concern with Al Qaeda terrorist threats—dramatically undermined this positive prognosis of Latin America.

In the Bush Anti-Terrorism Doctrine

The impact of geography on foreign policy has been profound since the 9/11 terrorist attacks on America. In a first phase of world reaction, much of the world sided with the United States in its war on terrorism—initially directed at the Taliban in Afghanistan, who had allowed Osama bin Laden and his Al Qaeda forces to train and to plan their attacks. In a second phase of the America-led war on terrorism, the global alliance began to unravel as differences in strategy and tactics widened the distance between the United States and its various allies. The Europeans differed sharply with the Americans, as did much of the Middle East, over the interpretation of the Israeli-Palestinian conflict, and notably with the U.S. reluctance to intervene directly and with its perceived pro-Israel bias. In a third phase of America's war on terrorism—as President Bush developed his perceptions of the "axis of evil" in his January 2002 State of the Union address—cracks between the United States and its previous allies opened still wider (see Chapter 4).

To return to the main point, geography has played a pivotal role in recent history, as in the past, in shaping the foreign policy of leaders. Land space—and who controls it—as a possible threat or opportunity may be viewed as a constant in foreign policy planning. At the same time, it more often than not is a key to understanding current trends toward centralization or decentralization in world politics. From Nazi *Lebensraum* and Truman's policy of containment to post–Cold War democracies and market economies, and the post-9/11 Bush Doctrine in an age of terrorism, geography stands out as a central piece in the politics and foreign policies of world affairs.

What Political Geographic Factors Help Explain the Terrorist War Against America?

Why do the Islamic fundamentalists in general—and Al Qaeda terrorists in particular—so hate the United States that they are prepared to attack Americans with suicide bombers and presumably by virtually any means at their disposal? This question has haunted Americans since 9/11, prompted a host of antiterrorist policies throughout the world, and launched new college courses throughout the United States on Middle East politics and America's war on terrorism. Much has been written and spoken on the subject, and much more will be written and spoken in the years ahead. The question brings us to political geography, which offers a frame of reference to help inform us about Al Qaeda terrorism and its pronounced anti-West, anti-U.S. posture.

While the subject commands more attention than we can give it here, we can at least provide a geopolitical framework. The key point is not to dismiss the terrorists as insane, or psychologically impaired, because rational reasoning—from their perspective—drives them. To explain their point of view, we must look at three dimensions: (1) the global level, (2) the regional level, and (3) the state level. Let us examine each of these in turn.

Global Factors

From an **international political system perspective** of geopolitics, the United States is number one in economic and military power. As the chief driving force in globalization and in cultural, economic, and military presence around the world, it

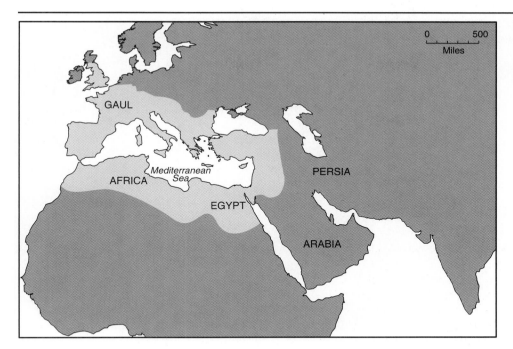

FIGURE 7.10

The Roman Empire at Its Greatest Extent (100 A.D.): Compare this map of the Roman Empire to that of the Arab Empire in Figure 7.11.

has drawn the ire of Al Qaeda terrorists—spurred on by Osama bin Laden, who operated originally from Afghanistan under the former Taliban's protection.

Yet, America's close links with the Saudi and Egyptian governments draw the ire of anti-U.S., anti-West Islamic fundamentalists, who see such Middle East rulers as wealthy repressive elites who have done little to help the impoverished masses living within their state borders. As one scholar points out, "For decades Arabs had been ruled by colonial governors and decadent kings," and when leaders like Egypt's Gamal Abdel Nasser came to power, it appeared that the Middle East was on the threshold of a new era of modernization and development.[34] Nasser argued for self-determination, socialism, and Arab unity, and for a time—as other Middle East regimes climbed on board, it appeared that indeed a new era had come. But instead it failed, and soon the newly "modern" republics atrophied into dictatorships, which have remained as such; several are backed by the United States. For this reason, many among the Middle East masses—watching the elite of their states squander oil's fabulous riches on lavish living while the poor grow poorer—have come to dislike the United States.

Finally, Islamic fundamentalists and many other followers of Islam are heirs to one of the great civilizations of the world (Arab). While today's Arab muslim and non-Arab muslim worlds are in a dire crisis of development, yesterday's Arab Empire was truly spectacular. It was larger than the Roman Empire (see Figure 7.10), for it included three continents (Asia, Africa, and Europe). (See Figure 7.11.) Its modern achievements, moreover, were legendary—in art, literature, architecture, mathematics, philosophy, medicine, trade and finance, reference for learning. Islamic fundamentalists declare that only a *jihad*, or "holy war," against the enemies of Islam will restore this former glory.

The Regional Level

A geopolitical regional analysis also helps flesh out key dimensions of the terrorist war against America. Southwest Asia—Afghanistan, Iraq, Iran, Saudi Arabia,

FIGURE 7.11

The Arab Empire at Its Greatest Extent (715 A.D.): Education flourished in the Arab Empire. Literature, philosophy, medicine, mathematics, and science became a part of the great Arabic pattern.

SOURCE: The National Geographic Society, Peoples and Places of the Past, 1983, p. 137.

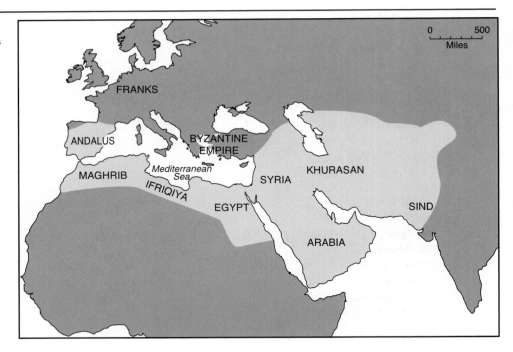

HISTORICAL PERSPECTIVE

The Arab World

A compelling case can be made that the Arabic Empire (seventh through eleventh centuries shown in Figure 7.11) was a good thing for many people, with its sense of pride and purpose, and power and dominion over much of the world. The Prophet Muhammad—who was born in Mecca and who died in Medina in today's Saudi Arabia—founded a religion that saw people of the Arab Empire as Allah's chosen people, with history on their side, yet quite willing at the time to allow coexistence with Jews and Christians as long as they paid a tax that assured them considerable freedom as well as cultural and intellectual autonomy. It was a time of political geography dominated by Islam.

Then came Western Crusades that began in the eleventh century, Western colonialism and violent European intervention in the Middle East, creation of the state of Israel in Palestine in 1947, Western-driven globalization, westernized greedy rulers and their police states, and U.S. military forces in Saudi Arabia. This history is a source of deep frustration and a feeding ground for terrorists bent on attacking the United States and other Western states.

This background forms a global perspective, because it is all about the Arab world's position of power in relation to the rest of the world.

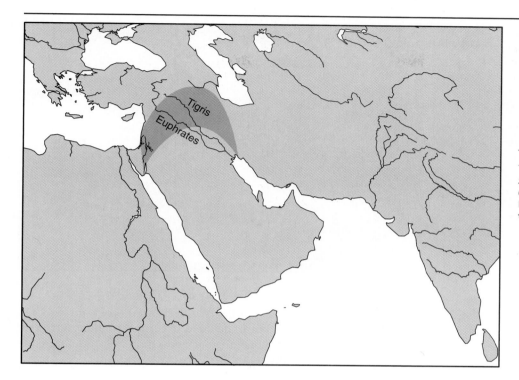

FIGURE 7.12

The Fertile Crescent:

The Fertile Crescent (see Figure 7.2) lies in Southwest Asia. Some of the best farmland of the Fertile Crescent is in a narrow strip of land between the Tigris and Euphrates—today's Iraq.

SOURCE: *The National Geographic Society, Peoples and Places of the Past, 1983, p. 26.*

Pakistan, and India—is the geopolitical world region that is the crossroads of three religious faiths: Judaism, Christianity, and Islam—spawned from 1200 B.C. to A.D. 1500. Each faith is based on the idea of a single, all-powerful God—the idea of monotheism—which distinguished Judaism, Christianity, and Islam from other religions of the time. The ideas of these three great religions—and their capacity to reach out to growing numbers of followers and spread to other areas of the globe— were in part shaped by the nature of Southwest Asia's location. (See Figure 7.12.)

The map of Southwest Asia shows this part of the world as being the location of the great Tigris-Euphrates river system and the Fertile Crescent—one of the world's earliest culture hearths, with its rich sources of food production, innovation and ideas, and traits and technologies that spread beyond the region. South of this area lies the bleak Arabian Desert (millions of square miles); west of the Nile lies the huge Sahara Desert, and in Southwest Asia's north are rugged mountain ranges. Much, although not all, of today's Arab world (see Figure 7.13) lies in this enclosed fertile area that spawned the three great religions and the powerful Arab Empire (see Figure 7.11).

Any regional analysis of terrorism's war against America must take note of this rich Southwest Asian history as the backdrop to what might be termed Southwest Asia's countries as the **volatile vortex.** The volatile vortex is a regional arena of income disparities, grinding poverty, elite rule, ethnic conflicts, unstable states, and divided Islamic loyalties—a volatile mix, as the name implies. The once powerful Taliban who protected bin Laden and provided a sanctuary for Al Qaeda terrorist training were originally from Pakistan. Pakistan allowed these militant students (the Taliban) to study and train within its borders, and not surprisingly remnants of the Taliban have returned to the northern tribal area of Pakistan following the U.S.-led attacks on Afghanistan. In addition to the Taliban, destitute followers of

FIGURE 7.13

Today's Arab World: Much of today's Arab world lies in the Southwest Asia region that spawned the once powerful Arab Empire.

SOURCE: Cassel & Co., Ltd., 1975

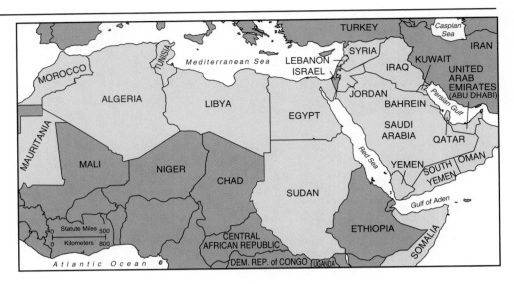

fundamentalist Islam come from this part of the world, spurred on by the actions, television appearances, and writings of bin Laden and other mastermind terrorists to hate America. Thus, this region contains ancient and complex roots that contribute mightily to terrorism against the West.

State-Level Factors

To do a thorough analysis of state-level factors that have contributed to anti-U.S. terrorism would require looking at each key state in Southwest Asia, as each state has its own unique set of circumstances. Pakistan's geographic proximity to Afghanistan, its role as a training ground for Taliban militants, and its turbulent tribal areas in the north that have served as a refuge for Taliban and Al Qaeda terrorists are all-important state-level factors. In addition, the multiethnic makeup of many of Afghanistan's neighbors is another state-level driving force toward volatility in the region. Because of its central role in the terrorist war against America, however, let's focus on Afghanistan, using the concepts introduced in this chapter.

To begin, Afghanistan is a land-locked country—253,000 square miles of foreboding terrain that borders on Iran, Pakistan, Tajikistan, Uzbekistan, Turkmenistan, and China. The population is composed of seven main tribes that historically have fought each other for dominance in the region. In the north towards the border with Tajikistan are the Tajiks, comprising about 25 percent of the population. Grouped around the border with Uzbekistan are the Uzbeks (6 percent). These two tribes formed the core of the Taliban opposition, the Northern Alliance that ultimately defeated the Taliban. In the northwest on the border with Turkmenistan are the nomadic Turkmens (4 percent). In the southwest are the Aimaq and Baluchi (8 percent). In the center are the Hazara (19 percent). The largest tribe is the Pushtun (known also as Pathans; 40 percent). The Taliban leaders and the majority of their supporters belong to this tribe.

Each tribe speaks a different language and has kin across the Afghan border: the Turkmens, Uzbeks, and Tajiks also live in the newly independent states of Turkmenistan, Uzbekistan, and Tajikistan. The Baluchi and Hazara have relatives in Iran and Pakistan, while some of the Baluchi and a large part of the Pushtun tribe live in neighboring Pakistan. So numerous are the Pathan, or Pushtun, that when Pakistan was forming in 1947, the Afghan government pushed for Pakistan's Northwest Frontier Province to be made the independent sovereign state of Pushtunistan.

This proposal soured Afghanistan's relations with Pakistan, and the division of the Pathan tribe has been a source of friction ever since. With the influx of some 2 million Afghan refugees into Pakistan, the Pushtun tribe has become a sizable force in Pakistani politics. Its political strength is probably the main reason why the Pakistani government chose, until recently, to support the training of Taliban mujahideen in Pakistan and the Taliban regime in Afghanistan. Keep in mind that none of these ethnic groups has an "Afghan" national identity. Their loyalty is not to Afghanistan; loyalty flows to ethnic group, tribe, or clan, rather than to the state or central authority.[35] Only a few times in its history was Afghanistan to unite around one leader. The most notable instance was in the eighteenth century when Ahmed Shah established a unified state in most of present day Afghanistan, under the Durani dynasty that lasted until 1826.

As mentioned before, owing to its territorial position on the map, the country's turbulent history is rife with foreign invasions and occupations. The 1979 invasion by the Soviet Union ended when it was forced out by anti-Soviet mujahideen guerillas, loosely organized under tribal leaders who were backed by Saudi Arabia, Pakistan, and the United States. When the Soviets departed, internal fighting erupted—a situation many observers fear will be repeated if a viable security establishment and political leadership do not emerge.

Besides being land-locked, Afghanistan is extremely poor, and a population of 25 million must struggle to survive. One out of every four children dies before the age of five. Life expectancy is about 43 years of age. Only 12 percent of the population has access to fresh drinking water, and barely 30 percent of the men and 15 percent of the women can read or write. The geography of Afghanistan is harsh and forbidding, and arable land is sparse, often ending only a few feet from riverbeds. Expanding desertification and environmental degradation exacerbate the terrible poverty and crumbling infrastructure. In addition, the whole population lives with the omnipresent danger of being blown up by antipersonnel mines, the enduring gift of the retreating Soviet army. All these problems underscore the scope of the Afghans' problem in finding the national unity, security, and sound economic base the country needs.

In terms of topography, the place is made for guerrilla war, tribal warfare, lawlessness, and defense against foreign invaders, including U.S. combatants—with its high mountains, deep valleys, and wide plains where land mines proliferate and knowledge of the terrain is in the hands of local inhabitants. Craggy cliffs and long tunnels hidden deep in the limestone rock offer unique hiding places. Ignorance of this land's topography is a serious danger to foreign invaders. Unpaved roads and steep mountain trails make vehicular traffic difficult at best, while steeply rising mountainsides frustrate troop movement. In addition, Taliban bases were difficult for the untrained eye to discern, because they often were located in caves in the mountains; while civilians and combatants were indistinguishable because they dressed and looked alike.

Afghanistan has been used in this discussion to illustrate many geopolitical concepts and the impact of geography on the state, region, and the world. That Afghanistan's geography—from location to topography—became the home of the Taliban and Al Qaeda terrorists who launched the 9/11 attacks vividly illustrates the continuing role of geography in world politics and how, in this case, it became a force for conflict and decentralization. Had we focused on today's Western Europe instead, we would have seen a different role of geography—one that has produced cooperation and centralization in the form of the European Union and North Atlantic Treaty Organization.

CHAPTER SUMMARY

What Are the Basic Elements of Political Geography?

Political geography—or *geopolitics* as some observers prefer to call it—is the study of how geography and international politics interact. It illuminates geography's impact on the driving forces in world politics—from national identity and nationalism to a state's power and development, to foreign policy and political decision making.

Three basic assumptions underlying political geography are:

- *Where humans live and what territorial states they occupy in great measure condition their level of development and power base vis-à-vis other humans in other states in other parts of the world.*
- *Humans, like most animal species, compete with each other for territory—and have been doing so since their inception.*
- *Human perceptions of the world comprise a kind of prism through which we interpret realities around us.*

A number of concepts and key terms, such as shatter-belt, are associated with political geography.

State and nation play key roles in political geography, as do intergovernmental organizations (IGOs), nongovernmental organizations (NGOs), and international law.

Today's political geography stems from a rich legacy of the past, dating back to the time of Aristotle.

What Geographic Factors Impact World Politics?

To understand the geographic factors that impact world politics, the subject can be divided into six domains: (1) location and development, (2) location and a state's territorial security, (3) landlocked states, (4) borders and boundary disputes, (5) transportation and communication channels and (6) oceans and air space. These domains are not necessarily mutually exclusive, but taken as a set of geographic factors they show the distinct imprint of geography on world politics.

How Does Geography Shape Human Perceptions?

Human perceptions drive world politics. Think of perceptions as the **mental processes of leaders and followers** from past to present.

- Perceptions are what humans think is true about the territorial world around them and their underlying assumptions about that world. Leaders act on these perceptions whether or not they actually reflect the "real" world.
- Unfortunately for world peace, cooperation, and stability, human beings are not as rational in interpreting the outside world as they might think. Humans have a limited capacity to remember and process information accurately.
- **Cognition** refers to how humans manipulate information and make decisions. Because humans are limited by what they know or can know, their perception and cognitive processes lead them to **simplify the outside world.**
- Perceptions and our cognitive processes lead to foreign policy based on biases, stereotyping, and prejudices relative to those who live elsewhere on the planet's real estate.

Perceptions have a profound impact in shaping: (1) national identity, (2) conflict in multinational states, (3) regional identity, (4) territory-linked religion, and (5) views of threats and opportunities.

How Are Maps Used in Political Geography?

Maps help us understand spatial relationships. Today's maps demonstrate advances in cartography that have been made by computer technology, sophisticated optics, satellite imaging, digital processing, global positioning systems (GPS) and remote sensing, and Geographic Information Systems (GIS)—complex databases that store data and create graphic outputs. Maps have become vital tools in foreign policy planning, wars, and in finding resources such as fish and oil to projecting crop production, identifying climate change and environmental deterioration, tracking the AIDS epidemic, or following refugee flows stemming from civil wars and repressive regimes.

Maps are associated with human perceptions, because they can be arbitrary in terms of what they illustrate, showing us what the mapmaker wants to emphasize—as demonstrated in Denis Wood's book *The Power of Maps*, which argues that many maps are a way to communicate selected perspectives and biases of the mapmaker.

Inaccurate maps can cause foreign policy disasters, as in the U.S. bombing of the Chinese embassy in Belgrade, Yugoslavia.

Maps are constantly in use in foreign policy planning, in shaping perceptions of those who read the maps, and in the U.S. war on terrorism.

What Is the Recent History of Geopolitical Thinking?

The twentieth century became known for Germany's *Lebensraum* theory, which influenced World War II, and the U.S. containment theory (also known as the Truman Doctrine), which shaped the Cold War.

- Geography has impacted strategic thinking in the post–Cold War period, notably in NATO's expansion and Russia's response—and in the U.S. approach to building democracy and market economies in the developing countries.
- The Bush Doctrine on antiterrorism is a reaction to the events of September 11, 2001. It identifies a number of countries with real or potential weapons of mass destruction (WMD) that must be confronted or even attacked, as in the case of Iraq. His "axis of evil" identifies these states on the world chessboard as North Korea, Iraq, and Iran, followed by Cuba, Libya, and Syria.

What Political Geographic Factors Help Explain the Terrorist War Against America?

Geographic factors that help explain the war against America can be classified in three ways: (1) global factors, (2) regional factors, and (3) state-level factors.

- At the global level the United States occupies the number one superpower position in economic and military power. It is the driving force in globalization around the world. As such, it has drawn the ire of Al Qaeda terrorists who see globalization as a threat to fundamental Islam, and who perceive the U.S. military presence in Saudi Arabia and the U.S. backing of Israel in the Palestinian-Israeli conflict as similarly ominous threats.
- Finally, from a global perspective, Islamic fundamentalists—like many followers of Islam—are heirs to one of the great civilizations of the world (Arab). While today's Arab muslim and non-Arab muslim worlds are in a dire crisis of development, yesterday's Arab Empire was spectacular both in size and in cultural richness.
- Any regional analysis of terrorism's war against America must take note of what might be termed the "volatile vortex" region of today's Southwest Asia, which includes Afghanistan, Iraq, Iran, Saudi Arabia, Pakistan, and India. Here is a regional arena of income disparities, grinding poverty, elite rule, ethnic conflicts, unstable states, and divided Islamic loyalties.
- State-level analysis examines each country that plays a role in the terrorist war against America. Afghanistan is a case in point. It is a land-locked country of 253,000 square miles of forebidding terrain that borders on Iran, Pakistan, Tajikistan, Uzbekistan, Turkmenistan, and China. Its population comprises seven main tribes that historically have fought each other for dominance in the region. Afghanistan's warlords and divided territorial loyalties—as in Pakistan—make tracking down Al Qaeda terrorists extremely difficult.

ENDNOTES

[1]See W. Gordon East, *The Geography Behind History* (New York: W.W. Norton & Co., 1965).

[2]Martin Ira Glassner, *Political Geography*, 2nd edition (New York: John Wiley & Sons, Inc., 1996), p. 11.

[3]Jared Diamond, *The Third Chimpanzee: The Evolution and Future of the Human Animal* (New York: Harper Perennial, 1992).

[4]Ibid., p. 219.

[5]Ibid., p. 236.

[6]Ibid., p. 2.

[7]See, for example, John T. Rourke, *International Politics on the World Stage*, 7th ed. (New York: Dushkin/McGraw Hill, 1999), p. 124.

[8]For more on this fascinating concept, see George J. Demko and William B. Wood, *Reordering the World*, pp. 31–32, 53–55.

[9]Robert I. Rotberg, "Failed States in a World of Terror," *Foreign Affairs*, July/August 2002, pp. 127–140.

[10]William B. Wood and George J. Demko, "Introduction: Political Geography for the Next Millennium," in Demko and Wood, eds., *Geopolitical Perspectives on the 21st Century*, 2nd edition (Boulder, Colorado: Westview Press, 1999), p. 8.

[11]World Council of Churches, Press Release, November 16, 2001.

[12]Aristotle, *Politics*, Book VII, Chapters 5–6.

[13]This point is made by Glassner in his superb book on *Political Geography*, (N.Y.: John Wiley & Sons, Inc., 1996) pp. 12–13.

[14]Ibid, p. 323.

[15]Spykman, a Yale University professor, published *America's Strategy in World Politics* (1942) and *Geography of the Peace* (1944).

[16]Jared Diamond, *Guns, Germs, and Steel: The Fates of Human Societies* (New York: W.W. Norton, 1998), Chapter 10.

[17]Ibid., p. 184.

[18]Inter-American Development Bank, *Facing Up to Inequality in Latin America: Economic and Social Progress in Latin America, 1998–1999 Report*, Distributed by the Johns Hopkins University Press for the Inter-American Development Bank, Washington, DC, 1999.

[19]Ibid., p. 98.

[20]See Emily S. Rosenberg, *Spreading the American Dream: American Economic and Cultural Expansion, 1890–1945*. (New York: Hill and Wang, 1982).

[21]Gal Luft, "The Palestinian H-Bomb," Foreign Affairs, July–August 2002, pp. 2–7.

[22]George B. Demko, *Why in the World*, p. 63.

[23]See Martin Ira Glassner, *Political Geography*, 2nd edition. New York: John Wiley & Sons, Inc. 1996, Chapter 36, for an excellent review of this subject.

[24]These observations are drawn from Guntram H. Herb and David H. Kaplan, eds., *Nested Identities. Nationalism, Territory, and Scale* (Lanham, MD: Rowman and Littlefield, 2000), pp. 16–19.

[25]John F. Burns, *The New York Times*, July 28, 2002.

[26]See Edward F. Bergman, *Human Geography: Cultures, Connections, and Landscapes* (Englewood Cliffs, New Jersey: Prentice Hall, 1995), Chapter 8.

[27]Ibid., p. 227.

[28]Denis Wood, "The Power of Maps (Maps are Subjective)," *Scientific American*, May 1993, p. 88.

[29]Ibid.

[30]*Reuters*, May 10, 1999.

[31]See Glassner, pp. 327–328.

[32]See James Dougherty and Robert L. Pfaltzgraff, Jr., *Contending Theories of International Relations*, 3rd ed. (New York: Harper and Row, 1990,) p. 63

[33]John Spanier and Steven W. Hook, *American Foreign Policy Since World War II* (Washington, DC: Congressional Quarterly Inc., 1995), p. 269.

[34]Fareed Zakaria, 'Why Do They Hate Us?' *Newsweek*, October 15, 2001, p. 26.

[35]Alvin Z. Rubinstein, "Afghanistan After the Taliban," *Foreign Policy Research Institute*, October 15, 2001, E-mail distribution.

CASE STUDY

Caspian Sea Region

The Caspian Sea region is important to world energy markets because it holds large reserves of undeveloped oil and natural gas. The Caspian Sea's mineral wealth has resulted in disagreements between the five countries that surround it, and the region's huge energy potential has sparked fierce competition—between producers as well as consumers—over the final export routes for this oil and natural gas.

Also, with the U.S. war on terrorism in full swing, the Caspian Sea region has taken on major significance for the United States. Central Asia, where the Caspian Sea is located, has become home to 60,000 American troops. One reason for these forces is containment of Islamic extremism, a goal shared by Russia, which sees its southern flank as vulnerable. Russia is also concerned, however, with protecting its economic interests in Central Asia and the Caucasus, which is crisscrossed by oil and gas pipelines. Some Russian leaders therefore view the new American presence as an imperialist interest in guarding Caspian energy resources for its own future needs. Others in Russia see a common U.S.-Russian interest in protecting oil routes and guarding against Islamic extremism. Whatever the case may be, Caspian energy supplies have made this region an emerging geopolitical hotspot.

Background

The Caspian Sea is located in central Asia, landlocked between Azerbaijan, Iran, Kazakhstan, Russia, and Turkmenistan. The Sea, which is 700 miles long, contains six separate hydrocarbon basins, although most of its oil and natural gas reserves have not been developed yet.

Proven oil reserves (defined as oil and natural gas deposits that are considered 90 percent probable) for the Caspian Sea region are estimated at 17–33 billion barrels, comparable to those in the United States (22 billion barrels) and the North Sea (17 billion barrels). In addition, the region's possible oil reserves (defined as 50 percent probable) could yield another 233 billion barrels of oil. Natural gas reserves in the Caspian Sea region are even larger than the region's oil reserves. Overall, proven natural gas reserves in the Caspian region are estimated at 177–182 trillion cubic feet (Tcf). Possible natural gas reserves in the Caspian region could yield another 293 Tcf of natural gas. Since they became independent in 1991, Azerbaijan, Kazakhstan, and Turkmenistan have sought to develop their national oil and natural gas industries. Over the past ten years, Azerbaijan and Kazakhstan especially, have received large amounts of foreign investment in their oil and natural gas sectors. With additional investment, the application of Western technology, and the development of new export outlets, oil and natural gas production in the Caspian region could grow rapidly.

Caspian Legal Status Remains Unresolved

Before 1991, only two countries—the Soviet Union and Iran—bordered the Caspian Sea, and the legal status of the Sea was governed by 1921 and 1940 bilateral treaties. With the collapse of the Soviet Union and the emergence of Kazakhstan, Turkmenistan, and Azerbaijan as independent states, ownership and development rights in the Sea have been called into question. Currently, no agreed-upon convention delineates the states' ownership of the Sea's resources or their development rights.

As a result, several conflicts have arisen, especially in the Sea's southern waters. In July 2001, Iranian military gunboats confronted a British Petroleum (BP) Azeri research vessel and ordered the ship out of waters Iran claims as its own. Azerbaijan, for its part, has objected to Iran's decision to award Royal Dutch/Shell and Lasmo a license to conduct seismic surveys in a region that Azerbaijan considers to fall in its territory. In addition, Turkmenistan and Azerbaijan remain locked in a dispute over certain fields.

These conflicts have hindered further development of the Sea's oil and natural gas resources, as well as the construction of potential export pipelines from the region. Negotiations between the countries have been slow; while Russia, Azerbaijan, and Kazakhstan have agreed on dividing the Sea by a "modified median" principle, Iran insists on an equal division of the Sea, and Turkmenistan agrees on the principle of dividing the Sea, but not the method. A proposed summit of the heads of states of the Caspian countries was postponed three times in 2001 when it became apparent that no final agreement could be reached.

Oil

Despite the lack of a multilateral agreement on the Sea, Azerbaijan and Kazakhstan have made substantial progress in developing their offshore oil reserves. Azerbaijan has signed a number of production-sharing agreements—both onshore and offshore—in order to develop its oil and natural gas industries. Although the country's oil production fell after 1991, in 1997, with the help of international investment in the sector, Azerbaijan's oil production rebounded in 2001.

Likewise, Kazakhstan has opened its resources to development by foreign companies. International oil projects in Kazakhstan have taken the form of joint ventures, production-sharing agreements, and exploration/field concessions. Boosted by foreign investment in its oil sector, Kazakhstan's oil production has increased steadily. In addition, preliminary drilling in Kazakhstan's offshore sector of the Caspian has revealed bountiful oil deposits, especially in the Kashagan field, raising hopes that Kazakhstan may become one of the world's largest oil producers.

Overall, oil production in the Caspian Sea region reached approximately 1.3 million bbl/d (billion barrels of oil per day) in 2001, and three major projects are currently under development in Azerbaijan and Kazakhstan:

- In April 1993, Chevron concluded a historic $20-billion, 50-50 deal with Kazakhstan to develop the Tengiz oil field, estimated to contain recoverable oil reserves of 6–9 billion barrels. Additional export pipelines likely will be needed, but given adequate export outlets, this joint venture could reach peak production by 2010.
  - In what was described as "the deal of the century," in September 1994 the Azerbaijan International Operating Company (AIOC) signed an $8-billion, 30-year contract to develop three Caspian Sea fields—Azeri, Chirag,

and the deepwater portions of Gunashli (ACG)—with proven reserves estimated at 3–5 billion barrels. Oil production at ACG is expected to reach 800,000 bbl/d by the end of the decade.

- Although signed with less fanfare in 1997, the offshore Kashagan block being developed by the Agip Kazakhstan North Caspian Operating Company (Agip KCO) may turn out to be more lucrative than both the Tengiz and the ACG deposits combined. Preliminary drilling has produced spectacular results, with analysts estimating possible oil reserves of up to 40 billion barrels (10 billion barrels of which are thought to be recoverable). Oil analysts are hailing the field as the largest oil discovery in 30 years.

These projects, along with others currently underway, could help boost Caspian Sea region production to around 3.7 million bbl/d by 2010. By 2020, production could increase by another 2 million bbl/d. Although not "another Middle East," as some analysts have claimed, the Caspian Sea region certainly is comparable to the North Sea in its hydrocarbon potential.

Natural Gas

The Caspian region's natural gas resources were extensively developed under the Soviet Union. After 1991, Caspian region natural gas, mostly from Turkmenistan, competed with Gazprom, the Russian state natural gas company. Since Gazprom owned all the pipelines, and export routes for Caspian natural gas were routed through Russia, Caspian natural gas was squeezed out of the hard currency market.

As a result, Turkmenistan's incentives for increasing production disappeared, and the country's output dropped throughout the 1990s. Now, however, with high world natural gas prices and a Turkmen-Russian agreement on Turkmen exports in place, the country's natural gas production has rebounded, and Turkmenistan has plans to boost natural gas output substantially over the next decade, contingent on securing adequate export routes, such as the proposed Trans-Caspian Gas Pipeline.

Uzbekistan is the third largest natural gas producer in the Commonwealth of Independent States and one of the top ten natural gas–producing countries in the world. Since becoming independent, Uzbekistan has ramped up its natural gas production nearly 30 percent. The country's natural gas reserves are estimated at 66.2 Tcf, with the richest natural gas district in the Uzbek section of the

Ustyurt Region. In order to offset declining production at some older fields, Uzbekistan is speeding up development elsewhere, as well as planning to explore for new reserves. Since Uzbekistan is land-locked and since its natural gas competes with Russian and Turkmen natural gas, Uzbekistan is limited in its ability to export. Instead, Uzbekistan has concentrated on supplying the Central Asian natural gas market.

With the emphasis on Azerbaijan's oil potential, the country's natural gas sector often has been overlooked. But the 1999 discovery of the Shah Deniz field will soon change that. The Shah Deniz field, which is thought to be the world's largest natural gas discovery since 1978, is estimated to contain between 25 Tcf and 39 Tcf of possible natural gas. Development of the field, which will cost upwards of $2.5 billion, should produce the first natural gas by 2004, making Azerbaijan a significant net natural gas exporter.

Overall, natural gas production in the Caspian Sea region reached 2.1 Tcf in 2000. Projects currently underway could help boost Caspian Sea region natural gas production to over 6 Tcf by 2010.

Export Issues

As increasing exploration and development in the Caspian Sea region lead to increased production, the countries of the region will have additional oil and natural gas supplies available for export. And with Azerbaijan's Shah Deniz field in development, along with increased investment to develop infrastructure and markets for the region's natural gas, Caspian natural gas exports could increase even further by 2020.

Lack of Transport Routes

In order to meet these export goals, the countries of the Caspian Sea region must address a number of transport issues. First, all oil and natural gas pipelines completed in the region (aside from those in northern Iran) prior to 1997 were routed through Russia and were designed to link the Soviet Union internally. When the Soviet Union collapsed in 1991, the republics that had been customers for Caspian natural gas were no longer able to pay world market prices for natural gas supplies due to the economic transition process. In addition, natural gas exports to other Newly Independent States (NIS) were limited because the pipelines pass through Russia and require agreements with Gazprom.

With a lack of export options, the Caspian region's producers have had two options: (1) sell their natural gas to Russia at below-market prices or (2) pay Gazprom a transit fee and export their supplies via the Russian pipeline system to ex-Soviet states that cannot pay fully in cash or are tardy with payments for supplies already received. In either case, things often do not go smoothly. For example, Turkmenistan's economy, which is concentrated mainly in oil and natural gas, experienced a huge 25.9 percent drop in GDP in 1997 when Gazprom denied Turkmenistan access to its pipeline network over a payment dispute. Although Gazprom and Turkmenistan resolved the dispute in 1998, in order to reach its full natural gas export potential, Turkmenistan and other Caspian region natural gas producers must solve the problem of how to pipe their natural gas to consumers and receive hard currency at market prices in return.

Similarly, prior to 1997, exporters of Caspian oil had only one major pipeline option , the 210,000-bbl/d Atyrau-Samara pipeline from Kazakhstan to Russia. In addition, smaller amounts of oil were shipped by rail and barge through Russia, as well as by a second small pipeline from Kazakhstan to Russia. In short, the Caspian region's relative isolation from world markets, as well as the lack of export options, has thus far stifled exports outside of the former Soviet republics.

Construction of New Export Routes

To handle all the region's oil that is slated for export, a number of Caspian region oil export pipelines are being developed or are under consideration. Likewise, several Caspian region natural gas export pipelines have been proposed. Still, many questions remain as to *where* all these exports should go.

West? The TRACECA Program (Transport System Europe-Caucasus-Asia, informally known as the Great Silk Road) was launched at a European Union (EU) conference in 1993. The EU conference brought together trade and transport ministers from the Central Asian and Caucasian republics to initiate a transport corridor on an West-East axis from Europe, across the Black Sea, and through the Caucasus and the Caspian Sea to Central Asia.

In September 1998, 12 countries (including Azerbaijan, Bulgaria, Kazakhstan, Romania, Turkey, and Uzbekistan) signed a multilateral agreement known as the Baku Declaration to develop the transport corridor through closer economic by integrating member countries, rehabilitating and developing new transportation infrastructure, and fostering stability and trust in the region. The planned Baku-Ceyhan Main Export Pipeline to transport oil from Azerbaijan to Turkey and then to European consumers is the main component of this cooperation.

In addition, the EU has sponsored the Interstate Oil and Gas Transport to Europe (INOGATE) program, which appraises oil and natural gas export routes from Central Asia and the Caspian, and routes for shipping energy to Europe. INOGATE is run through the EU's Technical Assistance to the Commonwealth of Independent States (TACIS) program.

East? Oil demand in Europe over the next 10 to 15 years is expected to grow by little more than 1 million bbl/d, while that of Asian markets is expected to grow by 10 million bbl/d over the next 10 to 15 years. Feeding this Asian demand, though, would necessitate building the world's longest pipelines north through the impassable mountains of Kyrgyzstan and Tajikistan and across the vast, desolate Kazakh steppe before heading east.

South? Caspian exporters could also supply Asian demand by piping oil and natural gas south, either through Afghanistan or Iran. The Afghanistan option, which Turkmenistan has been promoting, would entail building pipelines across war-ravaged Afghan territory to reach markets in Pakistan and possibly India. The Iranian route would pipe natural gas from Azerbaijan, Uzbekistan, and Turkmenistan to Iran's southern coast, then eastward to Pakistan, while the oil route would take oil to the Persian Gulf, then load it onto tankers for further transshipment.

However, any significant investment in Iran would be problematic under the Iran and Libya Sanctions Act, which imposes sanctions on non-U.S. companies investing in the Iranian oil and natural gas sectors. U.S. companies already are prohibited from conducting business with Iran under U.S. law.

North or Northwest? Russia has proposed multiple routes that would utilize Russian oil pipelines to transport oil to new export outlets on the Baltic and Black Seas. These pipeline systems would allow oil exports from the Caspian to run via Russia's pipeline system across Ukraine and Hungary, and then terminate at the Croatian deep-sea Adriatic port of Omisalj. In addition, Russia already has the most extensive natural gas network in the region, and the system's capacity could be increased to allow for additional Caspian region gas exports via Russia.

However, Caspian producers have political and security concerns about relying on Russia (or any other country) as their sole export outlet. In addition, most of the existing Russian oil export pipelines terminate at the Russian Black Sea port of Novorossiisk, requiring tankers to transit the Black Sea and pass through the Bosporus Straits in order to gain access to the Mediterranean and world markets.

However, the Bosporus Straits are already a major choke point for oil tankers, and Turkey has stated its environmental concerns about a possible collision (and ensuing oil spill) in the Straits as a result of increased tanker traffic. A number of options are under consideration for oil transiting the Black Sea to bypass the Bosporus Straits.

Regional Conflict

In almost any direction, Caspian export pipelines may be subject to regional conflict, an additional complication in determining final routes. Despite the ouster of the Taliban government in December 2001, Afghanistan remains scarred and unstable. Also, the Azerbaijan-Armenia war over the Armenian-populated Nagorno-Karabakh enclave in Azerbaijan has yet to be resolved. And separatist conflicts in Georgia flared in the mid-1990s. Moreover, Russia's war with Chechnya has devastated the region around Grozny in southern Russia. In addition, the Uzbek government is cracking down on rising Islamic fundamentalism in Uzbekistan, tensions have increased between rivals Pakistan and India, and the Caspian states themselves disagree over territorial claims in the Sea. Nevertheless, several export pipelines from the Caspian region already are completed or under construction, and Caspian exports are transiting the Caucasus. While the hope is that export pipelines will provide an economic boost to the region, thereby bringing peace and prosperity in the long run, the fear is that in the short-term, the fierce competition over pipeline routes and export options will lead to greater instability.

SOURCES: *Agence France Presse, BBC Monitoring Central Asia Unit, Central Asia & Caucasus Business Report, Caspian News Agency, Caspian Business Report, CIA World Factbook, DRI/WEFA Eurasian Economic Outlook, The Economist, Environment News Service, The Financial Times, FSU Oil and Gas Monitor, Hart's European Fuels News, Interfax News Agency, The Moscow Times, PlanEcon, PR Newswire, Radio Free Europe/Radio Liberty, Reuters, RosBusinessConsulting Database, The Times of Central Asia, Turkish Business News, Ukraine Business Report, U.S. Department of Energy, U.S. Energy Information Administration, and U.S. Department of State. This report is from U.S. Department of Energy, February 2002.*

QUESTIONS

Check Your Understanding

1. Fill in the following table about features of the countries of the Caspian Sea region:

Country	Status Regarding Oil	Status Regarding Gas	One Key Fact (geographical or other)
Azerbaijan			
Iran			
Kazakhstan			
Uzbekistan			
Turkmenistan			

2. Fill in the following table about the pros and cons of potential export routes in the Caspian Sea region:

Direction of Export Route	Pros	Cons
West		
East		
South		
North/Northwest		

Analyze the Issues

3. How could you apply Diamond's theories to the Caspian Sea region?
4. The chapter notes a number of geographic factors that impact world politics, among them (1) location and development; (2) location and territorial security; and (3) transportation and communication routes. How does each of these forces come into play in the Caspian Sea region?
5. Which geopolitical features of the Caspian Sea setting are likely to generate regional conflict? In contrast, which features might promote international cooperation in this part of the world?
6. In Chapter 3 we discussed the importance of natural resources as a power factor, and in Chapter 4 we focused on foreign policy as a means to translate power capabilities into policies in pursuit of core interests. Discuss the countries of the Caspian Sea region in terms of their political geography and how it affects their power capabilities, core interests, and foreign policy.

FOR FURTHER INFORMATION

To discover more about the geopolitics of oil in the Caspian Sea region, consult the following journal articles, newspapers, and Internet sites:

Edward Morse & James Richard, "The New Oil War," *Foreign Affairs* (March/April 2002), pp. 16–31.
Scott Peterson, "Terror war and oil expand US sphere of influence," *The Christian Science Monitor* at *http://www.csmonitor.com/2002/0319/p01s04-wosc.html*
Environmental Literacy Council "Geopolitics of Oil," at *http://www.enviroliteracy.org/article.php/303.html*
Institute of International Relations, "The Geopolitics of Oil in Central Asia," at *http://www.idis.gr/people/arvan2.html*
Constantine Arvanitopoulos, "The Geopolitics of Oil in Central Asia," Thesis, Winter 1998, at *http://www.hri.org/MFA/thesis/winter98/geopolitics.html*

CHAPTER 8

Nationalism and Regionalism

KEY QUESTIONS RAISED IN THIS CHAPTER

1. What is nationalism?
2. How does nationalism vary around the world?
3. How do leaders use nationalism in foreign policy?
4. How does regionalism impact on the international system?

Chapters 1 and 2 introduced the concepts of *state* and *nation.* You learned that each is unique, and that they differ in important ways, with powerful implications for the study and understanding of world politics. A state, you will remember, must not be confused with a nation, despite a frequent tendency by the media to use these terms synonymously—or to refer to *nation-states,* which only leads to more confusion. States include geographically bounded places, with governmental structures and sovereignty, such as the United Kingdom of Great Britain and Northern Ireland, France, Germany, Russia, China, and Japan.

A *nation,* on the other hand, is best understood as a group of people who consider themselves linked by various bonds. As much a psychological association as anything else, a nation is a group of people who consider themselves culturally or linguistically related.[1] Examples of nations are Palestinians, Serbs, Croats, Bosnians, and Russians. A nation constitutes a self-identifying group of people bound by language, culture, assumed blood ties, customs, religion, and territory. When "apprehended as an idea," to use Sir Ernest Barker's phrase, national identity becomes an exceptionally powerful force.

With these distinctions between state and nation in mind, this chapter examines how national identity becomes nationalism and how nationalism so dramatically impacts world politics—integrating people who comprise the nation, yet dividing the people of one nation from those of another and all too frequently leading to conflict—as vividly seen in Palestinian nationalism versus Zionism (Jewish nationalism) today. First we will look at the nature of nationalism and its world political consequences. Next we turn our attention to how nationalism varies from region to region of the world. With this understanding of nationalism we can then move on to learn how leaders have used nationalism as a powerful emotive force in domestic and foreign policy. Finally, this chapter will focus on regionalism as a psychological identity that, like nationalism, can work to both centralize and decentralize the world's population. Our case study on Nigeria underscores the dramatic role played by ethnic nationalism inside a sovereign state.

What Is Nationalism?

Identity with a homeland or a piece of territory is a key part of national identity. As Anthony D. Smith puts it, national identity has a strong spatial or territorial conception, where a "nation" of people possesses compact, well-defined territories.[2] National identity as it evolved from the late eighteenth century onwards also came to encompass the idea of a political community of laws and institutions, which reflect the national people's political will and express their political sentiments and purposes.[3] National identity, then, is a "we" feeling, a collective identity of "a people," bound by culture and a sense of shared territory. Rudyard Kipling's poem "The Return" captures the essence of national identity and nationalism as a people's perception:

> If England was what England seems
> An' not the England of our dreams
> But only putty, brass an' paint,
> 'Ow quick we'd drop 'er!
> But she ain't!

SOURCE: *Edward Bonver's Poetry Lovers' Page, http://www.poetryloverspage.com/poets/ kipling/return.html*

WHY IT MATTERS TO YOU

Nationalism

Nationalism has long been one of the most powerful forces in world politics—clearly reflected in German and Japanese nationalism that triggered World War II and in many Third World proxy wars linked to Cold War competition between the United States and USSR after World War II (see Chapter 4). Many of these wars affected U.S. citizens—directly through loss of life (World War II, Korea, Vietnam) or financially by war's costs to taxpayers. Nationalism remains a dramatically strong driving force. You experienced it in the religious nationalism behind 9/11 and in today's war on terrorism. Just think about how religious nationalism haunts your every day—in terms of its impact on the U.S. falling stock market, declining economy, undermined civil rights, restrictions on travel, and potential ill-health (a smallpox or anthrax attack). Nationalism is not just something "out there." It is here and now.

Anthony D. Smith's work on *National Identity* (1991) gives us a good summary of the underlying assumptions in a people's sense of *national identity:*[4]

1. A historic territory, or homeland
2. Common myths and historical memories
3. A common, mass public culture
4. Common legal rights and duties for all members
5. A common economy with territorial mobility for members

It would be difficult to overstate the powerful impact of nationalism on world politics (see box Why It Matters to You: Nationalism). As a remarkably potent magnet that crystallizes people's loyalty to a homeland and cultural hearth, its uniquely diverse faces have produced both centralizing and decentralizing consequences for the world political system.

As to its centralizing impact, nationalism has brought people with shared roots together inside new states, promoted unified democratic governments, challenged imperialism and spawned economic development. These impacts might well be classified as positive.

Yet on the negative, decentralizing, side, nationalism has led to horrific world wars (German and Japanese aggressive nationalism in World War II), unspeakable genocide of a people (German nationalism against the Jews in the 1940s), and harsh internal oppression inside a state by a majority nation over a minority nation (Croats over Serbs inside Croatia in the early 1990s).

So powerful is national identity and its nationalism counterpart that no matter how hard communist authorities tried to stamp it out inside the former Soviet Union during the Cold War, it tenaciously reappeared like spring flowers after winter. With the end of the Cold War, the many nationalisms of Eastern Europe and inside and around Russia have reemerged in spades.

Now let us look at the nature of nationalism. A close examination of this key driving force in world politics reveals that at heart, it is (1) a psychological group identity among people, (2) an emotional force that ignites people's passions; (3) a power factor with strong historic roots; (4) a driving force that leads to positive and negative impacts in international relations; and (5) an identity that competes with transnationalism for a people's loyalty. We can now probe each of these dimensions in turn.

A Psychological Group Identity Among People

From the psychological point of view, nationalism works as a bonding agent, tying people together in a common set of reference points and perceptions of reality. This group identity separates one national group from another across the world. It creates unity among groups members and separates them from others unlike them, through a particular language as well as art, culture, heroes, religion, and collections of customs. Originally confined to Europe and America in the later eighteenth and early nineteenth centuries, nationalism has spread around the world, uniting people around a multitude of flags and pieces of territory. The United Nations, with its original 54 nations, now includes over 187 countries—many of which have more than one national self-identifying group inside them.

Nationalism as an idea—the idea that those who share a common language, history, religion, and culture constitute "a nation" that commands individual loyalty and sacrifice—is so compelling that it is one of the greatest psychological forces at work in world politics today. Hans Kohn, one of the keenest observers of nationalism, describes it as "a state of mind."[5] Among the characteristics of a people that spawn the idea that they differ from others, language is one of the most common bonds—creating the feeling of sameness and of a "we" versus "them" syndrome. If you have traveled to another country and found yourself surrounded by people speaking a different language, you may have experienced great relief when you ran into somebody speaking your own language. But as noted above, unifying factors generating a sense of "a people" also include religion, history, culture (folk tales, dress, behavioral traits), and ethnic sameness. To pull it all together, a nation and its corresponding sense of nationalism may be defined as a "named human population sharing an historic territory, common myths and historical memories, a mass, public culture, a common economy, and common legal rights and duties for all members."[6]

Nationalist sentiments, as noted above, proved to be strong psychological forces in the Soviet Union after 1917. Throughout the Soviet years, Moscow wrestled with how to keep its restless nationalities under control and devised an elaborate federal political system to do so. In the end, such efforts proved useless. The Soviet Union broke up in 1991, which set the scene for geographically proximate Yugoslavia to follow a similar and far more violent path from 1991 onwards. As the twentieth century came to an end, Russia was still struggling with determined nationalist groups seeking autonomy, as was vividly demonstrated not only by the tenacious Chechnya nationalist breakaway movement in the Transcaucasian region—an area of many contentious nationalities—but also by restive militants in Dagestan.

Nationalism as a psychological force is fostered in a variety of ways. Mass media is perhaps the most effective means of triggering its appeal. In many countries, the government controls the instruments of mass media communication, such as mail, newspapers, telephone, telegraphy, and television, radio, and satellite transmissions. By promoting the symbols of the nation—such as flags, songs extolling the nation's virtues, stories of struggles of the past, reminders of times of defense against aggressors, and heroes who gave their lives for the nation—governments can motivate their people to all kinds of endeavors. Since 9/11, for example, Americans have come together in a psychology of defense against Al Qaeda forces—especially when they hang American flags in front of their homes or hear the national anthem with its words of unity:

> Oh, say does that Star-Spangled Banner yet wave
> O'er the land of the free and the home of the brave?

In contrast, a nationalism mural in Baghdad depicted Saddam Hussein fighting a three-headed serpent representing British Prime Minister Tony Blair, President Bush, and Israeli Prime Minister Ariel Sharon.[7]

An Emotional Force That Ignites People's Passions

Nationalism is a deeply felt emotional force. While we saw that emotion at work in Germany and Japan's drive for economic growth in post–World War II, darker sides of German and Japanese nationalism have appeared too. Arab identity and nationalist emotion have made Osama bin Laden popular in the Arab world following the catastrophic events of 9/11, and the emotional content of Palestinian nationalism drives Palestinians to blow themselves up along with as many members of the Jewish population as possible in the drive for an independent Palestinian state. Nationalist emotions are present in a national group's desire to win, as in the Olympic Games or world ice-skating competitions. Certainly nationalist feelings lie behind the drive of one national group, like the Serbs, to expand its territorial borders and gain more living space for its people at the expense of other national groups like Bosnians or Croats.

One striking aspect is how nationalism of the twentieth century has become more and more a matter of emotional *ethnic identity,* frequently expressed as bitter grievances against foreigners, passionate struggle for independence, and longing desire for a separate territorial state. We see this obsessive ethnic nationalism, for example, at the heart of the post–Cold War breakup of former Yugoslavia, in wrenching upheavals in the Transcaucasian region and in many other geographic regions of the world. American nationalism, as we shall see, is a bit different—characterized not by a particular ethnic group, but by a "melting pot" of ethnic groups. It too has strong emotive patterns, however, as evidenced when President Woodrow Wilson tapped into American nationalism as a reason for entering World War I. President Franklin D. Roosevelt also aroused American nationalistic feelings in support of U.S. entry into World War II—as did George Bush in the war against Iraq.

While new driving forces of globalization, interdependence, and the information revolution have been transforming the international political system, nationalism refuses to go away. Its power to mobilize people through high drama and intense emotions, and its presence from America to Asia, have left an unmistakable imprint around the globe throughout the twentieth century. Let's look at some specific examples of the effects of this emotive appeal.

Nazi Germany In the 1930s Adolf Hitler mobilized the German people, whom he referred to as the Aryan race (pure Germans, not Jews or Blacks) by using propaganda techniques. He touched a sensitive cord in Germans by his emotive speeches that argued that the Germans had been "stabbed in the back" by the peace settlement at the end of World War I. This settlement saddled Germany with the guilt and a huge financial burden for causing that war. In the midst of the severe postwar economic depression, Hitler gained a huge following by organizing high-stepping jackboot parades, mobilizing youth movements, and holding charismatic nighttime speeches attended by thousands of his compatriots. Month by month he laid out his plans for the "superior" German people to rule Europe. He envisioned

a hierarchy of peoples, with the Germans dominating everyone else, slaves at the lowest level, and Jews and Gypsies entirely eliminated. Passions released by his fiery **xenophobia,** or extreme nationalism, led to World War II, the Jewish holocaust, and the virtual destruction of his idolized Germany by Allied forces.

Xenophobia   *Ultranationalism,* also known as *xenophobia,* exploded during the mid-1930s, the period between World Wars I and II. It swept Japan, where the Ministry of Education published its *Principles of the National Policy* directed at school children. In it, service to the state was extolled, while individualism was discouraged; patriotism meant being against most things foreign. Just as Germany was trying to expand and dominate Europe under the powerful force of nationalism, the Japanese set out to create their "Greatest East Asia Co-Prosperity Sphere throughout the Pacific area." Whereas the Germans sought to exterminate the Gypsies and Jews, the Japanese—swept away by their own form of xenophobia—occupied parts of China and Southeast Asia and were ready to die for their emperor in absolute loyalty to the glory of Japan. The ultranationalist movement in Japan ended in disaster when the United States dropped atomic bombs on Nagasaki and Hiroshima, thereby ending the war.

Post-Colonial Nationalist Sentiments   After World War II, the emotive power of nationalism continued to mobilize people in all kinds of movements with all kinds of impacts on international relations. Much of the world colonized earlier by Great Britain, France, Holland, Germany, and Portugal, for example, began to break up into new sovereign states after 1947, largely as the result of pressure from nationalist movements throughout the Third World. India broke away from Great Britain. Pakistan, led by Pakistani nationalists, broke away from India. Bengalis inside Pakistan split off from Pakistan and formed the new state of Bangladesh. These

Xenophobia
Extreme nationalism that unleashes violent action—even "ethnic cleansing" (genocide)—toward other ethnic national groups.

For more information about Hitler's brand of xenophobic nationalism, go to **www.ablongman.com/duncan**.

movements resulted, among other things, from national identity and powerful nationalist pressures. Even the new postcolonial states had internal nationalist movements. Malays fought the Chinese in Malaysia over Malay government control and
the operation of Malaysia's commercial and financial operations. Ibo nationalists,
seeking to break away and form their own state of Biafra, fought the Yorubas and
Hausa in Nigeria (see this chapter's case study). Sinhalese battled the Tamils in Sri
Lanka (formerly Ceylon). Lebanon erupted in a violent civil war among competing
nationalities and religious groups. The people of Eritrea fought for their independence in Ethiopia in a bloody civil war, while civil wars between ethnic groups
caught fire in a number of other postcolonial states such as Angola, Burundi,
Congo, Somalia, and South Africa.

In Congo, Africa's third largest country—where at least seven nations and
three factions and rebel groups have been battling over diamonds, gold, timber,
and coffee—the civil war struggles have been so severe that observers call it
Africa's First World War. It continued fiercely even after a peace accord was signed
in August 1999. Meanwhile, the failure of Burundi's government and ethnic rebels
to end a seven-year civil war led its African neighbors to call a peace summit in
September 2000, which gave the parties 30 days to sign a cease-fire or face international sanctions.

Post–Cold War Europe has been the scene of new nationalism, too, where states
and minority ethnic national groups have come into conflict. One sees it in the collapse of Yugoslavia with its many national groups; in Germany's unification; in the
horrendous "ethnic cleansing" that went on inside Bosnia; in violence inside
Georgia; and in the alarming rise in neofascism and neo-Nazism in Belgium,
France, Germany, and Italy, where extreme right wing parties recently have gained
strength. Its presence is felt in western Russia, too, where Vladimir Zhirinovsky
heads up an ultranationalist party that threatens Russia's still-weak democracy and
Russia's neighbors as well. Indeed, with the collapse of communism, many scholars
have argued that the most powerful force in the minds of the world's population is
nationalism—with all the international security threats and problems for political
stability and economic growth it creates.

Nationalist Passion and World Politics   As noted, nationalism—once
sparked by leaders who have tapped into its psychological power—has made an
enormous imprint on the world stage. As such it ranks right up there with ideologies like communism or fascism, and it might in some cases be treated as a secular
moral religion. It has united people—and continues to do so—in a variety of causes
and movements that cover a wide range of possibilities in the international arena:

- Seeking territorial control over disputed land in order to create a new state for
  a stateless people (Palestinians in Israel).
- Fighting for independence against "foreign" oppressors (Vietnamese against
  their many "invaders" from China, France, Japan, and America).
- Holding out against imposed external ideologies (national groups against
  Marxism-Leninism in the former Soviet Empire).
- Eliminating "alien" national groups inside or in nearby states (Hitler's
  Germans against the Jews, and Serb ethnic cleansing of Croats and Bosnians in
  former Yugoslavia).
- Breakaway nationalist movements from inside an existing state to form a new
  state with its own sovereign institutions (Biafra in Nigeria; Chechnya in
  Russia; Quebec in Canada; East Timor in Indonesia; Eritrea in Ethiopia).

Web Exploration

For more information
on nationalism in
Africa, go to
**www.ablongman.com/
duncan**.

These are called **national self-determination** movements and frequently lead to bloodshed. For example, Indonesian militia groups went on a killing rampage against pro-independence people in East Timor after they voted for independence in 1999.

The manifestations of nationalism go on and on. The following brief list captures nationalism's wide-ranging possibilities and shows how over time it has united and divided peoples occupying the same territory in the international political system—and caused an immense amount of violence and bloodshed. It is a force at work at the global level, the state level and, most certainly, at the individual level of analysis. Studying nationalism helps us understand how and why:

- Violence and war occur in the international political system.
- People act as they do toward each other across state boundaries and within multinational states.
- Misunderstanding occurs so frequently in world politics—a result of differing perceptions of nationalist realities.
- Diplomatic negotiations can be so difficult over many issues.
- Perceptions form such an important element in assessing conflict and cooperation.
- Leaders manipulate masses.

To put it simply, understanding contemporary world politics requires a good look at nationalism's emotional content and how it shapes decentralization and centralization.

A Power Factor That Dates Far Back in Time

It would be difficult to pinpoint exactly when nationalism took form, but most historians and students of nationalism agree that as an idea that seized people's imaginations, nationalism became increasingly pronounced during the latter half of the eighteenth century in Western Europe and America. From this perspective, nationalism became a major force in world affairs well after the creation of states, which started to appear after 1648.

Other scholars argue that the way was paved for nationalism far in the past—by patriotic sentiments in Sparta, Athens, and republican Rome, "the models and exemplars of the public, and often heroic, virtues."[8] As we saw in Chapter 2, the printing press and newspapers also helped spawn nationalism in the late eighteenth century, as did the growth of towns and cities, an educated intellectual class who wrote about the virtues of civic patriotism, and a growing sense of nationality.[9] The American and French Revolutions reflect these forces, especially through the use of nationalism's symbols, such as the flag, patriotic songs, folk tales, ballads, poems—and even billboards and murals.

Spawned by these revolutions and by resistance throughout Europe to Napoleon's quest for empire, nationalism was an essentially French movement that appeared more and more in different countries in a variety of ways throughout the nineteenth century. For example, it gained strength in England and Prussia (via the Germans); among the Czechs, Slovaks, and Poles; in Italy and Spain; and within the Ottoman Empire from which the Greeks, Serbs, Bulgarians, and Rumanians became independent. By the late 1840s it was going strong, as a rash of nationalist movements broke out in Europe, notably in the vast Austrian Empire of the Hapsburgs. That empire was made up at the time by at least ten recognizable nationalities or language groups.

Nationalism Deeply Rooted in History: Archduke Ferdinand, heir to the imperial throne of the Austro-Hungarian Empire, and his wife Countess Sophia walk to their car in Sarajevo, June 28, 1914, just prior to their assassination. A 19-year-old Bosnian student, a member of the "Young Bosnia" movement dedicated to a Bosnia free of Austrian Hapsburg rule, assassinated them. The assassination ignited World War I.

By the late nineteenth century, large nations began to consolidate inside large states—in a new German empire, a unified kingdom in Italy, and in a large Austria-Hungary dual monarchy. So the principle of nations, with "a people" inhabiting states, was well in progress as the twentieth century began.[10] This was underscored by World War I, initiated when a young Bosnian nationalist, Gabriel Principe, chafing under Austrian rule, assassinated Archduke Francis Ferdinand, the heir to the Hapsburg empire. The assassination occurred in the streets of Sarajevo, Bosnia's capital, in the outlying Austrian Empire.

Most separatist movements at the turn of the twentieth century were based on ethnicity—the assumption that those seeking autonomy are a different people from those who rule them. So we find Basques and Catalans opposing the "Spaniards," Scots against the "English," or Albanians in Kosovo against the Serbs.

Today's ethnic claims to nationhood—and the right to a separate territorial state—should be distinguished from the versions of nationhood and nationalism that existed during the late eighteenth and early nineteenth centuries. Nationality as it first bloomed did not consider ethnicity as necessarily essential to the consciousness of "a people." The original "nations" of Europe—and America—had no unitary ethnic base, but rather based "national identity" on cultural and political perceptions, which therefore constituted what it meant to be British or French, German, Dutch, or Spanish.[11] Nor was "ethnicity" mandatory for the original American revolutionary nationalism that inspired the formation of the United States.

These earlier versions of nationalism were rooted in the eighteenth-century concept of *popular sovereignty,* the basic democratic principle that "the people" are the ultimate source of all legitimate authority. The idea in this brand of nationalism is that "the people" establish government and delegate powers to public officials through a social contract or constitution. This doctrine was expounded by the American and French revolutions of 1776 and 1789.

As we have seen, however, by the end of the nineteenth century and early years of the twentieth century, nationality and nationalism increasingly mirrored the ethnic component. Thus, when President Woodrow Wilson proclaimed the notion of "self-determination of nations" as a guiding principle for international relations at the conclusion of World War I, he opened the flood gates for any ethnic-national group to declare its "national" right to its own sovereign state. President Wilson's Secretary of State, Robert Lansing, worried that the idea of "national self-determination" was so "loaded with dynamite" that it might make the world dangerous.[12] He said, "It will raise hopes, which can never be realized. It will, I fear, cost thousands of lives . . . What a calamity that the phrase was ever uttered! . . . What misery it will cause."[13]

If Secretary Lansing could only see today's ethnic national conflicts and self-determination movements. President Wilson of course was using the "self-determination" phrase to mean "the consent of the governed." Unfortunately for stability in the international system, Wilson's phrase became interpreted as "national" self-determination. It became translated in the minds of many ethnic leaders as the right of ethnic national groups to have their own sovereign states. Thus many ethnic groups around the world began pounding the doors for their right to a self-governing state.

Lansing would have been doubly worried if he had considered the number of ethnic groups on the face of the earth and how many states there would be if every ethnic group had its own state. The world has an estimated six thousand separate indigenous nations, each with its own language, culture, and ties to an ancestral homeland. This translates into around 300 million indigenous people, over 5 percent of the world's population.[14]

Still, the existence of more than one indigenous ethnic national group inside a state does not mean an automatic breakup of the state. In many cases, what has happened is **devolution,** which takes place when a state's government grants more political and economic power to ethno-political national groups in order to hold the country together. This has happened in Italy, where Rome granted more minority power to Italy's separatist *Northern League* and in Spain, where the central government has been trying to hold the state together by giving more power to outlying ethnically or regionally identifying communities. The United Kingdom has done the same thing with Scotland, Wales, and Northern Ireland, as has France with its nationalist separatist movements.

A Driving Force with Positive and Negative Impacts

The negative aspects of nationalism, with its highly charged ethnic content and its influence on international conflict and decentralization, by now should be clear. As a negative force, it has created a security dilemma for the international community—namely, how to manage it or prevent it from spreading its wide range of accompanying problems, including the creation of scores of refugees. However, one caveat should be noted. Recent research by the World Bank on civil conflicts around the world shows that rebel fighting more often is motivated by the greedy pursuit of lucrative commodities—like diamonds and drugs—than by political, ethnic, nationalistic, or religious goals.[15] Still, nationalism has its benefits as well as its dangers.

Those who defend nationalist causes tend to be the defenders of what may be termed *liberal nationalism,* or the belief that every nation should have its own state

Web Exploration

For more information about Woodrow Wilson and nationalism, go to **www.ablongman.com/ duncan.**

Devolution

The process whereby regions within a state demand and gain political power and growing autonomy vis-à-vis the central government. Devolution can lead to self-determination movements, whereby ethnically identifying regions within a state break away and form their own independent sovereign new state.

and that one ethnic or cultural group should not collectively rule over another.[16] Those favoring this idea, however, do not suggest that every miniscule ethnic group, such as the Sorbs or Wends in Germany, or the Amish in the United States, should have its own state. Yet, they do believe that larger ethnic national groups, such as the Kurds, Ibo, or Tibetans, should be entitled to a state. This is so, the argument goes, in order to avoid the large-scale violence associated with life in many multinational states—such as Iraq, Nigeria, China, or Russia. Proponents of liberal nationalism also argue that democracy does not work in societies divided along linguistic and cultural lines. Examples cited include troubled Canada (the Quebec issue), the former Soviet Union, China (Tibet problem), Nigeria (three big ethnic groups, as discussed in the case study for this chapter), Angola, former Yugoslavia, India, Pakistan, South Africa, and Iraq. Switzerland, with three major cultural and linguistic groups, is a notable exception to this claim.

Given nationalism's liberal dimensions, as associated with the American and French Revolutions, let us consider its positive impacts:

- Promotes democracy.
- Stimulates the idea that political power legitimately resides with the people, and that political leaders exercise power only as agents of the people.
- Encourages self-determination and allows nationalities to preserve their cultures and govern themselves according to their own customs.
- Discourages imperialism by strengthening newly independent countries' resistance to outside occupation.
- Stimulates economic development by mobilizing people, as in Germany and Japan after World War II.

On the negative side, nationalism can:

- Lead to xenophobia, feelings of superiority (Serbs against Bosnians), and ethnic cleansing—or extermination of "foreign" ethnic national groups.
- Produce messianism—the propensity to think that one nation's duty is to "save" other nations.
- Stimulate violent self-determination movements and consequent bloodbaths.
- Spawn great conflict in world affairs, as between India and Pakistan, and North and South Korea, as well as generate suspicion, as with China's suspicion of Japan, or Russia's suspicion of the outside world.

Transnationalism
Transnational forces are those identities and movements that span a state's borders and affect more than one nation. They include such movements as feminism and Islam, to name only two of the more high-profile transnational forces today. Transnationalism dates back to the Greek stoics.

An Identity That Competes with Transnationalism for People's Loyalty

The concept of **transnationalism** refers to forces that cut across state boundaries. Transnational issues spring from ideologies, organizations, and systems of thought that affect people of different nationalities around the globe. Dating back to Greek *stoicism,* which made its appeal to people as members of humanity rather than as members of a nationality or political group, transnationalism is seen today in many forms, including those identified below:

- *Religions* such as Islam, Buddhism, Hinduism, Judaism, or Christianity, which are major sources of cooperation and conflict in the world. Religion increasingly plays a role in world politics, as in the liberation theology of Catholicism in Latin America, or the conflict of Protestants and Catholics in Northern Ireland. Note that religion can take an extremely militant form in the context of nationalism, as we saw with the Taliban in Afghanistan, and with the Muslim militants in Algeria and the Middle East. Arab-Israeli tensions, fundamentalist Islamic forces at work in Iran and Afghanistan, and Indian-Pakistani adversarial relations illustrate the power of religion to generate conflict in international relations.

- *Philosophies* like Confucianism, which affects the lives of many people in China, and the Falun Gong movement, which affects many others in that same country. The Falun Gong is a blend of traditional Chinese slow-motion exercises and Buddhist and Taoist principles that its adherents say promote good health.
- **Ideologies,** such as communism, which continues to shape politics and economics in China, Vietnam, and Cuba.
- *Transnational communications,* such as via CNN news; via transportation (sea and air); and via organizations, such as IGOs, NGOs, and MNCs (multinational corporation).
- *Feminism,* which has had an increased political impact in the world today, as evidenced by the increasing number of women occupying positions of responsibility in government, or conversely, by the women and children who make up a high percentage of the world's refugees.
- *Clash of civilizations,* as noted in Samuel P. Huntington's theory, discussed in Chapter 7. Huntington envisions conflicts arising from nations and groups of different civilizations—classified as Western, Confucian, Japanese, Islamic, Hindu, Slavic-Orthodox, Latin American, and possibly African.

Given the power of nationalism and transnationalism discussed in this section, you might wonder how multinational states hold together at all, especially given that nationally identifying people do not necessarily cluster in one part of a state's territory. They may live in different towns and regions, as was the case inside Croatia, Bosnia, and Serbia in former Yugoslavia. When Croatia and Bosnia separated from Yugoslavia to form new multinational states, their multinational groups were not clustered in one part of the new state's territory.

How do states adjust to multinational settings? States have made, tried to cope with, or govern, different national groups within their borders—in a variety of ways: Here are some of the tried methods:

- **Genocide:** Dominant groups seek to physically eliminate minority groups through violence, as in Hitler's Germany and Milosevic's former Yugoslavia.
- **Expulsion:** This occurs when a dominant group kicks out minority groups or scares them out. Milosevic also pursued this method, as did Idi Amin Dada in Uganda. Indonesia has acted similarly against the Chinese.
- **Federalism:** We see this form of government in Russia, India and Nigeria.
- **Integrationist nationalist ideology:** Mexico and Cuba have this kind of nationalism that attempts to bring together different ethnic groups into one identity, i.e. Blacks. Mulattos (black/white mix) and Whites as *Cubans;* Indians, Mestizos (Indian/white mix) and Whites as *Mexican.*
- **Devolution:** This occurs when national groups are given more autonomy, as with Great Britain's Scotland, Wales, and Northern Ireland.

Ideology
A set of political belief that serve to guide government policy and behavior.

For more information on ethnic nationalism in former Yugoslavia, go to:
www.ablongman.com/ duncan.

How Does Nationalism Vary Around the World?

Nationalist sentiment has varied over the years and from one cultural, economic, historical, political, and geographic context to another. The "melting pot" of American nationalism, for example, differs greatly from the racially charged Serb nationalism found in Yugoslavia. The *national self-determination* movement as exemplified by Canada's French-speaking population, has less ethno-racial and xenophobic content against "Canadians" than, say, that of the Chechens in Chechnya, who have been fighting Russians for hundreds of years. Canada's brand of nationalism, like that in some U.S. movements, emphasizes bilingual multiculturalism, while other brands of nationalism insist on one language, that of the dominant national group. Now let's take a closer look at some of nationalism's variations around the world.

Variations in History and Location

For more information on Indian nationalism in Mexico, go to **www.ablongman.com/duncan.**

The national identities found in the New World of North America, Central America, and South America have historically included a greater variety of ethnic groups than in the Old World, where the imprint of a single ethnic group has been more pronounced. The "Mexican" identity in the state of Mexico, for example, which came to the fore after Mexico's 1910 Revolution, includes *Indians* and *mestizos* (mixed white and Indian). The "American" identity encompasses a variety of ethnic groups, and the same holds true for "Canadian" nationalism. Cuba offers another New World brand of nationalism in which those of black, *mulatto* (mixed black and white), and white heritage all share the "Cuban" national identity.

Yet even in the post–Cold War New World, one sees the emergence of ethnic-based nationalism among Indian tribes in the United States, indigenous peoples in Canada, and the Maya in Mexico, who are part of the *Chiapas Zapatista* movement. America, if examined from the perspective of its Indian tribes and nations—many of whom assert their identity politically—must be considered multinational, although it harbors an overarching "American" national identity. In April 1999 Canada inaugurated a new native Indian Territory of Nanuvut, with Iqaluit its capital. Located between the Northwest Territories and Hudson Bay, this territory is home to the Inuit Eskimos.[17]

For more information on Inuit Eskimo nationalism, go to **www.ablongman.com/duncan.**

We can cite many illustrations in which a nation's location and history shaped its brand of nationalism. Russia, for example, has been attacked many times over the centuries—hence, its suspicion of the outside world. Since 1776, America has been isolated territorially from the power politics of Europe, which facilitated its growth as it pushed ever westward into its frontiers and gained more and more land. And because America is an immigrant nation, it does not show the same level of suspicion of the outside world that Russia does.

To summarize some of these differences between the United States and Russia, Russia's national image consists of the following elements:

- A sense of Russian culture as superior; a deep sense of community
- Defensiveness against foreigners, owing to so many past invasions
- Latent suspicions and fears of the outside world, due to past territorial vulnerability
- Sentimentality about the *Rodina* (Mother Russia) and Russian ethnic character

In contrast, American nationalism centers on the following core values:

- A creed of liberty and democracy, equality and opportunity
- Emphasis on the value of life and the pursuit of happiness
- An image as a land of promise and a destiny of prosperity
- An image of a land filled with diversity and numerous freedoms
- A place where constitutional rights and liberties flourish

Elsewhere in the world, such differences can be seen as well. For example, Pakistani nationalism has a built-in "anti-India" element stemming from past conflict and religious differences (Islamic versus Hindu). For India the situation is a mirror image, with built-in "anti-Pakistan" sentiments. Furthermore, separatists in India, such as the Sikhs, have their own nationalist identity and movement. An interesting footnote on nationalism is that people can change their nationalist beliefs over time. German and Japanese nationalism, once racist in nature during World War II, became distinctly less so in the post–World War II period.

For more information on national conflict between India and Pakistan, go to **www.ablongman.com/ duncan.**

Distinctions in Ethnic Nationalism

Ethnic nationalism refers to the identity of a people focused primarily on ethnic roots, such as Serb or Russian identity. Most of the world's countries have more than one ethnic national group living inside their boundaries. Many of these groups feel persecuted, most often because they are not granted major participation or representation in the states in which they live, which explains why ethnic nationalism has become such a driving force in world affairs at the outset of the new millennium. The discontent does not always translate into self-determination movements but takes many forms of political expression, not least of which is the struggle for land. In many cases this struggle is a reaction to state-sponsored *genocide*.[18]

A major characteristic of many ethnic national groups inside the world's states today is animosity toward neighboring ethnic groups, which leads almost automatically to conflict with the "outside" group. In this sense, identifying as a "Serb" in former Yugoslavia during that country's breakup beginning in the early 1990s produced routine hatred of Bosnians and Croats. The same might be said of the Tamils and the "Sinhalese" in Sri Lanka, the Tadjik or Uzbek and the Pushtuns in Afghanistan, or Yorubas toward Ibos in Nigeria. Such perceptions are born of geography, historical experiences, and cultural differences.

Yet, as mentioned earlier, ethnic nationalism also can lead to cooperation between groups—given appropriate economic and political conditions. When not manipulated by political leaders to serve their own drive for power—as so often happens (Nigeria and India are cases in point)—and when economic conditions benefit members of all or most of the ethnic groups inside a state, different ethnic nationalist groups experience—if not harmony—at least relative political stability. Malaysia—with its Malay, Chinese, and Indian groups—has a power-sharing arrangement that works most of the time, largely because the Chinese and Indian communities have accepted their subordinate role.[19] And many other states have used a federal form of government to hold together their multiethnic nationalist societies—as in Brazil, Russia, and China.

These opposite potentials for conflict (decentralization) versus cooperation (centralization) in multiethnic national settings have led to debate among scholars and policymakers over the causes of civil wars in developing countries. One group argues that ethnic hatred—frequently mobilized by political leaders for their own immediate advantage—makes stable democracy virtually impossible in multiethnic settings and violent conflict the natural outcome.[20] Others make the case that civil wars in poor countries are not due primarily to ethnic diversity, but rather to high levels of poverty, failed political institutions, and economic dependency on natural resources.[21] What is crucial, according to this view, are effective political institutions and economic opportunities for members of all the ethnic groups.

The terms *ethnic nation* and *tribe* are at times used interchangeably in the field of internationalism. You read in newspapers or textbooks about the Iroquois tribe or nation in America; Karen and Shan tribe or nation in Burma; or Ibo or Yoruba tribe or nation in Nigeria. Although the meanings of the two terms are very close, today we most often think of a tribe as a primitive group of people in a remote part of the world that is not so self-identifying and politically active as to constitute an ethnic nationality (as have the Kurds). Still, tribes can take on stronger and politically more powerful forms of national identity over time and become politically active, as demonstrated in the United States, Canada, and southern Africa. The term *clan*—a social group composed of several families with a common ancestor—represents another kind of social group. Clans are not limited just to Scotland; we also find them in Afghanistan, Iraq, and Somalia—where clan warfare has been devastating.

Religious Nationalism

For more information on religious nationalism in world politics, go to www.ablongman.com/ duncan.

Taliban
The name of the militant Islamic group that controlled Afghanistan until its defeat in the U.S.-led war in late 2001. The Taliban gave considerable support to Al Qaeda.

Hamas
"Islamic Resistance," referring to a Palestinian militant group that has employed terror systematically and regularly in Israel in an effort to promote the transfer of Gaza and the West Bank to a Palestinian authority.

Religious nationalism, found in many parts of the world, is a synthesis of religion and secular nationalism that merges cultural identity with the legitimacy of older religions.[22] Examples of religious nationalism—a basic fact of *contemporary* international politics—may be seen in Afghanistan, Bangladesh, India, Iran, Israel, Lebanon, Northern Ireland, Sri Lanka, and the Sudan. Indeed, its impact may be witnessed in U.S. domestic politics as well—as with the influence of the Moral Majority and related movements in American public life from the 1980s forward, including the 2000 presidential campaign. Religious nationalism spurred new levels of conflict in some parts of the world by 2001, as in Israel. In that troubled country, contending versions of how to create a Palestinian state have led to escalating conflicts between Palestinians and Jews, with many killed on both sides. Moreover, violent protests and widespread demonstrations by Muslim activists erupted in Bangladesh when a High Court verdict banned the use of *fatwas,* or religious edicts.

Some, if not many, religious nationals have been willing to resort to violence to make their point through terrorist activities, such as bombing everything from military installations to embassies, consulates, federal buildings, and airplanes. We see religious nationalism in the **Taliban** of Afghanistan, a militant movement of *Pushtun* Islamic students (see box Historical Perspective: The Taliban of Afghanistan). Its presence also is felt in Jewish extremism—as when Dr. Baruch Goldstein killed more than 30 Muslims in the Shrine of the Patriarchs in 1994. Actions of violent members of the Islamic **Hamas,** which wages war against Israel, provide another illustration.

India has also been the scene of rising Hindu nationalism pitted against Muslim nationalism. India's ruling party, the Bharatiya Janata Party (BJP) is based on principles of Hindu nationalism—one culture, one religion, and one language. Tensions between Hindu and Muslim nationalists erupted in February 2002 over the rebuilding of a Hindu temple, and in the state of Gujarat, Hindu nationalist extremism spiraled out of control and left at least 1,000 Muslims dead and 150,000 homeless after its anti-Muslim pogrom, as you read about in the case study for

HISTORICAL PERSPECTIVE

The Taliban of Afghanistan

Afghanistan's Taliban were deeply implicated in the 9/11 terrorist attack on America. They harbored and supported Osama bin Laden and the terrorist organization he founded, known as Al Qaeda, that the United States identified as responsible for the infamous attack. In October 2001, the United States began to bomb Taliban forces, and shortly thereafter the Taliban government collapsed. The word *Taliban* is from the Persian *Talib*, which means "religious student." Those who formed the Taliban studied in religious schools in Pakistan, where their families had taken refuge during the Soviet occupation of Afghanistan.

Members of the Taliban: Prior to their defeat by U.S.-led coalition forces in December 2001, in Afghanistan.

Violence in Gujarat, India: February—March 2002.

Chapter 1. Hindu nationalists have extended their influence through the education system, where a Hindu-extremist version of history is taught, and through recruitment of the youth and training in the martial arts.

Religious nationalism has created numerous problems in the international system—among them human rights abuses, new separatist movements, suicide bombings, and weakened states owing to terrorism and internal civil wars. **Human rights** are a big issue. When religious nationalists take power, they typically glorify their own religious communities as the true heirs of the state they occupy. This leads to poor treatment of minority groups and preferential treatment for the majority religious community. The religiously nationalist Taliban of Afghanistan insisted on the following rules in cities they captured:

- Female employment was restricted or banned.
- Women had to stay at home; when they left the house they had to be accompanied by a male relative and covered with an ankle-length veil.
- Nonreligious music, cassette tapes, TV, and movies were banned.
- Multicolored signs were prohibited.
- White socks were prohibited.

To enforce these rules, the Taliban employed a moral police force called *Agents for the Preservation of Virtue and Elimination of Vice* to search for violators. Offenders were brutally treated.

Violence associated with religious nationalism has been high in other parts of the world as well. Algeria has been the site of many violent attacks against locals and foreigners at the hands of Islamic extremists. Muslim factions also fought bitterly in Eritrea after the collapse of Ethiopia. Indeed, Islamic militancy has been active on the Horn of Africa—in former Ethiopia, Djibouti, and Somalia. Sudan, too, has been a major player in religious nationalism by spreading its brand of Islamic

Human Rights
Rights considered so fundamental that they belong to every individual on this planet. These rights include the basic political freedoms, economic rights—such as the right to work—and the right to leisure time. To date, women's rights are not considered fundamental human rights. The human rights upon which the states of the world are agreed may be found in the United Nation's Declaration of Human Rights, adopted by the UN General Assembly in 1948.

Divided Nationalism on the Korean Peninsula: A South Korean soldier looking at his North Korean counterpart through binoculars as the two stand guard across the borderline between two Koreas. While the Clinton Administration attempted to facilitate cooperation between North and South Korea, the Bush Administration has demonstrated more caution and restraint in dealing with North Korea and its traditionally militant brand of nationalism.

militancy. September 11, 2001, and Al Qaeda of course provide the most prominent example of the threat of extremism at the moment. But it is not Islamic extremism that presents the only danger to civilized life. Remember than many forms of nationalism can turn violent when they reach the stage of xenophobia. We have seen this violence in Serb "ethnic cleansing" of Bosnians, Hindu massacres of Islam's followers, and in the ferocity of interethnic national civil wars of all stripes within the world political system.

To summarize, nationalism has come in many shapes and forms over the years—and continues to drive world politics in many directions. On its positive side, it can unite people and propel them in directions that improve their lives, but when its dark side appears, it leads to massive instability, and the destruction of lives and a country's infrastructure. We have by no means seen the end of nationalism nor its replacement with some higher global unifying cause to bring together the people of the world. The big question is, what directions will it take us in the future—and to what extent will that future be one of centralization or decentralization? We can see some of the future possibilities of nationalism by examining how leaders have mobilized nationalism in the past, the focus of the next section.

How Do Leaders Use Nationalism in Foreign Policy?

The role of leaders in mobilizing and directing nationalist forces is extremely important. Nationalist sentiments, as you might imagine, offer an attractive source of power for leaders to use in pursuit of a variety of goals. Studies of ethnic nationalism point time and again to the multiple ways and extent to which politicians mobilize it for their unique political objectives. The origins of Nigeria's persistent political instability may be traced to this basic axiom of politics; political leaders have mobilized nationalized feelings, typically against other ethnic national groups, to advance their own interests, the consequences of which are rising tensions and decentralization. We see this phenomenon in India as well, where BJP leaders have tapped into Hindu nationalism in their attempt to mobilize political unity among the Hindu masses—unfortunately at the expense of its Muslim community.

When we probe into how leaders use nationalism in foreign policy, we find a number of answers. Some have used it to promote political unity and economic development, while others had tapped into its emotional appeal to urge national self-determination movements to break away from the current home state. In other cases, leaders have turned to nationalism to mobilize a country's population for war, and still other leaders have orchestrated an overarching brand of nationalism, hoping to surmount separatist ethnic national sentiments inside the country. We now examine these multiple purposes of nationalism more closely.

Seeking to Legitimize Power

Franjo Tudjman, who died in December 1999 at 77 years of age, led Croatia to independence from Yugoslavia in 1991. He did so by appealing to Croatian nationalism, insisting in Croatia's constitution of 1990 that it be "the national state of the Croatian nation," despite the presence of 600,000 Serbs, or 12 percent of the population. What makes his appeal to ethnic nationalism interesting is that Tudjman was previously a die-hard communist, and the separate ethnic groups in Yugoslavia lived in relative harmony before he used nationalism to stay in power after the Cold War ended. What followed was the wholesale dismissal of Serbs from civil service jobs, at which point the Serbs in Croatia began arming themselves. Civil war broke out, and Serbia's Serbs came to the aid of Croatian Serbs.

To fully understand this civil war, it helps to have some historical background. With Tudjman touting Croat supremacy inside Croatia, Serbs could not help but be fearful. They remembered Croat extremist nationalism and atrocities committed against them by the fascist *Ustasha* movement, which allied with Nazi Germany, during World War II and killed an estimated 200,000 to 750,000 Serbs. The Serbs formed irregular bands called *Chetniks* to retaliate against the Croats. As a result of this conflict, as many as one million Yugoslavians died at the hands of their own compatriots.

Serbia's Slobodan Milosevic is another example of a leader who used the passions of nationalism to promote his agenda. A committed communist during the Cold War, Milosevic shifted to the ideology of nationalism in order to legitimize his power and control over internal policy by mobilizing Serb masses against outside adversaries. Milosevic matched Tudjman in making inflammatory speeches, organizing demonstrations, and manipulating nationalist symbols—including historic incidents like the battle of Kosovo and images of the past's "Greater Serbia." Milosevic launched a secular but moralistic nationalist crusade to expand Serb territory and "ethnically cleanse" the "foreign" Bosnians who stood in the way. The result was four civil wars—in Slovenia, Croatia, Bosnia, and Kosovo—at a staggering cost in lives and infrastructure. Both Tudjman and Milosevic kept the violence going throughout the process by arousing ethnic-national passions.

Promoting State Political Unity and Economic Development

Fidel Castro is legendary for the way he has orchestrated revolutionary Cuban nationalism to stimulate unity and economic development. We find this approach in Castro's Revolution of 1959 and in the years that followed, and as expressed in his speeches and in the government newspaper, *Granma*. Castro overthrew the U.S.-backed dictator, Fulgencio Batista, notorious for his corrupt politics, and nationalized U.S. property used for sugar plantations and telephone and telegraph systems. He emphasized pride in Cuba's revolutionary past and its struggle for independence from foreign control dating back to its 1868 war with Spain. Cuban nationalism incorporated all racial and religious groups—white, black, and mulatto—and it became all inclusive in promoting a unique Cuban national/communist identity. Castro's charismatic appeals became the engines for self-sacrifice, defense of the homeland, and socioeconomic equality—helped along, it must be said, by Soviet economic, military, and technical support for many years.

Mexico's brand of revolutionary nationalism is in many respects similar to that of Cuba. Following the Mexican Revolution of 1910, Mexico nationalized U.S. oil property and promoted a racially inclusive type of nationalism that stressed the notion of all individuals in Mexico—white, *mestizo* (whites and Indians) and Indian—as belonging to the *patría* (homeland). The revolutionary "Mexican" nationalism stressed the rights of all Mexicans to education; working rights of women, children, and men; state control of Mexico's resources versus foreign control; presidential elections every six years with no re-election of previous presidents; right to vote; and pride in Mexico's heritage, including its constitution of 1917. Many problems

Revolutionary Nationalism in Cuba: Couple passing one of Cuba's many revolutionary billboards, this one at the Revolution Plaza in Havana.

remain, however, for Indians have not been fully incorporated into national life—as we have seen in the Maya Indian (Zapatista) uprising in the southern Mexican state of Chiapas. Indians are still deprived of land, while drug trafficking, illegal immigration, and corruption in government abound—despite the vaunted Mexican nationalism of unity and equality.

The kind of revolutionary nationalism found in Cuba and Mexico has been put into place not only to promote political stability and economic development, but, theoretically at least, to overcome separatist sentiments that run along racial lines. The Cuban and Mexican leaders' orchestration of nationalist symbols is designed to appeal to a people's higher sense of loyalty to the nation (patría) and to overcome those latent separatist sentiments based on racial identities. We find this use of nationalist ideologies also at work in "Malaysian" nationalist appeals, where Malay, Chinese, and Indian groups coexist, and in former Yugoslavia's efforts to appeal to a "Yugoslav" identity, which, as we know all too well, did not work.

Another brand of nationalism that is used to promote political stability and economic development is referred to as *National Communism*. This mix of capitalism, communism, and nationalism exists in countries like China and Vietnam—and ostensibly follows an ideology of communism with its accompanying single party system, elitist communist leadership, and state control of the economy. What has happened in the years following the Cold War, however, has been a turning to market incentives in former hard-line communist countries—in effect, a blend of communism with a national identity that promotes market economic incentives.

Promoting Self-determination Movements

Nationalism, as we have seen, finds classic expression when an ethnic national group, existing in a multinational state, asserts its right of national self-determination—in effect creating a movement to break away from its current state and form a new state. Such movements proliferate around the globe, as pointed out in Chapter 2. Cases in point: Eritreans in Ethiopia; Slovenes, Croats, Bosnians, Albanians (in Kosovo) in Yugoslavia; and Basques and Catalans striving for self-determination in Spain. In December 1999, the Basque separatist movement renewed its campaign of violence in its struggle for independence.[23] (See Chapter 6.)

A variation of this use of nationalism occurs when a leader mobilizes a minority segment of the population that feels disenfranchised inside a state in order to overthrow the government and establish a new regime. Examples include the Farabundo Marti Liberation Movement (FMLN) in El Salvador during the 1970s and 1980s, named after a national hero who resisted the United States in the early twentieth century, and the Sandinista Movement in Nicaragua in the 1970s and 1980s, also named after a national hero who resisted the United States earlier in Nicaragua's history.

Mobilizing for a War of Aggression or to Defend the Country

Throughout history, leaders have tapped into nationalism to gain followers in a quest for territorial expansion. Examples include German, Japanese, and Italian (Fascist) leaders in World War II, and Saddam Hussein's appeal to Iraqi nationalism to legitimize the attempted conquest of Kuwait.

Leaders also use nationalism to justify and legitimize a war in the name of a higher principle. Examples include the entry of the United States into World War I for the higher principle of making the world safe for democracy; the entry of the United States into World War II to fight the Axis powers; and the launching of the Iraq War of 2003 to defend America against weapons of mass destruction. But leaders may also use nationalist appeals to undermine another country's government without going to war. Examples of such nonmilitary appeals include broadcasting propaganda on television and radio into another country that appeals to that population's sense of national identity and points out what is "wrong" with their government. Illustrations include U.S. broadcasts into Cuba by way of TV and *Radio Marti,* and into East Europe and the USSR via *Voice of America* and *Radio Free Liberty* during the 1970s and 1980s, or East Germany's broadcasts into West Germany before the wall came down at the Cold War's end.

And leaders use nationalism to mobilize their people against possible "foreign" intervention, thus legitimizing their own leadership. International relations offer many examples of this use of nationalism. Fidel Castro, for one, has exploited the U.S. embargo. By "exploited," we refer to how Castro used the embargo to unite the Cuban people against a common threat (the United States as represented by the embargo) and to mobilize Cubans behind his brand of national communism. And when the U.S. Coast Guard rescued a five-year-old Cuban boy from the sea in December 1999 (the boat he was on sank and his mother drowned), he became a "nationalist" cause in Cuba because the United States refused to return him. Castro orchestrated protests in Cuba, placed Cuban troops around the U.S. mission in Havana, and made a fiery speech that aroused the nationalist passions of Cubans, who were already displeased with the U.S. presence in Guantanamo Naval Base. In this way, by emphasizing their unique strengths and struggles, nationalism becomes a force for uniting people within a state.

Before we turn to our next topic, regionalism, let's summarize this overview of nationalism. By now you know that since its emergence in the eighteenth century, nationalism has had a profound impact on world politics. It has provided the means for a nationally self-conscious people to resist perceived foreign oppression and has given rise to new governments and new territorial states for more than three hundred years. It spawned the American and French Revolutions, broke up past empires from the Austro-Hungarian to the Ottoman and the Soviet Union, and carved out new states from the colonial and imperialist conquests of England, France, Germany, Spain, and Portugal. As we have also seen, it has played a huge role in the life of the state and international affairs—from igniting national self-determination breakaway movements to sustaining revolutionary momentum in places like Cuba and Mexico, and inspiring Palestinians to fight for statehood.

Nationalism has spawned enormous international violence and conflict, and it continues to pose complex problems for the international community, such has how to control the violence it has spawned (as in Bosnia and Kosovo), and under what conditions international bodies such as the UN or NATO should intervene. In some cases, however, it can become the impetus for healthy democracy, self-government, economic modernization, and development. The bottom line is that nationalism is a vital part of the contemporary international scene. In the new millennium, we will continue to see nationalism at work. However, if every major ethnic national group in the world sees itself entitled to its own state and is unable to live peacefully in a multinational state, we likely will see many more national self-determination movements and violent breakaway efforts. With these thoughts in mind, we turn now to regionalism, a variation on nationalism.

How Does Regionalism Impact on the International System?

The term *regionalism* has many meanings in the study of international relations. It refers to a variety of institutions, organizations, movements, and identities that center on territorial regions of the world—all of which affect the life of the state in one way or another. The force of regionalism merits our attention, given its resurgence in the post–Cold War years and the many ways in which it has shaped international relations since then. The concept of region can be defined in any of the following ways:[24]

- **Functional region**—an area tied together by economic and trade relations, agricultural production, geographic characteristics, or other "functional" aspects. The U.S. corn belt in the Midwest is a case in point, as is Canada's fish-producing northeast maritime provinces.
- **Vernacular region**—an area where people are united by close identification with their culture, language, and history, as in the U.S. South.
- **Formal region**—an area tied together by a local government (like a city or town), but that often includes shared characteristics, such as language, economic identity, or an environmental property such as climate.

Let's look at each of these in turn.

Functional Regionalism

The importance of functional regionalism can be seen in the rise of regional trade organizations like NAFTA, MERCOSUR, or the EU. These organizations typically are viewed as a part of the **international political economy (IPE)** (see Chapters 5, 6, 11, and 12). IPE refers in part to industrial production zones linked by major cities that span state boundaries. In Western Europe two big zones of this type exist. Europe's industrial and commercial heartland, for example, appears to divide into two banana-shaped configurations.[25]

One "banana" region makes an arc from Catalonia out across France's Mediterranean coast and hinterland, into the Rhône-Alpes and from there into Lombardy and the Piedmont, then into Venice in Italy. The second carves out an area from southeastern England through northern France and the Benelux countries and down the Rhine Valley into Switzerland.[26] Figure 8.1 depicts these two regional industrial "bananas." The fascinating point is that European borders in some respects lose their meaning as cross-border regional interactions increase. One European employment region has emerged connecting Baden-Wurttemberg, Alsace, and Basel (Germany, France, and Switzerland), with a consequent growing regional identity.[27] Another regional identity in Europe connects Saxony, Eastern Germany, with Berlin. It extends into the Czech Republic and east to Poland.[28]

Another example of a functional region might be an agricultural zone, as in the U.S. Midwest, or where cocaine production is high, as in southern Colombia.

International Political Economy (IPE)
A field of study that explores economic and political links at the international level.

Web Exploration

For more information on Basque nationalism and separatism in Spain, go to **www.ablongman.com/ duncan.**

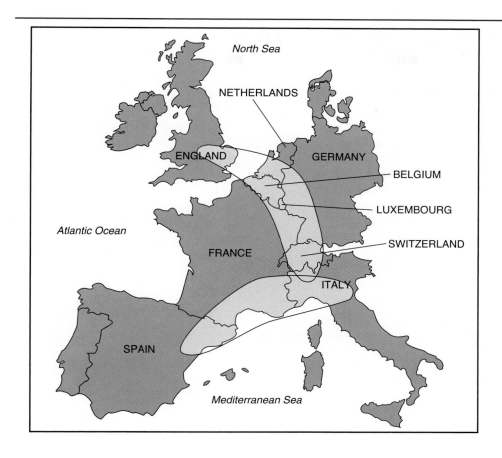

FIGURE 8.1
Europe's Industrial Production Zones: The Two Regional Bananas
SOURCE: John Newhouse, "Europe's Rising Regionialism," Foreign Affairs, January/February 1997, p. 70.

Over twenty thousand Marxist guerrillas control the vast south, including Colombia's borders with Peru. There they guard the coca harvest that becomes cocaine. At the same time, much of Colombia's north is ruled by right-wing paramilitary groups, which are notorious drug traffickers. The federal government and its military barely hang onto the country's mid-section.[29] Some observers see Colombia as a kind of Yugo-lombia—undergoing the kind of breakup experienced in Yugoslavia. In a discussion of commerce, trade, and economic development in different parts of the world, you will find much discussion of functional regionalism.[30]

Vernacular Regionalism

The term *vernacular* refers to a language that is native to a country or a region. A vernacular region, thus, describes an area where people live and closely identify with their culture, language, and history. People who live in such regions see their part of the earth as distinct from other parts. This type of regionalism highlights *self-identity* and *territory*. Across Europe these days, for example, one sees a rise in the use of local languages. They include Breton (a Celtic language spoken for over two thousand years that, until recently, had virtually disappeared), the language of the druids

HISTORICAL PERSPECTIVE

The Kurds and Kurdistan

In the 1920s, the Kurds lived in an independent state called Kurdistan. The European allies created it after World War I, when the old Ottoman Empire was carved up. Before the treaty creating Kurdistan was ratified, however, the Turkish leader, Kemal Ataturk, fought to expand the territory under Turkish control beyond the tiny region allocated by the allies. A new treaty established the modern state of Turkey in 1923—and Kurdistan disappeared as an independent state, much to the dismay of the Kurds. Since then the Kurds have been trying again and again, often by guerrilla war, to regain their independence.

The estimated Kurd population as of 1997 was as follows:

Country	Total Population	Kurds	Percent
Iran	65,000,000	6,500,000	10
Iraq	19,300,000	4,400,000	23
Syria	13,400,000	1,100,000	8
Turkey	65,000,000	14,300,000	22
Former USSR		500,000	
Elsewhere		1,700,000	
Total		**28,500,000**	

Web Exploration

For more information about the nature and consequences of ethnic national territorial regions, go to: **www.ablongman.com/ duncan.**

Kurdistan
The Kurds, around 25 million in number, have lived for over 3,000 years in a region today comprised of Turkey, Syria, Armenia, and Azerbaijan. A stateless nation, the Kurds dream of living in a free homeland one day called Kurdistan.

Catalonia
That region in Spain inhabited by Catalans.

(a Celtic religious order dating back to ancient Britian, Ireland, and France) and many other minority languages in France (Occitan, Basque, Corsican, and Alsatian); Gaelic in the schools in Scotland and Wales; Catalan rather than Spanish for all official business in Barcelona; and Basque in the Basque countries of Spain.[31]

At least two main types of vernacular regionalism can be identified. One type is the *ethnic national territorial region*, which, as its name suggests, develops based on ethnic national identity. A second is the *perceptual region*, with which people identify owing to its environmental, economic, and cultural features. Examples of the perceptual type are America's South and its southwest Sunbelt, Russia's Siberia, or China's thriving coastal area. We will examine each of these types of regionalism in more detail.

Ethnic National Territorial Regions   Ethnic national groups by nature identify with an ancestral homeland—a piece of Earth associated with their past, present, and future. Where ethnic nationalism is strong, it creates powerful regional identities within and across state boundaries; these configurations, in turn, have political consequences. We see this type of regionalism, for example, in the national identity and nationalism of the *Kurdish people* in Southwest Asia and the Middle East. The *Kurds* are a scattered nation without a state. Their heartland is a territorial area divided among Turkey, Syria, Iran, Iraq, and Armenia that they have been trying to establish as a sovereign state of **Kurdistan** (see box Historical Perspective: The Kurds and Kurdistan).

Ethnic national territorial regions abound in the world. In some cases, they are organized formally as autonomous republics or autonomous communities. *Spain* serves as a good example. It is the second-biggest country in Western Europe and has a rich regional variety to match. Its two most distinctive ethnic national regions are the *Basque country* and **Catalonia.** The power of these two regions is significant, because their presence—along with **Galicia,** another ethnic national territorial region—has undermined Spain's unity since the fifteenth century. Catalonia accounts for nearly 20 percent of Spain's GDP, although it has only 13 percent of Spain's population. Barcelona, a Catalan city, well might claim to be Spain's most successful urban center, with its new airport, new seafront, and thriving businesses. Catalan identity is strong at the turn of the century, and some authorities in France are concerned that a part of France's southwest will enter the Catalan sphere of interest. Catalan television is becoming popular in those French cities that were once the cultural pivots of Catalonia, and the area near Toulouse now conducts more business with Catalonia than with other French regions.[32]

The Basques, as we saw in Chapter 6, are extremely nationalistic, particularly regarding their language, which has no link to Spanish.[33] Basque nationalism has produced a Basque terrorist organization, the ETA, which originated in 1968. Both the Catalans and Basques have their own political parties that press for issues favoring their ethnic national groups and territories. Within Catalonia and the Basque country, however, people hold a range of views: Some are staunch defenders of independence movements, while other, more moderate, Catalans and Basques do not raise the question of separation from the state, yet argue for more autonomy and power for their region.[34]

But Spain has other regional political movements beside the Catalan, Basque, and Galician. Such movements have now arisen in the Balearic Islands, the Canary Islands, Andalusia, and Valencia. The input of each of these into Spain's political system is considerable, given their economic power, location, and numbers. Andalusia, for example, has a population of over 7 million people. Because of Spain's strong regional sentiments, especially the tenacious Catalan, Basque, and Galician ones, the Spanish Constitution of 1978 recognizes and guarantees the right to autonomy of all the nationalities and regions that comprise Spain—a clear decentralization of power. The map in Figure 8.2 shows Spain's "autonomous communities," which are political systems designed to hold the state together despite the multiple and strong regional identities.

Spain's devolution policy has since spilled over into international relations. After Spain granted autonomy to its regions, it joined the European Union. The European Union, for its part, makes clear its interest in negotiating directly with Spain's regions as well as with the Spanish state. By 1989 twelve of Spain's autonomous communities had opened an office in Brussels. By the early 1990s, the relationship between the EU and Spanish autonomous communities had grown more intense, as the latter expanded their role in the EU through its Committee of the Regions. That Spain's autonomous communities have exercised their own foreign policy stems in part from the open-ended devolution process in Spain.[35] In Great Britain the process has been more controlled relative to national communities like Scotland and Wales.

Perceptual Regions   Although they can exert strong political forces, perceptual regions tend to receive less attention than they deserve in the study of international relations. Most states around the world include or are included in perceptual regions, and in some places, the perceptual region of one state crosses over into another. Among the latter must be included Italy's Northern League, a region that sees itself as distinct from Italy's south and would like to go its own way. Its leader, Umberto Bossi, would like this area to break away from Italy and become a separate country—*Padania*—named for the Po River valley. Another breakaway region

Galicia
A region in Spain inhabited by an ethnically identifying group called Gallegos.

For more information on a functional region, go to **www.ablongman.com/ duncan.**

FIGURE 8.2
Spain's Autonomous Regions

Source: DeBlij and Muller, Realms, Regions, and Concepts, p. 90.

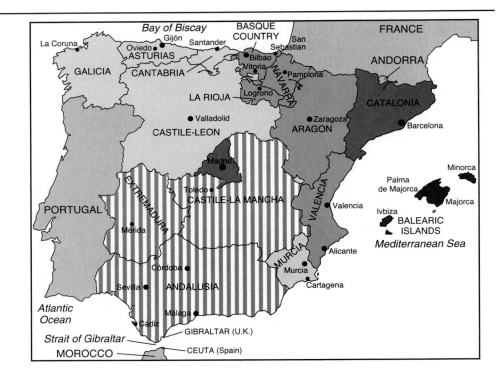

of this type lies in southern Brazil. There, three of Brazil's states, Paraná, Santa Catarina, and Rio Grande do Sul, make up a subregion. The three states have European standards of living, fertile and productive lands, and an affluent life style. The region, which has about 22 million people and an area the size of France, wants to break away to create a country called the *Republic of the Pampas.* In Africa in Sudan's south, the Sudan People's Liberation Army (SPLA), has claimed autonomy and set up an administrative structure—the National Liberation Council, which presides over an embryonic state known to the rebels as New Sudan.[36] All can be thought of as perceptual regions, because cultural, economic, and/or environmental features unite them.

Formal Regions

Formal Region
A type of region that reflects a high degree of homogeneity in one or several aspects.

In a **formal region,** people share a common government, and they frequently also have a common language and some environmental property, such as climate. Examples of formal regions are the autonomous communities, discussed earlier, in Spain, which are also ethnic national regions, suggesting that these categories are not mutually exclusive. In Russia, formal regions include both internal republics and autonomous regions, and China also has autonomous regions. Germany, in contrast, organizes its regional identities through its federal structure of *Lands,* where people identify themselves primarily as Thuringians, Bavarians, or Westphalians, and secondarily as Germans.[37]

Differences in standards of living have been prime movers in the alignment of people into formal, as well as vernacular, regional identities around the world. These differences help explain why Brazil's south wants to break away, just as Italy's

Northern League would like to separate from Italy's poorer south. Slovenia broke with Yugoslavia in 1991 largely because it saw its people carrying a disproportionate amount of Yugoslavia's economic weight. Today Russia is having a difficult time with its economy, in part because the governors of the internal republics and autonomous regions do not pay their taxes, preferring to keep the money closer to home. In China the growing economic gap between the thriving eastern coastal areas and the western interior has led to tensions with the minority people, who feel left out. China has around 55 minorities, such as the Hui (Muslim Chinese) and the Man (natives of Manchuria), Uighurs, and Tibetans. China's minorities are scattered around the sparsely populated frontiers of China, and many have cultural relationships with minority groups in neighboring states, including Kazakhstan, Kyrgyzstan, Russia, North Korea, Mongolia, Thailand, and Myanmar (former Burma). Should such groups become hostile toward the central government, they could impact China's national security. Such tensions can create separatist tendencies, which in turn threaten the ruling government.[38] Is regionalism of these types compatible with democracy?

Formal regions can cause serious problems for a state's political survival. In Russia, for example, a number of regions have become private fiefdoms, a kind of throwback to feudal days. These regions have exploited Moscow's weakness in order to conduct their own economic and—at times, foreign—policy. Their governors frequently refuse to pay the region's taxes to the central government, which they see as corrupt and inefficient.[39] China, as just mentioned, is facing similar problems with its autonomous regions.

CHAPTER SUMMARY

What Is Nationalism?

States, nations, and nationalism are key features and driving forces in today's international system. Whereas a state is a piece of territory with a government possessing sovereignty and inhabited by people, a nation is a psychological identity of people who see themselves as part of a common group. Nationalism springs from national identity.

- Nationalism of the twentieth century increasingly had ethnic identity as its base, and therefore was expressed frequently in terms of grievances against foreigners, struggles for independence, and the right to a separate territorial state.
- Ultranationalism is known as xenophobia—as in Germany, leading to the Jewish holocaust.

Nationalism can best be thought of as (1) a psychological group identity; (2) an emotional force that ignites people's passions; (3) a power factor that dates back in time; (4) a driving force with positive and negative impacts on world politics; and (5) an identity that competes with transnationalism for a people's loyalty.

How Does Nationalism Vary Around the World?

Eighteenth-century versions of nationalism were more inclusive than the post-colonial ethnic nationalism the world has seen in the post–World War II period. Both history and location shape nationalism, and we find numerous distinctions in ethnic identity—some leading to cooperation while others, more frequently, lead to tensions and conflict.

- American and Russian versions of nationalism illustrate vivid contrasts; for one thing, "American" nationalism is less ethnic-focused than "Russian" nationalism.
- Religious nationalism has demonstrated particular tendencies to violence and conflict.

Hindu and Muslim nationalists have clashed during 2002, causing much loss of life and leaving tens of thousands of Muslim refugees homeless in the wake of terror against them.

How Do Leaders Use Nationalism in Foreign Policy?

Some states try to control disparate nationalist forces inside their borders by creating a power-sharing federal form of government, as in the former Soviet Union and former Yugoslavia. The principle ways that leaders use nationalism are:

- Seeking to conquer perceived "enemy" ethnic groups
- Promoting state political unity and economic development by overcoming separatist sentiments within the state
- Promoting self-determination movements
- Mobilizing for war and defense of territory

When you examine these and other elements of nationalism, you realize just how significant the impact of nationalism has been on world politics. Nationalism helps us to understand the following:

- Why violence and war occur in the international political system.
- Why people act as they do toward each other across state boundaries and within multinational states.
- Why misunderstanding occurs so frequently in world politics—a result of differing perceptions of nationalist realities.

- Why diplomatic negotiations can be so difficult, since diplomats approach negotiations from different nationalist perspectives.
- How important perceptions are in assessing conflict and cooperation.
- How leaders manipulate masses.

How Does Regionalism Impact on the International System?

Regionalism has many meanings in the study of international relations. It denotes a variety of institutions, organizations, movements, and people's identities that center on territorial regions of the world—and that affect the life of the state in one way or another.

Any of the following types of regions can be studied:

- Functional regions, or areas tied together by economic and trade relations, agricultural production, geographic characteristics, or other functional aspects. The U.S. corn belt in the Midwest is an example, as is Canada's fish-producing northeast Maritime Provinces.
- Vernacular regions, or areas where people closely identify with a common culture, language, and history, as in the U.S. South.
- Formal regions, or areas tied together by local governments, but also often by shared characteristics, such as a common language, economic status, or environmental property such as climate.

ENDNOTES

1Walker Connor, "A Nation is a Nation, is a State, is an Ethnic Group, is a . . ." in John Hutchinson and Anthony D. Smith, *Nationalism* (New York: Oxford University Press, 1994), pp. 37–46.

2Anthony D. Smith, *National Identity* (Reno: University of Nevada Press, 1991), p. 9.

3Ibid., p. 10. Smith calls this element the national people's sense of *patria*.

4Anthony D. Smith, *National Identity*, p. 14.

5Hans Kohn, "Western and Eastern Nationalism," in John Hutchinson & Anthony D. Smith, eds., *Nationalism* (New York: Oxford University Press, 1994), p. 162.

6Ibid.

7*The New York Times*, September 18, 2002.

8Ibid.

9Carleton J. H. Hayes, *Modern Europe to 1870* (New York: The Macmillan Company, 1953), pp. 417–418.

10R. R. Palmer, *A History of the Modern World*, New York: Alfred A. Knopf, 1954, pp. 520–521.

11William Pfaff, "The Absence of Empire," *The New Yorker*, April 10, 1992, pp. 59–69.

12Robert Lansing, *The Peace Negotiations: A Personal Narrative* (Boston and New York: Houghton Mifflin Co., 1921), p. 97.

13Ibid., p. 98.

14Douglas Watson, "Indigenous Peoples and the Global Economy," *Current History*, vol. 96 (November 1997), p. 389.

[15]The World Bank studied 47 civil wars that occurred from Afghanistan to Zimbabwe between 1960 and 1999. Research indicates that the single biggest risk factor for the outbreak of war was a country's economic dependence on commodities. The drive for profits from coffee, narcotics, diamonds, and other gemstones both "prompts outbreaks of violence and determines their strength over time," says the study . . . diamonds are the guerrilla's best friend." The *New York Times,* June 16, 2000.

[16]Michael Lind, "In Defense of Liberal Nationalism," *Foreign Affairs,* vol. 73, no. 3 (May/June 1994), pp. 87–99.

[17]*The New York Times,* April 4, 1999.

[18]Ibid.; and Rudolph J. Rummel, *Death by Government* (New Brunswick, NJ: Transaction Books, 1994).

[19]Ted Robert Gurr and Barbara Harff, *Ethnic Conflict in World Politics* (Boulder: Westview Press, 1994), p. 114.

[20]Larry Diamond and Marc F. Plattner, eds., *Nationalism, Ethnic Conflict, and Democracy* (Baltimore: The Johns Hopkins University Press, 1994), pp. xix–xx1.

[21]Paul Collier, Ibrahim Elbadawi and Nicholas Sambanis, "Why Are There So Many Civil Wars in Africa? Prevention of Future Conflicts and Promotion of Inter-Group Cooperation," *Journal of African Economics,* December 2000.

[22]Mark Juergensmeyer, "Religious Nationalism: A Global Threat?" *Current History* (November 1996), pp. 372–376.

[23]*The Economist,* December 4, 1999, p. 48.

[24]These designations are derived from James M. Rubenstein, *An Introduction to Human Geography,* 6th ed., (Upper Saddle River, NM: Prentice Hall, 1994), pp. 29–30.

[25]John Newhouse, "Rising Regionalism," *Foreign Affairs,* vol. 76, no. 1 (January/February 1997), pp. 69–70.

[26]Ibid., p. 69.

[27]Ibid., p. 71.

[28]Ibid.

[29]Tim Padgett, "The Backyard Balkans," *Time,* January 18, 1999.

[30]The potential for development of another industrial-commercial cross-border zone exists in Northeast Asia, which ties together parts of Russia's far east and China's northeast.

[31]*The New York Times,* October 17, 1999.

[32]John Newhouse, "Rising Regionalism," p. 71.

[33]*Parliamentary Affairs,* vol. 51, no. 2 (April 1998), p. 259.

[34]*Publius,* vol. 27, no. 4 (Fall 1997), p. 138.

[35]*Parliamentary Affairs,* p. 266. Spain's constitution says little of how the region-building process will be restricted.

[36]*The Economist,* February 27, 1999, p. 43.

[37]John Newhouse, "Europe's Rising Regionalism," pp. 74–75.

[38]Dali L. Yang and Houkai Wei, "Rising sectionalism in China?" *Journal of International Affairs,* Winter 1996, pp. 456–476.

[39]*The Christian Science Monitor,* August 13, 1999.

CASE STUDY

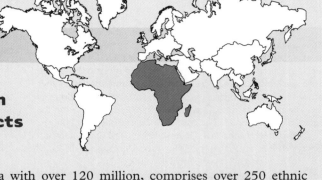

How Does Ethnic Nationalism Undermine Nigeria's Prospects of Achieving Democracy?

Nigeria, the most populous country in Africa with over 120 million, comprises over 250 ethnic groups. The dominant ethnic national group in the northern two-thirds of the country is Hausa-Fulani, most of whom are Muslim. Other large ethnic national groups in the north are the Nupe, Tiv, and Kanuri. The Yoruba people, about half of whom are Christian and half Muslim, predominate in Nigeria's southwest. The largest ethnic national group in the southeast is the Igbo, who are Catholic.

Conflict among these ethnic groups dates back to the early years following Nigeria's independence from Great Britain in 1960. In 1967 the Igbo launched a bloody civil war of secession and declared their independence, naming their territory the "Republic of Biafra." Hundreds of thousands were killed in a bitter struggle that ended with the defeat of Biafra in 1970. Since then rivalry between the Muslim north and Christian south has continued, with the appearance once again of a tentative Biafra movement.

Nigeria, it must be said, reflects a number of driving forces in today's Africa: (1) states that are weak owing to their multiethnic national composition, related interethnic tensions, and arbitrariness of borders drawn by Europeans to suit their own purposes; (2) conflicts derived from Muslim-Christian legacies of the past; and (3) widespread poverty. Conflict in Africa—represented by this Nigeria case study—is widespread. Conflict within the 36 Nigerian states subject to the country's federal form of government is aggravated by the adoption of Sharia (Islamic law) in a number of northern states, as opposed to Christian southern states—and by the struggle over the division of Nigeria's oil revenues. The oil-producing states lie in the southeast, including the Igbo states, and they clash frequently with the non-oil producing, non-Igbo northern states.

Nigeria faces challenging days ahead. It is still recovering from its many years of corrupt military rule under General Sani Abacha, who robbed the country until his death in 1998. Corruption still runs high, along with tax evasion and popular discontent between Muslims and non-Muslims. Personal and ethnic relationships dominate politics. In these respects, Nigeria resembles the Ivory Coast and Sudan. Still, Nigeria has not collapsed under ethnic-national civil war conditions—as have Somalia, Sierra Leone, and Democratic Republic of Congo. These states have been the scene of serious decentralization.

Now—keeping in mind what you have learned about nationalism in this chapter—let us turn to our case study on Nigeria. As you read the case study, note carefully what factors suggest promise for Nigeria's capacity to move toward democracy, even with its multiethnic national groups. Nigeria is an example of the challenges faced by developing countries coming out of a colonial-ruled past, where ethnic national groups have been forced to live within the same state, or territorial space, although they have little in common.

AFRICA'S CONTRADICTION

BY THOMAS TSAI

Nigeria on the Path to Democracy

Since Nigeria gained independence from Great Britain in 1960, democracy has had a difficult time taking root. The country's first post-colonial government was overthrown in January 1966 in a coup led by Major General Johnson Agiuyi Ironsi, who was later killed in a countercoup in July of the same year by officers loyal to General Yakubu Gowon. More coups followed in July 1975 and February 1976 and the brief interlude of democracy between 1979 and 1985 was ended by another coup. In the 1990s, democracy finally seemed to be emerging during the presidency of Moshood Abiola only to be reversed by the despotic rule of General Sani Abacha.

With the death of Abacha in 1998, Nigeria finally seemed to be heading toward peace. Garnering 62 percent of the vote in February 1999, current president Olusegun Obasanjo has pledged to enact economic and political reforms. With over 120 million people and a position of leadership in African affairs, Nigeria has become Africa's contradiction. It offers the best opportunity for democracy in Africa, yet it is beset by several internal problems that, if not addressed, will make it one of Africa's greatest failures.

Ethnic Tensions

Nigeria's most daunting challenge lies in overcoming the severe divisions among its competing religious and ethnic groups. In January 2002, clashes between the Hausa and Yoruba ethnic groups killed over 300 civilians in the chaotic aftermath of a deadly explosion at the Ikeja military barracks in Lagos.

In recent months the Tiv and the Jukun tribal groups of central Nigeria have engaged in genocidal tribal raids. Since the restoration of civilian rule in May 1999, a total of over 10,000 Nigerians have died in civil strife. These ethnic flare-ups revolving around the Tiv tribal group further highlight the flaws in Nigeria's government. On October 22, 2001, Nigerian soldiers drove into villages in the central Nigerian state of Benue, looting homes and murdering civilians. In that single episode more than 300 people were killed. Among the more prominent victims were relatives of a former army chief of staff, Victor Malu, whose house was also looted. The army attack was motivated by revenge; Tiv tribesmen had earlier ambushed and killed 19 soldiers. Instead of finding the murderers, the army launched indiscriminate reprisals, and underlying the army's actions was a strong undercurrent of ethnic tension. While Malu is a Tiv, many of the soldiers involved in the attack and the defense minister who dismissed Malu are Junkuns.

Perhaps due to Nigeria's history of coups, Obasanjo has remained silent regarding the abuses of the military. As shown by its involvement in the Tiv-Junkun massacres, the military is still very much motivated by ethnic loyalties, something that the government cannot erase by fiat alone. Many obstacles remain in the quest to construct a unified national identity.

Unstable Federalism

Further undermining national unity, Christian-Muslim antagonism runs deep in Nigeria, where the North is dominated by Muslims. The state of Zamfara in northwestern Nigeria overwhelmingly approved legislation extending the fundamentalist Islamic law code, Shari'a, to criminal cases. The Zamfara government established new Islamic courts and codes and justified the extension of Shari'a by pointing to section 277 of the 1999 constitution, which allows state level Sharia courts to "exercise jurisdiction in civil proceedings involving questions of Islamic personal law." Christians and other critics in the South have argued that the extension was not legitimate because the constitution forbids a state religion. Although condemned by the federal government in Lagos, other northern states, including Bauchi, Borno, Jigawa, Niger, Kano, Katsina, Sokoto, and Yobe, have followed Zamfara's example.

The Islamization of the northern states highlights important failures of Nigeria's democracy. Until the constitution itself is revitalized, many Nigerian states will continue to interpret the law as they wish. Although mandated by the constitution to hold elections in April 2002, numerous members of Nigeria's local government councils have decided not to relinquish their seats until 2003 due to confusion over the electoral laws. Moreover, the Senate's new legislation requires elections to proceed downward in the order of executive, senate, house, state, and local offices, raising the ire of Nigeria's 36 governors. The question of the sequence of elections is of little intrinsic importance, but the debate over the electoral act will have profound implications for legalism in Nigeria's burgeoning democracy.

Obasanjo, who faces re-election in 2003, is currently embroiled in a controversy regarding his own electoral prospects. In early April, scores of his supporters, including high officials in state and national politics, presented an official letter of support for Obasanjo's candidacy in next year's elections. This clarion call for Obasanjo's re-election may not seem egregious, but to many Nigerians it is too reminiscent of the Abacha past. Former minister of industry and current Senator Iyorchia Ayu remarked, "The president, if he truly wants to re-contest, should come out and then we will assess him critically. If we decide to vote for him, it would be on the basis that we believe in him, not because some people are instigating politicians to come and beg him to run. It is wrong; he should not take the Sani Abacha road." The recent actions of Nigeria's politicians raise the specter of Abacha's reign, during which regional leaders would formally declare their support of Abacha, essentially eliminating the populace from the electoral process.

The challenge of uniting the country still remains to be surmounted. In an episode indicative of the nation's polarized politics, northern governors have alleged that the western states of Oyo and Ogun alone have enjoyed federal projects worth U.S. $250 million while the 19 states of the North have yet to benefit from federal patronage. The northern governors have already rescinded their support for Obasanjo's reelection bid in 2003. Although the autonomy of state and local leaders is a vital component of federalism, Nigeria's harshly divisive regional politics still remains a major stumbling block on the road to democracy.

Economic Woes

Many had hoped that democratization in Nigeria would bring about an economic renaissance after the corrupt regime of Abacha, who reportedly took U.S. $4.3 billion from the nation's treasury. Despite Obasanjo's democratic credentials, he has not been immune to the grasp of corruption. Out of 91 nations surveyed by Transparency International's Global Corruption Report last year, Nigeria emerged second on its list of the most corrupt countries. Recurrent among the charges is Obasanjo's nepotism in elevating members of his ethnic group to high office.

Nigerian Senator Tokunbo Afikuyomi remarked last year that the "promises and prospects which the democratic experiment once held in view for most have given way to depression and despair. Some are

even tempted to conclude that it would have been better for us to have remained in the Egypt of militarism than the wilderness of democratization without dividends."

After three years of democracy, Nigeria's economy is still faltering despite its status as the world's sixth-largest exporter of petroleum, producing 1.9 million barrels a day, or 4.5 percent of the world's total production.

The government's handling of the economy has also been strongly criticized by the International Monetary Fund. Although Obasanjo stated that a tougher import inspection policy had raised customs revenue and limited fraud, the largest item in the 2002 budget is still expected to be military spending, with the defense budget amounting to U.S. $430 million. In this poverty-stricken country of more than 120 million people, the military has for years accounted for the largest share of government spending. According to most military analysts, the military has little to show for the funds it receives because much of the money is siphoned off into private pockets.

Some limited economic reforms have been made. According to Rotimi Subero, a senior lecturer at Nigeria's University of Ibadan, Obasanjo has ambitiously embarked upon exchange rate reform, the privatization of a few public enterprises, an increase in public wages, and the improvement of Nigeria's gross currency reserves. Nevertheless, Nigeria's external debt continues to be a manacle on the nation's economy. In 2002, Nigeria will spend U.S. $3.4 billion servicing its external debt of U.S. $28.6 billion.

Undermining these reforms is the lack of a coherent program and the continuing corruption of Nigeria's politicians, most noticeably in the National Assembly. In 1999 the president of the Senate and the speaker of the House of Representatives were removed from their positions for forgery and perjury.

Promising Trends

Despite Obasanjo's lack of resolve in his first three years in office, Nigeria remains one of Africa's great hopes. With the adoption of careful reforms, Nigeria can take on a vital role in the leadership of Africa. Last March, Obasanjo called on the presidents and diplomats of 19 African countries to decide on a unified code of conduct for African nations needing Western aid. The assistance plan, dubbed the New Partnership for African Development (NEPAD), calls for the establishment of an African peer-review mechanism and a "Council of the Wise" comprised of respected African figures who would monitor abuses of human rights and democracy. NEPAD has already been embraced by the international community; the inaugural meeting on April 15, 2002, in Dakar was attended by over 1,000 participants, including 20 African presidents and prime ministers, corporate leaders, and UN officials. As a primary architect of NEPAD along with Senegalese President Abdoulaye Wade, Algerian President Abdelaziz Bouteflika, and South African President Thabo Mbeki, Obasanjo has shown that regional cooperation can reap great economic and political dividends.

Another much lauded policy of Obasanjo is his recent commitment to initiate a program for comprehensive HIV testing of all Nigerians. By approving the budgetary establishment of over 300 primary health centers, Obasanjo has taken concrete steps toward stemming the AIDS epidemic in sub-Saharan Africa. Already, approximately 100 primary health care centers, vital additions to Nigeria's growing health care infrastructure, are ready for commissioning.

Professor Ibironke Akinsete, Nigeria's chairman of the National Action Committee on HIV/AIDS, has stated that "any country which aspires to lead Africa must take urgent and practical steps to reverse its . . . burden of HIV/AIDS." Nigeria has responded to the AIDS crisis by enacting vital measures to ensure the health of its people. In contrast to Mbeki's ignorance of the AIDS epidemic, Obasanjo and his administration have shown that Nigeria can become a leader in the struggle against AIDS in Africa.

Fresh Opportunities

If actually implemented and coupled with stable government, initiatives such as NEPAD would be a step toward achieving greater transparency and legitimacy for Nigeria. Echoing the general hope for the success of NEPAD, prominent Nigerian businessman Yemi Akeju declared, "With 700 million people, Africa is significantly a sector of the world that cannot be ignored. . . . But what we are now looking out for are the investors. Investors worldwide are looking for a place where they will have fresh opportunity to do business. With the new climate created in Africa by the NEPAD initiative, one would say there are fresh opportunities here."

Nigeria can provide the leadership that Africa needs to effectively address the issues of globalization and democracy, yet its own democracy is still threatened by corruption and ethnic strife. Nigeria has also shown that it can make changes to ameliorate the legacy of decades of military rule. Although ethnic tension still divides Nigerian society, Obasanjo has the opportunity to mend the divisions by strengthening a legitimate Nigerian democracy.

Among one of the most daunting challenges remaining to be addressed is the relationship between the police and military in Nigeria. Alhaji Ibrahim Coomasie, former inspector general of police, recently noted the Nigerian police "has been torn between the civil populace and the military, so much so that its civil traditions are almost lost to military authoritarianism." In contrast, the current inspector general has embraced the military as a partner in fighting crime, adding uncertainty to the future role of Nigeria's military. Despite the marriage of the police and military, nongovernmental organizations such as the Centre for Law Enforcement Education have fostered greater cooperation and trust between civilians and police through police-community partnerships. In order to ensure that the military does not become an agent of illegitimate power, it needs to be completely separated from the civilian police force. Increasing the size of the civilian police force from 180,000 to 577,000 officers, as Obasanjo has recently directed the inspector general to do, is no panacea. Nigeria must increase the transparency of its military and police forces to overcome the legacy of its military past.

Two futures for Africa are possible—one with a democratic and stable Nigeria, and one with a Nigeria stricken by autocratic rule, corruption, and intermittent coups. An entire continent awaits the result of the Nigerian experiment with democracy. Nigeria has the resources and can provide leadership to foster greater regional and international cooperation, leadership that many of Nigeria's neighbors need. A successful Nigerian democracy would provide hope for many of Africa's other burgeoning democracies.

SOURCE: Thomas Tsai, "Africa's Contradiction," Harvard International Review, Vol. 24, No. 3 (Fall 2002), pp. 32—35. Reprinted by permission of Harvard International Review.

QUESTIONS

Check Your Understanding

1. According to the article, what is the most daunting challenge Nigeria faces?
2. Why is Nigeria considered the "great hope" of Africa despite its many problems?

Analyze the Issues

3. Why make Nigeria relevant to the study of the impact of ethnic national forces within a state? What positive factors does it have going for it?
4. How does Nigeria's ongoing ethnic national setting act as a centralizing or decentralizing force in that region?
5. This chapter has looked at several aspects of nationalism. Among them were:
   - A psychological group identity among people
   - An emotional force that ignites people's passions
   - A power factor that dates back in time
   - A driving force with positive and negative impacts on world politics

   How does the case study illuminate these aspects of nationalism, with special attention to ethnic nationalism?
6. The case study points to two alternate and contrasting futures for Nigeria: (1) a democratic and stable Nigeria and (2) a Nigeria stricken by autocratic rule, corruption and intermittent coups. Which future do you think most likely? Why?

FOR FURTHER INFORMATION

To learn more about Nigeria's ethnic national groups, its problems of development and stability, and its political dynamics, take a look at the following books, new articles, and websites.

Godfrey Mwakikagile, *Ethnic Politics in Kenya and Nigeria,* Huntington, NY: Nova Science Publishers, 2002.

Toyin Falola, *Violence in Nigeria: The Crisis of Religious Politics and Secular Ideologies,* Rochester, NY: Univesity of Rochester Press, 1998.

Julius O. Ihonvbere, *Nigeria: The Politics of Adjustment and Democracy,* New Brunswick, NJ: Transaction Publishers, 1994.

"The Roots of Violence in Nigeria," *The Economist,* September 5, 2001, p. 58.

"Nigeria Ethnic and Political Groups," Visual Net, *http://www.fotw.calflagslng}.html*

"Ethnic Militias Guard Tribal Divides," *World Press Review,* September 2002, *http://www.worldpress.orglAfrical492.cfm*

CHAPTER 9

Global Violence: Wars, Weapons, Terrorism

KEY QUESTIONS RAISED IN THIS CHAPTER

1. What are the causes of war?
2. What are the weapons of war?
3. Why are there so many weapons and can they be controlled?
4. How can global violence be controlled?
5. What do we know about terrorism and terrorists?

etween the end of the Cold War and September 11, 2001, political attention began to move away from war-related concerns toward economic and social issues. For example, beginning with Bill Clinton's first presidential campaign, the phrase "It's the economy, stupid" became popular. In addition, the Clinton administration created a National *Economic* Council (NEC), an organ of the executive branch designed to parallel the National *Security* Council (NSC), which was created to deal with more "traditional" defense-related issues. The NEC symbolized this renewed interest in the importance of economics to the security of the country. Economic and social issues were also viewed as important in the 1990s because most people expected a "peace dividend" from the end of the Cold War. With the Soviet Union gone, there was no need to spend resources on containing communism. Also, throughout the 1990s, a quiet debate took place about using the services of the U.S. intelligence community (e.g., the CIA) for "economic espionage." Moreover, the relationship between the United States and the European Union grew strained in the 1990s, as one ugly trade dispute spilled over into another.

Despite all these economy-focused developments, for most of the world, war and the prospects for war were and are still as prevalent as ever. Violence around the world continued through the 1990s despite the end of the Cold War. In some places, violence actually increased because of the end of the Cold War. As we look to the future, the threat of *nuclear* war remains because of tensions between India and Pakistan, because of Russia's inability to control its vast supplies of nuclear materials, and because more countries seek to acquire "the bomb." Moreover, nonnuclear weapons are becoming more numerous, more widely available, and in some cases, more lethal than ever. Put these weapons in the hands of terrorists, and one can imagine a very dangerous world indeed (see the box Historical Perspective: War in Comparative Context). This chapter, then, revisits traditional subjects in the study of international relations. While economic and social issues are certainly important, the crucial topic of global violence still dominates international relations.

The first part of this chapter lays out a description and analytical framework for understanding why wars occur. The next section provides an overview of the tools of global violence, including weapons of mass destruction (nuclear, biological, chemical) and conventional weapons. This discussion is followed by a more general look at how global violence may be controlled. We will review the ability to eliminate the motivations for going to war, and—as an introduction to the next chapter—the ability (or inability) of international law and international institutions to keep the peace. The last section of the chapter focuses on the pressing issue of international terrorism.

All these topics were at the core of international relations in the twentieth century, and there is every reason to believe that they will remain pertinent throughout the twenty-first. It would surprise virtually every analyst of international relations if you, or even your children, lived to a ripe old age without having to confront the scourge of war. Interstate and civil wars occur on almost every continent, and the threat of terrorism increasingly confronts everyone.

What Are the Causes of War?

One of the most perplexing questions that has faced humanity is, Why are there wars? This simply stated question has no simple answer, but in the next few pages we will provide a framework for answering it. We begin by reviewing some of the major

HISTORICAL PERSPECTIVE

War in Comparative Context

It is vital to understand the political impact of war. As the famous Prussian military theorist Karl von Clauswitz put it, war is politics by other means. But it is also important to understand the immediate human cost of war for combatants. It is sometimes surprising to learn how many people died in a war, particularly if it did not get much press coverage or if it wasn't taught in schools (e.g., the Iran-Iraq war). It can also be surprising when the number of casualties is *relatively* low. For all the political ramifications, press coverage, and national soul-searching, the Vietnam War had *relatively* few casualties (for the American side, at least). Consider the comparative scope of human tragedy in the following examples:

- Almost 3,000 people died in the September 11, 2001, attacks on the World Trade Center in New York City.
- In the three days of fighting at Gettysburg in the U.S. Civil War, there were 50,000 casualties. In all, roughly 600,000 soldiers from the North and the South died in that war.
- Two million people were killed in the Thirty Years' War between 1618 to 1648.[1]
- At least 100,000 people died from the nuclear explosion in Hiroshima.
- One million people died in the eight-year war between Iran and Iraq in the 1980s.
- In World War I, 136,516 Americans were killed. In World War II, 405,399 Americans were killed.[2]
- At least 1.7 million Cambodians (or 21 percent of the entire population) were killed by the Khmer Rouge regime between 1975 and 1978.[3]
- Roughly 58,000 Americans were killed during the Vietnam War. Roughly 1.75 million military personnel were killed on all sides in the conflict in Vietnam from 1945 to 1975.[4]
- Roughly 42,000 people are killed on America's highways each year. About the same number of people are killed in highway accidents in the European Union each year.[5]

reasons for war. Since we will want to be more sophisticated than the average "armchair strategist," we will also look at some common mistakes people make about the causes of war, as well as the theoretical notion of immediate and underlying causes of war. Let's take a quick look at each in turn.

Desire for Territorial Gain and Independence

Two of the most obvious reasons for war are the desire to acquire territory and to achieve national independence. For example, two countries might fight over natural resources such as oil or access to the sea. Iraq's invasion of Kuwait was portrayed by the Iraqi government as an attempt to reacquire territory that should always have been (according to Iraq) a part of Iraq. Germany's invasion of Poland and later other eastern and western European countries during World War II was another clear example of a country's desire for territorial gain. In the future, we are likely to see conflicts over access to fresh water, conflicts that may see one country trying to absorb another.

Wars of independence may also start because one group of people may wish to govern themselves through the formation of a new state. The American colonists went to war with the British to gain their independence and form the United States.

Terrorists Attack the Pentagon: On September 11, 2001, a hijacked plane smashed into the Pentagon causing extensive damage. The Defense Department hoped to rebuild the affected section of the building by the one-year anniversary of the attack. Some Pentagon employees were able to get back to their new offices by mid-August 2002.

The bloody war between Algeria and France in the late 1950s and early 1960s is another example of a country (Algeria) going to war for independence.

Economic Causes

There are numerous economic causes of war. In the first Gulf War, for example, we can see economics at play in Iraq, the United States, and indeed in all members of the UN coalition. From the Iraqi perspective, Kuwait's oil fields and the Kuwaiti treasury enticed Saddam Hussein to go to war. From the United States and UN perspective, concern that a successful Iraqi invasion of Kuwait would leave too much oil in the hands of Saddam Hussein galvanized the UN to take Kuwait back from Iraq.

Economics can also be an important cause of wars involving smaller countries. The Red Cross has shown how corruption, banditry, and fights for diamonds, minerals, and timber fueled war in Liberia and Sierra Leone. And in Angola, a conflict with ideological roots was transformed into a battle over gold and diamonds. In addition, war can actually generate income. For example, weapons manufacturers can reap enormous rewards from ongoing struggles, and smugglers can evade blockades or sanctions so that they can charge high prices for their smuggled goods.[6]

Ideological Causes

Ideological differences have contributed to many wars of the past and are likely to be involved in future wars as well. The Korean War, for instance, can be portrayed as the attempt by democratic capitalist states to prevent the spread of atheistic, authoritarian communism. In fact, the entire Cold War—between the United States and the "free world" on the one hand, and Soviet-led communism on the other hand—represented a massive struggle between two competing ideologies that encompassed political, economic, philosophical, and religious differences.

Psychological Causes

Many psychological factors can be used to explain why wars occur. Some psychological analyses of war focus on *individual* psychology; others deal with *group* psychology. For example, we could say that an individual leader's thirst for power explains Adolph Hitler's decisions that led to World War II. We could also apply many psychological theories in attempts to understand the personalities and motivations of Franjo Tudjman and Slobodan Milosevic, who were responsible for starting the violence in Yugoslavia in the 1990s.

The field of psychology also informs our discussion by its efforts to explain how *groups* behave. Consider, for example, the notion of "mob mentality." When alone, individuals may act one way, but in a group they may act very differently. This idea has been expanded in the analysis of war. The most prominent approach is that of **groupthink.** As Irving Janis has pointed out, in groupthink, the motivation to achieve group unanimity overrides the motivation to appraise realistically alternative courses of action. Accordingly, group dynamics can lead to outcomes that don't fit rational expectations. This can happen for many reasons. Sometimes, for example, individuals in a group will not speak out (self-censorship) if their view deviates from the apparent group consensus. Direct pressure can also be applied to any member of the group who expresses strong opinions against what the group thinks is the consensus opinion. In other cases groupthink can lead to stereotyped views of enemy leaders as evil, weak, or stupid, or to an unquestioned belief in one's own inherent morality. The two most important results of groupthink for national decisionmakers is failure to consider a wide array of policy options and, ultimately, lower quality of policy decisions. A wide variety of political phenomena have been analyzed with regard to the impact of groupthink, including decisions by the Supreme Court (a group of nine justices), United States preparation prior to the Pearl Harbor attack by Japan, the escalation of the war in Vietnam, the Bay of Pigs fiasco, and the U.S. decision to attack Iraq in the Gulf War.

Another way in which psychological factors can explain war draws on insights from Chapter 2, where we saw that human nature has been used to explain the behavior of individuals and states. Some of the feminist approaches (elaborated in Chapter 10) for example, argue that men are more aggressive than women and that wars have always been a male enterprise. With only rare exceptions, men are terrorists, men are the main combatants in war, men direct wars, and men run the governments that decide to go to war.

Groupthink
A psychological theory applicable to many aspects of life, including foreign policy decision making. It suggests that the motivation to achieve group unanimity overrides the motivation to appraise realistically alternative courses of action.

Ethnic and Religious Differences

As we saw in Chapter 8, ethnic and religious differences can often lead to violence. Religious differences are at work in the wars between Israel (primarily a Jewish state) and many of its neighbors (which are primarily Islamic). Religious differences are also at the core of many internal conflicts, like the one between Catholics and Protestants in Northern Ireland (a part of Britain), and those between Hindus and Muslims in India, Pakistan, and elsewhere. Ethnic differences often lead to violence among groups as shown by the cases of the former Yugoslavia, the Trans-Caucasus region, Rwanda, and in the Middle East among Kurds, Arabs, and Turks.

Preemptive War

A country may also go to war if it expects to be attacked in the near future. In the early 1980s, for example, Israel attacked an Iraqi nuclear power facility because it feared that the facility would be used by Iraq to build nuclear weapons that could threaten Israel. A more recent example is the 2003 war in Iraq. The Bush Administration argued that Iraq's weapons of mass destruction (WMD) programs could only be shut down by military force. If left unchecked, Iraq would develop WMD and threaten Iraq's neighbors, Israel, and the United States. Thus, the United States and a coalition of countries achieved "regime change" in Iraq by force. Controversy persists over whether the Saddam Hussein regime would have ever used WMD—thus raising questions about the necessity of this preemptive war.

Domestic Political Causes

Sometimes wars occur not because of problems overseas (international) but because of problems at home (*domestic politics*). For example, considerable evidence suggests that Argentina went to war with Britain in 1982 because the political leaders in Argentina were struggling for popularity in the midst of an economic crisis. The Argentine leaders sought a popular issue that could save them politically; they found that issue in the public's desire to take back the Malvinas Islands (also known as the Falkland Islands). Was taking a couple of windswept, inhospitable islands at the southern tip of South America worth the risk of waging war with a great power like Britain? Most observers would say "no," but for some political leaders, the answer is "yes"—if going to war helps restore domestic political confidence in them.

Another example, although with less credible evidence, involves U.S. relations with Serbia in the 1990s. During the impeachment proceedings against President Bill Clinton in 1999—inspired by the Monica Lewinsky scandal—many people believed that the president tried to distract the American public by bombing Serb targets in Kosovo. During the same period, of course, the United States was also bombing targets in Iraq. Unfortunately, because of the time it takes for primary documents to become available and memoirs to be written, we may not know for a decade or more the extent to which the impeachment proceedings were relevant to U.S. foreign policy in Kosovo.

Misperception

Misperception
When applied to war and international relations, causes of war in which one or more countries in a dispute misinterpret the intentions of the other. The misunderstanding leads to a war that perhaps was not desired by any country.

Another complex but very important cause of war is **misperception,** which can take a variety of forms. One country may get the wrong signals from the adversary. One side could also incorrectly perceive either its own strength or the strength of the adversary. If one side is deluded into thinking that it has a superior military force, it may expect victory in a short war, but the mistake may prove disastrous. John Stoessinger, an international relations theorist, argues that the single most important reason for war is misperception. For Stoessinger the actual distribution of power or the actual strength of the enemy isn't what counts; it is the perception of these things.[7] Read box Historical Perspective: The Causes of the Gulf War to see how the issue of misperception can be applied to the Gulf War.

HISTORICAL PERSPECTIVE

The Causes of the Gulf War

The 1991 Gulf War, in which Iraq fought against a U.S.-led UN coalition, illustrates how misperception can contribute to war. The Iraqi leader Saddam Hussein had many reasons to invade Kuwait. After a war with Iran that lasted throughout most of the 1980s and which cost Iraq 400,000 lives, Saddam's political standing was tenuous. In addition, the war had helped deplete Iraq's treasury, which was $70 billion in debt. Saddam probably thought that a quick victory over Kuwait would help Iraq in two ways. First, Iraq would have access to Kuwait's rich oil fields. Second, it could loot the Kuwaiti treasury.[8] And of course, a successful takeover of Kuwait would make Saddam a popular figure at home and possibly elsewhere in the Arab world. But Saddam was subject to several misperceptions. First, he probably thought that the costs of the war would be low. Most important, he probably didn't expect the United States to get involved. In retrospect, this seems like an obvious mistake. At the time, however, Saddam and his advisors had ample reason to think that the United States would *not get involved.*

Saddam was aware of the Vietnam syndrome on the American psyche; that is, the American public was very sensitive about sending U.S. troops to far-flung places with the likelihood of major casualties. Another signal that Saddam received was that the United States was unlikely to get involved in the Middle East. In several instances, U.S. citizens or soldiers had been attacked in the Middle East but without a strong U.S. counterresponse. Consider the following examples:[9]

- In 1976 the U.S. Ambassador to Lebanon, Francis C. Meloy, was assassinated. The U.S. government covered it up to avoid public or congressional pressure to retaliate against those responsible for the murders.
- In 1983 terrorists bombed a U.S. Marine barracks in Beirut, killing 241 American servicemen. The United States "supinely withdrew," taking no military action. The United States didn't want to offend Syria, a client state of the Soviet Union.
- In 1985 CIA agent William Buckley was kidnapped and tortured to death by Syrian-backed terrorists. The United States averted its eyes.
- In 1989 Marine colonel William Higgins was killed by terrorists, who released a video of the corpse hanging from a rope.

None of these incidences generated much public outrage in the United States. Thus, Saddam was given the impression (or misperception) that the United States would not act in the Middle East. Compounding the impression of a gun-shy United States, as tensions rose before the invasion, the United States was told by Egyptian leaders and others in the Middle East that Iraq would not attack Kuwait. And when the U.S. ambassador to Iraq, April Glaspie, went to talk to Saddam, she didn't send strong signals to him to deter an attack.

Thus, a rational person might have drawn the same conclusions as Saddam. Unfortunately, Saddam incorrectly interpreted historical examples and failed to take into account the implications of the collapse of communism. For the United States, the costs of *inaction* were too great. If Iraq had been allowed to control Kuwait, Saddam would have controlled about 40 percent of the world's oil reserves. Without U.S. intervention, Saddam might have even taken over the lightly defended—and extremely oil rich—Saudi Arabia on Iraq's southern border. Iraqi leaders also didn't count on Mikhail Gorbachev's decision not to back Iraq, which the Soviet Union might have done during the Cold War. So, had Saddam better understood U.S. strategic interests, and had he been given a clear threat from the United States, he might never have invaded Kuwait.

The Structure of the International System

Yet another important cause of war can be the structure of the international system. In fact, most international relations scholars view this factor as a primary cause of war, but they disagree over how it operates as such. But what do we mean by *structure?* Most observers agree that three basic types exist, and you will be familiar with these concepts from Chapter 2.

- A *multipolar structure*, which has many great powers in the international system.
- A *bipolar structure*, which has two dominant countries.
- A *unipolar structure*, which has one country with predominant power.

In addition, most observers agree with the following three points—all of which should sound familiar. First, anarchy in the international system makes wars more likely because of the tension created by uncertainty over what other countries will do. Second, we live in a world where each country must rely on itself for survival (it is a self-help system). Third, as we saw at the beginning of this book, the world has no global police force to enforce international rules for keeping troublesome countries in line. Moreover, as the old saying goes, there are no permanent allies or enemies in this uncertain world. Differences of opinion appear, however, when analysts ponder whether the multipolar, bipolar, or unipolar structure is the most dangerous or most likely to produce peace.

Some people believe that multipolar systems are more peaceful because countries have more choices in forming alliances, and that they can better balance each other to prevent war. Others argue that bipolar systems (as during the Cold War) are safer because the two main countries (the United States and the USSR in that case) know that the risks of going to war are high, and therefore will avoid doing so. A major dispute revolves around the *unipolar* international system structure. Some analysts believe that since "power corrupts, and absolute power corrupts absolutely," a single country dominating the international system creates the most dangerous situation. In direct opposition to this view is **hegemonic stability theory,** which posits that international stability can be achieved when there is a *hegemon*—a single, dominant power. In many respects, the United States exhibits the characteristics of a global hegemon, the only superpower (uni-pole) in the international system. You may want to think about whether this bodes well for the world or whether, as the realists believe, the massive power wielded by the United States creates a very dangerous situation.

Why do wars start then? Unfortunately, scholars are often at odds about every aspect of this question. Take the example of gender. As we saw in Chapter 2, there are many strains of feminist thought in international relations. Some feminists believe that natural differences exist between the sexes. Others believe that the social environment in which people are raised—an environment which encourages males to be aggressive and violent, and females to be quiet and cooperative—is more important. Both the "nature" and the "nurture" feminists might agree that war is essentially a male enterprise, but they might disagree as to why. Wars start for many complex reasons. Two final cautionary comments: First, contrary to popular perception, not all wars are caused by the same thing, such as a thirst for power. One war may start because of religious differences, while another may start because of a dispute over territory. Second, people commonly believe that all wars are *offensive* wars. As we have mentioned, countries may go to war for *defensive* reasons (as Britain did in World War II because it was attacked by Germany) or for *national lib-*

For more information on how many people serve in the military, go to **www.ablongman.com/ duncan.**

Hegemonic Stability Theory
An international relations theory that argues that the political-economic stability in the world or in a region requires a strong power called a hegemon. The United States may be said to have provided hegemonic stability in Asia after the Second World War. This perspective disagrees with the realist notion that a unipolar structure to the international system is inherently dangerous.

eration (as Algeria did against France in the late 1950s and early 1960s). You are now better prepared to understand past wars and to consider why future wars may occur, but we need to add one more level to our thinking about why wars occur: the difference between immediate and underlying causes of war.

Immediate and Underlying Causes

The many causes of war can usefully be put into two categories. *Underlying causes of war* are generally long-term. For example, U.S. fear of the spread of communism led to U.S. intervention in Vietnam; U.S. dependence on foreign oil contributed to its involvement in the Gulf War. *Immediate, or proximate, causes of war* are generally short-term and applicable to a specific context. Think of them as the trigger that sets off a war. The immediate cause of World War I, for example, was the assassination of Archduke Ferdinand in Sarajevo. Which is better at explaining why there are wars—underlying or immediate causes? Scholars are split on this question.

To help demonstrate why, consider the causes of World War II. You will quickly understand why even very knowledgeable people disagree. Was World War II caused by the long-term attempt (underlying cause) by Germany to dominate Europe? Or was the war caused by Adolf Hitler's personal rise to power (an immediate cause)? Or was the war simply the second act of a two-act play (World War I and II) in which the land-based Germany attempted to challenge the global leadership of sea-based Great Britain (underlying cause)? An important point to keep in mind here is that a thorough explanation probably needs to include many causes.

Richard Ned Lebow applies this concept to the Cuban Missile Crisis.[10] In early 1962 Nikita Khrushchev of the Soviet Union sought to catch up with the United States in the nuclear realm by secretly placing missiles in Cuba, a communist country led by Fidel Castro. Khrushchev thought that if the USSR could not match the United States in terms of long-distance nuclear missiles, having a few Soviet missiles less than 100 miles off the American coast would be the next best thing. While the Soviets continued their construction of missile silos in Cuba, an American U-2 spy plane took pictures of the Soviet activity. For the next several days, President John F. Kennedy and his circle of advisors deliberated about the most appropriate course of action. They generally agreed that the Soviets shouldn't be allowed to set up the missiles, but how to prevent them was not clear. One plan called for the invasion of Cuba. Other plans were suggested, but all agreed that the confrontation between the United States and Soviet Union could result in a nuclear war. In fact, during the Cuban Missile Crisis, the United States went on its highest level of military alert, Defense Condition 2 (or Defcon 2). Defcon 1 indicates a state of war. In the end, the United States cut a deal with the Soviets. In return for the withdrawal of all Soviet missiles, the United States promised not to invade Cuba. Although this description of the Cuban Missile Crisis is only skeletal, what does it tell us about immediate and underlying causes?

Imagine that the crisis had spun out of control, and the United States and the Soviets had gone to war—let's call it World War III. Assuming anyone survived, what would historians of the future have said about it? Some would point to the *underlying* causes of the war as being most important. They would say that the ideological differences between the capitalist, democratic West and the communist East were too great to allow for compromise. They might also point to the protracted nuclear arms race between the United States and the USSR. Furthermore, they might say that the competition for spheres of influence around the world was

Anticipating the Results of World War III: This graffiti image painted on the Berlin Wall expressed the fear of a nuclear confrontation between NATO and the Soviet-led Warsaw Pact. The Berlin Wall symbolized the division between East and West during the Cold War. People in eastern Berlin were strictly forbidden from getting close to their side of the wall. This was not so in western Berlin, where graffiti thrived.

so dangerous that war was inevitable. Hence, historians would have portrayed World War III as a natural and inevitable extension of the 20 years of Cold War rivalry between the two superpowers.

A different group of historians would come up with a completely different explanation of World War III by emphasizing immediate causes. These historians would not have seen the outcome of the conflict in 1962 as inevitable. For example, they might focus on the particulars of the leaders in Moscow and Washington. It is possible, for example, that Khrushchev's rash decision to put missiles in Cuba might not have been made by any other Soviet leader. In terms of U. S. leadership, recall that in the 1960 presidential election, democrat John F. Kennedy barely beat republican Richard M. Nixon. Had one percent of the voters changed their minds, Nixon might have won the election and been at the helm in 1962. With Nixon's strong anticommunist reputation and solid background in foreign affairs, Khrushchev might never have attempted to go to the mat with the United States. As it was, Khrushchev viewed Kennedy as a weak president—someone who wouldn't stand up to aggressive Soviet behavior in Cuba.

A worse outcome than what actually occurred was also possible if one considers other potential immediate factors. For example, what would have happened if the Kennedy administration had opted for an air strike instead of the blockade of Cuba? Or during the tense days of the blockade (officially a "quarantine"), what would have happened if a subordinate from either military establishment had taken matters into his own hands and sparked a military confrontation that the political leaders didn't want? These are, of course, speculative questions, but they highlight how immediate factors can push a crisis closer to or further from war.

What Are the Weapons of War?

Global violence is affected not simply by the outbreak of war but also by the type and number of weapons involved. For example, the U.S.-led war in Afghanistan that began shortly after September 11, 2001, was essentially completed in short order because of the vast technological superiority of the U.S. military. This contrasts with the long, drawn out, and devastating Soviet attempt to subdue Afghanistan in the 1980s and early 1990s. This section of the chapter thus deals with the tools of global violence among states. Most people are aware, at least vaguely, of the destructive power of nuclear weapons. Increasingly, however, people are becoming aware of the threats posed by biological and chemical weapons. Compared to nuclear weapons, these weapons of mass destruction (WMD) are cheaper to make, easier to make, and easier to make in secret. They are often called the poor man's weapon of mass destruction. Atop a missile, fired from an advanced bomber, or even delivered by foot, biological and chemical weapons can have an enormous impact.

For more information on the effects of nuclear explosions, go to **www.ablongman.com/ duncan.**

Advances in weapons science will be critically important to diplomacy and military success in the future, as the war in Afghanistan showed. The country that develops weapons technology the fastest will have a real edge over the competition. This applies to both offensive weapons, such as smart bombs, and to defensive systems such as the proposed U.S. National Missile Defense (NMD). NMD aims to shield U.S. territory (or perhaps U.S. overseas targets) from a limited missile attack by rogue states—states that don't respect the rules of the international system, particularly from the U.S. perspective—such as Iran and North Korea.

For more information on national missile defenses, go to **www.ablongman.com/ duncan.**

The "smart" technologies in use today are not always as smart as they are purported to be. For example, in the Gulf War, 76 of 167 laser-guided bombs dropped by stealth fighters (F-117) in the first five days of the war missed their target.[11] Similar problems exist with weapons of less technological sophistication as well. For example, a third of the 65 Predator unmanned aerial vehicles—otherwise used so successfully in the Afghanistan war—were lost mostly because of operator errors.[12] Another example of the limits of contemporary weapons comes from the UN's Mine Action Coordination Center, which estimated that between 7 and 11 percent of the bomblets (about 20,000) dropped by NATO planes in the air campaign over Kosovo in 1999 failed to blow up.[13]

The United States, its allies, and its rivals are all heavily involved in research in or acquisition of weapons technology, with the hope of gaining the edge. Advanced technology will improve the force of explosives, make targeting more accurate, make information processing more efficient, and ultimately determine how well aggression is deterred and who wins a war. Let's now take a closer look at the weapons of violence in world politics.

Nuclear Weapons and Radiological Bombs

For most of the Cold War, only five countries *admitted* to having nuclear weapons (the United States, Britain, France, China, and the Soviet Union), although others have been suspected of having them for some time, including North Korea and Israel. The most recent members of the "nuclear club" are India and Pakistan, each

New Simple NATO Bombing Identification Chart: Despite enormous advances in weapon targeting, the most advanced laser-guided weapons can still miss their target. During the 1999 air war against Yugoslavia, NATO airplanes dropped most of their bombs from a high altitude in order to avoid being shot down. One of the results was less accuracy and the accidental bombing of civilians in rural and urban centers.

Source: Tribune Media Services, Inc.

TABLE 9.1   Worldwide Nuclear Stockpiles

Country	Total Nuclear Warheads
China	410
France	348
India	50–90
Israel	98–172
Pakistan	30–50
Russia	20,000
United Kingdom (Britain)	185
United States	10,700
Maximum Total	31,055

Source: Carnegie Endowment for International Peace, Deadly Arsenals (2002), www.ceip.org.

---

of which held nuclear blast tests in 1998. Table 9.1 shows the worldwide nuclear stockpiles by country.

The destructive power of nuclear weapons varies depending on many things, including the size and type of bomb. Although most people are aware of the damaging effects of the radiation from nuclear weapons, there are actually three other serious effects: blast, heat, and electromagnetic pulse (EMP). The blast of a nuclear explosion generates immensely powerful winds. Next, the heat generated from a nuclear explosion is comparable to temperatures of stars. From the Hiroshima bombing, potatoes baked in the ground. Finally, the EMP burns out transistors, overloads power supplies, and generally disrupts or destroys electronic equipment. Obviously, the combination of heat, blast, and EMP can have a devastating effect on life, yet those who survive must cope with the aftermath. In Hiroshima, for example, 65 of the 150 doctors in the city were killed, leaving roughly 8 doctors for every 10,000 survivors. Of the 1,780 nurses in the city, 1,654 were killed, and only

6 of the 30 Red Cross workers could function.[14] Moreover, the presence of tens of thousands of corpses created severe health risks. In all, about 100,000 died from the Hiroshima blast; roughly 70,000 people died from the nuclear bomb that exploded over Nagasaki.

Few expect nuclear weapons to be used any time soon, now that the Cold War is over. A more pressing concern is the use of nuclear material in radiological, or dirty, bombs. **Radiological bombs** involve conventional explosions that spread radioactive contamination. They are easier and cheaper to make than nuclear bombs, but they are not as devastating as nuclear explosions. There is a growing fear that terrorists could obtain nuclear material through theft or illegal purchases from many of the world's nuclear laboratories. The biggest source of "loose nukes" that could fall into the wrong hands is Russia. According to Matthew Bunn of Harvard University, 60 percent of all nuclear material in Russia remains inadequately secured.[15] Studies by the International Atomic Energy Agency reveal that thousands of radioactive sources worldwide, designed to generate high levels of radiation for industrial and medical equipment, are lying virtually unguarded in factories and hospitals, and more than 100 countries may have inadequate programs to prevent or detect thefts.[16]

Biological and Chemical Weapons

Like nuclear weapons, chemical and biological weapons can cause mass destruction. None, of course, has the ability to discriminate between soldier and civilian. **Biological weapons** contain living organisms. Such weapons developed by the United States and other countries include lethal agents such as Bacillus anthracis and botulinum toxin; incapacitating agents, including Brucella suis, Coxiella burnetii, and staphylococcal enterotoxin B; and anticrop agents such as rice blast, rye stem rust, and wheat stem rust.[17] **Chemical weapons** do not contain living organisms. They include harassing agents, irritants (e.g., tear gas), and casualty agents such as poison gas and nerve gas. Some nerve gases are so strong that a milligram is enough to kill a human being. Another category of chemical weapon includes incendiary devices such as napalm, antiplant agents such as defoliants, and anticrop agents such as soil sterilants.

Although both biological and chemical weapons have been around for a long time, and despite the efforts made after World War I to outlaw the use of such weapons, most people have only recently become aware that they could be used in war or on civilian populations. Iraqi leader Saddam Hussein ordered a chemical attack on the city of Halabja, a predominantly Kurdish city in northeastern Iraq, in 1988. An estimated 5,000 to 6,000 civilians were killed and another 10,000 injured. Today the people of Halabja still suffer from high rates of serious diseases such as cancer and birth defects. The Iraqi regime also killed thousands of Iranians with chemical weapons during the Iran-Iraq War in the 1980s.[18]

In the context of plans for war in 2002–2003, Iraq remained a concern as a source of biological and chemical weapons and materials. When United Nations inspectors were first allowed to review Iraq's weapons facilities (inspections that ended in 1998), they found a startling array of chemical and biological weapons. According to some estimates, there was enough to kill the world's population several times over. Included in the Iraqi stockpile were 480,000 liters of live chemical agents, 1.8 million liters of chemical ingredients, 30 chemical warheads for missiles, 19,000 liters of botulinum toxin, and 8,400 liters of anthrax.[19]

Biological Weapon
A weapon that has living organisms such as anthrax or botulinum toxin. It is a weapon of mass destruction in that it does not distinguish between soldier and civilian.

Chemical Weapon
A weapon consisting of harmful chemicals including tear gas, napalm, and poison gas. It is a weapon of mass destruction in that it does not distinguish between soldier and civilian.

Iraq's chemical and biological weapons capability is only one source of concern. For example, despite the end of the Cold War, the United States claims that none of Russia's reported 40,000 tons of chemical weapons has been destroyed.[20] And, in light of the inadequate surveillance of Russia's chemical and biological weapons, Senator Richard Lugar (R-Indiana) has described the threat of "catastrophic terrorism" from bioweapons as possibly the gravest challenge to global security.[21]

Since the anthrax letters sent through the U.S. postal system in the fall of 2001, much greater attention is now paid to the potential use of this and other biological weapons. Anthrax occurs naturally and about 2,000 people worldwide contract anthrax annually through the skin, mostly from handling contaminated wool, hides, or leather.[22] It is also developed in laboratories by several countries, including the United States. Anthrax spores can be released as a colorless, odorless, and invisible material over a large area or in small containers. Senator Patrick Leahy said that the letter sent to Senator Tom Daschle (discovered November 16, 2001) was so powerful that it could have killed 100,000 people.[23] And according to a Congressional report, if an estimated 100 kg of anthrax spores were released upwind of Washington, D.C., 13,000 to 3 million people could be killed.[24] Antibiotics can stop anthrax if taken in time. If not, the mortality rate is estimated to be 90 percent.[25]

Another dangerous biological weapons agent is smallpox, a virus that was essentially eradicated in the 1970s but maintained in Russia and the United States. Rogue states may also have it. Unlike anthrax, smallpox is highly contagious and kills one-third of the people it infects. The symptoms of smallpox appear within 12 to 14 days, but there is no effective drug treatment.[26] In 2002, in response to the threats posed by anthrax and smallpox, the United States began a serious debate of the merits of vaccinating the public, or at least health care professionals and others on the "front lines" of biological warfare. While it is hoped that anthrax and smallpox vaccines will work, they both pose risks as well. For example, the smallpox vaccine, if administered to all Americans, could result in 200 to 300 deaths and make several thousand people severely ill.[27] Table 9.2 provides more detail on the effects of attacks with various biological weapons.

For more information on anthrax vaccinations, go to **www.ablongman.com/ duncan.**

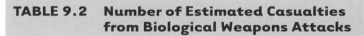

TABLE 9.2   Number of Estimated Casualties from Biological Weapons Attacks

Estimates of casualties from a hypothetical biological attack based on the release of 50 kilograms of various agents by an aircraft flying along at 2km path upwind of a city of half a million people.

Agent	Casualties	Fatalities
Rift Valley Fever	35,000	400
Tick-borne Encephalitis	35,000	9,500
Typhus	85,000	19,000
Bruxellosis	125,000	500
Q Fever	125,000	150
Tularemia	125,000	30,000
Anthrax	125,000	95,000

SOURCE: Ronald M. Atlas, "Table 1: Combating the threat of biowarfare and bioterrorism," *Bioscience*, June 1999, pp. 465–477.

Other biological weapons threats exist as well. Botulism (*botulinum toxin*), can be released in the air or used on food. It can cause severe food poisoning and even kill victims within a week through paralysis and respiratory failure. Like some biological and chemical weapons, it is considered to be ineffective at causing mass casualties.[28] Aflatoxin, produced by a mold that grows on peanuts, can incapacitate soldiers on a battlefield and cause liver cancer.[29] Pneumonic plague (*yersinia pestis*) can be distributed though the air and, if not promptly treated with antibiotics, can kill most of its victims.

How prepared is the United States or other countries for such attacks? By most accounts, civilian populations remain vulnerable. In October 2001 the executive director of the American Public Health Association, Mohammad Akhter, said that only half the states in the United States have federal experts specially trained to prevent or contain bioterrorism. In addition, only 24 states have Epidemic Intelligence Service officers from the federal Centers for Disease Control and Prevention.[30] Overall, the attacks of 9/11 gave the roughly 3,000 city and county public health departments in the United States—and as well as those in other countries—a wake-up call to address these threats. And to help counter the threat of biological attacks, Congress passed a $4.6 billion bioterrorism bill that will allow the government to provide better oversight of research facilities and to hire hundreds of new inspectors to verify the safety of the nation's food supply and drinking water.

Conventional Weapons Versus Unconventional Weapons

Any weapon that is not nuclear, biological, or chemical is typically considered a **conventional weapon.** However, a growing number of other weapons are quite unconventional. In the following paragraph we review several of these types of weapons.

Conventional Weapon
A loose term referring to any weapon that is not a weapon of mass destruction.

Most conventional weapons have been around for a long time or are simply modern variants of weapons that predate the twentieth century. For example, all the armed services make use of various kinds of guns, bullets, and bombs. Other common weapons include hand grenades, cannons, and artillery shells, as well as various "platforms" for firing weapons, such as submarines, planes, helicopters, and aircraft carriers. Furthermore, radar-evading cruise missiles guided by global positioning systems (GPS) can be launched from ships or jets. And "smart" bombs have sophisticated tracking and targeting systems, while dumb bombs (or gravity bombs) basically get dropped from a plane and land on their target by gravity. An unusual bomb is the Daisy Cutter, weighing 15,000 pounds, which was used in both the Vietnam and Gulf Wars and recently in Afghanistan.[31] It is the world's biggest conventional bomb and is designed to spread devastation over a broad area or penetrate "hard and deeply buried targets," like the caves of Afghanistan.[32]

Recent technological developments have led to the use of unmanned aerial vehicles (UAV) such as the Predator, which can track otherwise elusive targets and deliver missiles. Another UAV, the Global Hawk, is a reconnaissance aircraft (flying at 65,000 feet), which saw its combat debut in Afghanistan. Military planners in the United States and elsewhere foresee much greater use of these UAVs. John Warden, a former fighter pilot who helped plan the Gulf War air campaign, believes that by 2025, as many as 90 percent of all U.S. combat aircraft will be unmanned.[33]

The expression *light weapons* encompasses some of the weapons already mentioned, but characterizes those that are light in weight, such as pistols, rifles, and

Air Power Without Pilots: Unmanned aerial vehicles (UAVs), such as the Predator pictured here, began to prove their worth as reconnaissance and attack vehicles at the start of the 21st century.

hand grenades. Light weapons may not seem as effective as weapons of mass destruction, or as powerful and precise as cruise missiles, but they are often the weapon of choice in much of the Third World, and they can also lead to devastating results. In Rwanda in 1994, for example, about one million people were killed after the Hutu-dominated government spent millions of dollars on rifles, grenades, machine guns, and machetes. These were later used to slaughter Tutsi civilians.[34]

Yet another type of weapon that belongs in this loose category of conventional weapons is one designed to wipe out other weapons. For example, Ronald Reagan announced to a shocked world in 1983 that the United States was going to develop a space-based weapon system that could knock out any ballistic missile fired at the United States. Although the project—the Strategic Defense Initiative (SDI), or "Star Wars," as it was often called—was technologically unfeasible at the time, the notion of a protective shield for U.S. territory has remained an appealing objective, especially among Republicans. Over the past few years, tests have taken place of a less ambitious American missile defense program; specifically the goal is to wipe out incoming missiles with another missile fired from the ground (not space). Getting the missile defense program from its initial and only marginally successful testing phase to operational deployment will be difficult and take a long time. The program has been challenged by doubts about its cost (which could exceed $200 billion), its technical feasibility, and the reactions of potential enemies (e.g., they may build more missiles to overwhelm the system).

Keep in mind that not all the items purchased by military organizations are weapons specifically designed to kill or subdue an opponent. A large portion of a country's military budget involves things like salaries and benefits for soldiers and their families, maintenance, and research and development (R&D). And much equipment used by soldiers is for support. For example, transport planes like the

The Dangers of Light Weapons: A soldier looks at the skulls of victims of the 1994 genocide in Rwanda, which claimed the lives of over 800,000 people. Most of the deaths were caused by "light weapons" such as machetes, knives, and small firearms.

C-17 or C-130 are designed simply to move troops and equipment from one place to another. Computers and computer software help manage information on the battlefield and target certain kinds of weapons. They are not considered weapons but are vital to the efficiency of waging war. Other support items include everything from ready-to-eat meals to engineering equipment for building (or destroying) bridges or bunkers.

In brief, then, *conventional weapons* is a loose term encompassing a wide range of offensive and defensive weapons. All these weapons, however, differ qualitatively from "unconventional conventional weapons." The expression *unconventional conventional weapons* is not an official one or even one used very often, but it does help us make an important point. As a result of scientific and technological advances, scientists, engineers, and weapons manufacturers have become increasingly imaginative and innovative in finding new ways to subdue a foe. Some of the new or proposed weapons are designed to incapacitate a soldier while others are designed to render military hardware useless. Many are also being designed to help acquire battlefield intelligence. Consider how varied the following list of unconventional weapons is:

- Lasers weapons that inflict temporary or permanent blindness on the enemy.
- Nonilluminating paints to make military vehicles invisible to radar.
- Armor as flexible as skin, tough as an abalone shell, and enhanced with "living characteristics" such as the ability to heal itself when torn."[35]
- Insects (wasps, for example) that can sniff out land mines and chemical and biological warfare agents.[36]
- Acoustic generators that can send out high frequency sound waves to disorient and injure enemy soldiers.

- Stun-guns that can shoot electrified "nets" that trap an enemy. As domestic law enforcement officials have already found, stun-guns can also be used to shock the captured enemy if he or she tries to escape.
- Super caustic acids that weaken bridges and tunnels.
- High-powered microwaves that can "melt down" electronic systems on conventional weapons.

Some of these weapons will not be developed for technical reasons; others may not be developed for political or ethical reasons. For example, even though supporters of blinding laser weapons believe that the weapon is a nonlethal way of stopping an opponent, others—including the Red Cross—argue that such weapons should be outlawed because they are inhumane.

Land Mines: The World's Most Dangerous Weapons

When asked, What is the world's most dangerous weapon? most people quickly say, "nuclear weapons." One should keep in mind, however, that the degree of danger a weapon poses is determined in part by its destructive capacity but also by the likelihood of its use. A good case can be made for land mines being the world's most dangerous weapon. They have killed or maimed far more people than all victims of chemical, biological, and nuclear warfare put together. The production of land mines requires no fancy technology. Land mines are generally very inexpensive, and they are often hard to detect and eliminate. It has been estimated that between 80 and 100 million mines are still active, some in areas never identified as mine fields. Every 20 minutes someone around the world is injured by a mine, and every year 26,000 people are maimed or killed. Eighty percent of victims of land mines are civilians. In Cambodia, for example, 1 out of every 384 people is an amputee.[37] Afghanistan is the world's most heavily mined country in the world. Besides having to confront mines left over from the era of the Soviet invasion and before, Afghanistan's population must also contend with more recent problems such as unexploded cluster bombs. Each bomb scatters 202 bomblets, ten percent of which fail to explode. There are more than 230 areas hit by cluster bombs in the U.S.-led air war over Afghanistan.[38]

The 1980 Geneva Convention limits the use of weapons such as land mines, which are deemed to be "excessively injurious or to have indiscriminate effects." The International Committee of the Red Cross has also called for a complete ban on land mines. Moreover, in the last year of her life, Princess Diana worked to get the land mine convention ratified. The United States, however, is one of the few countries unwilling to sign an international convention that would ban the use of land mines. It argues that the dangerous border between North and South Korea makes land mines indispensable and that any treaty banning land mines would be impossible to monitor or implement.

International efforts to reduce the dangers of land mines have made some progress in recent years. A total of 138 countries have signed the Ottawa Treaty banning the manufacture, trade, and use of land mines; 110 of those countries have ratified the treaty. In addition, 22 million stockpiled land mines have been destroyed over the past three years by more than 50 nations. The number of countries producing mines has also dropped from 54 to 16. Despite these signs of progress, however, more than 250 million remain in the arsenals of 105 nations.[39]

For more information on weapons at **www.ablongman.com/ duncan.**

Why Are There So Many Weapons and Can They Be Controlled?

In this section of the chapter we will try to spell out the framework for answering the very difficult questions of why we have so many weapons and whether we can control them. To get a handle on these issues, it helps if we think in terms of both the supply of weapons and the demand for them. If the supply and demand are both high, controlling them will be all the more difficult.

Supply and Demand

Let's begin with the *demand* for weapons. A country, or its political leaders, have several reasons for wanting to be well armed. Consistent with the realist perspective, for example, politicians may believe that a well-armed country can deter potential aggressors. Another reason why a country may demand more weapons is that it is preparing an assault on another country. A country may also want weapons in order to keep up in an arms race.

The reasons for the massive *supply* of weapons are also numerous. For starters, when the demand for weapons is strong, supply is sure to follow, at least for national security reasons. To put it another way, when a country decides it needs weapons, it will try to obtain as many as it can afford. Another important reason for the wide availability (supply) of weapons is that the arms business can be extremely lucrative. Or, to put it another way, greed fuels much of the supply side of weapons. One thousand companies in 98 countries around the world produce small arms and ammunition, according to a study conducted by the Graduate Institute of International Studies in Geneva.[40]

In most countries—including the United States, which is by far the world's biggest arms exporter—the largest customer for weapons manufacturers is the government. As noted above, the U.S. government's demand for weapons during the Cold War was extremely robust. Ironically, when a government's demands for weapons is high, it creates the unusual situation in which taxpayer dollars (through the government) buy weapons, thus giving substantial profits to *private* arms companies.

Another reason for the large supply of weapons is the need to maintain a viable domestic arms industry. Just as no country wants to be dependent on another country for food, an independent arms industry is often a national priority—especially among the world's great powers. With the end of the Cold War, many American weapons manufacturers saw the number or size of their contracts drop precipitously. In some cases, companies were bought up by others as part of the post–Cold War consolidation process. Another response to the decrease in the government's demand for weapons is a more aggressive approach to the export of weapons. Many weapons makers in the United States, Europe, Russia, and elsewhere argue that if they cannot sell enough to their own governments, they'll go out of business. So they say they are forced to sell to other countries.

Most analysts of the global arms trade believe that it will be hard to stem the tide.[41] All the major industrial powers sell weapons, especially light weapons that are used in Third World conflicts where most of the world's turmoil is. In addition, many countries have military aid programs that foster weapons sales. Weapons purchases also take place on the global market—legally and illegally. It is also not uncommon for weapons to be stolen from government stockpiles.

For more information
on the diversion of
nuclear material, go to
**www.ablongman.com/
duncan**.

**Structural Arms
Control**
A type of arms control
designed to prevent the
spread (or proliferation)
of weapons to certain
countries.

For more information
on nuclear accidents
and which countries
have nuclear weapons,
go to
**www.ablongman.com/
duncan**.

For many people in the United States and elsewhere, a top national priority is control of the seemingly endless flow of weapons around the world. The weapons not only pose dangers to soldiers and, increasingly, to civilians, but also they can lead to costly arms races. Unfortunately, the task of arms control is more complicated than just limiting the number of weapons "out there," in part because the demand for weapons is so strong. Efforts to control the spread (or proliferation) of weapons fall into two general categories: structural and operational. We will explore these topics next.

Structural Arms Control

The concept of **structural arms control** is the one that most people are familiar with—that is, preventing the proliferation of weapons to certain countries. For example, it has been the stated policy of the five great nuclear powers (the United States, the United Kingdom, France, China, and Russia) to prevent the spread of nuclear weapons to other countries. Of course, their efforts have not always been successful, as the demonstration of nuclear explosions by India and Pakistan proved in 1998. Another example of structural arms control is the attempt to limit the use of land mines around the world, mentioned earlier. In general, structural arms control seeks to decrease the sense of instability or vulnerability that can be created by overly armed potential adversaries.

A familiar saying in international relations is "if you wish peace, then prepare for war." While this may make sense on the surface, preparing for war can increase tensions and make one's adversaries so nervous that war becomes *more* likely. For example, seeing one side prepare for war can make a potential adversary do the same, leading to a dangerous cycle: preparations designed to avoid war actually bring it on.

An instructive example of structural arms control is the Strategic Arms Limitation Talks (SALT), which began in 1969. As the United States and the Soviet Union realized the dangers (each side had enough nuclear power to destroy the planet) and financial costs of the nuclear arms race, they began the first major arms control efforts of the Cold War. SALT resulted in an agreement in which neither side would attempt to gain superiority over the other. It limited the number of nuclear weapons and ballistic missile launchers each country could have. In addition, the parties agreed that deployment would only be used for deterring war—not for aggression or victory in a war.[42] SALT also limited each side to only two Anti-Ballistic Missile deployment sites with no more than 100 ABM missiles at each. This was later changed to only one ABM site.

In 1991, SALT evolved into the Strategic Arms Reduction Talks (START). As the 1990s progressed, Russia and the United States were not just capping the number of nuclear weapons systems but were paring them down. START I set a limit of 1,600 on the number of deployed strategic nuclear weapons systems and 6,000 on the nuclear warheads. START II, begun in 1993, called for both sides to reduce their strategic nuclear warheads to no more than 3,000 to 3,500 by 2008. Illustrative of the difficulty of achieving structural arms control, the START treaty was never ratified by the United States Senate. When George W. Bush became president, he said that the United States would not ratify the START II treaty, and in 2002, the United States was pushing for important reductions but with the flexibility to keep almost 4,000 warheads available in storage.

Operational Arms Control

Almost as widely used as structural arms control, but without as much press coverage, **operational arms control** achieves greater security but without actually or directly limiting the flow of weapons. Operational arms control takes on many forms, including (1) keeping track of weapons and (2) notifying the "other side" of what you are up to. The principles which underpin both of these ideas are *good will* and *reputation*. If countries can learn to share information and build up at least some trust, the theory goes, then tensions should diminish and the odds of war should decline. Let's look at both aspects in turn.

Keeping Track of Weapons   When countries know what their potential adversaries have, they are less likely to make an unnecessarily dangerous decision based on limited information. Knowledge is power, as they say, but it can also reduce tensions between adversaries. With this in mind, the United Nations has developed a Register of Conventional Arms for the purpose of making more transparent who buys how much and from whom. Countries are supposed to furnish the UN with information about weapons sales and purchases by companies operating within their borders. In addition, the UN has considered tracking leases, grants, and long-term loans that are often part of arms transfers from one place to another. The UN's Register, however, has not been in use for long, and its effectiveness so far has been limited. Some countries have been reluctant to comply, and some have only complied partially. Asia and Africa tend to have the worst record of making reports to the UN.[43] After all, as Jordan Singer and others have argued, why should a country give out information when there is no guarantee that its adversary will do the same?

Notifying the Other Side   Countries often notify each other of troop movements and training exercises. The rationale is that if the countries regularly notify each other of such events, they will be less likely to perceive an adversary's "war games" or training exercises as a prelude to, or pretext for, war. In 1971 for example, the United States and the Soviet Union agreed to give advance warning on nuclear missile tests and to let each other know about any accidental missile firings. As part of the 1986 European Disarmament Conference, 35 countries pledged to give advance notification and allow international inspection of military maneuvers.

The Challenge of Verification   As we noted above, however, not all arms control plans work out. Sometimes it is hard to *verify* arms control agreements. Why sign an agreement with a potential adversary if there is no way to verify that the adversary is complying with the agreement? Negotiations on the UN's Convention on Biological Weapons, for example, have been stalled by disagreements over a system for verifying whether parties are observing. Lack of guarantees on verification also explains in part why the U.S. Senate has decided not to support the Nuclear Test Ban Treaty since 1999 (see box Historical Perspective: Reasons for Controlling the Spread of Nuclear Weapons, for more about this). Often, one side or another objects to strict verification procedures. As Sha Zukang, China's Director-General of Arms Control, put it, if verification procedures "are too intrusive and affect the legitimate security or economic interest of the states parties, or are too costly and impossible to sustain in a long run, they will not be able to get widespread support, and in the end the universality of the treaties will be undermined, which, in turn, will be detrimental to the strengthening of the nonproliferation regime."[44]

Operational Arms Control
A method of controlling weapons without actually or directly limiting the flow of weapons. It includes measures that foster trust among adversaries, such as notifying the "other side" of war games, hot lines, and public disclosure of weapons sales.

HISTORICAL PERSPECTIVE

Reasons for Controlling the Spread of Nuclear Weapons

For decades, the five major nuclear powers tried to prevent other countries from acquiring nuclear weapons. This was done in part for political reasons. If the "big five" could keep their club exclusive, they would retain a unique advantage over other countries. The five nuclear powers also tried to keep a lid on nuclear weapons proliferation because new nuclear powers were believed to lack safe command and control systems. For example, a country's structure for linking everyone involved with the decision to use the bomb may not be secure, or procedures for implementing that decision may not be safe. Main concerns focused on how new nuclear powers could ensure that their nuclear weapons wouldn't be fired accidentally, and that nuclear material wouldn't be sold to another country or wouldn't fall into the hands of terrorists. One keen observer of nuclear arms control, Scott D. Sagan, highlights six problems related to controlling nuclear weapons.[45]

First, emerging nuclear powers may lack the organizational and financial resources to produce adequate mechanical safety devices and safe weapons design features. After the Gulf War, for example, weapons inspectors found that Iraq's nuclear bomb design was highly unstable. It called for the bomb's core to be crammed with so much weapon-grade uranium that it would be perpetually on the verge of going off. As one weapons inspector put it, "I wouldn't want to be around if it fell off the edge of this desk."

Second, because the major world powers opposed nuclear weapons proliferation, emerging nuclear powers had to develop their weapons under conditions of great secrecy and thus without thorough monitoring of safety efforts. Public debate was less lively, making it more likely that a small number of bureaucratic and military interests would be in control and unchallenged.

Third, in countries with volatile civil-military relations, accidents are more likely to happen. In 1990, for example, the Pakistan air force may have loaded nuclear weapons on its F-16 aircraft without

How Can Global Violence Be Controlled?

Most observers of world politics believe that the twenty-first century is likely to be as violent as the last one. The decentralizing forces that affect more and more countries often lead to violent nationalist and separatist movements. In addition, with the greater ease of acquiring weapons and their increased lethality and variety, the potential increases for conflicts that stem from territorial disputes, personal ambitions, and religious and ethnic differences. If people are to reduce global violence, the motivations for going to war will have to be reduced. This chapter, as well as others in this book, suggests several ways of doing this. International law and international institutions, for example, are designed in part to help manage peacefully the relations among countries. But let's not forget the realist position that a strong country can deter aggression, thus contributing to peaceful (but perhaps tense) relations among countries. Let's look at this subject of deterrence first. Then we'll look at strengthening international institutions and international law.

informing Prime Minister Benezir Bhutto. As if this wasn't bad enough, the United States said that the F-16 hadn't been properly modified to carry nuclear weapons. In addition, this incident took place during a tense crisis over Kashmir.

Fourth, since countries seeking to acquire nuclear weapons often face adversaries that are geographically close, reaction time and margins for error narrow significantly. Between India and Pakistan, for example, there wouldn't be much time to determine whether an attack was real or not.

Fifth, "instant" nuclear powers may not have the benefit that the older nuclear powers had in learning about testing, training exercises, and deployments. In the early 1990s, for example, safety problems at military bases in Ukraine reportedly increased radiation levels at nuclear storage sites and produced violations of the schedules for technical servicing of missile warheads.

Finally, since political and social unrest are likely in the future in many emerging nuclear states, the risks increase for accidental and unauthorized weapons detonations. Disgruntled operators, for example, might engage in acts of sabotage that could inadvertently or deliberately produce accidents.

These problems need serious attention, but they neglect to mention the fact that even the major nuclear powers have not always been in complete control of their own nuclear weapons. Consider the following examples—not from India, Pakistan, Israel, or even Iraq—but from the United States. In Damascus, Arkansas, in September 1980, "during routine maintenance in a missile silo, a technician caused an accidental leak in a Titan II missile's pressurized fuel tank. Nearly nine hours after the initial leak, fuel vapors within the silo exploded. The pair of doors covering the silo, each weighing 740 tons, were blown off by the blast, and the nine megaton warhead was hurled 600 feet away. The warhead was recovered intact. One technician was killed in the explosion."[46] More recently, the U.S. General Accounting Office reported that the Los Alamos and Lawrence Livermore Labs were guilty of safety violations, including exposing their employees to radiation and inadequate monitoring of radiological contamination.[47] In a major effort to limit the development of nuclear weapons, most of the countries of the world have sought to implement a Comprehensive Test Ban Treaty (CTBT). The treaty's assumption is that if countries give up their right to test nuclear weapons, they will not try to develop them. By the end of 1999, 152 countries had ratified the global Comprehensive Test Ban Treaty. Bill Clinton signed the treaty in 1996, but the Senate has yet to give its approval.

Reducing Motivations: Deterrence

One of the most useful ways to prevent war is to make the potential aggressor think that an attack would be fruitless or worse. That is, a country can be *deterred* from starting a war if it thinks that its objectives won't be achieved or that the war will actually make things worse. Deterrence of a potentially aggressive country can be achieved in several ways. Being well-armed is the most obvious strategy. A well-armed defending country will not look like an attractive target to the potential attacking country. Some countries have followed this strategy by acquiring nuclear weapons, and some even seek deterrence by obtaining chemical and biological weapons. However, it takes more than just a good weapons arsenal to deter countries from attacking. In general, four major factors need to be in place for deterrence to work.[48] To help demonstrate why, let's take a look at the logic of *nuclear deterrence*.

First, the country hoping to deter a nuclear attack must have a **second strike capability.** This means that the defending country must be able to absorb an initial attack and *still have the capability* to inflict unacceptable damage on the attacker.

Second Strike Capability
The ability to withstand a nuclear attack and still retain the capability to retaliate with nuclear weapons.

For example, let's say that the attacking country (we'll call it Country A) knows that the defending country (Country D) has nuclear weapons. But Country A also knows that it can wipe out those nuclear weapons with its initial attack—a first strike. Country D's nuclear weapons will thus *not* serve as a deterrent. However, if at least some of Country D's nuclear weapons survive and can be used against A (in a second strike), A could be destroyed. Putting it in real-life terms, the Soviet Union may have resisted launching an all out war against the United States because it believed that the United States had a second strike capability—that is, the United States might have enough nuclear weapons left over after an initial attack to strike back. To help ensure second strike capability, the United States and the Soviet Union built both large numbers of nuclear weapons and different ways of delivering them. A **strategic nuclear triad,** for example, refers to the ability to launch a nuclear attack from air (e.g., bombers), land (e.g., missiles in silos), and sea (e.g., missiles launched from submarines). The submarine capability helped revolutionize modern warfare (and enhanced second strike capabilities) because submarines are so hard to find in the world's vast oceans.

Strategic Nuclear Triad
A nuclear force with the ability to launch nuclear weapons from sea, land, and air.

A second requirement for deterrence is the ability to inflict *unacceptable damage* on the attacker. There is no hard and fast definition of unacceptable damage. However, *complete* destruction of the attacker is not necessary for deterrence to work. "Unacceptable damage" could simply mean the loss of several major cities. Since "unacceptable damage" is a subjective notion, a country might be deterred from attacking if it believes that only *one* of its major cities could be at risk. This would especially be true of many Third World countries that have only a few population centers as, for example, Baghdad in Iraq.

Third, and just as important to the success of deterrence, is the psychological component. Basically, for deterrence to work, Country A (the attacking country) must *believe* that Country D will actually use its nuclear weapons to retaliate against Country A. This psychological component of deterrence gives the concept a seemingly illogical side effect. Normally, we tend to think that uncertainty in an anarchic world breeds tension among countries. Such tension is believed by many to make war more likely. (Recall how close we came to World War III during the tense days of the Cuban Missile Crisis.) Ironically, however, deterrence can actually be enhanced by psychological uncertainty. As we have said, if Country A believes that country D will retaliate, Country A will be deterred. This also works when Country A is uncertain about Country D's intentions. As the noted international relations theorist Kenneth Waltz put it, if you're not sure that the other side will use nuclear weapons, you won't want to take any chances; knowing that the other side *may* retaliate is enough to deter a potential attacker.[49] In short, maybe Country D won't use nuclear weapons in a counterattack, but maybe it will!

The fourth requirement for a country to deter an opponent is reliable command and control of the nuclear arsenal. In essence, Country D must be able to distinguish between an actual attack by Country A and a false alarm. Moreover, it also must not allow the unauthorized use of nuclear weapons.

One of the great historical questions for the second half of the twentieth century is, Why didn't the United States and the Soviet Union go to war? Most analysts believe that deterrence was the key—in particular, MAD, or *mutually assured destruction*. Both the United States and the Soviet Union had acquired enough nuclear weapons (with second strike capabilities) that an attack on one country would have led inevitably to the destruction of the other. Both sides had enough nuclear weapons to rain down destruction not only on the other but on the world as a whole. Hence, neither country initiated a war against the other.

It is possible to deter a country without assuring the total destruction of the attacker? Yes, because of the second requirement of deterrence: the ability to inflict unacceptable damage. This may explain why we will not see a war between India and Pakistan. Their nuclear arsenals are limited, but even a single warhead exploded in the other's national capital could inflict unacceptable damage. Would India risk a war with Pakistan if India knew that Pakistan could wipe out New Delhi? According to deterrence theory, that is unlikely.

Strengthening International Institutions and International Law

The question Why are there wars? has a parallel question that is just as complex: Why is there peace? The answer may be rooted in deterrence capabilities (nuclear or nonnuclear), but it may also lie in the strength of international law and international institutions. In short, global violence may be reduced thanks to the successful application of international law and the smooth functioning and effectiveness of international institutions. Each of these two methods of limiting global violence offers hope but also has major limitations.

The primary global security institution is, of course, the United Nations. As we saw in Chapter 5, the UN and other IOs can help states cooperate in a variety of ways. They can coordinate the interests of member states and interest groups. They can lower the administrative and political costs of making agreements. They can also promote compliance with (or enforcement of) agreements. However, IOs have not been particularly effective in preventing global violence in East Timor, Chechnya, Kosovo, Rwanda, and elsewhere. In addition, the UN has not been able to reduce tensions between many of the great powers. For example, the Russian-U.S. relationship is tenuous, as is the Chinese-U.S. relationship. Events and decisions made in this decade could turn either Russia or China into a hostile enemy. As long as relations among three of the five permanent members of the UN Security Council remain strained, the effectiveness of international institutions in limiting global violence will be impaired.

Countries that follow international law and accept rulings from international legal bodies gain a positive *reputation* as players who can be trusted. Such trust is important in the seemingly dangerous and anarchic world of international relations. The same may be said of *reciprocity*; good behavior on the part of one country may be reciprocated by another. When countries have good reputations and these countries expect reciprocal treatment, interstate tensions diminish and war becomes less attractive and less likely. If a strong enough consensus exists among countries to adhere to and enforce international laws, the future will likely be brighter than the past. Such an international consensus will, of course, be very difficult to achieve. Historical animosities between or even within countries cannot be eliminated easily. Religious differences are also difficult to resolve. History is full of ruthless leaders who spark wars for reasons of greed and personal aggrandizement. The current political, economic, and social trends do not indicate the disappearance of such leaders in the future.

International laws need compliance, but they also need enforcement. If the international community is unwilling to act, the laws become less effective in stopping violence. As you will see in Chapter 10, there are many examples of a lack of international consensus to enforce laws that members claim to support. Even among allies, getting agreement is difficult, as demonstrated by the U.S. unwillingness to go along with its allies and support the International Criminal Court (which became effective in July 2002), the Kyoto protocol, which deals with environmental destruction, and treaties or protocols banning land mines, torture, and even the death penalty.

The citizens of the twenty-first century, then, are likely to face many challenges. The tools of global violence are more available, more varied, and in some cases more lethal than ever, and the motivations for going to war will likely be similar to those of the past. The desire to prevent global violence in the twenty-first century may galvanize the world's states into forging stronger international institutions and laws, but much may depend on the traditional method of deterring aggression with strong militaries.

What Do We Know About Terrorism and Terrorists?

Terrorism is nothing new to international relations. In recent history, many countries have struggled with the threat of terrorist attacks. Besides the obvious case of the United States as a target, Britain, Spain, France, Columbia, Pakistan, India, Indonesia, Israel, and many other countries are often the targets of terrorism. This section of the chapter will explore types of terrorism, provide a description of who the terrorists are and what motivates them, and suggest ways in which terrorism may be stopped.

Types of Terrorism

Domestic Terrorism
Terrorism whose perpetrators are from the same country as where the terrorist act takes place; "home grown" terrorism.

International Terrorism
Terrorism involving citizens or the territory of more than one country.

In the 1990s Americans were reminded that terrorism need not be international in nature. The bombing of the Federal Building in Oklahoma City, which killed 168 people, was a striking example of "home grown" or **domestic terrorism.** In fact, historically, domestic terrorism has been a bigger problem than **international terrorism**. Domestic terrorism has taken a far higher toll than international terrorism in many countries, including Sri Lanka, India, and Pakistan.[50] In 1980, for example, neo-fascists exploded a bomb in a Bologna train station killing 85 and injuring 200.[51] One of the most serious sites of domestic terrorism has been in Algeria, where the government has been fighting what amounts to a civil war against Islamic extremists who are trying to overthrow the government. In the last ten years alone, almost 80,000 people have lost their lives either through terrorist attacks or government counterattacks.

What we are primarily concerned about in this chapter, however, are terrorist organizations with international reach; that is, terrorism involving citizens or the territory of more than one country. And the nature of international terrorism can be extremely complex. For example, the suicide attack at Israel's Lod Airport in 1972 was not simply an attack involving Palestinian terrorists and Israeli targets. Twenty-six people were massacred and 80 others wounded in an attack by Japanese terrorists who had gone to Israel on behalf of Palestinians to kill passengers on an inbound U.S. flight. Most of the people on the plane happened to be Puerto Rican pilgrims visiting the Holy Land.[52] Another example of the complex nature of international terrorism can be found in Bosnia, where former mujahideen (guerrillas who fought against the Soviet Union in Afghanistan with U.S. support) who originate from Tunisia, Sudan, Algeria, Afghanistan, Egypt, and other Middle Eastern countries have settled. They sometimes obtained Bosnian citizenship by marrying Bosnian women, many of whom were war widows.[53]

Terrorist Tactics

Terrorist tactics are varied, but they generally aim to put terror in the minds of the general public or a specific group of people—especially political authorities. In this respect, one could say that the *main weapon of terrorists is psychological*. The most common method of terrorism is bombing, such as the December 1988 bombing of Pan Am Flight 103 over Lockerbie, Scotland, that killed more than 200 people; the bombing of a tour bus near the ancient pyramids in Egypt in 1993 that killed 2 Egyptians and injured 15 others, including British tourists, Egyptians, and Syrians; or the almost simultaneous bomb explosions in Kenya and Tanzania in 1998. The attack on the U.S. embassy in Kenya killed 12 Americans and 201 Kenyans; several thousand others were wounded. The attack in Dar es Salaam, the capital of Tanzania, killed 11 Tanzanians and wounded more than 75, but no Americans.

Another terrorist tool is *arson* (deliberately setting something on fire), such as the 1993 attack against Turkish diplomatic and commercial facilities in six countries by the Kurdish PKK. Often terrorist groups take hostages with the hope of getting either money or political favors in return. This was the case in 2000, when militant Islamists in the Philippines extracted millions of dollars for their hostages; much of the money came from Muammar Qaddafi of Libya. Kidnapping also has been used to secure the release of fellow terrorists who are already in prison.

Other terrorist tactics include hijacking, sabotage, and threats that sometimes are not even carried out. And as 9/11 showed, terrorism tactics can be quite unusual. Hijackings of commercial jets and the use of jets or even crop dusters and other light planes for terrorism remain a concern not just for the United States but any country deemed a target by terrorists. Terrorists may also resort to biological attacks on the food supply, as did a cult in 1984 which contaminated restaurants in Oregon with salmonella, or the water supplies. The United States feared that an Al Qaeda cell may have been planning such a move (to poison water) in the Seattle Area in the summer of 2002. In addition, terrorists may resort to chemical attacks, as did the Aum Shinrikyo cult in 1995 when it released sarin nerve gas in Tokyo's subway. Oil pipelines have been attacked by terrorists in Columbia, and other such incidents could occur in the future because of the difficulty of protecting such long and remote targets. It is also possible that terrorists will try to disrupt or destroy electrical grids and transportation networks, in addition to the computer networks of their adversaries' businesses, interest groups, or government offices. Another form of terrorism, known as *environmental terrorism*, involves the targeting of hazardous waste disposal and even attacks on medical facilities that address health-related aspects of environmental pollution.

Let's take a closer look at a terrorist group in order to get a more concrete understanding of terrorism and to dispel certain myths about Islam-inspired terrorism. This example will also illustrate some of the aims and tactics of terrorists and show how governments react to those tactics.

One of the longest-lived terrorist organizations operates in Western Europe. **Basque Fatherland and Liberty** (Euskadi Ta Askatasuna or **ETA**) was founded in Spain in 1959 during the dictatorship of Francisco Franco. Its aims are to create an independent state in the Basque region of Spain and to unite with Basque-speaking counties (départements) in southwestern France. Figure 9.1 shows where roughly 2.5 million Basque people live. To achieve its objective, ETA has carried out bombings, assassinations, kidnappings, extortion, and other terrorist activities. Among its bombing targets have been key political figures in the Spanish

Basque Fatherland and Liberty (ETA)
A terrorist organization based primarily in Spain that seeks an independent state for the Basque regions of Spain and France.

FIGURE 9.1
Northern Spain and Southern France Highlighting the Basque Region

SOURCE: The Economist, March 18, 2000, p. 52.

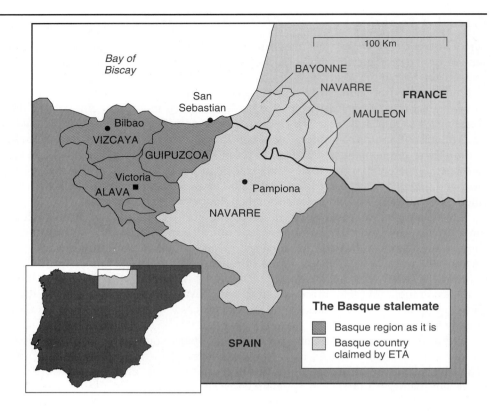

government as well as department stores, French car dealerships, and a McDonald's restaurant construction site, to name a few. ETA has also targeted Spain's tourist industry, which accounts for more than 10 percent of Spain's economy.[54] ETA has also been linked to violent organizations across Europe and in Algeria, Afghanistan, and Latin America. In addition, it has limited ties to a militant separatist group in Brittany, France. ETA is responsible for killing at least 835 people since it began its violent campaign in 1968.[55]

The Spanish government's response to ETA has been varied, including extradition of ETA fugitives from other countries, attacking ETA's financial infrastructure, and shutting down businesses with ETA involvement.[56] In the 1980s the Spanish government waged what has been called a "dirty war" against ETA members. The government established a secret organization designed to carry out assassinations and kidnappings in order to destroy ETA. The "death squads" that were created, however, were beyond full parliamentary oversight. Eventually, the government came under sharp domestic and international criticism, and 14 government officials were ultimately indicted for their part, including then Prime Minister Felipe Gonzalez (who was later cleared).[57]

In the history of ETA, 1998 seemed like a pivotal year. ETA was responsible for the deaths of at least six persons, but—under pressure on many fronts—the organization decided to call a cease-fire in November. In return, Spanish Prime Minister José María Aznar said he would even be ready to include ETA's political allies in discussions in a new peace process.[58] In addition, the Spanish government offered some relief for 530 ETA prisoners in Spanish jails and about one thousand exiles.[59]

THE VIEW FROM Saudi Arabia, Afghanistan, Pakistan, and Elsewhere

A Profile of Osama bin Laden

Since the end of 2001, no one has been sure of Osama bin Laden's location—or even if he is alive or dead. Nevertheless, he remains an important figure—continuing to be on the world's most wanted list, and heavily influencing events in countries as geographically dispersed as Pakistan, Saudi Arabia, Germany, Sudan, the United States, and Indonesia. Bin Laden was born in 1957, the seventh son among 50 brothers and sisters. He has 3 wives and 13 children. He is roughly 6-feet 5-inches tall and is believed to be suffering from kidney and liver disease. Bin Laden was a citizen of Saudi Arabia until the country revoked his citizenship in 1996, the same year he declared war on the U.S. in a *fatwa*. Bin Laden came from a large, wealthy family that has close ties to the Saudi royal family. His father, Mohammed Awad bin Laden, created the family's wealth in the construction industry.

Osama bin Laden received a degree in public administration in 1981 from King Abdul-Aziz University. In the 1980s, he was one of many mujahideen fighters (backed, in part, by the United States) who helped throw the Soviet Union out of Afghanistan. With the Soviet withdrawal in 1989, bin Laden set his sights elsewhere. From 1991 to 1992 during the Gulf War, bin Laden increasingly saw the United States as enemy number one. He vehemently opposed the presence of "infidel" American troops (there to deter an Iraqi invasion) on Saudi Arabian soil.

Bin Laden and Al Qaeda are linked to terrorist activity in Bosnia, Chechnya, Sudan, Yemen, Saudi Arabia, Egypt, Libya, Pakistan, and the Philippines, and he is wanted for the 1998 bombings of two American embassies (in Tanzania and Kenya), and, of course, for the 9/11 attacks.[60]

This anticipated peaceful era in Basque-Spanish relations fell apart completely after 14 months. In January 2000, ETA ended the cease-fire with a bomb explosion that killed an army officer. Two days later about a million people in Madrid protested against the attack. But another car bomb exploded in late February 2000, killing two people. Since then, ETA's new wave of terrorist attacks have spread throughout Spain. In September 2000 the Spanish government took another major step aimed at clamping down on ETA. Spanish authorities raided offices of suspected ETA supporters and arrested several key ETA members in Spain and France in a joint operation with the French police. In 2002, the Spanish government banned the Batasuna political party, a Basque nationalist party that seeks independence but which the Spanish government says has too many close ties to ETA. The central problem remains, however: the militant Basque nationalists want independence, while mainstream Spanish political leaders want the regions to remain a part of Spain.

Why Terrorists Stop Terrorizing

The scope of terrorist group activities varies from place to place and from time to time—as do the reasons why terrorist activities cease. In the late 1990s, at least in some places, terrorist activities declined for a variety of reasons. For example, many terrorist groups in the post–World War II era were Marxist,

Leninist, and Maoist inspired. Examples include the Red Army Faction (Germany), 17 November (Greece), the Red Brigades (Italy), the Red Army (Japan), and the Shining Path (Peru). With the collapse of the Soviet Union, however, such groups lost much popular support, and communist-oriented governments that once sponsored them were no longer around to provide financial or military support. In addition, in some instances, terrorist groups realized that their terror campaigns proved less effective than negotiations with established political authorities.

As we have seen, ETA declared a cease-fire on September 16, 1998, and began negotiations with the Spanish central government. This action was prompted by several factors. First, there was public outrage throughout Spain over the ETA assassinations of several local Spanish officials earlier in 1998. Second, the Spanish government had successfully infiltrated and dismantled several ETA "commandos." Third, the Spanish government was willing to grant some (but limited) powers to a Basque regional government. Finally, strong French legal pressure—brought about by ETA attacks in France—also eroded the ETA's support base in neighboring French provinces.[61] During the cease-fire, France collaborated with Spanish authorities to track down and arrest many ETA members. Unfortunately as we saw earlier, ETA relaunched its terrorist campaign; the above measures do not appear to have been strong enough to squelch ETA once and for all.

Another example of terrorists who chose to stop terrorizing, at least for the time being, comes from Great Britain. In Northern Ireland (a part of Britain, not the Republic of Ireland), the Catholic and Protestant communities, which had been fighting for two centuries, made a major commitment to end the violence by signing the Good Friday Accord in 1998. Under the leadership of the British and Irish governments, both communities and the political parties that represented them agreed to compromises that would create new, local governmental institutions for resolving conflicts. These compromises also mean turning away from terrorism as an accepted political instrument. In support of the peace process, most—but not all—paramilitary terrorist groups on both sides agreed to a cease-fire. The issue of "decommissioning" (destroying or turning in) the IRA's weaponry and bombs proved the major sticking point.[62] Nevertheless, motivating Catholic terrorist groups to choose more peaceful tactics was the growing public distaste for their violent attacks on innocent civilians. In addition, the British government had negotiated a shifting of powers away from London to Northern Ireland as part of the "devolution" process.

Implementing strong preventive mechanisms can also deter terrorists. For example, many ideas considered radical, politically impractical, or simply unnecessary before 9/11, are now becoming realities. The United States, for instance, has taken many steps to prevent and react to terrorist attacks, including the following:

- reorganizing bureaucracies that learn about, prevent, and respond to terrorist attacks (e.g., creating the Department of Homeland Security and overhauling the FBI and CIA, which failed to "connect the dots" of information that could have prevented the 9/11 attacks
- improving the ability of health care personnel to respond to large-scale attacks involving conventional, biological (e.g., smallpox), and chemical weapons (e.g., sarin gas)
- beefing up airport security

- shutting off terrorist organizations' funding sources from legal and illegal economic activities

Other countries are also hoping to prevent future terrorist attacks. Pakistan, for example, has taken a much tougher position with respect to militant Islamic groups within the country and is actively helping the United States and other countries track down Al Qaeda and former Taliban fighters.

Building on the above examples, we can begin to make a list of major reasons why terrorist groups stop terrorizing.

1. Poor leadership or internal power struggles can render a terrorist organization less effective or completely ineffective. Internal divisions, for example, helped weaken the New People's Army in the Philippines.
2. Domestic or international financial, logistical, or political support can decline significantly or be cut off completely. The lack of financial resources, in particular, makes it more difficult to train and transport terrorists, to acquire weapons, and so on.
3. The public may overwhelmingly oppose the tactics or the aims of terrorist organizations. This public opposition leads to pressure on governmental authorities to take action against terrorists.
4. Counter terrorist measures can succeed. Terrorist groups may be exhausted by government authorities through legal and sometimes extralegal means. Nonviolent antiterrorist measures can include improved intelligence, extradition, freezing terrorist assets, closing businesses linked to terrorists, closing newspapers that support terrorist organizations, and infiltration of terrorist groups. Some countries, such as Italy, also make it illegal to pay ransom for hostages.
5. Some of the terrorists' demands can be met. Such a situation can splinter a terrorist organization, with some members ceasing activities while others continue to wage their campaign of terror. A good example of this is the emergence of an independent Armenian state in 1991. Some Armenians, notably those left out of the new state of Nagorno Karabakh, started to fight for their independence, but international terrorism virtually ceased to exist.
6. All of the terrorists' demands can be met. In this situation, terrorist groups achieve their political aims, and thus no longer perceive the need to carry out terrorist activities.

International Control of Terrorism

Efforts at controlling terrorist organizations are still dominated by national governments. International forms of control include country-to-country cooperation as well as multilateral cooperation, such as through the international police agency known as **Interpol.** Unfortunately, Interpol's effectiveness is limited by several factors. First, although it maintains a data bank on criminal activity around the world, it is poorly funded and understaffed. Second, it is generally not supposed to get involved in political problems—and most international terrorist activities are highly political. The European Union has developed a European police force **(Europol)** with similar aims. However, it will be years before Europol has the political, technical, and financial support needed to tackle not only organized crime but terrorism as well. Despite the limited effectiveness of concerted international control of terrorism, the need certainly exists.

Interpol
An international police force that maintains a data bank on criminal activity around the world. It also fosters country-to-country and multilateral cooperation.

Europol
A European-wide police force that fosters country-to-country cooperation as well as multilateral cooperation.

Airline Passengers Carry Many Items That Can Be Used as Weapons: The photo, taken a week after the September 11, 2001, terrorist attacks, displays several items confiscated at the Los Angeles International Airport. In the weeks following 9/11, more than 5,000 items a day were seized from carry-on bags at the airport as tightened security measures were put in place.

Future Terrorist Threats

Terrorists pose many kinds of threats to countries around the world. Car bombings, kidnapping, suicide bombings, the use of radiological bombs, and cyber attacks on vital economic, administrative, and military computer networks are just a few. It is unclear how well prepared countries are to face the terrorist challenge, although many signs suggest that much needs to be done. One indicator of the lack of government control of dangerous material comes from a 2001 study by the International Atomic Energy Agency, which reported 175 cases of illegal trafficking in nuclear materials since 1993.[63] A 1999 study commissioned by the U.S. government to look into the threats posed by the proliferation of weapons of mass destruction around the world found that one of the most dangerous developments is the continued disintegration of Russia as a civil society. The commission also found that the U.S. government is poorly organized to combat the proliferation of such weapons. The report concludes that the United States lacks the necessary technology to protect soldiers from attacks involving such weapons. Of the thousands of possible chemical and biological threats, only a few can be detected by sensors, which have a very limited range.[64] An audit of both the Energy Department and Nuclear Regulatory Commission found that neither agency was keeping accurate inventory of nuclear materials loaned out for domestic research.[65]

As 9/11 showed, future terrorist threats could involve a variety of unexpected methods. For example, in October 2001, a drunken man with an extensive criminal background took a high-powered rifle and fired several shots at the Trans-Alaska pipeline. One shot punctured the pipeline's protective layer of galvanized steel and four inches of insulation, spilling over 285,000 gallons of oil. The pipeline, the most important link in the U.S. domestic oil network, is 800 miles long with about half of it above ground on open public land and thus difficult to protect.[66] In November 2001, U.S. Attorney General John Ashcroft warned about potential terrorist attacks on natural gas pipelines. Thousands of gas pipelines cross the United States and Canada, although most of them are buried.[67]

Another source of concern is the many ways weapons or terrorists might be smuggled into the target country. For example, in 2000 alone, 489 million people, 127 million passenger vehicles, 11.6 million maritime containers, 11.5 million trucks, 2.2 million railroad cars, 829,000 planes, and 211,000 vessels passed through U.S. border inspection systems.[68] The magnitude of the trade in goods and the mobility of people make it impossible to track everything. Roughly 18 million shipping containers enter U.S. ports in shiploads of up to 8,000 at a time.[69] In October 2001, an Al Qaeda suspect was found inside a Canada-bound container in an Italian port. The container had arrived from Egypt, and the man inside it was equipped with a laptop computer, a mobile phone, a bed, and food and water for the voyage to Halifax.[70] In March 2002 alone, some 25 Middle Eastern men were smuggled into the United States in shipping containers. According to one estimate, it takes five inspectors three hours to conduct a physical examination of a loaded 40-foot container or an 18-wheel truck, making it almost impossible to inspect everything.[71]

Other vulnerabilities exist as well. Less than one per cent of U.S. imported foods are tested by government authorities at the Food and Drug Administration (FDA). The Bush Administration proposed funding increases for both the FDA and the Department of Health and Human Services, but critics believe that the resource allocations to these organizations will still be inadequate to the task. The U.S. postal system—the vehicle for transporting anthrax in 2001—remains questionably secure. Yet another fear is that terrorists might strike some of the 15,000 chemical plants and storage sites that handle hazardous chemicals in the United States. According to a study by the Environmental Protection Agency, at least 123 chemical plants keep amounts of toxic chemicals that, if released, could form deadly vapor clouds that would put more than a million people at risk.[72] Even underground tunnels are a concern. In the past ten years, U.S. official discovered at least 16 tunnels along the U.S.-Mexican border. Five of these were started after the 9/11 terrorist attacks.[73] The tunnels were used primarily to smuggle drugs, but terrorists might use this method as well.

So, in terms of terrorist activities, what will we see in the twenty-first century? First, we can unfortunately be pretty sure that terrorism will play its part. Both old and new methods are available to terrorists with the motivation, money, and organizational skill to carry out attacks. Terrorists are likely to find ways of using "old" technology in new ways, just as they did for 9/11. For example, terrorists might use a "dirty" nuclear bomb which is believed to be easier to build and use than an actual nuclear bomb. Cyber terrorist attacks are also increasingly viewed as a threat to all countries, especially those heavily dependent on the Internet. Computer hacking can cause millions of dollars damage, shut down vital government websites, power grids, and so on.

The tentative efforts by the United States and other countries to prepare for future terrorist attacks have become significant efforts since 9/11. As we described earlier, many ideas considered radical, politically impractical, or simply unnecessary before 9/11 are now turning into reality.

But as long as potential terrorists believe that political authorities will yield to their pressure, terrorism will persist.

CHAPTER SUMMARY

What Are the Causes of War?

- Dominating the attention of those who study international relations is the vexing question of why there are wars. We concluded that wars are caused by many factors, and that not all wars are caused by the same things. These factors include the desire for territorial gain and independence, economic causes, ideology, psychological causes, ethnic and religious differences, domestic political causes, misperception, and the structure of the international system.

- Immediate causes of war are the short-term factors that give spark to the outbreak of war. Underlying causes of war are the long-term trends that create tension between countries.

What Are the Weapons of War?

- Weapons of mass destruction do not discriminate between soldier and civilian. Nuclear, biological, and chemical weapons can all be weapons of mass destruction.

- Weapons that are not weapons of mass destruction are called conventional weapons. Some conventional weapons are extremely dangerous. Land mines, for example, pose the greatest threat to the largest number of people on a day-to-day basis.

- New weapons inspired by high-tech advances are changing the face of warfare. These include unmanned aerial vehicles such as the Predator, lasers weapons that can inflict temporary or permanent blindness, and high-powered microwaves that can melt down electronic systems.

Why Are There So Many Weapons and Can They Be Controlled?

- The global demand for weapons has remained robust in the post–Cold War era. Countries want to be well armed for many reasons, including as preparation for waging offensive or defensive war. Countries also acquire weapons to deter potential attackers.

- The supply of weapons is driven in part because countries want weapons for the foreign policy reasons just noted. But the arms business is also very lucrative, attracting profit-seeking companies from around the world and thus contributes to supply.

How Can Global Violence Be Controlled?

- Arms control agreements attempt to stem the flow of weapons—either for two countries or many. Structural arms control focuses on numbers of weapons. Operational, or functional, arms control involves keeping track of weapons and notifying the "other side" of military training exercises, new deployments for defensive reasons, and other *confidence-building* measures.

- Countries may be dissuaded from starting a war because of deterrence. International institutions like the UN can help make countries see the merits of cooperation and, at the same time, provide a military response to those who engage in aggressive activities. Controlling global violence has never been easy. Deterrence can fail, and both international institutions and international law may be ignored by determined, aggressive countries.

What Do We Know About Terrorism and Terrorists?

- The short-term aim of terrorists is to inflict terror into a civilian population. Their longer-term objectives are almost always political in nature. This helps distinguish terrorists from (common) criminals.

- International terrorist organizations have been, and will continue to be, influential actors in the politics of many countries, as in the case of religious-inspired attacks in Northern Ireland, suicide bombers in Israel, ETA in Spain, and Al Qaeda in many parts of the world.

- All kinds of weapons, including weapons of mass destruction, appear to be easier to acquire, handle, and deliver than ever before. Future terrorist attacks could be on a massive scale.

ENDNOTES

[1]Jack Levy, "Theories of General War," *World Politics* vol. 37, No. 2 (April 1985), p. 344.

[2]American Battle Monuments Commission, *http://www.abmc.gov/abmc4.htm*.

[3]Cambodia Genocide Program, Yale University, *http://www.yale.edu/cgp/*.

[4]John F. Guilmartin Jr. and Kelly Evans-Pfeifer, "Casualties," in Stanley I. Kutler, ed. *Encyclopedia of the Vietnam War* (New York: Charles Scriber's Sons, 1996), pp. 103–104.

[5]"Getting There Safely," *Consumer Reports*, vol. 63, no. 4, April 1998, pp. 23–25; "42,116 die on highways in 2001; alcohol linked to 35% of deaths," *New York Times*, August 8, 2002; The United Nations quoted in *Time*, December 28, 1998, p. 59; "Highway Deaths Hold Steady," *Associated Press*, October 4, 2000; The European Conference of Ministers of Transport, as reported in "Please slow down," *The Economist*, February 9, 2002.

[6]*Forum: War, Money and Survival* (Geneva: International Committee of the Red Cross, March 2000).

[7]John G. Stoessinger. *Why Nations Go to War*, 7th ed. (New York: St. Martin's Press, 1998).

[8]Rick Atkinson, *Crusade: The Untold Story of the Persian Gulf War* (Boston: Houghlin Mifflin Company, 1993).

[9]John G. Stoessinger, *Why Nations Go to War*, p. 187.

[10]Richard Ned Lebow, *Between Peace and War* (Baltimore: The Johns Hopkins University Press, 1981), pp. 1–7.

[11]*The Wall Street Journal*, October 12, 1993, p.A 14.

[12]Alexander Nicoll, "Robot weapons convince skeptics," *Financial Times*, February 5, 2002.

[13]"Nothing's perfect," *The Economist*, November 10, 2001.

[14]John Hersey, *Hiroshima* (New York: A. A. Knopf, 1946), pp. 24, 56.

[15]Peter Finn, "Experts urge security at nuclear facilities," *The Washington Post*, November 3, 2001.

[16]Clive Cookson, "Security warning on radioactive materials," *Financial Times*, June 26, 2002.

[17]Ronald M. Atlas, "Combating the threat of biowarfare and bioterrorism," *Bioscience*, June 1999; pp. 465–477, see Table 2.

[18]See Christine Gosden, "Why I Went, What I Saw," *The Washington Post*, March 11, 1998; the State Department position from Richard Boucher, Press Statement: Anniversary of the Halabja Massacre." March 16, 2001, *http://www.state.gov/r/pa/prs/ps/2001/1322.htm*, and "Iraq's Weapons of Mass Destruction: A Net Assessment," International Institute for Strategic Studies, *www.iiss.org*, Sept. 9, 2002.

[19]Clive Cookson, "Hidden horror of Saddam's germ arsenal," *Financial Times*, February 12, 1998.

[20]Andrew Jack, "Warning of Soviet chemical weapons risk," *Financial Times*, May 24, 2002.

[21]Vladimir Isachenkov, "U.S., Russia working to protect bioweapons," *Associated Press*, May 28, 2002.

[22]"Anthrax effect depends on exposure," *Los Angeles Times*, October 13, 2001.

[23]"Leahy says anthrax letter could have killed 100,000," *Press Democrat News Services*, November 26, 2001.

[24]Alexander Nicoll, "Bioweapons set to dominate," *Financial Times*, July 10, 2002.

[25]Center for Civilian Biodefense Studies at John Hopkins University, Texas Department of Health, and the U.S. General Accounting Office. See also "Bioterror threats," *Knight Ridder Newspapers*, October 10, 2001.

[26]Ibid.

[27]Susan Oki, "The Smallpox Tradeoff," *The Washington Post National Weekly Edition*, May 13, 2002.

[28]Center for Civilian Biodefense Studies 2nd *Knight Ridder*, "Bioterror threats."

[29]Clive Cookson, "Hidden horror."

[30]Anjetta McQueen, "States lack bioterrorism plans," *Associated Press*, October 10, 2001.

[31]Alexander Nicoll, "US deploys old airborne toys—and tries some new ones," *Financial Times*, November 7, 2001.

[32]"Satellites and horsemen," *The Economist*, March 9, 2002. The daisy cutter is succeeded by the MOAB bomb.

[33]"A survey of the defence industry," *The Economist*, July 20, 2002.

[34]See, for example, Michael T. Klare, "The New Arms Race: Light Weapons and International Security," *Current History*, April 1997, pp. 173–178.

[35]Carl T. Hall, "Pentagon examines uses for biotech," *San Francisco Chronicle*, June 23, 2001.

[36]Jeff Nesmith, "Pentagon Recruiting Bees, Cockroaches and Wasps," *The Times-Picayune*, July 25, 1999, p. A32.

[37]Brochure from Campaign for a Landmine Free World, *http://www.vvaf.org*, 1998.

[38]Charles Clover, "Deadly race to clear Afghanistan of mines," Financial Times, August 6, 2002.

[39]Paul Donovan, "Making a killing," *The Guardian* (London), February 7, 2001.

[40]"639 million guns surveyed," *Press Democrat News Services*, June 30, 2002.

[41]On the impact of light weapons sales, see Michael T. Klare, "The New Arms Race: Light Weapons and International Security," *Current History*, April 1997, pp. 173–178.

[42]Seyom Brown, *The Causes and Prevention of War*, 2nd ed., (New York: St. Martin's Press, 1994), pp. 203–205.

[43]Jordan Singer, "A Watchful Eye: Monitoring the Conventional Arms Trade," *Harvard International Review*, Winter 1995/6, pp. 64–65, 83–84.

[44]Sha Zukang, "Thoughts on Non-Proliferation," *Presidents & Prime Ministers*, vol. 8, no. 2 (March 1999), p. 10.

[45]The following discussion borrows generously from Kenneth Waltz and Scott D. Sagan, *The Spread of Nuclear Weapons: A Debate* (New York: W. W. Norton and Company, 1995), pp. 80–85.

[46]CNN on line at *http://cnn.com/SPECIALS/cold.war/experience/the.bomb/*. CNN cites the following sources for this information: The U.S. Defense Department; *Arkansas Democrat Gazette*, September 20, 1981; Stephen Schwartz, letter to the editor, *Commentary*, January 1997.

[47]*Newsweek*, June 28, 1999, p. 4.

[48]Kenneth N. Waltz in Scott D. Sagan and Kenneth N. Waltz *The Spread of Nuclear Weapons*, pp. 20–29.

[49]Ibid.

[50]As reported in Tim Weiner, "Terrorism's Worldwide Toll Was High in 1996, U.S. Report Says," *The New York Times*, May 1, 1997.

[51]"Finding common cause," *Financial Times*, September 21, 2001.

[52]Brian Michael Jenkins, "Forward," in Ian O. Lesser et al., *Countering the New Terrorism* (Santa Monica, CA: The Rand Corporation, 1999), p. vi.

[53]R. Jeffrey Smith, "A Bosnian Village's Terrorist Ties," *The Washington Post*, March 11, 2000.

[54]Joshua Levitt, "Anti-Eta fight stepped up after Salou bombing," *Financial Times*, August 20, 2001.

[55]"Finding common cause," *Financial Times*.

[56]US State Department, "Patterns of Global Terrorism: 1998." *http://www.state.gov*

[57]"Spanish Court Clears Leader in 'Dirty War,' " *The New York Times*, November 6, 1996, p. A26.

[58]David White, "Eta ready for talks with Spanish government," *Financial Times*, December 23, 1998.

[59]U.S. State Department, "Patterns of Global Terrorism: 1998."

[60]Kathy Gannon, "Bin Laden Reportedly Ailing," *Associated Press*, March 25, 2000; PBS Online and WGBH/Frontline, 2001, *http://www.pbs.org/wgbh/pages/frontline/shows/binladen/who/bio.html*; the U.S. Department of State, 2002, *http://www2.fbi.gov/mostwant/topten/fugitives/laden.htm*, and Mark Huband, "Bin Laden's martyrs for the cause," *Financial Times*, November 28, 2001.

[61]U.S. State Department, "Patterns of Global Terrorism: 1998."

[62]Ibid.

[63]Peter Finn, "Experts urge security at nuclear facilities," *The Washington Post*, November 3, 2001.

[64]"U.S. ill-prepared for weapons proliferation, commission warns," *The Baltimore Sun*, July 9, 1999.

[65]John Heilprin, "Nuke inventory flaws revealed," *Associated Press*, November 7, 2001.

[66]Tim Woolston, spokesman for the Alyeska Pipeline Service Co., reported that the pipeline had been shot more than 50 times in the past, but never seriously enough to create an oil spill. See Maureen Clark, "Alaska pipeline continues to spew oil," *Associated Press*, October 6, 2001; Kim Murphy, "Alaska pipeline poses wide-ranging security risk," *New York Times*, October 14, 2001; and Maureen Clark, "Clamp slows leak in Alaska pipeline," *Associated Press*, October 7, 2001.

[67]Thirty interstate gas pipelines carry 90 percent of the natural gas transported, according to the Interstate Natural Gas Association of America. See H. Josef Hebert, "FBI puts U.S. oil, gas industry on alert," *Associated Press*, November 27, 2001.

[68]Stephen E. Flynn, "America the Vulnerable," *Foreign Affairs*, vol. 81, No. 1, January/February 2002, p. 64.

[69]"The Trojan box," *The Economist*, February 9, 2002.

[70]Ibid.

[71]See Stephen E. Flynn, "America the Vulnerable," p. 64; and James P. Pinkerton, "Ship ahoy, what evil lies in the cargo holds," *Newsday*, May 28, 2002.

[72]Eric Pianin, "Vulnerability of chemical plants causes worry," *Washington Post*, August 6, 2002.

[73]Julie Watson, "Tunnels along U.S.-Mexico border vex authorities," *Associated Press*, May 13, 2002.

CASE STUDY

Youth Turns to Terrorism

In the fall of 2001, 28-year-old Kamel Daoudi was arrested in England on suspicion that he was part of a plot by Al Qaeda to blow up the American Embassy in Paris. The Algerian-born computer specialist spent most of his life in France, where his hatred toward France in particular and the West in general solidified. Daoudi's experiences in France eventually led him to choose the path of terrorism. From his cell, Daoudi wrote three essays about his middle-class childhood, his turn to Islam, and his political radicalization. This case study begins with a brief background of France and Algeria and then presents excerpts from Daoudi's essays. The excerpts will give the reader insights into the mindset of a young, educated Arab who calls himself a terrorist, even though he denies involvement in any terrorist plot.

Background on France and Algeria

Life for Algerian descendents living in France can be difficult. The North African country of Algeria was once a colony of France until a bloody war of independence concluded in the early 1960s with an independent Algeria. But during the colonial period and the troubled years after the war, native Algerians moved in large numbers to France, seeking a shield from political turmoil but more often for economic opportunity. The urge to move to France persisted even into the 1990s as the Algerian government canceled democratic elections in 1992 out of fear that militant Muslims would gain control of the country through popular elections. French treatment of Algerian immigrants, as well as immigrations from other former French colonies in Northern and Sub-Saharan Africa, ran the spectrum from initial government support (France needed workers in the economic boom years following World War II) to racial hatred by various segments of French society. While many immigrants have adapted to French society and consider themselves—and are accepted as—fully French, many immigrants and their descendents suffer from both overt and subtle discrimination. Due in part to poor economic circumstances upon arrival, immigrants from North Africa often live in the worse parts of French cities. And Muslims in French society have had a harder time assimilating into French culture than other groups. Many non-Muslim French citizens, whose views are typified by far-right political parties such as the National Front,

blame the mostly Arab immigrants for the ills afflicting French society, especially crime. It is in this context that Kamel Daoudi found himself for most of his life.

Portrait of the Arab as a Young Radical

Childhood Experiences

Allah the Great says in the Koran that neither Jews nor Christians will ever be satisfied with you until you follow their religion. But Allah's way is the true way . . . This is without a doubt the verse of the Koran that sums up . . . the 28 years of my life.

My name is Kamel Daoudi. My first name means perfection in Arabic. My last name means coming from the tribe of the sons of David. I was born in Algeria on the third of August 1974. . . . My father was working in France to meet the needs of his large family . . . I only saw my father in the summer when he managed to save enough to pay for a ticket to take the boat or plane so that he could come and see my mother, his mother and me and leave us a bit of money. . . .

My childhood, in spite of my poor mother's poverty, was a happy one. I was spoiled by my maternal uncles and aunts who used to take me with them to the colorful sunny bazaars in the little town and bought me sweets and tried to make up for my father's absence. . . . In the summer of 1979, when I was about to turn 5, my father came to get us—my mother, my brother, who is two years younger than I, and myself—to take us to France . . . I was condemned to be my father's foot soldier while he was working. I was alternately an interpreter, guide and accountant for my poor mother, who had a great deal of trouble getting used to this new barbarian language. . . . Very early on I had adult responsibilities, which literally ate into my childhood, which I wanted to live in the same way as other children.

Mr. Daoudi describes how his father, a hospital worker, pushed him to excel in school and beat him with a wooden paddle when he failed to do so. During this period, his family was able to move from a working-class section of Paris to a middle-class neighborhood on the Left Bank.

There I started to discover the heart of Paris and real Parisians. My time was spent between school and play in the Jardin des Plantes. In school I was a brilliant student and I was often the only Arab in the class. People were jealous of me because of my good grades but they made fun of me for the way I acted and for my excessive modesty in the eyes of the French children. They made jokes about my first name. . . .

In junior high school I wanted to be Indiana Jones. I decided to learn as many languages as possible—English, then Spanish. I took courses in Arabic. . . . Then I went to senior high where I continued with Latin and also learned ancient Greek. At the end of 11th grade I gave up my adolescent dream to become an anthropologist or paleontologist. I knew that my country of origin had a greater need for engineers or doctors than Indiana Joneses. So I decided to make another dream come true. I wanted to be a pilot on a fighter plane. But I knew that my [poor] eyesight would never allow this. . . . So I decided to become an aeronautical engineer.

University and Paris Experiences

In 1992, while Mr. Daoudi says he was studying science and engineering at the University of Paris, the Algerian government canceled elections that the main Islamist party was poised to win. That set off a violent struggle between the government security forces and armed Islamic groups:

Just as I came close to achieving my dream I started to worry about religious and political questions. The context of the time was the war in Algeria, where they were about to set up a regime based on Islamic law.

The West hated us because we were Arabs and Muslims. France did everything possible to ensure than Algeria would not be an Islamic state. It backed an illegitimate and profoundly one-sided regime by sending weapons, helicopters and even the Foreign Legion (not many people know about that). The mas-

sacres committed by the Algerian army were the last straw for me. I could no longer study serenely. . . .

All of the pressure that had been put on me during my school years so that I would succeed at any price suddenly transformed itself into energy to challenge radically my environment and my father. . . . From that moment on I didn't want anything to do with the West.

Mr. Daoudi says he was further radicalized when his family was evicted from their apartment and had to move to a poor suburb of Paris:

That's where I became aware of the abominable social treatment given to all of those potential "myselves" who had been conditioned to become sub-citizens just good for paying pensions for the real French when the French age pyramid starts getting thin at the base. . . .

Making the Decision to Become a Terrorist

There were only two choices left for me, either to sink into a deep depression, and I did for more than six months at the end my second year at university, or to react by taking part in the universal struggle against this overwhelming unjust cynicism.

So I reviewed everything that I had learned and put all of my knowledge into a new perspective. I then understood that the only person worth devoting my life to was Allah. . . . Everything suddenly became clear to me and I understood why Abraham went into exile, why Moses rebelled against the Pharoah, why Jesus was spat upon and why Muhammad said, "I came with the sword on judgment day." My battle was and will be to eradicate all powers that are opposed to the law of Allah, the most high, whatever the price may be, because only our creator has the power to make laws and any system based on the laws of men is artifice and lies.

This glorious battle will not stop until the law of Allah has been re-established and applied by a just and honest caliph.

Empowered by his new perspective, Mr. Daoudi began to re-educate himself: "I had to succeed by acquiring enough political tools so that I could know my enemy well and fight back. I discovered the great contemporary writers of political Islam. . . . I read them in French or in English because my Arabic wasn't good enough. I knew that a victory of Islam over the West was possible.

I decided to go to Algiers in the middle of the war, with the curfew and the shooting that was taking place. For four months I saw the situation with my own eyes and I experienced the roadblocks. . . . and the intervention of the Algerian military security forces. Had it not been for my belief that armed groups had already been infiltrated by the Algerian security services, I would probably [have] joined up with the partisans who wanted to introduce Islamic law in Algeria.

France was a major protagonist in this conflict. . . . I could not accept the fact that the former colonial power was continuing to control my country's destiny when so many women, children and men had been tortured, massacred, raped and assassinated. . . .

The Algerian war, the Bosnian war, the gulf war, Kosovo, Afghanistan, Palestine, Lebanon—all of these events strengthen my conviction that the Judeo-Christian community influenced by atheism has a visceral hatred of the community of Muhammad. . . . For all these reasons and because of all these events which have left indelible wounds, I went over to the forces of the "dark side." . . .

I got married, thinking that marriage would regenerate me and make me more stable. But this was a mistake that made me want to escape the Machiavellian social trap that was closing in on me. My ex-wife, who I had met through an American chat room, . . . didn't live up to my dreams. In spite of her many qualities, she did not have . . . a taste for strong sensation and adventure. Seeing that my idea of life was not the same as hers I decided to leave her, leaving her everything I could.

Mr. Daoudi concludes his story by proudly accepting the label of terrorist: "My ideological commitment is total and the reward of glory for this relentless battle is to be called a terrorist. I accept the name of terrorist if it is used to mean that I terrorize a one-sided system of iniquitous power and a perversity that comes in many forms."

"I have never terrorized innocent individuals and I will never do so. But I will fight any form of injustice and those who support it. My fight will only end in my death or in my madness."

QUESTIONS

Check Your Understanding

1. Describe the positive aspects of Daoudi's childhood.
2. What experiences in Daoudi's life served to radicalize him?

Analyze the Issues

3. What is Daoudi's perception of France and of the French people? What is his perception of the West in general?
4. What is the role of religion in Daoudi's life?
5. How do the individual, state, and international system levels of analysis help explain Daoudi's turn to terrorism?
6. Given the decentralizing forces at work in world politics—including ethnic conflict and the fragmentation or failure of states—immigration from troubled regions of the world to the more stable and wealthy regions (e.g., Europe) is going to continue. Will this lead to more Kamel Daoudi's? If so, can anything be done?
7. Do you agree with the definition of "terrorism" in the last two paragraphs of the case? Explain.

FOR FURTHER INFORMATION

To find out more about Algerian, French, and Islamic terrorism, consult the following sources:

Africa Studies Quarterly (online): *http://web.africa.ufl.edu/asq*

Aussaresses, Paul. *The Battle of the Casbah: Terrorism and Counter-Terrorism in Algeria 1955–1957* (Enigma Books, August 2002).

Cornell University's Middle East and Islamic Studies web site devoted to Algeria: *http://www.library.cornell.edu/colldev/mideast/algeria.htm*

The North Africa Journal (various issues). The online version is located at *http://www.north-africa.com/one.htm*

Global Justice: Women, Poverty, and Human Rights

KEY QUESTIONS RAISED IN THIS CHAPTER

1. What do we mean when we talk about global justice and human rights?

2. What is the relationship between the history of women, global justice, and human rights?

3. How do feminist theories of international relations explain the relationship between discrimination against women, global justice, and human rights?

4. What is the relationship between poverty, global justice, and human rights?

5. How has the international community responded to state violations of global justice and human rights?

In India, husbands and mothers-in-law sometimes burn women if they do not give birth to a boy child or if their dowry is judged too small.[1] In China, women sometimes kill their girl children at birth or abandon them on the steps of orphanages, because China's one-child policy permits only one child per family, and most families want boys. In Iran and Afghanistan, women can be beaten to death because their dress—known as a burka, and legally required to cover them from head to toe—may be too short. In Nigeria a young divorced woman who gave birth to a child out of wedlock is appealing a sentence that she be stoned to death. It is not uncommon for husbands and neighbors to participate in the stoning to death of a woman whose husband has tired of her and falsely accuses her of adultery.[2] All over Asia and Eurasia, and in Central and Eastern Europe, women are being sold into slavery for the sex parlours of the prosperous industrialized countries. Our case study looks at the sex trade across the Burmese (Myanmar) Thai border and asks what the international community is doing to mitigate the suffering.

Women make up a little more than half of the world's population. However, in some countries they make up substantially less. In China and India, there are around 91 women for every 100 men. In populations of 1 billion or more (India's is 1 billion; China's is already 1.3 billion and climbing), these figures mean that there are 9 million fewer women than men in the total population. This huge gap spells lots of trouble for these states over the next few decades. With a shortage of women of marriageable age, there will be competition among males for wives. Those men who cannot find wives will leave for countries where women are more plentiful. Emigration may not hurt China as much as immigration to another country can cause problems for that country, especially if it faces large unemployment.

Women form the largest group of the poor and downtrodden. One out of every five people on the earth lives in abject poverty, on under one dollar a day, and one out of every two people in the world live on under two dollars a day.[3] Of those who live in abject poverty, 70 percent are women and children. They have little or no shelter over their heads—maybe just a section of corrugated tin or the side of a packing carton. Approximately 2.2 million of them die of infectious diseases every year because they have no clean water to drink. As water can be far away, women and girlchildren spend countless hours a year carrying water from distant sources.[4] If women are lucky, they may spend their days scratching out a meager subsistence from the land, or catch a tasty morsel that has fallen from a stall in the local farmers market. Please see box The View from the Slums: The Life of the Urban Poor for statistical evidence of the overwhelming numbers of female-headed households among the very poor.

The feminization of poverty is a growing global phenomenon because a society's attitudes towards women can deny them access to the natural resources, credit, technology and training that they need to find a job or open their own business. Nowhere in the world have women achieved equal opportunity with men in the marketplace, and the gap is widening.

Finally, for all the talk of human rights in the twentieth century, this era has been one of the most violently abusive, especially toward women. During the Second World War, the Japanese military practiced the mass rape of women as part of its strategy to subdue the country. During the Civil War in Bosnia-Herzogovina in the 1990s, the Serbian army systematically raped Bosnian Moslem women so their husbands and loved ones would reject them. As another way to keep their populations in line, predatory and unscrupulous rulers have used man-made famines. The most famous was the famine in the Ukraine in 1931–1932, engineered by Joseph Stalin, dictator of the Soviet Union, to eliminate all Ukrainian

THE VIEW FROM the Slums

The Life of the Urban Poor

The lack of affordable housing for low-income urban households in developing countries has resulted in a proliferation of slums (see Figure 10.1). There are many characteristics common to life in the urban poverty that spells reality for one-fourth to one-third of all urban households in the world. The United States Peace Corps sends out young Americans for two years to work in urban and rural areas where their skills can help local communities rise from poverty. If you want to help change the world, why not consider two years in the Peace Corps. It will change your life and those of others.

Numbers: 50 percent of the world's population now lives in cities. At the beginning of the twenty-first century there were 19 cities with populations over 10 million.

Roots: Most urban slum and shantytown dwellers were originally from rural areas and were driven to towns and cities by poverty.

Youth: Because rural migrants to cities and towns continue to have the large families common in the countryside, the average age of slum inhabitants is very low. Jobs are insecure and people tend to live from day to day. Such conditions foster resentment, frustration, and ultimately rage, which finds an outlet in murder, suicide bombings, and terrorism.

No services: Most slum households must fetch their water from a faucet standing some blocks away and deposit their waste in the street, in open sewers or, as in China, in pails to be picked up as night soil and spread on the fields for fertilizer.

Malnutrition and disease: Slum dwellers are dependent on cash to get food. Because incomes are very low and very uncertain, children are malnourished. Malnutrition is at the core of all preventable children's diseases in the developing world.

Premature adulthood: Children, especially girl children, often do not go to school because there is none or it costs too much, or they are pulled out of school to go to work for the family. Because raising children is a burden on ths household, many children are abandoned or leave home.

Polluted environment: Poor cities have some of the worst levels of air, water, and soil pollution in the world.

SOURCES: Facts drawn from United Nations Environment Program, United Nations Children's Fund and World Health Organization, *Children in the New Millennium: Environmental Impact on Health* on-line version, Nov. 2002; and United Nations, The Centre for Human Settlements, *State of the World Cities Report 2002*.

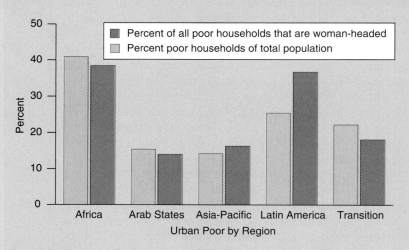

FIGURE 10.1

Urban Poor by Region

SOURCE: UN Centre for Human Settlements (Habitat), State of the World Cities Report 2001, *p. 18.pdf. Web address:* http://www.unchs.org/istanbul+5/statereport.htm

resistance to communist rule. Upwards of 40 million starved to death at that time. A similar planned famine occurred in Ethiopia in the 1980s with the same aim in mind, to eliminate resistance. A third massive famine is occurring in 2002 in Zimbabwe. Tragically, women and children bear the brunt of these cruelties. Tied down in one place by their children and family ties, women cannot easily move away to other communities or regions where food might be more plentiful. Worn down and weak, they easily succumb to starvation.

The twentieth century is also famous for its renovation of the practice of genocide. In the 1930s and 1940s, Adolf Hitler sent an estimated 5,693 851 Jews[5] to the gas chamber in an attempt to exterminate the Jewish people. In the Bosnian Civil War and the war in Kosovo, the Serbs tried to uproot all Bosnian Muslims and Kosovar Muslims by breaking and entering their homes, evicting the people living there, and burning the house down. In all these cases, the victims have largely been those people whom world politics has up to now considered "marginal": women and children. States that join the Union Nations must agree to its charter, at the end of which is the International Declaration of Human Rights. Yet, as we saw in Chapters 3 and 6, even states like the United States, that are in principle committed to upholding human rights, have been accused of serious abuses by international NGOs, like Amnesty International.

This chapter moves women, poverty, and human rights issues from the periphery to the center of world politics. The standard treatment of women in international relations considers how economic development or improved human rights can or will help women's second class status around the world. Women thus rarely receive separate treatment. The habit of putting women and men together in the theoretical pot rebounds to women's disadvantage.

For example, when we talk about human rights abuses in wartime, our attention is primarily turned to abuses against men. In 2001–2002, the world press published a mountain of material on United States abuses of human rights toward the Taliban fighters at Guantanomo Bay, Cuba, who were taken prisoner during the fighting in Afghanistan. The status of those prisoners provoked a torrent of concern among human rights advocates all around the world. We have not seen a similar outpouring of concern, however, over continuing abuses of women in Afghanistan or the fact that only upon international insistance did one woman make it into the new government of the country. The continued oppression of women in one of the world's most poverty stricken and devastated areas is not considered as salient as the status of members of the Taliban imprisoned in Cuba—even though those men deliberately and brutally forced Afghan women into the most conservative and confining way of life experienced by women in any Muslim country.

Do you see the problem? When our attention centers on poverty or human rights, women become marginal to the process of economic development or a state's cultural values. Women are placed at the center of the issue when we turn the question on its head to ask: How does the socially and culturally determined low status of women impact economic development and/or the promotion of human rights at the five levels of analysis we identified in Chapter 1?

In asking these questions, we follow the neoliberal paradigm, which includes the well-being of ALL humankind as a key value of international relations. Concerned as realism is with interstate relations in the global jungle and the dominant role power plays in that jungle, realists traditionally have not considered women and poverty as international problems. For the realist, these are domestic issues that national governments should solve within their own territory. Liberals, on their part, have taken a long time to place women and poverty in the forefront of the international agenda.

The attacks of 9/11 forcefully challenged liberal and realist assumptions. Political observers were unanimous in their opinion that endemic poverty and inequality were root causes of the tragedy. In post–Taliban Afghanistan, the international community not only insisted that women be given a role in the new government but also have complete access to education. In January 2002, the International Monetary Fund sponsored an international conference on poverty reduction strategies. Women still did not figure as a separate theme for discussion, but they were front and center in the sessions on poverty and inequality. If terrorism is rooted in inequality, then liberals or realists must eventually recognize that the abusive treatment of women in poor countries contributes, in ways we do not yet fully understand, to the formation of the terrorist mentality.

Our book's theme, centralization/decentralization plays loud and clear here. The 2002 Conference on Poverty Reduction Strategies started from the realization that in individual countries low income, societal attitudes, violence, malnutrition, lack of education, and inequality (including the women's lack of access to economic, social, and political opportunities) *taken altogether* fostered poverty. The international community has had a track record of helping states in the areas of economic development and health, but societal attitudes and inequality have traditionally been considered problems to be solved at the state level. Now, thanks to a strong NGO women's movement over the past two decades, the UN agencies have become convinced of the singular importance of women in the economic transformation of poor countries to modern states. From being a specific problem for each state to tackle as it saw fit (decentralizing tendency), women's issues have become a global problem under the UN. The attacks of 9/11 demonstrated that the time was either now or never to move women, poverty, and human rights to the center of the international stage.

This chapter is divided into five parts. It first examines the idea of justice and how the Universal Declaration of Human Rights fits into that concept. It is ironic that while the declaration satisfies no country, it is the best consensus the international community has been able to achieve on the subject. The chapter next tackles the subject of the nexus between women, poverty, and human rights. In this section, we first take a brief look at the status of women in the past and present, and at the strategic role women play in developing economies. The chapter then goes on to argue why a feminist perspective in international relations helps us to understand more clearly the need for more women in policy making and international policy analysis. In the fourth section, the chapter examines the statistical trends associated with global poverty and the widening gap between the haves and the have-nots. In the fifth and last part, we ask the question of whether it is appropriate for the international community to intervene in countries with flagrant human rights abuses. Who should decide whether it is appropriate to intervene, what form should the intervention take, and what countries should intervene?

What Do We Mean When We Talk About Global Justice and Human Rights?

Defining justice is very hard to do. One way of looking at it is to see it as a goal or objective. We could view the UN Universal Declaration of Human Rights as a set of common principles toward which humanity *ought* to strive in its everlasting quest for social justice. In this view, the signing of the Declaration might mean that a member state agrees that these principles are good to have around even if it has no intention of realizing them within its territorial borders. But are unachievable pie-in-the-sky goals all that we mean by justice? One would hope not.

Justice as Balance

Another way of looking at justice is as a sort of balance or equilibrium between a state's assets as compared to other states (wealth, power, status, health, welfare, education) and the distribution of these assets among its constituent groups. This definition gets at the fairness aspect of justice. Let's look a little bit more at this concept of justice.

First of all, let us look at justice as equal shares, for example, in the world's resources, as discussed in Chapter 7. In this case, we know that there is no such thing as equal shares. About a fourth of Russia is above the Arctic Circle, where farming is very difficult and where most people do not want to live. Canada also has large portions of its territory that are unsuitable for agriculture or for habitation by large numbers of people, while the African state of Chad is almost all desert. Less than 20 percent of China has naturally fertile soil, as compared to over 30 percent of the United States. Some states have seacoasts; others are completely land-locked. Some states are rich in natural resources, like Saudi Arabia or Venezuela; others, like Japan, have few natural resources.

Nor are states equal in size, in the educational achievement of their population, in technological development, or in economic prosperity. To realize justice as an equilibrium where every state is equal to every other state in even one dimension, such as per capita income, would mean a gigantic transfer of wealth from the rich industrialized states to the three-fourths of the world living in poverty.

Justice as Due Process

If justice is not about equal shares for all, what is it about? When we think about justice as a balance, two meanings of the word come to mind. The first is contained in the idea that *justice involves a process* that operates the same way for everyone according to a standard set of accepted rules and regulations. The second involves the idea of fairness, which we will discuss later. In the United States, the standard set of rules that defines the judicial process is contained in the first ten amendments to the Constitution. When we talk about *global justice* as "due process"—a process that considers everyone in the global community impartially on the same terms—we see immediately that there needs to be an accepted global standard or set of principles to enable due process to take place. We find this global standard in the UN Universal Declaration of Human Rights.

The UN Declaration sets forth general principles for a common judicial process that the member states assert to be universal and swear to uphold. A state cannot become a member of the United Nations without swearing adherence to the Universal Declaration. Some of the most significant human rights found in the document are discussed below.

The first set of principles assures equality before the law. Article 3 states that every human being has the right to life, liberty, and security of person. Article 7 says that all are equal before the law. Article 6 holds that everyone has the right to recognition everywhere as a person before the law. Equally important, everyone has the right to seek redress for a grievance at the appropriate national court-of-law (Article 8), and no one shall be subjected to arbitrary arrest or exile (Article 9). These concepts of justice are those Americans generally associate with the notion of a "fair trial."

Next in the Universal Declaration comes the set of principles associated with the building of democratic societies: the right to freedom of thought and conscience (Article 18), the right to freedom of peaceful assembly (Article 20), and the right to participate in government (Article 21). But the UN Declaration goes further in setting forth general principles regarding what all human beings have a right to. For example, everyone has a right to a nationality (Article 15), as well as the right to seek asylum (Article 14), the right to marry "without any limitation due to race, nationality, or religion" (Article 16), and the right to education (Article 26). The Declaration also asserts the right to work, and the right to rest and leisure (Articles 23 and 24), and contains particularly strong statements regarding the right to an adequate standard of living and the protection of motherhood (Article 25).[6]

These articles set the ground rules for all states that, if adopted, would lead to the development of legal processes that support the rule of law, democracy, and equal opportunity, as institutionalized in the Western parliamentary states.

Not all states adhere to the principles of the Declaration, even though their governments have put their signature of approval on it. Many countries today still do not assure the accused a fair trial, permit freedom of speech and assembly, or have a free and fair electoral system. In many states education remains the province of wealthy and privileged men. Women in most of Asia and Africa do not have the same rights as men either before the law, or in guarantees of equal access to education, health care, and work. In particular, women do not have the same rights as men to marry and have a family. We shall talk more about human rights and women later in the section.

Justice as Fairness

The second way to view justice is *as an equalizing factor for the human condition*. This aspect is going to make us think a little harder about the idea of "fairness." What do we mean when we say it isn't "fair" that some people are born into poverty and some into wealth? It isn't "fair" that there is no gender equality or that people are judged by their race. In these instances our talk of fairness refers to a condition that seems to exist in society or is inherent in the biological condition of a human being. In our best moments, we would like to even the odds a little. The U.S. Declaration of Independence rather grandiosely asserts that all men (and women) are born with the right to life, liberty, and the pursuit of happiness. That's a tall order for any country to deliver, let alone the international system. But the liberal and idealist side of us would like to believe that our institutions can and will rectify the most egregious inequities of the human condition.

In earlier times the question of fairness of condition did not arise. Prior to the nineteenth century, the distribution of wealth was pretty consistent. The world had only a few very wealthy people who enjoyed high social status and who were born into a high social class or caste. Much of their wealth took the form of land, crops or cattle. The wealth was transmitted from father to son, and this transmission of wealth served to entrench the power and status of the class. That everyone was born into a class based on what his or her father did was considered the natural order of things. In this system the vast majority had no money of any kind. Living was hard and insecure.

During the nineteenth century, the industrial revolution created more wealth in a few generations than had been created in the previous history of humankind. This wealth was "made," not inherited, and much of it came in a very negotiable form—money. Many individuals who started their lives in poverty, such as the great U.S. steel magnate Andrew Carnegie, ended their lives extraordinarily rich. In the wrenching upheaval of industrial change, the sight of some people becoming very wealthy raised society's expectations. The New World was the promised land where Horatio Alger reigned and impoverished urchins selling newspapers on a New York City street corner could rise to be industrial tycoons.

Over the course of the past two centuries, economic prosperity in the Western industrializing countries raised entire populations way above the levels of poverty typical of the non-industrialized world. As people began to notice the gap between those who made it and those who did not, they started to ask questions as to why some became rich and others remained poor. The industrial revolution was still very young when labor unrest and worker revolutions rudely shoved the question to the fore. In 1832 and 1848, European workers took to the barricades, demanding a change in their economic and social conditions to produce a more equal distribution of wealth. A studious young German named Karl Marx studied the worker's plight and came up with two answers. The first was the *Communist Manifesto*, published in 1948, which called on European workers to revolt. The second was *Das Kapital (Capital)*, Marx's explanation as to why workers lived in such abominable and depressing conditions. These two works influenced the course of the modern world perhaps more than any other books written during the nineteenth century (see Chapter 1 for a brief presentation of Marxism), and also played a seminal role in the European women's movement that will be discussed later in this chapter.

At the same time as Marx was writing his *Communist Manifesto*, women began noticing that the new industrial society did little for them. Like the old traditional society, the new kept wealth, status, and power in the hands of men. As Western women's movements demanded and achieved a relatively equal footing with men in Western society, the issue of ensuring that women made the same gains in the rest of the world became all the more salient.

The difficulties involved in trying to change the inequalities of condition that are determined literally by "the luck of birth" are considerable. *Social engineering*, or trying to create social justice by government directive, is a risky business. The leaders of the Soviet Union and China produced their version of equality of condition by vast projects involving murder, torture, starvation, and reeducation of millions of people. In so doing, they destroyed the educational and economic base on which the communist governments could have begun to build a modern industrialized society. It took decades before new generations could be born and educated to wipe out the negative consequences of this sweeping attempt at social engineering.

Despite the problems associated with changing inequalities of condition, disaffected human beings in all parts of our planet have shown a remarkable persistence in trying to "change the world," or at least the distribution of outcomes. The concept of justice as fairness lies at the foundation of such movements as national struggles for independence, ethnic and religious struggles for equal representation in political, social, and economic life, legislation outlawing discrimination and establishing a minimum wag, and the international women's movement. In every case, violence has failed to win the battle. History suggests that the only way to ensure fairness of any kind has been to assure due process through the guarantee of human rights.

What Is the Relationship Between the History of Women, Global Justice, and Human Rights?

The history of women makes it clear how left out they have been from these principles of due process and fairness. To understand just how global justice and human rights have passed women by, we will first look at their history of low political, economic, and social status. Until recently, international relations had little to do with women. They were invisible at the bottom of the pecking order. The international issues of war and peace were for men only. The following discussion of women's history, however, shows that individual women could and did exert enormous influence over the world politics of their generation. Indeed, the names of some of these women, such as Queen Elizabeth and Queen Victoria of England, now characterize a whole era. In addition, with the onset of early modern times in the seventeenth century, areas that had traditionally been women's preserve, like the household economy and care of the sick, moved out into the new public world of the economy and science dominated by men. Thus, the final section on women's history traces the origins of the women's movement from the growing realization, especially by middle-class women, that the much touted benefits of science and the industrial revolution had primarily benefitted men.

A History of Low Political, Economic, and Social Status

Throughout recorded human history, women have been treated as second-class subjects or citizens relative to men, regardless of race, religion, or geographic region.

Some evidence indicates that in ancient Crete prior to the arrival of the Indo-European conquerors, women as well as men took part in civic ceremonies and in the governance of society. There is no substantial evidence regarding other earlier civilizations elsewhere in the world. The one exception is in early accounts of the native tribes of North America, where women appear to have played a considerable role in decision making in the Iroquois and other tribal councils. However, whatever form of matriarchy or gender equality might have existed before the Mycenaeans and Dorians conquered Greece was destroyed or driven underground. Greek culture celebrated men. (See box Historical Perspective: How Greek Tragedy Merged Patriarchy with the Rule of Law.)

The Greeks saw women as highly emotional creatures, and philosophers like Aristotle were not sure that they were human beings like men. Greek women were not seen in public. When Plato dined with the young men of his Academy to discuss philosophy, women were conspicuously absent. At the height of the Peloponnesian War between Athens and Sparta (see Chapter 2), the great Greek writer of comedies, Aristophanes, wrote *Lysistrata*. The comedy suggests a slowly dawning awareness in Athens that women could and did exert influence in society. In the play, women refuse to have sexual relations with their men, unless the men stop fighting and bring peace between the two warring states of Athens and Sparta. Compare the thrust of this ancient comedy with the modern women's slogan, "If every woman stood up for peace, there would be no more war."

The Greeks thought so little of economic issues that they relegated *oikonomia* (whence our word economics), or the management of the *oikos* or household, to women and slaves. The standard Greek (and later Latin) word for human being was man. The Greek word for man, *anthropos*, lies at the basis of our word *anthropology*,

HISTORICAL PERSPECTIVE

How Greek Tragedy Merged Patriarchy with the Rule of Law

In his tragic trilogy, the *Oresteia*, Aeschylus, the first great Greek tragedian of fifth-century B.C. Athens, immortalized what then was probably the prevailing Athenian view of women in the Greek, male-dominated city-state. The first of the three plays, *Agamemnon*, begins as word comes from Troy to the Greek city of Mycene, that the Trojan War has ended and Agamemnon, Mycene's king, is about to return victorious. The Trojan War had begun some ten years earlier, when Agamemnon lay siege to Troy to reclaim his stolen mistress, the famed Helen of Troy. Agamemnon was prevented from setting sail for Troy, however, because the prevailing winds across the Aegean Sea were blowing away from Troy rather than toward it. To get the winds to turn in his favor, the king sacrificed his daughter, Iphigenia, to the sea god Poseidon. The murder enraged Clytemnestra, Agamemnon's wife, and she vowed vengeance when the king returns to Mycene. During his absence, Clytemnestra governs the city as its queen and raises the royal son, Orestes. When the royal ships dock in the harbor, Clytemnestra literally rolls out the red carpet for her lord and gives him a triumphant welcome. She holds a huge celebration, after which she and her lover, Aegisthos, follow the king into the royal bedroom and murder him. Orestes is sent to complete his education in exile.

The second play, *The Libation Bearers*, opens with Electra, the younger sister of Orestes, longing for his return. According to Greek custom, only the son can avenge a father's murder. The reunion of brother and sister takes place at Agamemnon's tomb. The longed-for meeting takes only a few lines in the play, but the discovery of a lock of Agamemnon's hair on the tomb covers 150 lines in which brother and sister give way to their grief and pledge their determination to avenge the murder. Indeed, Orestes has returned home to perform this very deed, accompanied by the goddess of wisdom, Athena. When Clytemnestra learns her son has returned, she knows the end is near. Orestes enters the palace by pretending to be a messenger with news of his own death and soon completes his mission. Almost immediately, Orestes rushes from the stage, pursued by the Furies, the goddesses of revenge, whose function it is to punish wrongs committed when kindred shed the blood of kindred.

The third play is called *The Furies*. When the play opens, the Furies, all of whom are women, are pursuing Orestes, driving him mad for his crime of matricide. In despair, Orestes prays to the sun god, Apollo, who tells him not to worry. Apollo will ask Athena, who has been with Orestes all along, to judge his crime. The trial takes place, and Athena hands down her judgment. The old Greek custom that one murder deserves another will end. The city of Athens will have law and a legal system that will judge the accused and only the accused, not a whole history of family feuds. The Furies are exiled to a cavern, escorted there by a procession of Athenians chanting Athena's praise. Orestes goes free.

The play celebrates the advent of the rule of law in fifth-century Athens. But under Aeschylus's hand, the rule of law, presented as a product of male reason (although it's Athena who guides it) and rationality, comes into being only with the banishment to the underworld of the Furies, portrayed as hysterical raving women, consumed by passion and rage.

or the study of human beings. The Latin word *homo* (man) is the same as the root in *human* and in such technical scientific terms as *hominoid*, or "like a human being."

The Roman world that followed Greece valued women primarily as mothers. One of the most important Roman gods was the Magna Mater, or Great Mother. Women were allowed to and did attend public functions, dinners, and parties. But they were admired chiefly as homemakers and mothers, and were celebrated in poetry and song as accomplished mistresses.

Neither Indian nor Chinese civilization treated women any better than did the Graeco-Roman world. In the Indian subcontinent and Chinese Empire, women were forcibly kept at home, despite the worship of Hindu goddesses in India and the spread from India throughout Asia of Buddhism, whose central figure, Buddha, exhibits the totality of all human qualities, both male and female.

After Confucianism triumphed in China in the seventh century of our era, women were totally shut out of public life. Of the three human bonds emphasized by Confucian philosophers, only one related to women—the bond of chastity on the part of wives to husbands, but not the other way round. The other two bonds were the loyalty of subject to ruler, and the obedience of sons to father. Throughout Asia when a woman married, she typically left her family forever to take up her home with her husband's family. She lived most of her adult life as a daughter-in-law under the control of her husband's mother.[7] If her husband was the firstborn son in the family, she might have some hope of rising to a position of influence as the reigning woman in the household, upon the death of her husband's father and mother. But that could only happen at the end of her life. While some may argue that women's subservient status contributed to the longevity of Chinese society and the strength and resilience of its family structure, a woman's life was consumed in hard work with little or no recognition from her family. In upper-class Chinese society, it was considered elegant for women to have small feet. While still toddlers, girl children had to submit to the painful practice of having their feet bound and their foot bones crushed, so that they would never again be able to walk freely. By hobbling women in this way, Chinese society ensured that they never would be able to leave home voluntarily and spontaneously, and so could not play any role in public without their family's knowledge. Foot-binding is one of the cruelest and most direct forms of human rights violation there is.

A History of a Few Influential Individuals

The Christian world that arose on the ruins of the Roman Empire assuredly found similarities between the Roman Magna Mater and Mary, the Mother of Christ. The two merged into a veneration of Mary throughout Christendom down to the end of the eighteenth century. Like religions everywhere else, medieval Christianity put women in second place, but the veneration of the Mother of God gave women a space or place where they could legitimately exercise power. During this long period, some women could and did—depending on their station in life—play extraordinarily influential roles. However, the lives of even the most fortunate depended ultimately on the character of the men in their lives.

The most influential and brilliant women of the Middle Ages were queens or rulers of feudal fiefdoms. Like men of the period, they acquired power through marriage or birth, and stayed in power by cunning, ruthlessness, and panache. In other words, they acquired and used power very much as did their male counterparts. Eleanor of Aquitaine (1122–1204) was the richest woman of her time and

Eleanor of Aquitaine: The most powerful ruler of her day.

ruler of her own kingdom of Aquitaine, now in France. She had a very checkered life. Her first marriage was to the King of France. Tiring of him, she then married the King of England. Avid for power, she plotted to murder her sons. Through her court in Aquitaine, she shaped much of the culture of her times, including the culture of courtly love. Eleanor's granddaughter, Blanche of Castille, became one of the great queens of France. She married Louis VIII when she was 12 years old. When he died she served as Regent of France. As Regent, she showed extraordinary financial ability and put France on a sound fiscal basis.

Isabel of Castile, (1451–1504) was the architect of the unification of Spain. Through her vision and the influence she exerted over her husband, Ferdinand of Aragon, she unified the small Spanish kingdoms into one state, and drove the Moorish rulers (Muslim Arabs) out of Spain forever. Ruthless to the core, she was also the prime mover in the expulsion of the Jews in 1492, the year of the unification of Spain. Americans remember her particularly because she helped finance the first voyage of Christopher Columbus to the New World. Without her appreciation of what the voyage could do for Spain and her taking of Columbus under her protection, the European "discovery" of America might have happened very differently.

The two greatest queens of the European Renaissance and early modern times were Queen Elizabeth I of England (1533–1603) and Catherine the Great of Russia (1729–1796). Elizabeth Tudor arguably was England's greatest monarch. Her name is associated with the English defeat of the Spanish armada in 1588, colonial conquests—particularly in America—and domestic prosperity. Her name is also associated with the golden age of English art and literature that produced William Shakespeare.

Catherine II, the Great, of Russia has the distinction of helping to murder her husband in order to ascend the throne of the Russian czars herself. She also has the distinction of bloodily putting down one of the largest peasant rebellions in Russian history. Through her great generals, who were also her lovers, she expanded the

Catherine the Great of Russia: Catherine the Great extended the territory of the Russian Empire to the Black Sea and, more than any other ruler since Peter the Great, made Russia a great power that the rest of Europe had to reckon with.

power of Russia west over part of Poland and south to the Crimean peninsula and the lands once ruled by the Turks.

All these women rose to power through their marital status or control of property. Some property was theirs by inheritance. Other times the husbands died, and the wife kept the property. Extraordinary individuals, they dominated the age in which they lived. Ordinary women had no hope of gaining sufficient status to match these achievements or to influence world affairs in such a way.

However, the attitudes and beliefs of these women were those of their times. None of them had any special policy toward women, or thought women were particularly maltreated. While the rights of Englishmen were very much under public discussion in Elizabeth's England, the question of rights for English women and all women was still at least three centuries away.

What may be less known about women in the Middle Ages is that despite their generally subservient status, a very distinguished group of philosophers existed among them. Thanks to feminist research, we are beginning to learn more about them. Although women in the Middle Ages could not become priests, they could and did enter nunneries in great numbers. Many did so to escape the inequities and harsh conditions of marriage, and many ended up writing or doing extraordinary things. Hildegard of Bingen (1098–1179) was a highly gifted woman in many fields. She wrote major works of theology, she was a mystic, and she wrote musical plays that were performed in the convent she founded. She also was an expert in medicinal herbs. Catherine of Sienna (1347–1380) was likewise a mystic, a philosopher, and a diplomat. Born into a poor family, Catherine became one of the Vatican envoys who went to the French city of Avignon and successfully persuaded the Pope to return the Papacy to its home at Rome. One of the most famous Spanish mystics was Theresa of Avila. Theresa started off her religious life in a fashionable nunnery. She then experienced a devastating illness. The illness led her to found her own religious order, based on the principles of simplicity, humility, and communion with God.[8] When her new monastic order became suspect to the Spanish Inquisition, she brilliantly defended herself and was let go.

To learn more about famous women in history who influenced world politics, go to **www.ablongman.com/ duncan.**

Joan of Arc: Depicted in the United States savings stamp series printed during World War II, "Women of America Save Your Country."

A History of Continued Subjugation and Discrimination

As we stated earlier, women like those we have just described were not very numerous. The dominant Western religious beliefs, whether Catholicism or subsequently Protestantism, always found cause to rationalize the ill treatment and abuse of women. Joan of Arc, the Maid of Orleans, is a prime example. She inspired a demoralized French army to win battles against better-armed and better-disciplined English soldiers and led the French troops to victory at the battle of Orleans in 1415. Captured by the English, charged with heresy and hearing voices, Joan was burned at the stake in 1415.

A century later, the founder of the Scotch Presbyterian Church, John Knox, vented his frustrations in trying to oust the Catholic Mary Queen of Scots from the Scottish throne through abusive attacks on women: "To promote a Woman to bear rule, superiority, dominion, or empire, above any Realm, Nation, or City, is repugnant to Nature."[9]

During the late Middle Ages, the study of alchemy, or making gold from base metals, was slowly transforming itself into what we would now term modern science and medicine. Men began to take the place of women in an area traditionally dominated by women: caring for the sick. Women would learn nursing skills from their mothers and grandmothers. The knowledge of herbal medicine was also transmitted from mother to daughter. In Italy, where women were allowed to attend university during the Middle Ages, there was a whole group of women doctors at Salerno. But by the end of the fourteenth century, women were forbidden to practice in most countries.[10]

THE WITCH No.3.

The Salem Witch Trials: These trials were made famous by New England writers such as Nathaniel Hawthorne. The trials became so notorious that when they were over, the New England governor ordered Salem to be abandoned and the town razed. At the time, the public viewed the trials more as a miscarriage of justice than an attack on women.

To find out more about the Salem Witch Trials go to **www.ablongman.com/ duncan.**

As the new medicine came into conflict with the old ways, women came under scrutiny as witches and persons who made bargains with the devil in which they abjured the Christian faith. The persecution of alleged witches began in the fourteenth century and reached its peak in the sixteenth and seventeenth centuries. In the American colonies, the most famous witchcraft trials were in Salem, Massachusetts, in 1692.

Why were women treated this way? How could any society relegate half of its population to these conditions? In the modern world, feminist philosopher of science Evelyn Fox Keller argues that modern scientific thought emerging from the Renaissance equated science with masculinity.[11] As science rose to be the dominant ideology of the Western world, maleness became equated with everything rational, and femaleness with everything irrational and emotional, taking us right back to where we started with Orestes, Athena, and the Greek Furies.

In other parts of the world, women's fortunes went up or down depending on lifestyle and religion. Women living in nomadic or seminomadic tribes tended to have more responsibility than women living in towns. Many believe that the myth of the female Amazon warrior came from the fierce Scythian horsewomen of the Central Asian steppe (200 B.C.). The Arab Bedouins also have a woman warrior tradition. Queen Zenobia of Palmyra (250 B.C.) is the best known to us from this tradition. In North America perhaps Sacajawea, who accompanied Louis and Clark on their famous Western Expedition in 1804, is the most famous example of strong, independent womanhood in Native American society.

When the nomads settled in cities, women's public status deteriorated. However, in Asia as in Europe, women of high class in the imperial courts of Persia, China, and Japan were able to exert enormous influence from behind the scenes. The first novel in the world was *The Tales of Genji*, written by Murasaki Shikibu, one of a group of talented Japanese women authors at the Japanese court in the tenth century A.D. And the last imperial image we have of China before the empire fell apart in 1911 is the Empress Dowager Cixi. The Empress vainly struggled to revive imperial power, as she coped with unrest at home and the virtual European takeover of her country under a humiliating treaty system. The historical image of the Empress possesses all the worst female characteristics. European historians of the time tended to see the Chinese Empire as a relic of the past in dire need of modernization. In this scenario, the Empress personified the bad woman holding progress back.

The famous women we have just described were not concerned with human rights, justice, or good deeds. They were concerned with power politics or the life of ideas. Their stories are exceptions to the general condition of women down to the nineteenth century. As such, they underscore the point that without a concept of justice and human rights that includes women as well as men, women historically had very tough going.

The Rise of the Women's Movement

The industrial revolution did little to change the status of women. Whereas the Greeks had left the economy (the business of the household) to women and slaves, the seventeenth century saw economics taken out of the private family sphere and elevated to the public domain of rational scientific knowledge, a domain, as we know, occupied by men. The Scotsman Adam Smith defined for the modern world how the invisible hand of the market worked under a capitalist system. The English economist Thomas Malthus was the first to warn of the dangers of population increases (see Chapter 13). Neither theory did any favors for women.

By 1800 women everywhere were legally considered the property of their husbands. Women could not own property except in some instances in the Far West of the United States. In both Europe and the United States they could not vote, nor could they make their own decisions regarding their future. The invisible hand of the market paid women what the early capitalists thought women were worth: very little. Women were indeed sought after in the early textile mills, but their lower education and limited skills put them at the bottom of the labor market. Men were the entrepreneurs, managers, scientists, and inventors. Poor men went into the risky jobs such as working in the mines or on the railroads, both of which paid better than women's work and were closed to women. In the middle and upper-middle echelons of society, women were not supposed to work. Instead they stayed at home to raise the family and look after the household. The sentimentalism of the Victorian era found its reflection in the newly popular St. Valentine's Day, where anonymous "lovers" sent women cards decorated with cupids and hearts, and gifts of flowers and chocolate.

The modern women's movement began in the middle of the nineteenth century and essentially evolved in two directions, reflecting the two meanings of justice discussed earlier in the chapter: The Anglo-American women's movement leaned more toward equating women's liberation with the achievement of equal rights under the law, or due process. The European variant emphasized the fairness aspect of justice and focused on equal conditions.

In the United States, justice as due process for (white) men was very much alive in nineteenth century capitalism, providing the legal underpinnings for the expansion of capitalism and democracy through the civil rights to own property, to enter into contracts, and to vote. By the end of the eighteenth century, women, like English author and feminist, Mary Wollstonecraft, who published "Vindication of the Rights of Women" in 1792, were already questioning the existing legal system. In 1848, Elizabeth Cady Stanton read a manifesto at a meeting of women in Senaca Falls, New York, demanding that women be given the same rights as men, particularly the right to vote. This meeting marked the founding of the women's suffrage movement in the United States. Women would not take no for an answer and organized throughout the United States and Great Britain. As the suffrage movement progressed through the nineteenth and early twentieth centuries, the authorities attempted to stop it with increasing cruelty and vindictiveness, particularly in Great Britain.

Perhaps because of their lower civil and political status, American middle-class women, and especially those who participated in the suffrage movement, were very sensitive to the immorality of slavery. The abolition movement produced some of the most determined and heroic women, both white and black, of that time who greatly influenced U.S. and European views on slavery and justice. Of particular mention are Sojourner Truth and Ida B. Wells, one of the first women editors anywhere in the world.

Sojourner Truth exposed all that was wrong with slavery in the United States, and she became a living legend for her work in the Underground Railroad. Ida Wells literally risked her life to make public the injustices of the Southern Jim Crow laws, and fought throughout her long lifetime for equality of blacks under U.S. law. To publicize the difficulties blacks were having in the South, Wells traveled to London where she was given a hero's welcome by the suffragettes. Under Wells's strong influence, the Anglo-American women's movement decided that black women's right to vote was a matter of women's rights as much as it was a matter of racial discrimination. From then on, the movement fought for the right to vote for all women, regardless of color. Unfortunately, when civil rights is mentioned today, our minds go immediately to issues of racial discrimination rather than women's rights. Most people do not realize the close connection between the two movements. Women took the lead in advancing the cause of anti-slavery and racial injustice in the South. Is it any wonder that their next step was to march for their own rights?

In France and the rest of continental Europe, the women's movement joined forces with the socialist movement with a focus on obtaining justice as equality of condition. By coincidence, Karl Marx's *Communist Manifesto* came out in 1848, the same year as Stanton's *Manifesto on the Rights of Women*. Marxism, as we know from Chapter 1, teaches that history is the history of the class struggle. According to Marx, the first class division and thus the first class struggle was between men and women in the family. Marx developed the concept of "exploitation," whereby the ruling class in society deliberately keeps the underclass in line by permitting it a subsistence living only, whether as slave, serf, or worker. Under the capitalist system, the capitalist pays the worker just enough to keep him alive and creams off the difference between the low wage and the actual market price of the commodity manufactured by the worker as profit.

Marx held that women were among the worst exploited, since their unpaid work in the home made them totally dependent on their husbands for every material good. A large number of highly educated and intelligent European women were

Sojourner Truth: Celebrated activist on the Underground Railroad, depicted in the United States postage stamp series. *"Famous African Americans."*

To find out more about famous black women in American history, go to **www.ablongman.com/ duncan.**

persuaded that emancipation from such intolerable conditions was the only way to women's liberation, and they worked actively under the socialist aegis throughout the nineteenth and twentieth centuries. Russia in particular after 1861, produced an extraordinary group of women reformers and revolutionaries who sacrificed family, easy living, and money to teach reading to the illiterate newly freed serfs, or to spread the word about women's emancipation in the factories and sweatshops, where Russia's new urban proletariat worked.

Wherever European women traveled during the nineteenth century, they brought their ideas of emancipation with them. In India, English women were appalled at the practice of *sati*, where the wife is burned with her husband on his funeral pyre. In the Islamic countries, they were shocked by the practice of polygamy, by the seclusion of women in the harems of the rich, and by the mandatory dress of long black robes from head to foot among poor women. In Africa and the Middle East, Western women were horrified by the practice of female circumcision, where the clitoris is cut and the entrance to the vagina sewn up only to be unsewn for intercourse. Even Western women raised in non-western cultures never quite seemed to adjust to non-Western practices. Pearl Buck, an American writer of the twentieth century who was very sympathetic to China, the land of her birth, nevertheless could not come to terms with the Chinese practice of foot-binding.

Thus, as women—especially middle- to upper-class women—became more involved in the suffrage or socialist movement at home, their peers were experiencing culture shock in the European colonies in Asia and Africa and demanding equal rights for all women everywhere.

Sad to say, women's demands were not answered quickly. New Zealand was the first country to give women the right to vote in 1893. Norway was the first European country to give women the right to vote in 1913. Women got the right to vote in the United States in 1919, about the same time as in the United Kingdom. Women did not get the right to vote in France or Germany until after the Second World War, and only gained this right in Switzerland in 1971.

The socialist-communist women's movement flourished in Germany, Central and Eastern Europe, and the young Soviet Union. It went underground in Germany when Hitler came to power. As long as the Father of Russian Communism, Vladimir Ilych Lenin, lived, the Russian women's movement had the protection of Lenin's wife, Nadezhda Krupskaya. When he died, his successor, Josef Stalin, took steps to gut the movement of all political power. Experience dies hard, however. With the collapse of the Soviet Union in 1991, the women's movement came to life once again. Russia is the only country today where women have founded their own political party. The party may not get many votes at the polls, but its existence tells the other parties that they neglect women's issues at their peril.

After the Second World War, many of the newly independent states in Asia took steps to improve the status of women. The most active women's movements are probably in the Philippines and India. In India, women lawyers have been untiring in their attempts to stop bride burning and to generate more respect for the girl child. In the Philippines, women's groups have struggled to end the smuggling of young women to the brothels of Southern Asia, Canada, and the United States, and to give these women some legal protection from pimps [see case study].

Japanese women only began to organize in the last decade of the twentieth century. But already they have been able to file lawsuits for age discrimination in hiring and firing women and have made sexual harassment a major issue in Japanese boardrooms.

Women's Rights as Human Rights

More than a century and a half has passed since the women's movement began, but the worldwide implementation of numerous fundamental human rights is still incomplete. The problem is that many do not view women's issues as human rights issues. The fact remains that women's rights, including women's right not to be beaten, to marry by choice, to be educated and to receive equal pay, are not yet part of the Universal Declaration of Human Rights.

Despite setbacks, women have not given up on their agenda. However, they realize that without political pressure, all the ideas about equality, justice, and democracy—even those agreed upon in the Universal Declaration of Human Rights—are mainly talk. To quote the Executive Summary of the UN Womenwatch Working Groups, formed to evaluate progress in implementing the Action Platform approved at the UN Fourth World Conference on Women in Beijing in 1995, "There is an absence of political will necessary to undertake action that will achieve lasting change."[12]

At the 1995 Beijing Conference on Women, Hillary Rodham Clinton, U.S. Senator from New York, was considered *militant* by the media and many of the African and Asian delegates to the conference when, in her opening remarks to the conference, she called for the inclusion in the UN Universal Declaration of Human Rights of the sentence "*Women's rights are human rights.*"

In the 1970s, the Equal Rights Amendment that proclaimed that women and men had the same rights in the United States was defeated. And today, despite talk, education, and legislation, women in the United States still earn on the average 75 percent of what men earn, and are breaking the glass ceiling of higher management only with small pinpricks. In Europe, the Scandinavian countries have gone furthest in requiring the state to provide equal opportunity for women. Yet, the international media gives small coverage to such an extraordinary event as Finland's 2000 presidential election. Three of the four candidates were women, the two front runners were women, and Tarya Halonen went on to become Finland's first woman President.

Outside the industrialized nations, women's progress has been even slower. Women have advanced furthest in Latin America, particularly in Chile, Argentina, and Mexico. Educational levels of women throughout South America, with the exception of Ecuador and Peru, are surprisingly high. Much remains the same, however, in Africa and Asia. The practice of genital mutilation has now jumped the Atlantic. Immigrants from Africa and the Middle East bring their customs with them. Since women who have undergone the painful procedure rarely go public with their experience, it is hard for the U.S. courts to bring the perpetrators of genital mutilation to justice, and it is equally hard to get exact figures on the extent of the practice.

Africa is also suffering from an AIDS epidemic, where women constitute the largest number of victims. HIV is now infecting women more rapidly than men. AIDS workers say the increasing infection of women is due among other things to poor education, poor protection, and the habit of men going off to the city to work and returning to wife and family on the weekends. An entire middle generation of Africans, and especially women, is at stake.

Women's condition in most of the Muslim countries has not noticeably improved despite these countries' adherence to the UN Declaration. As mentioned earlier in this chapter, women suffer most severely in Afghanistan, where the Taliban imposed extremely harsh laws and men are reluctant to abandon tradi-

To find out more about The Beijing Conference and its follow-up, go to **www.ablongman.com/ duncan** and **http://www.iisd.ca/ linkages/4wcw/ other.html**

To find out more about the spread of AIDS among women and hope for cures, go to **www.ablongman.com/ duncan.**

A Pro-Taliban Woman: This woman holds a copy of the Koran and a toy rifle at a protest in Lahore, Pakistan, against the U.S. invasion of Afghanistan. Why would she support a male-dominated society and play the terrorists' game?

tional practices. Women in Iran are just beginning to protest against the government's restrictive female dress code and the rules and regulations preventing women from moving about freely without male attendants. A growing bone of contention between Saudi Arabia and the United States is the refusal of the Saudi government to let a young girl abducted to Saudi Arabia by her Saudi father, but a U.S. citizen, return to her American mother in the United States.

In India, women remain at the bottom of the social ladder. Men prefer boy children to carry on the family and to work the farm. If a woman does not produce a boy, she is ostracized by her husband and can eventually be burned by him. A can of kerosene is cheaper than sending the woman back to her family and having to repay the bride's family her dowry.

In China, the government has taken a highly rational approach to trying to decrease the rate of population growth. In the early 1980s the government announced a policy of only one child per family. The policy was enforced by carrot-and-stick tactics. The carrot was a large apartment in which to raise the child, a guaranteed free education for the one child, and special bonuses at work to help raise the child. The punishments ranged from reducing wages and cutting apartment size to forced abortion, no matter what the age of the fetus nor the desire of the family.

The policy has appeared to succeed in the cities. It is rare to find any adult with more than one child riding on the back of his or her bicycle. The policy, however, has been harder to enforce in the large open rural areas where there are fewer law enforcement officers. The rapid and extraordinary economic development of China has been blighted, however, by the specter of girl babies left on orphanage doorsteps or

Web Exploration

To find out more about violence against women, go to **www.ablongman.com/ duncan.**

just plain murdered at birth. Desperate parents have taken desperate measures to ensure the desired boy, despite official assertions of equality of the sexes.

In practice, then, we can see that women's rights are NOT yet seen as human rights. Hillary Clinton was thought militant because she attempted to bring the issue of women's rights to the forefront of international politics. Women have been given a raw deal, she argued. States ought to sign on the dotted line. Yet, throughout the world, women continue to be thought of and treated differently from men, and their rights remain less than fully human.

How Do Feminist Theories of International Relations Explain the Relationship Between Discrimination Against Women, Global Justice, and Human Rights?

Feminist Theory of International Relations
An approach that believes that gender is the key to our understanding of international relations. The aim of feminist theory is to uncover the gender dichotomies that mainstream international relations conceals or rejects and to lay these bare before the public eye.

When confronted with the global circumstances of women, many of us will shake our heads: "That's too bad. We're sorry women suffer so much around the world. That's life, I guess." But we need to make sense of this situation, and making sense leads us directly into theory. Theory, as we saw in Chapter 1, enables us to put the many parts of a picture into a frame. The obvious question is why women continue to be second-class citizens. Feminists do not buy the argument normally advanced by men that equality is merely a matter of economic development and education. Feminists know that even in the developed countries, women are not equal to men. How, then, do feminist theories explain the inequality?

The **feminist theory of international relations** is what many call a *sex-neutral theory of international relations.* According to feminist theories, men interpret history primarily in terms of wars, weapons, and conquests, whether military or economic. Mainstream international relations theorists generally term these issues *high politics.* Women set history in a different light. Wars bring destruction, and women tend to gain least from wars. Their husbands may be killed, their sons may die, and their homes may be destroyed. War brings enslavement and hardship to all its victims, but the physical violation of women is generally considered a conqueror's right. The Serbian rape of Bosnian Muslim women in the mid-1990s was a repetition of the legendary rape of the Sabine women by Roman soldiers in the early days of Rome, or the rape of Chinese women in Nanking by Japanese soldiers in 1937.[13] In all these instances, men went on an orgy of cruelty. Women were raped not once but by whole gangs of soldiers. They were totally dehumanized. In some cases, a pregnant woman was cut open and her child pulled from her belly. With these brutal images in mind, let's take a closer look about what feminist theory has to say about the way women are treated in international politics.

Five Kinds of Feminist International Relations Theory

Rather than give wars primacy, feminist theories consider a whole range of factors that mainstream IR theorists, realists and idealists alike, have termed *low politics.* These factors include the role of culture, economics, religion, globalization, and the concept of gender in denigrating women's experience. As a result, when we use the term *feminist theory,* we actually refer to multiple strains of feminist scholarship in international relations. Virtually all of the theories agree, however, that male IR theories artificially separate men and women's spheres of activity into a male public sphere of production and economic development and a female private and thus, unmentioned, sphere of reproduction and the role of the home in raising and feeding children. Some feminist theorists concentrate on overcoming this gender division that crosses society at all levels of the international system. Others question the relevance of the division to women's rights, while still others advocate a radical separation of male and female culture and activity. V. Spike Peterson and Anne Sisson Runyan group these strains of theory into five general categories:[14]

1. *Radical feminists* focus on the role of culture in denigrating women's experience and women's ways of acquiring knowledge. Radical feminists hold that the division between public production and private reproduction is a deliberate male construct designed to keep women in their low status place. Some members of this group go so far as to advocate complete separation of women from men as the only solution to the achievement of total gender equality between the sexes.

2. *Socialist feminists* stress the importance of economic issues in achieving equality and their relationships to power and culture. They agree with the radical feminists that the division between public production and private reproduction is the cornerstone of patriarchy. Their aim is to show how the private reproductive sphere that was considered traditionally female interfaces with and relates to the public, productive sphere considered traditionally male. Far from advocating total separation of the spheres, they argue that each complements the other and that neither would be economically viable in isolation. The socialist feminists thus argue for using the same criteria of value on women's unpaid work in the home as is done in the public economy. Until recently, no state carried economic data that even mentioned the contribution of women's unpaid work at home, particularly in child-rearing and subsistence farming, let alone tried to set a value on it. Many mainstream economists appreciate the socialist feminist argument, and the UN, in particular, is trying to derive a formula that can be used worldwide to calculate the value of women's unpaid work.

3. *Liberal feminists* are the most active in equal rights movements. They seek to overcome the gender dichotomies of public and private by replacing the concept of gender difference with the concept of gender sameness. Women have the same capabilities as men, they assert. They see U.S. Army privates Jessica Lynch and Shoshana Johnson—who served in Iraq, were captured by the Iraqis, and subsequently liberated—as prime arguments for mixed sex combat units, where women fight alongside of men. In response, other feminists argue that in emphasizing sameness, liberal feminists run the risk of taking masculine traits and abilities as the norm to which women should aspire. How are we then to evaluate uniquely women's work like childbirth and childrearing?.

4. *Postcolonial feminists* focus on the experiences of women of color. This group sees globalization as a continuation of the process known as colonialism in previous centuries. Specifically, the fall of the Soviet Union and advances in communication technology have enabled global corporate and financial institutions to bypass state regulations, while the greater permeability of state borders has aided and abetted transnational organized crime. The net result, according to this theory, has been to make the Northern states more responsive to corporate interests than to their voters, and Southern states more reliant on foreign direct investment and criminal pay-offs at the expense of their citizens, particularly the weakest among them, women. Postcolonial feminists contest the Western feminist description of the division between the public and private sphere as a male construct. For Third World women, they argue, a clear division does not exist.

Men dictate all cultural and societal values. And women have virtually no privacy to where they can retreat. Most women in the developing world work in the public sphere to keep their families alive. In the public sphere, women are told how to behave in culturally "authentic" ways, if they want to work. For example, in Muslim countries, women must wear the burka or a suitable head covering. A man can stone his wife to death with little or no evidence and have the backing of his community. The wife has no private support at all. In some parts of India, women must not be seen in public alone without their husbands around. Once so seen, a woman immediately earns the reputation of being loose. The women in her town or village will shun her as readily as the men. In Bosnia, a Bosnian Muslim woman raped in public by a Serbian soldier is considered worthless by her family and community. Thus, for women of color, the private per se does not exist but is always understood by what is happening in the public world, whether it be renewed outbreaks of racism, sexism, or ethnic or religious violence. As a consequence, post-colonial feminists place great emphasis on grass root movements that try to reach women where they are living to build up private support groups and sustain the membership when one member experiences family rejection or economic hardship. One area where grass roots groups have been particularly effective is in reaching women caught up in the transborder sex trade, as you will see in the case study for this chapter.

5. *Postmodern feminists* take issue with the very concept of gender. They argue that like the concept of sex, the concept of gender contains within it biological determinism. Sex is determined by biology, male or female. Gender is culturally determined by society. It embodies how society expects men and women to behave. Gender thus emphasizes relations between men and women that are not biologically determined. However, according to the post-modern feminists, the continued cultural assertion in many societies that men and women's roles are unchangeable or established by God leads those societies to believe these roles are determined by one's sex, that is, by biology. The post-modern feminists urge us to rethink all our gender-based concepts and attitudes and to see that they are social constructs that are created and embedded in interlocking systems of male-dominated power. Post-modern feminists disagree with the post-colonial feminists that there is a sisterhood of all women. Rather they insist that any and every action that a group of women takes must arise from struggle and consensus within that particular group. Rather than looking at women's situation with global concepts and global instruments of change, these theorists assert, we should concentrate on the discrete and individual action of particular groups.

As you can see, each of these five approaches has its strengths and weaknesses. You will have to decide for yourself which approach offers you the best explanation for women's continuing low status in the world today. To help you decide, let's now take a look at how these approaches can be applied to international relations.

Feminist Explanations of Gender Bias in International Relations

All these theories agree that *gender,* the culturally defined roles society imposes upon us, *provides the key to our understanding of international relations.* Broadly speaking, the aim of feminist theory is to uncover the gender dichotomies that mainstream international relations conceals or rejects. The feminist goal is to map the subconscious male dominant underside of world politics and to bare it before the public eye. To understand what these theories do, we'll look at three core areas of IR: international security, international economics, and environmental security.

International Security How can we understand violence in the world today? Feminist theory says that understanding starts with the acknowledgment that virtually all cultures reward men for violence. In the public space that men dominate, violence is celebrated. Realism, feminists argue, is really the strategy and practice of using violence judiciously to achieve a state's goals. *High politics* has always been dominated by men, and since the nineteenth century, the international arena has been perceived as a dog-eat-dog no-man's-land characterized by a Darwinian fight for the survival of the fittest. In Chapter 7, one concept of geopolitics presented involved the struggle for territory typical of all male creatures in the animal world. Mao Zedong liked to say that "Revolution [i.e., *male violence*] is not a dinner party [i.e., *female activity*]." In mainstream IR, consideration of questions associated with *low politics*, such as international development, world poverty, women's issues, and human rights comes *after* the issues of war and security have been exhaustively discussed. High politics, feminists argue, is to international relations what the public production or male sphere is to domestic politics. Low politics corresponds to the female or reproductive sphere.

Feminist theorists are united in the conviction that this distinction between high and low politics must go. They argue that the traditional high politics of international relations is largely irrelevant to today's security concerns. The modern world is highly interdependent and faces multiple threats from so many sources that state independence may no longer be possible or desirable. Will the Balkans be more secure with an independent Kosovo? How sovereign is Afghanistan under virtual occupation by UN-provided troops? What fresh insecurities will the new citizens of East Timor face when their independence from Indonesia has been fully realized? The Palestinians have been fighting for independence for over a century. Yet their fundamental insecurity is not a military threat from Israel but their own desperate need for economic betterment, a process that can only be successful in association with Israel, not against it.

The attacks of 9/11 taught the lesson that *national* defense against terrorism is meaningless. The U.S. government has even dropped the term "national," and now speaks of *homeland* defense. Feminist theorists argue that terror can strike any time any place with any means. There is no one state enemy out there whose military and economic strength can be targeted and destroyed by the U.S. government in order to improve national security.

Arguing from the liberal IR feminist approach, J. Ann Tickner questions the relevance today of the distinction between *state* (public) security and *individual* (private) security. In her view, the "heavy emphasis" on militarily defined security, common to the practices of the modern states, does not always ensure, and "may even *decrease*," the security of individuals as well as their natural environments. Individuals, she says, face many forms of insecurity: ethnic conflict, poverty, natural catastrophes, local terrorist acts, unemployment, family violence, and environmental degradation. None of these kinds of security are commonly linked with what states have traditionally defined as their national security goals.

Moreover, she continues, traditional definitions of security rely on gender inequalities. Security based on military might elevates masculine characteristics and endows men with first-class citizenship as virile soldiers who protect the weak. Masculine traits likewise inform the basic assumptions of economic security, where states have promoted a concept of economic development that has primarily bene-fited men. The traditional association of women with nature, which places both in a subordinate position to men, mirrors and supports the exploitative attitude toward nature that has typified the past two centuries. The vast gender gap in who controls and may access wealth is a driving force in economic insecurity today. In like fash-ion the view of nature as there for the taking has contributed to our growing envi-ronmental insecurity.

If the world's multiple insecurities are to be addressed, virtually all the femi-nists approaches agree that international relations must be reformulated.[15] In this reformulation, the male emphasis on a state's independence, sovereignty, and na-tional or racial distinctness from other states has to go. The post-colonial feminist perspective sees striving for attachment and community—concerns associated gen-erally with women—as much a part of politics as is the desire for independence and self-identification. Building community from the grass roots up is a dimension of international behavior in its own right.

The proliferation of community-building regimes like the European Union in the last half of the twentieth century, and even trade agreements like the World Trade Organization and NAFTA, provide evidence of the significance of the femi-nist analysis. We may indeed be moving toward types of international organization that demand different, more inclusive definitions of national sovereignty then we now have. Feminists find it significant that Europe is the continent that is moving fastest toward a new form of state integration and that its integrated institution, the EU, is one of the most aggressive agencies in promoting gender equality.

Second, feminists argue, there is a need to modify the realist and liberal views of the world that are based on assumptions of rigid boundary distinctions: levels of analysis, domestic versus foreign policy, internal versus international violence, and the ordered domestic life of the state versus anarchy in the international arena. Post-colonial, socialist, and postmodern feminists alike posit the need to identify interrelationships among all kinds of international actors at all levels of society. Conceptualizing violence as permeating all levels of society can help us rethink our traditional definitions of the state and lead to models that might, for example, pro-vide ways to link domestic violence with regional and world wars. For example, the Serb-Christian rape of Muslim women and the Japanese rape of the Chinese women of Nanking represent individual acts by individual people. They took place in a climate of war, where such acts were praised and celebrated by their respective national governments. The government's support of such behavior led to interna-tional outrage and eventual retaliation on the part of the international community.

Feminists argue that the war on terrorism, though seemingly focused on the high politics of national defense and secure state borders, relies more than ever be-fore on low politics for victory. Traditional "women's issues," like culture, educa-tion, and sense of community at the local level, determine the origins of terrorism and are among the most powerful weapons we have to reduce the probability of the emergence of new terrorists.

International Economics   In the economic sphere, the socialist feminists ar-gue that current models of economic development have not taken into account women's particular needs nor the role that women play in the development process. It is abundantly clear that the exploitation of women's unpaid labor in the home and local community, and their lower paid and underpaid labor in the monetary economy have been crucial for the expansion of the global economy. As noted ear-lier, until recently, world economic data made no effort to assess women's unpaid

WHY IT MATTERS TO YOU

Terrorism and the Subjugation of Women

Terrorism provides a fine example of violence linked to the subjugation of women. In Chapter 6 you read a short biography of Osama Bin Laden. Consider that same biography from the feminist perspective.

Bin Laden was one of fifty siblings in a wealthy Saudi family and not being the firstborn, he was forced to adjust and fit into the family culture or fight for domination. He chose the latter. In his youth, he challenged the Saudi authorities for leadership, and when his challenge failed, he turned against his country and created a formidable and ruthless international terrorist network. One way that we can understand the origins and practice of terrorism is to learn more about the level of violence

within bin Laden's family, and how it reflects the level of violence used in Saudi Arabia to keep the population, particularly women, in their place. The neocolonial feminists' perspective seems right on target when it argues that in developing countries, there is no such thing as privacy, and no distinction between public and private. Publicly endorsed behaviors mold individual actions.

What do you make of an authoritarian family structure rooted in an authoritarian state structure that resorts to violence to enforce a rigid social agenda, and a charismatic leader who creates a rigidly controlled terrorist underground organization that keeps all its parts in line?

contribution to a state's economy. The UN is working on models to get at these kinds of statistics now. Yet, it has long been evident that women's unpaid labor is the sustaining factor in the nonmonetary subsistence economies of the developing states, providing food and survival for the family.

Because women have been marginalized in the international economic system, most feminist theorists, but especially liberal and socialist feminists, prioritize international issues associated with the achievement of social justice for women. One of the most important objectives of the world women's movement is to overcome women's exclusion from the halls of economic and politic power and to promote new forms of economic production based on women's needs and requirements. To use Tickner's words once more, "Social justice, including gender justice, is necessary for an enduring peace."[16]

Women are at the forefront of most social justice movements precisely because they feel their exclusion from productive society. Through the Internet, women have found and maintained contact with women in similar situations all over the globe. For example, today when the World Bank mishandles small loans to women in Ghana, women throughout Africa and Asia know about it. News of a trial in the Philippines that vindicates a woman accused of a crime by her pimp owner quickly finds its way to multiple websites that address women's problems.

Feminists argue that the presence of more women in high places in the international world can bring to international decision-making this sense of social justice for the marginal and peripheral. If the new global market system is to work and, as we have seen, some feminists who adopt the postcolonial point of view sincerely doubt that it will, it has to redress inequities of economic and educational opportunity throughout the world. Women are at the bottom of both hierarchies.

Environmental Security   As in the economic area, women have shown themselves to be the chief organizers and participants in local environmental organizations. In India, Vandana Siva became world famous overnight when her group of women, known as Treehuggers, hugged trees they did not want logged in their local community, and stopped the logging. These tactics have now spread worldwide. Men, say the feminists, *do* things to nature. Men decide to log, build dams, or turn wetlands into farmland. Men like to leave their legacy on the earth. So they construct huge projects like dams, level mountains to build roads, turn rivers around, or drain lakes.

Women, ecofeminists argue, think and act differently. (We will discuss more about ecofeminism in Chapter 13.) They could bring to international decision-making a sense of the oneness of humankind with our planet, and a sense of the need for caring and maintaining this planet for the next generations. It perhaps was not by accident that a former Norwegian woman prime minister, Gro Harlem Brundtland, headed the UN World Commission on Environment and Development that in 1987 published its findings in a report entitled *Our Common Future*.[17] The report mentioned for the first time the need for *sustainable development* if the human species was to survive on our earth. Norway is one of the most active countries in the world today in terms of promoting gender equality.

In summary, the main contribution of women to international relations theory and practice lies in a sense of self that is of and with this earth: a sense of interrelatedness that moves beyond boundary lines and frontiers, a sense of our commonality with the rest of humankind regardless of state borders, and a sense of our being an integral part of the natural world.

Why is it that we view these values as women's values? The answer lies in the background and history provided in this chapter. Traditionally, social justice and equality have not been the primary concerns of international relations and arguably are not yet at the top of today's agenda. We contend that these are becoming major issues on the world agenda for two reasons: The first is the visibility of a whole host of new insecurities promoted to the forefront of the international agenda by 9/11. These insecurities relate *vertically* to individuals, families, and communities more than to the traditional *horizontal* concept of national security as borders that are militarily safe from another state. These inse-

Vandana Siva: Indian feminist environmentalist and fighter for the rights of India's poor.

curities are forcing the world's leaders to rethink the traditional essentially masculine concepts of power, national security, and the anarchy of the international arena. The second is that women, through their international organizations and individual spokespersons, have become leading advocates of social justice, clearly articulating the relationships between social justice, women's rights, and economic fairness. In so doing, they have moved beyond the neoliberal belief in cooperation as a means to ensure global justice to a broader focus on achieving a more equitable world.

What Is the Relationship Between Poverty, Global Justice, and Human Rights?

To understand this relationship, we must first look at the nature of poverty in our modern world. Many of us may think of poor people as simply those who are unfortunate enough to have little or no money, and the very poor as those 1.2 billion people in the world living on less than one dollar a day. But poverty is not just the absence of money; it is a condition, a way of life that affects more than half the human beings on this planet. In this section we will look at the five indicators of poverty developed by the international organizations most concerned with poverty and use them to understand the specific characteristics of poverty in different states. We then turn to the causes of poverty and finally to international responses to poverty

Five Indicators of Poverty

In Chapters 2 and 3 you learned about the North-South gap, and the difference between the First, Second, Third, and Fourth Worlds. You will learn more about the gap in Chapter 12. The North-South gap refers to the strong economic conditions in the industrialized countries (mostly found in the northern hemisphere) and the weak economic conditions in the world's poorer countries (mostly found in the southern hemisphere). The gap is caused by a combination of factors. In 2000, the large international organizations most concerned with poverty, like the World Bank, the United Nations Development Program (UNDP), and the Organization for Economic Cooperation and Development (OECD) identified eight international development goals to be achieved during the next twenty-five to fifty years. These goals are listed in Table 10.1. Note how many of these goals link progress to improvement of women's condition in society. Goals 3 and 5 refer directly to women, while goals 2, 4 and 6 require the active enlistment of women to achieve them.

TABLE 10.1   Millenium Development Indicators

Millennium Development Goals

1. Eradicate extreme poverty and hunger
2. Achieve universal primary education
3. Promote gender equality and empower women
4. Reduce child mortality
5. Improve maternal health
6. Combat HIV/AIDS, malaria, and other diseases
7. Ensure environmental sustainability
8. Develop a global partnership for development

SOURCE: World Bank, Worldview.pdf, p. 3 http://www.worldbank.org/data/wdi2000/worldview.htm

To measure global progress towards these goals, the IGOs developed a series of 48 indicators, ranging from the proportion of population below $1.00 a day and prevalence of underweight children to HIV prevalence among 15- to 24-year-old women and land area protected to maintain biological diversity. To illustrate how these indicators can develop a rounded view of poverty, we have chosen the five most relevant indicators that OECD originally identified as critical to the world's understanding of the nature of poverty. The first indicator, "incidence of extreme poverty," refers to the proportion of people in the state population living on less than one dollar a day. The number represents the percentage of the very poor in the total population. The second indicator involves access to primary and secondary education and the adult literacy rate, or the ability to read a local newspaper. The third indicator, mortality rate of children under five years of age, refers to the number of children per thousand in that age cohort who have died in a given year. The fourth indicator, the fertility rate, refers to the number of children born in any one year per thousand of women in the childbearing age. And the last indicator, population with access to safe drinking water, represents the percentage of people in the entire population, who have clean water to drink.

These indicators are all linked. To understand the linkages, the United Nations has sorted the states of the world into five groups or quintiles, with the first quintile being the set of poorest states, and the fifth quintile the set of richest states. Poverty exists in all states but manifests itself in each one in different ways. In the poorest states, or first quintile, all the indicators have high numbers, indicating that people there suffer severe poverty on multiple dimensions. In the next to poorest quintile, the under-five mortality rate, access to education and the literacy rate, and the incidence of extreme poverty receive high scores. In the fifth, or most wealthy, quintile, the percentage of the population with access to safe drinking water and access to education receive the highest scores. What does this variation in the poverty indicators tell us? The indicators give us a statistical representation of what the poverty problem is in a given state, and enable us to compare poverty conditions across states at different levels of economic development. Finally, the indicators point us to areas where we might be most effective in alleviating poverty in the different groups of countries. In the developed states, for example, we probably should attack poverty by working on education and clean drinking water. In the poorest states of the world, we need to consider all the indicators, but we probably should focus first on relieving the incidences of extreme poverty, lowering the fertility rate and reducing the under-five mortality rate.

Figure 10.2 indicates which countries have the highest percentage of their population living below the general UN indicator of poverty, $1.00 a day. On that map, 14 states are colored light green, indicating that more than 40 percent of the population *earns less than this amount.* However, most of the states in southern Africa are colored white, meaning that they did not send in any data. The data the UN has collected indicate that in sub-Saharan Africa, the poverty rate has stayed at 48 percent over the past decade, while the number of people living in poverty *has grown* from 220 million in 1990 to 300 million in 1998![18] You will also see that all of North America and most of Western Europe are left white. Does this mean that Canada and the United States did not provide data? Not at all. What it means is that a very, very few people, if any, in these countries earn less than $1.00 a day. Extreme poverty does not exist in North America or in Western Europe. The poverty threshold for a family of four in the United States is $17,000 a year, an unobtainable fortune to the poorest of the poor living in Africa or India.

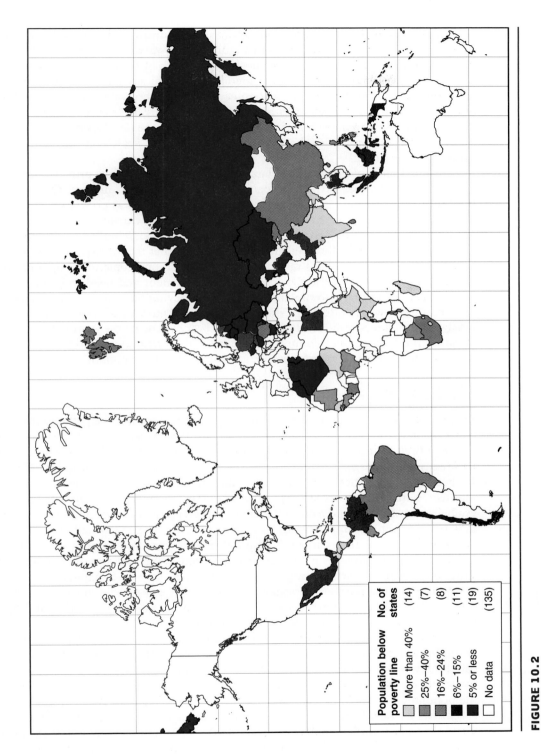

FIGURE 10.2

Incidence of Extreme Poverty: Under $1.00 a Day

Source: http://www.cgiar.org/tac/meetings/meet0100/maps.pdf

Population below poverty line	No. of states
More than 40%	(14)
25%–40%	(7)
16%–24%	(8)
6%–15%	(11)
5% or less	(19)
No data	(135)

Huge gaps between rich and poor in the same country are not just characteristic of the poor Third World states. In Figure 10.3, you will note that the United States joins a whole group of states whose poorest fifth of the population consumes only 9 to 10 percent of the national income. Can you say in which areas of the world the poorest fifth of the population consumes 11 percent or more? How does the African continent compare to North America in this regard? As evidence piles up that the gap between rich and poor is increasing in the developed world as well as in the developing world, the industrialized states are searching for answers to remedy the situation.

We must remember that most data on poverty are *static*. They provide only one snapshot, so to speak, of poverty conditions—not a motion picture. One of the hardest factors to assess is how many of the people counted as poor at one time in one country are still poor 15 or 20 years later. What are the *dynamics* of moving out of poverty? In the United States the percentage of people living below the poverty line may hold rather steady. But this does not mean that the same people are listed as being poor at every census taking. We know that some people move up and out, but we know little about the dynamics of this movement and need to know more.

To sum up, poverty is not simply a matter of having no money. It manifests itself in different ways in different states. The five indicators of poverty represent the most salient factors contributing to poverty everywhere in the world. By understanding the linkages and connections between the factors, we can begin to map out the causes of poverty for an individual state or an entire region.

Causes of Poverty

Why are the poor countries so poor, and why do they appear to be getting relatively poorer? Many attribute their problems to globalization. Most of these states have few or no natural resources to speak of. Thirty-three of the resource poorest nations are in Africa; nine are in Asia, five in the Pacific, and one in Latin America (Haiti). Because these countries are so poor, they have no private capital to invest, and having few natural resources, they have difficulty attracting foreign investment. Globalization further undermines indigenous entrepreneurship because local products simply cannot compete in quality and price with the mass-made goods marketed by the global corporations. Those individuals who used to produce products for the local market simply go out of business. Finally, the poorest counties seem to suffer most from conflict. During the 1990's, for example, Sub-Saharan Africa experienced the highest number of casualties from interstate and civil wars, over 1.5 million victims.[19] Conflict may be seen both as a cause and a result of political and economic instability, and discourages foreign investment.

Other causes of poverty may be derived from a closer look at the five indicators. Doubtless, Third World countries are aiming to achieve the level of well-being typical of the wealthiest states. In this wealthiest group of states, 39 percent of the population does not have access to safe drinking water as compared to 92 percent of the population in the poorest states. Access to clean water is one of the prime measurements of health delivery. And yet, 1.1 billion people, or 18 percent of the world's population, does not have it, and over 2.4 billion lack access to adequate sanitation.[20] How can a child learn at school or a mother care for her children, if they are suffering from water-borne diseases?

Let's take another indicator, access to education. Those countries with a low rate of access to education have low literacy rates, especially among women. In

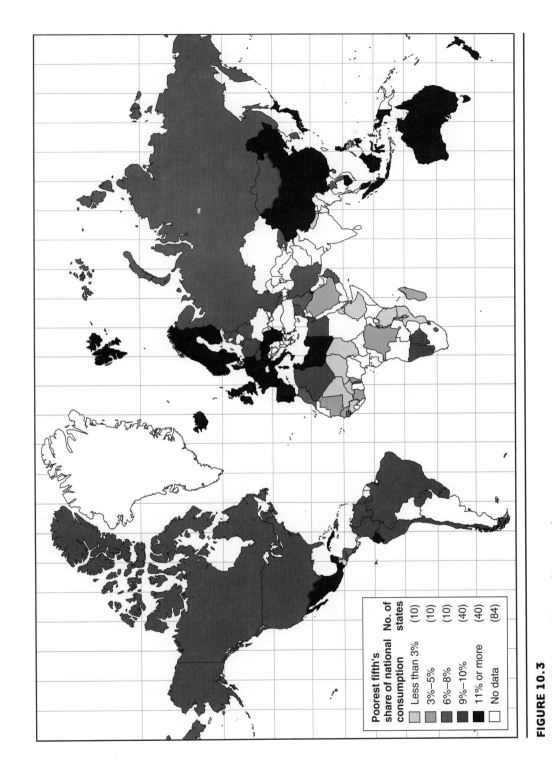

FIGURE 10.3

Poorest Fifth's Share of National Consumption

SOURCE: Organization for Economic Cooperation and Development (OECD) http://www.oecd.org/dac/Indicators/htm/map3.htm.

Poorest fifth's share of national consumption	No. of states
Less than 3%	(10)
3%–5%	(10)
6%–8%	(10)
9%–10%	(40)
11% or more	(40)
No data	(84)

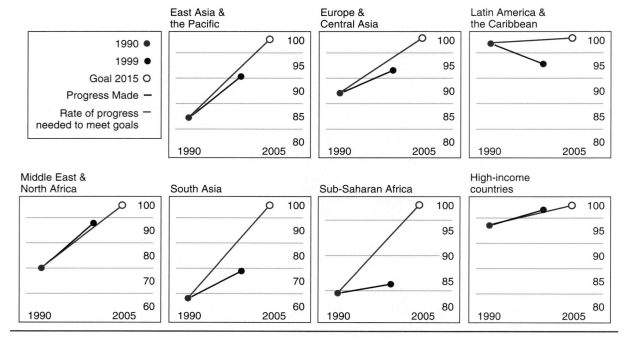

FIGURE 10.4

Ratio of Girls to Boys in Primary and Secondary Education (%)

SOURCE: http://www.developmentgoals.org/Gender_Equality.htm

Niger, for example, for 100 literate males in Niger, there are only 65 literate females. No matter what proportion of the population can actually read, there will be 3 men for every 2 women who can read. In India the proportion is 3 literate women for every 4 men. To illustrate what these figures mean, in 1995, the adult literacy rate in India was 54 percent. Of this percentage, about 36 percent would be male and 27 percent would be female. By contrast, in the whole of Northern Eurasia, including Russia and China, the literacy rates of men and women are essentially the same. However in China, OECD data indicate that only 50 percent of the entire population could read in 1995.[21]

The relevance of education and literacy in today's technological economy is easy to see. Virtually all learning today takes place with the help of the printed word, or with a picture and words projected on a screen. Almost everything modern society does requires learning to read, from reading instructions on your washing detergent, to playing the stock market. The lack of universal access to education in some African states, India, and Pakistan means that only the very few will enter the rich world of the global economy. While some wealth may trickle down, the trickle down effect is by no means guaranteed. Without education, it is becoming harder and harder for a person to advance up the wealth ladder.

The gender gap shows up very well in data on enrollments in primary schools (see Figure 10.4).

The figure shows that between 1990 and 1999, progress in enrolling girls in school was most positive in two regions of the world: East Asia and the Pacific, and the Middle East and North Africa. By contrast, ratio of enrollment of girls to boys has fallen in Latin America and the Caribbean and has barely moved forward in Sub-Saharan Africa. During the same period the high-income countries made steady progress towards the goal of universal enrollment in primary and secondary education.

To understand the problem facing the women in the poorer countries of the world, let us compare data from African countries that have provided statistics on female enrollment in primary education as a percentage of all females of school age. In every case, we find that severe poverty is associated with low female enrollment. In Ethiopia only 19 percent of school-aged girls are enrolled in school; in Mozambique, 35 percent; in Eritrea, 30 percent. Of all the states in that first quintile on the poverty indicators, only Malawi indicates that all its girl children are in school. By contrast, in those states in the medium human development range, the lowest ratio of girl pupils to total girl population was 70 percent in Oman; in the states with high human development, the lowest was 85 percent in Chile. You may be surprised to find a relatively high ratio of girls to boys in school in a Muslim country like Oman, but the data suggest that poverty is at least, if not more, of an important a factor than culture in impeding women's progress in society

Our final indicators of poverty have to do with life expectancy, infant mortality, and fertility rate. Let us look at life expectancy first.

You will see in Figure 10.5 that all the Central African states have a life expectancy lower than 55 years of age. These states are also where the lowest number of people has access to safe drinking water. In addition, these countries have the lowest literacy rates and the highest indices of severe poverty. The prime killer in Central Africa is AIDS. Until this epidemic is brought under control, the life expectancy of Central Africans can be expected to continue to fall. India and the Central Asian republic of Kazakhstan have life expectancies between 55 and 64 years of age, while all the republics that constituted the Soviet Union except Kazakhstan have life expectancies only between 64 and 69 years of age. The drop in life expectancy in Russia today is one of the most terrible things to have happened to that country and indicates how health care has fallen off since the end of the Soviet regime. Indeed, a middle-aged man in Russia will probably die before a middle-aged woman in India. Only the developed northern countries, including Japan, have life expectancies above 74 years of age.

In general, women tend to live longer than men. However, earlier in the chapter, we discussed the troubling tendency in some countries to murder girl babies and girl children in favor of having more boys to increase the wife's status in her home. So life expectancy data from states where we know boy children are prized, pampered, fed, and schooled in the place of girl children will show fewer women living into old age, because child mortality rates greatly influence life expectancy rates.

Table 10.2 provides child mortality rates for selected countries. If life expectancy in Niger and Nigeria is so low, one explanation is that many children die of disease before they reach the age of five, possibly from AIDS, another disease or malnutrition. Another reason may simply be they die because they are girls. In the Central African states, child mortality reaches over 20 percent in many areas. That means that in the population under five years of age, two children in ten may be expected to die before they reach five years of age, and if the statistics are accurate, more girl children than boy children may be expected to die. As Table 10.2 shows, in India 13 more girl children per 1000 under five die than do boy children. In Nigeria, 84 more girl children than boy children per 1000 die before they reach five.

These figures bring out more than any others the close connection between global justice, human rights, the status of women, and poverty. Niger and India,

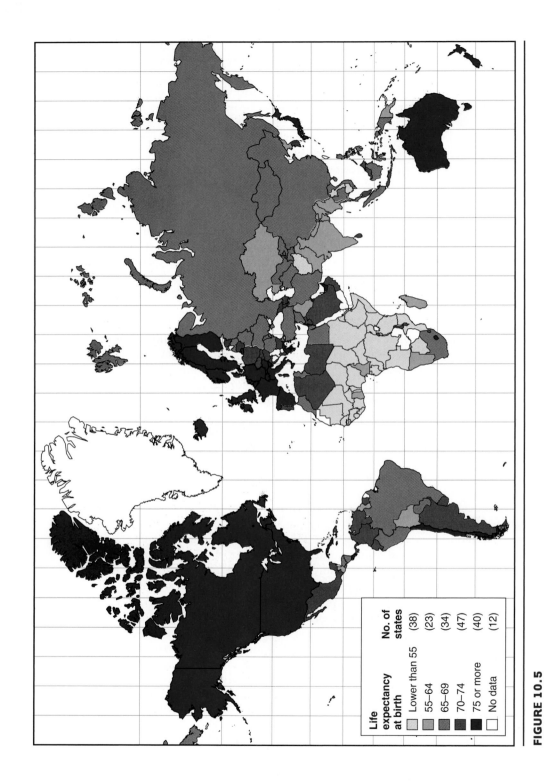

FIGURE 10.5

Life Expectancy at Birth

Source: http://www.worldbank.org/depweb/english/modules/social/life/t-map.html *(OECD).*

Life expectancy at birth	No. of states
Lower than 55	(38)
55–64	(23)
65–69	(34)
70–74	(47)
75 or more	(40)
No data	(12)

TABLE 10.2 Child Mortality Rate—Selected Countries, 1988–1998		
Country	**Male per 1,000**	**Female per 1,000**
Bangladesh	37	47
Bolivia	53	47
Chad	106	99
China*	10	11
India	29	42
Niger	212	232
Nigeria	118	202
Pakistan	22	37
Togo	75	90
Tunisia	19	19
Turkey	12	14

* Official figures

SOURCE: United Nations Development Program (UNDP), *World Development Indicators*, Table 2.18.

as we know, have some of the poorest populations in the world. In both countries the dominant religion values males over females. All families, especially poor families, prefer boys to girls. Boys stay with the family, while girls leave at marriage to become part of a new family. If a family is poor, it can ill afford to raise many children. In Niger, where food is scarce, it is easier to neglect the girls and give the boys food so that they have a better chance of staying alive. As we reported earlier, in India if a wife fails to deliver a boy, the husband can set fire to her to get rid of her and take a new wife who might bear him the desired son. The situation is so tense that pregnant women are using the modern technology of ultrasound, not to determine the health of the fetus, but to determine its sex. If the test reveals a boy, the woman is happy. If it is not a boy, the woman will abort it. Indian medical practitioners find gender-selective abortion abhorrent. But unless attitudes and economic conditions change, the practice will continue.[22]

If we add the high child mortality rates to low enrollment rates of girls in primary and secondary school, we can expect to find a relatively low number of women in the poorest countries employed in the paid labor force. In India for example, there are two men working for every woman. In Niger the statistic is about the same. While women in most South American countries participate in the paid labor force at about the same rate as in the industrialized states, the same is not true in Central America. There, because of extensive poverty, women must work in their own small plots to raise enough food to enable their families to survive.

Our last poverty indicator is the fertility rate, or the average number of children a woman bears in her lifetime. You have probably guessed that if poverty is associated with high child mortality rates and low literacy rates, particularly among women, then it is also associated with a high fertility rate. A large number of growing babies clearly makes many mouths to feed and bodies to care for, and places large demands on weak educational systems. In some cases, the data justify this assumption; in other cases not. In virtually every country in the world the fertility rate has dropped. Yet it is still very high in the poorest states of Africa, and highest of all in the somewhat better-off Middle East. In Central Africa the fertility rate in most of the states runs between 6 and 6.7 births per woman. In the Muslim Middle East,

Oman has the highest fertility rate of 7.2 per woman. Saudi Arabia is next with 6.1 and Iraq third with 5.5. However, if we turn to the states with the largest populations, India and China, we find that the fertility rate is now relatively low. In India women today bear on the average fewer than 3 children per family. The fertility rate has been brought down by an aggressive government policy to sterilize women after they have had three children and of course, women's interest in killing their girl babies in the hopes that next time it will be a boy. In China the one-child policy has resulted in a fertility rate of 1.9.[23] This rate is still almost twice as high as that desired by the Chinese authorities, whose goal is one woman, one child. As you might expect, neither China nor India is included in the group of poorest countries.

A final relationship between women and poverty that bears mention here is the global trafficking in women and girls for prostitution. Trafficking in human beings, or slavery, is as old as the human race and has experienced a marked increase in the past decade in response to the expansion of the global economy. Chinese hidden in sealed containers in a cargo ship pay thousands of dollars to risk their lives to get to the New World. Mexicans and others from Central America run the gauntlet of fences, dogs, and police on the Mexican/U.S. border. However, 80 percent of the traffic is in young women and girls under 18!

To find out more about global trafficking in women and girls for prositution go to **www.ablongman.com/duncan.**

Unscrupulous businessmen purchase daughters of poor parents in Southeast Asia, or simply "shanghai" or kidnap them to work as indentured servants in underground textile factories in the United States. An estimated 500,000 women are trafficked from Eastern Europe and the former republics of the Soviet Union. Most of these end up in Western Europe, many in the German and Dutch red light districts. In the Netherlands, Dutch data indicate that most of these women are under 21 and are being recruited at progressively younger ages.[24] Canada and the United States also engage in this kind of traffic, with women coming from South America, Thailand, and the Philippines. By 1998 the problem had become so serious that in the fall, the Boston-based newspaper *The Christian Science Monitor* ran a ten-part exposé. For these women, globalization has become a nightmare. You will learn more about this terrible problem in the case study at the end of the chapter.

This section has covered the problem of poverty as defined by the UN's five indicators. As you have read, the causes of poverty are multiple and linked, making it difficult for the poorest countries to improve their situation. Women are the most affected by poverty because society in a large part of the world values male children over girls, gets rid of unwanted girl children, forbids girls to attend school, and treats mothers cruelly if she fails to give birth to a boy. Unwanted teenage girls may be sold into prostitution by desperate parents or tricked by clever traffickers into becoming another number in the growing number of high-jacked prostitutes. The failure of many countries to support girl children and to provide education to lift them out of poverty thus multiplies the problems the governments of the lesser developed states (LDCs) have in surmounting poverty and achieving sustained economic development.

With the millennium development goals and their indicators, the international community has developed a solid statistical approach to clarifying our understanding of why there is poverty and why it is so difficult to eradicate. It is time now to look at international efforts to address the problem in all its urgency and complexity.

International Responses to Poverty

International attempts to alleviate poverty have had varied success. We will begin this discussion by looking at the kinds of programs that did not succeed. In general, the most unsuccessful programs have been large-scale projects, such as dam building, water treatment plants, hospital construction, large industrial facilities, and energy infrastructure. In Africa and Central America in particular, attempts to pursue development policies that had proved effective in the West fell short of expectations. Large injections of aid did not produce commensurate improvements in income or living conditions. Substantial international private investment, even when linked with international aid or loans, was similarly ineffectual in bringing large numbers out of poverty. Even in those cases where the national government of a poor state consciously adopted an export-oriented or **import-substitution** economic development strategy, little occurred to modify the conditions of the poor.

The West has been preaching the benefits of population control and family planning to the rest of the world for a long time now. Reduce the number of births and family incomes will rise, we say. However, even when fertility rates go down, the numbers living in absolute poverty seem to grow. Development experts have thus turned to other answers to the stubborn problem. The first step, they decided, was to get as accurate a picture as possible of the problem. As things turned out, data collection proved one of the more successful approaches to alleviating poverty, as we shall see in the next section.

Data Collection   As development experts tried to understand why earlier policies had not worked, they saw a need to create a *measurement system* that would more accurately assess poverty within countries and provide a more precise comparison of poverty between countries. The result was the development in the 1990s of five indices related to poverty and development. These *indices* differ from the five *indicators* of poverty discussed earlier in that the indicators measure the most salient aspects of poverty. The *indices* combine these indicators with other criteria to develop an entire measurement structure or system, as shown in Table 10.3. Each index ranks states according to its selected criteria. A given state may have a slightly different rank on another index. We can thus see immediately where every state is in relation to all the others across all the development indices.

The first three indices of Table 10.3 focus on the positive side of economic and social development. The **Human Development Index (HDI)** provides a comparative measure of a state's economic development. Previously, a state's economic development had been primarily measured by its gross domestic product (GDP) per capita. But by 1990, there was general agreement that factors other than making money contributed to development. HDI is thus a mix of many factors related to development: (1) GDP and GDP per capita, as measured on purchasing power parities between states (PPPS) and (2) three of the five poverty indicators: life expectancy at birth; combined enrollments in elementary, secondary, and university education; and adult literacy rate. When all these factors are thrown into the hopper, mixed, and sorted, we find that in 1999, Canada and Norway come out at the top of HDI, followed by the USA, Japan, and Belgium. At the bottom of the list of 174 countries is Sierra Leone, with Niger, Ethiopia, Burkina Faso, and Burundi ranking only slightly higher. China ranks 106 as a medium development country, while India falls into the low development category with a rank of 139.

The **Gender Development Index (GDI)** for the first time puts the achievements of women into the measurement of human development and illustrates how cultural or economic bias against women depresses a state's overall level of economic development. Essentially, the index uses the same data and same statistical measures as HDI but also captures inequalities in achievement between women and men. GDI is HDI adjusted downward for gender inequality. A third new index, called the

Import-Substitution
The development of national industries to produce products that might be expensive to purchase and import from the global marketplace. A prime example is the former Soviet Union's automotive industry.

Human Development Index (HDI)
An index that provides a comparative measure of a state's economic development. It is used in UN comparative economic databases.

Gender Development Index (GDI)
An index that puts the conditions of women into the measurement of human development. Essentially, the index uses the same data and same statistical measures as HDI but captures inequalities in achievement between women and men.

TABLE 10.3 Top and Bottom Five Countries in the UN Human Development Indices

Index	Top Five	Bottom Five
HDI	Canada	Burundi
	Norway	Burkina Faso
	United States	Ethiopia
	Japan	Niger
	Belgium	Sierra Leone
GDI	Canada	Guinea-Bissau
	Norway	Burundi
	United States	Burkina Faso
	Australia	Ethiopia
	Sweden	Niger
GEM	Norway	Jordan
	Sweden	Mauritania
	Denmark	Togo
	Canada	Pakistan
	Germany	Niger
HPI-1	Barbados	Central African Republic
	Trinidad and Tobago	Ethiopia
	Uruguay	Sierra Leone
	Costa Rica	Burkina Faso
	Cuba	Niger
HPI-2	Sweden	New Zealand
	Netherlands	Spain
	Germany	United Kingdom
	Norway	Ireland
	Italy	United States

SOURCE: United Nations Development Program (UNDP), *Human Development Report 1999* (New York: Oxford University Press, 1999), p. 128.

Gender Empowerment Index (GEM)
An index that measures the extent to which women have become equal participants with men in leadership positions in the social, economic, cultural, and political life of their country.

Human Poverty Index (HPI-1) and (HPI-2)
An index that measures the proportion of people living in a developing state (HPI-1) or an industrialized state (HPI-2), who are affected by three key deprivations: longevity or life expectancy, knowledge, and a decent living standard.

Gender Empowerment Index (GEM) measures the extent to which women have become equal participants with men in leadership positions in the social, economic, cultural, and political life of their country. The **Human Poverty Index (HPI)** measures just what its name suggests, poverty. The index reflects the distribution of economic and social progress and measures the backlog of deprivations that still exist within and between states. There are two versions of this index, one for developing countries (**HPI-1**) and one for industrialized countries (**HPI-2**).

HPI-1 reflects the proportion of people living in a developing state who are relatively deprived of three key factors: longevity or life expectancy, knowledge, and a decent living standard. Estimates of HPI-1 have been worked out for 77 countries. At the top of the list are two Caribbean Islands, Barbados (with a value of 2), and Trinidad and Tobago. The last entry in HPI-1 is Niger, with a value of 62 preceded by Burkina Faso, Sierra Leone, and Ethiopia. China is number 16 on the list, while India is 47.

Comparing the HPI with the HDI tells us how well the achievements of development are distributed in a country. For example, while China and Guyana are very close on the HDI index (98 and 99 respectively), China ranks thirtieth on the HPI index, while Guyana ranks eleventh. The gap between HDI and HPI tells us that the availability of those factors essential to economic development and better living conditions are more equally distributed in Guyana than in China.

HPI-2 provides the same type of measurement for the industrialized countries. You will recall that on HDI, the top ranking countries were Canada, Norway, the United States, Japan, and Belgium. On the HPI-2 index, the countries at the top of the list are Sweden, Netherlands, Germany, Norway, and Italy. France is seventh, and Canada, tenth. The United States is in last place with a rank of seventeen! Yet, the United States ranks third on HDI, and is in first place as regards GDP per capita. These rankings tell us that income and access to knowledge, longevity, and income are very unevenly distributed in the richest country in the world.

The GDI and GEM round out our picture of poverty, social justice, and gender equality in the world. The GDI tells us that only a very few countries have a systematic practice of breaking down the barriers to gender equality. It further shows that wealth or poverty is not everything. Some countries, like Sierra Leone, can improve the lot of their poorest women while remaining among the desperately poor states. The Gender Empowerment Index shows us that in the last analysis, attitude counts for something. The Scandinavian states have done most to bring women into the decision-making process and rank highest on the index. In the bottom rankings we find once again those state with a societal bias against women and girls.

The Indices of Human Development have given us a more refined and accurate comparative picture of social, economic, and political conditions around the world than we ever had before. Next we will see how these indices have contributed to a change in the design of programs to alleviate the misery they attempt to measure.

Targeted Microinvestments   More accurate information on the multidimensional character of poverty has changed and continues to change the way international and national organizations respond to global poverty. At the present time, the richest 20 percent of the world's population control 86 percent of the world's GDP, engage in 82 percent of the world's exports of goods and services, control 68 percent of foreign direct investment, and have 94 percent of the world's Internet users.[25] With such global domination, it would seem easy for the wealthy states to allocate large sums of money to alleviate poverty and distribute global wealth more equally. But throwing billions of dollars everywhere around the world where poverty was diagnosed did not happen nor is it going to happen. The wealthiest nations spend less on domestic programs and health and nutrition than they spend on cosmetics, cigarettes, pet foods, alcohol, drugs, and the military. And in the past decade, these same states dropped the amount of aid they gave to the least developed countries by 23 percent.[26] From 1990 to 2000, official development assistance (ODA) of the donor states fell steadily from 0.33 percent of donor country GNP to 0.22 percent, a far cry from the 0.7 percent UN Secretary General Kofi Annan would like to see.[27] In 2001, for example, the U.S. government spent approximately $10 billion on ODA, the largest amount of any state, but this money came out of a total federal budget of $1.9 trillion! The picture becomes a little brighter when you consider that that same year, Americans gave to charitable organizations and international NGOs some $34 billion to help combat poverty overseas.[28] Even $44 billion, however, is a far cry from the billions of dollars needed to combat the multiple dimensions of poverty. What then are the options?

To find out about the current international approach to women's issues, go to **www.ablongman.com/ duncan.**

Muhammed Yunus: Founder of the microcredit movement and the Grameen Bank.

The indices we have just reviewed are pointers to where international assistance and investment could be most effectively targeted. A more equal distribution of wealth requires empowering people at the local level to go into business and produce something for sale. With the money they earn, they can buy consumer items they need or want at the local market, thereby building up the local economy.

Foreign direct investment (FDI) is a traditional option and since 1990, private financial flows to developing countries have increased a little over five times. However, 80 percent of these investments went to just 10 developing countries and represented only 2.5 percent of all FDI flows.[29] Still, investment is a very important and necessary option.

In addition, the international financial community seems to be settling on two other complementary and more innovative responses. The first is to empower individuals at the local level to become entrepreneurs by providing capital up front. The poorest states support this objective but add that reconstructing the local economy will not work unless the industrialized countries abolish all tariffs for the 48 poorest countries so that the local products of these states can reach the global market. The second answer is to focus on women, the poorest adult members of every society, as the vehicle to turn poverty around.

The change in the world financial community's attitude from "big is best" to "small may be better" is largely attributable to the work of Muhammad Yunus and his invention of **microcredit.**

Microcredit
The provision of small loans by a lending institution to individuals.

Born in what was then the State of Bengal, India, Yunus in 1975 returned from a Fulbright fellowship with a doctorate in economics earned in the United States to confront perhaps the world's worst poverty conditions in the newly independent country of Bangladesh. Being a professor of economics at the country's best university, Yunus decided that he could do more for his country researching the causes of poverty than teaching abstract economics to a privileged few. For two years he walked about his province with his graduate students searching for answers. He conceived of the idea of microcredit one day in 1976 when he was interviewing a woman who made bamboo stools. He learned that since she had no capital, she borrowed the equivalent of $.50 to buy the raw materials for the stools. After repaying the middleman she had $.01 left after all her work and the sale of the stools. Yunus found 42 other women in the same situation. These women were not lazy, he realized; they simply lacked capital. He reached into his own savings and lent each Bangladeshi Taka 317, or $5.50 USD. He knew he had to institutionalize this lending process for it to expand and grow, and when no bank would work with him, he started his own experimental project, staffing his "bank" with his graduate students.

In 1979 the Central Bank of Bangladesh was won over and arranged for the Grameen project, as it was called, to be serviced from the branch offices of the seven state-run banks, first in one province of the country, and by 1981, throughout the country. Grameen was incorporated as an independent bank in 1983. The bank now has over 2.5 million borrowers with 500 Grameen spin-offs, including the Full Circle Fund on Chicago's south side. Here, the large majority of borrowers, like the first Grameen borrowers, are women. They are mostly welfare mothers who borrow as little as $300 a month.

One of the two extraordinary things about the bank is that loan repayment is extremely high, putting the lie to the financial world's traditional perception that the poor do not repay their debts. The other amazing part about the bank is that most of its clients have been women. Loaning to women, even in the United States in 1976, was considered in bank circles to be a risky business. Many states required a male co-signer of the loan. Yet virtually all the women who borrowed from the Grameen project repaid their loans.

Grameen's success made the world financial community sit up and take note. While more conservative bankers insisted that large infrastructure projects like sewage and water systems were the best investment for poverty, many others caught Yunus's vision and saw possibilities in providing capital to the poor. The World Bank has turned its attention in earnest to what it calls microfinancing and microcredit with extraordinary success. A group called International Financing and Development (IFAD) has only good news to report from its microfinancing in Ghana. The United States has a small commercial and private loan program in Russia to assist people who are too poor to qualify for a loan from a regular Russian bank. Repayment of these loans, including two-year car loans, has been in the ninety-seventh percentile.[30]

In recent years the world community has started a systematic program of targeting women for special grants and loans. Some of these programs may seem very strange in the Western world but perfectly normal where they are implemented. In a competition called "Development Marketplace," held by the World Bank in February 2000, a project entitled "Ending Genital Cutting"—focused on women in the West African state of Guinea—was among the winners. The project director explained that female circumcision provides the women who perform it an income of sorts. The award-winning project aims to provide 10 women with capital so that "they can turn toward more entrepreneurial pursuits."[31]

In the second area of deprivation, access to knowledge, global financial institutions as well as national governments have developed many programs. Some of the most successful provide student loans to finance higher education to complement the traditional system of scholarships and stipends. A recent major success story was the World Bank's financing of student loans in the African state of Namibia. Loan repayment was very high, and university graduates were able to find better opportunities than they would have had with less education.

Many literacy programs and education projects have been targeted specifically at women to help them escape from poverty. A full list of these programs may be found on the UN's Womenwatch website.

In the third area of deprivation, longevity, the World Health Organization and humanitarian NGOs, in cooperation with national health organizations, have eradicated some of the worst communicable diseases and provided minimal health care to the very poor. For example, today, over 90 percent of the world's children have been vaccinated against tuberculosis and the major childhood diseases. Smallpox has been eradicated. These are huge steps forward in improving life expectancy for the most vulnerable of the world's poor.

Sad to say, tuberculosis made a comeback in the last five years of the twentieth century and has reached epidemic proportions in Russia. A second serious threat to the health of the poor is the AIDS epidemic raging throughout Central Africa, Thailand, and Southeast Asia. States in sub-Saharan Africa may be losing most of their most active and educated population (over 25 million live with HIV/AIDS), a loss that helps explain the persistent instability, violence, and economic problems in that region. What is less known is that in Africa, the most vulnerable are women of childbearing age. The UN estimates that AIDS has orphaned some 13.2 million African children.[32] Moreover, without treatment, infected women give birth to infected children, continuing the epidemic. While great advances have been made in the treatment of HIV, the medications are very costly, and thus largely inaccessible to people in Africa.

We should not leave the subject of caring for the world's poor without mention of one of the most famous women of our time, who was widely revered as a saint in her lifetime: Mother Teresa.

Born in Albania at the beginning of the twentieth century, Mother Teresa committed to the vocation of nun as a teenager. After serving the poor in various countries, she was sent to Calcutta, India. There she was appalled by the sheer number of poor people who were dying on the streets with no one to care for them. The hospital and sisterhood she founded in Calcutta to accompany the dying on their final journey raised the world's consciousness about human dignity and global poverty. When she died in 1997, millions of grateful Indians and other nationalities accompanied her coffin to its final resting place, proving how much one dedicated caring individual can do.

You may think that with so much poverty in the world, thinking smaller as the World Bank and the U.S. government seem to be doing is a further abandonment by the rich countries of the world of their poorer neighbors. The jury is still out on the question. We now know that the some of the vast development schemes of the second half of the twentieth century produced unintended consequences: agricultural pollution of water basins, industrial and automobile pollution in cities, and soil erosion and depletion. One thing is certain: If the world is not to be divided between the very, very rich and the very, very poor, with women marginalized as they have been at the edge of the monetary economy, we have to develop programs that reach the poor where they are and provide them tools for self-improvement. These tools are capital to raise their living conditions, education to advance, health services for a healthy life, and all three to strengthen their human dignity.

How Has the International Community Responded to State Violations of Global Justice and Human Rights?

Our last section turns from the intersection of human rights, women's rights, and poverty to look at human rights issues alone. What can or should the international community do when the Security Council agrees that rights are being violated? First we will look at the historical record of international intervention and then turn to a discussion of the pros and cons of such action.

The Historical Record on International Intervention

In December 1945, as allied victory in Europe seemed certain, the allied powers met in London to determine the procedure for prosecuting and punishing persons charged with crimes committed during the Second World War. The resulting Control Council Law No. 10 identified three kinds of international crimes: crimes against peace, war crimes, and crimes against humanity. On December 11, 1946, the newly constituted General Assembly of the newly formed United Nations affirmed these principles. Among the crimes identified as crimes against humanity were enslavement, torture, rape, other inhumane acts committed against a civilian population, and persecutions on political, racial, or religious grounds, whether or not these acts violated the domestic law of the country where the acts were perpetrated.

Up to the 1990s, the United Nations tended to emphasize economic sanctions, and economic and humanitarian aid to bring about a state's voluntary compliance with UN human rights and criminal principles. The best-known example is the 43-year embargo against South Africa to force the South African government to end its policy of apartheid.

In the 1990s, the UN position markedly changed. In 1996, President Clinton agreed to a UN force to maintain peace between the warring ethnic and religious parties in Bosnia. When the UN effort broke down, the United States with Security Council agreement led a NATO force to Bosnia. In 1999 evidence of Serbian attempts to ethnically cleanse the Kosovar population in the Serb province of Kosovo encouraged President Clinton to ask the Security Council for another peacekeeping force. His proposal was stiffly resisted by Russia and China and the United States put together another NATO military initiative. In 1999 as well, the UN formally sent a peacekeeping force to East Timor under Australian leadership to stop the killing of East Timorese by Indonesian militia following the vote for independence. In 2003, France unilaterally sent troops into the Ivory Coast to stop a civil war. That same year, President George W. Bush requested Security Council agreement to send troops to Iraq to effect Iraqi regime change and force Saddam Hussein to give up his weapons of mass destruction (WMD). Opposition from France, Germany, and Russia ruled out any Security Council agreement. Agreement within NATO was also impossible. The United States put together what it called "a coalition of willing states" and invaded Iraq without UN approval.

These five events suggest that the UN has moved away from its voluntary compliance position but only so long as the big five in the Security Council are in consensus on military intervention. The Security Council was irreparably split on Iraq. France urged giving more time for voluntary compliance while the United

States argued that Security Council resolutions not backed by the real threat of force were meaningless and irrelevant.

Current Arguments For and Against International Intervention

Today, there seems to be no international consensus on UN intervention. Before the invasion of Iraq, most nations thought that intervention to stop flagrant human rights abuses was appropriate even if it that intervention violated the sovereignty of UN member states. But opposition to this policy was building up with the U.S. decision to bomb Serbia and invade Kosovo.

One of the staunchest defenders of the right of UN intervention has been UN Secretary General Kofi Annan. On a number of occasions, he has offered a persuasive vision of world community that sets human rights equal to or above the right of state sovereignty. In his view, the Charter of the United Nations empowers the Security Council to use force in the *common interest*. What is the common interest? The UN Charter says that it is *human security*. Annan argues the world cannot stand idly by when people are suffering from the "scourge of war."[33] Annan sees global human security linked to individual security, which in turn is linked to good governance and respect for human rights.[34] Nevertheless, despite knowledge of Saddam Hussein's cruelty, Annan was adamantly opposed to the U.S. war in Iraq on the grounds that Iraq was trying to comply with the UN order to give up his weapons of mass destruction (WMD), and war was unnecessary.

Others point out that UN interventions have been few and highly selective. All involved small states but not all small states with severe human rights violations. There was no invasion of Rwanda, for example, when the Hutsi and Tutsi tribes practiced genocide on each other. Of the states the UN did take military action against, one involved an entity that was a non-functioning new state, and two were states with severe economic and social problems: Yugoslavia and Indonesia. Of the non-UN military actions against sovereign states, human rights were secondary considerations. The Americans unilaterally invaded Afghanistan in 2001, not because of that country's human rights violations but because it harbored terrorists suspected of involvement in the 9/11 attacks. Regime change may have been the main goal in Iraq, but the United States primary publicly stated reason for invading Iraq was because Sadam Hussein had not complied with UN resolutions.

When Russia sent troops back into Chechnya in the Fall of 1999, the West immediately accused the Russians of human rights abuses. British Prime Minister Tony Blair went so far as to insist that the West do something. But outgoing Russian President Boris Yelstin sternly warned the West that it could not push Russia around because Russia had nuclear bombs. Yeltsin's successor Vladimir Putin reinforced this message by declaring that Russia was renouncing its non-first use of nuclear weapons. The hard truth may be that the UN took no action against Russia because it knew the cost was too great.

Women ask why no UN action is taken against countries that permit or condone violence against women. They are quick to answer their own question. Violence against women is not universally considered a violation of human rights. Besides, who would go to war with China or Saudi Arabia on the issue?

The accuracy of the feminist insight was borne out by a BBC reporter commenting on Russian cruelty in Chechnya in February 2000. Asked about reports of multiple rapes of young Chechen women, he replied that these reports were true. But, he added, there were rapes in Bosnia. The Americans raped in Vietnam, and there were rapes during World War II. The rapes in Chechnya were nothing out of the usual.

Some argue that the UN Charter empowers the world community to take up arms in cases of serious violations of human rights. The other side argues that the more things change, the more they remain the same: The interests of the dominant, stronger state(s) rule the world as they always have. The stronger states will pick and choose what instances of human rights violations they will act upon, based on the relative power capability of the state so accused. Can you identify the liberals and the realists in the argument?

CHAPTER SUMMARY

Women, poverty, global justice, and human rights are interrelated global problems.

What Do We Mean When We Talk About Global Justice and Human Rights?

Justice may be seen as balance or as an equilibrium involving equal distribution.

Justice may also be seen as due process, with its emphasis on a legal system in which everyone is treated equally under the law regardless of wealth, race, sex, or religion.

Human rights are the principles upon which due process is built. Justice as fairness seeks to redress the inequality of condition that human beings experience when they enter this world.

What Is the Relationship Between the History of Women, Global Justice, and Human Rights?

Women's history is one of almost universally low political, economic, and social status. No culture has considered women "human" in the same way men are human.

In women's history, there have been a few influential individuals, most of whom were upper-class women, women rulers, or in rare cases, philosophers and writers.

The industrial revolution initially did little to alleviate the continued subjugation and discrimination of women.

In 1800, women in Europe and America—with few exceptions—could not own property, had no civil rights, and were considered the property of their husbands. They were also the lowest paid workers.

Western women were appalled at women's status in non-Western countries.

The women's movement dates from 1848. It had essentially two branches: The American and British movement focused on due process, and the continental European movements focused on equality of condition and utilizing Marxism as a tool to advance their cause.

Both the suffrage movement and the women's socialist movement experienced increasingly severe repression up to the First World War.

Today, the international community does not yet agree that women's rights are human rights. While the modern-day women's movement has helped achieve economic progress and human rights for women in many countries, the United Nations has yet to endorse the statement that women's rights are human rights.

How Do Feminist Theories of International Relations Explain the Relationship Between Discrimination Against Women, Global Justice, and Human Rights?

Feminist theories of international relations help us uncover the gender bias in world politics.

There are five kinds of feminist international relations theory: radical feminism, socialist feminism, liberal feminism, postcolonial feminism, and postmodern feminism.

We used these approaches to uncover gender bias in three areas of international relations:

1. In the area of international security, feminists argue that the mainstreaming of feminist theory in international relations would do away with the rigid male conception of the international world as states with fixed borders operating in an anarchic world. Feminists see the international world as multilayered and multidimensional, composed of many levels of government and many kinds of issues. National security today has been replaced with the concept of homeland security, which involves the whole international system at all its levels of administration.
2. In the area of international economics, feminist theorists argue that current models of economic development have not taken into account women's particular needs nor the important role they play in the development process. Women's unpaid work is not part of global economic statistics, yet is an essential contribution to a state's economic development.
3. In the area of environmental security, feminists argue that men act without regard to the effect of those actions on nature. Women, in contrast, live in nature. The UN Commission on Environment and Development, headed by a woman, published *Our Common Future*. It was the first study to make mention of *sustainable development*.

What Is the Relationship Between Poverty, Global Justice, and Human Rights?

Poverty is a multidimensional condition that the international community has defined by a set of five indicators. The first indicator is the incidence of extreme poverty defined as earning under one dollar USD a day. The second is a state's literacy rate. The third is a state's mortality rate for children under five years of age. The fourth is a state's fertility rate, and the final indicator is the percentage of a state's population that has access to safe drinking water

The causes of poverty are multiple. These include lack of natural resources and low ratings on the five indicators, with the lowest ratings of all for women in the states that rank lowest on the five indicators. The indicators suggest that the continued discrimination against women in many countries is a main cause of poverty.

There have been essentially two types of international response to poverty:

1. The first is the refinement of methodology in the collection of data on poverty. In the past ten years, the UNDP has developed four kinds of measurements of economic development for any state. These are the Human Development Index (HDI), the Human Poverty Index (HPI; with one scale for developing nations and one for developed nations), the Gender Discrimination Index (GDI), and the Gender Empowerment Index (GEM).
2. The second is the elaboration of investments and aid programs specifically targeted toward poor people, especially women.

In the past few years, there have been two shifts in the world community's approach to end poverty.

1. The first is the shift from the financing of projects on the macrolevel to the financing of microprojects on the local level. The most salient success story of this shift is the Grameen Bank.
2. The second is the shift from considering women's problems secondary to the problems of economic growth to mainstreaming women in economic growth projects.

How Has the International Community Responded to State Violations of Global Justice and Human Rights?

In preparation for the international trials that took place after World War II, the allied powers drew up three kinds of international crimes that they considered appropriate for an international court to prosecute. These were crimes of war, crimes of peace, and crimes against humanity.

The newly constituted United Nations affirmed these categories in 1946.

Up to the 1990s, the main approach to persuading states to comply voluntarily with UN human rights principles was to use economic sanctions, alienation from the international community, and humanitarian aid.

Since the 1990s, there have been four cases of UN intervention on charges of a state's violation of human rights and commission of crimes against humanity, and three instances of non-UN sanctioned intervention.

Current arguments for and against a state's intervention set issues of human rights against state sovereignty. There is a growing consensus that in states where human rights abuses have occurred, the UN and NATO have a right to intervene. Those in favor of intervention argue that it is the duty of the international community to safeguard human rights. Those opposed say that interventions have been highly selective, based both on the relative foreign policy interest in the intervention and on the relative power capability of the accused state.

ENDNOTES

[1] National Public Radio devoted a section of its news coverage on June 8, 2000, to reports of continued bride and wife burning in India. The report especially stressed the role of the mother-in-law in wanting to be rid of her daughter-in-law.

[2] Senior paper by Gerry Lemcke, SUNY Brockport, 1998, is an exhaustive analysis of Internet data on the maltreatment of women, especially in Afghanistan. The interested student is urged in particular to go to the following web pages: the Feminist Majority webpage (*http://www.feminist.org/afghan0*) and the Revolutionary Association of Women of Afghanistan (*http://www.rawa.org*). Further data may be found in the U.S. Department of State's Annual Report on International Religious Freedom for 1999: Afghanistan. (*http://www.state.gov/www/global/human_rights/irf/irf_rpt/*)

[3] Vincent Châtel and Chuck Ferre, "The Victims of the Holocaust: An estimation", *http://www.jewishgen.org/Forgotten Camps/General/VictimsEngl.html*

[4] United Nations, World Summit, "Facts about Water."

[5] Vincent Châtel and Chuck Ferre, "The Victims of the Holocaust: An estimation", *http://www.jewishgen.org/Forgotten Camps/General/VictimsEngl.html*

[6] UN Universal Declaration of Human Rights, *http://www.un.org/right/50/dclara.htm*

[7] John King Fairbank, *China: a New History* (Cambridge, Mass: The Belknap Press of Harvard University, 1992), pp. 18–19.

[8] Teresa of Avila's best known work is *Interior Castle*, a mystical account of the turning of the soul to God.

[9] John Knox (1558), "First Blast of the Trumpet Against the Monstrous Regimen of Women," as cited in *The Los Angeles Times*, June 29, 1993.

[10] Elise Boulding, *The Underside of History*, rev. ed., vol. 2 (Newbury Park, CA: Sage Publications, 1992), pp. 60–63.

[11] Evelyn Fox Keller, *Reflections on Gender and Science* (New Haven: Yale University Press, 1985).

[12] Executive Summary, Women Watch Working Groups, *http://un.org/womenwatch*

[13] Iris Chang, *The Rape of Nanking* (London: Penguin Books, Ltd., 1997). The Japanese have never apologized for what happened.

[14] The classification of feminist theory is grounded in the analysis found in V. Spike Peterson and Anne Sisson Runyon, *Global Gender Issues*, 2nd ed. (Boulder, CO: Westview Press, 1999), pp. 165–177.

[15] The following discussion is based on J. Ann Tichner, *Gender in International Relations: Feminist Perspectives on Achieving Global Security* (New York: Columbia University Press, 1992), pp. 127–144.

[16] Ibid., p. 129.

[17] United Nations, World Commission on Environment and Development, *Our Common Future* (New York and Oxford: Oxford University Press, 1987).

[18] United Nations, World Summit, "Facts about Africa."

[19] OECD, Human Development Report 2002 (New York: Oxford University Press, 2002), p. 17.

[20] United Nations, World Summit, "Facts about Water."

[21] UNDP, *Human Development Report 1998* (Oxford: Oxford University Press, 1999), pp. 145–146.

[22] Of some 8,000 abortions performed in a clinic in Bombay, India, in 1993, 7,999 were of female fetuses. As long as women are rejected and abused for giving birth to girl children, this practice will continue. See John Ward Anderson and Molly Moore, "The Burden of Womanhood," *The Washington Post National Weekly Edition*, March 22–28, 1993.

[23] *Human Development Report 1998*, pp. 176–177.

[24] UNDP, *Human Development Report 1999* (Oxford: Oxford University Press, 1999), p. 89.

[25] The data for the following pages has been taken from *Human Development Report 1999*, pp. 134–150.

[26] OECD, *World Development Report 1999*, p. 2.

[27] "Study: Poor Countries Marginalized" (Bangkok, Thailand, AP, 5:15 PM ET 02/13/00)

[28] United Nations, World Summit, "Facts about Finance and Trade."

[29]Carol Adelman, "America's Helping Hand," *Wall Street Journal*, August 21, 2002, p. 12. Federal budget data is from Congressional Budget Office, "Historical Budget Data, 1960–2001," Table 1. *http://www.cbo.gov/showdoc.cfm?index=1821&sequence=0#t6*

[30]For more information, see The Russian Microcredit Project, Document 42, a US Department of State /NISCUP Funded Partnership Among the University of Washington-Evans School of Public Affairs, the Siberian Academy of Public Administration, and Irkutsk State University, the Russian Microfinance Group, "Curriculum, Research and Outreach" at Microfinance.ru.pdf. and "From Hope to Harvest-Microcredit-IFAD's 20th Anniversary, *http://www.ifad.org/events/past/anniv/co.htm.*

[31]Steven Pearlstein, Staff Writer, 'World Bank Rethinks Poverty, Report Finds Traditional Approach Fails' *Washington Post*, September 13, 2000, p. E01.

[32]United Nations, World Summit, "Africa."

[33]Kofi Annan, Address at the United Nations University, "Japan's World Role in the 21st Century," Tokyo, November 11, 1999. (*http://www.un.org/News/ossg/sgcuff99.htm*)

[34]Kofi Annan, Remarks at the World Bank, "On Peace and Development: One Struggle—Two Fronts," Washington D.C., October 19,1999. (*http://www,un.org/News/ossg/sgcuff99.htm*)

CASE STUDY

The Global Sex Trade: A Violation of Human Rights or a Business with Globalization Problems?

This case study puts into sharp relief the major issues discussed in this chapter: global justice; global resistance to acknowledging and granting women's rights; the relation between women's rights, human rights, and global poverty; and the case for international intervention in states documented to have serious violation of human rights. Sex trafficking is as old as organized human society, but it increased astronomically in the last decades of the twentieth century as a result of forces we have discussed throughout the book: the increase in the movement of goods, people, and money across borders; and the global scope of problems such as poverty, crime, and terrorism.

This case study includes four readings. The first provides an overview of the sex trade and is drawn from a Congressional Report written in 2000. The second reading comes from the *Philadelphia Inquirer,* describing the reaction of a Burmese mother when she learns that the daughter she sold into sex slavery is not working in a small border village in Thailand but has been sent for bigger profits to the Thai capital of Bangkok. The Thai village lies across the Mai Sai River on the Thai/Burmese border, just a short distance from the famous Golden Triangle formed by the conjunction of Burma (today called Myanmar by its military rulers), Thailand, and Laos at the northern rim of the Indochinese Peninsula. The Golden Triangle is a center of the global heroin trade. In this article, you will see how poverty influences family values and decisions in a country (Burma) that has been closed to the world since 1988 and governed by a military junta. We have no accurate data on the country's real gross domestic product because of the high volume of black-market, illicit border trade. But Burma is considered one of the poorest Asian countries. AIDS is so serious that the mortality rate now exceeds the birth rate. Recently, it has opened its border with Thailand at Mai Sai, where trade in everything, including human beings, has increased significantly.

The third article focuses on the sex trade in the Canadian city of Toronto. The article comes from one of the city's main alternative entertainment weeklies. The fourth reading summarizes the propositions approved in the UN Protocol to Prevent, Suppress, and Punish Trafficking in Persons, Especially Women and Children, supplementing the United Nations Convention Against Transnational Organized Crime, approved in November, 2000.

Note that there is an NGO defending the rights of women on both sides of the sex trafficking issue. How do you feel about that?

SEX TRADE: THIRD WORLD TO FIRST WORLD

1. Overview: Trafficking in Women and Children: The U.S. and International Response

Scope of the Problem Worldwide

The trafficking of people, especially women and children, for prostitution and forced labor is one of the fastest growing areas of international criminal activity and one that is of increasing concern to the U.S. Administration, Congress, and the international community. Although men are also victimized, the overwhelming majority of those trafficked are women and children. According to official estimates, between 1 and 2 million women and children are trafficked each year worldwide for forced labor, domestic servitude, or sexual exploitation. An estimated 50,000 persons are trafficked each year to the United States. Trafficking is now considered the third largest source of profits for organized crime, behind only drugs and guns, generating billions of dollars annually.

Trafficking is a problem that affects virtually every country in the world. Generally, the flow of trafficking is from less developed countries to industrialized nations, including the United States, or toward neighboring countries with marginally higher standards of living. Since trafficking is an underground criminal enterprise, there are no precise statistics on the extent of the problem and estimates are unreliable. But even using conservative estimates, the scope of the problem is enormous. The largest number of victims trafficked internationally still comes from Asia, with over 225,000 victims each year believed to be coming from Southeast Asia and over 150,000 from South Asia. They usually end up in large cities, vacation and tourist areas, or near military bases, where the demand is highest.

Causes of Rise in Trafficking

The reasons for the increase in trafficking are many. In general, the criminal business feeds on poverty, despair, war, crisis, and ignorance. The globalization of the world economy has increased the movement of people across borders, legally and illegally, especially from poorer to wealthier countries. International organized crime has taken advantage of the freer flow of people, money, goods and services to extend its own international reach.

Other Contributing Factors Include:

- The continuing subordination of women in many societies, as reflected in economic, educational, and work opportunity disparities between men and women. Many societies still favor sons and view girls as an economic burden. Desperate families in some of the most impoverished countries sell their daughters to brothels or traffickers for the immediate payoff and to avoid having to pay the dowry to marry off daughters;
- The high demand, worldwide, for trafficked women and children for sex tourism, sex workers, cheap sweatshop labor, and domestic workers. Traffickers are encouraged by large tax-free profits and continuing income from the same victims at very low risk;
- The inadequacy of laws and law enforcement in most origin, transit, and destination countries, hampers efforts to fight trafficking. Even in the United States, more effective legal remedies are only now being considered. Prostitution is legal or tolerated in many countries, and widespread in most. When authorities do crack down, it is usually against prostitutes themselves. Penalties for trafficking humans for sexual exploitation are often relatively minor compared with those for other criminal activities like drug and gun trafficking.
- The priority placed on stemming illegal immigration in many countries, including the United States, has resulted in treatment of trafficking cases as a problem of illegal immigration, thus treating victims as criminals. When police raid brothels, women are often detained and punished, subjected to human rights abuses in jail, and swiftly deported. Few steps have been taken to provide support, health care, and access to justice. Few victims dare testify against the traffickers or those who hold them, fearing retribution for themselves and their families since most governments do not offer stays of deportation or adequate protection for witnesses.
- The disinterest and in some cases even complicity of governments is another big problem. Many law-enforcement agencies and governments ignore the plight of trafficking victims and downplay the scope of the trafficking problem. In some cases, police and other governmental authorities accept bribes and

collude with traffickers by selling fake documentation, etc. In addition, local police often fear reprisals from criminal gangs so they find it easier to deny knowledge of trafficking. Many countries have no specific laws aimed at trafficking in humans.

Traffickers and Their Victims

Traffickers acquire their victims in a number of ways. Sometimes women are kidnapped outright in one country and taken forcibly to another. In other cases, victims are lured with job offers. Traffickers entice victims to migrate voluntarily with false promises of good paying jobs in foreign countries as au pairs, models, dancers, domestic workers, etc. Traffickers advertise these phony jobs, as well as marriage opportunities abroad in local newspapers. Russian crime gangs reportedly use marriage agency databases and match-making parties to find victims. In some cases, traffickers approach women or their families directly with offers of well-paying jobs elsewhere. After providing transportation and false documents to get victims to their destination, they subsequently charge exorbitant fees for those services, creating lifetime debt bondage.

While there is no single victim stereotype, a majority of trafficked women are under the age of 25, with many in their mid-to-late teens. The fear among customers of infection with HIV and AIDS has driven traffickers to recruit younger women and girls, some as young as seven, erroneously perceived by customers to be too young to have been infected.

Trafficking victims are often subjected to cruel mental and physical abuse in order to keep them in servitude, including beating, rape, starvation, forced drug use, confinement, and seclusion. Once victims are brought into destination countries, their passports are often confiscated. Victims are forced to have sex, often unprotected, with large numbers of partners, and to work unsustainably long hours. Many victims suffer mental breakdowns and are exposed to sexually-transmitted diseases, including HIV and AIDS. They are often denied medical care and those who become sick are sometimes even killed.

Francis T. Miko, Foreign Affairs, Defense, and Trade Division with Grace (Jea-Hyun) Park, Research Associate

---

SOURCE: *Excerpts from U.S. Congressional Research Service Report 98-649 C, May 10, 2000*

2. Thai Village a Sex-Trade Hub as Families Sell Off Daughters

By Andrew Perrin

MAE SAI, Thailand—Ngun Chai sold his 13-year-old daughter into prostitution for the price of a television set.

He had no regrets. His wife, Lu, had one. When she discovered that her eldest daughter wasn't working in a bar in a nearby city—as the agent who bought the girl had promised—but was selling her body in a Bangkok brothel to as many as eight men a day, she wept.

The tears were not for her daughter.

"I should have asked for 10,000 baht [$228], not 5,000," she said. "He robbed us."

The Chai family lives in a thatched hut in Pa Tek village on the outskirts of Mae Sai, a bustling township on Thailand's northern border with the military state of Myanmar, formerly known as Burma.

Tensions here can run high between the rival armies, and bullets sometimes are traded across the Mae Sai River, which separates the two countries. Yet the sporadic hostilities have done nothing to hinder trade in the town's two chief commodities—drugs and daughters.

The smuggling of vast quantities of heroin and amphetamines from Myanmar and Laos through Thailand has made this region, called the Golden Triangle, infamous. But it is the explosion in recruitment of young girls for the international sex industry that has put Mae Sai on the map.

There are no reliable statistics on the number of children working in the sex industry worldwide, but the lowest figure generally cited is one million. The United Nations Children's Fund estimates that a third of all sex workers in Southeast Asia are between the ages of 12 and 17. Many are bought and sold in Mae Sai.

Every year hundreds of young girls in the town—and thousands from neighboring Myanmar and Laos, and Yunnan province in southern China—are sold into prostitution and taken to brothels in Bangkok, to feed the multibillion-dollar sex industry. Sex tourists come to Thailand from all corners of the globe, and Thai men are reliable customers as well.

Few villages in the region have contributed as many daughters as Pa Tek.

Most residents are Burmese immigrants who came to escape poverty and persecution by Myanmar's military junta; while they are permitted by the

Thai government to live here, they have no legal status. Many are farm workers earning less than $150 a year.

Such poverty makes Pa Tek's daughters easy pickings for brothel agents—"aunties," as they are known. The Development and Education Program for Daughters and Communities (DEPDC), a Mae Sai township-based organization, estimates that of Pa Tek's 800 families, close to 600 have sold at least one daughter to the trade.

"Agents will come to the village with orders to fill," said DEPDC director Sompop Jantraka. "The people in Bangkok, mostly foreigners, can order girls like they order pizza. They will say 'I want a girl with thin hips and big bosoms and a round bottom' and the agents will come up here and find her. And they always deliver."

Virginity is highly prized. Fueling the demand for young girls is ignorance about HIV/AIDS transmission and myths about the curative powers of virginity. Some brothel clientele—particularly men from Taiwan, Hong Kong and the Middle East - believe that sex with a child is less risky because she is more likely to be "clean."

In reality, said Phil Marshall, manager of a Bangkok-based UN interagency project on trafficking women and children, children are more prone to bleeding, infection and disease: "Biologically, children are more vulnerable to HIV. Clients are less likely to use a condom on a 15-year-old girl."

Somporn Khempetch, coordinator of the Child Protection and Rights Center in Mae Sai, has seen the resulting devastation. Last year, she said, 50 girls in Pa Tek died of AIDS.

Yet despite the risks, there is no shortage of parents willing to sell their children. With prices ranging from $115 to nearly $1,000—six years' wages for many families—parental bonds are easily broken. So well-established is child trafficking that many of the brothel agents are villagers and often friends or relatives of the people from whom they buy girls.

"We tend to think of trafficking as involving sophisticated crime networks, but much of it is really a cottage industry involving small-time profiteers," Marshall said.

A new report from the International Labor Organization, in conjunction with the U.N. Development Project, supports his claim, saying that most girls leave their villages through informal networks.

What's more, it says, many leave willingly.

"What we have found is that many girls want to leave home and work elsewhere, preferably in cities,"

said Hans van de Glind, deputy project manager for the International Labor Organization in Bangkok, and one of the report's authors. "They don't want to work in agriculture like their parents, and are bored with village life.

"It's not so much a poverty issue, because we found that girls from one village would migrate while girls from another, equally poor village wouldn't," van de Glind said. "Consumerism plays a part. A girl with access to a television, who lives close to a road, is more likely to migrate. Suddenly they want to have nice clothes, a motor bike and an entertaining life like the people on TV."

Yet even the impact of modern communication technology is secondary to the power of traditional values that say children must support their parents by any means available. In Thai, it is called *todtan bunkhun,* or "repaying the breast milk."

"When I was at work [in a Chiang Mai brothel], 50 percent of me hated what I was doing," said one 14-year-old girl, now housed at the DEPDC, who said she had mixed feelings about being "rescued" during a police raid. "But the other 50 percent wanted to stay so that I could earn money for my parents.

"My father cannot work. He is very old and I must support the family. It is my job."

DEPDC director Sompop insisted that education is the key to keeping girls from prostitution. He pointed to the success of the 1997 Thai constitution that stipulates 12 years of free education for citizens. Before that, he said, the majority of girls leaving Mae Sai were Thai; now, he said, Thais account for less than 2 percent.

So agents are casting their nets wider. Hundreds of girls from Myanmar and China's Yunnan and Guangxi provinces cross the Mae Sai River bridge into Thailand every month.

"How can we stop it?" asked Wichai Promsilpa, Mae Sai's police chief. "This is an open border. Thousands of people cross here every day. We cannot tell the difference between a girl coming here to buy eggs and a girl coming to work as a prostitute."

He said the trade has exploded since Thailand opened its borders with Myanmar. "When I was based here 10 years ago and the border was closed, there was no people trafficking," he said.

SOURCE: *"Thai Village a Sex-Trade Hub as Families Sell Off Daughters" by Andrew Perrin,* Philadelphia Inquirer, *March 25, 2002 (http://www.philly.com/mld/philly/news/ 2930614.htm).*

3. Sex Slaves or Harassed Toronto, Canada Sex-trade Workers?

By Vern Smith

Being 'Rescued' by Police Means Imprisonment

Kita never considered herself a "sex slave." So when police raided the massage parlour where she was working in 1994—located near Sherbourne and Dundas—she didn't consider herself "saved" either. In fact, languishing for 18 months in custody was pretty much the worst thing that ever happened to her as she waited to get over a bawdy-house charge accompanying her so-called rescue. Of her former massage-parlour employer, Kita says, "Everything was fine. The boss—she took care of everything. At that time, I got $90 out of every $120 we charged customers."

One reason Kita wasn't complaining about her job is because of where she comes from. She's a refugee from Burma, a war-torn country where she was impoverished. Speaking through an interpreter, Kita says, "You asked me if I was a slave of my employer here, and I say no."

But police and immigration officials are saying yes. Increasingly, migrant sex-trade workers are spending months in jail after being charged with prostitution and immigration offences during raids on megacity strip clubs, brothels and massage parlours. Although police often claim they are rescuing migrant sex workers, advocates say the women are less free after being saved.

"The women do report that the worst thing that happened to them during their stay in Canada was being arrested, strip-searched, then being held in detention for three months to a year," says Kara Gillies, a spokesperson for the Migrant Sex Workers Advocacy Group. "I just don't understand how charging people, arresting them from their working environments, then putting them in cells is helpful. This is the justification for going in and disrupting people's lives and livelihoods. It's on these grounds that police are rescuing these women.

While sex-trade workers are feeling the long lash of the law, their employers are lining their pockets by exploiting things like NAFTA to bring in more strippers and dancers from developing countries. The upshot is that sex-trade workers are suffering, but not necessarily because of their working conditions.

This appears to be true of Kita, now 22, who is married and pregnant and attempting to become a Canadian citizen. She asked to be interviewed under her former work name.

Following the 1994 raid, she spent six months at Metro West Detention Centre, then another year at Celebrity Inn—an immigration holding tank on Airport Road. Unable to post a combined $7,000 for her criminal and immigration bonds, Kita remained in custody. "The guards would be yelling at the children to stop crying," she remembers, "and I had to be there for a year. I had one set of clothes—the one I wore when I was busted. I didn't have any clothes to go to court. I didn't kill anybody. I didn't use heroin or sell heroin or have any serious charges."

The definition of a sex slave is an indentured person held against his or her will and forced to perform sex for no pay. Reports claim that women are bought and sold among gangsters as sex slaves. Gillies says that's not quite accurate, and is co-writing a report on the matter funded by Status of Women Canada. "It's not sex slavery," she says. "The problem is that they have no redress when it comes to contract violations. Women's groups tend to equate prostitution with human trafficking, deeming sex work in general inherently exploitative. There's no question that many of these women are very vulnerable, often because of their status as migrant workers. Domestic workers, factory workers and seasonally employed workers all have very little access to redress when they aren't paid on time."

Gillies sees this a lot with dancers and prostitutes. "They've come in on their own volition only to end up in exploited work conditions, and it's, 'Oh well, screw you, bad whore.' But when we see the exploitation, it would be more accurately defined as a labour issue."

The women often come to Canada through underground routes with expenses paid by agents. Upon arrival, Gillies says, they've incurred debts of anywhere from $5,000 to $30,000. "In most situations the women know this in advance and agree to work a certain number of hours or see a certain number of clients," she says. "They run into difficulties when they agree to see 400 clients in advance and then someone on this end changes it to 500. The situation is compounded by the fact that their business is undervalued in terms of social perspective, and—in the case of prostitution—criminalized."

Bonds for both criminal and immigration matters can exceed $7,000. Some women can't pay, remaining in jail until they are either deported or they get money from "unscrupulous sources."

"It varies," says Gillies. "Some will have money that hasn't been seized by police, in which case they can post bond. But in many situations the women have been sending money to their families or paying a huge percentage of their earnings to their agents."

A Thai woman, who worked in a North York massage parlour as Amy, says she didn't happen to have

$3,500 handy when 68 people were arrested on prostitution charges in December 1998. Along with 24 other women and one man, she was charged under the Immigration Act. "There was no crime," says Amy. "Only the women, and they pointed guns at us."

More recently, the focus has changed from massage parlours to strip clubs, where police are arresting migrant dancers without proper paperwork. Project Almonzo—a year-long blitz leading to some 700 prostitution-related charges at GTA strip joints—found immigration officials and police working in tandem. A number of migrant women have been found to be working on expired paperwork, and others on tourist visas that provide no labour rights. Mercier says Immigration Canada doesn't keep statistics on migrant sex-trade workers, but if more are plying their trade here it's because they've been invited.

Claiming a shortage of homegrown talent, strip clubs have used NAFTA to find new recruits in Mexico. Last spring, strip clubs began lobbying Ottawa to let more foreign dancers work legally—offering to pay for immigration spot checks and a free hotline for dancers. Failing such a move, the industry claims scores of clubs will close.

Mary Taylor, outreach coordinator for the Exotic Dancers Alliance, disputes this claim. "How can there be a shortage if some clubs have between 80 and 100 girls Thursday through Saturday?" she asks. "They want more because they're charging the dancers a fee to work in the clubs. The more girls they have, the more money they make. Each girl is paying more than $40 a night, and they're swarming to clubs that turn a blind eye, because that's where the money is."

The industry's plea for outside help coincides with the arrest of more than 100 migrants during the year-long Almonzo blitz, leaving the dancers to fend for themselves in court. "Clubs take the girls' money and they don't provide anything for that money—nothing," says Taylor.

While Almonzo targeted sex in strip clubs, police say the project was not intended as a hooker sweep, but as a crackdown against human traffickers.

"We're not here to change the system," says Peel constable Don Ross. "A lot of the people who you call migrant sex workers have been dealt with, and I think they are treated very fairly. We put them in contact with social services and they're treated as victims. They're not treated as bad people. They're not treated as accused people."

Whatever the focus, to Mook Sutdhibhasilp it sounds like another 'rescue.' "Recently, they haven't been using the term 'rescue,' but that's how it started," says Sutdhibhasilp, an activist on the migrant sex

workers issue who's co-writing the report with Gillies. "Thai women busted as part of Project Trade and Project Orphan were supposed to be part of an alleged sex-slave ring, too. There are still raids at massage parlours, but it's not news anymore. They're talking about sending a message to traffickers."

"Local sex workers will be fined, but they won't be deported and they won't be jailed. Once migrant women get busted, they are held. They call it detention—right, to protect the women—but all the women just call it jail."

SOURCE: *Sex Slaves or Harassed Toronto, Canada Sex-trade Workers?* by Vern Smith, Eye, August 10, 2000 (an alternative Toronto, Canada news and entertainment weekly). http://www.eye.net/eye/issue/issue_08.10.00/news/sex.html

4. Summary of Basic Provisions of U.N. Protocol to Prevent, Suppress and Punish Trafficking in Persons, Especially Women and Children

Each State Party shall adopt legislative and other measures to make trafficking—as defined in the protocol—a crime when committed intentionally.

Each State Party shall protect the privacy and identity of trafficking victims to the extent possible under domestic law.

Each State Party shall ensure that its domestic legal or administrative system contains measures that provide to trafficking victims:

- information on relevant court and administrative procedure,
- assistance to enable the victim's views and concerns to be presented during criminal proceedings in a manner that will not prejudice the rights of the defence, and
- appropriate treatment for the physical, psychological and social recovery of victims.

Each State Party shall take measures that permit victims of trafficking to remain in its territory in consideration of humanitarian factors, including the possibility of compensation for damage suffered.

Each State Party must facilitate and accept the repatriation of a victim of trafficking to the victim's country of nationality or permanent residence without undue or unreasonable delay.

State Parties shall establish comprehensive policies, programs and other measures to prevent and combat trafficking in persons and to prevent victims of trafficking, especially women and children from revictimization. These measures include:

- information and mass media campaigns,

- cooperation with non-governmental organizations, and
- bilateral or multilateral cooperation to alleviate poverty, lack of equal opportunity and economic underdevelopment.

Each State Party shall adopt or strengthen laws or other measures to discourage the demand that fosters trafficking.

Law enforcement, immigration and other relevant authorities of State Parties shall cooperate with one another by exchanging information in accordance with their domestic laws.

State Parties shall provide or strengthen training for law enforcement, immigration and other relevant officials in the prevention of human trafficking.

To the extent possible, State Parties shall strengthen border controls to prevent and detect human trafficking.

At the request of another State Party, a State Party shall, in accordance with its domestic law, verify within a reasonable time, the legitimacy and validity of travel or identity documents purported to be issued in its name and suspected of being used for trafficking.

SOURCE: As Adopted by U.N. and 80 Other Nations, November 2001. United Nations, "Protocol to Prevent, Suppress and Punish Trafficking in Persons, Especially Women and Children, Supplementing the United Nations Convention Against Transnational Crime" adopted by General Assembly resolution 55/25 of 15 November, 2000, Official Records of the General Assembly, Fifty-fifth Session, Supplement, No. 49 (a/45/49), vol. 1.

QUESTIONS

Check Your Understanding

1. According to the articles, why does the flow of sex trafficking generally run from less developed to more developed parts of the world?
2. What state- and regional-level economic and political factors make the Golden Triangle area of Southeast Asia a center for sex trafficking?

Analyze the Issues

3. Explain the relationship between sex trafficking issues: historical subjugation of women, as discussed in the chapter; and access (or lack of access) to education and economic opportunity for women.
4. The articles portray women in the sex trade from several viewpoints: as victims, beneficiaries, and dutiful daughters. How do you see them? Which cultural and economic factors contribute to your answer?
5. Two NGOs are mentioned in the readings, one that is concerned over the fate of young girls in Burma and Thailand, the other that serves as an advocate for sex workers in Canada. How do you see them as promoting the interests of women worldwide?
6. In your opinion do the provisions of the UN Protocol Against Trafficking in Persons adequately address the issues women might have with the sex trade? If so, which provisions are most germane to addressing these problems? If not, what else would be needed? Consider needed reforms at the individual, local, state, and global levels.

FOR FURTHER INFORMATION

The full text of the UN Protocol to Prevent Trafficking in Persons may be found in pdf format at *http://www.uncjin.org/Documents/Conventions/dcatoc/final_documents_2/convention_%20traff_eng.pdf*.

For a complete discussion of U.N. measures to abolish slavery in all its forms, see U.N., Office of the High Commission on Human Rights, David Weissbrodt and Anti-Slavery International, *Abolishing slavery and its Contemporary Forms* (New York and Geneva: United Nations, 2002).

Trafficking in Persons Report, June 2002 at *http://us.state.gov*
> *http:://usinfo.state.gov/topical/global/traffic/crs0510.htm*. Congressional Research Service Report
> 98-649 C, Francis T. Miko, Specialist in International Relations, Foreign Affairs, Defense and
> Trade Relations with Grace (Jea-Hyun) Park, Research Associate, Foreign Affairs, Defense,
> and Trade Division, "Trafficking in Women and Children: The U.S. and International
> Response," May 10, 2000.
> *http://www.unhchr.ch/women/focus-trafficking.html*. "Trafficking in persons, Information Note"
> (March 2001)
> *http://www.unifem-eseasia.org/Gendiss/Gendiss2.htm*. "Trafficking in Women and Children,
> Gender Issues Fact Sheet 2"
> *http://www.swimw.org/orgs.html*. List of International Sex Workers' Rights Organizations. The list
> supports the legalization of prostitution.
> *http://con.law.harvard.edu/vaw02/mod3-1a.htm* Donna Hughes Modules on Violence Against
> Women that she developed for a course on the subject at Harvard Law School. It is well worth
> reading the material assigned for the course.

Judith Mirkinson, "Red Light, Green Light: The Global Trafficking of Women" originally
> published in *Breakthrough*, Spring, 1994, published by Prairie Fire Organizing Committee at
> *http://deepthought.armory.com/~leavitt/women.html* and at
> *http://eserver.org/feminism/gender/trafficking-of-women.txt*. This is one of the shocking early studies
> of the sex trade that helped put the issue on the international political and legislative agenda.

Information on Burma and Thailand may be found at
> *http://www.cia/gov/cia/publications/factbook/geos/bm.html* and
> *http://www.cia.gov/cia/publications/factbook/geos/th.html*

CHAPTER 11

International Political Economy I: The Advanced Industrial Countries

KEY QUESTIONS RAISED IN THIS CHAPTER

1. How do experts view the international political economy?
2. What are the arguments for free trade and protectionism?
3. Who manages global trade?
4. How does the global financial system operate?
5. What is the role of international businesses in world politics?

Intellectual Property Rights
Rights given to persons over the creations of their minds. They are customarily divided into two main areas: copyright and rights related to copyright; and industrial property which includes protection of distinctive signs—particularly trademarks—and industrial designs and trade secrets.

No major event around the world can be explained without considering the links between politics and economics. Economics influences every politics issue, and every economic issue takes place within a political context whether the event involves war, trade disputes, international loans, the expansion of a security organization, or the decision to create a single currency for many countries. (See, for example, box Why It Matters To You: Intellectual Property Rights.) Surprisingly, though, undergraduate students majoring in economics do not receive much training in politics. Likewise, political science or government majors do not have to take much economics. What's more, few undergraduate political science *and* economic majors learn very much about political-economic links *at the international level*. Unfortunately, the real world is not divided as neatly as it is for many college majors.

The field of study that explores economic and political links at the international level is called *international political economy*, or IPE. Some IPE analysts focus on the way international influences affect domestic politics and economics; others focus on the impact of domestic forces on global political and economic relations. Either way, IPE is clearly an *interdisciplinary* field of study.

A theme that permeates this entire book is that the world at the start of the twenty-first century is undergoing extremely interesting developments; the centralizing and decentralizing forces that we have discussed in each chapter are at work in the international political economy as well. Some decentralizing forces are; that the global capitalist system has recently been rocked by oil price spikes; antiglobalization protesters are lamenting the way rich companies exploit people in poor countries; questions are being raised about the value of international institutions such as the World Bank and International Monetary Fund; and the United States appears much less willing to take on the role of global economic and political leader. Centralizing forces are that twelve European countries now have a single currency, and that certain groups of countries seem more interested in improving trade relations among themselves than encouraging a better global economy. The case study at the end of the chapter explores these centralizing and decentralizing dynamics in more depth. The way these economic developments play out will differentiate the twenty-first century from the past.

IPE is an extremely comprehensive field. To make sense of its complexity, scholars have developed several theoretical frameworks. Remember that without theory, we would be wandering aimlessly in an ocean of seemingly unconnected ideas, facts, and figures. In this chapter, therefore, we revisit some of the theories already covered in this book as well as introduce you to three major IPE approaches: economic liberalism, neomercantilism, and the rational choice approach. The first of these approaches will be introduced in the first section of the chapter, which deals with international trade relations. A central issue for this part of the chapter centers on the merits and shortcomings of free trade and its opposite: protectionism. The next section of the chapter builds on the first by looking at how global trade is, or is not, managed. Particular attention will be devoted to the World Trade Organizations. The focus of the next section of the chapter is how the global financial system operates. We will explore the value of currencies and exchange rates, and describe the roles of the World Bank and International Monetary Fund. The chapter concludes with a look at the importance of international businesses in international relations, many of which have, as we saw in Chapter 6, more economic weight than many countries. Since IPE is too large a topic to condense into one chapter, this chapter will emphasize the political-economic relationship among well-to-do countries, while Chapter 12 complements this one by focusing on the international political and economic relationship between the world's rich and poor countries.

WHY IT MATTERS TO YOU

Intellectual Property Rights

It is difficult to separate political forces from economic forces. This is true with respect to any activity within a country or between countries, and it is true in the case of trade in intellectual property.[1] According to the World Trade Organization, **intellectual property rights** are the rights given to persons over the creations of their minds.[2] They usually give the creator an exclusive right over the use of his/her creation for a certain period of time. Intellectual property rights are customarily divided into two main areas: copyrights and industrial property, which includes protection of distinctive signs, particularly trademarks, and industrial designs and trade secrets.

Computer software, prerecorded music, and movies are all examples of intellectual property. U.S. companies are major producers of high technology products and services that depend on intellectual property. These industries are important because of their economic size and relatively high profits, and because they tend to spur growth throughout an economy.

The creators of software, music, and movies—all based on intellectual property—believe that when people steal their work, their rights are being violated. It can takes years and millions of dollars, for example, to research and develop such software programs as Windows or Lotus, but it can take only minutes to copy them illegally. Sometimes a newly released film in the United States can be seen illegally in another country the very same day. For many people—and students—using software from someone else or listening to prerecorded music (say, through Napster or a similar company) is considered acceptable, but the people who created the intellectual property argue that "using" or "listening" without paying is really a form of stealing.

The scope of the industries related to intellectual property (and its theft) is impressive. According to the International Intellectual Property Alliance, for example, the U.S. copyright industries in 2001 accounted for over $535.1 billion in sales, exceeding 5 percent of the economy and one-half

Applying Pressure to Violators of Intellectual Property Rights: A steamroller crushes some of the half a million compact disks at a dump site northwest of Moscow. Such efforts to crack down on companies who steal intellectual property are gaining momentum but still have a long way to go, particularly in the Third World.

trillion dollars for the first time. These industries also achieved estimated foreign sales and exports of $88.97 billion in 2001.[3]

As robust as these sales figures are, pirating is also big business. For example, in the past five years, about a third of the Windows and Office software used, worth about $12 billion, is used illegally.[4] According to the Software and Information Industry Associate and the Business Software Alliance, business software makers overall lose $12 billion a year from piracy. In addition, such piracy costs 100,000 jobs and $5.8 billion a year in wages in the U.S. alone.[5] In November 2001, the largest software police sting in U.S. history netted $100 million worth of counterfeit computer software in the Los Angeles area.[6]

(continued)

(continued)

Some companies in many countries are actually quite active in pirating intellectual property. In every case the piracy rate is declining due to a growing awareness of the value of intellectual property rights. Nevertheless, piracy rates are still very high in some countries. According to the Business Software Alliance, China's piracy rate, for example, is 90 percent or more. In Israel, the piracy rate is 60 percent or more.[7] Several *political* ramifications arise from the theft of intellectual property, which translates into lost revenues for the businesses that produce it. First, these businesses put pressure on their governments to crack down on countries that allow such piracy. Many businesses are trying to fight back on their own as well. Facing the piracy problem in China, Microsoft initiated a program to reward people who turn in offenders. As Microsoft put it, this was "really just the first prong of what will be our overall grand antipiracy programme here and in Thailand."[8]

So why does all this matter to you? First there is the negative impact on the economy of countries that rely on intellectual property rights. Pirated intellectual property can result in lost revenues and the elimination of jobs, which always has the potential to trickle down to you, your friends, or your family. The pirating of computer software and music, from disk or over the Internet, is also an issue for students in First World countries. Because technology makes copying of these things so easy, companies and individuals find the temptation hard to resist.

How Do Experts View the International Political Economy?

Since we know that the international political economy is extremely complex, how should we go about trying to understand it? There is no single answer to this question. With a topic as comprehensive as IPE, it is not surprising that scholars differ in their approaches. Of all the theoretical attempts at understanding IPE, three have risen to the top as either the most popular or the most useful. Each theory begins with different assumptions, explains events in different ways, offers different policy prescriptions, and makes different predictions about the future of the international political economy. A fourth approach, the Marxist and neo-Marxist, has also garnered support. This approach is taken up in Chapter 12 because of that chapter's emphasis on relations between the First World and Third World countries and its exploration of why there are rich countries and poor countries. The other three are introduced here and will be amplified as the chapter proceeds.

1. *Economic liberalism* grows out of the classical economics tradition. Students who have taken a basic microeconomics course will find many elements of this approach familiar. For example, it assumes that human beings are rational actors and that they try to maximize their satisfaction (in terms of profits, for example). This approach assumes that the government should play a minimal role in regulating the economy and that countries should be free to trade with each other. Note that *economic* liberalism should not be confused with *political* idealism, which was initially described in Chapter 1.

2. *Neomercantilism* is associated in part with the realist tradition in international relations. It emphasizes the role of the state in helping to guide a country's economy in one direction or another so as to increase the power of the state. Neomercantilism does not necessarily support the idea that countries should be free to trade with each other. Neomercantilists would recommend that the

	TABLE 11.1 Theoretical Approaches to Understanding IPE			
	Economic Liberalism, Classical Economics	**Neomercantilism, Mercantilism, Realism**	**Rational Choice, Public Choice**	**Marxism & Neo-Marxism**
Position on free trade	Free trade is good.	Free trade is good if it serves state interests.	Free trade may be good for some groups in society but not all.	Free trade is bad.
General comments about the political economy	Free market principles should dominate the political economy. Note: This "liberalism" is different from political liberalism (which grew out of political idealism).	The state uses the economy to increase its power.	Individuals in the market and the state are rational actors seeking to improve their satisfaction (utility).	Economic factors dominate politics and society.
Most important unit of analysis	The individual or the firm.	The state.	Interest groups, individuals, (demand) and government officials (supply).	Class (capitalist and proletariat) or the international capitalist system.
Expectation about the IPE	Harmonious and self-regulating; international economic integration through the world market.	Inherent struggle among states; regulated by a balance of power.	Cooperation or conflict, depending on the demands for either alternative.	Inherent conflict, especially class conflict; revolutionary change until Marxist utopia.

country export as much as possible while protecting its companies by creating barriers to trade from other countries.

3. *The rational choice* approach, like the economic liberalism approach, is based on microeconomic assumptions about human behavior, but it emphasizes the domestic political sources of international economic policy making. The rational choice approach looks at not only what motivates individuals (e.g., profits) but also at which interest groups in society benefit or lose from different government economic policies.

As you might have guessed from the brief summaries of these approaches, a common theme running through all theories of IPE is the interaction of states and markets.[9] The term *states* refers to the governmental or public aspects of IPE issues, while the term *markets* reflects the economic and private elements. Thus, the IPE theories covered in this chapter deal, in different ways, with the interaction of states and markets. Table 11.1 provides a comparison of these approaches to IPE. As this chapter progresses, you will learn more about each of them in turn.

HISTORICAL PERSPECTIVE

The Legacy of Bretton Woods

In order to introduce the first IPE theory—liberal, classical economics—a bit of historical background is in order. As with much of our understanding of contemporary international relations, we begin with the pivotal period right after World War II. In 1944 the United States and its World War II allies met at *Bretton Woods*, New Hampshire, to discuss how to regulate the international political economy. The principle philosophy that infused the discussions was the idea of establishing a *liberal* global economy. Essentially, postwar political and economic leaders drew the lesson from the 1930s and 1940s that economic policies that limited free trade (i.e., protectionism) were chiefly responsible for both the Great Depression and World War II. Thus, they believed, establishing fixed rules in international economic relations would create a more constructive environment. Instead of each country looking out purely for its own economic interest and seeking its own benefit at every corner, special codes should be established covering a wide variety of trade and monetary issues and specific economic sectors. In light of our discussion about national sovereignty and international organizations in prior

chapters, it is worth emphasizing that the founding countries of the Bretton Woods system decided to be bound by international rules even if this sometimes meant unfavorable rulings.

And out of the Bretton Woods agreement were born the main global trade and financial organizations we have today. In the international monetary area, the Bretton Woods delegates set up the *World Bank* (formally known as the International Bank for Reconstruction and Development) and the *International Monetary Fund (IMF)*. In the trade area, the General Agreement on Tariffs and Trade (GATT) was established.[10] GATT would be transformed in the 1990s into the *World Trade Organization*. The key points of the liberal **Bretton Woods system** are summarized below.

- U.S. leadership would ensure the smooth functioning of international trade and monetary relations.
- International monetary relations should be based on a fixed convertibility into gold. That is, a specific amount of gold (one ounce) could be exchanged at a fixed rate against the U.S. dollar ($35).

Bretton Woods System

An international political-economic system of rules, procedures, and institutions designed to foster a liberal global economy through more cooperative trade and monetary policies; named after the location of the original meeting in Bretton Woods, NH.

In the next two sections of this chapter, we will take a look at the product of the Bretton Woods system and the liberal economic philosophy that dominated the immediate post–World War II era. We will look first at the international trading system and then at the international monetary system.

What Are the Arguments for Free Trade and Protectionism?

Since World War II and before, scholars and political leaders around the world have debated the merits and shortcomings of a global free trading system. Our theories of IPE take conflicting positions in this debate, and politicians rarely agree among themselves as to the ultimate costs and benefits of free trade and protectionism (restrictions to trade). We begin our exploration of this debate with the rationale for global free trade. This follows with a discussion of the rationale for protectionism. Along the way, we will look at how countries protect their companies and workers,

- International institutions were established to encourage both international free trade (e.g., GATT) and stable monetary international relations (e.g., World Bank and IMF).
- Free trade among countries was to be encouraged, and protectionist barriers to trade were to be minimized.

Thus instead of each country going it alone, as was done prior to World War II with disastrous consequences, countries would trade more freely with one another. The system put in place at Bretton Woods in 1944 still impacts worlds politics and economics at the start of the twenty-first century.

In the end, how successful was the Bretton Woods system? The answer depends on one's time frame. Through the 1950s and 1960s, the world experienced a historically unprecedented economic boom. In the late 1960s and early 1970s, however, the Bretton Woods system frayed and then eventually was torn apart by economic strains in the United States and changes in the rest of the international political economy. Mounting U.S. budget deficits—made worse by the costs of the Vietnam War, a declining U.S. balance-of-payments position, and greater competition from Europe and Japan—all combined to weaken the ability of the United States to continue as leader of the Bretton Woods system. Because of a lack of faith in the United States, countries were less willing to hold on to dollars and more interested in holding gold. The fixed link between the U.S. dollar and gold had thus been broken Summarizing this period in time, David Balaam and Michael Veseth of the University of Puget Sound point out that by the late 1960s, the United States "was faced with a domestic war on poverty, an international war on communism (in Vietnam), and the burden of Bretton Woods hegemony, which called for greater financial discipline. Eventually, U.S. leaders were forced to choose between national interest and international responsibility, which is a fundamental tension in IPE. The key decision was made in 1971, when President Richard Nixon formally broke the link between the dollar and gold. The world slowly shook off its system of fixed exchange rates. By the oil shocks of 1973–1974, a system of flexible exchange rates had been established."[11]

Despite the collapse of the Bretton Woods system, two important features are still very much alive, and they both maintain an important place in the international political economy. First, the notion of an open, liberal international economy still has considerable appeal around much of the world. For example, many of the former communist countries in Eastern Europe have made so many market-oriented changes that they are poised for membership in the European Union. Second, the international institutions set up to help manage global trading and monetary relations still have critical roles to play.

whether regional trading blocs are good or bad for the global economy, and whether protectionism is on the rise around the world.

The Rationale for Free Trade

People who grow up in capitalist countries are typically raised to believe that companies should be allowed to buy and sell good with other countries without government interference. Although they may not understand why this is the case, they generally feel strongly that trade among companies in different countries should be possible. Below, we offer two theoretical underpinnings of this belief.

The Economic Liberalism Approach   According to the economic liberalism approach to IPE, global free trade benefits big states and small states, the developed countries and developing countries. According to supporters of this view, many benefits that come from an open international trading system derive from competition. For example, competition among companies for your hard-earned dollars leads to several advantageous outcomes. First, it can help reduce the *price* of

For more information on the WTO, go to **www.ablongman.com/ duncan.**

goods and services. Second, competition can help increase the *quality* of goods and services available. Third, competition can increase the *variety* of goods and services. Competition among businesses can also make companies more *efficient*. These benefits can occur at both the domestic economic level and at the international level.

An example of global competition involves two of the world's largest airplane producers. In late 1998 United Airlines threatened its main airplane supplier, Boeing, with going to the competition, Airbus Industrie of Europe. According to Andy Studdert, United Airline's senior vice president for fleet operations, United told Boeing to improve "quality and support or United will be forced to use Airbus." In the case of airplanes, such threats can matter a lot because planes cost so much and because the number of planes ordered in one deal can reach as high as $75 million.[12] Threats of going to the foreign competition should occur more often in the future if the globalization process continues throughout the twenty-first century.

At the opposite extreme, where there is *no* competition, a *monopoly* situation exists in which only one company makes the goods or provides the services. If consumers are forced to buy from only one company and have no alternatives, the company doesn't feel the pressure to innovate or lower prices. As economists would say, it has no *incentives* to become more efficient or provide better goods more cheaply. In this situation as well, consumers are at a major disadvantage.

Comparative Advantage   There is a common saying among neoliberal economists about global free trade: a rising tide lifts all boats. No matter how big the boats are, everyone will be better off with free trade. This notion is linked to two important concepts in economics and IPE. First, since a rising tide lifts all boats, free trade is considered to be a *positive-sum game*; it is a game in which all players can win. As in any game, two or more countries play against each other in the international political economy, and since this is a positive-sum game, there are more winners than losers. This contrasts with protectionism, which (according to economic liberalism) is a *zero-sum game*—a win for one company (or country) must mean a loss for another company (or country).

The second important concept is the notion of **comparative advantage**, popularized by nineteenth century British economist David Ricardo. In a liberal international economy, the theory goes, if countries specialize in what they do best, and if no barriers to trade exist, then everyone will be better off. In such an environment, free trade will lead to the best use of resources and an optimum distribution of wealth among countries. To demonstrate this key point, imagine a country that excels in making computers and another that excels in growing wheat. Comparative advantage tells us that if both countries specialize in what they do best and then trade with each other, they will both be better off than if they didn't trade with each other. This even holds true if one country is better at making computers and at growing wheat. In the end, remember that for comparative advantage to work, trade between countries must not be hindered.

The Rationale for Protectionism

Convinced of the merits of free trade? Most people are not. In fact, many argue, if global free trade is so beneficial, why do countries create so many barriers to free trade? In this section of the chapter we offer several theoretical rationales and examples of the protectionist tools that governments use.

For more information on countries' level of globalization, go to **www.ablongman.com/ duncan.**

Comparative Advantage
In a liberal international economy, countries should specialize in what they produce most efficiently and/or at lowest cost compared to other countries.

For more information about David Ricardo, go to **www.ablongman.com/ duncan.**

The Neo Mercantilist Approach **Mercantilism** and its modern variant, **neomercantilism,** offer some insights into the question of why so many protectionist policies exist. They are approaches to the international political economy that emphasize the power of the state, assume that a strong economy is vital to the strength of the state, and that, as a result, the state should play an important role in guiding the economy. This contrasts with the economic liberalism approach, which calls for minimal state intervention in the economy. Mercantilist policies were used in Europe in the seventeenth and eighteenth centuries to solidify national unity and increase the wealth and power of the state. These policies included the acquisition of precious metals and the implementation of protectionist measures such as tariffs, both of which helped fill state treasuries. The mercantilist approach helps explain the rise of the German state in the nineteenth century. Feeling the need to catch up with its rivals, especially France and Britain, the German *state* organized the economy and society in order to develop a more competitive industrial base.

Neomercantilism in the twentieth century evolved from the Great Depression, the end of the gold standard, and a general disillusionment with global free trade that had set in by the 1970s. In the post–World War II era, states exhibited elements of neomercantilism because they feared that other countries would prosper more and hence become more powerful—especially through intense competition at the global level. Consistent with mercantilists, neomercantilists called for *the state* to overcome the economic problems of the day. The recommendation for a neomercantilist state is to try to manage trade with policies that protect the state and minimize the relative economic gains of other states.[13]

As previously noted, the case for international free trade is a good one, and much of what is taught in typical economics departments in American colleges emphasizes this case. However, many countries around the world strongly support protectionist policies, or policies that restrict free trade among countries. Why? We offer two broad answers.

First, some countries say that it is dangerous to abandon the production of a certain product because another country does it more efficiently. (This is a criticism of comparative advantage.) For national security reasons, for example, a country may want to produce certain things no matter what. Food security and the guarantee of home production of weapons for national defense offer two good examples. In addition, with free trade, countries may end up specializing in economic sectors that are not very helpful to their overall economy. For example, if a country specializes in tourism, it may have little industrial or high-tech development, and although the tourism industry might create many jobs, the jobs would generally be low paying. Specializing in agriculture or raw materials can make a country particularly vulnerable to price fluctuations over time. Countries that rely too heavily on oil exports—from Russia to Norway to Mexico—have at times also had trouble because of sustained periods of *low* oil prices. Nigeria, for example, lost over $2 billion in a ten-month period in 1998 due to low oil prices. This drop in oil revenue was a major blow to the government's budget and planning. The budget, for example, was based on $17 per barrel, but prices eventually fell to as low as $9. This led to a budget shortfall of 46 percent.[14] Such vulnerability to global market prices can also take place within certain regions of a single country. If there is a glut in the global market for wheat, for example, Nebraska and Kansas would likely take a considerable hit. In short, some countries (and regions within countries) believe that specialization can threaten their economic security.

Second, countries seeking to diversify their economies (not rely on only one or two products) may want to use protectionist policies. One specific reason why states

Mercantilism
An approach to the international political economy that emphasizes the power of the state. A national strategy developed in the seventeen century to increase state power and wealth, primarily through the accumulation of precious metals.

Neomercantilism
A more contemporary form of mercantilism in which the state plays an important role in ensuring economic growth and stability. It is normally associated with protectionist policies and may involve import substitution and export promotion strategies. The mercantilist focus on precious metals is of much less importance for neomercantilism.

French farmers worried about a loss of income protest in Brussels, Belgium: The farmers, like those across the European Union (EU), are integrated into the EU's Common Agricultural Policy. So, protests are often directed not just at the French government in Paris, but against EU officials in Brussels.

Infant Industry
A government and business strategy in which a new industry is granted protection from foreign competition so that it will eventually be able to compete internationally on an equal footing.

adopt protectionist policies is to help out an **infant industry.** A country considering building a national car company from scratch, for example, might feel that international competition is too stiff. Trying to enter the global car market from scratch is almost impossible, given the General Motors, Fords, Toyotas, Daimler-Chryslers, and Volkswagens of the world. The idea behind the "infant industry argument" is that the government should provide temporary help until the infant industry grows up. In the 1970s and 1980s, for example, the Japanese government helped block imports to strengthen the Japanese telecommunications and computer manufacturing sectors.[15] When the infant industry is mature enough to compete on its own internationally, the government aid is supposed to stop. Often it does not, however, and the "infant industry argument" is just a cover for good, old-fashioned protectionism.

Rational Choice Approach
An approach to IPE based on microeconomic assumptions about rational human behavior and emphasizing the domestic political sources of international economic policy making.

The Rational Choice Approach   Another reason why countries use protectionist policies is offered by the **rational choice approach** (also called the public choice approach). According to the rational choice approach, protectionist economic policies are heavily influenced by *domestic political factors*. Instead of looking at a nation-state as a single unit, national government policies are really the work of individuals and groups struggling for influence at the apex of the political system. The rational choice approach borrows many ideas from microeconomics, which assumes that people are rational beings in both the marketplace and in politics. Rational choice theory posits that individual consumers, workers, managers, and company owners all weigh the costs and benefits of the available alternatives with the aim of improving their satisfaction (or "utility," as economists would say).

A similar kind of rational reasoning occurs at the government level as well. Politicians support or oppose policy alternatives by weighing their costs and benefits. However, they weigh the costs and benefits in terms of what is rational for them. Since they are not running businesses, profits are not what matter. What matters most to a politician is getting elected or reelected. So, politicians trying to maximize their satisfaction will support the policy that best guarantees their electoral success—whether or not it is good for the country as a whole. Consider the controversial case of abortion and U.S. foreign policy. Pressure from interest groups (particularly antiabortion and religious groups) on the U.S. Congress has led the Bush administration (as well as the two previous Republican administrations) to deny funding to certain international agencies out of concern that the agencies provide abortion services. Abortion foes, of course, are glad that no U.S. tax dollars are going overseas to help women in developing countries get abortions. Pro-choice advocates, however, oppose the Bush Administration's policies in part by noting that the U.S. shouldn't force its views on other countries and because overpopulation can contribute to misery, poverty, and disease in developing countries.

The idea that politicians are more interested in getting elected than doing what may be right for the country, of course, goes against much of what people are raised to believe in democracies. Elected officials in the rational choice world are driven more by the desire to hold office than by any ideological stance or concern for the good of the country. If this is true, what one can hope for is that the elected official will choose policies that are both self-serving and country-serving at the same time.

Most important for our purposes, the rational choice approach suggests that government officials will create or maintain protectionist policies if enough pressure is brought to bear on them. Elected officials, after all, need to keep their important constituents happy. If enough of the constituents *demand* protectionist policies, the government is more likely to *supply* them.

Let us now briefly summarize the theoretical rationales for protectionism. As we have seen, free trade can create both winners and losers in the competitive economic struggle. For at least three reasons, countries seek protection. According to the neomercantilists and consistent with much of realism, states try to protect certain aspects of their economies on the grounds of national security. Second, states may also want to minimize their economic vulnerability by diversifying their economies through the development of new sectors, which requires protecting infant industries. Third, the rational choice approach tells us that countries use protectionist foreign policies if political leaders are concerned about getting into office (or staying in office) and when enough protectionist pressures come from important interest groups in society.

Protecting Jobs, Companies, and Industries   Two goals of protectionist strategies are securing profits for local companies and jobs for local workers. Countries also try to balance the value of goods coming into and going out of the country. This refers to a country's *balance of trade*. A country's balance of trade is said to be in deficit when more money is leaving the country than coming in (see Figure 11.1). Trade deficits can be manipulated with protectionist policies. Whether using protectionism is a good strategy in the long run has been debated for centuries and will continue to occupy international relations students throughout the twenty-first century.

Governments that wish to protect their companies or industries have many tools at their disposal. The most common, and the most obvious, protectionist tools are tariffs and quotas. **Tariffs** act like a tax on imports. For example, say that the

Tariffs
A form of tax on all goods being imported into a country. Compare with *quotas.*

FIGURE 11.1

Balance of Trade: Impact on a Country's Reserves

SOURCE: *Adapted from Joshua Goldstein, International Relations, Second Edition (New York: Addison Wesley Longman, 1997), p. 324.*

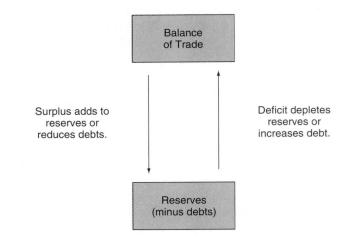

Balance of Trade: 1. By selling exports abroad, money comes into the country.
2. By buying imports, money goes out of the country.

Balance
of Trade

Surplus adds to
reserves or
reduces debts.

Deficit depletes
reserves or
increases debt.

Reserves
(minus debts)

Koreans wish to sell their cars in the U.S. market. Each car originally costs $20,000. However, imagine that the U.S. government has imposed a tariff of $1,000 on every Korean car imported into the United States. This makes the same Korean car now cost $21,000. What does this mean for Americans and what does it mean for Koreans? For American car *companies*, the tariff is beneficial. With the tariff, Korean cars are now more expensive, and Americans will be less likely to buy them—and more likely to buy American cars. The U.S. government also benefits because the tariff revenues ($1,000 on each car imported into the United States) fill government coffers. American *consumers*, however, do not benefit from the tariff. Either their choice is effectively limited or they have to pay more for the Korean car they really want. Korean car companies will obviously be adversely affected by this situation.

Quotas are quantitative restrictions or numerical limits on the number of items that can be imported. Using the Korean car example, imagine that the United States has a quota on Korean cars set at 5,500. This means that Korean companies can only send 5,500 cars to the U.S. market. In the case of quotas, there is no "tax" on the cars, simply a limit on the number that can be imported.

The winners and losers are basically the same with quotas as they are with tariffs. American auto makers know that only a few Korean cars will be on the road competing with their cars. American consumers, if they don't act quickly, will not be able to buy a Korean car. Korean car companies and their employees will also be hurt because they won't be able to make and sell as many cars as they want to in the United States. Note that, unlike tariffs, the U.S. government does not collect revenues with quotas. Overall, however, the costs to consumers of import quotas tend to be much higher than tariffs. In the United States, for instance, the import quotas and price supports for sugar producers allow American companies to control about 90 percent of the market. The peanut quota system only allows 1.7 million pounds of imports each year. This represents only a tiny fraction of U.S. consumption. James Mac, a lobbyist for the Peanut Butter and Nut Processors Association, said that this translates into a "virtual embargo" on foreign peanut exporters.[16] Finally, whether a tariff or a quota is used, consumers seem to be the losers.

Quotas

A limit on the number of items that a country can export to or import from another country. Compare with *tariffs*.

From the end of World War II through the 1970s, the use of tariffs and quotas dropped dramatically, thanks in part to global acceptance of the liberal philosophy of trade (that it should have few barriers) and to the policies adopted by GATT and the WTO. However, because of two oil price shocks in the 1970s, the decline in U.S. global economic leadership, and the uncertainty that followed, countries began to find new ways to protect their companies. Since GATT had generally rendered tariffs and quotas off-limits, the protectionist tools of choice became **nontariff barriers,** or **NTBs.** Compared to tariffs and quotas, NTBs are much more difficult to eliminate because they are much more subtle. Often countries can make a strong case for restricting free trade. The examples that follow will help demonstrate why.

NTBs generally fall into three categories: fiscal barriers, physical barriers, and technical barriers.[17] **Fiscal barriers to trade** involve different tax rates on goods and services. Often, goods are exempt from tax when sold in the country of origin but are subject to tax in the country that imports them. In addition, tax breaks are sometimes granted to local firms, which makes it harder for foreign goods to compete. *Physical barriers* are those arising from delays at borders for customs reasons (e.g., excise duties) and administrative burdens, such as checking forms, collecting statistics, and complying with complicated import licensing procedures. *Technical barriers* may involve the need to comply with particular technical regulations within a country. A wide variety of technical barriers exist, as the following examples illustrate.

- *Product safety standards:* For years the French government required that cars purchased in France be equipped with yellow headlights. The official reason was that yellow would be less likely to blind oncoming traffic. Despite the fact that the rest of the world seemed to get by with white headlights, this regulation forced other car company to pay the extra cost of making their cars with yellow headlights just for France.

- *Health standards:* The United States could not ship beef to Europe if the cows were fed special hormones. Are the hormones safe? The United States says, "yes," the EU says, "no," and in the end, the European beef industry gets its protection.

- *Public procurement:* This term refers to the contracts that are established between governments (hence "public") and private companies. Governments sometimes rely on private companies to provide services such as road building and setting up telecommunications systems. *Protectionist* public procurement policies are those that discriminate against foreign companies. For example, the U.S. government might prefer to give contracts to American companies as opposed to Canadian, Belgian, or Taiwanese companies. On the one hand, such policies limit competition. On the other hand, American companies and their workers can benefit greatly.

- *Voluntary export restraint (VER):* Not much is voluntary about a VER. A country such as Japan will "voluntarily" decide not to export as many cars to Europe as it can because the Europeans say that Japanese competition is too stiff. Japan is unlikely to restrain itself out of the goodness of its own heart. Behind Japan's "voluntary" action is a tacit *threat* by the Europeans that they would take drastic action (e.g., quota restrictions) against Japanese auto exporters if the situation didn't improve. This actually occurred at the end of the 1980s and early 1990s. Japan voluntarily agreed to restrain its exports to Europe because this was a better alternative than having the Europeans crack down even harder on Japanese car companies.

Nontariff Barriers (NTB)
Methods of restricting foreign imports that are neither tariffs nor quotas. Examples include subsidies or tax breaks for domestic companies and relatively rigid health and safety standards for foreign competitors.

Fiscal Barriers to Trade
Government tax policies affecting goods and services that discriminate against foreign companies. For example, goods in the home country may be exempt from taxation while goods from a foreign country are subject to taxes on their exports of goods or services.

Public Procurement
The acquisition by governments of goods or services from private companies. Governments sometimes rely on private companies to provide services such as road building and setting up telecommunications systems.

Voluntary Export Restraint (VER)
A strategy of avoiding the imposition of trade restrictions by self-limiting the level of exports to the country or countries threatening trade restrictions. The belief is that the level of exports "voluntarily" restrained from within will be better than the level of exports imposed from without.

WHY IT MATTERS TO YOU

Restricting Trade for Unacceptable Labor Practices

Opponents of free international trade often include labor organizations in the industrialized countries. In 1998, for example, Charles Kernaghan of the National Labor Committee (NLC), a New York worker rights group, argued that most of the private label clothing and shoes sold at Wal-Mart stores were made in Third World countries "renowned for abhorrent labor practices."

Wal-Mart is the world's largest retailer and turns over around $130 billion a year globally—which is close to the GDP of Greece. According to the NLC, Wal-Mart allowed its suppliers to hire young girls to work for up to 14 hours a day. At factories in China, the NLC found that employees worked 7 days a week, 10 hours a day for 12.5¢ an hour. In addition, they were forced to live in dorms (at a cost of $3.44 a week). They were also under surveillance at work and in the dorms. Similar discoveries were made at factories making clothes under the Kathy Lee label (for Kathy Lee Gifford). Wal-Mart, by the way, is planning on expanding its overseas operations so that a third of its sales will come from outside the United States by 2003. As of the late 1990s, Wal-Mart already had over 600 stores outside the United States.

In order to avoid the bad publicity of unacceptable labor practices, some companies have created "codes of conduct." According to *Consumer Reports*, a typical code of conduct "says that any factory with which the company does business must pay wages legal in the local country, including overtime; maintain a safe workplace; and refrain from abusing employees or employing children." One of the problems with codes of conduct, however, is that they are sometimes difficult to implement. Despite Liz Claiborne's code of conduct, for example, the National Labor Committee met with employees of contractors working for Claiborne in El Salvador and found women working 85 hours a week, 7 days a week. None of the employees had seen Liz Claiborne's code of conduct.

In 1999 the American shoe company Nike was so concerned about public perceptions of its overseas operations that it offered all-expense-paid trips to about a dozen college students to visit Nike plants in 2000. At several college campuses in the United States, students have protested what they claim are sweatshop conditions and low pay at Nike's factories, which produce college-licensed goods.

So, you may want to consider whether or not you care that the clothes you wear are made by a company that allows sweatshop working conditions in its factories. You also might want to think about what you would be willing to pay for your clothing if good working conditions around the world raised labor costs and, hence, prices.

SOURCES: Lorrie Grant, "Wal-Mart Yearns for Global Market Domination," *Democratic and Chronicle* (Rochester), November 8, 1998; Nancy Dunne, "Wal-Mart Attacked for Supplier Labor Standards," *Financial Times*, July 31, 1998; and *Consumer Reports*, "The Shame of Sweatshops," August 1999, pp. 18–20; "Nike Invites Students to Visit Plants," *The Associated Press*, November 12, 1999. Regarding European Companies, see William Echikson, "It's Europe's Turn to Sweat About Sweatshops," *Business Week*, July 19, 1999, p. 96.

Regional Trading Bloc
A loose expression that may encompass both free trade areas and customs unions. These are political-economic arrangements that seek to foster greater trade cooperation among member states.

Other types of NTBs include low interest loans to local companies and export financing assistance. Sometimes people even call for protectionism because of unacceptable *labor standards* (see box Why It Matters To You: Restricting Trade for Unacceptable Labor Practices). Again, the aim of these policies is to protect employment levels and domestic firms or industries from international competition.

Trading Blocs   A check of the political-economic arrangements of countries around the world will quickly yield a long list of **regional trading blocs**—often re-

TABLE 11.2 **Key Regional Trading Arrangements**			
Name of RTA	**Acronym**	**Founded**	**Members**
Free Trade Area of the Americas	FTAA	1995	15
Southern Common Market	MERCOSUR	1995	5
North American Free Trade Agreement	NAFTA	1992	3
Asia Pacific Economic Cooperation	APEC	1989	18
Association of Southeast Asian Nations	ASEAN	1967	10
Latin American Free Trade Association	LAFTA	1960	11
The European Union	EU	1958	15

ferred to as *regional trading arrangements (RTAs)*—many of which have come into existence in only the past 10 to 15 years. Most of the world's major and minor countries are members of one type of trading bloc or another. RTAs are found on every continent of the world, and sometimes membership crosses oceans, as in the case of the Asian Pacific Economic Cooperation (APEC). See Table 11.2 for a list of some of the key RTAs. One key question for observers of the international political economy is whether RTAs are good or bad for global free trade. Before we get to this question, however, let's look at several types of RTAs.

One type of RTA is called a **free trade area (FTA),** whose aim is to reduce trade barriers across the borders of participating countries. Canada, the United States, and Mexico, for example, have eliminated or plan to eliminate hundreds of tariffs, quotas, and nontariff barriers to trade as part of the NAFTA agreement.

A **customs union (CU)** is like an FTA except that it has the added element of a *common external tariff.* If NAFTA were to become a customs union, for example, the three countries would give up their own tariff rates and settle on *one* rate acceptable to all three countries. Why does a common external tariff matter? Let's say that you are a Japanese car manufacturer and wish to export to Europe. Imagine that the French tariff rate is 25 percent; thus, every car you send to France costs consumers there 25 percent more than it would with no tariff. Let's say, though, that the British tariff rate is only 6 percent. As a Japanese exporter, what is the more appealing place to send your cars? Britain. Once your cars are in Britain, you can easily move them across the border (in this case the English Channel) at no cost because of the free trade area agreement between the France and Britain (as EU members). The French government, of course, loses out in such an arrangement because they don't get *any* benefit from their 25 percent tariff. In order to avoid this sort of problem, the countries of the EU decided to establish a common external tariff rate in 1968. So no matter where your first point of entry is for your Japanese cars, you will always pay the same tariff rate.

The degree to which states in a trade bloc wish to cooperate depends on many political and economic factors. Figure 11.2 illustrates the options that states have in deciding how much economic policy coordination to have. At one extreme (the left side of the diagram), states and their companies behave like separate states normally do. As one moves to the right, states increase their degree of economic cooperation or market integration. Customs unions are more developed arrangements than FTAs, for example. It is rare, but some countries go even further than CUs and seek monetary union, where the member states give up their own individual national currencies for a common, or single, currency. As we saw in Chapter 5, the

Free Trade Area
International trade among countries that is devoid of tariff and nontariff barriers.

Customs Union (CU)
A free trade area in which all member states agree to a common external tariff.

FIGURE 11.2
Degrees of Economic Policy Coordination

Completely Separate Countries	FTA	Customs Union	Monetary Union	One Country

EU is the best example of this phenomenon. At the extreme right side of the diagram, countries have coordinated their political and economic policies so much that they have effectively merged into a single country. Different trade blocs, thus, have different institutional structures ranging from the relatively well-coordinated EU to the loosely organized and politically ineffective APEC.

As we saw in the box Historical Perspective: The Legacy of Bretton Woods on p. 446, GATT and WTO systems are based on the idea that members should cooperate in a multilateral, not unilateral or bilateral, way. However, because of the increased use of protectionist policies, especially nontariff barriers, some IPE observers are nervous that the rising number of trade blocs will harm the global, multilateral free trade approach of the WTO. The worst case scenario is a world of belligerent trade blocs in which a "Fortress Europe" competes against a "Fortress North America," which competes against a "Fortress Asia." Other opponents of trade blocs focus on the potential for job losses for some of the countries within a trade bloc. For example, Ross Perot and others in the United States fear that NAFTA will encourage U.S. companies to move their operations to Mexico, where the wage rate can be five times less than in the United States. Why pay workers $20 an hour in the United States when you only have to pay them $4 an hour in Mexico?[18]

Also in the case of NAFTA, other people worry that many American and Canadian companies set up shop in Mexico to evade the more stringent environmental standards in the north. *Maquiladora* factories allowed mostly American companies to invest in plants in Mexico, ship raw materials there, and then export finished goods back to the United States without customs duties. The maquiladora program was so successful that by 1999, there were 3,050 factories—a third more than when NAFTA took effect.[19] (See Chapter 13 for more on environmental aspects.)

Exactly why trade blocs form is a controversial issue. Six explanations are given below, and although each differs from the others, you will see that they also have areas of overlap.

1. Hegemonic stability theory (see Chapter 1) suggests that since we are in an era of declining hegemony (i.e., the United States is no longer as powerful as it was in the 1950s and 1960s), protectionist trade blocs are more likely to form. In the heyday of American hegemony, the United States took the lead in keeping the international trading system open. Since the United States is no longer willing or able to play this role, hegemonic stability theory would predict that no other state or international organizational will be able to fill the void. It also predicts that greater instability will follow.

2. Some economists suggest that trade blocs form to achieve traditional trade gains such as increased competition, more efficient use of resources, and greater access to markets in member countries. Among NAFTA countries, for instance, the free flow of goods is enhanced.

3. Trade blocs are useful in shielding members from global competition. Once in a trade bloc, countries that do not feel their industries are ready for the onslaught of global competition can enjoy the fruits of free trade on a regional scale.

4. Because of the increased use of protectionist policies, some countries view trade blocs as insurance in case the multilateral trading system fails. This explanation was particularly relevant during the tumultuous final years of the last comprehensive round of global trade talks, the Uruguay Round, that took place in the early 1990s. We will touch on this issue later in the section on the World Trade Organization.

5. Trade blocs may form to further national security goals that favor allies and hurt enemies. The United States, for example, encouraged the formation of the European Union because an economically strong Europe would be better poised to confront the challenge of Soviet Communism.

6. Trade blocs may also form for reasons related to domestic politics. National politicians, for instance, may wish to undertake important economic reforms (e.g., eliminating protectionist policies) *through regional means* that may not be politically popular back home. Then when faced with opposition at home, the politician can claim that his or her *hands are tied* and that "the regional institutions require that we take these steps." For example, national politicians in the European Union might like to reduce the amount of government aid that goes to farmers but be reluctant to do so because they fear the wrath of the powerful farm lobbies. However, because the European Union is considering expanding to central and eastern European countries, these politicians can now more safely claim that reduction in farm assistance is required to accommodate the new countries (see Chapter 5 for more details about EU expansion).

The rational choice approach that we described earlier in the chapter, which uses the concept of "supply and demand," can also be used to understand aspects of regional trading blocs. First, government officials *supply* policies to constituents. The *demands* come from businesses, labor groups, or other constituents who want government policies that favor them. For example, U.S. labor unions and environmental groups are generally opposed to NAFTA. If they were to get highly organized, they could send lobbyists to Washington and state capitals and put political pressure on legislators across the country with the aim of ending NAFTA. The interest groups applying pressure to government officials are *demanding* that the government *supply* a policy that is more favorable to them—in this case the end of NAFTA, which these groups feel is either bad for American workers or for environmental conditions.

Is the World Becoming More or Less Protectionist? The answer to this question has seemingly opposite answers. In some respects the world is indeed closing up. Since the 1970s, global economic troubles have built momentum as exemplified by the increased use of nontariff barriers. In addition, in the wake of the Asian financial crisis of the late 1990s, many countries have resorted to a variety of protectionist policies. Nevertheless, the desire is still there to maintain and even strengthen global free trade and the multilateral approach. Compared to GATT, for instance, the WTO breaks new ground in the elimination of barriers to free trade. For example, talks are under way in the so-called "Doha Round" of WTO meetings to tackle some of the persistent trade barriers as well as newer ones. Thus, the development around the world of regional trade blocs highlights the dual trend toward greater protectionism *and* further opening of global trade. In some ways trade blocs help limit the free flow of goods globally, but in other ways trade blocs may be seen as building blocks to a more open international economy. Moreover, the countries in the key trade blocs are also the key players in the WTO, an organization

FIGURE 11.3
Share of World Trade by Country
SOURCE: Data from Eurostat.

Share of World Trade
Exports of goods (1998)

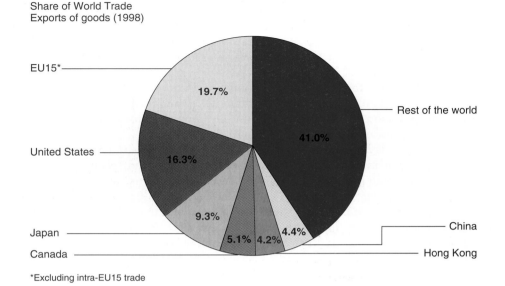

EU15*

19.7%

Rest of the world

41.0%

United States

16.3%

China

Japan

9.3%

5.1% 4.2% 4.4%

Canada

Hong Kong

*Excluding intra-EU15 trade

FIGURE 11.4
The EU's Main Trade Partners
SOURCE: Data from Eurostat.

EU15 Main Trade Partners
Exports by region 1998

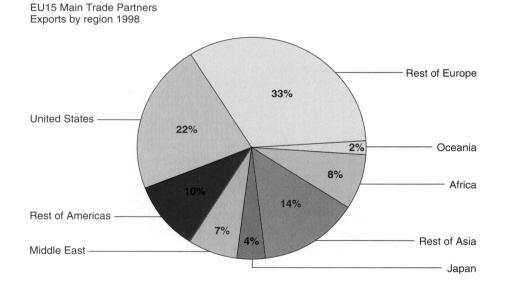

Rest of Europe

33%

United States

22%

Oceania

2%

Africa

8%

Rest of Asia

14%

Rest of Americas

10%

Japan

Middle East

7%   4%

committed to global free trade. Trade between the United States and the EU is enormous, and many jobs on one side of the Atlantic are dependent on what happens on the other side. For example, 6 million U.S. jobs are supported by European investment, and another 1.5 million U.S. jobs are connected to American exports to Europe. Moreover, EU countries invest about $150 billion in the United States, while the United States invests about $120 billion in Europe.[20] These two major trading bloc partners have a strong stake in keeping trade flowing (See Figure 11.3, which shows the share of world trade by country, and Figure 11.4, which illustrates the EU's Main Trade Partners by region).

The World Trade Organization: The WTO consists of over a hundred member states, but the dominant players in the WTO are the United States and the countries of the European Union. While most of the trade between the United States and EU is carried out routinely, some high-profile disputes have disrupted relations between the two trading partners and have caused problems within the WTO itself, as portrayed in this cartoon.
Source: Satoshi Kambayashi, UK.

To summarize this section, the forces for global free trade tend to be associated with the centralizing tendencies around the world. The forces of protectionism can lead to fragmentation on a regional level (more protectionist trade blocs) or on a state-by-state level, where countries struggle against each other with competitive protectionist policies. But as we have seen, support for both global free trade *and* greater protectionism is at work. Both forces will likely continue through the beginning of the twenty-first century, barring any economic, military, or other catastrophe.

Who Manages Global Trade?

Whether you support free trade or protectionism of one kind or another, you may wonder how it is that almost 200 countries and their millions of companies do business every day. In many respects, global trade may appear not to be "managed" at all. The forces of supply and demand regulate who buys and sells the multitude of products and services out there. We know that governments impose rules (such as tariffs, quotas, and nontariff barriers) to help manage the impact of participation in the global economy. In addition, thanks to a historical convergence of circumstances, one of the most important international institutions in the world is actually designed specifically to help manage global trade. We now turn to this institution, the World Trade Organization—its mission, its contributions, and its critics.

The World Trade Organization

As we discussed in Chapter 5, *international organizations* are a major force in determining the direction of the international political economy. The global economy is not ruled completely by the "invisible hand" of self-interest. It is influenced by the most powerful countries in the world and by the rules and institutions that they helped create. In the area of international trade, the major international organization that buttresses the relatively liberal trading system is the *World Trade Organization (WTO)*, the offspring of the General Agreement on Tariffs and Trade (GATT).

One early goal of GATT was to create a productive economic environment that would help countries rebuild from both the Great Depression and the destruction of World War II. Similar to other international organizations established by the Bretton Woods system (see box Historical Perspective: The Legacy of Bretton Woods on p. 446), GATT created a permanent forum where countries and companies could discuss issues that concerned them. This forum was designed to be *multilateral* in nature; that is, it involved many countries, unlike the more cumbersome and historically protectionist *unilateral* or *bilateral* trade arrangements.

At the heart of GATT's (and the WTO's) foundation was the desire to foster freedom of trade by the systematic and long-term strategy of lowering trade barriers. GATT focused at first on the most serious and common barriers to trade: tariffs and quotas, discussed earlier. For nearly two decades (the 1950s and 1960s), thanks in part to GATT, the world experienced a historically unprecedented economic boom. By the early 1970s, GATT could confidently say that its basic aims had been achieved. Although it faced rising protectionism after that, it still was a significant factor in freeing up international trade. Between 1950 and 1996, for example, world exports rose 16 times and world output rose 5 times. World export of manufactured goods rose 31 times, while manufacturing output rose by a factor of 9.[21] In addition, GATT had only 23 countries when it was founded in 1947; now WTO membership stands at 132 with 31 countries waiting to join.

One of the free trade elements of the Bretton Woods system that remains today is the **most-favored-nation principle (MFN).** Members of the WTO, according to the MFN, are supposed to grant tariff or other barrier reduction to *all* other WTO members. A second important principle of the WTO is *reciprocity*. Reciprocity bolsters the MFN because it implies that a country's reduction in tariffs, for example, will be reciprocated by other WTO members. A third principle is *nondiscrimination*, which means that foreign goods will be treated the same as domestic goods, that is, foreign goods will not be discriminated against. GATT and later the WTO were highly successful at reducing trade barriers among members through the global economic boom years following World War II.

In the 1970s and 1980s, the world economy faced serious challenges. The response by many countries, including the United States, was to reestablish or enhance existing barriers to foreign competition. Since GATT had made most tariffs and quotas off-limits, countries devised new forms of protectionism by using **nontariff barriers,** as discussed earlier in the chapter. In the late 1980s and early 1990s, GATT members held a long series of trade talks, known as the **Uruguay Round** (the talks began in Punte del Este, Uruguay), which attempted to tackle some of the nontariff barriers that were increasingly hindering free trade. It was at the conclusion of the Uruguay Round in December 1993 that GATT was retired and the WTO was born.

The WTO was given many new responsibilities, increasing its potential influence as an international organization. For example, it now has an expanded scope of responsibility beyond GATT's to include not just goods but services as well. Thus, over the next several years, the WTO will be addressing trade disputes in *consumer* services, which cover such things as restaurants, hotels, and travel agencies. The WTO will also address problems in *producer* services, which involve investment and banking, insurance, intellectual property rights, advertising, data processing, and so on. Moreover, the WTO plans to integrate into its multilateral framework certain economic areas that were previously not a part of GATT. These include agriculture, textiles and clothing, telecommunications, and even labor stan-

Most-Favored-Nation Principle (MFN)
A pillar of GATT and now the WTO, in which imports from one state are granted the same degree of preference as imports from the most preferred states.

Uruguay Round
A series of negotiations as part of GATT that lasted between 1986 and 1994. The aim of the round, begun in Punte del Este, Uruguay, was to tackle global trade barriers, especially non-tariff barriers that were increasingly hindering free trade. It addressed seriously for the first time services and agricultural goods.

dards and the environment. Another major new development in the WTO is a much more effective and timely *dispute-resolution mechanism*—that is, a more efficient way for companies and countries to resolve their problems quickly and in an orderly way. Finally, the WTO is being given greater powers to enforce its own rules. Like GATT, the WTO can rule against a country for unfair trade practices, but the WTO is now less likely to be ignored by the offending country.

Just how effectively these WTO rules will be enforced is still to be determined. Why aren't the rules clear-cut and completely enforceable? Opposition from member states and the public to an expanded role for the WTO puts pressure on governments to avoid rules that would allow them to be overruled by the WTO.[22]

Positive Contributions of the WTO   How well has the WTO worked so far? By the 1990s the WTO was in many ways very successful. For example, most of the 163 cases brought to the WTO between 1995 and the end of 1998 were settled without the need for arbitration. When the WTO was called upon to adjudicate disputes, no government defied any of its rulings. Even though some countries were short-term losers in particular cases, they still abided by the WTO because of the broader and long-term benefits of WTO membership. The United States, for instance, was a short-term loser when the WTO forced it to lift illegal restrictions on imports of Costa Rican underwear. In another case, Japan was forced to reform its alcohol tax policies after complaints were made by the United States, the EU, and Canada.

Challenges Facing the WTO   As we look to the future, what are some of the major challenges facing the World Trade Organization? First and foremost, the WTO must deal with the question of what type of organization it will be. Most observers agree that the WTO will continue to be dominated by governments seeking to hold on to as much national sovereignty as possible. Most of its members are not very interested in granting the WTO too many powers. Second, WTO member states rarely come to any real consensus about how policy problems should be dealt with. The WTO members even had a hard time deciding who should lead the organization. One should not get the impression, however, that the WTO is totally hampered by the whims of nation-states. Its members do understand the need for cooperation, and the WTO is heading into an increasingly large number of new areas. Third, as the box The View from the Demonstration: Violent Protests Against the WTO on page 463 points out, the WTO faces considerable opposition regarding its effects on the environment and job security.

Although environmental issues are dealt with in much more detail in Chapter 13, the crux of the protesters' *environmental complaint* runs along these lines. For most people, there seems to be a trade-off between the environment and the economy; what is good for one is bad for the other. For example, the conservationist group the World Wildlife Federation (WWF) argues that trade has a destructive impact on the environment because it facilitates the overconsumption of natural resources. "Increased trade in natural resources is one of the biggest driving forces in deforestation, soil degradation, water overuse, marine pollution and ultimately species extinction." The WWF also believes that strengthening environmental regulations worldwide should take place *before* seeking greater trade liberalization.[23] Another point made by many environmentalists is that companies will try to evade costly environmental standards in one country by setting up shop in a country that has lax standards.

The WTO's environmental position is, naturally, quite different. Mike Moore, the WTO's former general secretary, has stated that there is not necessarily a trade-off between the environment and the economy, as in the example of lower trade

FIGURE 11.5
The Relationship Between Environmental Degradation and Poverty

SOURCE: World Trade Organization (WTO).

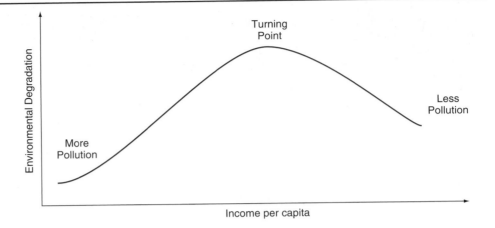

barriers to environmentally friendly goods and services. Another example of policy that is good for both the environment and the economy is the elimination of fishery subsidies (a form of government assistance) that encourage overfishing.[24] In addition, Moore argues that the real cause of environmental degradation is poverty, not trade (see Figure 11.5). Chapters 10 and 12 go into further detail regarding global poverty. The WTO also argues that very little evidence suggests that companies seek locations where environmental standards are lowest. Few economists argue that high environmental standards hurt the competitiveness of companies. In countries with strict standards, the costs of complying represent only a tiny fraction of the total production cost.[25]

The *labor complaint* of the WTO protesters like those at the "Battle of Seattle" focused on the wages of workers in the Third World, where in some places, transnational corporations pay workers a dollar an hour or less, and where working conditions are often inhospitable and even dangerous. Of particular concern to the labor protesters is the apparent trend of international businesses to set up factories in countries with very low wages. Lower wages in the Third World, they believe, end up affecting wage levels in the United States. In essence, American workers must settle for lower wages in order to keep their jobs from being sent overseas. In the long run, then, the labor protesters worry that U.S. jobs will be lost and that worker standards and wage levels in the United States will decline.

Supporters of global free trade, however, are quick to point out several important points. According to Laura D'Andrea Tyson, a former top Clinton economic advisor, there is no evidence that trade liberalization encourages a "race to the bottom" in labor standards. Indeed, the opposite is true. Trade actually encourages economic development, which in turn enhances labor standards.[26]

Was the failure of the WTO talks in Seattle a result of both the peaceful and violent demonstrations in Seattle? Many protesters believed so. In one of its articles, *Newsweek* even referred to the "protesters who shut down the World Trade Organization meeting."[27] Upon further analysis, however, the source of the failure lies elsewhere. We need to look at two important conclusions about Seattle. First, the WTO talks failed because of issues unrelated to the concerns of the protesters. Compared to previous WTO (and GATT) meetings that attempted major reforms, the Seattle meeting had a much larger number of member states participating (135), many of whom were new to multilateral trade talks.[28] The complexity of the

THE VIEW FROM   The Demonstration

Violent Protests Against the WTO

In November 1999 Bill Clinton gave a speech hoping to gain widespread support for the WTO and global trade in general. He said that he wanted everyone who thought that global trade was a bad thing to go to Seattle, Washington. "I want everybody to get all of this out of their system.[29] Clinton, the WTO, and the Seattle Police Department, however, got much more than they bargained for when, one month later, thousands of anti-WTO protesters hit the streets of Seattle during the WTO summit meeting. While most of the protests were peaceful, the media were enthralled, as for days they covered the violent demonstrations, which were sometimes met with harsh police crackdowns.

An unusual mix of individuals and organizations came to Seattle to protest all sorts of things, including environmental degradation, lost jobs, and the lack of accountability of the WTO. Doctors Without Borders was there, as was the Sierra Club, those in favor of freeing Tibet, French farmers, and even anarchists and the Seattle Lesbian Avengers. One common denominator of the protesters was that they were upset about the globalization process. And the WTO was simply the most visible symbol of that process.

More specifically, the two biggest complaints against the WTO were related to environmental and labor issues. Environmentalists and labor unions typically don't have much in common, but they found the Seattle WTO meeting a cause for cooperation. One union organizer put it this way, "I saw a sign on the street that said it best: 'Teamsters and Turtles.' We have been united in our fight against the WTO."[30]

Violent Protests: Riot police guard the front of a Nike store from looters and vandals in downtown Seattle during the protests against the World Trade Organization in November 1999.

issues involved also contributed to the talks' failure. The agenda was very crowded, and many issues were highly technical. In addition, the United States was also relatively unwilling to make concessions in negotiations with other WTO members as a result of the 2000 presidential election campaign.[31]

Second, the protesters may have been making their case at the wrong place. For most WTO supporters, the WTO is not the correct forum for dealing with many of the issues that brought the protesters to Seattle. What appears to be the overall concern among protesters wasn't free trade per se, but the globalization process in general. As Fareed Zakaria put it, "the purpose of trade agreements is to lower trade barriers. There are other methods, treaties, and organizations aimed at pursuing environmental and labor goals."[32]

Perhaps the most important outcome of the Seattle protests may be that the protesters ironically got a psychological boost from the "Siege of Seattle."[33] In the future, they may look back at Seattle as the spark that triggered more effective protests, public opinion more favorable to their concerns, and ultimately more favorable legislation.

How Does the Global Financial System Operate?

The political ramifications of monetary relations are evident at both the global and national levels. At the national level, for example, deficits and surpluses affect a country's prosperity and ultimately its power and influence in the world. Global financial interactions can even threaten the sovereignty of states. In our increasingly interdependent world, *autonomous* national economic policy making is not really possible—especially for smaller states. Any state's monetary relations are really international monetary relations. As a result, many people argue that at least some international cooperation is needed. The trouble, however, is that international cooperation is difficult to achieve.[34] In the following discussion of monetary relations, we'll explore how currencies are valued, we'll discuss one of the most interesting experiments in international monetary relations in a long time (Europe's single currency, the euro), and we'll explore the efforts at international cooperation in financial matters by looking at the International Monetary Fund and the World Bank.

Placing a Value on Currency

Throughout the centuries, money has taken a variety of forms. The first types of cash were metal or clay. At various times, barley and other goods were also used as currency. In Mesopotamia, we see the beginning of casting and coiling as the world's first cash appeared in the form of rings of silver. China developed the world's first paper currency, and the first government outside China to issue paper currency was the Massachusetts colony in 1690 for a military expedition ordered by London. The first modern, preprinted checks, which depositors could use to pay anyone, appeared in England in 1781.[35]

For money to be useful—no matter what it is made of—it must be able to store value, that is, it must be valuable in some way. The value of a country's currency depends on many things, including the economic health of the country issuing the money, the confidence that people have in the currency, and how much people demand the currency. (Like other goods, there is a supply and demand for money.) For much of the post–World War II period, the U.S. dollar was the most stable and desired currency in the world. It was also easy to tell how much it was worth. The

The Euro: The new currency for 12 of the 15 European Union countries.

Bretton Woods system fixed the value of the dollar to a certain amount of gold: one ounce of gold was worth $35. As discussed earlier, however, the dollar left this gold standard in 1973. The value of currencies compared to one another thus became flexible; currencies were allowed to float against one another without the link to gold.

Determining Exchange Rates

To help demonstrate the effects of allowing currencies to fluctuate against each other, consider the following example. Imagine that on July 22, you wanted to buy a British jacket that costs £100, roughly the equivalent of $160. However, you couldn't get to the store until the end of September. By then, unfortunately, the value of the dollar had dropped. This is called devaluation. Because of the devaluation in the dollar, your original $100 is not as "valued" as it used to be. At the end of September, it will take more dollars to buy the jacket. Now you have to pay $180 for the jacket—even though it is still priced at £100. What do you do now? Instead of paying more money, you could decide to buy an American sweater for $160. What are the political economic implications if everyone else in the United States did what you did? Obviously, more American sweaters would be sold and fewer British jackets would be sold. In addition, more jobs would be supported in the United States, since you and everyone else "bought American." Since fewer British goods are sold, the job situation gets worse in Britain. So, British export companies won't do as well as they would have before the dollar devaluation. Ultimately, the trade balance shifts in favor of the United States.

Changes in the value of a country's currency can have a profound impact on the employment rate and the country's trade balance. Consider these issues when

For more information on the origins, purposes, and types of money, go to **www.ablongman.com/ duncan.**

you read about Europe's single currency; with one currency, there are no longer any currency fluctuations! See the Web Exploration for an illustration of the value of foreign currencies.

Unifying a Region: Europe's Single Currency (the Euro)

For more information on the value of foreign currencies, go to **www.ablongman.com/ duncan**.

One of the most important new developments in the international monetary system is the advent of the European Union's single currency, the euro. Unprecedented in history, the euro replaces 12 national currencies, including the German mark, the French franc, and the Italian lira. Because the European Union has a population and combined economy larger than that of the United States, many have speculated about the impact on EU-U.S. relations as well as on the international monetary system in general. Will the euro rival the U.S. dollar as the currency of choice around the world? Foreign banks, companies, and individuals will likely hedge their bets (and spread out their risk) by diversifying their currency holdings with euros as well as dollars. Although it is still too early to tell, the U.S. voice in determining the direction of global monetary relations may soon not be as loud as it once was.

What drove the EU countries to create the euro? First of all, not all EU member states have adopted the euro. Britain, Denmark, and Sweden opted out of the "euro-zone" for a variety of reasons. But for those that opted in, one of the main reasons was a desire to create a more stable monetary environment in Europe. The roots of this desire go back decades but particularly to the 1970s. After the United States abandoned key elements of the Bretton Woods system, and after a series of wars in the Middle East and the OPEC oil shocks, the international monetary system was highly unstable. Leaders in France and Germany spearheaded the establishment of the European Monetary System (EMS) to help coordinate several major European currencies. The EMS helped achieve a certain degree of monetary stability in Europe. This rudimentary form of monetary cooperation, however, was deemed insufficient for handling many problems facing Europe.

Second, many Europeans felt that the European single market, although quite a success, was hampered by varying currency values across the continent. One of the most obvious problems with 15 currencies for 15 EU countries was that converting currencies was costly and time consuming. A person who began with the equivalent of $100 in Spain and who then spent a few days in France, Belgium, and Denmark had to convert the dollars into each of the countries' currencies—and keep track of what all the different numbers meant. In addition, banks and currency offices charge fees, or commissions, for making the currency conversion. Such *transaction costs* are now eliminated within the euro-zone.

Third, EU members wanted the benefits from competition that would emerge from the *transparency* of prices. In theory, it should be easy to compare the costs of goods from one part of Europe to the next. In practice, however, before the euro, this seemingly simple exercise was anything but. "Should I buy a new Volkswagen here in Germany or would it be a better deal in Italy? Now if I add in the transportation costs and the different taxes I would have to pay, and then take into account the currency conversion. . . ." This arrangement was obviously more complicated than it is for, say, someone in Kansas looking to shop across the border in Missouri or for a Virginian to consider buying a car in Maryland.

Finally, Europe had a variety of *political* reasons for establishing the single currency. For example, establishing the euro was intended to create a viable alternative to U.S. hegemony in global monetary relations. By working together, the

12 (and eventually more) European countries have more clout in global monetary dealings than they had individually. Another political reason is that many Europeans felt that the European Union needed a boost to keep its momentum going. They feared that without this major policy initiative, the entire EU would atrophy. A third, more concrete, political reason goes back to the 1989–1991 period of German unification. A loose agreement was struck between Germany and the other major European powers: on the one hand, East and West Germany were allowed to unify; on the other, Germany—led by Helmut Kohl—committed itself to furthering EU economic and monetary union.

One of the most important actual and symbolic losses to national sovereignty is the elimination of a country's currency. The EU with its euro is extremely unusual in this respect. But if the EU countries can do it, why not other trading blocs? MERCOSUR (a customs union made up of Brazil, Argentina, Paraguay, and Uruguay) has considered—albeit not extensively—creating a common currency for some of the same reasons. ASEAN—the South East Asian nations—and Japan, China, and South Korea are considering, at least hypothetically, the idea of a single currency in South-East Asia.[36] And what about the NAFTA countries? The idea of Mexico, Canada, and the United States sharing the same currency may sound outlandish, but it is actually being considered.[37] The idea is that the U.S. dollar (or some completely new currency) would become the currency for the three NAFTA countries. Proponents of the idea suggest that Canadian and Mexican businesses could benefit from currency stability; that is, they could avoid sharp drops in the value of their own currencies compared to the dollar. This is already being done in some countries where the dollar is a key currency. In Peru, Russia, and Turkey, for example, where people don't trust their own money, the U.S. dollar is highly valued. Argentina is already heavily "dollarized." According to one estimate, by 1995 about half of Argentina's bank deposits were in dollars. In 2000 Ecuador adopted the U.S. dollar as its *de facto* currency.

Others have even suggested that by the year 2030, there will only be two major currencies in the world: the euro and the dollar. Zanny Minton Beddoes, a correspondent with the British magazine *The Economist*, for example, predicts that by that year, the euro will be used from France to Romania and that the dollar will be used from Alaska to Argentina and perhaps even in Asia.[38] Critics of the idea of a

Fake Argentina Dollar: Argentina's currency is linked, or pegged, to the U.S. dollar. As the dollar rises and falls in value, so does Argentina's currency, the *real*. Some have suggested that Argentina simply adopt the U.S. dollars as its national currency.

common NAFTA currency—let alone a dollar-denominated Western hemisphere—however, believe that the resulting loss of economic sovereignty will discourage countries from taking that path. The Canadians and Mexicans, for example, would be particularly worried about being dominated by the much more politically and economically powerful United States. Both countries have a long tradition of trying to resist the clout of the United States.

In general, though, no one is expecting a currency union in NAFTA any time soon. In addition, Alan Greenspan, chairman of the Federal Reserve Board, has argued that Mexico or any other country thinking to dollarize shouldn't expect that all their problems will disappear once they adopt the dollar. Improvements in their economies depend just as much, if not more, on policies the foreign governments choose—not which currency they use. Nevertheless, it is interesting to speculate that if the EU's euro proves successful in the long run, more and more people are likely to consider the prospects of a NAFTA currency. It will, of course, take time for this to occur. One thing is certain from this discussion about single currencies: the link between economics and politics is extremely important.

The International Monetary Fund and the World Bank

International Monetary Fund (IMF)
A United Nations agency responsible for overseeing the entire international monetary system by promoting exchange rate stability and orderly exchange relations among its member countries.

World Bank
A United Nations agency designed to promote the economic development of the world's poorer countries and to assist these countries through long-term financing of development projects.

The international monetary system has several major players. In addition to the world's major countries and financial companies, international institutions are vital to the management of global financial relations. The two main international institutions that help oversee global monetary relations are the **International Monetary Fund** (IMF) and the **World Bank.** Both are part of the United Nations framework.

The IMF was created to oversee the international monetary system by promoting exchange stability and orderly exchange relations among its member countries. When addressing economic troubles in particular countries, the IMF seeks to achieve economy-wide financial stability. The aim of the World Bank, by contrast, is to promote the economic development of the world's poorer countries by financing specific projects that could achieve institutional and structural economic changes.[39] In short, the IMF normally handles macroeconomic and currency liquidity problems while the World Bank addresses individual projects and programs. (See Table 11.3, The IMF and the World Bank Compared, for a closer comparison of these two organizations.)

The IMF and World Bank claim some credit for the progress made in helping the troubled economies of the world since the 1950s. As the World Bank has noted, more progress has been made in reducing poverty and raising living standards since World War II than during any other period in history. Life expectancy has increased from 55 to 65 years, incomes per person have doubled, more children are attending schools (from less than half to more than three quarters), and infant mortality has been reduced by half.

Although the objectives of the World Bank and IMF are laudable, not everyone is happy with their policies. By the late 1990s, the two institutions had acquired a long list of detractors. One criticism came from those who saw an inefficient overlap evolving between the IMF and World Bank. Jessica Einhorn, a former managing director of the World Bank, has described how in recent years, the World Bank "has been called on for emergency lending in wake of the Asian financial crisis, for economic management as part of Middle East peacekeeping efforts, for postwar Balkan reconstruction, and for loans to combat the AIDS tragedy in Africa," in addition to a role in such areas as biodiversity, ozone depletion, narcotics, crime, and

TABLE 11.3	The IMF and World Bank Compared	
	International Monetary Fund	**World Bank**
Goals	• Oversees the international monetary system	• Seeks to promote the economic development of the world's poorer countries
Main Functions	• Assists all members—both industrial and developing countries—that find themselves in temporary balance of payments difficulties by providing short- to medium-term credits • Promotes exchange stability and orderly exchange relations among its member countries • Supplements the currency reserves of its members through the allocation of special drawing rights (SDR); to date, SDR of $21.4 billion has been issued to member countries in proportion to their quotas	• Assists developing countries through long-term financing of development projects and programs • Provides the poorest countries whose per capita GNP is less than $865 a year special financial assistance through the International Development Association (IDA) • Encourages private enterprises in developing countries through its affiliate, the International Finance corporation (IFC)
Source of Funding	Principally from the quota subscriptions of its member countries	Primarily from borrowing on the international bond market
Amount of Funding	About $215 billion	$184 billion, of which members pay in about 10%
Size of Staff	2,300 drawn from 182 member countries	7,000 drawn from 180 member countries

SOURCE: World Bank Website (http://www.worldbank.org) August, 1999.

corruption.[40] This widening agenda, according to critics, has led to ineffectiveness and a lack of focus.

Another general criticism is that the World Bank and IMF are tools used by the Northern industrialized countries to dominate the South. The World Bank, for example, requires that countries receiving its loans make economic policy changes through *structural adjustment programs* (SAPs). SAPs often require countries to cut social spending to balance government budgets. Cuts of government programs put a heavy burden on the poor, who depend on social services. In addition, when countries receiving World Bank loans were asked about the results of implementing such policies, the answers were not always positive. Some people complained that policies mandated by the World Bank destroyed local jobs and industries.[41] The World Bank began a program in 1998 to reevaluate the consequences of its SAPs. One cosmetic result was that in 2000, the World Bank changed the name *SAPs* to *Poverty Reduction and Growth Facility*. At this point in time, it is too early to tell if new World Bank policies have significantly altered the situation.

Others criticized the lack of compliance with IMF's and World Bank's own rules, the inability of the institutions to address serious problems like the Asian financial crisis that began in 1997, the two organizations' failure to address the important role of women in the development policies of Third World countries, their disregard for the environment in favor of economic growth, and their lack of public transparency (i.e., their rather secret way of conducting business).

The United States, as the twin institutions' most influential member, has recently been contemplating major changes to the duties of the IMF and World Bank. One congressional commission proposed that the IMF be limited to short-term financing to resolve crises in emerging economies and that the World Bank focus on providing poor countries with grants rather than loans. Another proposal was to have the World Bank pull out of Asia and Latin America so that two *regional* institutions can take over: the Asian and InterAmerican Development Banks.[42] But, the direction of IMF and World Bank reform is not yet clear. One reason is the lack of consistency in U.S. policy. When the Bush administration began in 2001, it argued that it was a bad idea for the IMF to make loans to countries with serious economic troubles because this would, in effect, reward economic failure. In financial-speak, this was a "moral hazard" to be avoided. But, as Harvard professor Ricardo Hausmann points out, if the IMF is not supposed to help very troubled economies, in the end, the world would not really need the IMF.[43] By the second year of the Bush administration, the United States had chosen not to accept its own rhetoric, as it encouraged the IMF to make large loans to several countries, including a $30 billion loan to Brazil in the summer of 2002. As in previous financial crises, the United States and the IMF decided that it was important to calm markets down and establish a stable economic environment that could attract more investors and entrepreneurs.

While the IMF and the World Bank are the primary intergovernmental organizations for managing international monetary affairs, other organizations and banks exist as well. The *Group of Eight* (G8), for example, is a coordinating body made up of the governments of the seven leading industrial countries plus Russia (which was included for the first time in the 1990s). The G8 holds economic summit meetings that include not only high-ranking financial and economic ministers but heads of state and government as well. The aim of the G8 is to address in a coordinated manner the current trade and monetary problems.

Another important organization that helps coordinate global financial relations is the *Organization for Economic Cooperation and Development* (OECD). This international organization was created in 1961 to replace another IO that distributed Marshall Plan funds in Western Europe. Today, the OECD's membership includes the world's advanced industrialized countries. It differs from the EU in that it has very few ties to the public in member countries.[44] The OECD has many links to the G8, which also has many ties to the IMF. Since the OECD and G8 have some common members, they are often viewed as a club of the wealthy states that fails to address the economic concerns of the developing countries. One response by the G8 to the apparent lack of focus on the Third World is the establishment of a new "talking shop" to be comprised of both industrial and developing countries.[45]

What Is the Role of International Businesses in World Politics?

You will recall from Chapter 6 that multinational corporations differ from transnational corporations, but that most people use the term *MNC* to refer to any large companies with operations in two or more countries. MNCs have grown enormously in the past two decades in terms of their geographic scope and their economic influence. As we saw in Table 6.1 in Chapter 6, many corporate actors have more economic clout than most countries. Wal-Mart, for example, controls almost the same economic resources as all of Greece. The 1990s even witnessed the merger of MNCs, thus creating even larger companies. Exxon acquired Mobil, Travellers Group acquired Citicorp, Daimler Benz acquired Chrysler, and so on.[46] The size and nature of these international businesses have profound political implications, but observers strongly disagree over whether MNCs are ultimately good or bad for the international political economy. We conclude this chapter with a brief discussion of the contributions and criticisms of MNCs.

According to the economic liberalism approach, MNCs provide many benefits to the company *and* the home and host countries. Because of their size, MNCs can exploit economies of scale and thus increase economic efficiency enormously. In addition, they can create new jobs in both home and host countries. MNCs can also teach workers and managers in the host country about efficient methods of production, management skills, and the transfer of new technologies and processes. As we saw in the case of NAFTA, the economic liberalism approach predicts that, because of the presence of more MNCs, Mexico will have more well-off consumers interested in buying American products. Other benefits should result from the increased global competition that is fostered by MNCs. Instead of each country having a **national champion,** for example, foreign companies can compete with domestic companies for the consumers' money. Competition from Japanese carmakers in the 1980s and 1990s most likely prompted increased productivity in the U.S. auto industry and eventually higher quality in American-built cars.

Critics of unrestrained MNCs, by contrast, point to a variety of features they view as detrimental. For example, they say that because capital is more mobile than labor, MNCs move to where costs are low *at the expense of their workers.* As the case of Wal-Mart illustrated, many opponents of MNCs decry the conditions in which host employees must work. Others point to the limited degree to which foreign knowledge or technology is passed on or adapted in the host country. Sometimes the MNC retains the more advanced business aspects of the company for home employees, while host employees are left with the blue-collar jobs. Another complaint is that once a large MNC sets up shop in the host country, local competitors face bankruptcy because they cannot compete with the vast economic resources of the large foreign company. Host countries can try to regulate the foreign company (e.g., by requiring that a large percentage of the workers be local), but if host countries push MNCs too much, the foreign companies can simply threaten to pull out of the host country and go somewhere else. This is particularly relevant when cheap labor is vital to the company's operations, and there is plenty of cheap labor in many, many countries.

Are MNCs actually good or bad for the global political economy? As the previous paragraphs suggest, the answer is "it depends." The opportunity exists for MNCs to have both positive and negative consequences. Much depends on the company and the relationship between the company and the home and host countries. One thing is certain, however: MNCs will be a permanent and growing feature of the international political economy in the twenty-first century.

National Champion
A company or industry, supported in various ways by the government, that dominates the home market. Both business and government interests lie in making the company competitive internationally.

CHAPTER SUMMARY

How Do Experts View the International Political Economy?

International political economy is the study of the interaction of political and economic forces at the international level. It is a critical field of study because every major, and even most minor, issues have both economic and political elements. To get a better understanding of the complexity of IPE, several theories offer us considerable guidance, but they do differ in the explanations and prescriptions for change.

- *Economic liberalism* assumes that because rational human beings—as business owners, workers, consumers, and so on—try to maximize their satisfaction (in terms of profits, for example), the most efficient economic outcomes will result. Government is supposed to play only a minor role in regulating the economy, and free trade should be encouraged among countries.
- *Neomercantilism* emphasizes the role of the state in helping to guide a country's economy in one direction or another so as to increase the power of the state. Neomercantilist policies often involve protectionist policies such as the use of tariffs, quotas, and nontariff barriers to trade.
- *The rational choice* approach emphasizes the domestic political sources of international economic policy making. It looks at not only what motivates individuals (e.g., profits) but also which interest groups in society benefit or lose from different government economic policies. If enough groups in society demand protectionist government policies, politicians (seeking to maximize their votes at election time) will supply those policies.

What Are the Arguments for Free Trade and Protectionism?

According to the economic liberalism approach, a rising tide lifts all ships. If countries keep down their trade barriers to each other, everyone should be better off. If countries specialize in what they do best, comparative advantage suggests that national economies and the global economy as a whole can be run as efficiently as

possible. Those who favor protectionism say that countries sometimes want to advance a particular industry (or company) for economic reason (e.g., the "infant industry" argument), for national security reasons (e.g., no country wants to depend on another for food or weapons), or for the protection of jobs.

Who Manages Global Trade?

Global trade may appear not to be "managed" at all, but several forces act on the apparently chaotic international trading system. As in domestic economies, the forces of supply and demand play their part in regulating who buys and sells what to whom. In addition, governments impose rules (such as tariffs, quotas, and nontariff barriers) to help control the impact of their countries' involvement in the global economy. One of the world's most important international organizations is the World Trade Organization, which, inspired by the economic liberalism approach, seeks to encourage global free trade.

How Does the Global Financial System Operate?

Several elements drive the global financial system. Modern economic systems depend on currencies that are accepted by everyone. In the past, currencies have sometimes been linked directly to the price of gold. Today, the value of a currency depends on many factors, including the health of the country's economy and how strong that economy is compared to the economies of other countries. This combination of factors establishes a country's exchange rate.

One of the most important developments in IPE in a long time is the establishment of a new currency in Europe, the euro. Twelve European countries, including Germany, France, and Italy, have chosen to eliminate their own national currencies in favor of a single currency for all. Just as Americans can easily use the same currency in California as they can three thousand miles away in New Hampshire, Europeans (in the euro-zone) can use the same currency to make purchases in most countries across Western Europe.

The two most influential international organizations in the global financial system are the IMF and World Bank. The IMF is designed to stabilize the overall health of a country's economy or a geographic region that has been hard-hit financially. The World Bank was established to promote economic development in the world's poorer countries by financing specific projects.

What Is the Role of International Businesses in World Politics?

International businesses, or multinational corporations (MNCs), have a large and growing impact on the political economy of the home and host countries. Some MNCs are so big that they have a larger economic presence than most countries. Whether the influence these companies wield is constructive or destructive depends on the viewpoint. The economic liberalism approach believes that these companies can transfer skills and knowledge as well as provide jobs to poorer parts of the world. Opponents of MNCs claim that these economic behemoths trample local competition, take away jobs, and pollute the environment. See Chapter 12 for more details about MNC's in the third world.

ENDNOTES

[1] Business Software Alliance, Software Publishers Association, as quoted in Avi Machlis, "Soft talk masks a harder line against high-tech piracy," *Financial Times*, May 27, 1998.

[2] World Trade Organization, *http://www.wto.org/wto/intellec/intellec.htm.*, August 14, 1998.

[3] Steven E. Siwek, "Copyright Industries in the U.S. Economy: The 2002 Report," International Intellectual Property Alliance, *http://www.iipa.com/*. See also the "U.S. Software State Piracy Study," Business Software Alliance, *www.bsa.org.*

[4] Paul Abrahams, "Microsoft's copycat and mouse war," *Financial Times*, June 2, 2002.

[5] Robert Jablon, "Authorities get record haul of fake software," *Associated Press*, November 7, 2001.

[6] Ibid.

[7] Business Software Alliance, Software Publishers Association, as quoted in Avi Machlis, "Soft talk".

[8] "Microsoft opens informers' hotline," *Financial Times*, November 10, 1998.

[9] See, for example, David N. Balaam and Michael Veseth, *Introduction to International Political Economy* (Upper Saddle River, NJ: Prentice-Hall, Inc., 1996).

[10] A more comprehensive International Trade Organization (ITO) had been proposed in the late 1940s, but it was opposed by the U.S. Congress. The ITO was never submitted for ratification, and the less substantial GATT emerged by default. See Don Babai, "General Agreement on Tariffs and Trade," in Joel Krieger, ed., *The Oxford Companion to Politics of the World* (Oxford: Oxford University Press, 1993), pp. 342–348.

[11] David N. Balaam and Michael Veseth, *Introduction to International Political Economy*, p. 139.

[12] Bloomberg News, "United tries 'tough love' to correct Boeing issues," *US Today*, October 26, 1998.

[13] The U.S. Super 301 provision of the Omnibus Trade and Competitiveness Act of 1998 is viewed by many as an example of a managed trade tool that allows the United States to retaliate against countries that *the United States* deems to be trading unfairly.

[14] "Hit by dwindling oil revenue, Nigeria slashes public workers' pay," Agenu France Press, December 28, 1998.

[15] Joan E. Spero and Jeffrey A. Hart, *The Politics of International Economic Relations*, 5th edition, (New York: St. Martin's Press, 1997) p. 66.

[16] Gerald M. Meier, *The International Environment of Business* (Oxford: Oxford University Press, 1998), pp. 84–85.

[17] Klaus Heidensohn, *Europe and World Trade* (London: Pinter, 1995), pp. 32–33.

[18] Basic trade theory helps explain these phenomena. The Heckscher-Ohlin theorem of factor price equalization posits that free trade will cause all factor prices (wages in this case) to equalize across countries. In the case of the United States and Mexico, for example, the lower Mexican wages will eventually rise and the American wage level will eventually drop. Such a development, of course, is not very appealing to American workers and labor unions. In addition, the Stolper-Samuelson model suggests that free trade will benefit the abundant factor of production and harm the scarce one. In the case of NAFTA, the United States has an abundance of capital and is scarce in unskilled labor compared to Mexico. So over time, one would expect unskilled American workers to be hurt most by the greater free trade between Mexico and the United States.

[19] Christopher Parkes, "Mexico's free trade zone may be victim of its own success," *Financial Times*, June 1999.

[20] See European-American Business Council, 1998. *The United States and Europe: Jobs Investment and Trade*, 5th ed., as quoted in Stephen Fidler, "Millions of jobs depend on Europe, says study," *Financial Times*, November 19, 1998; and Tony Barber, "EU investment level in U.S. rises sharply," *Financial Times*, July 28, 2000.

[21] Martin Wolf, "Wealth of Nations," *Financial Times*, May 19, 1998.

[22]"The beef over bananas," *The Economist*, March 6, 1999 p. 65.

[23]Frances Williams and Vanessa Houlder, "WTO defends record on the environment," *Financial Times*, October 15, 1999.

[24]Ibid.

[25]Ibid.

[26]Laura D'Andrea Tyson, "What Really Sabotaged the Seattle Trade Talks," *Business Week*, February 7, 2000.

[27]Michael Elliott, "Lessons from the Battle of Seattle," *Newsweek International*, January 1, 2000.

[28]Laura D'Andrea Tyson, "What Really Sabotaged the Seattle Trade Talks."

[29]Mark Suzman, "US domestic concerns sank Seattle," *Financial Times*, December 6, 1999.

[30]See several articles that covered the WTO meetings in Seattle in *Newsweek*, December 13, 1999, pp. 31–40.

[31]The United States and the EU were at odds over agriculture, and the United States put labor and environment on the agenda and kept antidumping off. In addition, the United States pushed a multilateral process to address labor issues despite nearly unanimous opposition—especially in the Third World. The United States also delayed compromises on U.S. antidumping laws and textile quotas in return for concessions on trade in agriculture and services from the developing countries. See Mark Suzman, "U.S. domestic concerns sank Seattle," *Financial Times*, December 6, 1999; and Laura D'Andrea Tyson, "What Really Sabotaged the Seattle Trade Talks."

[32]Fareed Zakaria, "After the Storm Passes," *Newsweek*, December 13, 1999, p. 40.

[33]The "Siege of Seattle" is the lead article in *Newsweek's* coverage of December 13, 1999.

[34]Joan E. Spero and Jeffrey A. Hart, *The Politics of International Economic Relations*, p. 30.

[35]See Paul Krugman, "Greasing the Wheels," *Discover*, October 1998; and Heather Pringles, "The Cradle of Cash," *Discover*, October 1998.

[36]Edward Luce, "Asia pact aims to avoid further currency crisis," *Financial Times*, May 10, 2001.

[37]Robert J. Samuelson, "Dollarizing—A Black Hole," *Newsweek*, May 17, 1999, p. 55.

[38]Zanny Minton Beddoes, "From EMU to AMU? The Case for Regional Currencies," *Foreign Affairs*, vol. 78, Number 4, July/August 1999, pp. 8–13. Note also that Robert Mundell, recently awarded a Nobel price for economics, has called for a common currency for South America. He recommends initially that South American countries link their currencies to the U.S. dollar to lock in monetary stability. See Geoff Dyner, "'Father of euro' stirs up currency debate in South American family," *Financial Times*, May 9, 2000.

[39]World Bank, *http://www.worldbank.org/*, August 1998.

[40]Jessica Einhorn, "The World Bank's Mission Creep," *Foreign Affairs*, September/October 2001, vol. 80, No. 5, pp. 22–35. For another critical review of the World Bank, IMF, and other aid agencies, see William Easterly, "The Cartel of Good Intentions," *Foreign Policy*, July/August 2002.

[41]Nancy Dunne, "World Bank policies 'boosting poverty,'" *Financial Times*, August 14, 1998.

[42]Stephen Fidler, "Call for overhaul of IMF and World Bank expected," *Financial Times*, February 24, 2000.

[43]Ricardo Hausmann, "Baffled by Brazil," *Financial Times*, August 22, 2002.

[44]Craig N. Murphy, "Organization for Economic Cooperation and Development" in Joel Krieger ed., *The Oxford Companion*, pp. 664–665.

[45]Robert Chote, "G8 plans new financial 'talking shop,'" *Financial Times*, June 19, 1999.

[46]"The Year's Biggest Deals," *Business Week*, January 11, 1999, p. 8.

[47]Guenter Burghardt, "New Challenges for the Transatlantic Partnership," The World Affairs Council/World Boston, June 27, 2002. *http://www.eurunion.org/News/speeches/2002/020627gb.htm*

[48]*The Times* (London), 21 May 2002.

[49]Edward Alden and Michael Mann, "Brussels plans sanctions on U.S.," *Financial Times*, April 20, 2002.

CASE STUDY

How Do Countries Manage a Trade Dispute?

Trade relations between the European Union and the United States are simultaneously cooperative and hostile. According to Guenter Burghardt, EU Ambassador and Head of the European Commission Delegation to the United States, "trade and investment have long been regarded as the basis for the transatlantic partnership, and increasingly determine the well-being of the entire global economy. Over time, our bilateral cooperation has become even more crucial given the sheer size of our respective economies." In fact, the economies of the EU and the United States account for roughly 56 percent of the world total, and the EU-U.S. trade relationship accounts for over 40 percent of world trade. To put the trade relationship into a different perspective, the bilateral dimension of EU-U.S. trade is a $2 billion-a-day relationship. And from a political perspective, no fundamental progress can be made on global trade issues without the European Union and the United States working together.[47] As evidence of the cooperative nature of the relationship and of the at least partial commitment to global free trade, both trading partners agreed in November 2001 to a new round of global trade talks.

Nevertheless, tensions across the Atlantic have mounted over the past decade as one high-profile trade dispute follows another. There have been disagreements over bananas, subsidies for Boeing and Airbus, special treatment offered to U.S. exporters under Foreign Sales Corporations (FSC) tax provisions, and agricultural subsidies, to name a few. EU Trade Commissioner Pascal Lamy has declared that "we are reaching a critical point as far as the prospects for world trade liberalisation and transatlantic relations go."[48] The case study for this chapter takes a look at one of the trade disputes in the transatlantic relationship: steel. The case was triggered by the Bush Administration's imposition of tariffs on imported steel in March 2002. The steel dispute affects not just the EU but large steel exporters like Japan, Russia, Ukraine, and South Korea. The case demonstrates the complex trade relationship among political allies and raises important questions about the commitment to free trade, the role of international institutions (in this case, the WTO), and the impact of domestic politics on foreign economic policy.

THE CASE OF STEEL

The United States Imposes Tariffs on Steel Imports

By Bronwen Maddox

WELL, the steel wars have become more formal, and probably, more serious.

If the United States agrees by today to compensate the European Union for its new tariffs on steel imports, the EU will drop its threat of a trade war.

Otherwise it will look to hit back by slapping sanctions—maybe as soon as June 18, 2002—on a list of American products. It sent that list—two lists, in fact—to the World Trade Organization this week. In retaliation for a move by the Bush Administration which it sees as driven entirely by the demands of the November congressional elections, the EU has hand-crafted its list of targets to cause as much political pain as possible to the Bush Administration and Republicans in Congress.

Although this is just the opening dance, nothing about the steel wars suggests that they are about to end quickly and amicably. Intensely politicized on each side, with highly visible jobs in each continent at stake, it ranks as one of the nastiest transatlantic trade wars to break out in years.

There are signs of a desire for conciliation on the European side, but fewer on the American one, at least this side of the elections. In fact, the U.S. farm bill last week has only made the war of words this week more ill-tempered.

When the Administration slapped tariffs of up to 30 percent on a range of steel imports in March—hitting Europe and Japan hard but deliberately sparing its neighbors Canada and Mexico—it surely knew that a European counterattack would follow. After all, the tariffs affect about 1 percent of the EU's $220 billion trade with the United States each year.

The United States claims that its action is legal under WTO "safeguard" rules, allowing it to protect its struggling industry while it restructures. The EU, proud possessor of a more modern and efficient steel industry, says this is nonsense.

Today Japan will follow suit and tell the WTO that it plans to retaliate, the first time it has done so, and even the first time it has lodged such a notification with the WTO. The move came after Takeo Hiranuma, the trade minister, failed to find a solution in a telephone conversation with Robert Zoellick, the U.S. trade representative, early yesterday.

Today's deadline marks the end of the two-month period under WTO rules for governments to settle a dispute before the formal machinery gets into gear. Now, things get more serious.

The EU has sent the WTO two lists of American products that it wants to hit in return. There is a "short list" which represents the quick fix of immediate retaliation, and a longer list which it will submit for formal arbitration, a process which could take two years.

The short list identifies U.S. products sold in Europe worth $364 million. With WTO approval, the EU might slap 100 percent tariffs on these from June 18. Fruit juices are prominent in this list—a direct strike at Florida, where President Bush's brother Jeb is running for re-election as governor in November.

[The EU strategy is designed to "hit the United States where it hurts" by targeting exports from states crucial to the re-election of president George W. Bush. These include citrus fruits from Florida, apples and pears from Washington and Oregon, and steel from Pennsylvania, Ohio, and West Virginia.[49]

The longer list identifies U.S. exports to the EU worth $583 million last year, including steel, textiles, clothes and fruit.

For goods on this "long list," the EU suggests a range of tariffs of between 8 percent and 30 percent. The list includes men's and women's coats, toilet paper, yachts, women's panties, as well as "stockings for varicose veins."

Although the WTO panel will meet for the first time on May 22, it is not expected to reach a decision before the end of next year.

Will the row blow over? On the optimistic side, the EU feels it made some progress on the compensation issue at the EU-US summit ten days ago. Anthony Gooch, spokesman for Pascal Lamy, the EU trade commissioner, said this week that if the United States compensated the EU for lost market share, that "would obviate the need to take counter-measures."

Clearly, this is a plea for a truce. Cut us a bit of slack and we will back off, is the European message. The trouble is that there is no sign that the Bush Administration intends to back off, given the all-pervasive influence of the congressional elections, and the Republicans' bid to regain control of the Senate, now hanging by a single vote.

For Bush, those elections are crucial to his ability to get legislation through Congress for the remainder of his term. It is hard to see the niceties of U.S.-European relations weighing more in his calculation.

For its part, Congress agrees. President Bush is seeking "trade promotion authority" to give his administration the power to negotiate trade agreements that can be approved or rejected by Congress but not changed, as Bill Clinton enjoyed through much of his presidency.

But the request has run into opposition in Congress, to put it mildly. Congress has no intention of giving Bush room for maneuver if that could be exercised against local interests.

What is more, the EU negotiators voiced their optimism before the U.S. farm bill, which Bush signed this week, raised the temperature. The bill grants an extra $190 billion in subsidies to American farmers in the next decade.

That has triggered renewed, bitter criticism in the EU this week. The United States was frankly "hypocritical" on free trade, declared Guy Verhofstadt, the Belgian prime minister.

More seriously for Bush, the United States was also attacked in Paris yesterday at the OECD meeting of industrialized countries. Mike Moore, the WTO head, warned of protectionist "stormclouds" threatening free trade.

Glen Hubbard, President Bush's chief economist, was left limply declaring that "the U.S. administration is incredibly committed to free trade." He said: "Indeed, it's probably the president's greatest single priority other than the prosecution of the war on terrorism."

Before the farm bill, the United States's antagonists in the steel wars might have listened silently if sullenly. Now, they find that claim frankly incredible.

SOURCE: Bronwen Maddox, "EU Throws Down Gauntlet to Bush as Steel Wars Heat Up," The Times, May 17, 2002. Copyright © Times Newspapers Limited, London. Reprinted by permission.

Looking for a Solution to the Steel Trade Dispute

By Paul Meller

Dateline: Brussels, Sept. 25, 2002.

The European Union is poised to drop its threat of rapid retaliation against United States tariffs on imported steel imposed in the spring, senior officials said today.

The European Commission, the union's executive body, has drafted a recommendation that sanctions involving over $300 million of goods should be shelved until after a ruling by the World Trade Organization, which is expected next year. The Europeans' retreat on steel comes after the Bush administration scaled back its proposed tariffs on steel imports, exempting a further 178 steel products and largely defusing the dispute.

In March 2002, when the United States announced import tariffs of as much as 30 percent, the European Union was concerned that Europe would be flooded by steel imports from other coun-

tries that had been priced out of the United States. But this side effect "has not been so dramatic," a top commission official said today.

Since March, the Bush administration has narrowed the product categories of steel that would be subject to the tariffs to the point where more than half the European steel exports to the United States are now exempt.

And steel prices have stabilized recently, weakening the case for an immediate retaliation.

"All these things together led us to the conclusion that sanctions are not necessary at the moment," the commission official said.

But some diplomats representing the 15 member nations of the European Union in Brussels said the commission was backing away from unilateral sanctions because it would not get the majority support for rapid sanctions it needs from the member states.

The commission will present its recommendation to foreign ministers of the member state governments on Monday.

"The threat of sanctions has been enough to force the Bush administration to water down its steel tariff regime," said one diplomat, who spoke only on the condition of anonymity. "Why crank up the pressure now?"

When the commission first considered sanctions against the United States, it drew up a list of products including citrus fruit, textiles and steel products with the intention of hitting American industries in states that are important for the White House in next month's Congressional elections.

In addition to the exemptions already granted to European steel producers, the Bush administration has said it is considering reining in the tariffs even more. United States officials have said that a new round of exemptions will be considered between November and next March.

SOURCE: Paul Meller, "Europe Is Set to End Threat on Steel Tariffs," The New York Times, September 26, 2002. Copyright © 2002 by the New York Times Co. Reprinted with permission.

QUESTIONS

Check Your Understanding

1. Why did the U.S. impose tariffs on steel imports? In what ways did the Europeans threaten to retaliate against the United States?
2. What is the role of the World Trade Organization in the steel dispute?

Analyze the Issues

3. How do domestic politics in the United States affect the trade dispute in steel?
4. Why didn't the dispute over steel become a full-blown trade war between the United States and the EU? Were concessions made by either side, and if so, why?
5. How well does the steel case fit the liberal economic approach to international political economy? Assess the actions of the United States and the EU in terms of their consistency with neomercantilism and the rational choice approach.

FOR FURTHER INFORMATION

To find out more about the steel issue, consult the following journal articles, newspapers, and Internet sites:

Alan Cafruny, "Transatlantic Trade and Monetary Relations: The Nature and Limits of Conflict," an article prepared for the New International Challenges: Reassessing the Transatlantic Partnership conference organized by the IAI in Rome on 19/20 July 2002 and sponsored by the German Marshall Fund of the United States, the Institute for Security Studies of the European Union, and the U.S. Embassy in Rome.

Steven Everts, "America and Euroland," *World Policy Journal*, Winter 1999/2000.

"Steel Global Safeguard Investigation," United States Trade Commission, October 9, 2002, *http://www.usitc.gov/steel/*.

G. Tarr D., "The steel crisis in the United States and the European Community" in Baldwin, R. E., Hamilton, C. B. and Sapir, A. (eds.), *Issues in US-EC Trade Relations* (The University of Chicago Press: Chicago and London, 1988).

Williams, B. (2002) 'EU-US trade war looms over steel tariffs' *The Militant*, vol. 66, no. 4, 28 January.

CHAPTER 12

International Political Economy II: The Politics of Development

KEY QUESTIONS RAISED IN THIS CHAPTER

1. What is meant by development?
2. What theories explain rich and poor countries?
3. What factors impact the politics of development?
4. What is the connection between democracy and economic development?
5. What are the prospects for future Third World development?

Many people, especially Americans, are generally optimistic when they discuss the development of the world's poorer countries—loosely called the Third World. Actually, conditions in the world's poorer countries have almost always been bad. They are bad today, and for most countries in the Third World, things are likely to be bad in the future. As you learned in Chapter 10, about 75 percent of the world's population lives in abject poverty; with women and children in especially bleak situations, and over a billion people living on only a dollar a day (see Figure 12.1 and Table 12.1). In many countries, the literacy rate is only in the 40 percent range and life expectancy in the least developed countries is in the low 50s compared to the upper 70s in the advanced industrial democracies.

This chapter will look not only at the issues facing the Third World but also at the reasons why there are poor (and rich) countries. In addition, we will explore a variety of policy recommendations for improving the political and economic conditions of the world's less developed countries. Since there is much disagreement as to which paths successfully lead to development, we will rely on several different theoretical approaches to guide us. Fortunately, the theories discussed in previous chapters give us a solid foundation from which to start. With this chapter overview in mind, the sequence of topics is as follows. We first look at the politics of development concept and what is meant by development—followed by a focus on theories that explain why some countries are poor while others are rich in standards of living. Next we study the factors that impact the politics of development, by which is generally meant whether countries are governed in ways that initiate and sustain the process of development or hold it back interminably. We then explore key links between democracy and development and tie in that subject with today's remarkable march toward increasing globalization. This chapter's case study on the pros and cons of globalization and its effect on development carries that discussion more deeply into the sphere of development—with its overall impact on centralization and decentralization.

What Is Meant by Development?

Given the scope of poverty in the world and the large numbers of countries whose populations fall into the category of "developing" countries, students of world politics have devoted much attention to developing the world and the political dynamics that drive it. Certainly it is a tough place to live, as you might well imagine, given the grind of daily life, struggle to make ends meet, and fine balance between life and death. To borrow a phrase from Thomas Hobbes (1588–1679), life in the Third World can be "nasty, brutish, and short."[1] In the developing world, tens of thousands of individuals are illiterate, lack access to health services, do not have safe drinking water, are malnourished, and die young. Given this dour perspective, the obvious question to ask is, how does a country develop? We will explore this question in the following sections by looking at what we mean by development.

A Transformation of a Country's Underdevelopment

Fortunately, Hobbes's pessimistic predictions and observations do not apply to everyone in every country. First, not all poor countries today were always poor. For example, China at one time was the richest country in the world, and India was thriving up to the end of the eighteenth century. Second, and more important, some countries have made great strides in the past 50 years—a relatively short time.

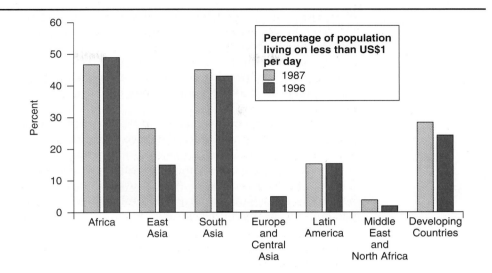

FIGURE 12.1

Poverty Headcount Index: The graph compares 1987 with 1996 for seven regions. The table looks at other indexes of poverty in developing countries.

SOURCE: World Bank as reported in "Old Battle; New Strategy," *The Economist* January 8, 2000. The graph is entitled: "Always with Us."

TABLE 12.1 Human Poverty in Developing Countries

Region or Country Group	Illiterate Adults 1995	People Lacking Access to Health Services 1990–1995	People Lacking Access to Safe Water 1990–1996	Malnour-ished Children under 5 1990–1996	Maternal Mortality Rate (per 100,000 live births) 1990	People Not Expected to Survive to Age 40[a] 1990s
All developing countries	842	766[b]	1,213	158[b]	471	507
Least developed countries	143	241	218	34	1,030	123
Arab States	59	29	54	5	380	26
East Asia	167	144	398	17	95	81
Latin America and the Caribbean	42	55	109	5	190	36
South Asia	407	264	230	82	554	184
South-East Asia and the Pacific	38	69	162	20	447	52
Sub-Saharan Africa	122	205	249	28	971	124

[a] Among population aged 0–39.

[b] Excludes Cyprus and Turkey.

SOURCE: *Human Development Report, 2000*. Copyright © 2000 United Nations Human Development Program. Used by permission of Oxford University Press, Inc.

With luck, more countries will solve such seemingly intractable problems as poverty, political instability, illiteracy, discrimination against women and other minorities, child-labor practices, and even slavery. Along the way, however, Third World countries will face many *internal* obstacles (such as lack of social cohesion and problems determining effective governmental policies) as well as *external* obstacles (such as global economic competition and political pressure from other countries).

Despite a tremendous interest in development over the past half century, the concept of development does not have a common definition. This is true even with the post–World War II explosion in numbers of newly independent countries in Africa, Asia, and Latin America. Still, we know for certain that at minimum, development is a process of change over time. When people speak of development, they are talking about purposeful change in a specific direction—like human beings growing, or developing, into mature adults.[2] By thinking of some kind of finish line in the process of development, we can begin to measure actual development in a country's economy, polity, or society—as opposed to wandering, aimless change.[3]

An Improvement in Economic, Political, and Social Life

Economic Development
The use of land, labor, and capital to produce higher standards of living, typically measured by increases in gross national product (GNP) and more equitable distribution of national income.

Development, more specifically, is an improvement in a country's economic, political, and social life. Economists look at **economic development,** which is the easiest to follow, because it involves physical progress in standards of living that can be empirically measured. Political scientists emphasize political development, which is harder to measure. The latter is of course linked to history and culture. Sociologists and anthropologists write about social and cultural development, which are equally difficult to chart and measure.

Given these three types of development in poor countries, how can we make sense of the changes taking place in the world's poor countries? First, we know *under*development when we see it in Africa, Asia, and Latin America, because poverty conditions are crystal clear—as indicated in Chapter 10 and in the data presented in this chapter. Yet debate still surrounds how one measures overall development—especially in the political and social realms. Some observers, for example, criticize modern concepts of political development that stress democracy and that emphasize the creation of market economies by a country's political leaders. They say that such concepts are Western-based in that they reflect experiences and values of Western Europe and the United States. As such, the argument is that they may not reflect the culture, religion, attitudes, and values practiced in a so-called "developing" country. Afghanistan's Taliban and Iran's conservative Muslim leaders come to mind, with their intense opposition to Western concepts and to globalization in the economy.

Second, we know that rates of development, as in economic development, vary greatly from one country to the next. China is moving rapidly in economic development, while Haiti and Africa south of the Sahara are not. South Korea is far ahead of North Korea in economic growth, while Mexico is ahead of Guatemala, and Taiwan is doing much better economically than the Sudan. Rates of development are by no means the same throughout the developing countries. Think of the Soviet Union's former two key client states: Vietnam and Cuba. Vietnam embraces market economic principles while hanging on to its single Communist Party rule; Cuba has tinkered with market economics and yet is still ruled by the Communist Party and its aging leader, Fidel Castro.

Third, some developing countries are pressing for economic and political development at the same time. Russia's quest is for better standards of living in its economy, while it tries to push ahead with democratizing its government. China, in contrast, strives for economic development but not political development, seeking instead to retain its authoritarian single-party, communist-controlled, political way of life—akin to that of its neighbor, Vietnam.

Fourth, when development occurs in one sector of a country, such as its economy, that sphere of development tends to change other sectors, like the political and social systems. Indeed, many political economists believe that economic development is a precondition for political (democratic) and social development (a growing middle class). If standards of living go up and an economy becomes more modern and diversified, it can generate movement toward a more democratic system—as occurred in Mexico during the late nineteenth and early twentieth century.

Such a political transition might occur because a more diversified economy can produce more interest groups and political parties, higher literacy, and the spread of mass communication media like newspapers and televisions. These emerging factors can produce more organized pressure on, and inputs into, government decisions; in short, increased political participation by the people. A thriving economy, moreover, should generate more opportunities for upward mobility and higher standards of living—for women as well as men.

The fascinating idea is that development is an interlinked process of change, where change in one arena—economic, political, or social—impacts conditions in another arena. For example, some observers believe that China's authoritarian political system could erode under pressures from economic development.

Fifth, most of the developing countries have been impacted by *globalization*. If you travel through developing countries—from China and Vietnam to Mexico and Guatemala—you can see the presence of Internet Cyber Cafes, IGOs, NGOs, MNCs, and global banking and financial institutions. Coca-Cola and Pepsi Cola have been globalized, along with McDonalds and Kentucky Fried Chicken. Even Comandante Marcos, leader of the Zapatista Revolution in Chiapas, Mexico, uses the Internet to propagate his revolutionary ideology. Still, violent opposition on the part of the conservative Taliban in Afghanistan vividly demonstrates that developing countries react in different ways to Western globalization. Nor should we forget that globalization in the developing countries can backfire. In May 2000 a computer hacker in the Philippines unleashed the "I love you" computer virus, which in a few hours wiped out about a billion dollars' worth of files on over 10 million computers all over the world.

Development, then, is movement toward higher standards of living, widening opportunities to live a better life, upward social and economic mobility, and expanding participation in government. We now turn to explicit definitions of economic, social, and political development.

For more on the China-U.S. crisis of April 2001 and China's quest for legitimacy, go to **www/ablongman.com/ duncan.**

An Analytical Framework to Evaluate Change

Development has traditionally been defined in economic terms, first in terms of overall economic growth (as measured by GNP or GDP) and later in terms of economic growth per person (e.g., GDP per capita). Such measurements are useful but very incomplete, as we will see. They are useful because they indicate which countries are doing well economically and whether the same country is doing better or worse over time. However, a country could have a rising national income but still have much of its population excluded from the political process. Or, a country may be growing economically in the short run while destroying its environment in the process—thus hurting long-term economic growth. To encompass these and other definitional problems, we build on Chapter 10 (see discussion of the five indicators of poverty and the five indices of poverty) and propose five components to the definition of development.

The first component is *economic*. Since the equitable distribution of wealth (equity) matters just as much as overall economic growth, we use the notion of economic health as measured by GDP per capita. It matters that we focus on not only the size of the economic pie, but on how the pie is divided as well. For example, a country's development would be very restricted if only 1 percent of the population benefited from 99 percent of the economic growth. A second component of development includes the *health of the population*. The most useful measurement is the infant mortality rate, which taps into such things as the quality and quantity of food, the availability of housing, and the quality of and access to medical care. A third indicator of development is *literacy*. A country's literacy rate is a useful indicator of development because it measures quality and access to education. Most people in the rich, industrialized countries take for granted the ability to read and write, not to mention basic math skills. Imagine what it would be like trying to get a decent job without being able to read or write. Illiteracy is a terrible problem in many countries. Around the world, about 1 billion people are illiterate. In most of the First World countries, the literacy rates are in the high 90 percent range. For other countries, however, the rates can be as low as 40 percent (e.g., Mali) and even 20 percent (e.g., Nigeria).[4] For most countries, the literacy rates are lower—and sometimes substantially lower—for women than for men.

The remaining two components of development are not yet widely accepted among mainstream political scientists and economists. Historically, few people paid attention to these two issues, and there is still reluctance to include them. But for our discussion, we include *environmental sustainability* as the fourth indicator of development. This concept refers to the ability of a country to advance in economic development without destroying the environment in the process (see Chapter 13 for more details). The fifth component of development deals with *civil rights, particularly gender rights*. In most countries, women play a relatively small role politically as well as economically (by traditional measurement). Thus, improvements in this area would see greater participation of women in political and economic life. Some analysts hope to define development as freedom. The economist Amartya Sen, for example, suggests that development requires the removal of major sources of "unfreedom: poverty as well as tyranny, poor economic opportunities as well as systematic social deprivation, neglect of public facilities as well as intolerance or overactivity of repressive states."[5] In short, then, development has come to encompass many elements besides economic progress.

A Concept Used to Classify Groups of Countries in the World Political System

By using each of one or more indicators, it is possible to rank countries in terms of development. A relatively complex system of ranking countries was presented in Chapter 10: the Human Development Index (HDI). As you learned, a variety of political, economic, and social elements are factored in for each country so that countries can be compared by their HDI score.

The most common way of categorizing countries, however, is also the most problematic. If you will recall from Chapter 2, *First World* countries are rich and democratic. The *Second World* refers to the world's communist countries. These countries are also referred to as "countries in transition." The rest of the world's countries are described as the *Third World*—those that are relatively poor and politically unstable. A common expression that encompasses Third World countries is the global *South*, where most Third World countries are located. This term contrasts with the *North*, where most of the First World countries are found. Other terms commonly used to describe the Third World are: *less developed countries (LDCs)*, *underdeveloped*, and *undeveloped*. The term *Fourth World* is sometimes used to refer not to countries but to indigenous peoples, such as the Tamils in Sri Lanka and the Mayans of Guatemala. It is important to note that there is no progression from Fourth World to First World; that is, it doesn't make sense for countries to go from fourth to third to second to first world status.

This system of categorizing countries is a useful shortcut for making sense of over 185 different countries, but it is full of nagging problems. First, some countries do not fit neatly into one category. China, for example, may be classified as a Second World country from a political perspective because a single political party— the Communist Party—dominates it. However, China has introduced so many capitalist elements into its economic system that the term Second World no longer makes perfect sense.

A second problem is with the term *Third World*, because some countries, such as Russia, are unique enough or so peculiar that they almost need their own category. Third, it makes sense to create certain exceptions to the First, Second, and Third World categorization system. This is often done for oil-rich countries such as Saudi Arabia and Kuwait, and for the **newly industrializing countries (NICs)** such as South Korea, Taiwan, and Singapore. Fourth, many people oppose the term *Third World* because it has a negative or pejorative connotation; it is viewed as implying inferior status. A fifth problem with this commonly used category system is that some Third World countries have regions that could well be defined as "developed." India, for example, would be considered more developed than China in some ways but not in others. India is much more democratic than China and has a much freer press. It also has a much lower literacy rate than China. Likewise, some developed countries (that is, countries in the First World) have regions that by many definitions would be defined as "Third World." Consider, for example, which parts of the United States may have Third World features. Thus, the terms *First, Second*, and *Third World* are useful but crude shortcuts for categorizing the world's countries; they are helpful, but only to a point.

For more information on Guatemala's highly divided population, go to **www.ablongman.com/ duncan.**

Newly Industrializing Countries (NICs)
Those countries previously classified as lesser developed countries (LDCs), but which have raised significantly their levels of production and wealth—typically through export-led growth.

What Theories Explain Rich and Poor Countries?

In many of the chapters of this book, you have considered some extremely difficult questions, such as, Why are there wars? in Chapter 9. In this chapter, you will consider an equally daunting question: Why are there rich, politically stable countries and at the same time, poor, politically unstable countries? This question leads to a host of other challenging questions. How can poor countries improve their economic situation? Must countries trying to develop economically also be democratic, or can a country be too poor to be democratic?[6] Should the state play a dominant role in the economy, or should a hands-off approach, such as "let the market drive

HISTORICAL PERSPECTIVE

Three Theoretical Approaches to Development

	Economic Liberalism	Mercantilism, Economic Nationalism	Neo-Marxism Dependency
General comments about the political economy:	Free market principles should dominate the political economy.	The state uses the economy to increase its political power.	Economic factors dominate politics and society.
Most important unit of analysis:	The individual or the firm.	The state.	Class (capitalist and proletariat) or the international capitalist system.
Expectation about the IPE:	Harmonious and self-regulating; international economic integration through the world market	Inherent struggle among states; regulated by a balance of power.	Inherent conflict, especially class conflict; revolutionary change until Marxist utopia.
Main obstacles to development:	Mostly internal.	Internal and external.	Mostly external.

the economy" be chosen? Should all states try to develop by creating a U.S.-style economy? Unfortunately, there are no easy answers to these questions; nor is there a consensus among academics or practitioners. We can, nevertheless, make significant progress in addressing these questions by building on our theoretical foundations from earlier chapters.

The three approaches that follow offer different explanations for why there are rich and poor countries. They also offer different prescriptions—or policy recommendations—for helping Third World countries improve their lot. Chapter 11 has given us a head start in understanding the following theories. Specifically, we will briefly review the economic liberal and neomercantilist approaches. We then will explore in more depth neo-Marxism and dependency theories. (See box Historical Perspective: Three Theoretical Approaches to Development.)

Economic Liberalism
An approach to IPE based on free market principles and open international trade and monetary systems. Founded in part on the belief that the role of the state should be minimized because of the inefficiency that may result as well as the fear of states abusing their power.

Economic Liberalism

As we saw in Chapter 11, **economic liberalism** (*neoliberal economics*) grows out of the classical economics tradition. According to this approach, free market principles should dominate a country's political economy. Domestically, the state should limit its regulation of the economy. Internationally, the state should not construct barriers to trade and investment with other countries. When individuals can buy, sell, and trade freely across borders, everyone will be better off in the long run. Since the

1960s, U.S. foreign policy toward Third World countries has essentially relied on this approach. A look at Walt W. Rostow's 1971 *The Stages of Economic Growth*[7] shows how little the approach has changed since then. The **Modernization School** espoused by Rostow and others attempts to modernize "backward" countries by encouraging the kinds of policies that helped the United States become so successful.

How does the neoliberal economic approach answer the question "Why are there poor countries?" The primary response is that Third World problems are created or made worse by *failed government policies*. Policies that restrict trade, for example, can lead to what economists call "market imperfections" that hinder the efficient use of land, labor, and capital. In some countries, government policies tend to favor the small minority of the well to do. "Kleptocracies," for example, are governments that essentially steal from the people; this was the case in the Philippines under Ferdinand Marcos (1917–1989). Proponents of the neoliberal economic approach admit that the international political and economic environment is competitive and sometimes even hostile. In the long run, however, there is no substitute for sound domestic policies. This point was recently echoed by the United Nations, which argued that effective governance—in conjunction with sound international assistance—is essential for development. As Mark Malloch Brown, head of the UN's Development Program put it, "governance is a critical building block for poverty reduction."[8]

Neomercantilism and Economic Nationalism

Mercantilism, neomercantilism, economic nationalism, realism, and "statism" have in common the belief in the primacy of the state. In the seventeenth and eighteenth centuries, *mercantilist policies*, followed especially by Spain and Portugal, were used to increase national unity and the power and wealth of the state. These policies primarily involved the acquisition of precious metal (bullion) and protectionist trade policies (e.g., tariffs). *Neomercantilism* evolved in the nineteenth century, as Germany sought to build a stronger industrial capacity through protectionist policies—but without the reliance on bullion. Neomercantilists believed that the state should be the main determinant of organized political, economic, and social activity.[9] Neomercantilism remained highly relevant through the twentieth century, when the international political economy was hit by the 1930s Great Depression as well as the collapse of the gold standard and the oil shocks of the 1970s. As a response to these devastating events, many countries soured on the neoliberal belief in an unfettered international market economy. Like earlier mercantilists, they saw the need for the state to resolve the country's problems through various forms of trade protection. Many of today's neomercantilists, or economic nationalists, use the term *managed trade* to describe increased government regulation of global trade.

What is the neomercantilist explanation for underdevelopment? Consistent with its emphasis on the power of the state, neomercantilism contends that international power struggles will make political and economic life harder for weaker countries. This idea is, of course, consistent with *realism*. Domestic policies that allow too much foreign domination of the economy can be harmful to the country's development. The neomercantilists thus often oppose the prescription of neoliberal economists. Instead of letting market forces drive the economy, neomercantilists argue that as long as market forces hurt a country, those forces should be curbed through the kinds of protectionist policies described in Chapter 11. Instead of having the

Modernization School
An approach to development that seeks to modernize "backward" countries through the adoption of policies consistent with economic liberalism and free trade. The United States is usually seen as the successful model to emulate.

state relatively aloof from the economy, the state should take on an active role in guiding the economy. Note, however, that neomercantilists do not call for a totalitarian state. The state is to serve as a guide—not a dictator—of economic affairs.

Neo-Marxism and Dependency

As with mercantilism and neomercantilism, we need to explain what makes the "neo" version of Marxism new. *Marxism*, as developed by Karl Marx, Friedrich Engels, and others in the nineteenth century, focused primarily on the struggle between the capitalist and proletarian classes *within a country*. Marxists predicted that domestic (or internal) economic crises in individual states would result in the revolutionary and violent overthrow of capitalists in favor of a dictatorship of the proletariat (working classes). This movement *on a national scale* was eventually expected to sweep the globe as country after country succumbed to the "inevitable logic" of Marxist socialist development. *Neo-Marxism*, which developed in the early part of the twentieth century due to the influence of V. I. Lenin and others, had a much more *international focus* to it. *Imperialism*, as we learned in Chapter 1, was seen as the most advanced stage of capitalist development by which rich (primarily European) countries sought cheap raw materials in the undeveloped parts of the world. Rich countries created colonies in the world's **periphery** (a process known as **colonialism**) and then geared those colonies' development to the benefit of the home country or to the small number of local capitalists. Neo-Marxists predicted that the oppressive capitalist class eventually would be overthrown and that poor countries would similarly throw off the oppressive influences of rich countries. Neo-Marxists thus built on Marxism by grafting on this international element. In short, the primary neo-Marxist explanation for political and economic problems in Third World countries is their exploitation by rich countries.

Neo-Marxism became especially prominent after World War II. Thanks to the works of Latin American scholars in particular, the *dependency approach*, a variant of Neo-Marxism, became standard fare in college courses on development. The basic point of dependency theories is that if development were to occur at all in the Third World (or the periphery), it would be dependent on an exploitative relationship with First World (or **core**) countries. An interesting example of this is France's efforts to create an economy in Algeria (North Africa) that would serve French—not local—needs. This included the production of wine, which was in high demand in France but of little value to the local Muslim population.[10]

Some of the main targets of the dependency approach were multinational corporations from rich core countries that invested in the periphery. It was believed that the vast majority of the profits generated by MNCs in the periphery were simply sent back to the core country, thus enriching the wealthy at the expense of the poor. Figure 12.2, The Dependency Explanation, illustrates how this process works.

Like the neo-Marxists, proponents of dependency theories believe that the structure of the international system is biased against poor counties. For example, the trading relationship between core (First World) and periphery (Third World) countries is often lopsided in favor of the core. These poor terms of trade result in income being transferred from the periphery to the core.

The neo-Marxist approach offers a variety of policy prescriptions for dealing with the external forces hindering development.[11] It begins with the premise that if the right changes can be made to the international political-economic structure, the

Periphery
In the international system, that region or substate entity that is not part of the central decision-making group of states. Kosovo, Chechnya, Kashmir, and East Timor may be considered part of the periphery. Africa has been, up to now, a peripheral region of the international system.

Colonialism
Control of territories in what is now considered the Third World by rich, mostly European countries with the aim of gearing the colonies development to the benefit of the home country.

Core Countries
In the language of the dependency approach, these are the world's rich countries: First World countries.

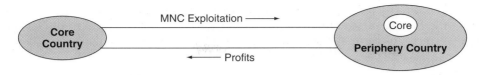

FIGURE 12.2

The Dependency Explanation for How the Rich Exploit the Poor: As the diagram suggests, multinational corporations from rich countries set up shop (invest) in Third World countries, usually with assistance from wealthy Third World capitalists (the "core in the periphery"). Profits from the MNC operations in the periphery are then sent back to the home country leaving the peripheral country no better (or even worse) off than before the investment.

situation will improve for the world's poor countries. Some people believe that if the North were simply to increase aid and provide better market access for the South, things would improve for the South. Neo-Marxists, however, believe that these are only partial measures that won't significantly alter the dependent relationship between the core and periphery. They argue that periphery countries should sever political and economic ties with core countries. By cutting the links to the exploitative core countries, development will no longer depend on the demands of core countries. One method of severing ties is to *nationalize* a foreign company, that is, take over the factories and facilities of the MNC. On their own, periphery countries could then diversify their economies (become less dependent on a few exports) and avoid having to spend scarce cash on expensive imported goods. These prescriptions were the centerpiece of the most important policy adopted by developing countries after World War II: **import-substituting industrialization.**

Another neo-Marxist, dependency-inspired strategy culminated in the 1970s with the establishment of the **New International Economic Order (NIEO).** For a time it seemed as if the South was finally gaining some leverage over the North, especially after the oil shocks caused by OPEC. Third World countries were essentially demanding a restructuring of the international system so that it was no longer biased against them. By the 1980s, however, it was clear that the NIEO had failed. The neo-Marxist policies (such as import-substituting industrialization) adopted by many developing countries, especially those in Latin America, contributed to huge governments budget deficits, enormous debts, and rampant inflation. The NIEO also failed because the much more powerful North was unwilling to cede significant influence to the world's poorer countries.

Even though these shortcomings, as well as the collapse of communism in 1989–1990, largely discredited dependency notions, similar ideas persist to this day. Opponents of global capitalism made disruptive appearances at the WTO meeting in Seattle in 1999 and at meetings of the IMF in Washington in 2000. While many of today's anticapitalists may not call themselves neo-Marxists, they do share some common assumptions. Modern capitalism and globalization, for example, are believed to be responsible for a massive concentration of corporate power within and across national boundaries, a concentration supported by the World Bank, the IMF, and other international organizations dominated by First World countries.[12] The cartoon, depicting the IMF's treatment of Argentina during its 2001–2002 economic unraveling is in this spirit.

Import-Substituting Industrialization
Policies designed to increased national political-economic independence by building up national industries so that the country will not have to rely so much on expensive imports. Examples include nationalizing foreign companies, trade barriers on foreign goods, and diversifying the national economy in order to reduce dependence on a few exports.

New International Economic Order (NIEO)
The effort by Third World countries to alter the rules of the international system, especially with respect to trade and financial structures.

SOURCE: © StudioBendib/www.bendib.com/Inkcinct Cartoons, 2002.

Complaints against the North-dominated capitalist system can also get very specific. In May 2000, for example, international groups of environmentalists and scientists challenged a company in the First World over a patent for a fungicide made from a tropical tree. According to some of the campaigners, the patent in question typifies the way First World companies are plundering the genetic resources of the Third World by claiming "ownership" of applications known to developing world farmers and doctors for centuries.[13] The notion of rewriting the rules of the international system also persists. In April 2000, for example, the Group of 77 (Third World countries) called for a "new global human order." They specifically asked the world's rich countries to open their borders to Third World imports, to forgive debts, to increase aid to poor countries, and to share new technologies. In addition, the Group of 77 called for a stronger voice in the decision-making powers of the World Bank and the International Monetary Fund. Furthermore, the United Nations was also asked to play a bigger role in economic aid, rather than channeling it through organizations controlled by rich nations.[14]

Theory and Practice of Third World Cooperation

It would seem logical that if Third World countries can band together, they may be able to put more pressure on the world's rich and politically powerful countries and thus alter the rules of the international system in their favor. The New International Economic Order was one such attempt (that ultimately failed). Another option for Third World countries is to cooperate when certain products that they possess are in high demand by the rest of the world, especially the First World. The best example of this is the formation of OPEC, which was discussed in Chapter 5.

Until the early 1970s, seven major Western multinational corporations, known as the Seven Sisters, dominated the international oil industry. These included Standard Oil of New Jersey (now Exxon), Gulf (Chevron), Standard Oil of California (Chevron), Mobil, Anglo-Dutch (Royal Dutch-Shell), Texaco, and British Petroleum. The countries that hosted the Seven Sisters, however, resented the fact that the foreign oil companies were benefiting from oil profits more than they were. These oil-producing countries took control of the American and European oil companies. OPEC now has eleven member states: Saudi Arabia, Iraq, Iran, United Arab Emirates, Venezuela, Kuwait, Libya, Nigeria, Algeria, Indonesia, and Qatar. These OPEC countries supply more than 40 percent of the world's oil and possess about 78 percent of the world's total proven crude oil reserves.[15]

Although OPEC may appear to be a purely economic organization, the implications of its actions can have a significantly political impact. In 1973 OPEC raised oil prices from roughly $3 a barrel to $12 a barrel, which sent shock waves around the world. Another shock came in 1978, when it again raised the price of oil; it seemed that OPEC was clearly in the driver's seat in this most critical of industries. These two events in the 1970s represented the best opportunity yet for Third World countries to gain leverage over First World countries, most of which were highly dependent on oil imports—particularly those from the Middle East. The benefits from this new-found power were not equally distributed throughout the South, and in some cases, the oil shocks actually hurt countries in the South. Of course, the oil-producing countries benefited most. Many non-oil-producing Third World countries suffered the same problem as First World countries: they had to pay much higher prices for oil.

As you read in Chapter 5, OPEC's influence on the world stage did not last. Through most of the 1980s and 1990s, not only was more oil found (increasing world supply), but most First World countries became more efficient energy consumers (decreasing demand). In addition, OPEC's member states started cheating significantly on their output targets; they pumped more oil than they said they would, thus creating an oversupply. The incredibly low oil prices of 1998 and early 1999 made some observers wonder whether OPEC would ever play the kind of role it did in the 1970s. But it was those low prices that galvanized OPEC and even non-OPEC members to work together to stabilize and thus raise world oil prices. This effort led to the doubling of oil prices in the United States within a year from 1999 to 2000.

The lesson of OPEC—as a group of Third World countries banding together to leverage First World countries—is difficult to apply within other contexts. First of all, OPEC's successes have been limited, and oil has not been the cure-all for its members' economic and political woes. Second, most countries in the Third World do not possess raw materials or manufactured goods or services that are as high in demand in the First World as oil. As a result, efforts to form cartels in other commodities have generally failed.

After reviewing the above theoretical approaches to development, we can see that Third World countries have generally followed three different strategies, based on theoretical ideas and actual experience.[16] First, some countries have tried to detach themselves from the international political economy (the neo-Marxist and dependency recommendation). For the most part, these efforts have failed. The change in attitude toward contact with First World countries is exemplified by the attitudes of Brazil's President Henrique Cardozo. Cardozo had been a leading proponent of the dependency approach and has denounced U.S. multinational corporations as instruments of American imperialism. However, by the 1990s, he had come to believe—like many leaders in the Third World—that MNCs can provide the capital and technology necessary for economic development.[17]

A second strategy for some Third World countries was to change the international political-economic order. The most prominent attempt was the NIEO. This strategy thus far has also failed. The 1980s and 1990s saw a major ideological shift in the Third World as more and more countries adopted neoliberal economic policies (e.g., less regulation, favoring foreign investment). This offers a partial explanation for Mexico's decision to support NAFTA. The third strategy of developing countries has been to adopt neomercantist domestic policies and to maximize the benefits of participation in the international political economy. Almost every country in the world has actually supported the neomercantilist prescription of protecting domestic industries from foreign competition.

What Factors Impact the Politics of Development?

Directly related to the previous discussion about strategies for development is what may be called the "politics of development." This term refers to how developing states are governed, how their political leadership operates in terms of launching and sustaining economic growth, how political elites allocate their country's scarce resources, and how the international political economy affects political and economic decisions in the host developing country. Generally speaking, the "politics of development" concept spotlights the overall realm of politics as it bears on the economic, political, and social lives of everyone who lives inside the state and is subject to its rule.

Politics—both domestic and international—can contribute to development or hold it back, in which case the rich are allowed to get richer and the poor to become poorer. In many parts of the developing world, a few people in control of the political system use it to enhance their own personal wealth rather than to advance the interests of their people. Such was the case in the Congo under the late Mobuto Sese Seko, or within Cambodia's dictatorial regimes. Elsewhere the nature of politics is associated more with economic and social development, as in Costa Rica, Singapore, Taiwan, and Vietnam.

The politics of development studies who gets what, when, where, and how in a developing country. Politics and governing, then, are intimately tied into all those decisions and outcomes that affect whether a country is moving toward improved standards of living for more and more people and toward wider popular participation in government.

Several key questions come to mind. How do political decisions affect a country's **capital formation**—that is, how land, labor, and physical capital (like factories for manufacturing) are developed to generate income in the country? What political decisions are made that impact on a country's vital **social overhead capital,** such as *education and health?* Who gets educated? What do they study? How do politics determine whether roads, bridges, schools, dams, and communication facilities get built—and if so, whether they are built in the right places to benefit the whole country? Where do politics come into the equation in terms of how much public spending supports the military versus schools, hospitals, and public health programs?

Let's look more closely now at the factors that shape the politics of development.

For more information on Vietnam's economic and social development, go to **www.ablongman.com/ duncan.**

Capital Formation
The process by which land, labor, and physical capital (like factories for manufacturing) are developed to generate income in a country.

Social Overhead Capital
A term in economic development studies to indicate factors such as a population's health, education, and welfare that contribute to economic growth.

Mobuto Sese Seko (1930–1997): Mobuto ruled Zaire (now the Democratic Republic of the Congo) with absolute authority. Concentrating power in himself through a one-party state, in reality a cult of personality, Mobuto amassed a huge personal fortune through economic exploitation and corruption. Since his overthrow and subsequent death in 1997, ethnic civil war (over 200 ethnic groups) and foreign armies seeking to exploit the country's wealth (cobalt, copper, petroleum, industrial and gem diamonds, gold and silver, for example) have devastated this struggling Third World state. Its authoritarian rule and instability vividly illustrate development difficulties in a postcolonial setting. Zaire was formerly the Belgium Congo, ruled by Belgium and granted independence in 1960.

The Colonial Legacy

You can see from the previous discussion on mercantilism, neomercantilism, and dependency that many of these countries are states that have been created from former colonial European empires. As such they have inherited economic, social, and political systems from the colonial era, during which they were essentially exploited as regions of cheap labor and raw materials to fuel the manufacturing industries back home for those countries that dominated them—Britain, France, Germany, Portugal, Spain, and other European states.

The colonial legacy has left a distinct imprint on Third World politics of development. It led to great shifts of wealth from today's developing countries to the industrialized European part of the world, thereby contributing to today's poverty and population growth. Colonialism also left in its wake state boundaries with no cohesive national territories. Other consequences of colonialism were:

- *Political institutions* designed on European models, created for colonial rule of the countries rather than linked to traditional cultural norms of the colonized area. In many cases this has resulted in unworkable postcolonial settings, with the military emerging as the only institution with enough power to maintain order and stability.[18]
- *Economic systems* geared to exploit raw materials and cheap labor for the benefit of the mother country rather than for sustainable economic development in the colonized country.
- *Inadequate infrastructures* for successful economic development, including low literacy rates, poor housing and health facilities, and inefficient transportation and communication.

- *Ethnic, caste, tribal, religious, and linguistic divisions* among the colonized state's population, which have contributed to chronic postcolonial instability.

Economic and Human Factors

Today's postcolonial politics of development in poor states is affected by the basic lack of economic and natural resources, extensive poverty and inequality, and comparatively weak power compared to the developed countries within the international system.[19] Remember that 80 percent of the world's population lives in countries that generate only 20 percent of the world's total income.[20] (But see the discussion that follows on measuring economic assets in developing countries). This means that political leaders have fewer resources available to initiate positive change and respond to growing demands from an expanding population with high birth rates. Added to this situation is the persistence of high-level government corruption, which we will examine in more depth, resistance to change from entrenched elites who live the sweet life, and a willingness to resort to violence by the haves and have nots in order to make their positions clear. Remember that corruption diminishes available economic assets that otherwise could find their way into development projects.

Human Underdevelopment In terms of human underdevelopment impacting the politics of development, Sub-Saharan Africa, for example, enters the twenty-first century with lagging school enrollments, high mortality for its children, and widespread endemic diseases like malaria and HIV/AIDS. Such diseases cut life expectancy by 20 years or more and undercut rates of savings and growth. In addition, many of this region's countries—as is the case elsewhere in the Third World—are plagued by an inability to produce sufficient food to feed their people. Add to this the lack of other economic resources (in addition to arable land) such as those linked to energy (oil, natural gas, coal), and you can see how the problems of development magnify.

Income Inequality Income inequality is extremely high in the developing states, where top income earners receive far more than the low-income earners. Latin America illustrates this point. The ratio of income of the top 20 percent of earners to those at the bottom is around 16 to 1; in Brazil it is nearly 25 to 1, compared to about 10 to 1 in the United States and 5 to 1 in Western Europe.[21] Needless to say, a country's top dogs do not want to give up their privileged position. This breeds a political system of, among other things, *uncollected taxes*, thus depriving the state of money that could be invested in development projects; minimal political change, which impedes the incorporation of more people into national political life so that their interests may be represented; and siphoned-off state funds for personal use. A classic case in point is Mexico, where corruption has held back a more effective allocation of the state's resources to improve human development at a time when peasant groups are demanding more land and labor is striving for higher wages. Indeed, in Mexico the ruling party, the Institutional Revolutionary Party (PRI), has been accused of channeling public funds to election campaigns.[22] In a recent survey of high-ranking public officials and key leaders of civil society in over 60 developing countries, the respondents rated public sector corruption as the most serious obstacle to development and growth in their countries.[23]

Another Look at Economic Assets in Developing Countries

Hernando De Soto, a leading scholar of economic transformation has made a compelling argument that developing countries have far more economic assets than people think—assets they need to make a success of capitalism. De Soto is President of the Institute for Liberty and Democracy (ILD), which is headquartered in Peru and regarded by *The Economist* as arguably the most important think tank in the world. De Soto himself was recently named one of the five leading Latin American innovators of the century by *Time* magazine. What is his argument? De Soto has shown through extensive research that most of the poor in Asia, Africa, the Middle East, and Latin America actually possess the assets required to make capitalism work. In fact the value of wealth that the poor have accumulated is worth five times all the foreign aid received throughout the world since 1945.[24] But, to use De Soto's words, the poor hold these resources in forms that they are unable to use as capital:

> Houses built on land whose ownership rights are not adequately recorded, unincorporated businesses with undefined liability, industries located where financiers and investors cannot see them. Because the rights to these possessions are not adequately documented, these assets cannot readily be turned into capital, cannot be traded outside of narrow local circles where people know and trust each other, cannot be used as collateral for a loan, and cannot be used as a share against an investment.[25]

This fascinating research points out that the poor people of the world in fact have capital assets, but lack the processes that give them meaning within the capitalist system. Their houses do not have titles, their crops do not have deeds—and thus, they have been unable to make their domestic holdings work within capitalist society and produce additional value. Despite their wealth, they are not within the world of legally enforceable transactions on property rights. In Haiti, for example, untitled rural and urban real estate holdings are together worth around $5.2 billion, while the value of rural and urban real estate held outside the normal legal realm amounts to about $74 billion.[26] In this sense the apparent but illusory lack of economic assets reflects the political world of development, in which elites have not moved the political/legal system forward to allow the poor to participate in national and international economic life. As far as globalization goes, since most poor people cannot participate in an expanded market within their own countries, they are excluded from the positive sides of globalized international market life in which their country participates. That is, the property rights systems that link their country up to international monetary and investment opportunities is a world apart from the so-called poor people in developing states.

Government Factors

Any discussion of lagging economic resources, as is clear in the preceding discussion, naturally brings into focus other issues of government in the developing countries. One of the big issues within that realm is the lack of government legitimacy. Let's take a closer look.

Lack of Government Legitimacy   Many countries face a lack of legitimacy of their governments.[27] By this is meant that most of the population of the state has little faith in their government and how it makes decisions, or they may simply not identify closely with the government, which they see as having virtually no effect on their lives. Many reasons account for this situation, including abject poverty of the lower classes, vast income inequalities, populations living in the hinterlands—far from the capital city and other large population centers, and ethnic diversity—with its distinct cultural preferences and linguistic differences. For example, there are ethnic tribal groups in the jungles of Guatemala who do not speak Spanish—the language of Guatemala and its government: As a result, these groups barely identify with their government.

This is not surprising, because the Guatemalan military has been responsible for killing scores of peasant Indians at random over recent years.[28] Where ethnic groups are numerous inside a state—as in Nigeria—it is difficult for any government to gain the respect and support of those ethnic groups who are not represented in the government's instruments of power. A review of the differences between ethnic nations and states in previous chapters will highlight this point for you.

Lack of Government Power and Authority in the Countryside
Governments in developing countries simply may not have the power and authority to affect the lives of people in the countryside, who are far from the capital city where the center of government resides. If the state's central administrative apparatus does not extend much beyond the capital city or one or two other large cities, its power is noticeably limited. In this situation—which is quite clear in parts of Africa and Latin America—even if a government were dedicated to mobilizing its human and material resources in support of modernization and development, it would be difficult to do so. Not far from La Paz, the capital of Bolivia, paved roads become dirt roads and rope-pulled ferries are used to transport local buses across rivers. In other parts of Latin America, it has been common for large landowners in rural areas to drive their farm workers (campesinos) to the city at election time and force them to vote for the landowners' preferred candidates.

Violence Within and Between Developing Countries
Causes of violence within and between developing countries are many, as you learned in Chapter 9. One such cause is the lack of democratic institutions to resolve conflict between groups, including ethnic national groups. Another is poor economic conditions and the stresses of economic transformation. Economic inequalities, discriminatory economic and political practices, ethnic minority status, and political alienation all contribute to violent conflict. Leaders bent upon the quest for power frequently fan violent conflict—as the world has seen time and again.[29] See box The View from Bosnia: Civil War's Impact on Development.

Civil war—a product of political decisions to make war against another group (typically another ethnic national group inside the state)—is catastrophic for economic development. Infrastructure such as roads, bridges, railways, telegraphs, schools, hospitals, and dams are destroyed, the importance of force over peaceful conflict resolution is promoted, and the government's legitimate power is virtually destroyed.[30] In addition, domestic and foreign investment are deterred. A look at what has happened in Angola, Chad, Sudan, the Congo, Ethiopia, Sierra Leone, and Somalia in the last decade of the twentieth and onset of the twenty-first century illustrates this point. Figure 12.3 depicts how turbulent the politics of civil wars have been in Africa. Keep in mind that one of the root causes of civil wars in developing countries is the intense identification with ethnic nationality rather than with the government of the state in which such ethnic groups live.

The Impact of Military Elites
Military elites remain strong in a number of developing countries and, as such, undermine economic development, hold back

THE VIEW FROM Bosnia

Civil War's Impact on Development

- Bosnia entered its postcommunist era of economic and political development in a state of civil war. In 1992, when the war began, it was trying to make a market economy and democracy work simultaneously, set against its legacy of communism and authoritarian rule. Now, UN and NATO forces are prominent everywhere, with each country housed in its own compound—37 military groups from 37 countries.

- Bosnia's leaders and their followers have been severely divided by ethnic identity and conflict both before and after the Dayton Peace Accords of 1995 that ended its civil war. Divisiveness remains high, and only international forces keep the peace.

- Government corruption remains extensive—owing in part to a virtually nonexistent judicial system. Unemployment is extremely high, about 40 to 50 percent, with incomes averaging only around $2,000 per year! Children sell mushrooms and berries by the road, trying to earn something . . . anything, for the family. Inflation is high: a pair of Levi's cost $80.00

- Bosnia's young and old alike are pessimistic about the future.

- Physical destruction is overpowering—broken shells of homes and office buildings, totally destroyed parliament and newspaper buildings in Sarajevo, broken roads, and more. It is a heartbreaking sight.

- Bosnians, albeit Muslim, have long identified with the West, because they were part of the Austro-Hungarian Empire, while Serbs have identified with Eastern Orthodox religion, the Cyrillic alphabet, and Russia.

- A strong criminal element runs public services in Sarajevo. The day after the 1999 Summit Meeting was held there, during which Western countries pledged more millions to help Bosnia, Ray Duncan and two of his students were mugged in a public Sarajevo trolley by three thugs posing as "trolley security." They relieved them of $45 in return for the passports they had confiscated. They left the trolley and divided up the money down the street. This happened just a few blocks from where Western dignitaries, including President Clinton, were departing the country amidst a gala display of flags at the Sarajevo International Airport.

human rights and social justice, and inhibit the growth of more democratic government. Pakistan is a case in point, with its frequent coups, low economic growth, and ineffective civilian political institutions. Pakistan's military simply has outstripped fledgling civilian institutions, leaving the legislative branch of government weak, the judiciary underdeveloped, the press stilled, and one prime minister after the other dependent on the military to sustain public order.[31] Economic growth has suffered under military-dominated conditions, made more difficult by an annual population growth of about 3 percent. Algeria is another case of politics dominated by the military, a place where the government implements policies selected by the army.[32] Military power still remains behind the scenes in parts of Latin America—as, for example, in Argentina, Chile, Colombia, Peru, and Venezuela.

The Diversity of Governing Systems   Day-to-day politics of development take dramatically different forms throughout the Third World. Here the nature of a country's leadership comes into play. In China, Vietnam, and Cuba, for example, leaders have focused on achieving market socialism (see box The View from China on page 300).

For more information on development and Castro's Cuba, go **to** **www.ablongman.com/ duncan.**

FIGURE 12.3

Turbulent Africa

SOURCE: *From* Foreign Policy, *Spring 1999, volume 114, p. 15.*

Turbulent Africa
- ■ Civil conflicts
- ▢ Countries where conflicts could easily start up again
- ■ Civil conflicts that entail military intervention by other African countries
- ▨ Interstate conflicts

Mexico's leaders, in contrast, have pursued a more open market economy, where one party, the PRI, has dominated for years, but now increasingly faces stiff competition from other parties. Unlike China, Vietnam, and Cuba, Mexico enjoys membership in a free trade organization, NAFTA. Bosnia, meanwhile, is trying to develop with generous international grants and loans, but in a situation where political order is maintained exclusively by international military forces (NATO). Government corruption remains extensive—owing in part to a virtually nonexistent judicial system. Bosnia's civil war in the early 1990s devastated its infrastructure, as you read.

Cultural Factors

Not all the problems and issues associated with how Third World countries govern themselves are due strictly to colonialism—or to economic or government issues. In analyzing today's politics of development, a number of scholars increasingly have turned their attention to traditional attitudes and values embedded in a developing country's culture as one of the major obstacles to development. Let's look at why this might be so.

The bomb-damaged building that housed the liberation newspaper Oslobottenje *in Sarajevo.*

Traditional Cultural Values and Political Culture   In his 1994 book
The New World of the Gothic Fox, Claudio Veliz argues that Latin America has been
held back in terms of modernized democratic and advanced economic development by its culture. In making his argument, Veliz contrasts the Anglo-Protestant
and Ibero-Catholic legacies in the New World. Latin Americans, he says, tend to be
populist and oligarchic, or absolutist, collectivist, or dogmatic—and flawed by their
social and racial prejudice and intolerance toward political adversaries. In contrast,
the Anglo-Protestant is more egalitarian, pragmatic, innovative, and adaptable to
the compromise and bargaining inherent in democratic governance. In "The View
from Latin American: Fragile Democracies," you will see how The Ibero-Catholic
culture has been expressed in Latin America's political instability and upheaval.[35]

African writers, too, such as Daniel Etounga-Manguelle, an economist from the
Cameroon, attribute Africa's poverty, authoritarianism, and social injustice primarily
to traditional cultural attitudes and values. He focuses on African culture as one that
suppresses individual initiative, achievement and saving, and that promotes jealousy
of success and a high degree of fatalism.[36] While such views will be debated, they do
offer a window onto the world of culture that drives the way people think and act.

A number of cultural traits have been linked to economic and political development. Some of the more notable attitudes and values may be summarized as follows:[37]

- **Time orientation.** A progressive culture stresses the future, while a static culture focuses more on the present or past.
- **Work and achievement.** The culture that values hard work as a key to the
  good life progresses, while the static culture focuses less attention here.

Market Socialism

China practices a different version of market socialism from India. In market socialism, the state monopolizes political power, typically in a single party system like the Communist Party, while slowly releasing the screws of control on the economy. Since the late 1970s China—with its huge population of over 1.3 billion—has allowed more free enterprise and economic freedom while still retaining a large number of state-owned firms, political control by the communists, and protection of its internal markets from foreign competition. By late 1999, in an effort to gain admission to the World Trade Organization, China made clear that it was now prepared to throw open its agricultural and industrial markets to foreign competition—a remarkable change from its protectionist past.[33] Still, *China faces gigantic challenges to development*. Among such obstacles must be included income inequalities between the developed coastal areas and the underdeveloped western regions, plus ubiquitous corruption, scores of inefficient and unproductive state-owned firms, and horrendous pollution. A field trip to China in 1999 by one of the authors of this book produced the following observations about China's development:

- Signs of high economic vitality flourish in the coastal cities like Shanghai and Beijing, eastern inland cities such as X'ian and Wuhan, and other big cities like Chengdu and Chongqing. One sees omnipresent cell phones, high-rise buildings and industrial complexes under construction, the huge Three Gorges Dam project, and ubiquitous foreign investment, as evidenced by Canon, Sanyo, McDonalds, and CNN news.

- China's youth are on the move, acquiring higher education, becoming technologically sophisticated, and learning English as their preferred second language. This is a country that is distinctly developing and a far cry from what one would have witnessed back in the early 1980s. Many signs, advertisements, and museum placards are in Chinese and English.

- Shanghai is especially astounding in its frenetic construction activity, with high-rise apartments and giant cranes silhouetted against the skyline. One-third of the world's cranes are located in Shanghai. People in Shanghai see themselves as hard-working and industrious, while they view Beijing as the "government city," a place of politicians and bureaucrats. Each big city's population in China see itself as superior to others.

- Pollution is rampant everywhere—Beijing, Shanghai, Wuhan—and is extremely bad in X'ian. China is one of the most polluted countries in the world.

- Despite rapid development and industrialization concentrated in the western coastal areas, China is still a living museum in terms of ways of life that date back hundreds of years. Hong Kong's new modern airport and New York–style skyline stand in sharp contrast to peasant agriculture and over fifty indigenous ethnic groups living as they did centuries ago.

Type of Corruption	Costs (billion Yuan)	As a Share of Gross Domestic Product
Kickbacks from government purchases	46	.63
Kickbacks from construction contracts	50	.68
Tariff losses from smuggling with official involvement and support	25	.34
Tax evasion by state-owned enterprises and entities	105	1.43
Lost interest income from public funds illegally deposited in private accounts	6	.08
Uncovered illegal use of extra budget revenues	17	.23
Entertainment (mainly meals)	100	1.4
Total Paid with Public Funds	**343**	**4.79**

Source: *Foreign Policy*, Fall 1999, No. 116, pp. 98–99. Copyright © 1999 by The Carnegie Endowment for International Peace. Reprinted with permission.

THE VIEW FROM India

Market Socialism

India has embarked since the early 1990s on a dismantling of its cumbersome state bureaucracy and planning system. It has begun cutting red tape, simplifying taxes, and reducing the state sector in an effort to liberalize foreign investment and increase exports to reach out to the world in spirited competition. Some observers have described India as a "New Tiger" out in Asia.[34]

- **Frugality.** Investment and a frugal approach toward financial security tend to characterize progressive cultures; in static cultures, the values represent a threat to the egalitarian status quo, and one person's gains are thought to occur at the expense of another.
- **Education.** Although the trigger for advancement in a progressive culture, education is of marginal importance, except for the elites, in static cultures.
- **Merit.** An emphasis on merit and achievement are extremely important for advancement in a progressive culture, while connections to family are more important in the static culture.

Resistance to Western Versions of Change   The impact of globalization has been dramatic around the world, and the spirit of development has fired the imaginations of many Third World leaders. In addition, the Western world's international financial institutions like the World Bank and the IMF have pressed for development along with the idea that a state's people should be able to exercise more control over government decisions. Yet despite all this, older traditional ways of thinking and self-identifying continue to be powerful forces affecting the politics of development.[38]

While key cultural values in the West—from whence the development idea has sprung—have been individualism, market economies, and political democracy, the non-Western world tends to embrace other values. Since the West makes up only a small percentage of the world's population but promotes its values almost everywhere, cultural clashes seem inevitable. As Harvard's Samuel P. Huntington argues, the key distinctions among people in the post–Cold War world are not ideological, political, or economic, but cultural, and in many parts of the developing world, people are attempting to answer the question. Who are we? Their traditional way of answering this question is to identify not with a market economy or democracy, but with ancestry, religion, language, history, values, customs, and local institutions.[39]

To summarize, then, a state's politics of development is held back or spurred on by a multiplicity of factors, including the following:

- Its colonial legacy.
- The strength of its state institutions.
- The legitimacy of its government.
- Its ability to govern beyond the capital city.
- The honesty of its leaders, or their corruption in diverting economic assets.
- Its tax base and ability to collect taxes.

- Openness or resistance to westernized versions of change, including legal systems to represent the poor population's economic assets.
- Ethnic, caste, tribal, religious, and linguistic divisions within the population.
- Modes of development, as in the varieties of market socialism in China, Vietnam, and Cuba.
- Levels of violence within the state and between it and others.
- Strength of ruling military elites.

Now let's look beyond the politics of development to see how politics and economics interact.

What Is the Connection Between Democracy and Economic Development?

To begin, democracy is not required for economic development. During the latter part of the twentieth century, economic development occurred throughout the Third World, in various stages and at different rates of speed, in countries without democratic governments. In Chile, for example, the military authoritarian regime of General Augusto Pinochet promoted economic growth in the 1970s and 1980s, as did China and Vietnam's centralized Communist Party. Still, most scholars agree that *economic development is tied to the transition to democratic institutions over time*, although democracy does not automatically secure sustained economic growth at the outset.[40] For economic development to occur, the country's political elites must provide law and order, property rights, and macroeconomic stability. They will do even better if they go beyond these requirements and prevent monopolies, corruption, and vast income inequalities through appropriate tax structures and other public policies such as education.[41]

The Role of Democracy in Developing Countries

How strong is democracy in the Third World? Democratic government caught fire in the 1970s and swept parts of the Third World during the 1980s, spreading through Africa, Eastern Europe, Latin America, and Asia. But by the 1990s the idea that democracy was the wave of the future began to cool, because it proved less strong in many countries than first imagined—in the sense that elections had not guaranteed consolidation of democratic processes. In sub-Saharan Africa the surge to democracy fell apart, and in Latin America it produced a mixed picture.[42] (see box The View from Latin America: Fragile Democracies).

Today many developing countries engaged in economic development projects profess to be democratic while they in fact remain highly authoritarian. Many resist the complex transition to democracy; it threatens the privileges of the powerful and arouses distrust in the disenfranchised. The big point here is that elections do not guarantee democratic rule, because traditional political cultures can get in the way.

Links between economic development and democratic development are revealed in the very practical aspect of how a country prioritizes its policies. Many scholars have pointed to the trade-offs in the development process, and they note that no country will be able to achieve all its development goals at the same time. Thus, they must establish priorities. Let's look at two important countries to see how they have addressed perhaps the broadest trade-off in development: whether economic development precedes or follows political development.

THE VIEW FROM   Latin America

Fragile Democracies

Peruvians elected President Alberto Fujimori to an unprecedented third term in May 2000. Peru's constitutional tribunal had ruled in 1997 that a third term would be illegal, and the May election came amidst demonstrations against Fujimori, while 30 percent of the ballots were blank, and international condemnation plagued the election's legitimacy.

Ecuador suffered a military coup during 1999. Venezuela's government became increasingly authoritarian. Paraguay had to impose a state of siege in May 2000 after a military coup attempt. In Mexico, the ruling party, the PRI, held the country's 2000 presidential election campaign amidst allocations of corruption. Colombia was mired in a war against guerrillas which it eventually lost.

As you've read elsewhere in this book, since the late 1970s, China has chosen a path of economic development while the government keeps a firm political grip on the country. China still has only one political party, the Chinese Communist Party, and it is not very tolerant of opposition.

In contrast, Russia has attempted to change its politics and its economics at the same time. Since the collapse of the Soviet Union in the early 1990s, Russia has thrown off most of its communist-era economic structures while at the same time destroying the tight grip of the Communist Party and internal security forces that dominated society.

How has Russia faired in its attempt to avoid the dilemma of whether to prioritize economics versus political change? The answer is, so-so. Compared to other countries making the transition out of communism, Russia seems to be experiencing some of the slowest progress. While high-tech start-ups thrive in big cities like Moscow and St. Petersburg, oligarchs and criminal elements known as the Mafia run much of the Russian economy, and the country is in dire need of loans from the international community. Politically, the 1990s did see free presidential and parliamentary (Duma) elections, but they were not completely free of governmental meddling, especially with respect to control over the media. Much of the Russian population feels left out of the political process, which hurts the legitimacy of the government. The tie between the oligarchs and the Mafia is long-standing and was cemented in the last decade of the Soviet regime. Putin's challenge is to break that tie and to create law and order without destroying the free press or stifling economic growth. In short, Russia has tried revolutionary changes in both the political and economic spheres with very mixed results.

The trade-off over development priorities leads to some serious dilemmas. As a national leader, what would *you* recommend? One path you might take is to prevent the introduction of democratic reforms (as China did) while the economy is being reformed. It has been said that when economic conditions are terrible, people will tolerate limited political freedoms; in other words, "what is economically correct cannot be morally wrong."[43] A second path you might take is to implement policies based on the idea that a sound economy depends on democratic openness. Mancur Olson has argued against the idea that democracy is a luxury only rich countries can afford. Instead, he says, the dispersal of political power and the emergence of representative government have often been the triggers for faster economic growth.[44]

The Role of Non-Western Political Thought

Non-Western modes of political thought exist throughout the developing countries of the world. These in turn shape the nature of decision making, goals and objectives, and the overall political process—and, in turn, economic and social development. We find such non-Western modes of thought vividly expressed in the pronouncements of Islamic fundamentalists, Arab nationalists, Hindu fundamentalists, Iran revolutionaries, Chinese Marxists, Chiapas leaders, and the Shining Path movement of Peru, as well as by South American novelists, Caribbean political theorists, and Indian film makers. As one student of non-Western thought aptly pointed out, the values of the non-Western world are widespread and should be considered when we think about the politics of development.[45]

Non-Western political thought has a number of dimensions that condition the politics of development. Preoccupied with what they see as a threat to traditional cultures and religions, its radical proponents tend to indict the West as neoimperialists and neocolonialists who exploited their countries in the past, "ripped away the cultures, silenced the languages, belittled the religions and denied the histories of native peoples. Imperialism was more than alien rule; it was cultural annihilation."[46] Beyond resenting imperialism, radical upholders of non-Western political thought tend to be highly suspicious of perceived continuing Western hegemony, while stressing themes of cultural and economic emancipation from Western dominance. In what we think of as non-Western thinking, communitarian values and responsibilities take precedence over individualism. "Progress," defined as moving toward a Westernized world of globalized market interdependence with its secular materialist utopia, is not desirable. Progress instead is measured in terms of the principles of, for example, Islam, Confucianism, or Buddhism.

The Role of Globalization

Globalization at best has been a mixed blessing in the developing world. It has had widely different impacts, uplifting some parts of the developing world and leaving others in economic stagnation and human deprivation.[47] The problem has been that international flows of capital, emergence of a globalized economy, and globalized financial markets have increased the income inequalities between the richest and poorest parts of the Third World and within many developing countries themselves. To be sure, in a select group of countries—China, other countries in East Asia, and Chile, for example—the number of poor people has declined. Yet in much of the Third World, poverty and income inequalities have continued to grow. Countries that have fared best in the globalized economy have moved toward less state intervention and higher export growth, especially in manufactured goods. Africa has not done well in either regard and has been left behind.

Globalization came under siege, as noted in Chapter 11, in late 1999 and early 2000. Huge public protests were mounted in the streets of Seattle, Washington, during WTO meetings, and in Washington, D.C., in May during IMF proceedings. Protests represented the growing sentiment among labor unions, environmentalists, human rights activists, and others that the world capitalist and market economy models of development backed by the WTO and IMF were laissez-faire doctrines that were spreading more poverty than progress in the Third World. The development concepts promoted by the WTO and the IMF were privatization, deregulation, and open capital markets to create jobs, stimulate competition among companies, and supply foreign capital and technology to poor countries. These approaches, WTO and IMF backers argued, would best promote the prosperity and competition in which democracy and respect for human rights would flourish. Not so, say their critics, who point to the record in Latin America and elsewhere. Instead, they believe that reform of the WTO and the IMF is needed to promote people and the environment over profits. The case study at the end of this chapter is instructive on the pros and cons of development.

The Role of Ethnic and Religious Conflict

Ethnic and religious conflicts have contributed greatly to many development problems, including the following: (1) weak states lacking legitimate institutions; (2) corruption; (3) undermined democratic institutions; (4) poor economic development; and (5) high violence and loss of life. Still, for a number of scholars and policymakers who have studied this problem, it is not ethnicity and religion per se that spawn mass violence, as witnessed in the former Yugoslavia or as generated by Islamic fundamentalism in Iran or Afghanistan.

Some observers argue that the impact of ethnic and religious differences is linked to how a country's leaders manipulate ethnicity and religion to their own ends—and whether they ignite ethnic and religious passions of one group against another. Such conflicts are also, of course, generally fueled by poor economic and social conditions.[48] Widespread violence among ethnic groups in former Yugoslavia, for example, was promoted by worsening economic conditions and a scarcity of resources, coupled with leadership styles of men like Franjo Tudjman of Croatia and Slobodan Milosevic of Serbia. Other leaders fueling violence include religious nationalists such as Saudi exile and Islamic militant Osama bin Laden, and leaders of militant Palestinians in the Hamas and in Islamic Jihad organizations who oppose the Palestinian-Israeli peace process.

What Are the Prospects for Future Third World Development?

The end of the Cold War has spawned a number of crosscutting forces that have both helped and hindered the prospects for development by way of intelligent political decision making in the Third World. *On the positive side*, a peaceful end to the nuclear rivalry between the world's superpowers brought growing agreement on the need for cooperative management of Third World conflicts, and widening consensus about the importance of human rights and democratic governance. The end of the Cold War also provided the opportunity to decrease military spending by the Great Powers, with added attention to providing economic resources and promoting democratic rule and market economic growth in the developing world. Indeed, military authoritarianism began to decline in parts of the Third World as market economic growth caught fire—as in Latin America.

On the negative side, however, violence has increased throughout much of the developing world, most notably via civil wars. While the causes of these internal conflicts vary, as we have seen throughout this book, the end of the Cold War has played its part. This is so largely because during the Cold War, many Third World regimes managed to stay in power as a result of substantial aid from either Western countries—including the United States—or the Soviet Union and its East European allies. Angola, Central America, and the Horn of Africa are cases in point. Once the Cold War ended, outside powers withdrew their support, which left a vacuum of power and a no-holds-barred fight to the finish. Classic examples are Angola and Ethiopia, where violence and war became the tools of power-seeking leaders, and where death rates among civilians have been higher than among soldiers.

The end of the Cold War has also seen the end of checks against the power of ethnic and religious nationalism as forces shaping the politics of development. The rise of both forms of nationalism has been pronounced around the world—and expressed in many ways, from the assassination of Israeli Prime Minister Yitzhak Rabin to car bombings in New Delhi, Bombay, and Karachi, to the emergence of the Taliban in Afghanistan, and to the Islamic leadership of Hasan Turabi in Sudan. One finds religious nationalists in the Muslim countries of Saudi Arabia, Pakistan, and Turkey—where Islamic revolutionaries perceive moderate Muslim leaders as obstacles to progress.[49] In India the Bharatiya Janata Party (BJP) has become the largest religious nationalist movement in the world. Scholars believe in general that while the West can live with some of the tenets of post–Cold War religious nationalists—the importance of morality, for example—other aspects are more contentious. These include the identification with particular pieces of territory as the strict province of one religion and the contention that democratic institutions should be non-secular, that is, based on divine justification.[50]

As this chapter illustrates, a country's prospects for development turn on many external (international) and internal (domestic) factors, such as its colonial legacy, its core-periphery relationships, the nature of its leadership, its levels of corruption, its ability to collect taxes, and its degree of ethnic and religious conflict. Leaders are especially important. Given the diversity of Third World economic, social, and political circumstances, it would be foolish to try to predict the future for states from Latin America to Asia. What we know for certain is that the post–Cold War era has unleashed enormous forces for change toward democratic politics and market economies—forces that have been both embraced and condemned in the Third World. Globalization and interdependence seem here to stay, and they increasingly link domestic and international factors in a close embrace. Yet, they have produced a mixed record of good and bad at the level of standards of living and human development.

So many questions about a state's prospects for development are linked to it leaders—what their perceptions are, what relations they expect to have with the external world, and how they plan to use the country's natural resources in the process of development. Important also are the degree and scale of ethnic national harmony or conflict and the leaders' role in that mix. Bosnia's ethnic national conflict stands in sharp conflict, for example, to Costa Rica's relatively stable political leadership. China and Vietnam, both following models of market socialism, offer a different brand of leadership than that found in Cuba; not surprisingly, the former two countries promote different brands of market socialism than that of Cuba as well.

In trying to build a profile of any specific country's prospects for development, the best we can do is to ask a series of questions based on many of the forces examined in this chapter. A good question to begin with is this one: Does the country's

Rebuilding Afghanistan...

INKCINCT

"The first thing they want us to build is a bomb shelter!"

SOURCE: Copyright John Ditchburn.

political system enjoy legitimacy among the broader population? If it does not, you might well expect a high degree of military spending, instability, and lack of investor confidence in risking capital in that country. A second key question is, Who is running the country and what are the guiding developmental perceptions of those in control? The answer to this question will tell you whether or not, and to what extent, the country is trying to build democratic political institutions and a fairer distribution of national income. Another important factor is infrastructure. Solid economic infrastructure facilitates a smooth functioning economy, but when a country starts out underdeveloped, then is bombed to pieces as in the U.S.-led war against Afghanistan's Taliban, those who are left face a daunting task in moving in a development direction. This is especially so, as bombs continue to fall after the major war—as the Inkcinct cartoon above illustrates.

As we look to the future, then, we do have a few reasons to be optimistic about development in the Third World, although a lot will depend on the particular circumstances in each country. The development optimists emphasize the following trends. First, with the end of the Cold War, countries in some parts of the Third World will no longer need to spend scarce cash on defense expenditures. Second, as the North increasingly realizes the effects of global interdependence, it may take a greater stake in maintaining the stability and economic viability of the South.

For more information on international aid and development, go to **www.ablongman.com/ duncan.**

Resolving certain pressing global problems—such as drug trafficking, illegal immigration, and pollution—will require cooperation between First and Third World countries. Third, while there have been setbacks, democracy is being practiced increasingly throughout the Third World, thanks in part to the end of the Cold War.[51] What Third World leaders do to respond to changes in international forces will be critical. As Monte Palmer of Florida State University put it, international trade and aid "cannot compensate for confused leadership, self-serving bureaucracies, communal conflict, and mass alienation."[52]

CHAPTER SUMMARY

What Is Meant by Development?

Development is a transformation in a country's poor living conditions that leads to a higher quality of life. It may also be viewed as an improvement in economic, political, and social life for men, women, and children. Certainly the concept offers an analytical framework to evaluate whether, and to what extent, a country is exhibiting progress in its economic, political, and social life.

- Development has traditionally been defined in economic terms.
- However, there is much more to development than how much a country's economy is growing. Just as important is how equitably income is distributed throughout the country.
- Political participation, presence of human and civil rights, and ecological conditions are also factors of development.

What Theories Explain Rich and Poor Countries?

This chapter explored three major approaches to answering this question:

- The liberal, neoclassical economics approach recommends capitalist, free trade principles as the way out of poverty.
- The neomercantilist approach emphasized the role that the state should play in fostering development.
- Neo-Marxism and dependency theory emphasized exploitative capitalist relationships between rich core countries and poor periphery countries as the causes of poverty.

- Some theories focus on the idea of greater cooperation among Third World countries.

What Factors Impact the Politics of Development?

The "politics of development" refers to how developing states are governed, how political leaders' actions encourage or impede growth, how political elites allocate their country's scarce resources, and how the international political economy affects political and economic decision in the host country. Factors that impact the politics of development are:

- Colonial legacies.
- Economic forces—such as lack of economic resources, poor human development, and gross income inequality. But De Soto has documented the fact that poor people's property is not represented in the legal system, and thus, their combined vast wealth is restricted from the realm of capitalism.
- Governing forces—like insufficient government legitimacy, corruption, ethnic and religious violence, and military elites.
- Cultural forces—including traditional culture and resistance to Western versions of development.

Politics—both domestic and foreign—can contribute to development or hold it back. In many parts of the developing world, a few people in control of the political system use it to enhance their own wealth rather than to advance the interests of their people. The types of politics that advance or hold back development in the Third World vary significantly from country to country. China, Vietnam, and Cuba practice different versions of market socialism. In market socialism, the state monopolizes political power, typically in a single party system such as the Communist Party, while slowly releasing the screws of control on the economy.

What Is the Connection Between Democracy and Economic Development?

Democracy is not required for economic development. During the latter part of the twentieth century, we saw economic development occurring throughout the Third World in various stages and at different rates of speed in countries without democratic governments from Chile to China.

- Democracy is less strong in developing countries than it may seem.
- Non-Western political thought is now frequently at work during development.
- Globalization is a mixed blessing
- Ethnic and religious conflicts undermine democratic development.

What Are the Prospects for Future Third World Development?

The Cold War's end produced both positive and negative impacts on development. The prospects for development will depend on many factors. Worth remembering are the following:

- While democracy is not required for economic development, economic development is tied to the transition to democratic institutions over time.
- Democratic government, as an idea, caught fire in the 1970s and swept parts of the Third World during the 1980s. But by the 1990s, the idea that democracy was the wave of the future began to cool off as it became clear that it might not be as strong in many countries as first imagined.
- Non-Western modes of political thought are currently at work throughout the Third World, with sometimes violent results.

ENDNOTES

[1] Hobbes was actually referring to man in the state of nature, not to conditions in the Third World.

[2] Monte Palmer, *Political Development: Dilemmas and Challenges* (Itasca, Illinois: F.E. Peacock Publishers, Inc., 1997), pp. 14–15.

[3] Ibid., p. 15.

[4] United Nations Educational, Scientific, and Cultural Organization. *http://www.unesco.org/*

[5] Amartya Sen, as quoted in Richard N. Cooper, "The Road from Serfdom," *Foreign Affairs*, vol. 79, no. 1 (January/February 2000), p. 164.

[6] Robin Wright, "Freedom's Formula," *Los Angeles Times*, February 25, 1992.

[7] W. W. Rostow, *The Stages of Economic Growth*, 2nd ed. (Cambridge: Cambridge University Press, 1971).

[8] Barbara Crossette, "U.N. Says Bad Government Is Often the Cause of Poverty," *The New York Times*, April 5, 2000.

[9] David Sylvan, "The Newest Mercantilism," *International Organization*, vol. 35 (Spring 1981). pp. 375–9.

[10] Mahfoud Bennoune, *The Making of Contemporary Algeria: 1830–1987* (Cambridge: Cambridge University Press, 1988), pp. 176–195.

[11] Joan E. Spero and Jeffrey A. Hart, *The Politics of International Economic Relations*, 5th ed. (New York: St. Martin's Press, 1997), pp. 154–155.

[12] Robert Gilpin, *The Challenge of Global Capitalism* (Princeton: Princeton University Press, 2000), p. 300.

[13] Michela Wrong, "Challenge to patent on neem tree oil," *Financial Times*, May 10, 2000.

[14] The Associated Press, "Poor Countries Draft Proposal on Poverty," *The New York Times*, April 12, 2000.

[15] OPEC, *http://www.opec.org*.

[16] Joan E. Spero and Jeffrey A. Hart, *The Politics of International Economic Relations*, p. 151.

[17] Robert Gilpin, *The Challenge of Global Capitalism*, p. 172.

[18] Randal L. Cruikshanks and Earl D. Huff, "Prospects for the Future," in Joseph N. Weatherby et. al., *The Other World: Issues and Politics of the Developing World* (New York: Longman, 1997), pp. 274–275.

[19] William A. Joseph, Mark Kesselman, and Joel Krieger, *Third World Politics at the Crossroads* (Lexington, Massachusetts: D.C. Heath and Co., 1996), p. 11.

[20] Nancy Birdsall, "Life is Unfair: Inequality in the World," *Foreign Policy*, no. 111 (Summer 1998), pp. 76–77.

[21] Ibid.

[22] *The News*, Mexico City, March 28, 2000, p. 12.

[23] Cheryl W. Gray and Daniel Kaufmann, *Finance & Development*, March 1998, pp. 7–10.

[24] Hernando De Soto, *The Mystery of Capital* (New York: Basic Books, 2000), pp. 4–5.

[25] Ibid, p. 6.

[26] Ibid, p. 33.

[27] William A. Joseph, Mark Kesselman, and Joel Krieger, *Third World Politics*, p. 11.

[28]Stephen Connely Benz, *Guatemalan Journey* (Austin: University of Texas Press, 1996), Part II.

[29]Carnegie Commission on Preventing Deadly Conflict, *Preventing Deadly Conflict*, Final Report, Carnegie Corporation of New York, 1997.

[30]For further discussion of this and related points, see Marina S. Ottoway, *Democracy Challenged: The Rise of Semi-Authoritarianism.* (Washington, D.C.: Carnegie Endowment for International Peace, 2003).

[31]Sumit Ganguly, "Pakistan's Never-Ending Story," *Foreign Affairs* vol. 79, no. 2 (March/April 2000), pp. 2–6.

[32]Labouari Addi, "Algeria's Army, Algeria's Agony, *Foreign Affairs*, vol. 77, no. 4 (July/August 1998), pp. 44–53.

[33]Edward S. Steinfeld, "Beyond Transition: China's Economy at Century's End," *Current History* vol. 98, no. 269 (September 1999), pp. 271–275.

[34]Steven Strasser and Sudip Mazumdar, "A New Tiger," *Newsweek*, August 4, 1997, pp. 42–44, 46.

[35]Claudio Veliz, *The New world of the Gothic Fox* (Berkeley: University of California Press, 1994), prologue and chapter 1.

[36]Daniel Etounga-Mangvelle, "Does Africa Need a Cultural Adjustment Program?" in Lawrence H. Harrison ed. *Culture Matters* (New York: Basic Books, 2000).

[37]This list is drawn from an article published by Lawrence E. Harrison, in the journal *The National Interest*, Summer 2000. Mr. Harrison directed United States Agency for International Development missions in five Latin American countries between 1965 and 1981. He is a senior fellow at Harvard University's Academy for International and Area Studies, and is coeditor of *Culture Matters: How Values Shape Human Progress* (Basic Books, 2000).

[38]Ibid.

[39]Samuel P. Huntington, "The Many Faces of the Future," *Utne Reader*, no. 81 (May/June 1997), pp. 75–77, 102–103.

[40]Ronald L. Tammen et. al., *Power Transitions: Strategies for the 21st Century* (New York: Chatham House Publishers, 2000), p. 123.

[41]Blanca Heredia, "Prosper or Perish? Development in the Age of Global Capital," *Current History*, November 1997, pp. 383–388.

[42]Thomas Carothers, "Democracy Without Illusions," *Foreign Affairs*, vol. 76, no. 1 (January/February 1997), pp. 85–99.

[43]Robin Wright, "Freedom's Formula," *Los Angeles Times*, February 25, 1992.

[44]See Mancur Olson, *Power and Prosperity: Outgrowing Communist and Capitalist Dictatorship* (New York: Basic Books, 2000), and "Out of Anarchy," *The Economist*, February 19, 2000.

[45]Donald J. Puchala, "Some Non-Western Perspectives on International Relations, *Journal of Peace Research*, vol. 34, no. 2 (1997), pp. 129–134.

[46]Ibid.

[47]Blanca Heredia, "Prosper or Perish," pp. 383–388.

[48]Carnegie Commission, *Preventing Deadly Conflict*, pp. 26–27.

[49]Mark Juergensmeyer, "Religious Nationalism: A Global Threat?" *Current History*, November 1996, pp. 372–376.

[50]Ibid.

[51]Monte Palmer draws these conclusions in *Political Development*, Chapter 9.

[52]Ibid., p. 281.

Is Globalization Good or Bad for Developing Countries?

This case study is structured around an intellectual give-and-take between two well-known observers of the less developed regions of the world. Thomas Friedman, author and columnist with the *New York Times*, argues optimistically that globalization can be a vital force for progress in developing countries. Author Robert Kaplan contends that globalization actually makes world politics—and the domestic politics of developing countries—more unstable. Both authors draw upon a wide variety of historical and contemporary examples to support their positions, and yet they come to very different conclusions. Along the way, though, the case study explores several issues raised in Chapter 12, including the importance of both internal (domestic) and external (international) factors that affect a country's development.

THE PROS AND CONS OF GLOBALIZATION

Thomas Friedman: Techno Logic

What is globalization? The short answer is that globalization is the integration of everything with everything else. A more complete definition is that globalization is the integration of markets, finance and technology in a way that shrinks the world from a size medium to a size small. Globalization enables each of us, wherever we live, to reach around the world farther, faster, deeper, and cheaper than ever before and at the same time allows the world to reach into each of us farther, faster, deeper, and cheaper than ever before.

I believe this process is almost entirely driven by technology. There's a concept in strategic theory—the sort of things Bob Kaplan has written about—stating that capabilities create intentions. In other words, if you give people B–52s, they will find ways to use them. This concept is quite useful when thinking about globalization, too. If I have a cell phone that can call around the world at zero marginal cost to 180 different countries, I will indeed call around the world to 180 different countries. If I have Internet access and can do business online, a business in which my suppliers, customers, and competitors are all global, then I will be global, too. And I will be global whether there is a World Trade Organization agreement or not.

Since September 11, 2001, many people have asked me if terrorism will stop the process of global-ization. I had often wondered about this sort of situation: What would happen if we did reach a crisis moment, a crisis like terrorism, or a major financial crisis, and things started to go in reverse? People would say "Bring back the walls!" but I knew that was going to be a particularly defining moment for us, because that's when we were all going to wake up and finally realize that technology had destroyed the walls already—that the September 11 terrorists made their reservations on Travelocity.com.

Robert Kaplan: Bad News Is Next

Let me try to give a slightly richer definition of globalization. The best historical metaphor I can come up with is China in the third century B.C., when the Han overlordship replaced the period of the warring states (following the short interlude of the Qin dynasty). Think of it: You had this massive mainland China, thousands of miles across, with little states constantly coalescing into bigger states over the centuries. And then, for a long period, you had six or so major states fighting each other. Finally, they were unified by a series of balance-of-power agreements, by an embryonic bureaucracy developing in all of them, and by the Chinese language. What the Han dynasty represented was not a single state; it was a serious reduction of conflict among the warring states, so that the highest morality was the morality of order, with everyone giving up a share of their independence for the sake of greater order. I'm not talking about some sort of "world government" over China. It was just a loose form of governance, where everything affected or constrained everything else.

Today, too, everything affects everything else—we're affected by disease pandemics in Africa, by *madrassas* (seminaries) in Pakistan—but there is still nothing like a global leviathan or a centralizing force. The world is coming together, but the international bureaucracy atop it is so infantile and underdeveloped that it cannot cope with growing instability.

And more complexity does lead to more instability. Today, we have several factors driving this relationship. First, we are seeing youth [population] bulges in many of the most unstable countries. Big deal if the world population is aging; that doesn't interest me for the next five or ten years. I care about the many countries or areas like the West Bank, Gaza, Nigeria, Zambia, and Kenya where over the next 20 years the population of young, unemployed males between the ages of 14 and 29 is going to grow. And as we all know from television, one thing that unites political unrest everywhere is that it's carried out by young males. Another factor is resource scarcity—the amount of potable water available throughout the Middle East, for instance, is going to decrease substantially over the next 25 years. When you put them together, these driving forces lead to sideswipes, such as the September 11 attacks. Another sideswipe could be an environmental event like an earthquake in an intensely settled area, like Egypt or China, that could lead to the removal of a strategic regime.

In *The Lexus and the Olive Tree*, Tom [Friedman] wrote that globalization doesn't end geopolitics. That's the key. Globalization is not necessarily *good* news; it's just *the* news. And the news could get scarier and scarier, because more interconnections will lead to complexity before they'll lead to stability.

Thomas Friedman Responds: State of Progress

Bob [Kaplan] brought up the role of the state and of governance; these are absolutely crucial issues. Some people believe that the state will wither away and matter less in an era of globalization. I believe exactly the opposite; the state matters much more in a globalized world.

Why? Well, the first thing we have to understand about globalization is that, oddly enough, it's not global. It affects different regions in different ways, and it links different countries in different ways. Yet every part of the world is directly or indirectly being globalized in some way. In this context, the state matters more, not less. If I could just use one image to describe the state—including political institutions, courts, oversight agencies, the entire system of governance—I would say it's like a plug, and it's the plug that your country uses to connect with globalization.

If that plug is corroded, corrupted, or the wires aren't connected, the flow between you and that global system—what I call the "electronic herd"—is going to be very distorted, and you are going to feel the effects of that distortion. But if the plug works well, the flow between you and the global system will be much more enriching.

The dirty secret about globalization—and it takes a lot of countries a long time to figure it out—is that the way to succeed in globalization is to focus on the fundamental. It's not about the wires or the bandwidth or about modems. It's about reading, writing, and arithmetic. It's about churches, synagogues, temples, and mosques. It's about the rule of law, good governance, institution building, free press, and a process of democratization. If you get these fundamentals right, then the wires will find you, and the wires will basically work. But if you get them wrong, nothing will save you.

Consider Botswana and Zimbabwe. Both countries have problems, but Botswana was probably in the top 20 percent of countries last year in per capita income growth. Zimbabwe was, I dare say, certainly in the bottom 20 percent. These two countries are right next to each other. Botswana has its problems, to be sure; it's not some ideal paradise. But it has decent democratization, decent institutions left over by the British, decent free press, and decent oversight and regulatory bodies.

And Zimbabwe? Zimbabwe has President Robert Mugabe. Now, if you told me right now that in five years I'll be able to get a fair trail in Zimbabwe, I'd say that Zimbabwe is going to be fine. But if you tell me I won't get a fair trial in Zimbabwe in five years, then it doesn't matter if everyone in Zimbabwe has an Internet address, a personal computer, a Palm Pilot, and a cell phone. If the institutions through which people have to operate to generate growth and interact with the global system are corrupted and corroded, then all the gadgetry in the world won't make a dime's worth of difference.

Or just compare Egypt and the East Asian countries. They started out with about the same per capita income in 1953, but now there's huge disparity between them. People who have studied these parts of the world point to two fundamental differences: One is the value placed on education. The other is how leaders justify their rule.

In Asia, which had autocratic regimes for several decades, leaders tended to justify their rule with a simple trade-off: Give me your democracy and I will give you prosperity. And people gave up many democratic rights and they got prosperity. The more prosperous they became, the more the relationship between them and the regime changed, until ultimately, you had a tip-over point, and these became democratic countries in almost every case. But what happened in Egypt? The leader said, don't judge me on whether I brought you a better standard of living; judge me on how I confronted the British, how I confronted the Americans, and how I confronted the Israelis. Give me your rights, and I'll give you the Arab-Israeli conflict. That was a bad trade. As a result, we see a huge gap between the two.

That's why with globalization, leadership matters more, not less. If you have the calcified Brezhnevite [referring to Leonid Brezhnev, a leader of the former communist, highly bureaucratic, Soviet Union] management that Egypt has, then it's no wonder that the Cairo skyline has barely changed in 50 years. But if your management "gets it"—as a corporation or a country—then you'll benefit from globalization.

Robert Kaplan Responds: State of War

I agree that good things are going to happen in a more global world (and humanists will duly celebrate them), but foreign policy crises are about what goes wrong. In the short run, I'm pessimistic. Remember that poverty does not lead to revolutions—development does. The revolutions in Mexico and France were preceded by years of dramatic and dynamic economic development, as well as urbanization and population movements. And what have we seen for the last 10 years? Incredible dynamics, with the middle classes emerging in China, Indonesia, and Brazil. But this development will not automatically lead to West Germany–style democracies. They may eventually, but for the next 20 or 30 years, they will experience more and more turbulence.

Of course, part of the trouble with some states is that they are states in name only. North Africa exemplifies this problem. In North Africa, you have three age-old civilization clusters: Egypt, Tunisia, and Morocco. They all have their problems, but all three are far healthier as states than, say, Algeria or Libya. Why is that? Why did Algeria and Libya get so radical and suffer through civil wars? Because they were never states to begin with.

Tunisia has been a state since Roman times. There's a state mentality there, even without democracy. Citizens argue about the budget and about education. The leader does not have to be oppressive, because a state community already exists. But Algeria and Libya are geographic expressions that were not cobbled together as states until relatively recently. The only institutionalizing force there is radical ideology.

Certainly, you could argue that Africa is in a class by itself. But consider the European Union. Despite its fits and starts, if you look at the European Union emerging out of a coal and steel consortium in the early 1950s, which includes France, Germany, the Benelux countries, and Italy, and then expanded to [Britain], etc., you see a gradual superstructure growing. At the same time, however, localism emerges. You see Catalonia and the German *lander* (states) reasserting themselves. And yet, I must ask, who today would fight for Belgium? Who would fight for Germany So, on balance, I think the state is weakening in Europe. But here's where Tom is right: States make war. And they make war because they have political accountability to people who are stuck in geographic space and because they must defend their citizenry and are therefore willing to take big risks on military strikes. The United Nations would never do that. To have the guts to make war, you have to have your own citizenry on your back; you must be physically responsible for them. I believe that, in the next 10 years or so, major wars will be very state-driven.

SOURCE: *Excerpt from Thomas Friedman and Robert Kaplan, "States of Discord," Foreign Policy, March/April 2002, pp. 64–70. Copyright 2002 by Foreign Policy. Reproduced with permission.*

QUESTIONS

Check Your Understanding

1. What do Friedman's and Kaplan's definitions of globalization have in common?
2. Why does Friedman describe the state as a plug?

Analyze the Issues

3. Which factors shaping the politics of development (pp. 492-502 in Chapter 12) were mentioned in the case study?
4. Why is Friedman optimistic about globalization and Kaplan is not? Did their arguments make you more or less optimistic about countries in the developing world?
5. According to the authors, why are some developing countries worse off (or better off) than others?
6. Explain the notion that complexity leads to more instability. Do you agree with Kaplan's position that an increasingly complex world, made worse by globalization, will in fact lead to more instability?
7. Which, if any, of the theoretical approaches described in the chapter—notably, economic liberalism, neomercantilism, and neo-Marxism—fits Friedman and which, if any, fits Kaplan?

FOR FURTHER INFORMATION

To find out more about the globalization and development, consult the following sources:

William Pfaff, "For Latin America, Globalization Has Not Been Paying Off," *International Herald Tribune*, August 31, 2000.

Marc Plattner and Zaki Laidi, "Is Globalization Good for Democracy?" *Journal of Democracy*, vol. 2002, vol. 13, no. 3 (July 2002), pp. 54–79.

John T. Rourke, ed., "Is Economic Globalism a Positive Trend?" in *Taking Sides: Clashing Views on Controversial Issues in World Politics* (New York: McGraw-Hill/Dushkin, 2002), pp. 1–18.

James N. Rosenau, "The Complexities and Contradictions of Globalization," *Current History*, November 1997.

Tina Rosenberg, "Globalization," *New York Times Magazine*, August 18, 2002.

CHAPTER 13

The Global Environment and the Population Problem

KEY QUESTIONS RAISED IN THIS CHAPTER

1. What environmental factors help explain how human society began?

2. How have the industrial and scientific revolutions internationalized environmental problems?

3. What are the Earth's most serious environmental problems?

4. What is the international community doing to mediate global water problems?

5. What are the green and biotech revolutions?

6. Why can't we agree on a common strategy for protecting the global environment?

—The sedge is wither'd from the lake and no birds sing.

—JOHN KEATS

There is a lot of talk about saving planet Earth. But the Earth has gotten along a long time without us, and will get along a long time after we have gone. The main concern of the human race today is to keep the earth sufficiently people-friendly so that the 11 billion or so human beings we expect to inhabit the planet by 2050 will be able to survive. Keeping the planet people-friendly means repairing environmental damage that now threatens human and other forms of Earth life, and developing sustainable forms of agriculture, animal and fish husbandry, industry and lifestyles that can accommodate increased numbers of humans without breaking down the earth's ecosystems. These tasks are global in scope. They cannot be accomplished by single states acting alone but require—perhaps more than any other global problem—dedicated, focused, long-term international cooperation.

Human beings have caused and overcome environmental problems since the dawn of the human race. The first humanoids may have come down out of the trees looking for food when their harvest of fruits and nuts became scarce. Certainly, the first hunter-gatherers moved from place to place following the seasons or looking for new sources of food as weather changes, overgrazing, or hunting reduced their local food source. Early in their settlement of Central America, the Amerindians exhausted the animal protein available and so had to turn to the arduous work of domesticating wild corn and beans to maintain their protein intake. Humankind's shift to agriculture so increased available food that agricultural populations grew and attracted the envious attention of hunting tribes that had not yet made the shift. Successful agriculture required water. Thus, the first city-states, followed by imperial systems of government, arose to manage the huge task of irrigation construction and maintenance. Walled cities, like Jericho in Israel, came into being to protect the settlers and their water supply from predatory nomads, and with the cities came trade, civilization, and environmental problems. We know from the historical evidence that the first city-states between the Tigris and Euphrates rivers, and along the Ganges River between India and Pakistan, ceased to exist because of the salting of the irrigation channels caused by primitive ditch construction, and erosion from the cutting of forests ever further up the river banks. Archaeology tells a similar story of environmental degradation as the key to the collapse of the Mayan civilization in Central America.

Desertification
The process of becoming desert from land mismanagement or climate change.

The difference between the impact of earlier human societies on the environment and the impact of modern society today is one of scale. Today *deforestation* and **desertification** occur on a global scale. In early human history, tribes settled on bottom land along the rivers. Large portions of the planet were either hostile to human habitation or required a great deal of effort to cultivate. So environmental damage was local, and frequently could be remediated by a local solution or by migration to another location. In the twentieth century, the human race spread all over the globe, and except for the high mountains and the Arctic regions, humans now dominate the planet. As a result, problems such as water, air pollution, and soil degradation have become global in scale, requiring solutions at a global level that address specific ecological conditions at the local level. This chapter talks about these global problems.

Not only are the problems global in scale, many of them concern chemicals and man-made materials that have only recently been developed. The United States dropped the first atomic bombs on the Japanese cities of Hiroshima and Nagasaki in 1945. This action ushered in the atomic age. Instead of being the age of unlimited energy, as it was once thought it would be, the atomic era has raised the twin horrors of planetary collapse through nuclear war and the danger of worldwide radioactive fallout through nuclear accident or through the improper storage of nuclear waste.

As you saw in your case study in Chapter 1, the possibility of nuclear war can never be ruled out. Even more frightening, accidents at nuclear power plants have already occurred and can easily occur again. The world has experienced at least three major accidents. The first occurred in September 1957, with the explosion of an underground liquid waste container at a place called Mayak in Chelyabinsk Province in the central Ural Mountains of Russia. The explosion sent a radioactive cloud over 20,000 square kilometers. In the years following the blast, 10,000 people were relocated.[1] The second accident occurred in 1976 in the United States in the state of Pennsylvania, at a nuclear power plant called Three Mile Island. The third accident took place in 1986 in the town of Chernobyl, about 38 miles from the capital of Kiev in the then Soviet Republic of the Ukraine. The accident caused the roof to blow off of one of the six nuclear power plants there, immediately killing the 17 persons in the building and the firemen who went to put out the fire. In the immediate aftermath of the explosion, another 43 people died. Radiation fallout flew around the world, borne aloft by the prevailing winds. Radiation effects were observed in sheep in northern Scotland and along the coast of California. The whole world realized that a nuclear accident is a global affair with global implications.

Nuclear accidents are not the only modern man-made disasters affecting our planet. When the chemical DDT was first developed, it seemed the salvation of humankind from insect-borne diseases. The insecticide was first used during World War II to eradicate mosquitoes in the Asian tropics, where malaria, as well as yellow and dengue fever, were rampant, and where American soldiers were fighting. DDT came into widespread public use after the war. The chemical was to a large extent responsible for killing the mosquitoes that brought the polio epidemic to the U.S. East Coast in the late 1940s. By the 1950s, however, people began noticing that where DDT had been sprayed, there was no bird or insect life.

It took a courageous and determined scientist, Rachel Carson, to collect the data and do the research that proved just how toxic DDT was to the environment. Carson's book *Silent Spring,* published in 1961, turned America on to the extent and scope of our current environmental problems and marked the beginning of the modern environmental movement.

Since then the world has seen an ever-growing number of toxic chemical incidents. In 1979 a serious outbreak of anthrax, which took 64 lives, occurred in the city of Yekaterinburg, the home of former Russian president Boris Yeltsin.[2] On December 3, 1984, a toxic cloud of methyl isocyanate (MIC) gas enveloped the hundreds of shanties and huts surrounding a Union Carbide plant producing pesticides in Bhopal, India. Four months after the accident, the Indian government reported that 1,430 people had died. In 1991 the government reported 3,800 more dead and 11,000 more with serious disabilities. And most Americans know of Agent Orange, another Union Carbide chemical compound that was used to defoliate the forests in Vietnam.

People all over the world have become increasingly concerned with the impact of pesticides and herbicides on human health. Thus, you may have an "organic" food shop in your neighborhood, serving people who wish to avoid food that has been sprayed with herbicides. The most recent global outcry has been over advances in biotechnology that change gene systems in plants and that clone animals.

To find out how a nuclear power plant works, go to **www.ablongman.com/ duncan.**

To find out more about the nuclear tragedy at Mayak, go to **www.ablongman.com/ duncan.**

For a blow by blow account of the nuclear accident at Three Mile Island, go to **www.ablongman.com/ duncan.**

For an account of the accident at Chernobyl, go to **www.ablongman.com/ duncan.**

For an account of the chemical accident in Bhopal, India, go to **www.ablongman.com/ duncan.**

For more information on Agent Orange, go to **www.ablongman.com/ duncan.**

To date, every scientific advance in warfare, agriculture, and health has brought heretofore unknown consequences. The question is: Can the peoples of the earth, represented by the international community, learn to alleviate old environmental threats and at the same time respond effectively to new, as yet unknown, environmental challenges?

This chapter is designed to start you thinking about how you would answer that question. The human race now dominates the planet. Most other flora, fauna, and inert matter are under our control. We would like to be wise stewards, but international stewardship over the whole world so far requires more cooperative intent and desire than we have yet demonstrated. As this text has shown, decentralizing forces like ethnic nationalism, religious conflict, unresolved demands for independence, and fears of attacks from uncontrolled terrorist NGOs occupy our full attention. To understand the scope of this dilemma, we will first review how the initial interactions between human beings and their natural surroundings were shaped by environmental factors that continue to shape human society today. The next section looks at the impact on planet Earth of the industrial and scientific revolutions of the past two centuries, followed by a brief review of our planet's most serious environmental problems caused in large part by those revolutions. We then turn to ways in which the international community is trying to alleviate these problems. Our final section as well as the chapter's case study explore the so-called green and biotech revolutions and the pros and cons of the application of genetic engineering to agriculture and human reproduction. As you go through the chapter, you will see that although it seems obvious that the international community has to cooperate to safeguard its future, the drive to secure the short-term economic and political survival of individual states and substate units (ethnic groups) has brought the negative decentralizing tendencies to the fore.

What Environmental Factors Help Explain How Human Society Began?

In Chapter 7 you learned that geography has had a profound impact on human development. The territories that people inhabit condition their level of development and their ability to become a great power. In Chapter 10, you learned that one of the greatest inequities among states is the unequal distribution of natural resources. Now we will turn the discussion on its head. Instead of looking at potential territorial power bases, we ask what environmental factors favored the formation of human society and remain essential to the life of any community. Although every society faces certain environmental restrictions, for some regions, notably in Saharan Africa, in Siberia, and the Canadian Arctic, the environmental conditions are so unfavorable as to make sustaining human life very difficult.

The first factor probably any of us would mention is water. A steady and dependable source of water was crucial for the emergence of settled human society on this planet. Farming demands a lot of water, so river basins were the logical locations for the first agricultural communities.

Second, early human society needed a moderate climate where it was relatively easy to keep warm. Until recently, no humans lived on Antarctica, and only a few hardy tribes lived in the Arctic. And until very recently, there were no large cities in the Arctic. Even now the populations of the largest Arctic cities do not exceed the populations of medium-sized cities in the rest of the world. They never will. The living conditions in the Arctic simply do not encourage large numbers of people to move there.

The tropics also were not densely settled until recent times. While their warm climate is favorable to human beings, it is also favorable to disease-causing microbes. Neither the Congo River basin nor the Amazon River basin was densely settled until modern times. The indigenous tribes that formerly occupied the tropics were largely hunter-gatherers who had, over the millennia, adapted to a climate that carried lethal infections and where crop growing was difficult. Today, as many parts of the Amazon forest are being cut down and replaced with large plantations, we have learned that those early peoples were very wise. The soil of the rain forest provides few of the nutrients for its trees and plants and hence few nutrients for an agricultural crop like corn. Essential to the survival of tropical trees is the rain forest *canopy,* the huge leafy green treetops that umbrella-style cover the forest.

So with these two essentials—access to freshwater and a moderate climate—we look for the origins of settled human society along the Earth's big rivers, like the Nile and the Ganges, and on the land between the Tigris and Euphrates rivers (Mesopotamia). But perhaps you will ask, Why along those rivers? Why not along the Mississippi? Why not in a location with temperate climate in the Americas, like San Diego or Mexico? Read the story of Mesopotamia on the Web Exploration in the margin, and see if you can find the answers.

The story of Mesopotamia points us to another vital factor in any society: ease of communication. From the very beginning, internation communication was crucial to societal development. In the Americas, the basic direction of transportation is from north to south. East-west or west-east movement in the Americas is foiled by the Rocky Mountain/Andean range, which runs the length of the hemisphere; by desert in both North and South America, and inland from the coastal mountains in California; and by the tropical rain forest of the Amazon River basin and Central America. However, if you travel from north to south, you travel away from a cold climate through a temperate, subtropical, and eventually tropical climate, and then back to a cold climate. Although the north-south route might have been the least arduous in terms of human effort, in terms of moving the cultural and eating habits acquired in the north to a southern locality or vice versa, such a move would have been very difficult.

The Incas, for example, built their empire on the cool mountaintops and plateaus of the Andes. Beyond these mountains to the north lay the thick, disease-ridden forests of Central America. Having adapted very successfully to the Andean climate, the Incas had little urge to penetrate the Central American tropical forests. Deserts and tropical forests likewise discouraged the Amerindian tribes of North America from moving south.

By contrast, as you learned in Chapter 7, the main direction of movement across Eurasia is horizontal, east-west or west-east. Human beings, animals, and plants were able to move across the central section of one huge land mass and remain essentially in the same climate. Thus, as they moved, they could expect to plant the seeds they brought with them and obtain similar results as in the last place they lived. In this way, a favorable geography enabled a great deal of sharing of information and technology across Eurasia at a very early stage of human development. The settlement of the Americas, with their natural barriers to movement, came much later, and the sharing of information and technology occurred on a much more restricted scale.

To learn more about Mesopotamia go to **www.ablongman.com/ duncan.**

These factors had an enormous impact on where and how humans first developed, and they still do today. The coming of the Europeans to the Americas transferred the accumulated experience of Europe to the temperate zones of the New World in a very short time. Today all around the globe, the temperate lands retain their geographic and ecological advantages over areas of climate extremes. The most trade and sharing of information occurs between states in the temperate climate zones. And the states located in the tropics continue to have difficulties with disease (AIDS), agricultural and industrial development (land reform, technology), and the establishment of permanent forms of government.

We see then that the temperate lands offer the most favorable environmental conditions for a state to grow and prosper. But no location, no matter how well endowed by nature, can offer unlimited advantages. Sooner or later, human societies will exhaust the resources closest to them or easiest to obtain and will need to find new ways to exploit resources that might be farther afield. The invention of these new methods and their practical application we call technology. While the simple tools that humankind used throughout most of its history did over time cause environmental stress, the new technology has caused more environmental damage in a single generation than the old ways had produced in several centuries. It also has created huge economic inequalities between those countries that started the revolutions and systematically improved the technologies and those countries that had to import the technologies from abroad. To understand the impact of science and technology on the natural and man-made world, we turn to the next section.

How Have the Industrial and Scientific Revolutions Internationalized Environmental Problems?

The terms *industrial and scientific revolutions* refer to a historical process whereby human beings, by applying science and ingenuity, created tools and instruments that enable us to do things we otherwise would not be able to do.[3] We use the word *revolution* to describe the process because technological inventions and their incorporation into daily life literally revolutionized the way people live. For example, before the wheel was invented, humans could only travel on foot or on the backs of animals. The wheel made it possible to move much larger loads than could be moved on the back of one person or animal. The wheel also transformed the art of pottery making and the method for moving water from an irrigation canal to the fields where it was needed. The mass use of gunpowder as a weapon in the fifteenth and sixteenth centuries made the fortress-like medieval stone castles irrelevant. As a result, small dukedoms and earldoms were unable to withstand the power amassed by a wealthy monarch. Medieval Europe gave way to modern Europe with its nation-states, as castles gave way to country estates and urban palaces.

We talked in Chapter 2 about the dramatic changes in the human condition brought about by Gutenberg's invention of movable type. When railroads first made their appearance, people said that traveling at 20 miles an hour would ruin one's health or cause a heart attack. Who could then have foreseen the change in the national landscape produced by the mass adoption of the automobile as the chief mode of transportation in the United States?

Technologies not only transform our way of life, they change the way we think about our world. Fifteenth-century Europe was recovering from a terrible plague that had decimated the human population. Many areas had long since run out of wood, and most of the gold and silver mines on the continent had been mined to the technological limits of the mining machinery at the time. Environmental degradation was becoming increasingly visible. At the same time, the Chinese compass, the European invention of the astrolabe, and scientific proof that the earth was round brought together a set of technologies that gave the European sailors confidence to sail across unchartered oceans. The knowledge they brought back of the lands they had found changed the way Europe thought about itself and the world. In a single century, Europe leaped from a musty backwater of the planet to the center of global activity. During the next two centuries, the application of technology for industrial purposes, known as the industrial revolution, enabled Europe and then the United States to take the lead in the expansion of international trade and the conduct of international affairs.

The Industrial Revolution

We tend to divide the **industrial revolution** into a series of phases based on energy use and type of human labor replaced by machines. (See Table 13.1).

The first phase, the preparatory period, ran from the mid-eighteenth century into the nineteenth century. All products were literally made by hand. The period was marked by a shift from wood as the primary energy source to coal. By the eighteenth century, wood was a scarce resource in Europe. Virtually all the original European forest had been cut down and replanted. Demand for wood was a driving force behind the English encouragement of colonies in the New World, where logging proceeded at an unprecedented pace. By the Battle of Yorktown in 1783, the last battle of the American Revolution, the once heavily wooded seaboard of the original colonies had become open fields. England turned to coal.

The mining and use of coal demanded a much higher concentration of resources. This brings us to *the second phase* of the industrial revolution, the take-off,

Industrial Revolution
A rapid major change in the economy of a country or region characterized initially by the general introduction of power-driven machinery and later by significant changes, usually through automation, of existing types and uses of machines; the replacement of first physical and then mental forms of human labor by machines.

TABLE 13.1   The Four Phases of the Industrial Revolution

Phase	Name	Energy Source	Dominant Technology
1	Preparatory	Wood; Shift to coal	Handwork, "putting out" of or the subcontracting production, to households, beginning of small factories (mainly in textiles)
2	First industrial or take-off	Coal	Steam engine, mechanization of simple kinds of labor, mechanized looms, the railroad, smokestack industries
3	Second industrial or automation revolution	Gasoline, electricity	Automobile, airplane, electric light; complex forms of labor replaced by automated programs
4	Third industrial or information revolution	Electricity, natural gas, wind, solar	Computer, fiberoptic cable, TV, cellphone, biotechnology, automated processes that replace linear forms of human thought

Ford Model T: The car that, for better or for worse, made automobile transportation accessible to the masses.

where coal is king and mass production comes into being. The key invention, the steam engine, made mass production economical by dramatically reducing the cost of land and sea transportation. The steam engine pumped the water out of the coal mines, transported the mined coal to smelters over the new railroads, and powered the smelters. Smelters provided the iron for construction of the steam engine, the rails on which the trains traveled, the mining equipment, and ultimately, the ships that rapidly distributed the new products such as textiles and iron implements. Thus, the second phase of the industrial revolution involved the replacement of human labor by machine labor. The prime example of this process was the development of the mechanical loom, which replaced cottage handwork with linen and cotton goods woven on mechanical machinery in factories.

The third phase of the industrial revolution saw the beginning of *automation*. It began at the end of the nineteenth century, with the successful harnessing of electricity, petroleum and natural gas through the use of fossil fuels and hydropower. The technological inventions and developments that accommodated these new energy types were the internal combustion engine, and the chemical and metallurgical industries. Chemical processes synthesized man-made fabrics, replaced natural dyes made from flowers and minerals with chemical dyes, and produced the first chemical pharmaceuticals. Metallurgy made possible the mass production assembly line first put into place by Henry Ford.

The age of the automobile and airplane saw a network of railroads and roadways leading into and around cities, and later to and from airports. To escape the pollution of the inner city, the better-off moved out, first along the railroad lines and then along the newly built roads. By the last quarter of the nineteenth century, the suburbs had come into being. In the United States, the flight of the middle and upper class brought urban blight and inner-city ghettos.[4] The new kinds of energy required even greater outlays of capital than that needed for coal, to build pipelines and power lines to transport fuel to the new sprawling **megalopolis** or mega-city. Slowly but surely the spaces between the cities filled in. Much of the east and west coasts of the United States and most of Western Europe became one vast suburbia. And the development of plastics generated the throwaway society.

The microchip, biotechnology, and advanced materials ushered in the *fourth phase* of the industrial revolution, often called the **information revolution.** In a few decades the computer has revolutionized society. As we saw in Chapter 1, the microchip globalized national economies by enabling us to transmit data around the world in seconds. We went to the moon and saw "spaceship earth" in its entirety from afar. No longer is the earth our sole reference point. The universe has become our yardstick and the biosphere is now the dominant image.[5] Technology has forged a global interdependence that has undermined our concepts of national sovereignty and international behavior, and has heightened our vulnerability as passengers aboard a fragile and unique planet.

Most of you grew up in the fourth phase of the industrial revolution. Your great grandparents lived through the second and third phases. Today about three-quarters of the globe is making the transition to the second and third phase. The important point is that as the revolution has progressed, it has spread further and further around the globe until in the information revolution, the economies of individual regions and countries have become globalized. The result has been the almost total destruction of pre-industrial society, accompanied by a very uneven distribution of economic and environmental costs among the wealthy industrialized states and the poor developing states.

The Benefits and Costs of Technology

The uneven distribution of technology creates distortions in technology use and consequently in the consumption of energy and other natural resources. First, the concentration of technology use in the northern industrialized states produces one set of benefits and costs in terms of environmental pollution. Second, the continuation of traditional lifestyles on the edge of the more technologically advanced cities in the less developed countries (LDCs) poses costs and benefits associated with public health and the control of disease. We shall look at the benefits and costs of technology first and the benefits and costs of applying science to public health in the next section.

Technology has arguably raised the standard of living in virtually every country on the globe. Modern conveniences have made life easier for all of us fortunate enough to have them and are sought after by people in countries that are striving to industrialize. Throughout the world, the cell phone and E-mail have become the most common modes of communication. As a matter of principle, most agree that everyone ought to share the benefits that technology has brought, and we believe in *la dolce vita* (the sweet life) for all. The problem is that the application of technology does not bring only benefits. It also brings unpleasant environmental surprises.

The first major problem with technology, as Canadian scientist H. Brook explains,[6] is that the benefits of an invention increase linearly in proportion to its scale of application, whereas environmental and social problems resulting from the

Megalopolis

A huge city. The term is used to describe a vast human settlement that transcends original city limits and spills over into the city's suburbs and the city beyond. The entire East Coast of the United States may be described as a megalopolis.

Information Revolution

The explosion in information that has become available to people across the world in the form of television news (CNN) and cyberspace (fiber optics, satellites, Internet, and World Wide Web).

SOURCE: *Mike Thompson,* Detroit Free Press, *Copley News Service.*

application increase nonlinearly or geometrically as the scale of application rises. By the time the negative consequences of the technology register in the public consciousness, society can no longer do without it. Take the automobile, for example. Despite the old timers teasing, "Why don't you get a horse!" the benefits of driving a car so clearly outweighed the problems of caring for and feeding a horse that purchases of new cars steadily increased in the early years of the twentieth century. With the arrival of Henry Ford's mass production assembly line, cars became affordable for everyone. What freedom, what speed! The road opened up before the motorist! And as fast as they could think them up, the new automobile companies provided innovations and adapted their product to the public's needs. Paved roads came into being. As the numbers of automobile owners increased, the automobile industry consolidated. Firms that could not keep up with the competition went out of business or were bought up. Today three major U.S. auto firms control all U.S. production of automotive vehicles: General Motors, Ford Motor Company, and Chrysler-Daimler Benz.

Success froze companies into a particular mode of operation that discouraged risk taking and new ventures. Why change behavior if you already dominate the market? Change risked jeopardizing capital investment, marketing structure, and supporting bureaucracies. In the early days of the automobile, manufacturers offered many options and choices. Gradually one variant of the internal combustion engine predominated, driving the other options out of the market. The logic of mass production and economies of scale to beat the competition forced companies to cut back on technical options and limit research leading to improvements.

In 1972 when Congress passed the Clean Air Act requiring automobile producers to clean up pollution emissions from automobiles, General Motors was unable to provide a quick fix. It took the company more than ten years to get a catalytic converter onto its passenger cars. Meanwhile, the still-growing, more competitive, and more flexible Japanese carmakers had a converter on their models in half that time. The U.S. car companies used their economic clout to prevaricate, object, and complain. Their major coup was to prevent Congress from mandating pollution controls on the really big polluters: small trucks, pickups, and what later came to be called SUVs.

Technological Monoculture   The term used to describe a combination of market domination and political, economic, and social influence is **technological monoculture**, and as noted, the auto industry is an excellent example. The annual income of General Motors is larger than the GDP of all but the wealthiest countries. Furthermore, the auto industry has tight links with the petroleum, synthetic, and natural rubber industries. It has extended its production network worldwide. In order that we may use the automobile efficiently and safely, the U.S. government has paved the nation from one end to the other with four-lane highways. To service the cars, small businesses have set up public parking lots, repair shops, delis, and foodmarts at the gasoline stations that line the streets of our towns and villages. Auto travel takes off where air travel ends through the car rental business anchored at the airport. The automotive industry with its supporting systems now constitutes a more and more self-contained social system that is unable to adapt to the changes brought about by its success.

> **Technological Monoculture**
> The domination of the market by one variant of a technology utilized in a specific industrial sector by a company or group of companies and the use of this domination for political, economic, and social influence.

After Mexico City, Los Angeles is probably the most polluted city in the world.[7] While the Los Angeles government can crack down on gasoline-powered lawn mowers and the types of machines and chemicals used by your corner dry cleaner, it has proved ineffective in cracking down on gasoline-powered cars. Millions of people need to get here from there every day. Their needs keep millions of other people employed maintaining roads, selling gasoline and groceries, and building malls where you can park your car and shop. Short of a major economic collapse, the prospects are dim that Americans will be able to adapt their car-based life style to the exigencies of global climate change and the rise in global consumption of energy. Our whole social system is built on it. When the price of gas goes up at the pumps, pressure is put on OPEC countries to produce more oil. Few in number are the voices that suggest turning to smaller cars or using alternative transportation.

Reduction in Variability   Technological monoculture leads to the second problem with technology: *reduction in variability,* both within human society and in the environment where that society is situated. Just as the domestication of plants and animals thousands of years ago led to the concentration of certain flora and fauna on human-managed land to the exclusion of other species, so technology is a selective process. By contrast, healthy natural ecosystems are marked by high variability. Human activity impacts on these systems in ways that only now are beginning to be understood. All human management of the environment, whether it be the city, farm, or wilderness, provokes a response from the ecosystem as it tries to adapt to the impact of human disturbance. (See Figure 13.1 for a visual model of the process.)

In the figure, human-managed society is shown as interacting with the earth's ecosystems and the global biochemical cycles that moderate our atmosphere. Human society takes from those ecosystems the renewable and nonrenewable resources humans want, thereby changing the original ecosystems in that location. However, this ecosystem over time has found a stable equilibrium between its diverse elements through its intersection with the global biochemical cycles in what is

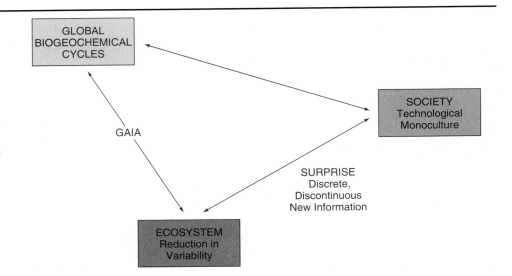

FIGURE 13.1

Model of the Gaia Principle and Environmental Surprise

SOURCE: *Barbara Jancar-Webster, "Technology and Environment in Eastern Europe" in James R. Scanlan (ed.), Technology, Culture, and Development: The Experience of the Soviet Model (Armonk, NY: M. E. Sharpe, 1992), p. 178.*

called the *gaia* (from the ancient Greek word for earth) principle. You may pick up a handful of dirt and see only dirt, but it contains a diverse array of bacteria that sustain each other and the soil around them in innumerable ways. When human activity intrudes upon that stable equilibrium formed from all those varied patterns, the ecosystem is not passive. It responds to reach a new equilibrium based on its interactions with the global biochemical cycles and the extent and intensity of the human impact. The reaction is always a reduction in the variety of patterns and in the number of plants and animal species.

Hawaii provides an example of the consequences of human management of the environment that led to reduction in variability. Because of its inaccessible location in the middle of the Pacific Ocean, Hawaii had perhaps the most diverse plant and animal life of any place on earth. Two thousand years ago the first humans arrived from Polynesia bringing their plants, animals, and agricultural technology. These *exotic* or foreign species thrived in the Hawaiian climate, having left their natural competitors behind. By contrast, the weaker Hawaiian species became extinct. The process was accelerated after the arrival of Americans and Europeans in the nineteenth century with their industrial enterprises and the practice of covering large amounts of land with only one crop. Today, very few native species of plant or animal survive in the entire archipelago. The rich ecosystem reacted to human intrusion with a reduction in variability. What took millions of years to evolve became extinct in two centuries—its original web of biodiversity supplanted by an imported human management that favors urban complexes, suburban land use, and agricultural monoculture.[8]

Reduction in variability has speeded up even more in the twenty-first century because of the huge capabilities of our earthmoving and construction technology, the high speed of travel, and the numbers of people on the move in the world. We have become a species on a planet at risk. When the human impact is too strong, nature reacts to the stress through the element of surprise. Let us look at some examples of this phenomenon.

The Yorkshire countryside in England was once covered with temperate forest, filled with varied species of hardwoods including oaks, maple, and beech. But it has been grazed over for so long that all the roots of the original trees have died, leaving a barren moor. The moor is one of the happier results of reduction in variability and an example of an ecosystem that appears to have adjusted to human intrusion with minimum surprise. Covered with heather and rich in peat, the moor has traditionally provided fuel for the local farmers and food for their sheep.

Flooding is another example of surprise. Deforestation on hillsides exposes the soils on the hills to the elements. With no trees to hold the soil in place, the rain washes the soil down hill. When deforestation is combined with agriculture on this marginal land, rain washes away both the homesteads and the planted areas with the rest of the soil. People not only lose their homes and livelihood, thousands can die, as they did in the catastrophic floods in China in 2001. Similarly, the deserts in Africa, expanding due to overgrazing of marginal grassland and the absence of rain, have contributed to waves of famine in Saharan Africa. Problems like famine and floods have necessitated the mounting of global efforts to rescue the victims, feed the hungry, and tend the sick. Surprise in the world today moves quickly from the local to the international system level.

Environmental Surprise   Why does society experience surprise, and can it learn to avoid those consequences? Yes and no. Humans can predict some consequences of human management of the environment but not all of them. Because our management is selective and rigid, and nature's response adaptive and resilient, we can never be sure how or when nature will react. Surprise can come in several forms. Desertification is one form of surprise. Other times surprise can occur as an individual event, like the nuclear power plant explosion at Chernobyl or the outbreak of foot and mouth disease in Europe in 2001. Sometimes a consequence becomes obvious as a result of the buildup of certain phenomena over a long period of time, like dangerous levels of sulfur dioxide or lead in the air, deforestation, or the ozone hole. Sometimes surprise can come from the emergence of new information such as that concerning global warming, acid rain, and the development of more precise methodologies and instruments to measure toxicity in water. The long-term buildups may not manifest themselves in a single generation. Our children or our children's children may be required to devise solutions to problems we, our parents, or grandparents set in motion.

Until recently, states and international organizations tended to downplay the obviously negative relationship between industrialization and environmental pollution. They no longer do so (see box Why It Matters to You: Needed—More Miles per Gallon). Industrialization has produced and continues to contaminate those environmental factors that this chapter argued were vital for continued human existence: access to fresh water, moderate climate, and ease of communication.

If we understand the process by which a technology produces environmental surprise, the international community has a faint chance of anticipating that surprise and perhaps heading it off in another part of the world. However, the more the world adopts certain forms of technological monoculture, the more difficult it is to change the system under increased environmental stress.

To learn more about "future shock" and human ability to adapt, go to **www.ablongman.com/ duncan.**

The Benefits of Applying Science to Health

As with technology, applied science has also proven to be a Pandora's box of benefits and costs. While its benefits were first applied in Europe and the United States, its major contribution today has been to the improved health of Third World states.

WHY IT MATTERS TO YOU

Needed—More Miles per Gallon

Understanding how technology impacts the environment is of tremendous importance in today's world. From the first part of this chapter, you may have deduced that the United States has one of the best mixes of environmental factors in the world, which significantly contributes to the well-being of its citizens. It also has one of the most advanced levels of applied technology. Worldwide, the greatest increase in energy use in the past ten years has occurred in transportation, with the United States leading the way in consumption of gasoline per capita. The U.S. consumption of gasoline makes this country number one in production of CO_2, one of the greenhouse gases contributing to global warming. High gasoline consumption also has created the permanent smog belts along the west and east coasts, and is a major contributor to acid rain and pollution of lakes in the northeast and Canada. Yet we did not become aware of the environmental surprise lurking in the gasoline engine until several generations of Americans had grown accustomed to its use.

Gasoline use in Asia is expected to increase twice as fast as our use in the next ten years. Where will the energy come from? Will automobiles have to be rationed? Who will decide whether you can have two cars or no car? How will the fumes from millions of more vehicles affect our planet's atmosphere? What alternative modes of transportation can the world adopt? How can we ensure that these modes will be available when we need them? All these questions require an international response that so far has been weak. If having a car matters to you, how about considering or an engineering career in alternative fuels or hydrogen engines?

Probably the most significant application of science to human health has been the understanding and prevention of disease. Epidemic disease has been the scourge of humankind since the dawn of civilization. Up until the nineteenth century, the world's population had been hostage to the seemingly random and ferocious outbreaks of epidemics, which frequently killed 60 to 70 percent of a city's population. Typhus, cholera, schistosomiasis, tuberculosis, smallpox, yellow fever, influenza, and malaria have been the perennial diseases of humankind. When humans lived an essentially rural existence, the customs and rituals developed over the centuries to prevent infection or limit the spread of disease worked remarkably well. Most traditional religions have rituals and practices that effectively limit either the growth of a population to the critical mass beyond which epidemics occur, or that prevent a disease from spreading through some kind of quarantine or specific taboo. All religions, for example, insist on the institution of marriage—with the bride a virgin—and condemn adultery, especially on the part of the woman. Traditional societies further encouraged women to breastfeed their children for three years, as breastfeeding women tended to be less fertile and children who were breastfeeding gained immunity from most infectious diseases. These practices worked to limit population growth and to minimize infection. In Asia today, many women are denied the right to remarry if widowed. We are used to thinking of these practices as dehumanizing to women, as indeed they are. But they also constitute a form of birth control that may also be seen as a form of disease control.

In the cities, custom and habit work less well, particularly during times like today, when migration to urban centers occurs on a mass scale. The very density of ur-

HISTORICAL PERSPECTIVE

How Sanitation Eradicated Cholera in Europe

An outbreak of cholera in England in 1832 brought about the establishment of local boards of health. The terrifying news that a new outbreak was moving across Europe in 1848 caused Parliament to authorize a Central Board of Health to supervise and manage the local boards. The Central Board wasted no time enacting far-reaching programs of public sanitation that reformers had advocated for over a decade. The Board was given legal powers to enforce its regulations. It thus removed innumerable sources of filth from British towns and cities, and began to install water and sewer systems all over the country.

France and Germany followed England's example. In Germany, however, Hamburg remained self-governing and refused to go to the expense of a modern sewer system. Not convinced that untreated water had anything to do with cholera, the city took its water from the Elbe River without special treatment. Downriver, in the Prussian city of Altona, however, the Prussian government installed a water filtration system. The Hamburg city fathers had reason to regret their failure to act. In 1892 cholera came back to Europe. Altona was spared the epidemic while Hamburg bore its full force.[9] Thus, by the end of the nineteenth century, all of Western Europe implemented water treatment systems, including sewage plants.

---

ban populations has historically made the city a perfect target for epidemic disease. So destructive of human life was the Black Death that raged through Europe in the fifteenth century that many scholars believe it undermined the sociopolitical system and contributed to the rise of new forms of government and religion that did not insist on absolute authority. The increase in size of European cities in particular during the seventeenth century created optimum conditions for the spread of plagues. The seventeenth-century plague memorials all over Europe testify to the virulence of epidemics. Advances in the science of medicine eventually brought the dreaded epidemics under control. Let us take a look at three of the most significant advances.

New Medical Technology   The invention of the microscope (in 1610) enabled European scientists for the first time to see organisms invisible to the naked eye. In due time, the bacilli causing the major epidemics were identified. Even more remarkable were the discoveries of how to prevent various diseases or render the bacilli impotent.

Sanitation   With the new weapon of science, Europe departed from the traditional approaches to treating disease. The progressive enactment of sanitation and water treatment programs in all of Europe's major cities and eventually in the countryside brought epidemics under control for the first time in history and made cities safe for habitation. (See box Historical Perspective: How Sanitation Eradicated Cholera.)

During the nineteenth century, Western colonial administrations helped spread scientific medical practice around the globe. As the world's regions adopted Western sanitation measures and used vaccines to inoculate their populations against disease, the death rate of both Western and non-Western countries dropped.

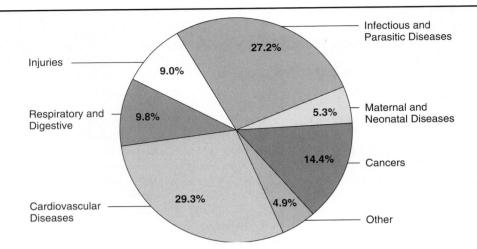

FIGURE 13.2

Leading Causes of Death, 2001

SOURCE: The World Health Organization, World Health Report, 2002, Annex: Table 2 "Death by Cause, Sex, and Mortality Stratum in WHO Regions," http://www.who.int/whr/en/ or http://www.who.int/whr/2002/en/

Vaccines, Antibiotics, Insecticides   In the twentieth century, science turned its attention to the eradication of disease. At the turn of that century, yellow fever was the focus of U.S. military attention because the disease threatened U.S. expansion into the Caribbean. Although yellow fever was a viral disease, Walter Reed went to Cuba and proved that mosquitoes spread it. In 1901 a campaign was launched to eliminate yellow fever from Havana by attacking mosquito-breeding places. Forty years later, the invention of DDT contributed to the U.S. victory over Japan by protecting U.S. troops from malaria and yellow fever. In 2000 New York City health officials used the same approach to limit the spread of the West Nile virus as was used in Havana 100 years earlier. They attacked mosquito-breeding places. Only this time they used highly sophisticated bioengineered chemicals.

In the twentieth century, most of the scientific work on disease has been performed at the national level: in the medical research community, in university and government laboratories, and in hospitals. The U.S. Center for Disease Control in Atlanta, Georgia, has been a key player in collecting data and providing timely warnings of the path of an epidemic. Since World War II, the World Health Organization has led the way in distributing the results of this research—the vaccines and medications— and in providing the health workers to deliver the medication to afflicted countries, particularly the LDCs. When the discovery of penicillin during World War II led to the virtual eradication of TB in the 1950s and 1960s, it looked as if international cooperation in science had conquered all the world's major diseases.

Then came AIDS in the 1980s. AIDS is now of epidemic proportions, particularly in Russia and China. The 1990s saw the emergence of a more deadly TB bacillus, the West Nile virus, Ebola Hemorrhagic Fever, and other new diseases. In 1991, cholera swept down the west coast of South America, the first such outbreak in nearly a century in the Americas. Between 1991 and 1995 it infected 1 million people and killed 11,000.[10] In 2003, a killer virus known as severe acute respiratory syndrome (SARS) was first identified in Hong Kong and in a very short time had infected people all over the planet sowing panic in its path. Figure 13.2 shows that infectious diseases represented over 27 percent of the leading causes of death in 2001—83 percent of these deaths occurred in the LDCs.

Why have old diseases returned, and why do new viruses keep appearing? The immediate answer to that question is found in the substandard living conditions

THE VIEW FROM Africa and the Developing World

Selected Facts

- In Africa, 30 percent of the rural water supply systems are not functioning at any one time. In Latin America and the Caribbean only 4 percent are not functioning.
- Only a negligible percent of urban wastewater was reported treated in Africa in 1998.
- Diarrheal diseases claim the lives of nearly 2 million children every year and have killed more children in the past 10 years than all people lost to armed conflict since World War II.
- Nine out of ten malaria cases occur in Sub-Saharan Africa.

- HIV/AIDS is the leading cause of death in adolescents aged 15 and older in the LDCs.
- Children constitute half of the world's 10 million environmental refugees displaced by natural catastrophes, degraded land, or armed conflict and land mines.
- In the past decade 2 million children have been killed in armed conflict.

SOURCE: United Nations Environment Programme, United Nations Children's Fund and World Health Organization, *Children in the New Millennium: Environmental Impact on Health*, (UNEP, UNICEF and WHO, 2002), pp. 22, 38 and 47.

and malnutrition that set entire populations at risk in LDCs. Insufficient and contaminated water supplies are highways carrying waterborne infections and disease to populations whose immune systems are already weakened from malnutrition brought on by the farming of lands degraded by overuse, drought, and pesticides. As thousands migrate to cities in search of a living, they are unable to find affordable housing, and so are forced to live in shacks put together from scrap metal, wood, and cardboard. These homes have inadequate waste disposal, no plumbing, and are often close to open waste dumps that create hazardous environmental conditions to those living nearby. The newcomers, like the relatives they left behind in the country, have no money and few resources to obtain food. In the barrios surrounding the major cities of the LDCs (as we know from Chapter 10), sanitation and clean water are very difficult to come by, and in these conditions, insects and rats multiply. The overtaxed urban administration finds itself without sufficient resources to confront the problem properly. And the epidemics return (see box The View from Africa and the Developing World).

The second answer lies in the millions of people who are on the move in our modern world. Driven out of their homes by famine, joblessness, and low pay, people can become desperate enough to brave any odds to live their dream of a better life in the United States or Western Europe. Wherever these people move, they carry with them whatever infections they may have at the time, thus globalizing disease.

Figures 13.3A and B give a picture of the outflows and inflows of migration around the world. Annual net migration means that the total outflow or inflow of individuals from an area has been added up and then divided by the number of years the study was underway, in this case five. The net migration from Asia thus has averaged about 1.3 million persons a year, and from Latin America around 600,000 persons a year. However, if you look at the rate of migration, you get a different picture. Because the Asian population is so large, the migration *rate* is a mere

FIGURES 13.3A & B

Net Annual Migration Totals and Rates, 1995–2000

SOURCE: *Data derived from United Nations, Department of Economic and Social Affairs, Population Division, International Migration Report 2002 (New York: United Nations Presss, 2002) pp. 11–15 and UN Wall Graph, "International Migration, 2002."*

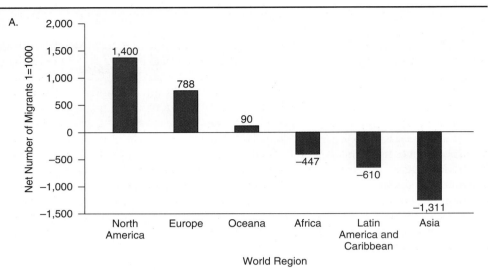

A.

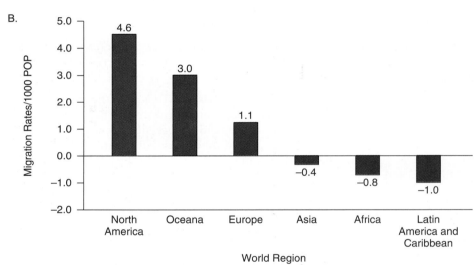

B.

0.4 individuals per 100,000 population, while Latin America's a minus 1. Put simply, these populations are so huge that even when a very large number of people emigrate, their emigration has little impact on overall regional population size. By contrast, Europe and North America have experienced substantial net inflows of population. Immigration now accounts for 89 percent of Europe's population growth and is the substantial reason why the population growth rate in the United States is a positive number. Airplane travel facilitates this movement of population, since you can fly from Asia to Europe or North America in less than a day.

However, as shown by the catastrophic die-off of the Amerindian from infectious disease brought by the Europeans, a microbe that has stabilized and been rendered relatively harmless to its home population can decimate a population on another continent. And so, at the beginning of the twenty-first century, the first world finds that it is no longer safe from the spread of contagious diseases but must now seek to reduce the risk of infection by going abroad to solve public health problems in the developing countries.

This section has pointed out that while science was first applied to health problems in the West, it proved to be a major benefactor of the developing world when it was applied there. After World War II, it looked like the major infectious diseases were about to be eradicated worldwide. However, mass migration to the cities as the LDCs developed industry, the inability of the LDC governments to provide adequate sanitation and housing, and the rapid movement of large numbers of peoples by air have brought the old diseases back with greater virulence than ever, and introduced new ones. Once again, the containment of disease must be found at the international level. Disease has become a global problem, and governments can no longer ensure the health of their citizens without cooperation from other states. The international community showed its understanding of the globalization of public health issues when it made water (sanitation), health, and sustainable development, especially in the Third World, the major themes for the Earth Summit at Johannesburg, South Africa, in August 2002.

The Costs of Applying Science to Health

One of the clearest results of improved public health around the world has been the increase in the world's population. Population size and growth trends have been a global concern every since Thomas Malthus (1766–1834) compared European population data with European agricultural production at the beginning of the nineteenth century and determined that population tended to increase at an exponential rate (10^1, 10^2, 10^3), while agricultural production increased only at a linear rate (1, 2, 3, 4). He warned that it would not be long before Europe's population had outgrown its capacity to feed itself and mass starvation would result. Fear of running out of food to feed the world's growing numbers has thus been with us for almost 200 years. The newer aspects of concern over population size and growth rate relate to recent trends for the growth of population to occur in the lesser developed countries, the concentration of huge masses of people in large urban areas and the impact of those concentrations on the global environment. We will discuss these three issues in the next sections.

Increased Global Population While population growth rates remained more or less stable until the beginning of the eighteenth century, they took off at the end of that century, and by the beginning of the twentieth century, growth rates formed an almost vertical line straight up on a population growth chart. The world population passed the one billion mark around the end of the eighteenth century. In 1950, the world population was 2.5 billion. It had doubled to 5 billion by 1985 and passed the 6 billion mark in 2000.[11] There is little question that the healthier a population, the longer it lives. Moreover, the more women who live to childbearing age, the greater the increase in the birth rate. The enormous improvements in the health of the global population that occurred in the nineteenth and twentieth centuries were key factors in the explosion of population that became manifest in the last quarter of the twentieth century. By contrast, the data presented on human poverty in Chapter 10 confirms the fact that the less science is practiced, the lower the longevity and the greater the incidence of infant mortality. There is also a connection between high poverty, low development, and high incidence of disease. We do not yet know enough about this relationship to understand why this is so, but certain facts seem to stand out.

We can take Africa as an example. AIDS, as we know, is fast becoming a catastrophic pandemic there because Africans have few human or material resources either to research a cure for the disease or to purchase the expensive medications produced by the high-tech science of the high-development world. In addition, a low literacy rate means that few of the continent's inhabitants have the minimum scientific skills to understand the basics of preventing the disease or how it is transmitted. Like many of us, in times of crisis, they tend to adhere to their traditional practices even if science suggests that a change is required.

The other side of this picture is that Africa has a very high average annual population growth rate. From 1980 to 1995 Africa's average annual growth rate was 2.92 percent, the highest of any continent. As a comparison, the whole of Europe, excluding the former Soviet Union, had an average annual growth in population of 0.29 percent, and North America's, including the Caribbean and Central America, was 1.69 percent. Africa's high birth rate means that despite disease, wars, and famine, its population is steadily increasing.

Africa's growth in population necessarily is related to improved health care and the efforts of the international community to vaccinate entire populations. From 1980 to 1995, Africa's infant mortality rate dropped from 135 babies per 1,000 born to 95, while the under-five mortality rate fell from 147 per 1,000 to 67 per 1,000 children—a remarkable feat.[12] Between 1950 and 1990, the population of Rwanda expanded 4 times, the population of Nigeria 3.8 times, and the population of Ethiopia almost 3 times, despite record famine. However, increased population creates ideal environments for microbe, which prefers many hosts to a few. Increased population also puts tremendous pressure on governments to provide for basic human needs, not to mention education and health. Given Africa's disease-prone semitropical climate, epidemics and social conflict may be expected to keep returning to the continent. One way of looking at Africa's predicament is to see it as a closed circle: improved health, more people living to old age, increased birth rate, high population growth, return of epidemics and social unrest.

The data seem to confirm what we have called the Pandora's box effect of the impact of science on the health of Third World populations. Improved health leads to more children, which strains a developing state's economic and social resources, and so infection and disease return. Countries like India and China that have worked hard to reduce their population growth rate, have been able to maintain an adequate public health system to keep their people in relatively better health.

Reduced Birth Rates in the Industrialized States   A second major influence of science on population growth involves such developments as the pill and amniocentesis. In Chapter 10, we mentioned the negative side to amniocentesis as used by women in India and Pakistan to practice gender-selective abortion. The pill has its two sides as well. On the one hand, it has altered dramatically the facts of human reproduction, by separating the act of procreation from the sexual act. Where the pill is used, fear of pregnancy has almost become obsolete. Women can have children when, if, and as often—or as infrequently—as they please. The pill took a long time to reach Africa, which is another important reason why the population increased so rapidly. But the pill quickly conquered the Western world and much of Asia, where it played a big role in reducing and keeping the birth rate down. Women's right to say when, like all technological and scientific advances, brought enormous immediate benefits to women. They enthusiastically entered the business and professional world—long the domain of men.

The pill also produced its brand of environmental surprise where it was adopted. With decreased social stigma, intercourse before marriage increased, especially among teens, with a concomitant rise in communicable sexual diseases. The pill also dramatically affected adult women's lifestyles. With the choice of childbirth theirs, most women in the industrialized world preferred to have no more than two children. Children become a burden in the work world, and the birth rate in all Western countries, with the exception of the United States, has dropped. Today European states, and especially Russia, with few exceptions, have a *negative population growth* (0.29/1,000 population growth rate). This means that there are not enough new people born to sustain the current numbers of people. Eighty percent of the population growth in Europe is from immigration. While we cannot fault the pill totally for this trend, it certainly aided women in their choice of how many children to have. This trend of negative population growth has not yet reached the United States. Interestingly enough, although the U.S. birth rate turned down in the 1970s, it showed a surprising rise in the 1990s.

Increased Population Density   A final major impact of science on population growth has been the rapid increase in population density. We saw how the third phase of the industrial revolution brought the megacities into being. But the large cities of that time such as London or New York were small compared to the size of Shanghai or Mexico City today. We do not know how many people the planet can

FIGURE 13.4
Global Population Trends, 1950–2050

SOURCE: World Resources Institute, World Resources 1998–1999, (http://www.wri.org/ powerpoint/trends). *Data from United Nations Population Division,* Long Range World Population Projections: Two Centuries of World Population Growth 1950–2000, *Table 6, p. 22.*

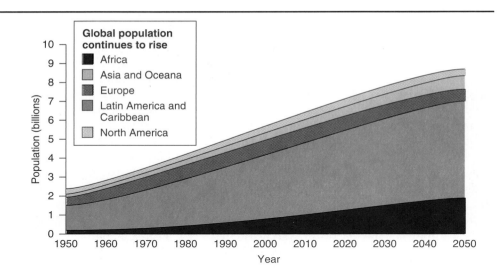

sustain, and to date, the earth's population continues to grow. More significantly, it is becoming more urbanized, with people living closer together. The following two graphs from the World Resources Institute suggest that the problem of world population growth may still be with us but that it has taken a different turn.

Figure 13.4 shows the upward trend in population growth, and also the differences in growth rates between major regions. At the same time, the band representing the European growth rate gets smaller towards 2040, while the band representing Latin America and the Caribbean gets wider and wider as does the band representing Africa. Can you explain why the band for Africa is so small despites its having the highest birth rate in the world?

The global population cannot level off permanently unless the global birth rate equals the global mortality rate and population growth *stabilizes.* Figure 13.5 explains why it is so difficult to predict a definite date for this occurrence. As the chart indicates, the achievement of population stabilization of any of the world's regions occurs when the line showing the ratio between birth and mortality rates reaches 1, because 1 = no population growth; for example, a 3 percent birth rate with a 3 percent mortality rate = 1. This ratio is called the *stabilization ratio.* The graph shows that between 1950 and 2000, the trend in four regions of the world has been for the stabilization ratio line to move toward one. Only the ratio of Europe and North America, however, has reached 1. The Asian stabilization line shows a sharp drop from 1980 on, due in large part to the Chinese birth control efforts that dramatically decreased the Chinese birth rate. By contrast, Africa's stabilization ratio is predicted to continue to rise until around 2010 and then start down toward one. The ups and downs you see in the stabilization ratio lines describe or trace what is now accepted as a normal demographic process: namely, since the exponential upswing in the nineteenth century, the population stabilization ratios of all the regions of the world first curve generally upward, as birth rates are higher than death rates. As industrialization takes root, the curve starts down. Africa is expected to be the last continent to follow this pattern.

It must be emphasized that the graph in figure 13.5 is based on current figures. Looking at it, we can hypothesize that when Africa stabilizes its population, the

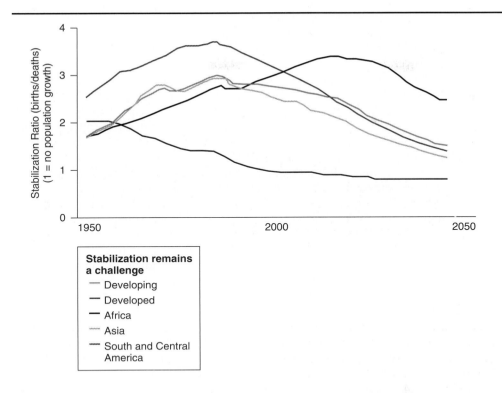

FIGURE 13.5

Stabilization Rate Data and Predictions, 1950—2050

SOURCE: *World Resources Institute,* World Resources 1998—1999, *(http://www.wri.org/ powerpoint/trends). Data from United Nations Population Division,* World Population Prospects 1950—2050 *(1996 Revision).*

world will have achieved population stabilization. But we cannot be sure that that will be the case. In the industrialized countries of Europe and North America, the population growth rate has turned negative: that is, the birth rate has reached negative numbers, meaning that more people are dying than being born. The population ratio in Asia might also go into negative numbers—so much that some experts are warning of a "population crunch!" And so the leading industrialized countries of the world—together with the world's economic powerhouse, China—may be heading into a population decline. What effect might these developments have on the world economy and the environment? Whatever else happens, we can be sure that most of the population growth that will occur in the next fifty years will be in the LDCs and in Asia. Virtually no growth will be taking place in Europe. Although the Chinese rate of population growth is slowing, there are still 1.2 billion people, or a third of the world's population, living there now. So China will continue to be major player in the world.

From this brief study of two graphs, we can risk making the conclusion that population issues of the twenty-first century will focus less on country growth rates and more on the very uneven distribution of people. First, since all the population increase in the next twenty years will be in the developing countries, these will have young populations. Europe, by contrast, will have a steadily aging population, and will continue to experience overall population decline. Second, 50 percent of the global population today lives in cities. Population densities are the highest in Asia and are increasing even though the birth rate is declining. To get a picture of how densely populated some areas of the world are, take a look at the dark red clusters on the map, World Population Density, at the front of this book. The urban population—the number of people living in cities—is expected to double by 2030. Already cities of 25 million people are a fact. By 2025, 5 billion people are expected to live in urban areas, 4 billion of whom will live in cities in the developing world. *Urbanization,* or the movement to the city, can bring improvements in health through sanitation and safe drinking water. But, as we just saw, urban poverty can also bring epidemics of new diseases caused by the slum conditions the new migrants from rural areas all around the globe are compelled to accept (see Chapter 10). Moreover, the crowding of migrants from different ethnic groups with different cultures speaking different languages is likely to bring increased violence, as each group struggles for its share of material goods already in scarce supply in the LDC megacities. Third and finally, as the densely populated megacities spread, the amount of arable land available to feed the enormous numbers of urban mouths steadily decreases. Feeding the urban hungry in developing countries will increasingly depend on food imports from the developed world.

Let us summarize our discussion of the interrelationship of the industrial revolution, science and technology, population growth, environmental pollution, and international politics. First of all, technology has improved the conditions in which vast numbers of people on our planet live, and in the process has contributed to the rapid growth of the world's population. The cost of improved health and well-being has been an explosion of population that, despite a current decrease in rate of growth, is nevertheless projected to rise to 11 billion in 2050 before population stabilization is achieved. On the other hand, the development of the pill coupled with the attractive values of a First World kind of lifestyle have caused a sharp reduction in the birth rate in all regions of the world, with the possible exception of Africa. The jury is still out on the impact of technology and science on population growth, but they appear to be important factors in limiting family size.

Second, every new scientific or technological advance has an upside and a downside. The upside is immediately visible, and it lures people to want the advance. The downside is not always as immediately obvious. But, as noted in the discussion of technological monoculture and environmental surprise, if the entire world follows the American way, the global population will be in a technological straitjacket risking an environmental surprise from which it may not easily escape. Most of the natural disasters at the end of the twentieth century, including floods, hurricanes, and earthquakes, could have been mitigated if the global community had been more aware of the phenomenon of environmental surprise and taken collective measures to ensure environmental sustainability.

Finally, the interconnectedness of science, technology, population, and the environment extends over the entire planet. The international community can no longer let each state do as it pleases. The solutions to the problems posed by increased population, megacities, and environmental surprise have a global reach and are now among the most critical issues of international politics.

What Are the Earth's Most Serious Environmental Problems?

The next part of the chapter will briefly consider the major environmental problems of our time: global warming, air pollution, global water problems, and the green and biotech revolutions. The section concludes with a discussion of how the world is organizing to address the problems, using water as an example.

Global Warming

The consensus among scientists is that our planet is warming. The evidence shows that at the earth's surface, the average temperature is 1.5 degrees Fahrenheit warmer than it was a century and a half ago. In fact the earth has steadily become warmer since the "little ice age" that occurred in the late Middle Ages, causing the Vikings to give up Leif Erickson's attempt to establish a settlement in North America.

The Evidence   Although scientists generally agree that this warming trend exists, they do not agree on its cause. Ice ages and warming trends have occurred throughout earth's history, many point out. The dinosaurs, for example, lived in a warmer climate than most of us do now. Then came an era in which ice moved all the way down to the middle of the North American continent. The ice receded, and the earth again warmed. *Paleoclimatologists,* scientists who study climate change in the far distant past, have examined ice cores from Greenland and there found a story of abrupt climate shifts from hard ice to ice-sheet collapse and climatic warming. The big question is *why?* Scientists have been taking meteorological data for only the past 150 years or so. Considering the age of the earth, that is an insignificant data base from which to make major predictions. As noted, **paleoclimatology** has evidence of what we might call "natural" periods of warming and cooling throughout earth's history. But we do not know whether natural warming gives us the entire explanation. Many scientists believe that human activity has made a major contribution to the currently rising temperatures.

Paleoclimatology
The study of climate variations in the far distant past.

An authoritative study published by the Intergovernmental Panel on Climate Change (IPCC) in 1990 came to the following conclusions:

1. A natural greenhouse effect already keeps the earth warmer than it would otherwise be without it.
2. Emissions resulting from human activities are substantially increasing the atmospheric concentrations of greenhouse gases, contributing to the earth warming more than may be good for its ecosystems and creatures, including humans. The greenhouse gases include carbon dioxide, methane, chlorofluorocarbons (CFCs), and nitrous oxide.

Figure 13.6 will help you understand global warming and the possible contribution of human activity. In the lower right of the figure, infrared radiation is emitted from the earth. Going higher up the figure on the right hand side, we see that some of this infrared radiation is absorbed by the greenhouse gasses and re-emitted back to earth. The effect is to warm the earth. If human activities are producing emissions that substantially increase the atmospheric concentrations of greenhouse gases, then human activity has a lot to do with the greenhouse gases portrayed in the figure that absorb and re-emit the infrared radiation back to earth. Some scientists disputed the IPCC finding, particularly its relative certainty that human activity, if not stopped, could increase the global mean temperature by about 0.2 degrees Fahrenheit by the year 2023. These scientists argued that there is more evidence that the earth will be cooler by that time. Roy W. Spencer, senior scientist for climate studies at NASA's Marshall Space Flight Center in Huntsville, Alabama, summed up the counterargument as follows:

> There remain substantial uncertainties in our understanding of how the climate system will respond to increasing concentrations of carbon

FIGURE 13.6

Model of the Greenhouse Effect from IPCC Study

SOURCE: *From J. T. Houghton, et al. (eds.) Climate Change the IPCC Scientific Assessment (Cambridge: Cambridge University Press, 1990).*

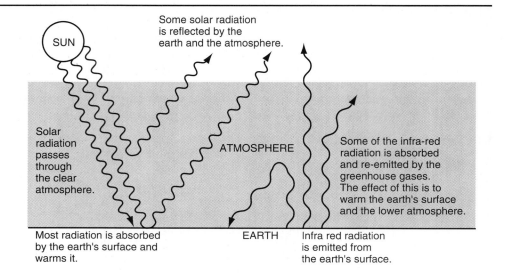

dioxide and other greenhouse gases. The popular perception of global warming as an environmental catastrophe cannot be supported with measurements or current climate change theory. . . . I believe that any warming will likely be more modest and benign than had originally been feared. Even if warming does prove to be substantial, the time required for it to occur (many decades) will allow us considerable time to better understand the problem, and to formulate any policy changes that might be deemed necessary.[13]

In 2001, the IPCC revealed new findings that indicated the earth was indeed warming and that the cause was in large part attributable to man-made greenhouse gas emissions. Paleontologists once again argued that calving and melting of polar glaciers is a cyclical affair and the fact that glaciers seem to be retreating faster than previously is not unusual. And so it goes, on and on.

What is a layperson to make of these arguments? Certainly we can see signs of climate change all around us. Many parts of the world, including much of the United States, have been experiencing drought in the past few years. Yet, 2002 saw heavy rain in Europe that caused catastrophic floods in Prague, the Czech Republic, and in Dresden, Germany. How should we interpret these signs? Should we wait and see? Should we begin to deindustrialize immediately? Should we drastically curtail our use of fossil fuels? Let's look at some attempts to answers.

The International Response   The prudent course is to take whatever precautions are necessary to mitigate the impact of human activity on global warming. In 1982 as information hardened that the release of CFCs into the environment might erode the protective ozone layer, Mostafa K. Tolba, the skillful and energetic executive director of the United Nations Environment Program (UNEP), positioned his organization to initiate the effort to develop a global convention on the ozone layer. Five years later, the UN convention on the ozone layer was ratified at Montreal, Canada. The convention signers agreed to phase out CFCs. A subsequent meeting in Helsinki in 1989 set the year 2000 as the deadline for the phase-out, and at the further urging of Tolba in London in 1990, the industrialized countries agreed to contribute $240 million to help the developing countries comply over the next three years.[14] Meanwhile, at the national level, the states of the European Union, the United States, and other countries passed laws aimed at reducing the emission of greenhouse gases.

The trail of international activity next led to the UN Earth Summit held in Rio de Janeiro in 1992, where a framework agreement on the reduction of greenhouse gases was signed. Under Rio's inspiration, the states of the European Union, the United States, and other states passed laws aimed at reducing the emission of greenhouse gases. The signing of more detailed protocol in Kyoto in 1998, defining specific emission reduction targets for the world's 39 industrialized nations, stalled on the refusal of developing countries like China to become part of the regime. Without China's participation, the U.S. Congress would not consider ratification. A meeting in The Hague in 2000 broke up over disagreements between the countries of the European Union and an umbrella group led by the United States over emission target policy. The European countries urged specific, quantifiable cuts in greenhouse gas emissions, while the umbrella group wanted a trade-off between amounts of greenhouse gas emissions and greenhouse gas sinks, such as forests and oceans (see Chapter 1). In March 2001, following the IPCC announcement that the global warming trend was serious, the rift between the industrialized nations was somewhat patched up. Ministers from eight industrialized nations, including Russia, issued a joint declaration in Trieste, Italy "to strive to reach agreement on outstanding political issues" and "appropriate environmental strategies."[15] A short time later, the U.S. unilaterally withdrew from the treaty. The U.S. withdrawal sparked sharp controversy over whether the implementation of the agreement would have actually reduced greenhouse gasses, proving once more that without international agreement on the nature of the problem and its solution, nothing gets accomplished.

Many people applaud national and international efforts to reduce greenhouse gas emissions. But no country and no international organization has yet proposed a radical change in lifestyle that might actually reduce the amount of greenhouse gases emitted in the atmosphere. The international answer to "What should we do about the situation?" seems to be the age-old human response to things we don't want to think about: Wait and see.

Pollution from Energy Sources

Energy consumption is a central issue in world politics (see Chapter 7), and as we showed in our discussion of the stages of energy use, crucial to industrial development and to our survival on this planet.

So why can't we use lots of energy? The obvious answer is that the kinds of energy we use most—fossil fuels (coal, oil, gas)—are nonrenewable resources, meaning that the earth contains a fixed amount that we are fast using up. Plutonium and uranium are also nonrenewable resources.

The second reason we need to take care with energy use is that *most kinds of energy are heavy polluters.* As we saw earlier in the chapter, the burning of fossil fuels, such as coal and petroleum, contributes to the emission of carbon dioxide—one of the greenhouse gases—and possibly to global warming. The burning of coal produces sulfur dioxide, one of the airborne pollutants that can be borne long distances by the wind and that can return to Earth as acid rain many miles from the source of the burn. The subject of acid rain will be taken up later in the chapter. It is a major culprit in the die-off of lakes and forests in many regions of the world.

Nuclear energy burns clean, but if something goes wrong at the plant, the accident can cause a major disaster, as it did at Chernobyl and in the central Urals. Even if we could make nuclear power plants 100 percent safe, we would still need to know how to dispose safely of the spent nuclear fuel rods, and to store them for hundreds, and perhaps thousands, of years.

Wood and biomass burning also contribute to greenhouse gases. Over 2.5 billion people in developing countries depend on firewood, animal dung, or crop residue for cooking. In 1999, Indian scientist Veerabhadran Rtamanathan led a team of researchers that discovered a huge blanket of soot and smoke nearly two miles thick hanging over the Indian Ocean. Nicknamed the "Asian brown cloud," the discovery suggested that soot may be as critical a factor in climate change as CO_2.[16] A second problem with burning wood is that you have to cut down trees to do it. Deforestation is a crucial global environmental problem, as the tropical forest stands in Asia, Africa, and Latin America are essential to the absorption of CO_2 from the air and its storage as energy-producing material.

"The oxygen released as a by-product of photosynthesis provides most of the atmospheric oxygen vital to respiration in plants and animals."[17] In other words, we need forests so that we can keep breathing. We also need forests along rivers and streams and on hillsides to prevent soil erosion. When the trees are gone, catastrophic flooding and mud slides caused by heavy rain, such as have occurred in Costa Rica and on the coast of California, are the inevitable consequence.

Of all the nonrenewable energy sources, natural gas is the cleanest and is being adopted for public municipal transportation. Next time you visit a major European or North American city, take a good look at the city buses. You may see a sign on them that proudly signals "We burn only natural gas." The problem with natural gas is the problem of all nonrenewable energy sources, however: once the gas is gone, it is gone—maybe not forever, but for a very, very long time. Fortunately, new discoveries of gas reserves have greatly increased the availability of natural gas, and for the short term, gas seems to be the best answer to energy pollution. Unfortunately, our consumption of gas is far less than our consumption of oil.

As Figure 13.7 shows, oil represents around 40 percent of the world's total energy supply, or what is currently on hand for distribution. In addition to this supply, there are *proven reserves* (we know roughly how much oil is in the ground at a certain location) and *potential reserves* (we can only guess how much is there). Most of the easily obtainable oil lies under the Arabian Peninsula and in Iran and Iraq. Mexico has some excellent reserves off its coast in the Gulf of Mexico. But the rest of the easy-to-extract oil has already been taken out of the earth. Finding and extracting more oil is a job for the big petroleum companies. A single person sinking a well can no longer do it. The process is long and costly, and frequently leads to no commercial results. When the Soviet Republics in Central Asia gained their independence in 1991, the global oil companies jumped at the possibility of getting in on the ground floor of an oil boom (for more on this subject, see the case study that accompanies Chapter 7). Ten years later there is still no boom, and companies are warning that there might not be enough oil in the ground to justify the huge cost of building a pipeline out to the Mediterranean Sea to transport the oil where it is most needed. We know oil supplies are limited. We do not know exactly how limited, but clearly the supply cannot go on forever. The same is true for coal and natural gas that are in second and third place after oil in global energy consumption.

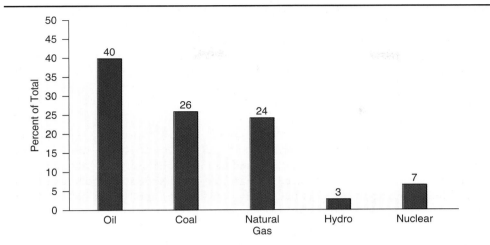

FIGURE 13.7

World Commercial Energy Supply, 1998

SOURCE: http://www.wri.org/powerpoints/oil/sld001.htm

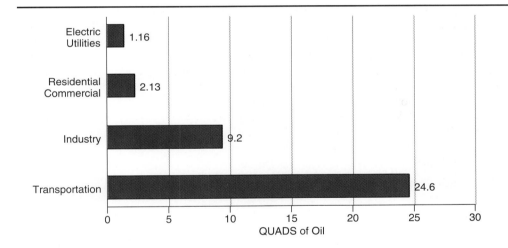

FIGURE 13.8

Global Oil Consumption by Sector, 1998

SOURCE: World Resources Institute (http://www.wri.org/powerpoint/oil/sld014.htm).

We talk most about the limitations of oil because oil is the major fuel of our modern transportation system, as illustrated in Figure 13.8.[18] Obviously motor vehicles are the primary beneficiaries of this consumption. Oil keeps our buses, trucks, SUVs and fast cars running, the number of which has increased *NINE times* since 1950 (see Figure 13.9)! To date most of the motor vehicle registration is in the industrialized world. But China is undergoing a huge economic boom, and its population of 1.3 billion is becoming increasingly prosperous. Can you imagine what will happen to oil consumption when every Chinese has a car? Will there be enough oil to go around? What if India becomes a car-crazy society at the same time? Today the developed countries consume about 53 percent of all energy produced in the world (see Figure 13.10). If China and India adopt the energy-profligate lifestyle of the West, we shall almost certainly experience a dramatic change for the worse in our own lifestyle. What this will be we can only guess. Most analysts doubt there is enough energy for the whole world to consume at the rate the industrialized world does today.

FIGURE 13.9

Motor Vehicle Trends, 1946–1995

SOURCE: World Resources Institute, World Resources 1998–1999, (http://www.wri.org/ wri/powerpoints/ trends/sld026.htm). Data from American Automobile Manufac- turers Association, World Motor Vehicle Data 1993, p. 23 and Motor Vehicle Facts and Figures 1996, p. 44.

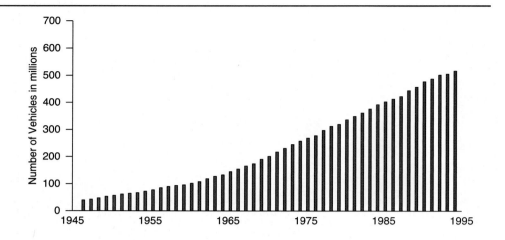

FIGURE 13.10

Regional Shares of Global Energy Consumption

SOURCE: Compiled from World Energy Organiza- tion, World Energy Out- look: 2002, Figure 2.3: "Regional Shares in World Primary Demand" (http://www.world energyoutlook.org/ weo/pubs/weo2002/weo 2002.asp).

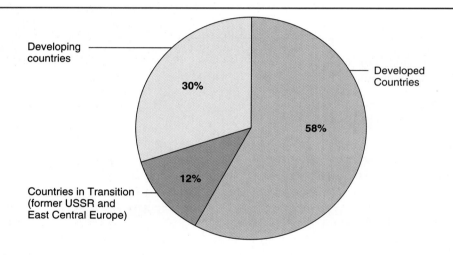

If fossil and nuclear fuels are in such a crisis, why don't we go right to renew- able energy sources like solar, wind, and geothermal power? As economists Jerry Taylor and Peter VanDoren put it, the main obstacle to the use of all renewable en- ergy sources is cost. Generating electricity from solar power costs between 11 and 12¢ per kilowatt hour as compared to 3¢ per kilowatt hour for "clean-burning" nat- ural gas. If you include in your calculation the short lifespan of a photovoltaic cell that converts sunlight into electricity, borrowing costs, and equipment costs, you are talking about 30¢ to $1.00 per kilowatt hour. Taylor and VanDoren calculate the real cost of wind power at 10¢ a kilowatt hour.[19] The up-front cost of installing a geothermal or passive solar heating system may be four to six times the installation cost of a natural gas or oil furnace. The breakeven point, where costs for geothermal heating equal costs for oil or gas heating, is projected at 20 years. If you take into consideration maintenance and possible replacement costs, that point could recede far into the future. At present, the cheapest form of renewable energy is wind power. The problem with wind power is that you need some 50 square miles of wind turbines to generate electricity for around 70,000 homes. Many people do not like the looks or sound of so many wind turbines so close to their houses. In sum,

Air Pollution in Europe: Urban smog, very small particles, and toxic pollutants pose serious health concerns to millions of people. Air pollutants are also carried hundreds of miles by winds and thus affect areas far-removed from the source of the pollution, often in another state, in the form of acid rain.

people are not rushing to use *renewable,* or *"soft," energy* sources because so far they are either too expensive or not very aesthetically pleasing to have around.

The high cost of soft energy today does not mean it will not become more attractive tomorrow. But some things will never change. Solar energy demands continuous sunlight. Wind power needs constant wind. So far, these events do not occur on a regular basis anywhere in the world. We are left with our reliance on fossil fuels, particularly natural gas, and on *energy conservation.* The more we make our energy-consuming products work efficiently, the more we reduce the amount of energy needed to run them.

Securing energy is a global problem that is likely to become worse. In 2001, California, which has the fifth largest GNP in the world, experienced rolling blackouts. The shortage of electric power was attributed to low electricity production in the state, and predatory electric power companies' flawed regulatory policies. For many countries, such blackouts have long been routine. They simply do not have enough energy available to keep the lights on all the time. As we saw in previous chapters, the need for access to secure sources of energy drives the foreign policies of most of the world's states. The pervasiveness of this need—and the limits of the resources—call for extensive international problem solving.

Air Pollution

The air we breathe is a global commons. The air belongs to all of us and belongs to no one. It is what might be called the common property of humankind. But if the air is free to everyone to breathe, it is also free to everyone to pollute. Let's look at various aspects of this issue.

Air as a Global Commons   The concept of a *global commons* derives from the concept of *the common,* or commonly used land that was situated at the center of rural towns in England and New England two centuries ago. Because the land was held in common, everyone who had cattle or sheep and no pasture of their own could graze their animals there. It does not take a lot of imagination to see that what belongs to everyone also belongs to no one. Thus, every animal owner wanted to use the commons as much as possible to make sure his stock was fed. The inevitable results were overgrazing and the destruction of the commons. Garrett Hardin drew the world's attention to this dilemma in 1968 with his article "The Tragedy of the Commons," published in *Science* magazine.

In the box Why It Matters to You: Commons Thoughts from Barry Commoner, you will see how one guru of the environmental movement looks at the commons problem.

Global Commons
Areas of the earth's biosphere that are shared by all the world's population, such as oceans and the atmosphere.

The **global commons** are those parts of the biosphere that are held in common by all humanity. These include the oceans, outer space, the seabed, Antarctica, the electromagnetic spectrum, and the atmosphere. One major problem of the oceans and the atmosphere is that they are fast becoming pollution dumping grounds for everyone in the world. In his book *The Endangered Atmosphere,* Marvin Soroos argues that humanity "faces the daunting challenge of constraining its releases of air pollutants to preserve the essential qualities not only of the atmosphere but also of the larger Earth system."[20] (Please take another look at Figure 13.1, the Gaia figure.) The model tells you that human society, the natural ecosystem, and the atmosphere are all interconnected. Without the Earth's unique atmosphere, there would be no life on Earth. The emission of greenhouse gases threatens the life-saving layer that protects us from the sun's lethal rays.

To play the game of "Tragedy of the Commons," go to **www.ablongman.com/ duncan.**

Air Pollution and the International Response   As discussed earlier, polluted air contributes to the greenhouse effect through the emission of carbon dioxide and other greenhouse gases. The long-range transport of air pollutants, such as sulfur dioxide (SO_2), also produces the phenomenon of acid rain, although just how this occurs is not yet completely understood. Air pollution has an important impact on public health, as the increase in asthma and respiratory ailments indicates. Whereas a century ago, air pollution was largely an urban phenomenon that people could escape by going to the country, the industrialization of most of the globe has made air pollution a global phenomenon.

To the credit of the world's states, atmospheric pollution has now been recognized as a serious problem, and the international community has passed major treaties to reduce the emission of air pollutants worldwide. These include the Transboundary Air Pollution (LRTAP) Convention (1979), Partial Test Ban Treaty (1963) against nuclear testing in outer space and on the seabed, the Montreal Protocol for the Protection of the Ozone Layer (1987), and the Kyoto Framework Convention on Climate Change (1992).

Regime Theory
Developed by Oran Young; holds that international cooperation depends on well-designed regimes. If a treaty promotes a well-designed regime, the chance of the treaty being implemented is much greater than if it designates a flawed regime.

Each of these major treaties establishes what is called an *environmental regime.* Typically, the treaty sets up a *goal* to be reached, a *process* by which to reach the goal, a time line, and some kind of *permanent organizational framework* to monitor progress. In the early 1990s **regime theory,** developed by international relations scholar Oran Young, was thought to be the up-and-coming way to get the world's states to move from signing treaties to implementing them.[21] The evidence today is ambiguous.

If we take the LRTAP Treaty (1979), the evidence indicates that ambient concentrations of SO_2 have declined in many cities of Western Europe and North America, countries that signed the treaty. But SO_2 concentrations remain high in

WHY IT MATTERS TO YOU

Common Thoughts from Barry Commoner

Environmental scientist Barry Commoner joined the faculty of Washington University in St. Louis in 1947. In 34 years there he explored viral function and led cellular research with implications for cancer diagnosis. Alarmed in the early 1950s by the health risks posed by atomic testing, Commoner helped found the St. Louis Committee for Nuclear Information. In 1966 he established the Center for the Biology of Natural Systems to study man's relationship with the environment. The author of nine books and the 1980 Citizens' Party presidential candidate, Barry Commoner, a pioneer in the creation of the environmental movement, was termed the "Paul Revere of Ecology."

Barry Commoner has developed a set of laws on ecology that tell you in no uncertain terms that when it comes to the environment, everything in this world is connected with everything else in a constantly evolving dynamic that we will never completely understand—in other words, the earth is our "commons," and its care and maintenance matter to all of us. You can deny or ignore these realities, or you can adapt your lifestyle and work for a healthier planet. Here is an assortment of his thoughts on our natural environment and why it must matter to you:

The first law of ecology is that everything is related to everything else.*

When you fully understand the situation, it is worse than you think.*

No action is without its side effects.*

If you see the light at the end of the tunnel, you are looking the wrong way.#

Sooner or later, wittingly or unwittingly, we must pay for every intrusion on the natural environment.*

Barry Commoner: One of the most influential of the generation of environmentalists that jump-started the modern environmental movement in the 1970s. At first, mainly concerned with the overall impact of human activity on the environment, he later became convinced that poverty was an inseparable part as well as consequence of environmental pollution.

Sources: * Aapex Software Corporation, Great Quotations Library CD Collection, Las Vegas, 1994. # [equals] Robert Byrne, ed., 1,911 Best Things Anybody Ever Said (New York: Fawcett Columbine Books, 1988). From the St. Louis Walk of Fame website (http://www.Stlouiswalkoffame.org/inductees/barry-commoner.html). Reprinted with permission.

Asia, Latin America, and Eastern Europe, where coal continues to be used and where there is a great deal of diesel traffic. Forest dieback caused by acid rain is still a serious problem in Eastern Europe and the Eastern Canadian provinces while the Northeastern states of the United States continue to suffer the death of lakes from acid precipitation. A World Bank calculation of the health costs to China from its increased use of coal and increased number of motor vehicles runs into the tens of billions of cases of respiratory damage.[22]

Despite the phasing out of CFCs required by the Montreal Protocol (1987), ozone pollution has continued to rise in cities in Europe, North America, and Japan as auto and industrial emissions have increased. Nitric oxide emitted by motor vehicles is the major culprit in the creation of the yellow smog over Los Angeles. Ozone pollution can cause breathing difficulties, impair lung function, and cause shortness of breath, asthma attacks, and chest pain.[23]

As we saw earlier, the climate change regime is already in serious trouble at a very young age. Whether there will further attempts to reconstitute the Kyoto regime or whether the nations of the world will be able to agree on a new regime covering every state remains to be seen. The War on Terrorism has taken many governments' attention away from global environmental issues. Without a resurgence of popular interest in the global commons, the future of a global warming regime remains in doubt (see Chapter 1).

In summary, the atmosphere is a global commons that every state uses as a dump for air pollutants. The increased concentration of these pollutants is a major contributor to global warming and is creating global health problems, most of which are beyond the resources of one country to resolve. To date, the international community has yet to agree on measures to reduce greenhouse gasses. It has dealt more effectively with transboundary air pollution that crosses state frontiers.

Water Scarcity and Water Pollution

Of all the global environmental problems, as we discussed in Chapter 10, water scarcity and absence of clean water probably present the most immediate threat to humans in the next century. Figures 13.11 graphically summarizes the problem.

World water demand is growing, but supplies are limited and are distributed in a chaotic fashion around the globe. A 1997 United Nations assessment of freshwater resources found that one third of the world's population lives in countries experiencing moderate to high water stress. Moderate to high **water stress** refers to consumption levels that exceed 20 percent of available supply. The UN study made it clear that matters are going to get worse.[24] As Figure 13.11 indicates, by 2025 one half of the world's population, including that of the United States, will be experiencing water shortages, and two-thirds will be living in areas undergoing moderate to high water stress.[25]

Why is this happening? For one thing, as the world population increases, the demand for food increases. Agriculture accounts today for about 70 percent of water consumption around the world (see Figure 13.12). Increasing amounts of this water are being distributed to fields by irrigation. And the UN expects a 50 to 100 percent increase in irrigated water by 2025. The negative effects of irrigation are clearly seen from the drying up of the Aral Sea in Central Asia. At one time, two great rivers flowed into this land-locked sea, the Amu Darya and the Syr Darya. In the desire to turn Central Asia into one of the world's leading cotton-producing regions, the former Soviet government paid for the construction of huge irrigation systems. Pesticides and herbicides followed. By the end of the 1980s, the Aral Sea had lost a third of its size. The rivers had stopped flowing into it. By the 1990s the sea was down to half its size. Fishing boats lay useless in heaps of sand blown up by the desert wind. The sand blew back onto the fields and its inhabitants, bringing salt and residue from the pesticides and herbicides that had been used on the fields. In Australia, overirrigation of land has brought salt to the surface, endangering the entire future of agriculture in a large part of that continent.

Water Stress
A term used by the United Nations to indicate consumption levels that exceed 20 percent of available water supply.

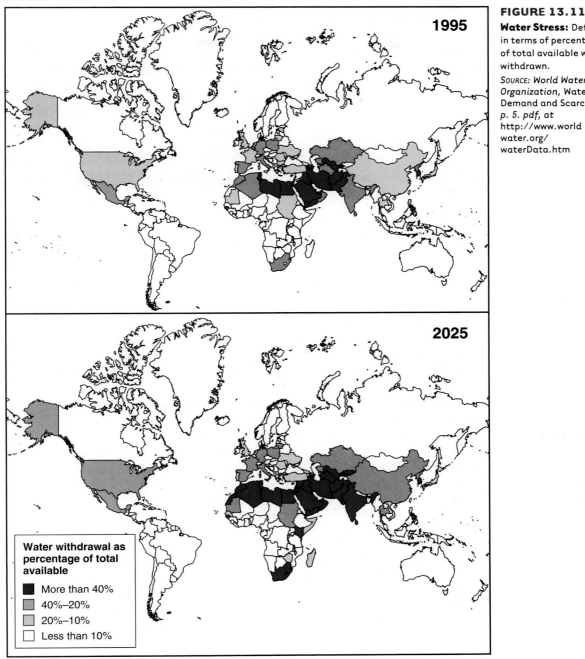

1995

2025

Water withdrawal as percentage of total available

- ■ More than 40%
- ▨ 40%–20%
- ▨ 20%–10%
- □ Less than 10%

FIGURE 13.11
Water Stress: Defined in terms of percentage of total available water withdrawn.
SOURCE: World Water Organization, Water Demand and Scarcity, *p. 5. pdf, at* http://www.world water.org/ waterData.htm

FIGURE 13.12

World Water Use by Consumption Category and Region

SOURCE: World Resources Institute, 1998–1999 World Resources (New York and Oxford: Oxford University Press, 2000), p. 188.

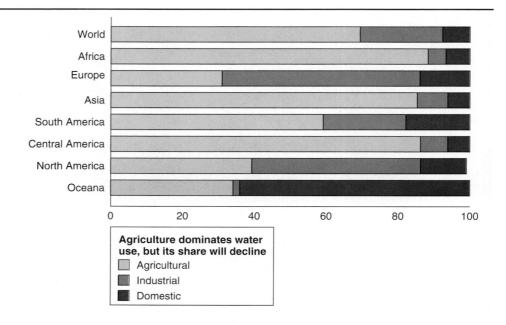

China presents another illustration of what happens to rivers when a country turns to irrigation to water its fields. Slowly but surely the northern part of China is drying out. In one year alone, 1999, the water table under Beijing, the Chinese capital, fell 8 feet. In all, it has dropped nearly 200 feet since 1965. The Yellow River is simply being overused for irrigation. In 1972 the river stopped running to the sea for 15 days. In 1997, a drought year, it stopped running for 226 days. As more and more water is diverted to industry and cities upstream, there is less available for use downstream.[26] But China must face hard facts. Water scarcity means the country must, in the future, import grain to feed its vast population.

As one more example, one major obstacle to the solution of the Israeli/Palestinian conflict is the finding of an equitable allocation of the waters of the Jordan River. Until recently, Israel controlled the river from its source to its termination in the Dead Sea. With its withdrawal from Lebanon in May 2000, Israel gave up control of the river's source but not its status as major user of the Jordan's water. During those years, Jordanians learned to live on less than 8 gallons per family per day.

Pollution further contributes to the water crisis. Outbreaks of water poisoning are becoming common in the United States. In 1998 the city of Milwaukee, Wisconsin, experienced water poisoning, although the city's water treatment system met U.S. Environmental Protection Agency (EPA) regulations. In May 2000 an E. coli outbreak in the water system in Walkerton, Canada, made 1,000 people sick and killed 17. The green revolution in agriculture, with its extensive use of fertilizers, pesticides, and herbicides, has dumped a whole range of pollutants into river basins. And wherever industry exists, toxic chemicals and heavy metals seep into waterways. Some of the worst landfills in the United States are around Niagara Falls, New York, where the conversion of water to electricity at the turn of the century made possible the development of the petrochemical industry. Because of the cost and difficulty of cleaning up the heavy metals, most rivers will never be free of them. Fishermen on Lake Ontario in the Great Lakes region of

Wu Gorge in China: The water here will rise 300 feet when the Three Gorges Dam is completed.

North America are told not to eat the fish they catch. The land around the lake is home to some of the largest industrial polluters in America.

Finally, the damming of rivers for water power has contributed to water shortages and changed river basin environments. Damming has further impacted human health. The newest case is the Senegal River development project in West Africa. Predicted to stabilize water supply, increase the fish population, furnish energy, and improve public health, the dam has failed to live up to its promise. A World Resources Institute study found the age-old diseases of schistosomiasis, malaria, Rift Valley fever, and diarrhea only modestly improved in the region below the dam, because improved sanitation and water treatment failed to materialize.[27]

In another part of the world, the huge Three Gorges Dam, under construction on the middle reaches of China's Yangtze River, promises to save the farmland and population of the lower Yangtze from severe river flooding. It also promises to alleviate the water shortage in North China by transferring water from the Yangtze via canal to the Yellow River. If the dam is to live up to its promise, however, the Chinese must relocate some one million inhabitants and build a huge canal to carry water north toward Beijing. The Chinese government is determined to see the project through. It hopes to relieve the growing water shortage in the north and produce clean energy through the hydropower station being built at the dam. Environmentalists worry about the tremendous loss of land that will be permanently flooded, downriver silt, increased use of fertilizers, the displacement of population, and the potential salting of the aquifer carrying water north. On balance, dams may be more of a contributor to water problems, rather than their solution.

Poor countries are particularly vulnerable to the dangers of water scarcity. The majority of countries where high water stress and low income come together

To learn more about water pollution and water scarcity, go to **http://www.ablongman /duncan.** **(http://www.epa.gov/ water)**

Mother and Child in Ethiopia: At the turn of the twenty-first century, Africa is a catastrophe of poverty, famine, disease, violence, and ecological degradation. Each of these problems feeds off the rest. Research is beginning to clarify the links between them, opening a whole new area in international relations called ecological security.

are found in the arid regions of Africa and Asia. We are all too familiar with pictures of drought-stricken Ethiopia, where a mother scoops up water from what looks like a mud puddle and gives the contaminated water to her anemic child.

In sum, water scarcity and water contamination affect every continent and most states. The problems are caused by overuse of existing water supplies, industrial pollution, and to some extent damming of rivers. Because few rivers are located wholly within one state, the regulation of waterways is necessarily a task for the international community. Let us see what success it has had in ensuring water security.

What Is the International Community Doing to Mediate Global Water Problems?

To understand the nature of international regulation of waterways, let us first take a look at available freshwater around the world. Virtually all the industrialized countries in the north have access to fresh water. The situation is far different in the southern half of the globe. This unequal access is compounded by the fact that almost all major global waterways cross national borders. Few countries have the luxury of using water that originates and ends solely within their boundaries. So what are their options?

International Water Treaties

Probably the most common way to solve the problems of use of international waterways is the water treaty. Water treaties exist in all parts of the world. The two best known in North America are the treaties on the Columbia and the Colorado rivers. Downriver users tend to get the worst of a river treaty. Excessive damming of the Colorado as well as U.S. federal allocations of water to the seven signatory states have left Mexico with the leftovers of the river. In 1905 a levee on the lower Colorado broke, and water poured into the Salton Sink, 240 feet below sea level in California's Imperial Valley. A lake was formed and trapped the waters. As a result, the Colorado effectively ceased to flow out to the Gulf of California, and California gained a huge territory for agriculture.

International river treaties are especially difficult where there are multiple users. Both the Danube and the Rhine rivers in Europe are the subject of international treaties. In February 2000 a cyanide spill at the Baia-Mare gold mine in northwestern Romania turned the Tisza River into a death trap for fish and aquatic life. Rising high in the Romanian mountains on the border of Romania and Ukraine, the Tisza winds its way through Hungary until it reaches the Danube, downstream from Novi Sad in Yugoslavia. The cyanide spill followed the river's course until it too reached the Danube. The Yugoslav government raised a loud protest and demanded compensation, as did the Hungarian government. The international community wrung its hands. UNEP conducted an investigation. The European Union promised to help, and there the matter rested. Apparently, the international treaty governing the Danube does not apply to this case, and thus, neither the Hungarians nor the Yugoslavs had legal recourse to compensation. Treaty or no treaty, less powerful states have a difficult time getting the more powerful cosigners of international treaties to act.

The UN Regional Seas Programs

International water treaties also exist to govern the world's regional seas and oceans. The UN's Regional Sea Programs are perhaps the most active of the water treaty regimes. Examples are the Regional Seas Program for the Mediterranean, the Caspian, and the Black Sea. Regime-creating treaties have been signed, as we know, in the areas of global warming and transboundary air pollution. How effective is this kind of international response to environmental problems?

Water treaties, like all other international treaties, depend on the voluntary compliance of the states that sign them. Liberal proponents of regime theory argue that having a regime in place binds the signatory states into a centralizing system from which they can extricate themselves only with difficulty. Those who question the usefulness of regimes argue that a treaty that is on paper only, with few states in compliance, is not a treaty at all. What do you think? How effective a solution do treaties offer to our environmental problems? In the final section of this chapter, we will examine an alternative approach to solving environmental problems: the application of science and technology. The green and biotech revolutions that we will discuss next represent this approach.

What Are the Green and Biotech Revolutions?

The **green** and **biotech revolutions** involve the application of science to agriculture and animal husbandry with the aim of improving crop yield and crop resistance to pests and climate variation. The green revolution started in the 1920s and continues today. The biotech revolution extends the application of biological science to the breaking of the animal and plant gene codes and the human gene code. Let's first look at the green revolution—how it began, what it consists of, and how it is viewed today.

Green Revolution
The great increase in yield of grain crops, such as corn, rice, and wheat, due to the development of high-yielding hybrids, the use of fertilizers and pesticides, and the implementation of more efficient land management. The father of this revolution was Iowa-born Henry Wallace.

Biotech Revolution
The widespread application of bioengineering to increase food production and improve plant and animal strains.

Origins of the Green Revolution

The trigger for this revolution was the energetic and resourceful research of Henry Wallace, a genius from Iowa, a former U.S. Secretary of Agriculture, and a candidate for president of the United States in 1948. Wallace tried mating or crossbreeding different kinds of corn to produce more prolific plants. He kept exact records of his trials. When he thought he had good results, he took his hybrid corn seeds to the Iowa farmers. At first, he had great difficulty getting them interested in buying his seeds and applying his methods. But Wallace's powers of persuasion were superb. Some farmers bought his seeds. They talked up their excellent results to friends and neighbors, and the green revolution was launched.[28]

To increase further corn yield per acre, Wallace and his assistants conducted experiments using various kinds and amounts of fertilizers. To record his results accurately, he taught himself the then new science of statistics, a feat that compelled all future generations of students to master the science. During World War II, the green revolution gave agricultural production in the United States sufficient stability that the country never had to fear food scarcity.

To learn more about Henry Wallace, go to **www.ablongman.com/duncan.**

After World War II, another native Iowan familiar with Wallace's research, Dr. Norman Borlaug, carried the green revolution to Asia. He was given the Nobel Prize in 1970 for his work in reducing food shortages in India and Pakistan in the 1960s. Like Wallace, Borlaug has remained relatively unknown for his scientific work, because of the serious concerns that were first raised at that time about the environmental surprise contained in the green revolution. Nevertheless, the revolution's success in Asia provides one of the major explanations for the ability of that continent, with the exception of Japan, to feed itself today without major imports of food.

To learn more about Norman Borlaug, go to **www.ablongman.com/duncan.**

Pros and Cons of the Green Revolution

The major criticism of the green revolution is that it has destroyed local knowledge and local culture and made formerly self-sustaining regions dependent on the global market and international corporations. There is truth in this criticism. Until recently, the world did not give much thought to the disappearance of local cultures and lifestyles. Now we no longer deny the importance of this loss.[29] Totally focused on the small world around them, the people of a particular culture know local plants and their uses as no scientist can know them. Much of this information is handed down orally from generation to generation. Scientists are eager to identify all the kinds of plants that might be helpful to humanity, but they cannot do this without the help of the local people who know them. As the local cultures disappear, this knowledge disappears as well, possibly forever.

In addition, local cultures are the expression of a way of life that has evolved to make life in the local environment sustainable. When this culture is destroyed by the green revolution, humanity loses a storehouse of knowledge on sustainability. What science must learn by trial and error, these indigenous cultures have learned through centuries-old oral traditions. Once destroyed, those options for sustainability may be lost forever.

A second complaint against the green revolution is that it makes the local farmer dependent on the global market. Hybrid seeds do not reproduce themselves. To produce high yields, they require large amounts of fertilizers. They are also vulnerable to pests and crop diseases and hence require pesticides and herbicides. Seeds and fertilizers cost money. Thus, the green revolution is largely for the larger farmer, who has sufficient managerial capability and resources to profit from it. The smaller farmer is driven out of business or left to till marginal lands.

Again, there is truth in this complaint. The loss of self-sufficiency occasioned by the green revolution is a serious loss. The small farmer is driven out of business because he has no money. The farmer who survives depends for his livelihood on the global export market. His choice of what to grow is driven by what can bring the most profit from sales abroad. No longer is he concerned with feeding his locality or bringing local food to the local market. Unless the international market has a demand for it, local produce becomes increasingly rare, as the world shifts to a standardized food menu, dictated by **agribusiness.**

A final argument against the green revolution is that growing for the global market requires a lot of land. As more and more acreage is planted to global standardized crops, **biodiversity,** or the maintenance of the extraordinary diversity nature has given us, is put increasingly at risk. Whether it be the cutting down of the Amazon forest or expanding cropland in Southeast Asia to plant export crops, the expansion of cultivated land reduces the diversity of plant and animal species where it occurs.

This argument has a stronger counterargument. The green revolution has brought with it a trend toward harvesting more from fewer acres. Experts have calculated that India's transition to high-yield farming spared the country from having to plough an additional 100 million acres of virgin land, an area equivalent to California. And high-yield crops have contributed to India's ability to slow and, in some places, to halt deforestation of its timber. These are hopeful signs. While it may be true that standardized crops planted over large acreages reduce the biodiversity of that area, it is also true that fewer American farmers produce more food on less land for more people than ever before.

Fortunately, we have becoming increasingly aware of the impact of losing local cultures rooted in prescientific ways of managing the land. As one of the most basic components of economic development, the green revolution has caused artificial job scarcity, driving the less successful off the land and raising the level of conflict in regions where formerly different ethnic or religious groups lived peacefully side by side. The enormous plus side of the revolution is that it has enabled the world to feed millions, and perhaps billions, more than it could have using the old methods.

Also on the positive side, indigenous knowledge and ways of living may yet converge with modern science despite the many obstacles. Dr. Walter Lewis, a biologist at Washington University in St. Louis, Missouri, first went to the Andean foothills of Peru in 1982. Over the years, he and his team built up strong ties with the Aguaruna and Achuar tribes of the Jivaro people, who were very familiar with all the fauna in their region. In times gone by, they had developed a medical practice utilizing some 500 of the region's identified 10,000 plant species—an astonishingly high number. Dr. Lewis was particularly interested in remedies for malaria.

Agribusiness

The totality of industry engaged in the operations of a farm, the manufacture and sale of farm equipment and supplies, and the processing, storage, and distribution of farm products. Agribusiness may also refer to one giant multinational corporation engaged in one of these farm operations, such as Arthur Daniels Midland (ADM).

Biodiversity

Short for biological diversity—the number of different species of plants and animals inhabiting a specific ecosystem, such as the Amazon Forest or the Mediterranean region.

After years of working together, the Aguaruna led the team of biologists to ten anti-malarial plants and taught the scientists how to prepare the medicine from them. Dr. Lewis readily admits he would never have found the plants by himself. To realize the benefits of their joint work, Dr. Lewis helped the tribe develop nurseries to grow medicinal plants. The nurseries have meant the abandonment of a semino-madic lifestyle for the group.[30] While Dr. Lewis's story suggests that modern scientists can successfully learn from an indigenous group, one wonders how long the Aguaruna will survive as a people after their lifestyle has been so radically changed by economic success.

Another area where scientists are pushing the agricultural frontiers is in turning to sea plants to find new medicines. Again, this type of research raises environmental concerns about reducing biodiversity of the world's oceans or of harming endangered species, such as coral reefs. But the benefits promised include a cancer therapy made from algae and a painkiller taken from snails.[31]

The big question is how to manage the demands and promises of modern medicine with the desire to keep some part of our planet out of reach of human manipulation. These and questions like them are ones you in the next generation will have to face.

The Biotech Revolution

Throughout agricultural history, fields planted with the same kind of plant tend to attract pests and disease. The biotech revolution enables domesticated plants to resist disease and pests through the introduction of pest-resistant genes from an alien life form. Thus, this revolution may be seen in large part as a continuation of the green revolution.

Critics wonder about the effects of this genetic engineering on the plant produce. We do not yet know what long-term impact on health genetically engineered food will have. However, given the known dangers of pesticides and herbicides, it seems to make sense to pursue a path where none of the polluting chemicals would come into play. Integrated pest management is one variant of the biotech revolution, where plant and insect species are utilized to control each other.

Cloning
The growing of an individual from a single cell of its parent. The individual generally is considered an identical copy of the parents; for example, Dolly the sheep.

Another more controversial aspect of the biotech revolution is **cloning.** In 1999 British scientists produced the first cloned sheep. Since then, cloning has taken off. There are cloned monkeys and cloned pigs. The time is coming when there will be cloned humans. The ethics of cloning will surely be one of the most critical issues of the twenty-first century.

Thus far, science has trumpeted its biotech achievements to a world that has responded rather conservatively. When the United States tried to market hormone-treated meat and genetically engineered soybeans and corn to the European Union, the reaction was a mass public boycott of all produce imported from the United States. Europeans demonstrated by the thousands to prevent the import of genetically engineered food. The protest was so strong and sales so poor that in 2000, mid-western farmers returned to the old kinds of soybean rather than risk even poorer sales and possible bankruptcy. In 2002, Robert Mugabe, the dictator of the African state of Zimbabwe, refused to accept the United States offer of American corn to feed his starving population on the grounds that the corn was genetically engineered and thus unsafe to eat (see the case study at the end of this chapter for more on this issue).

On their part, the big agricultural companies argue that genetic engineering poses no danger. On the contrary, it opens up enormous opportunities for improvements in human health and well-being. Cloning pigs makes possible organ transplants from our closest animal cousin. People needing a liver transplant will no longer have to wait in line for a human liver. Cloned animal livers will be immediately available.

So far, most people remain skeptical. Perhaps that is the appropriate attitude to take. The history of technology tells us that if the benefits are already here, environmental surprise cannot be far behind. Nature is not passive. And how nature will react to genetic engineering, we cannot know until later.

The above discussion indicates that what is grown and sold on the world's markets is most certainly going to become an international problem requiring international regulation. To date, each country within the European Union has regulations about what foods may be imported. If biotechnology circles the globe, regulation will have to be international.

Why Can't We Agree on a Common Strategy for Protecting the Global Environment?

If all these environmental problems are so serious, why can't we listen to the scientists and agree on the right solutions? This chapter has suggested many answers to that question. Let us summarize them here.

1. Environmental problems are not equally distributed and affect each region and country differently. While water scarcity may be a world problem, its effects will be less severely felt in North America than in China or the deserts of Africa, the Middle East, or Central Asia.
2. Reasonable people, including scientists, differ about the severity and cause of environmental problems. There may be general agreement that the world may be warming. There is less agreement as to why it is warming.
3. Every environmental remedy has its cost. The closer you come to really clean air and really clean water, the higher the cost. How clean is clean is thus not a scientific question but a political question demanding a political solution. When the Clean Air Act Amendment of 1990 required car owners to test annually the catalytic converter in their car and to pay to have it put in the proper condition if it failed the test, car owners protested. Car owners did not think clean air meant cleaning up their car. The requirement was tacitly dropped.
4. Every state has a different capacity to pay the cost of environmental remediation. The United States, Western Europe, and Japan can afford to undertake costly pollution control programs. Most other states cannot. These poorer states accuse the rich states of having caused the problem and demand that the rich states pay for the damage. Many states refuse outright to pay for pollution control.
5. The industrialized states already have laws and regulations in place that they are reluctant to let an international treaty force them to change. If the United States is already reducing its emissions of CO_2 as a result of the 1990 Clean Air Act, why should it sign the Kyoto Convention forcing U.S. industry to undergo higher costs for more radical emission control?

6. States like to point fingers, as we all do. The developed states look at the developing states and say, "Don't do as I do, do as I say. We'll help you, too." The developing states, including China, say, "We refuse to risk our development by putting on pollution controls that are very costly and will limit the global marketability of our goods. You, the industrial states, got to where you are because you polluted. Now you are rich and can afford to clean up your act. We'll clean up ours when we become as rich as you."

7. Some nations may benefit from the ecological downturn of others, just as some ecological disasters make good TV viewing but occasion low public reaction. If the earth really is warming, then Canada and Russia—cold countries—stand to benefit. If the seas rise, people living in regions toward the middle of the world's continents will be better off than those along the coast. Upstream water-users have an easier time imposing their views of water allocation upon downstream users. Why should Americans care if a cyanide spill killed all life in the Tisza River? Do New Yorkers do anything about an ecoli outbreak in Canada?

8. Environmental problems are highly complex. Most scientific answers are shrouded in uncertainty. Our knowledge of how nature responds to human activity is too limited to be able to predict her future response. We have only recently moved from the mindset that nature was neutral and that we could manage our fields and forests as we wanted and everything would be fine. We now know that nature responds to every situation, but we do not know how she will respond to a given set of circumstances.

9. Last but not least, we are all part of the problem. Most people are locked into a culture of denial.

"And may we continue to be worthy of consuming a disproportionate share of this planet's resources."

This chapter has told you that planet Earth sets the limits on human activity. We cannot run the planet the way we run a corporation or even a university. Planet Earth has its own ways of acting and will let you know when it is put upon. In earlier civilizations, religion indicated the appropriate parameters of human behavior toward nature. The lesson from the industrial and scientific revolutions is that we cannot continue to define technological change as progress, as we have in the past two hundred years. More is not necessarily better. Over 6 billion of us are traveling together on spaceship earth. Soon there will be more. In 2002 the international community assembled to discuss sustainable development and poverty, the same topics that the UN environmental conference discussed in Rio de Janeiro in 1992. And that meeting built on the UN environmental conference in Helsinki in 1972, where these issues were first raised in an international forum.

The time for talking may be running out on us. The clock is counting down the hours and minutes that the international community may have left to make and implement life-saving programs for the people of planet Earth. Here's where you can help. Only you as a voter and a concerned citizen of an individual state can bring pressure to bear on the international representatives appointed by your state to make the hard global decisions necessary to ensure the survival of the human race. The motto of the environmentalist represents the positive vector of the decentralization/centralization continuum: Act locally, think globally. More than any other issue before the world today, environmental concerns challenge each one of us to work on all levels of the international system (within our local communities, at the state and regional levels, and at the international system level), to promote the common interest of us all, the health of the planet.

Web Exploration

To find out what pollution is in your backyard go to **www.ablongman.com/ duncan.**

CHAPTER SUMMARY

The main concern of the human race today is to keep the earth sufficiently people friendly so that the 11 billion or so human beings we expect to inhabit the planet by 2050 will be able to survive.

What Environmental Factors Help Explain How Human Society Began?

The same factors that explain why human society first arose are critical to humanity's continued survival today: a steady and dependable source of water, a moderate climate, and an easy migration movement in the same or similar climate zone.

How Have the Industrial and Scientific Revolutions Internationalized Environmental Problems?

The industrial and scientific revolutions refer to historical processes whereby human beings, by applying science and ingenuity, created tools and instruments that enable us to do things we otherwise

would not be able to do. Inventions such as the steam engine and the automobile revolutionize the way society lives, creating a new socioeconomic order that cannot be reversed.

The history of energy use can be seen in the four phases of the so-called industrial revolution, which are based on the type of energy that predominated during that period.

The *preparatory period,* marked the shift from wood to coal. The *first industrial revolution* saw the automation of simple tasks, with coal as the main energy source. The *second industrial revolution* involved the automation of more complex tasks and the development of the petrochemical and automotive industries. Petroleum and natural gas are the main sources of energy. The *third industrial revolution,* called the information revolution, witnessed the automation of basic human thinking skills via the computer. There is no single energy source, but oil and natural gas predominate in the generation of electricity. As the revolution progressed, the use of technology expanded and covered increasing portions of the globe. In the fourth phase of the revolution, the rapid pace of communication globalized national and corporate economies.

The uneven distribution of technology creates distortions in technology use and consequently in the consumption of energy and other natural resources. Technology has, however, arguably raised the standard of living in virtually every country on the globe.

The benefits of technology come with costs. By the time the negative consequences of the technology register in the public consciousness, society can no longer do without it.

- The first cost is *technological monoculture*. A technology's benefits are understood long before we gain an understanding of its problems. By the time we do, and that may come a generation later, the technology has become locked into the economic and social fabric of society in a way that cannot be changed.
- Technological monoculture leads to the second problem with technology: *reduction in variability,* both within human society and in the environment where that society is situated. Nature is eclectic. Technology is selective.
- *Environmental surprise* is nature's reaction to technological change. The reaction can be a one-time event, like Chernobyl. Sometimes the surprise becomes obvious over a long period of time, like the ozone hole. Sometimes surprise can come from the emergence of new information, like global warming. If we understand the process by which a technology produces environmental surprise, there is a faint chance the international community can anticipate that surprise and perhaps head it off in another part of the world.

As with technology, applied science has also proven to be a Pandora's box of benefits and costs. While its benefits were first applied in Europe and the United States, their major contribution today has been to the improved health of Third World states.

Prevention of disease. Probably the most significant application of science to human health has been the understanding and prevention of disease.

New medical technology. Advances in medical technology have helped scientists see the mi-

crobes that cause disease and developed the medical instruments to save lives.

Sanitation. Major improvements in sanitation, such as water treatment and sewage systems, occurred largely within the last two hundred years.

Vaccines, antibiotics, insecticides. In the twentieth century, science turned its attention to the application of chemistry to the eradication of disease. The research has been done mainly at national laboratories and research centers while the World Health Organization has been the lead organization in carrying the vaccines to every country to eradicate infectious diseases. In the 1980s, despite WHO work, old infectious diseases, like TB, are coming back, and new diseases, such as AIDS and West Nile disease have reached epidemic proportions.

Today, the containment of disease must be found at the international level. Disease has become a global problem and governments can no longer ensure the health of their citizens without cooperation from other states.

Increased global population. One of the clearest results of improved public health around the world has been the increase in the world's population, which is expected to grow to 10.5 billion in 2050 before it levels off.

Reduced birth rates in the industrialized states. A second major influence of science on population growth involves such developments as the pill and amniocentesis. The birth rate in all Western countries, with the exception of the United States, has dropped. Today the birth rate in the European states, and especially Russia, has fallen below the replacement level.

Increased population density. Population issues of the twenty-first century will focus on the very uneven distribution of people.

- Almost all the population increase in the next twenty years will be in the developing countries, while Europe will experience a steadily aging population.
- Fifty percent of the global population today lives in cities. Population densities are the highest in Asia.
- The number of people living in cities is expected to double by 2030. By 2025, 5 billion people are expected to live in urban areas, 4 billion of whom will live in cities in the developing world.

What Are the Earth's Most Serious Environmental Problems?

Global Warming   The evidence shows that at the earth's surface, the average temperature is 1.5 degrees Fahrenheit warmer than a century and a half ago.

Scientists do not agree on the evidence, however. Some say it is definitely warmer, while others say it may even be getting colder. In the absence of certainty about what is happening, the international response has been to prevent the world from warming further or faster. These steps include the Montreal Protocol for Protection of the Ozone Layer (1979) and the Kyoto Framework Convention on Climate Change (1992).

Pollution from Energy Sources   Most energy sources are polluters. The world today is dependent on fossil fuels as its major energy source. Fossil fuels are the principal contributors to the greenhouse gases that produce global warming.

While nuclear power emits no pollutants in the air, Chernobyl showed us that using that power is very dangerous; moreover, the world has yet to find permanent deposition sites for spent nuclear fuel rods.

The burning of firewood and biomass contributes to the greenhouse effect; releases smoke, carbon monoxide, and other air pollutants that are harmful to human health; and leads to deforestation.

Solar, wind, and geothermal energy are renewable energy sources. While their use is increasing, they are still too costly to persuade the average person to select them as their fuel of choice.

Air Pollution   The air we breathe is a *global commons.* Like oceans, the seabed, and outer space, it belongs to no one and belongs to everyone. Air pollution problems are global problems because:

- emissions of air pollution from any one country contribute to the formation of greenhouse gases that can cause the warming of the whole earth;
- emissions of air pollutants from one country can be borne by the wind and air currents to another country far away. These emissions combine with other atmospheric factors to produce acid rain. Acid rain can cause forest dieback and dead waterways.
- The emission of chlorofluorocarbons (CFCs) into the atmosphere has contributed to the deterioration of the ozone layer that is vital to the maintenance of life on Earth.

The international response to global air pollution problems include the Transboundary Air Pollution (LRTAP) Convention (1979), Partial Test Ban Treaty (1963) against nuclear testing in outer space and on the seabed, the Montreal Protocol for the Protection of the Ozone Layer (1987), and the Kyoto Framework Convention on Climate Change (1992).

- Each treaty establishes a *regime,* or treaty system, that promotes compliance with the treaty but cannot compel compliance.
- The international community has been more effective in handling transboundary air pollution problems than the issue of global warming.

Water Scarcity and Water Pollution   Water problems constitute perhaps the most serious environmental threat to the world today. By 2025 one half of the world's population will be experiencing water shortages and two-thirds will be living in areas undergoing moderate to high water stress. One billion people in the world live without access to clean drinking water; 2.5 billion do not have proper sewage and water treatment facilities.

The causes of the world's water problems include the high demand for water required by agriculture, widespread irrigation projects, and pollution of water systems by industrial and agricultural run-off.

What Is the International Community Doing to Mediate Global Water Problems?

The international response to water scarcity includes

- international water treaties whose purpose is to allocate water use of multinational or international rivers equitably to all the states along the river
- major efforts of the international community, specifically the United Nations, to prevent inappropriate uses of waterways (building dams) and to bring water where it is needed.

Solutions to global water pollution problems fall heavily on the international financial institutions to provide funding for water treatment plants and urban sewage systems. The international water treaties in place do not safeguard the riverine rights of the less powerful treaty signers.

What Are the Green and Biotech Revolutions?

The green revolution is the application of the scientific method to seed production to produce more prolific plants and increase crop yield per acre. The revolution began in the United States in the 1920s with the work of Henry Wallace. It was carried abroad to India and Pakistan by Nobel Prize winner Norman Borlaug. The green revolution has helped prevent starvation in Asia and Africa, but it has many opponents. It allegedly has encouraged the spread of agribusiness at the expense of the small farmer and has been accused of being a major player in the elimination of biodiversity.

The biotech revolution involves the decoding of the genetic code and the genetically altering of plants and animal species so that they can resist disease or increase in size and yield. A second aspect of the biotech revolution has been the development of the ability to clone animals and eventually human species. Medical science has been enthusiastic about genetically modified (GM) foods and cloning. GM foods enable plants to

fight disease and insects and bring higher yields without reducing the application of pesticides and fertilizers. Cloning and the use of animal organs in modern medicine will resolve the tragic shortages of human organs for transplants and help find cures to now incurable diseases. Detractors argue that humans should not play God. Cloning may seem beneficial and harmless at the present time, but the environmental surprise will eventually come.

Why Can't We Agree on a Common Strategy for Protecting the Global Environment?

Environmental problems are hard to resolve for a variety of factors.

- A long period of time elapses between a technological innovation and its environmental surprise.
- There is much scientific uncertainty surrounding every environmental problem.
- Governments are reluctant to take action that may undermine economic growth or destabilize society in the absence of strong public pressure or clear scientific evidence.
- We are locked into a culture of denial.

ENDNOTES

[1] For a brief description of the event, see Anna Scherbakova and Scott Monroe, "The Urals and Siberia," ed. Phillip R. Pryde, *Environmental Resources and Constraints in the Former Soviet Republics* (Boulder, CO: Westview Press, 1995), pp. 70–71. See also Zhores Medvedev, *Nuclear Disaster in the Urals*, trans. George Sunders (New York: Vintage Books, 1980).

[2] Anna Scherbakova and Scott Monroe, p. 69.

[3] See the discussion of technology in Rudi Volti, *Society and Technological Change*, 3rd ed. (New York: St. Martin's Press, 1995), Chapter 1, pp. 3–15.

[4] J. Wreford Watson and Timothy O'Riordan, eds., *The American Environment: Perceptions & Policies* (London and New York: John Wiley & Sons, 1976), pp. 79–92.

[5] P. Timmerman, "Mythology and Surprise in the Sustainable Development of the Biosphere," ed. W. C. Clark and R. E. W. Munn, *Sustainable Development of the Biosphere* (New York and London: Cambridge University Press, 1986), pp. 435–454.

[6] H. Brooks, "The Typology of Surprises in Technology, Institutions, and Development," In W. C. Clark and R. E.

Munn, eds., *Sustainable Development of the Biosphere* (New York and London: Cambridge University Press, 1986), p. 329.

[7] See World Resources Institute, *World Resources 1994–1995*. Table 11.2 (New York: Oxford University Press, 1994), p. 199.

[8] See Edmund O. Wilson, *The Future of Life* (New York: Alfred A. Knoff, 2002), pp. 42–54.

[9] William J. McNeil, *Plagues and Peoples* (New York and London: Doubleday, 1976) p. 242.

[10] World Resources Institute, "Cholera Returns," *World Resources 1998–1999*, p. 22.

[11] SOURCE: U.S. Census Bureau, Historical Estimates of World Population and Total Midyear Population for the World 1950–2050 downloaded from *http://k12science.ati.stevens-tech.edu/curriculum/popgrowthproj/worldpop.html*.

[12] World Resources Institute, *World Resources 1994–1995* (New York: Oxford University Press, 1995), pp. 270–273.

[13] Roy W. Spencer, "How Do We Know the Temperature of the Earth? Global Warming and Global Temperatures," ed.

Ronald Bailey, *Earth Report 2000: Revisiting the True State of the Planet* (New York: McGraw-Hill, 2000), p. 39.

[14]Robert C. Fleagle, *Global Environmental Change: Interactions of Science, Policy, and Politics in the United Nations* (Westport, CT: Praeger, 1994), pp. 183–185.

[15]Communique cited from the Environmental News Service, March 2001 (*http://ens-news.com/ens/mar2001/2001L-03-05-01.html.*)

[16]John J. Fialka, "Soot Storm: A Dirty Discovery Over Indian Ocean Sets Off a Fight," *The Wall Street Journal,* CCXLI, 88 (May 6, 2003), pp. A1 and A6.

[17]See "photosynthesis," in *Columbia Encyclopedia,* 9th ed., William Bridgewater and Seymour Kurtz, eds. (New York and London: Columbia University Press, 1968), p. 1957.

[18]A quad is a unit of energy equal to one quadrillion British thermal units. A British thermal unit is the amount of heat required to raise the temperature of water 1 degree Fahrenheit.

[19]Jerry Taylor and Peter VanDoren, "Soft Energy versus Hard Facts: Powering the 21st Century," *Earth Report 2000,* pp. 135–139.

[20]Marvin Soroos, *The Endangered Atmosphere* (Columbia, SC: University of South Carolina Press, 1997) p. 3.

[21]See Oran Young, "The Politics of International Regime Formation: Managing Natural Resources and the Environment," *International Organization* 43 (1989), 349–376; and Oran R. Young and Gail Osherenko, eds., *Polar Politics: Creating Environmental Regimes* (Ithaca: Cornell University Press, 1993).

[22]The World Bank, *Clear Water, Blue Skies: China's Environment in the New Century* (Washington, DC: The World Bank, 1997), Table 2.1, p. 19.

[23]*World Resources 1998–1999,* Data from Box 2.6, pp. 64–65.

[24]World Watch Institute, "Water: Critical Shortages Ahead," *http://www.wri.org./trends/water2.html*

[25]World Summit on Sustainable Development, "Freshwater," *Global Challenge Global Opportunity: Trends in Sustainable Development,* p. 10. Downloaded pdf file from *http://www.johannesburgsummit.org/index.html*

[26]Lester R. Brown, "Falling Water Tables in China May Soon Raise Food Prices Everywhere," message sent by *Infoterra@cedar.at* May 3, 2000.

[27]"Regional Profiles: Senegal," *World Resources 1998–1999,* p. 114.

[28]For a layman's account of Wallace's contribution to the green revolution, see John C. Culver and John Hyde, *American Dreamer: A Life of Henry Wallace* (New York: W. W. Norton, 2000), pp. 3–108.

[29]See, for example, Darrell A. Posey, *Traditional Resource Rights: International Instruments for Protection and Compensation for Indigenous Peoples and Local Governments,* "IUCN Biodiversity Programme," Gland, Switzerland and Oxford: IUCN, The World Conservation Union, 1996.

[30]Bernice Wuethrich, "The Changing Landscape of Knowledge," Smithsonian Institution, *Forces of Change: A New View of Nature* (Washington, DC: The National Geographic Society, 2000), 190–191.

[31]John Henkel, "Drugs of the Deep: Treasures of the Sea Yield Some Medical Answers and Hint at Others," *http://www.fda.gov/fdac/features/1998/198_deep.html*

CASE STUDY

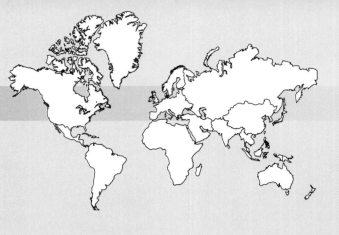

Should the International Community Regulate Genetically Modified (GM) Foods?

The ability to genetically modify food, as discussed in this chapter, represents a dramatic technological and scientific breakthrough. Genetic modification, as defined by the U.S. Department of Agriculture, is a special set of technologies that alter the genetic makeup of such living organisms as animals, plants, or bacteria. Combining genes from different organisms is known as recombinant DNA technology, and the resulting organism is said to be "genetically modified," or "genetically engineered."[1]

The appearance of GM foods and their indiscriminate sale in the marketplace has aroused increasingly strong public opposition. Oregon is the first of the 50 states of the United States to put the issue to a public vote, asking voters' opinion on a measure that would require all foods containing at least one-tenth of one percent of genetically modified material to be labeled as such.[2]

However, nowhere has the issue aroused a more strident protest than in Western Europe, particularly in the United Kingdom. By 2001 opposition had grown so strong that the German Ministry of Agriculture stopped all research into GM foods. Opponents say that transgenic plants growing in fields beside a wild area risk transmitting mismatched genes into wild plants and destroying the earth's precious store of biodiversity. These skeptical scientists and environmentalists argue that a GM product could end up poisoning those who eat it, causing international catastrophe on the scale of the mad cow disease in Europe in 2000–2002.

Scientists who favor GM research say the protest is misplaced, that transgenic produce will be the solution to famine for the growing human population that has run out of agricultural space. They point to the chronic hunger problem around the world and argue that the only solution is to develop plants that produce more but require less land, less water, and fewer fertilizers and herbicides.

In the summer of 2002, Southern Africa experienced severe drought, and hundreds of thousands of people risked starvation. The United States offered to send corn (maize) to alleviate the situation. As discussed in Article B, Zimbabwe, Malawi, Zambia, and Mozambique initially refused. The United States was taken by surprise. The European Union, and especially the United Kingdom that has been most outspoken regarding the dangers of GM food—as you will see from the readings—openly accused the United States of wanting the deliberate death of large numbers of Africans. A survey of Asian consumers taken in 2002 indicated that they looked favorably on GM foods but would welcome regulation.

In the interests of relieving global hunger and solving the problems of failed agriculture, what actions can the United Nations take in this matter? Should the UN regulate the quality and production of GM foods? Do you see this type of action as part of the UN mission? (See Chapter 5). Should the UN as a world body take a vote on whether or not UN agencies may distribute GM foods? How can the UN serve as a centralizing agency promoting the good of all humankind and at the same time accommodate the concerns and interests of the individual states?

---

[1]See http://www.ornl.gov/hgmis/elsi/gmfood.html

[2]Reuters News 10/03/02 http://www.packaging-technology.com/informer/breakthrough/break306/

To help you think these questions through, this case study provides four articles on the subject. The first briefly describes the pros and cons of the controversy. The second expresses the attitude of the Southern African countries. The third, from *The New Scientist*, a British publication, argues that skepticism about the benefits of GM foods in the UK is not just confined to the consumer or environmental activist but extends to the scientific community while the fourth, from *The New York Times*,

makes no bones about calling the European attitude "imperialist."

Here is a brand new technology that appears to have potential to free the world from hunger, yet it is under attack as a corporate deception that will globalize agribusiness, promote U.S. hegemonic ambitions, and murder biodiversity. If you were a representative from the United States, the UK, or one of the Southern African countries, what action would you urge the UN to take?

DEBATE ABOUT GM FOODS

A. Controversies Surrounding the Risks and Benefits of Genetically Modified Food

The appearance of genetically modified foods in the marketplace has resulted in a firestorm of public debate, scientific discussion, and media coverage. A variety of ecological and human health concerns come with the new advances made possible by genetic modification.

What Are the Benefits?

Genetically modified foods (GM foods or GMF) offer a way to quickly improve crop characteristics such as yield, pest resistance, or herbicide tolerance, often to a degree not possible with traditional methods. Further, GM crops can be manipulated to produce completely artificial substances, from the precursors to plastics to consumable vaccines.

What Are the Risks?

The power of genetic modification techniques raises the possibility of human health, environmental, and economic problems, including unanticipated allergic responses to novel substances in foods, the spread of pest resistance or herbicide tolerance to wild plants, inadvertent toxicity to benign wildlife, and increasing control of agriculture by biotechnology corporations.

SOURCE: *Science Controversies On-Line Partnerships in Education (SCOPE) Forum (http://scope.educ.washington.edu/gmfood).*

B. Divergent Views on Modified Foods Delay Food Aid

Divergent views on gene-altered foods are delaying the shipment of food aid to millions of starving southern Africans, a senior official said on Sunday.

Prega Ramsamy, CEO and Executive Secretary of the 14-member Southern Africa Development Community (SADC), said in Angola the absence of a clearly defined regional response to genetically modified (GM) food relief was a serious problem.

"The absence of a harmonised regional position on GMOs is creating operational problems with regard to movement of food and non-food items which may contain GMOs.

"This is particularly serious given the current humanitarian crisis," Ramsamy said. "The food crisis in southern Africa remains a grave concern to all of us.

"What SADC has been urging member countries to do is to accept milled GMOs, but of course each government must make its own choice," added the Botswana-based Ramsamy.

Ramsamy, in Angola for the annual SADC summit starting this week, said the issue would be high on the agenda. Foreign and trade ministers were gathering in the capital Luanda for the meetings which Angola hopes will showcase its return to peace after a costly civil war.

Angola faces severe food problems of its own because of its 27-year war. But it is not listed by the UN among the six southern African countries worst hit by shortages which analysts blame on capricious weather and poor food management.

Around 13 million people in the region are facing severe food shortages, which could persist for the next seven months at least, and urgently require 1.2 million tonnes of cereals if famine is to be averted, SADC food security experts said.

Zimbabwe, Malawi and Mozambique say they accept milled GM food relief, but Zambia has completely outlawed GM relief and says it is working on non-GM commercial imports to plug its food gap. Lesotho and Swaziland, the other countries facing food shortages, have not said whether they readily accept GM relief.

Ramsamy said SADC's council of ministers would create an advisory committee to develop guidelines to safeguard members against potential risks in the areas of food safety, contamination of genetic resources, and consumer concerns.

SADC officials said that the committee could meet as early as next week. Zambian officials said they were pressing for conclusive research on GM-foods before they could be allowed.

The spread of AIDS in the region had compounded the food misery. "Healthcare workers emphasised the lethal combination of hunger and HIV—how the convergence of the two calamities sharply increases people's vulnerability to infection and disease," Ramsamy said.

Africa is the continent hit hardest by AIDS. The members of the SADC, South Africa, Zimbabwe, Zambia, Swaziland, Lesotho, Botswana, Mozambique, Namibia, the Democratic Republic of Congo, Angola, Tanzania, Seychelles, Mauritius and Malawi.

SOURCE: *The Daily News*, Harare, Zimbabwe, The Famine in Southern Africa October 1, 2002 (http://allafrica.com/stories/200210010545.html). *Copyright © 2002 The Daily News. All rights reserved. Distributed by AllAfrica Global Media (allAfrica.com).*

C. The British Perspective: Worlds Apart

The Planet Has Never Been More Divided Over Transgenic Crops

Anyone who thought the inexorable rise of genetically modified crops had been body-checked by consumer pressure and green opposition is wrong. According to figures out last month, 5.5 million farmers worldwide—mainly in the United States, Argentina, Canada and China—now grow GM crops covering more than 50 million hectares. That's an area the size of Spain. And with vast countries like Indonesia about to join the GM club, next year's leap could be bigger still.

Yet in Britain, where there is still no commercial growing, the GM industry's prospects have taken another dive. A report on the potential health impacts of GM foods slams the current system of safety screening—developed in the United States—as flawed and subjective, and calls for better tests (see "Good enough to eat?"). The fact that existing GM crops haven't harmed anyone is no reason for complacency, the report warns. The next generation will be more complex, and even subtle changes in foods could have an impact on people dependent on single food sources—such as babies fed formula milk.

Just another gloomy warning from green consumer activists? Far from it. The report comes from a panel of scientists set up by the Royal Society in London, and is an astonishing sign of how far Britain's scientific establishment has moved on this issue. A few years ago, senior scientists were wont to dismiss public concerns about GM crops as hysteria. Now they are telling regulators to get tougher.

The report rightly has no truck with the more lurid fears about GM technology—such as the idea that the DNA that is added to food crops could create dangerous viruses. But as it points out, inserting genes into plants is not yet an exact science, so unforeseen side effects on a plant's biochemistry are a real possibility. Toxins normally present in a plant at harmless levels might increase. Nutrients important to a balanced diet might decline.

Yet all companies have been required to do so far is show that their GM food crops are "substantially equivalent" to non-GM breeds. And that phrase has never been properly defined. Must the plants look and smell about the same? Must they contain the same levels of starch, protein and fibre? Must they be equally well liked and tolerated by rats? Or pigs? There's no consensus among companies and regulators, and the panel is right to say that must be fixed.

It would be naive, though, to see this as the key to hearts and minds. In Britain, neither big business nor its regulators is trusted on GM foods and consumers cannot yet see this technology giving them anything they want. Reforming the idea of substantial equivalence will not change this.

Nor will it make the environmental concerns go away. A couple of months ago, we reported on a worrying phenomenon in Canada: GM crops cross-pollinating with each other to produce "bastardised" strains. Resistant to more than one herbicide, such crops could in time behave like super-weeds.

The GM industry may be making a killing in certain parts of the world. But in sceptical countries it has a mountain to climb—and in Britain the mountain just got bigger.

SOURCE: *The New Scientist, Editorial, 09 February 2002* (http://www.newscientist.com/hottopics/gm/gm.jsp?id=23290100).

D. The Pro-GM Food Perspective

Critics of Biotechnology Are Called Imperialists

By Andrew Pollack

Tribal herders in Kenya, driven out of the countryside by drought and failed crops, brought their cattle into Nairobi last year. With five million people in Kenya facing starvation because of a severe drought, opponents of agricultural biotechnology urged the Kenyan government to reject corn donated by the United States and Canada because some of it was genetically modified. And when the United States sent corn and soy meal to India after a 1999 cyclone that killed 10,000 people, a prominent biotech critic in that country accused Washington of using the cyclone victims as "guinea pigs" for bio-engineered food.

Such actions raise a troubling question about the critics of biotechnology. Are they so against it that they are willing to let people die? Indeed, the critics, most of whom live in wealthy countries, are increasingly being called imperialists for opposing a technology that could be used to develop improved crops for poor nations.

"To deny desperately hungry people the means to control their futures by presuming to know what is best for them is not only paternalistic but morally wrong," Hassan Adamu, until last week Nigeria's minister of agriculture and rural development, wrote in an op-ed piece in *The Washington Post*.

Until now, the debate about biotechnology has focused on whether modified crops are safe for consumption and for the environment. And it has largely pitted the United States against anti-biotech Europe, neither of which faces much risk of hunger.

But there is a growing recognition that the Third World might have the swing vote on whether genetically modified agriculture succeeds or fails. So both sides are courting developing countries—though some experts say the poor are being used as pawns.

Focusing on hunger rather than safety could help the beleaguered biotechnology industry because it emphasizes the potential benefits, not the risks. The critics say the industry is using the poor to justify selling their products to the rich.

"The feeding-the-world argument is a very carefully engineered P.R. exercise to create some moral legitimacy for this technology," said Brian Halweil, an analyst at the Worldwatch Institute in Washington. He points out that the industry concentrates on crops like herbicide-resistant soybeans for farmers in the Midwest, not drought-tolerant millet for subsistence farmers in Africa.

Not all critics want to stop biotechnology; some just want to increase testing and regulation. But the most zealous seem to say that virtually no benefit could outweigh the risk of genetic pollution from transferring genes between species. In remarks to reporters last year, Benedikt Haerlin of Greenpeace dismissed the importance of saving African and Asian lives if it meant unleashing the technology.

In fairness, most critics contend that biotechnology won't alleviate hunger in the first place. The world already produces enough food, they say, but the poor can't afford to buy it. And they note that peasant farmers in India have destroyed fields of genetically engineered crops, so it is not only well-fed environmentalists who oppose them.

Many critics see biotechnology as the latest incarnation of corporate agriculture, which is heavily dependent on pesticides and which replaces diverse crops with single varieties. Such an approach, they say, is antithetical to lower-tech sustainable farming practices, like better crop rotations, which in some cases can produce dramatic gains at lower cost. There is also a fear that poor farmers, who often save seeds from one year's crop to plant the next, will have to buy expensive biotech seeds every year, making them dependent on multinational companies or driving them off their land if they cannot afford the costs.

Biotechnology companies "don't really want to get to the crux of the matter, which is about control of the food system," said Anuradha Mittal, co-director of Food First, a food-policy research institute in Oakland.

Biotech backers, and many other food experts, say that for some farmers and some regions, absolute shortages of production are a problem. And while early efforts were indeed aimed at crops for rich countries, there are now numerous projects to develop third world crops that are resistant to pests, drought or poor soil. Such crops could lessen, not increase, the need for expensive inputs like pesticides and water. And in any case, farmers are free not to use the new seeds, if they choose.

"For us to take an attitude that these farmers are gullible and ignorant and we have to take care to protect them from Western influences is absurd," said C. S. Prakash, a professor at Tuskegee University who is developing genetically modified crops for the Third World. He accuses biotech opponents of romanticizing the old ways that left people in poor health and abject poverty.

The poster crop in this debate is "golden rice," which contains bacterial and daffodil genes that allow it to make a nutrient that the body converts to vitamin A. Such rice could help alleviate a vitamin deficiency that blinds and kills millions of people each year.

Developed by public sector scientists in Switzerland and Germany, the rice seed is to be given free to poor farmers in developing countries.

But some critics have denounced golden rice as a Trojan horse aimed at winning acceptance of genetically engineered food. They say the rice doesn't contain enough of the vitamin-A precursor to make a difference and that, anyway, the diet of hungry children lacks the fat and protein needed to convert the precursor into vitamin A. They say that solving just one vitamin deficiency won't make much difference for children who suffer from multiple nutrition problems. They also say there are other ways of providing vitamin A, like vitamin capsules or unpolished rice.

Some proponents agree that it is unclear how much vitamin A the rice can provide. But, they say, why does trying it preclude other approaches—which obviously haven't solved the problem yet—from being pursued as well?

Ingo Potrykus, the Swiss scientist who led the development of golden rice, said opponents have a "hidden political agenda." In an article to be published in the journal *In Vitro Plant*, he writes: "It is not so much the concern about the environment, or the health of the consumer, or help for the poor and disadvantaged. It is a radical fight against a technology and for political success."

In fighting to keep golden rice from the poor in developing countries, he adds, the opposition "has to be held responsible for the foreseeable unnecessary death and blindness of millions of poor every year."

SOURCE: *New York Times in Review, February 4, 2001*

QUESTIONS

Check Your Understanding

1. In your own words, summarize the arguments for and against the use of golden rice.
2. Why are the African countries reluctant to accept GM corn even if acceptance might ward off or mitigate the famine?

Analyze the Issues

3. What environmental and health risks, such as loss of biodiversity and cancer, are presented as arguments against GM foods? Do you think they are serious enough to promote a refusal to use them when starvation threatens?
4. How is the GM issue a product of the internationalization of the scientific and technological revolution? (Think about technological monoculture, environmental surprise, biodiversity, and water and agricultural land shortages around the world)
5. Based on what you have read in this chapter, what options does the international community have to mediate the problem? How can the United Nations accommodate the concerns and interests of its diverse membership and still fulfill its mission of bettering the lives of all humankind?
6. Represent a delegate from the United States, the U.K. or one of the Southern African countries to the UN. What arguments would you make for or against centralized UN regulation? How vigorously would you argue for decentralized regional or individual state controls on GM?

FOR FURTHER INFORMATION

To find out more about the international politics of genetically engineered foods, consult the following journal articles, maps, Internet sites and films:

The New Scientist Special Report on genetically engineered foods provides readers with letters and scientific comment of all kinds. The address of the journal is *http://www.newscientist.com/nsplus/insight/gmworld/gmfood/gmfood.html*

Robert Paarlberg, "The Global Food Fight," *Foreign Affairs*, vol. 79, no. 3 (May/June 2000), pp. 24–38.

C. Ford Runge and Benjamin Senauer, "Removable Feast," *Foreign Affairs*, vol. 79, no. 3 (May/June 2000), pp. 39–51.

Michelle Marvier, "Ecology of Transgenic Crops," *American Scientist,* vol. 89, no. 2 (March–April 2001), pp. 160–167.

The National Academies of Science maintains a website on biotechnology and genetic modification at *http://www4.nas.edu/onpi/webextra.nsf/web/web_extra_crops?OpenDocument.* The site has links to many other sites.

Two other excellent U.S. government sources are the U.S. Department of Agriculture (*www.USDA.gov*) and the U.S. Department of Energy *www.energy.gov.*

Map showing distribution of biodiversity around the globe can be found at this website: *www.nhm.ac.uk/science/projects/*

Glossary

Agribusiness: The totality of industry engaged in the operations of a farm, the manufacture and sale of farm equipment and supplies, and the processing, storage, and distribution of farm products. Agribusiness may also refer to one giant multinational corporation engaged in one of these farm operations, such as Arthur Daniels Midland (ADM).

Anthropogenic: Caused by humans or originating from human actions.

Balance of power: A foreign policy principle that world peace and stability is best preserved by way of a basic equilibrium among the world's major actors—typically states.

Balance of power theory: Posits that peace and security are best preserved by a state of equilibrium between the major players in a potential war.

Balance of trade: An economic term referring to the value of goods coming into, and going out of, a country.

Basque Fatherland and Liberty (ETA): A terrorist organization based primarily in Spain that seeks an independent state for the Basque regions of Spain and France.

Basques: An ethnic group with its own language and cultural roots located in northern Spain and southern France.

Biodiversity: Short for biological diversity—the number of different species of plants and animals inhabiting a specific ecosystem, such as the Amazon Forest or the Mediterranean region.

Biological weapon: A weapon that has living organisms such as anthrax or botulinum toxin. It is a weapon of mass destruction in that it does not distinguish between soldier and civilian.

Biotech revolution: The widespread application of bioengineering to increase food production and improve plant and animal strains.

Bipolar system: A balance of power system in which states are grouped around two major power centers.

Bretton Woods system: An international political-economic system of rules, procedures, and institutions designed to foster a liberal global economy through more cooperative trade and monetary policies; named after the location of the original meeting in Bretton Woods, NH.

Capital formation: The process by which land, labor, and physical capital (like factories for manufacturing) are developed to generate income in a country.

Carrying capacity: A natural ecosystem is determined by its maximum sustainable yield and this yield is the products of the size of the ecosystem and its ability to regenerate itself.

Catalans: A self-identifying ethnic group in Spain.

Catalonia: That region in Spain inhabited by Catalans.

Chemical weapon: A weapon consisting of harmful chemicals including tear gas, napalm, and poison gas. It is a weapon of mass destruction in that it does not distinguish between soldier and civilian.

Cloning: The growing of an individual from a single cell of its parent. The individual generally is considered an identical copy of the parents; for example, Dolly the sheep.

Coercive diplomacy: The threat and use of force in tandem with diplomatic pressure by one actor on another. The UN's coercive diplomacy on Saddam Hussein to reveal more information on Iraq's WMD in 2003 is a good example. (Coercive diplomacy failed in this case.)

Cold War: The great ideological and power conflict between the Soviet Union and its allies and the United States and its allies, which lasted roughly from 1946 to 1991.

Collective security: A concept of world order maintaining that aggression could be deterred by promising overwhelming collective retaliation by the combined power of the world's states against any community member that pursued aggression. In other words, an attack against one is an attack against all. Collective security first took form in the League of Nations—which the United States refused to join—immediately following World War I.

Colonialism: Control of territories in what is now considered the Third World by rich, mostly European countries with the aim of gearing the colonies development to the benefit of the home country.

Comparative advantage: In a liberal international economy, countries should specialize in what they produce most efficiently and/or at lowest cost compared to other countries.

Comparative government: The study of the interactions of actors within state borders.

Containment: A U.S. foreign policy pursued during the Cold War that aimed at preventing the Soviet Union from expanding into Western Europe, Asia, and other regions of the Third World. President Harry S. Truman announced it in 1947.

Conventional weapon: A loose term referring to any weapon that is not a weapon of mass destruction.

Core countries: In the language of the dependency approach, these are the world's rich countries: First World countries.

Core objectives: A term used in foreign policy to underscore a state's primary objectives (or interests), such as pursuit of its physical (territorial) security, economic vitality, and sovereign political independence.

Corporate actors: Businesses and business associations; a catchall term for multinational and transnational corporations.

Customs Union (CU): A free trade area in which all member states agree to a common external tariff.

Deep ecology: A world view that promotes a reverence for nature, a concern for ecological principles such as complexity, diversity, and symbiosis, and that sees human beings in a living relationship with their environment. The environment is not there for human use alone. We gain our identity from it. Deep ecology proposes to reconnect humankind with nature.

Dependency theories: A set of related theories that have in common the belief that less developed countries can never develop because they are dependent upon the industrial states for capital and technology. An approach that argues that foreign investment in developing countries is a means to dominate and extract capital from weaker states.

Desertification: The process of becoming desert from land mismanagement or climate change.

Deterrence: A defensive strategy to dissuade, without the actual use of force, another country from attacking. Normally used in the context of nuclear deterrence.

Devolution: The process whereby regions within a state demand and gain political power and growing autonomy vis-à-vis the central government. Devolution can lead to self-determination movements, whereby ethnically identifying regions within a state break away and form their own independent sovereign new state.

Diplomacy: The negotiating process by which states and other international actors pursue international relations and reconciliation of competing interests by compromise and bargaining.

Domestic terrorism: Terrorism whose perpetrators are from the same country as where the terrorist act takes place; "home grown" terrorism.

Ecofeminism: Argues that women are more closely associated with the natural world than men. Men have an instrumental attitude towards nature and ask, How can I use it? Women have a reverence and empathy for nature, since they contain within themselves the secrets of birth and regeneration.

Ecojustice: Since environmental quality is not equally distributed around the world, there is a need to develop methodologies and procedures to address the environmental inequalities that are the result of lack of natural resources, poor location, and poverty.

Ecological paradigm: The approach to international relations that assumes that the world of humans cannot be studied apart from its natural environmental contact, and that sees the human world as a subset of the global ecosystem. Central to this paradigm is the view that planet Earth with its surrounding atmosphere represents a finite ecosystem.

Economic development: The use of land, labor, and capital to produce higher standards of living, typically measured by increases in gross national product (GNP) and more equitable distribution of national income.

Economic liberalism: An approach to IPE based on free market principles and open international trade and monetary systems. Founded in part on the belief that the role of the state should be minimized because of the inefficiency that may result as well as the fear of states abusing their power.

Ethnic nationalism: Identity of a people—focused essentially on ethnic roots, such as Serb or Russian identity—expressed in behavior ranging from peaceful to violent.

Ethnology: The branch of anthropology that deals with the comparative cultures of various peoples, their distribution, characteristics, and folkways.

European Union (EU): A multipurpose international organization comprising fifteen western European countries and that has both supranational and intergovernmental characteristics.

Europol: A European-wide police force that fosters country-to-country cooperation as well as multilateral cooperation.

Feminist Theory of International Relations: An approach that believes that gender is the key to our understanding of international relations. The aim of feminist theory is to uncover the gender dichotomies that mainstream international relations conceals or rejects and to lay these bare before the public eye.

Fiscal barriers to trade: Government tax policies affecting goods and services that discriminate against foreign companies. For example, goods in the home country may be exempt from taxation while goods from a foreign country are subject to taxes on their exports of goods or services.

Formal region: A type of region that reflects a high degree of homogeneity in one or several aspects.

Free rider problem: A form of cheating, like an individual riding a bus for free, associated with countries benefiting from a stable international system or from membership in an international organization without having to pay any of the political, military, or economic costs.

Free trade area: International trade among countries that is devoid of tariff and nontariff barriers.

Free Trade of the Americas (FTAA): A proposed free trade area extending throughout the Americas, first announced at a Summit of the Americas in Miami in December 1994. Signatories designated 2005 as the deadline for conclusions of negotiations for the FTAA. Implementation was to follow in subsequent years.

Functionalism: A theory that states can promote cooperation by working together in selected areas (such as coal and steel industries) and that the ties they build will compel them to cooperate in other areas as well.

Galicia: A region in Spain inhabited by an ethnically identifying group called Gallegos.

Gender Development Index (GDI): An index that puts the conditions of women into the measurement of human development. Essentially, the index uses the same data and same statistical measures as HDI but captures inequalities in achievement between women and men.

Gender Empowerment Index (GEM): An index that measures the extent to which women have become equal participants with men in leadership positions in the social, economic, cultural, and political life of their country.

General Assembly: A branch of the United Nations in which each member state of the UN is allotted one vote, regardless of size. It is heavily involved in social welfare and economic matters, and it acts as the focal point of activity for the many agencies, committees, and institutes that deal with United Nations matters.

Geopolitics: The study of the geographical distribution of power among states throughout the world, with specific attention to the rivalry between the major powers.

Geostrategy: Foreign policies pursued by states or intergovernmental organizations (such as NATO) that focus on territory and the geographic distribution of power. The U.S. post–World War II policy of containment of the Soviet Union illustrates geostrategy.

Global Civil Society: The term given to the emergence of a great deal of interaction of NGOs with international organizations as they lobby and seek to have their views represented or endorsed by the United Nations and world financial institutions.

Global Commons: Areas of the earth's biosphere that are shared by all the world's population, such as oceans and the atmosphere.

Globalization: The process of becoming worldwide in scope. When we speak of the globalization of industry, we refer to the process of industries going worldwide in scope; the internationalization of industry. The effects or consequences of globalization include the reduction of regional differences in lifestyle and the loss of distinctive regional identities.

Green Revolution: The great increase in yield of grain crops, such as corn, rice, and wheat, due to the development of high-yielding hybrids, the use of fertilizers and pesticides, and the implementation of more efficient land management. The father of this revolution was Iowa-born Henry Wallace.

Groupthink: A psychological theory applicable to many aspects of life, including foreign policy decision making. It suggests that the motivation to achieve group unanimity overrides the motivation to appraise realistically alternative courses of action.

Hamas: "Islamic Resistance," referring to a Palestinian militant group that has employed terror systematically and regularly in Israel in an effort to promote the transfer of Gaza and the West Bank to a Palestinian authority.

Heartland Theory: A geostrategic theory first constructed by Sir Halford Mackinder, which states that Eurasia will have ultimate strategic advantage over sea power in competition for control of the world.

Hegemon or **Hegemonic State:** A country with overwhelming military, political, and economic power, and with the ability to write and enforce the rules of the international system. A powerful state in a region that tries to use its military or economic power to dominate countries in the region.

Hegemonic Stability Theory: An international relations theory that argues that the political-economic stability in the world or in a region requires a strong power called a hegemon. The United States may be said to have provided hegemonic stability in Asia after the Second World War. This perspective disagrees with the realist notion that a unipolar structure to the international system is inherently dangerous.

Home Country: The country of origin, or home base, for an international company.

Host Country: The country that hosts an international company. For the company, it is a foreign country.

Human Development Index (HDI): An index that provides a comparative measure of a state's economic development. It is used in UN comparative economic databases.

Human Poverty Index (HPI-1) and (HPI-2): An index that measures the proportion of people living in a developing state (HPI-1) or an industrialized state (HPI-2), who are affected by three key deprivations: longevity or life expectancy, knowledge, and a decent living standard.

Human Rights: Rights considered so fundamental that they belong to every individual on this planet. These rights include the basic political freedoms, economic rights—such as the right to work—and the right to leisure time. To date, women's rights are not considered fundamental human rights. The human rights upon which the states of the world are agreed may be found in the United Nation's Declaration of Human Rights, adopted by the UN General Assembly in 1948.

Idealism: A philosophical position that argues that human beings are basically good. War can be prevented when the proper international institutions are created. States can cooperate to solve problems and improve the existing world order under the right institutions.

Ideology: A set of political belief that serve to guide government policy and behavior.

Imperialism: A theory developed by Vladimir I. Lenin, who argued that it was the highest stage of capitalism (see Marxism). Under imperialism, national states driven by economic success and the need for more and more raw materials, acquired colonies that they proceeded to exploit for cheap labor and natural resources, and which they used as an expanded market where they could sell their goods.

Import-Substituting Industrialization: Policies designed to increased national political-economic independence by building up national industries so that the country will not have to rely so much on expensive imports. Examples include nationalizing foreign companies, trade barriers on foreign goods, and diversifying the national economy in order to reduce dependence on a few exports.

Import-Substitution: The development of national industries to produce products that might be expensive to purchase and import from the global marketplace. A prime example is the former Soviet Union's automotive industry.

Industrial Revolution: A rapid major change in the economy of a country or region characterized initially by the general introduction of power-driven machinery and later by significant changes, usually through automation, of existing types and uses of machines; the replacement of first physical and then mental forms of human labor by machines.

Infant Industry: A government and business strategy in which a new industry is granted protection from foreign competition so that it will eventually be able to compete internationally on an equal footing.

Influence: The capacity of one actor to change or sustain the behavior of another actor in the global system.

Information Revolution: The explosion in information that has become available to people across the world in the form of television news (CNN) and cyberspace (fiber optics, satellites, Internet, and World Wide Web).

Intellectual Property Rights: Rights given to persons over the creations of their minds. They are customarily divided into two main areas: copyright and rights related to copyright; and industrial property which includes protection of distinctive signs—particularly trademarks—and industrial designs and trade secrets.

Interdependence: States do not live in isolation from one another. Increasingly, the new driving forces in world politics—such as international finance, trade and commerce, environmental pollution, the information revolution, transnationalism, intergovernmental organizations (IGOs), and nongovernmental organizations (NGOs)—are linking states together in a web of wide-ranging interactions.

Intergovernmental Organizations (IGOs): An international grouping of states.

International Monetary Fund (IMF): A United Nations agency responsible for overseeing the entire international monetary system by promoting exchange rate stability and orderly exchange relations among its member countries.

International Organizations (IOs): A catch all term that refers mostly to intergovernmental organizations but that can also apply to nongovernmental organizations.

International Political Economy (IPE): A field of study that explores economic and political links at the international level.

International System: A concept that includes a number of key actors (states, nations, IGOs and NGOs) and the patterns of actions among those actors that can be explained by the distribution of power and other factors. The state plays a pivotal role within this system, because the system has no central authority to maintain order and dispense justice.

International Terrorism: Terrorism involving citizens or the territory of more than one country.

Interpol: An international police force that maintains a data bank on criminal activity around the world. It also fosters country-to-country and multilateral cooperation.

Irredentism: When a state wishes to push its boundary lines farther out to include some population that it believes belongs within its boundaries. Irredentism can lead to war when one state claims the people and a part or the whole of the territory of another state.

Kurdistan: The Kurds, around 25 million in number, have lived for over 3,000 years in a region today comprised of Turkey, Syria, Armenia, and Azerbaijan. A stateless nation, the Kurds dream of living in a free homeland one day called Kurdistan.

Kurds: A stateless nation of people, who live in four states: Turkey, Iraq, Iran, and Syria. They have strived for years to create a state of Kurdistan.

Landlocked State: As the term suggests, a state surrounded by other sovereign states and shut off from easy access to the sea—such as Paraguay and Bolivia in South America.

League of Nations: An international organization established in 1918 to maintain peace and security. Although it did not prevent the outbreak of World War II, it did have a significant influence on the creation and structure of the United Nations.

Lebensraum: The German word for "living space." A geopolitical concept touted by Adolph Hitler, it was one justification given to Nazi territorial expansion.

Levels of Analysis: A method of classifying the players and how they relate to one another in the international system on five different levels.

Liberalism: A philosophical approach that argues that human nature is basically altruistic and that human altruism enables us to cooperate. In the international arena, compassion and caring for the welfare of others should motivate state actions. War is not a certainty because violence and selfishness are not the only part of the human condition but rather the result of flawed institutions. In addition, all wars are a matter of collective concern.

Majority Voting: A voting rule in which the majority of states (or individuals) must agree.

Marxism: The theory that history is a one-way street from the past into the future. As history progresses, we find that there have been thresholds in human experience that mark a turning point in terms of socioeconomic and political organization. These changes are always a change forward and indicate a progressive betterment of the human condition. The engine driving the change is the class struggle—the tension between the class that possesses the means of production in a given society and the class that works for the ruling class. Marx identified the human race as having gone through prehistoric society, slave-holding society, feudal society, capitalist society. The end condition of human society was the classless society of communism.

Megalopolis: A huge city. The term is used to describe a vast human settlement that transcends original city limits and spills over into the city's suburbs and the city beyond. The entire East Coast of the United States may be described as a megalopolis.

Mercantilism: An approach to the international political economy that emphasizes the power of the state. A national strategy developed in the seventeen century to increase state power and wealth, primarily through the accumulation of precious metals.

Microcredit: The provision of small loans by a lending institution to individuals.

Misperception: When applied to war and international relations, causes of war in which one or more countries in a dispute misinterpret the intentions of the other. The misunderstanding leads to a war that perhaps was not desired by any country.

Modernization School: An approach to development that seeks to modernize "backward" countries through the adoption of policies consistent with economic liberalism and free trade. The United States is usually seen as the successful model to emulate.

Most-Favored-Nation Principle (MFN): A pillar of GATT and now the WTO, in which imports from one state are granted the same degree of preference as imports from the most preferred states.

Multinational or **Multiethnic State:** A state such as Nigeria, the United States, Russia, or India, which contains more than one nation and/or ethnic group within its territory. Most states are multinational in nature.

Multipolar System: An international system based on three or more centers of power (poles) that may include states or IGOs, such as the European Union. The nineteenth-century international system may be described as multipolar.

Mutually Assured Destruction (MAD): In the context of the rivalry between the United States and the Soviet Union, both sides were deterred from attacking each other because they believed that the destruction of both countries would be assured if one of them initiated a nuclear attack upon the other.

Nation: A group of people linked together in some manner, such as by a common territory, with a common culture that may or may not be based on religion, a common language, a common history or understanding of the past, and a general desire for independence.

National Champion: A company or industry, supported in various ways by the government, that dominates the home market. Both business and government interests lie in making the company competitive internationally.

National Interests: The principal priorities pursued by states in the international arena. Territorial security, political independence, and economic vitality are a state's key national interests.

National Self-determination: The right of all people to determine their own government.

Nationalism: A strong emotional attachment to one's nation that can be expressed in a range of behavior from peaceful to violent.

Natural Resources: A state's basic resources that spring from its physical setting, such as oil, gas, uranium, coal, and arable land so vital to agricultural productivity.

Neoliberalism: A philosophical position that argues that progress in international relations can only be achieved through international cooperation. Cooperation is a dynamic rather than a static process. By focusing on understanding the dynamics of the web of relationships driving the international system, states and other international actors can effectively use the international institutions spawned by the system to promote peace and cooperation.

Neomercantilism: A more contemporary form of mercantilism in which the state plays an important role in ensuring economic growth and stability. It is normally associated with protectionist policies and may involve import substitution and export promotion strategies. The mercantilist focus on precious metals is of much less importance for neomercantilism.

Neorealism: An approach to international relations developed by Kenneth N. Waltz, which argues that while humans may be selfish by nature and driven by a lust for power, power is not the true end. States really pursue power in order to survive. The end goal is national survival.

New Diplomacy: The style of diplomacy that has evolved since World War I, with emphasis on open—as opposed to secret—negotiations, summit meetings, and in which nationalism has a greater impact on the negotiating process.

New International Economic Order (NIEO): The effort by Third World countries to alter the rules of the international system, especially with respect to trade and financial structures.

Newly Industrializing Countries (NICs): Those countries previously classified as lesser developed countries (LDCs), but which have raised significantly their levels of production and wealth—typically through export-led growth.

Nonaligned Countries: A term used to designate those developing countries that tried to avoid siding with either the West or the East during the Cold War years.

Nongovernmental Organizations (NGOs): An international organization made up of groups or individuals recruited across state boundaries, either by profession or interest.

Nonstate Actors: Important players in international relations who are not nation-states.

Nontariff Barriers (NTB): Methods of restricting foreign imports that are neither tariffs nor quotas. Examples include subsidies or tax breaks for domestic companies and relatively rigid health and safety standards for foreign competitors.

North: A term loosely referring to the advanced industrial democracies of the northern hemisphere.

Old Diplomacy: The form of diplomacy that characterized the era prior to World War I. European-centered, it emphasized secrecy and was generally devoid of nationalism.

Oligopoly: A limited number of companies that can control most of the supply—and hence price—of one or more products.

Operational Arms Control: A method of controlling weapons without actually or directly limiting the flow of weapons. It includes measures that foster trust among adversaries, such as notifying the "other side" of war games, hot lines, and public disclosure of weapons sales.

Paleoclimatology: The study of climate variations in the far distant past.

Palestine Liberation Organization (PLO): The major Islamic national liberation movement dedicated to achieving a Palestinian state in what have been Israel's Gaza Strip and West Bank.

Peacebuilding: A peacekeeping operation that includes UN efforts to oversee the development of democratic institutions.

Peacekeeping: A military operation, normally associated with the United Nations, whose aim is to provide a buffer between warring parties who allow a neutral force to carry out peace plans.

Periphery: In the international system, that region or substate entity that is not part of the central decision-making group of states. Kosovo, Chechnya, Kashmir, and East Timor may be considered part of the periphery. Africa has been, up to now, a peripheral region of the international system.

Political Geography: A field of study that looks at the geographical consequences of political decisions and actions, the geographical factors that were considered during the making of any decisions, and the role of any geographical factors that influenced the outcome of political actions.

Political Realism: A philosophical position that assumes that human beings are imperfect with an innate desire for power. The international system is composed of states and other actors whose primary interest is to survive and thrive in an anarchic jungle of competing actors where there is no higher authority to mediate their actions. The fundamental purpose of the state is to use its power to further its interests while containing the power of other states that might prevent this from happening.

Prisoners of Conscience: People imprisoned because of peaceful expression of their beliefs, politics, race, religion, color, or national origin.

Public Procurement: The acquisition by governments of goods or services from private companies. Governments sometimes rely on private companies to provide services such as road building and setting up telecommunications systems.

Qualified Majority Voting (QMV): Associated with the European Union, a voting rule in which the larger countries have more votes than the smaller countries and no country has a veto.

Quotas: A limit on the number of items that a country can export to or import from another country. Compare with tariffs.

Race: A division of humankind possessing biological traits that are transmissible by descent and that are sufficient to characterize it as a distinctive human type. Color is the major trait identified with race today.

Rational Choice Approach: An approach to IPE based on microeconomic assumptions about rational human behavior and emphasizing the domestic political sources of international economic policy making.

Realpolitik: A term coined by the German Chancellor of the nineteenth century, Otto Von Bismarck, to describe his foreign policy for Germany; namely, the building up of Germany's military to make Germany one of the leading European powers, rivaling Great Britain.

Regime: The process or procedure that is born of a treaty that the treaty signatories agree to follow. The treaty usually sets up a goal, a process by which to reach the goal, a time line and some kind of permanent organizational framework to monitor progress.

Regime Theory: Developed by Oran Young; holds that international cooperation depends on well-designed regimes. If a treaty promotes a well-designed regime, the chance of the treaty being implemented is much greater than if it designates a flawed regime.

Regional Trading Bloc: A loose expression that may encompass both free trade areas and customs unions. These are political-economic arrangements that seek to foster greater trade cooperation among member states.

Religious Extremism: The use of religion to rationalize extreme actions, such as terrorism; militancy against a recognized government.

Second Strike Capability: The ability to withstand a nuclear attack and still retain the capability to retaliate with nuclear weapons.

Security Council: The most important branch of the United Nations. It deals primarily with peace and security issues, and can authorize the use of military force. The Security Council consists of 15 countries: 5 permanent members (Britain, China, France, Russia, and the United States) and 10 others that rotate periodically.

Social Overhead Capital: A term in economic development studies to indicate factors such as a population's health, education, and welfare that contribute to economic growth.

South: A term loosely referring to the less developed countries of the Southern hemisphere.

Strategic Nuclear Triad: A nuclear force with the ability to launch nuclear weapons from sea, land, and air.

Structural Arms Control: A type of arms control designed to prevent the spread (or proliferation) of weapons to certain countries.

Supranationalism: An arrangement whereby national governments transfer a significant amount of sovereignty to an international governing body. This body is an autonomous authority that is above the state and that has designated powers of coercion that are independent of the member states. Supranationality, however, does not mean that these institutions exercise total authority over national governments.

Sustainable Development: In the interests of its own survival, the human race must not undertake any economic development that leaves a larger footprint on the environment than the ecosystem can successfully accommodate without breaking down. What this concept means in practice is still being worked out.

Taliban: The name of the militant Islamic group that controlled Afghanistan until its defeat in the U.S.-led war in late 2001. The Taliban gave considerable support to Al Qaeda.

Tariffs: A form of tax on all goods being imported into a country. Compare with quotas.

Technological Monoculture: The domination of the market by one variant of a technology utilized in a specific industrial sector by a company or group of companies and the use of this domination for political, economic, and social influence.

Temperate Zone: Two (north and south) areas of the globe that lie between 23 degrees and 60 degrees north and 23 degrees and 60 degrees south. They are temperate in climate and said to be prime territorial areas conducive to economic development owing to temperature and other climatic factors.

Terrorism: Politically motivated violence usually perpetrated against civilians. Terrorists and terrorist groups normally want to change by force or by threat of force a political context that they do not like.

Transnational: Going beyond state borders or unstoppable at state borders. Air pollution, for example, may be confined within the boundaries of one state, or it may be transnational, crossing state boundaries. We call this instance transboundary air pollution.

Transnationalism: Transnational forces are those identities and movements that span a state's borders and affect more than one nation. They include such movements as feminism and Islam, to name only two of the more high-profile transnational forces today. Transnationalism dates back to the Greek stoics.

Treaty of Westphalia: The treaty signed at the close of the Thirty Years War in 1648 that called for the recognition of territorial entities that could no longer be dominated as sovereign states and which had fixed borders, a recognized population, and an acknowledged government.

Truman Doctrine: A foreign policy announced by President Harry S. Truman in 1947, which declared that the United States would defend free people everywhere against the threat of communist aggression.

Unanimity Voting: A voting rule that requires a unanimous decision. This type of voting rule gives each person (or country) a veto; that is, it takes only one "no" vote to nullify the vote.

Unipolar System: When power in the international system revolves around a single superpower.

Uruguay Round: A series of negotiations as part of GATT that lasted between 1986 and 1994. The aim of the round, begun in Punte del Este, Uruguay, was to tackle global trade barriers, especially non-tariff barriers that were increasingly hindering free trade. It addressed seriously for the first time services and agricultural goods.

Voluntary Export Restraint (VER): A strategy of avoiding the imposition of trade restrictions by self-limiting the level of exports to the country or countries threatening trade restrictions. The belief is that the level of exports "voluntarily" restrained from within will be better than the level of exports imposed from without.

Water Stress: A term used by the United Nations to indicate consumption levels that exceed 20 percent of available water supply.

World Bank: A United Nations agency designed to promote the economic development of the world's poorer countries and to assist these countries through long-term financing of development projects.

Xenophobia: Extreme nationalism that unleashes violent action—even "ethnic cleansing" (genocide)—toward other ethnic national groups.

Photo Credits

Name Index

Subject Index